THE
AMERICAN
PLANNING
TRADITION

Provided by
The Journal of Planning Education and Research

THE
AMERICAN PLANNING TRADITION

::

CULTURE AND POLICY

Edited by
ROBERT FISHMAN

Published by
THE WOODROW WILSON CENTER PRESS
Washington, D.C.

Distributed by
THE JOHNS HOPKINS UNIVERSITY PRESS
Baltimore, Maryland

Editorial offices:
The Woodrow Wilson Center Press
One Woodrow Wilson Plaza
1300 Pennsylvania Ave., NW
Washington, D.C. 20004-3027
Telephone 202-691-4010

Order from:
The Johns Hopkins University Press
Hampden Station
Baltimore, Maryland 21211
Telephone 1-800-537-5487

Library of Congress Cataloging-in-Publication Data

The American planning tradition : culture and policy / edited by Robert Fishman.
p. cm.
Includes bibliographical references and index.
ISBN 0-943875-95-1 (hard : alk. paper) — ISBN 0-943875-96-X (pbk. : alk. paper)
1. City planning—United States.   2. Land use, Urban—United States.
3. Land use—United States—Planning.   4. Urban renewal—United
States.   I. Fishman, Robert, 1946–
HT167 .A5769 1999
307.1′2′0973—dc21
99-050614

Frontispiece: Metropolitan Landscape. "City of Towers," the New York Regional Plan's depiction of an ideal downtown for Manhattan showing Art Deco towers widely spaced in an open streetscape. (From *Regional Plan of New York and Its Environs,* vol. 2, *Building the City,* 1931)

ABOUT THE CENTER

The Center is the living memorial of the United States of America to the nation's twenty-eighth president, Woodrow Wilson. Congress established the Woodrow Wilson Center in 1968 as an international institute for advanced study, "symbolizing and strengthening the fruitful relationship between the world of learning and the world of public affairs." The Center opened in 1970 under its own board of trustees.

In all its activities the Woodrow Wilson Center is a nonprofit, nonpartisan organization, supported financially by annual appropriations from the Congress, and by the contributions of foundations, corporations, and individuals. Conclusions or opinions expressed in Center publications and programs are those of the authors and speakers and do not necessarily reflect the views of the Center staff, fellows, trustees, advisory groups, or any individuals or organizations that provide financial support to the Center.

Contents

CONTENTS

Foreword

■■
■■

"The world of public affairs is so old," Woodrow Wilson once observed, that no person can know it "who knows only that little segment of it that we call the present." In keeping with this point, the American Program of the Woodrow Wilson International Center for Scholars, the nation's official memorial to Wilson as a scholar and a statesperson, is concerned mainly with research on the history of American society and politics. It is devoted to furthering critical reflection on the relations between ideas and institutions in modern America, particularly the institutions of government. It provides a forum in Washington, D.C., for the presentation and assessment of new scholarly perspectives on the American experience, and does what it can—through its fellowships, scholarly working groups, conferences, and publications—to develop our knowledge of those long-term, fundamental, underlying issues and problems that shape our understanding of the national community, past and present.

The progress of scholarship requires collaborative creativity. One of the duties of the American program is to facilitate collaborative creativity by providing administrative leadership for cooperative projects that arise from time to time out of the scholarly discussions that take place among the Center's staff, its fellows, and its advisers. This book is an example. It had its origins in debate between former Center Fellows John L. Thomas and Robert Fishman over what to make of the deep-seated bias in the history of America's regional cultures against the rise of the modern metropolis that grew up to dominate each of them. Their discussions helped to isolate themes that had not been properly investigated and subjects that promised to repay the effort of fresh reconsideration in light of today's concerns. Thus others were brought into the discussions and persuaded to make their own contributions, and so slowly the book took its present form. Along the way, all who were involved in the meetings of what became a workshop group learned a good deal from one another. Thanks are due to all of the authors, and especially to Robert Fishman, the book's editor, for the care that has been taken to make the results of this work available to the reader.

MICHAEL J. LACEY
DIRECTOR, AMERICAN PROGRAM
WOODROW WILSON INTERNATIONAL CENTER FOR SCHOLARS

Main waiting room, Union Station, Washington D.C., 1908, designed by Daniel H. Burnham. This monumental space, pictured here in its beaux-arts splendor soon after its completion, aptly embodies that assured mastery of efficiency and grandeur that characterized the American planning tradition at its height. After scandalous neglect (also typical), the main waiting room and the rest of Union Station were partially restored in 1988. (Library of Congress Prints and Photographs Division, Detroit Publishing Company Photograph Collection)

CHAPTER ONE

The American Planning Tradition

An Introduction and Interpretation

■ ■
■ ■

ROBERT FISHMAN

The last half-century has seen a radical transformation in American cities and regions, but paradoxically, this transformation has stimulated our interest in the older forms of cities and increased our respect for the planning tradition that created them. For example, the tidal wave of single-family suburban tract development after World War II has led to a new understanding of older residential areas where a pedestrian scale and a dense, complex mixture of housing types and other land uses seemed to lead to better opportunities for community. The revolutionary decentralization in retailing and the rise of "Mallopolis" on every major highway has made the surviving older Main Streets a focus for civic pride and redevelopment. And the dispersal of office employment to anonymous office parks has taught us the special value of the central regional downtowns, with their irreplaceable heritage of diversity, public space, historic structures, and regional identity.

Indeed, as everything that is either "urban" or "public" now seems in perpetual crisis, we look back with new respect on a planning tradition that helped to shape cities whose vitality astonished the world. With far fewer resources, these planners of America's great cities left a magnificent legacy of public spaces, public transit, public parks, public libraries, public schools, public health, and public safety. Merely preserving this legacy sometimes seems beyond our present capacities. No longer can we view these figures from the past merely as necessary precursors who prepared the way for the full revelations of "modern planning theory" that we now finally possess. Instead, we must view the leaders of the planning tradition as contemporaries and even as prophets. They are colleagues who struggled with many of the same problems of urbanism that afflict us today, and dealt with those problems with more vision, confidence, and hope than seems possible today.

In this spirit of renewal and respect, the contributors to this volume have attempted to re-evaluate the American planning tradition. No one of us could have mastered the synthetic vision that Lewis Mumford once brought to this field. Instead, under the auspices of the Woodrow Wilson Center, we have tried to bring the specialized scholarship of many disciplines together. This volume is the product of not only individual research but lengthy discussions of common problems and central themes.

These discussions were especially necessary because, for the purposes of this volume, we have consistently defined "planning" in broad terms. For us, planning is collective action for the common good, but particularly action that concentrates on building and shaping the shared physical infrastructure for present needs and future growth. Although planning necessarily looks beyond city boundaries, its main tasks historically have been creating an urban infrastructure and linking cities to the rural hinterland. In this sense, the archetypal planning act in the American tradition remains what it has been since Aristotle in *The Politics* identified Hippodamos as the first planner: the establishment of a city plan.[1] For laying out a network of streets means establishing the public framework for complex communications, which are the essence of urbanity: density and exchange.[2]

Thus, the original icons of the American planning tradition remain those defining grids that were so often copied on the face of North America: the Spanish Law of the Indies (1573), which prescribed a central plaza surrounded by a grid of streets; William Penn's plan for Philadelphia (1682), in which the grid is interrupted by a central square and a park in each of the four quadrants; James Ogelthorpe's plan for Savannah (1733); Pierre Charles L'Enfant's combination of the grid and the diagonal for Washington, D.C. (1791); and the genesis of the greatest of all

the urban grids, the Commissioners' 1811 Plan for New York City, which laid a massive grid on Manhattan. To these we must add their rural counterpart: the grid of six-mile-square townships and mile-square sections established by the Land Ordinance of 1785, which formed the basis for the survey and sale of public lands in the nineteenth century (figs. 1–5).[3]

Although grid plans have been ubiquitous in cities from ancient Greece to the Forbidden City in Peking, the architectural historian Witold Rybczynski has recently emphasized two particular meanings of the American grid: land speculation and pluralism.[4] The grid, of course, remains the most obvious and most convenient way to turn acreage into building lots. As the New York commissioners explained in 1811, "a city is to be composed principally of the habitations of men and that strait sided and right angled houses are the most cheap to build, and the most convenient to live in."[5] But Rybczynski also relates the grid to American pluralism, for the pure grid provides no privileged locales for the cathedral square or government center around which European cities had been organized.

Pluralism is perhaps the best way to begin to define the American planning tradition, but I would go further by identifying three elements that distinguish American planning, especially from its European counterparts:

1. The extraordinary scale of the tasks of planning;
2. The persistent obstacles that American society and politics put in the way of effective planning; and
3. The remarkable flexibility and creativity that American planning in the past has shown in overcoming these obstacles and achieving results worthy of the scale of the tasks.

The tasks of American planning have been nothing less than to provide the necessary framework for the settlement of a continent and for the creation in less than three centuries of a new network of major cities. In the civilizations of Europe, Asia, and Africa, the basic settlement patterns were worked out over three millennia or more.[6] In the United States, not only did a city like Chicago grow from a village to a world city in less than fifty years, but a complex new urbanity grew up with the city: a web of rail lines connecting Chicago to a "hinterland" as large as the Austro-Hungarian empire; an innovative urban economy that provided markets for foodstuffs and raw materials on a scale never before seen; an urban infrastructure that could provide water, sewage, police, fire, and other vital services for a population that could double in a single decade; and parks, schools, churches, museums, newspapers, department stores, and theaters that established a new kind of urban culture. And Chicago was only one American city.[7]

These enormous tasks had to be accomplished in the absence of a strong state to direct them, and in the context of a society in which the rights of private property put strict limits on whatever powers the state did possess. Throughout the nineteenth century the "model" state for planning was Napoleonic France. There one saw a centralized government that could exercise its control at all levels, from the city block to the whole nation. This state was led by skilled and dedicated bureaucrats pledged to uphold the prestige and power of the government. The French state could utilize a corps of experts trained at the great state schools to follow consistent doctrines of engineering and urbanism.[8] As we shall see, none of these conditions for power obtained in the United States.

And if state power was weak here, private property was correspondingly strong. All physical planning ultimately involves the control of land use, and hence a limitation on the rights of private property. In Europe these limitations were consistent with an older, feudalistic concept of property in which property rights were always limited by the claims of superiors. In most nineteenth-century English cities, for example, the most valuable land was still owned by aristocratic families who clung tenaciously to their "freehold" by selling only long-term leases (ninety-nine years, typically) that imposed strict controls on whoever built on and occupied these sites. Whatever the social inequities of this system, it made possible the squares of London's West End, which remain models of urban order and decorum.[9]

In the United States, all such "feudal" systems of land tenure lost out to a democratized freehold system in which both farmland and urban lots were sold outright to purchasers. Sam Bass Warner, Jr., co-author of Chapter 10, has characterized this system as "land as a civil liberty," for "it meant freedom for even the poorest farm family to win autonomy, freedom to profit from rising land values in a country teeming with new settlers, and freedom to achieve the dignities and prerogatives that went with the possession of even the smallest holding."[10] But, as Warner indicates, the ideal of autonomy was inevitably linked to the freedom to speculate on land for future gain. In the countryside, the American "yeoman farmer" was often as much a land speculator as an agrarian, as he mortgaged his land to the limit to maximize his profits when he sold out and moved on. Loyalty to the community and the locality was always counterbalanced by the competitive individualism inherent in the capitalist marketplace. As Richard Hofstadter put it, "What developed in America was an agricultural society whose real attachment was not to the land but to land values."[11]

This speculative freedom grew even more intense in the cities, where planning and indeed any kind of long-term perspective seemed lost in the frantic efforts to maximize gains. We often think of American cities following already-established patterns of frontier settlement. In fact, as Richard Wade observed, "the towns were the spearheads of the frontier";[12] that is, in order to persuade settlers to buy land in a locality, the locality needed first a viable city that could provide a convenient market for the farmer's crops and a source of credit, supplies, and services. Thus, the American city was always a kind of double speculation—the effort to lure a critical mass of capital and skills to a speculative urban center in order to open up the surrounding territory for speculative sale as farmland. In these "city speculations," geography alone was rarely the determinant, especially when one enters the era when canal and railroad connections determined the extent of a city's hinterland. Cities rose and fell based on the luck and tenacity of their founders, and even when a city had established its place in the urban hierarchy, the financial history of land within each city was a set of boom-and-bust cycles in which wild inflation gave way suddenly to an even more destructive deflation. We need not be surprised that in Herman Melville's *Confidence-Man,* a dark fable of American greed, the Confidence Man (who takes on a variety of swindler's roles) appears once in the guise of a land speculator offering lots in "the new and thriving city, so called" of New Jerusalem, located somewhere in northern Minnesota: "Here, here is the map. . . . There, there you see are the public buildings—here the landing—there the park—yonder the botanic gardens—and this, this little dot here, is a perpetual fountain."[13]

It would seem that American society inherently lacks the stability for long-term planning or the social solidarity for collective action. The contributors to this book will provide ample evidence for the failures of American planning, but paradoxically, they also provide more significant evidence for the power of American planning—even under the most difficult circumstances. Perhaps the greatest analyst of this paradox was Alexis de Tocqueville in *Democracy in America.* With centralized France as his point of comparison, Tocqueville immediately sensed the messy pluralism of American cities. As he observed, "No sooner do you set foot upon American ground than you are stunned by a kind of tumult; a confused clamor is heard on every side; and a thousand simultaneous voices demand the satisfaction of their social wants."[14] Yet Tocqueville also understood that the result of this pluralism was not merely anarchic individualism but a surprising amount of planning: collective action for the common good. "Everything is in motion around you: here, the people of one quarter of a town are met to decide on the building of a church; there, the election of a representative is going on; a little further, the delegates of a district are posting to town in order to consult some local improvements; in another place, the laborers of a village quit their plows to deliberate on the project of a road or a public school."[15]

Tocqueville's explanation of this paradox goes to the heart of the American planning tradition. As he argues, the very power of a European centralized government tends to produce apathy and passive resistance among the governed because it operates without public knowledge or discussion. By contrast, the absence of a controlling central power invites collective action outside a bureaucratic hierarchy. "Under [democracy's] sway, the grandeur is not in what the public administration does, but what is done without it or outside of it. Democracy does not give the people the most skillful government, but it produces what the ablest governments are frequently unable to create; namely, a superabundant force, and an energy which is inseparable from it, and which may, however unfavorable circumstances may be, produce wonders."[16]

As we shall see, the "wonders" of American planning almost invariably take place outside any well-defined administrative structure. They are the product of ad hoc commissions, special authorities, private-public partnerships—all of which tend to blur the lines between federal, state, and local jurisdictions and between the private and the public. Indeed, the very difficulty of public planning imposed by the federal system has often spurred a more effective effort, because action always requires extensive public discussion and alliance-building rather than simply a fiat from an all-powerful government. Similarly, the deep regard for private property has often strengthened planning by forcing activists to better define the benefits of collective action. As Tocqueville says, the feeling the American "entertains toward the state is analogous to that which unites him to his family, and it is by a kind of selfishness that he interests himself in the welfare of his country."[17]

The most powerful focus of "selfishness" in planning has been the city itself, where the material interests of both the elite and the common citizen are bound up with the future of their city in an intense competition with other cities. The spur of self-interest has always been the key to the power of what I would call "the urban conversation": the intense and impassioned discussion of urban and regional strategies. Although the specific planning problems differ, the basic themes of the urban conversation are always the same: how to justify public action to a society that is deeply individualistic; how to support long-term investment strategies in a society built on short-term gains; how to justify the taxation of private profit for the common resources and the common good. This urban conversation—rather than any centralized

government—has been the ultimate source of the authority that generated the outpouring of investment in roads, bridges, waterworks, schools, libraries, and other public facilities that so astonished Tocqueville. It showed, he acknowledged, "a power, which, if it is somewhat wild, is at least robust."[18]

If the wonders of American planning have been less in evidence in recent years, and if its powers have been less robust, one explanation is that planning has forsaken the language and strategies of the urban conversation for the technical discourse of the academy and the bureaucracy, and abandoned the strategy of public persuasion for a delusive centralization that sought to bypass the need for public support. As I shall argue, there is evidence that the urban conversation is finally being revived in response to the regional challenges of urban decay, suburban sprawl, and ecological crisis. Perhaps this book will make a modest contribution to that conversation.

In the rest of this introduction, I have used my (undemocratic) powers as editor to expand my remarks to be both a summary of the chapters that follow and also an interpretation of some of the main themes of American planning history. This interpretation was motivated by my need to explain a contradiction that seems to underlie the historiography of this field. For my colleagues in this volume and indeed in my own chapter on "The Metropolitan Tradition" (chapter 3), the manifest content of American planning history emerges as a record of missed opportunities and partial successes punctuated by outright failures. But I also firmly believe that this seemingly impoverished tradition is somehow responsible for the "wonders" that impressed Tocqueville and the legacy that inspires us today.

This paradox stems, I think, from the role of "planning" within the larger "urban conversation" I have described. Planning thought at its most complex and ambitious is necessarily outside the structures of power that control massive investments. Its real successes are always partial and slow, and even some of its failures have more significance for the future than was recognized at the time. Indeed, when there is too comfortable a fit between planners and power, as in Robert Moses's ascendancy over New York, the results are invariably oversimplified in theory and disastrous in practice.[19] Some of the complex ideas that Moses once elbowed aside as impractical are finally finding their place in the revived urban conversation. I have therefore tried to put the strengths and the limitations of the American planning tradition in their larger context of American urban and regional history.[20]

The Urban Era in American Planning, 1830–1930

One persistent misunderstanding of American urban and planning history is that this nation is inherently "anti-urban." The archetypal American, we are told, is the pioneer agrarian, and American culture therefore has always been deeply suspicious of urban forms and urban values.[21] The American urban crisis of today stems from this anti-urban bias that somehow unites the colonial frontiersman with the contemporary suburbanite. We are all Huck Finns, constantly "lighting out for the territories."

I would argue that a more realistic view of American history would show that in no other society since the European Middle Ages have cities played such a formative role in creating the national economy and culture. During our "urban century" from 1830–1930 the power to shape the American economic system lay not with the federal government or the states but with the cities. These cities operated in ways that recalled the

independent city-states of the Middle Ages: they pursued their separate economic interests in intense competition with other cities. The American planning tradition evolved as a formidable weapon in this system of "urban mercantilism."

American planning took on its definitive form at the beginning of the nineteenth century in response to an overwhelming challenge. The emerging nation had been organized economically and spatially around the Eastern seaboard ports that were connected to their hinterlands by river systems that drained into the Atlantic.[22] After the Revolution it became obvious that the great task ahead was to link this coastal system to the massive new lands opening up on the other side of the Alleghenies. Unfortunately, water flowed downhill even in the New World; hence there were no convenient rivers that crossed the Alleghenies to connect the Eastern seaboard with the Great Lakes, the Ohio River valley, or the Mississippi River valley.

Colonial settlement along the Atlantic coast had necessarily taken advantage of the opportunities that nature provided: finding the best natural ports with rivers that gave free access to the interior. Now human action would have to create a transportation system that went where the natural flow of water could not go and thereby open the continent to development. And human action would have to locate and create the centers of trade—the great cities—that could properly focus and manage this development. The history of American planning and of American society was profoundly shaped by the fact that the power to respond to this great challenge devolved from the federal government and the states to the American cities. As we shall see, the urban elites of Boston, New York, Philadelphia, and Baltimore seized the initiative that the federal government and the states were unable to exercise. The motive of these urban elites was clear: to direct the maximum amount of trade to their own cities; to create great hinterlands far beyond what "natural" geography would have given them; and, not least, to deprive rival cities of their potential share in the bounty.

This outcome meant that any broader co-ordination and cooperation that the federal government or the states might have managed was rendered impossible. But it also meant that economic development would not have to wait for the federal government to work out the nation's sectional quarrels or for the states to work out the inevitable urban-rural divisions. Instead, power and resources were concentrated in the hands of those quickest to use them. In the fashion that Tocqueville had analyzed, the absence of a controlling central authority mobilized competitive energies in the rival cities. The emerging technologies of the canal and especially the railroad were immediately pressed into use. Just as important, the urban elites were forced to pay attention to creating an urban infrastructure capable of handling rapid growth, and ultimately to underwriting an "urban vision" for their cities that went far beyond the functional.[23]

This "urban era" was certainly not envisioned by the authors of the federal Constitution, who never mention cities at all. And, for the first half-century of the new republic, the assumption persisted that only the federal government had the resources and scope to lead national planning. This assumption was reflected in Alexander Hamilton's plans of the 1790s to use federal power to promote American manufacturing. It was also embodied in the complex series of land laws that sought to give substance to Thomas Jefferson's vision of the agrarian "yeoman republic." Finally, as we see in Michael Lacey's chapter (chapter 4), a whole series of federal initiatives envisioned a national system of transportation and communication to open up the interior. These began with Albert Gal-

latin's 1808 plan for a federal system of canals and roads and came to a halt with the rejection of Henry Clay's "American System" of internal improvements in the 1830s.

As Lacey shows, all these initiatives led nowhere because the federal system then lacked the executive power to overcome sectional divisions and make the crucial choices that any planning system demands. Nor was the federal government any more successful in using control of public lands to create a "yeoman republic." Despite the Jeffersonian rhetoric, the grid system proved better suited to the needs of large-scale land speculation than to those of the prospective small farmer.

With the federal government on the sidelines, the initiative temporarily passed to the states, which pressed ahead with fragments of the "national system"—mostly canal projects—designed to advance the interests of their own people.[24] The great monument of this era was New York State's Erie Canal (built during 1817–25). At a time when the longest operating canal in the United States was 28 miles long, New York State's engineers and merchants resolved to take advantage of the gap in the Alleghenies to push a great canal 364 miles west from the Hudson at Albany through unsettled wilderness to connect with Lake Erie below Buffalo. When the canal was finished in 1825, New York City, the greatest natural port on the Atlantic, now possessed a direct water link west to the Great Lakes and the emerging Midwest. It was an achievement that decisively altered the economic geography of the United States and laid the foundation for New York City's dominant position in the twentieth century.[25]

But the Erie Canal and the canal era in general were far from simply projects to benefit the largest cities. Canal transportation created a complex network of new cities and towns that tended to spread development throughout whole regions. As other states attempted to repeat New York's success, the nation embarked on a "canal era" in which water transport and water power produced a pattern of dispersed settlement that Lewis Mumford in the twentieth century recalled as "the golden day" of balanced regional growth and vital local culture.[26] But this era of state initiative soon came to grief on over-ambitious projects that plunged many states into bankruptcy in the 1840s.

With both the federal government and the states now on the sidelines, the main actors in this drama—the cities—were now ready to step forward. The key initiative had been taken by Baltimore, a city whose growth-oriented merchants had won a major place in the international coffee and tobacco trade, but also a city with very restricted natural water routes to the interior. While Philadelphia and the Commonwealth of Pennsylvania were pouring millions into a "Main Line" canal that would somehow connect Philadelphia and Pittsburgh, Baltimore merchants quickly identified the steam railroad as the means that would enable them to surmount the Alleghenies and reach the Ohio River valley.[27] In 1829 they chartered the Baltimore & Ohio (B & O) Railroad. Although the B&O would not actually reach the Ohio River until 1853, Baltimore had pioneered the definitive instrument of urban-centered national planning: a private railroad corporation controlled by an urban elite and run in the interest of the city's economy.[28]

This "private" control not only allowed but in fact required massive public subsidies: the B&O got essential capital from both the city and the state treasuries. In 1850, the Illinois Central Railroad, which connected the emerging railroad metropolis of Chicago with the South, pioneered the definitive form of public railroad subsidies: federal land grants comprising alternate sections of land on each side of the right-of-way. These land grants, which would eventually total 141 million acres, were the great engine that would

carry the railroads across the continent.[29] This "private-public partnership" effectively enlisted the federal government and its public lands in the service of urban capitalism. Far more than the canals, the railroads tended to concentrate first trade and then manufacturing at those few strategic junctures where extensive rail and water transportation routes came together. The railroad was the instrument that the urban elites needed to inscribe their commercial geographies on the American continent (figs. 3, 4).

The railroad boom initiated the "boomer era" in American urbanism. As the frontier of settlement moved inexorably west, it became obvious that all aspiring cities must now be railroad "junction cities," on the model of Chicago, and also that a city must spend generously, on the model of Baltimore, to secure the best rail connections. These expenditures were a challenge even for long-established cities, but soon the "boomers" discovered the financial mechanism that could provide capital not only for railroad connections but for all the urban infrastructure needed for future growth: a city is a legal corporation that can borrow based on the security of its tax base.[30] Since the boomers always assumed that their cities were destined for explosive growth, money borrowed today could be paid back easily when a city's tax receipts had doubled or quadrupled. This technique of borrowing against future growth became the "enabling act" for nineteenth-century urban planning.[31]

Cities borrowed to their limits to subsidize rail links and thus make themselves transportation centers. They borrowed for docks, warehouses, and other aids to trade and manufacturing. They borrowed for street paving to make internal transportation efficient. They borrowed to bring running water, gas, electricity, and transit to their people. Above all, cities could borrow to pay for a wide range of public works that could combat the deleterious effects of urban crowding produced by their success. As Frederick Law Olmsted observed in 1870, it had long been taken for granted that "the larger the population of a town should be allowed to become, the greater would be the inconvenience and danger to which all who ventured to live in it would necessarily be subject, the more they would be exposed to epidemic diseases, the feebler, more sickly, and shorter their lives would be; the greater the danger of sweeping conflagrations; the larger the proportions of mendicants and criminals; and the more formidable and dangerous the mobs."[32]

So urban elites, utilizing the most advanced technology of the time, launched major projects to prevent cities from destroying themselves with their own growth. Thus, Olmsted could assert in 1886 that for major American cities it was "now a matter of course" and "little more than a question of time

when and how the port should be provided with docks, basins, elevators, and better general water-side facilities for commerce; when certain streets should be widened; when rapid transit for long, and street cars for short, transportation, a civilized cab system, telegraph, telephones, and electric lights should be introduced, better conveyances across the rivers gained, better accommodations for courts provided, the aqueduct enlarged, public schools multiplied, graded, and made more educational, industrial and night schools started, public museums of art and natural history founded, the militia made more serviceable, the volunteer fire department superseded, and a strong police force organized.[33]

In effect the cities took on the responsibility for creating the infrastructure for the emerging industrial society. Under nineteenth-century conditions the massing of people and productive facilities in dense urban locales still brought a significant increase in economic growth rates. City governments in ef-

fect borrowed against their future growth to provide the collective resources necessary to support rapid growth in private enterprise and to reduce the social costs of such growth. This investment involved risks—some cities wound up with massive debts and little growth—but the intense competition between cities tended to overcome doubts. Cities could take on these risks only because the economic benefits of urban growth were perceived to extend far beyond the urban elite. The "urban conversation" that necessarily accompanied a ballot measure to pass a new bond issue always emphasized these shared benefits to secure voter support. Even a working-class taxpayer saw himself as a potential homeowner—and thus someone who could eventually share in the general increase in land values created by the city boom (figs. 6–10).[34]

Yet precisely when the cities became the controlling centers of the national economy, the urban elites lost control of city governments to professional politicians and their "machines" that could mobilize working-class and especially immigrant voting blocs.[35] The resulting conflict between the urban political "machines" and elite "reformers" would provide the main drama in urban political history for a century. But behind these well-publicized conflicts we can now discern a larger area of agreement and compromise. The machines as much as the elites were dedicated to a growth policy that could support population increases, ever-larger city payrolls, and massive borrowing for public works.

The elites feared with some reason that the urban machines would stifle growth by increasing taxes, and that their corruption and inefficiency would constitute a further tax on urban enterprise. But by the 1890s the "good government" forces were able to put a de facto ceiling on urban property taxes and to use the state legislatures to enforce limits on municipal debt. For major projects and for long-term planning the elites were able to go outside the normal channels of municipal government to utilize state-appointed commissions, such as the one responsible for Central Park in New York City. At the same time, elite control of newspapers, banks, and insurance companies enforced minimum standards of efficiency in such key municipal departments as fire, water, and public health.[36]

Machine politicians, by contrast, told the voters with some reason that "good government" forces were obsessed by low taxes and cared little for municipal services beyond those useful for business or those that adorned the affluent neighborhoods of the city. As the machines strove for their own survival to provide those jobs and services for their constituents, they ensured that public services in American cities would necessarily be distributed far more equitably than the elite might have wanted—and indeed far more equitably than in the supposedly better-run cities of Europe. Jon Teaford's illuminating comparisons show American cities at the turn of the twentieth century significantly ahead of the much-praised German cities in such measures as water and sewerage, streetcar service, fire protection, parks, and public libraries.[37]

The single figure who best embodies the strengths of the American planning tradition in the urban era—indeed, I would argue, the single most important figure in all of American planning—was Frederick Law Olmsted.[38] For all his discontents with the American city, he never doubted that the urbanization of the United States was our path to a true civilization. His emphasis was on creating complexity within the booming cities, where rapid growth tended to produce an inhuman uniformity. Where the nineteenth-century city grew as a solid mechanical expanse of buildings, Olmsted wanted to open up the city to nature. Where the city gave priority to the needs of production and moneymaking, Olmsted sought to make a place for healthful leisure and civilized contemplation. Where the city tended to brutally segregate rich and poor, Olmsted wanted to bring them together in harmony and beauty (fig. 2).[39]

Olmsted had no formal training in landscape architecture or any other specialization. His considerable authority stemmed from his broad mastery of "the urban conversation," his ability to articulate the cultural ideals of the urban elite and translate them into a convincing language of park and suburban design.[40] He valued his independence and preferred to be a consultant rather than a member of any city administration. Government meant to him the brutal and incompetent Surgeon-General Clement Finley, who refused to implement reforms when Olmsted was executive secretary of the (voluntary) Sanitary Commission during the Civil War, or the corruption of Tammany Hall and other city political machines. Great projects were best left to the direction of "the best men."[41]

Nevertheless, Olmsted was a democrat—after his own fashion. Roy Rosenzweig and Elizabeth Blackmar, Olmsted's most determined scholarly critics, point out that he stubbornly resisted any attempt by ordinary people to use his parks for sports and other boisterous recreation rather than the quiet contemplation he thought was appropriate.[42] Yet Olmsted was particularly proud that in Central Park in New York, Prospect Park in Brooklyn, and his other great parks "the poor and the rich come together . . . in larger numbers than anywhere else"[43] and "you may thus often see vast numbers of persons closely brought together, poor and rich, young and old, Jew and Gentile."[44] He delighted that a rich New Yorker of his acquaintance complained that Central Park was too good for the people. "Why," he quotes the man as saying, "I should not ask for anything finer in my private grounds for the use of my own family."[45]

The American Planning Tradition at Its Height, 1900–1930

If Olmsted was the single greatest figure in the American planning tradition, that tradition arguably reached its height only in the three decades after Olmsted's death in 1903. In part those were the years when Olmsted's complex legacy was assimilated by that group of architects, engineers, landscape architects, and reformers who would in the early twentieth century establish themselves as the planning profession. But the strengths of American planning went well beyond even the best of the Olmsted legacy. Newly equipped with a professional organization—the American Institute of City Planners, founded in 1917—and an emerging university curriculum, American planning nevertheless retained its flexible, interdisciplinary status. The leaders of the profession still worked as independent consultants outside the constraints of full-time government employment. And planning theory warded off orthodoxy by maintaining its links both to the aesthetic imagination and to social reform.[46]

For planners primarily interested in the aesthetics of cities, this was the "City Beautiful" era, the attempt to adapt the European design vocabulary—especially the formal achievements of French Beaux Arts classicism—to American cities.[47] With the magnificent Court of Honor at the 1893 Chicago World's Fair as the model, City Beautiful planners concentrated on creating grand public spaces: civic centers, boulevards, and parkways.[48] For planners interested primarily in social reform, the key issue was housing. Reformers recognized that the crucial weakness of the early twentieth-century industrial city was the burden of inhuman overcrowding it placed on its poorest residents. The "housers" experimented with a wide range of remedies, from tenement regulation to slum clearance to model housing, and joined forces with social reformers to sponsor the settlement-house movement.[49]

Nevertheless, the main planning achievements of this era, in my view, involved neither City Beautiful designs, which remained isolated "showpieces" within the city, or social reform, which remained a marginal concern for most planners. The main achievements, rather, were to translate the technology of the "second industrial revolution" into urban forms that expressed the promise of modern urban living. The American city experienced what might have been a paralyzing combination of stresses: the high tide of immigration in the years just before the First World War coincided with a burst of new technologies that also had to be assimilated if the American city were to prosper.[50] First among the technologies was electricity in all its protean forms: first as urban lighting, then as power for factory machinery, as electric traction for trolley systems and subways, and finally as long-distance radio communications. Cast-iron construction gave way to steel and reinforced concrete, and the central machine-system of the nineteenth century—the steam engine and the railroad—found a powerful rival in the internal combustion engine and the automobile.[51]

Yet the result was not paralysis but an unprecedented urban vitality.[52] The American metropolis became the world heartland of mass production and other advanced industrial techniques, while creating a built environment that embodied "the landscape of modernity." Planning at its most effective was a multifaceted enterprise to provide the public and collective undergirding for the new building types that now defined American urban culture: the skyscraper, the department store, the vaudeville and movie palace, the sports arena, the mass-production factory, and a range of housing types from the humble working-class row house to the upper-middle-class suburban villa. Yet the "power" of planning in this era was not derived from any solid institutional base. As in Olmsted's time, planning remained dependent on the strength of the consensus generated by the "urban conversation."[53] For the urban elite and the new immigrants alike, a great city—that is, an economically strong and growing city—was one that had an impressive and lively central business district, an efficient "factory zone," and a plethora of healthy neighborhoods for every income and ethnic group.

For the skyscraper downtowns that astonished the world, planning meant creating the concentrated infrastructure to support what Rem Koolhaas has called "the culture of congestion."[54] This required massive construction projects for subway and other mass transit lines coordinated with equally massive electric, gas, water, sewage, telephone, telegraph, and other utilities—all focused in the service of unprecedented concentration and communication in the booming central business and "bright light" districts. For the urban factory districts, planning meant upgrading freight rail and water transportation, providing cheap water and power, and creating mass transit links for an urban working class.[55]

Although the upper-middle-class bedroom suburbs from this era remain enduring ideals for suburban living, the more modest middle-class and working-class urban neighborhoods that took shape on the periphery were, in my opinion, an even more impressive achievement.[56] Following the expanding systems of city services and transportation, a host of small-scale speculative builders created a varied environment based on what Sam Bass Warner, Jr., has eloquently termed "an intricate weave of small patterns."[57] What had only recently been luxuries for the few became standard services for the many: running water, electricity, gas, paved roads, sewers, police and fire protection, parks, public schools, and a mass transit system that connected the neighborhood to jobs in the factory district and to downtown. Although cramped by the standards of post-1945 suburbia, these modest neighborhoods were often genuine communities where density supported an active street life and local centers. The neighborhoods were the necessary counterweight to downtown, and urban life unfolded between the two poles of the neighborhood community and the cosmopolitan downtown.[58]

If planning worked at the modest level of the neighborhood, it also began to confront the far more difficult problem of "the urban region." At the turn of the twentieth century, when central cities in the East and the Midwest began to lose their ability to annex their smaller suburban neighbors, planners and reformers realized that "the American metropolis" extended beyond any realistic political boundary. But for this metropolis to achieve civilized standards of health and efficiency, it needed regional coordination of city, suburb, and rural periphery. The urban conversation must become a regional conversation.

The model region for this broadened conversation was Boston. As early as the 1880s, the pollution of the Charles River led to the creation of the Metropolitan Sewerage Commission. In 1893 two reformers, the landscape architect Charles W. Eliot (significantly, a former associate of Olmsted) and the journalist Silvester Baxter, built on the success of the Sewerage Commission and persuaded the state legislature to create a Metropolitan Park Commission to purchase and preserve the region's vital open spaces from the high ground at the edge to the beaches at the core. Like so many other creations of the Progressive Era, this proposal bypassed the presumed patronage and parochialism of the municipal governments of Boston and its suburbs to put key planning powers in the hands of an appointed board. In treating both the aesthetics of open space and the engineering of sanitary facilities on a regional scale, these two commissions built an awareness that the flow of clean water defined the ecology of the region and was the key to its future. Although the Massachusetts Legislature in 1896 rejected an even more ambitious proposal to create a single "super-county" for Boston and its suburbs, the Sewerage and Park Commissions made the essential point that "Boston" was now a regional and ecological unit.[59]

This regional perspective then became the basis for the two great monuments of American planning in the early twentieth century, Daniel Burnham and Edward Bennett's *Plan of Chicago* (1909) and the *Regional Plan of New York and Its Environs* (1929).[60] Both these massive plans were privately funded from elite sources to provide a detailed yet comprehensive vision for the two largest American metropolitan regions. Both sought to become in effect regional governing commissions—not by assuming any real governing powers but by setting the agenda for each region's municipal governments. Both plans were distinguished not only by their scale, ambition, and confidence, but by their remarkable ability to integrate the best planning thought on all aspects of metropolitan development (figs. 11, 12, 14, 15).

This increasingly intense regional conversation inevitably broadened still further toward a national conversation. If urban reformers were concerned with the relationship of each growing metropolis to its regional hinterland, they were also necessarily concerned with the impact of the cities as a whole on the rest of the nation. The "urban era in planning" had tended to treat the natural resources of the country as mere commodities to be delivered by the railroads as quickly as possible into urban markets. Olmsted, as always, had been ahead of his time in foreseeing that urban planning must develop its necessary counterpart: rural conservation.

As Michael Lacey and James Wescoat, Jr., show in their respective chapters for this volume (chapters 4 and 5), the emerging conservation movement necessarily meant a greater planning role for the federal government, a role that the federal government had shirked since the failure of Henry Clay's American System in the 1830s. For both Lacey and Wescoat, Theodore Roosevelt with his "New Nationalism" was the key figure in what Wescoat calls "a time of great reports and conferences" headed by the *Report of the Inland Waterways Commission* in 1908. If the metropolitan region had become the chosen unit for the most comprehensive visions of urban planning, the "river basin" would now serve a similar integrative function for federal planning. As WJ McGee, author of the Inland Waterways Commission's report, argues, mastering the great rivers through dams, canals, irrigation systems, and other massive construction projects was an undertaking that only the federal government could attempt. With federal multipurpose planning, the great rivers could become a national transportation system to balance the power of the railroads; a source of water and hydroelectric power that could develop the impoverished regions of the South and the arid regions of the West; a standard for conservation, as forest protection in the uplands helps to prevent floods in the plains.

There is no better sign of the vitality of planning during this era than the fact that planning theory never hardened into a single dogma but instead broadened into a great debate over the future form of the nation. In this volume the debate is represented by the contrasting positions espoused by the protagonists in my chapter on "The Metropolitan Tradition in American Planning" (chapter 3) and by John L. Thomas's chapter on the regionalist tradition (chapter 2). The "metropolitanists" in my terms were planners like Daniel Burnham or the authors of the 1929 *Regional Plan of New York*, who believed that the basic urban form established in the nineteenth century would persist into the twentieth, even if "the metropolitan area" grew to twenty million people and stretched fifty miles or more from its historic core. This giant city would still be defined by its downtown, the overwhelming economic and cultural focus of the metropolitan area. The bulk of the population would still cluster relatively tightly around the downtown in a massive "factory zone" which would be the productive heart of the metropolis. Beyond this zone would be the residential suburbs—still a refuge for a relatively small elite—and beyond that the "outer zone" of farms, forests, and parklands (figs. 16, 17).

For the metropolitanists, the main challenge of planning was to create a monumental downtown worthy of a great urban civilization; to construct a massive network of rail transit to connect all the residents of the metropolis with the downtown; to make the "factory zones" not only the most efficient places on the planet for industrial production but also decent places for the bulk of the city's population to live; and finally to maintain the outer zone as a source of fresh air, fresh water, and open space for the metropolis, to establish parks and other recreational facilities there and to build the transit lines and parkways that would enable urbanites to experience unspoiled nature.[61]

As Thomas shows, the "regionalists" took a more radical view of the prospects for the city in the twentieth century. Led by such notable designers and social critics as Lewis Mumford, Benton MacKaye, and Clarence Stein, the regionalists saw the crowded cities of the nineteenth century as a temporary phenomenon, the inhuman result of the backwardness of nineteenth-century technology and the concentration of power in the hands of a metropolitan elite. In the new age of electricity and the automobile, the big city was, in Stein's phrase, a "dinosaur city" whose crowding and inefficiency consumed society's resources and stunted its residents' lives (figs. 18, 19).

The twentieth century would see a return to the dispersed settlements characteristic of the canal era, but with regional networks of highways and electrical power that would bring the benefits of advanced technology to every point in the region.[62] The regionalists criticized infrastructure investments designed to maintain the crowded urban cores, and called for a decentralized highway system that would serve a regional network of planned "New Towns." As central cities shrank, the "urban region" would consist primarily of New Towns located throughout the region and set in an open, green environment, each combining both work and residence. This true "regional city" would occupy, in Thomas's phrase, the "middle ground" between the old, crowded cities and the old, isolated rural areas. This middle ground could combine all the economic benefits of living in a technologically advanced society with the human scale, local identity, and community of small-town America.

Both the metropolitanist and the regionalist visions embodied the core belief of the American planning tradition at its most confident: that intelligent, imaginative, collective action could genuinely shape cities and regions that met the highest ideals of the nation. This core belief would be sorely tested over the rest of the twentieth century.

The Crisis of the American Planning Tradition, 1930–70

The 1929 stock market crash undermined the faith in enlightened capitalism on which so much of American planning had been based.[63] The skyscraper downtowns were beset with vacancies, homeowners saw their dream houses threatened by unpaid mortgages, and local governments were paralyzed by tax shortfalls. The principal institutional legacy of the 1920s for planning had been "zoning": the legal capacity to segregate land uses in the interest of protecting residential neighborhoods from encroachment by industry, and indeed in maintaining the value of land throughout the city.[64] But zoning proved to be of no use against the devaluation of all property in the Depression. Nevertheless, the election of Franklin D. Roosevelt rapidly revived the sense of mission in American planning. For a time it appeared as if all the varied strands of the American planning tradition would find a home within the capacious structures of the New Deal.

For the cities, the early New Deal employment programs promised the labor and resources to reconstruct aging public urban infrastructure and to replace slums with decent housing. As Gail Radford has shown, the first New Deal housing projects were based on the ideal of "modern housing," which would replace speculative, piecemeal development with planned designs that would raise housing standards not only for the poor but for the urban working and middle classes as well.[65] Meanwhile, the New Deal "Greenbelt" program of suburban New Towns seemed to embody regionalist hopes for a planned decentralization of metropolitan population. With private suburban development at a standstill, the experimental Greenbelt towns promised to provide a model for bounded, coherent communities that would preserve the open space at the edge of the region. Still further from the cities, the Tennessee Valley Authority and other major water and power projects seemed to validate the 1908 Inland Waterways Commission's perception that controlling the great river basins would be the strategic point for the federal government to begin a new era of conservation and rural community development.

But this planning utopia failed to materialize. Instead, the American planning tradition entered a period of prolonged crisis that negated its historic strengths and stymied effective action. As we have seen, American planning drew its main support from its role in furthering the ambitions of the largest American cities. But even at its most pro-urban, the New Deal had a bittersweet message for the cities: the era of urban leadership in national planning was over. For the first time since the 1830s, the cities and their infrastructure projects no longer determined the basic directions of national economic development (to the city's advantage). Only the federal government now possessed the tax base and borrowing capacity for the major tasks of planning. The federal government had a different agenda from that of the cities, and this divergence would grow more obvious as the reform impulse in the Roosevelt administration diminished.

In Chapter 6, Alan Brinkley has identified the rise and fall of the National Resources Planning Board (NRPB) as a key episode in the New Deal's transformation. By the late 1930s, the NRPB had emerged as the most strategically placed planning organization in the federal government, reporting directly to the president. Its corps of expert planners wished to coordinate not only the federal government's investments in urban, regional, and conservation projects, but also to coordinate this full range of physical projects with the federal government's new responsibilities for the performance of the American economy. But precisely these ambitions made the

NRPB a convenient target for the opponents of planning in Congress. The NRPB was defunded by Congress in 1943. In Brinkley's view federal planning after World War II lost the comprehensive scope that the NRPB had attempted to establish and focused instead on the use of tax and fiscal policy to promote rapid growth.

One can observe that "planning for rapid growth" meant in practice the federal government directing infrastructure investment outside the central cities, either to the suburban fringe of urbanized regions or to hitherto underdeveloped sections of the South and West.[66] The urban housing programs lost their comprehensive ideals and instead became narrowly defined as housing for poor people. Meanwhile, the Federal Housing Administration (FHA) sponsored long-term, low-interest mortgages and other incentives for new suburban housing and thus established a nationwide system that "redlined" (i.e., excluded) the older urban neighborhoods. The federal highway programs created a whole new transportation network that served the suburbs and the outlying regions far better than it served the cities, while neglecting the urban-centered rail and mass transit systems.[67] Massive federal water and power projects ensured that the developing regions would have the cheap power, water, and other resources to compete effectively with urban factory districts.

These programs in effect severed the link between economic development and the growth of cities that had held true since the 1830s. Industrialization, especially, was no longer tied to the rail-based infrastructure centered in cities. National corporations could thus move production from these older cities to the cheap land and nonunion labor that the suburbs and the Sunbelt provided in ample quantities. Even though these national corporations were still mostly based in the downtowns of the older cities, the corporate

leadership's attachment to these cities was now divided at best. Whereas local elites had once looked to the total development of their central cities and surrounding regions, business-sponsored urban planning after World War II now concentrated on the downtown alone. Pittsburgh's Allegheny Conference, the model organization for business planning, brought together the city's industrial and financial establishment to sponsor the redevelopment of the downtown as a suitable setting for corporate headquarters. Meanwhile, this same establishment oversaw the dismantling of Pittsburgh's industrial base.[68]

As postwar growth accelerated, American planning found itself unable to conceive a coherent strategy in the face of destructive fragmentation. Suburbs used their political independence to wall themselves off from the central city's problems while continuing to avail themselves of federal largesse in highways, sewer projects, and other infrastructure improvements; suburban real estate entrepreneurs took advantage of these improvements to construct shopping centers and industrial and office parks that competed directly with the city; and the FHA continued to favor new suburban housing over urban renovation. But the most damaging fragmentation was the great divide of race.[69]

Between 1940 and 1960 more than four million Southern blacks migrated to Eastern and Midwestern cities, a "Great Migration" that dwarfed the earlier "Great Migration" of blacks during and after World War I.[70] The new migrants inevitably pressed against the boundaries of the "color line" established in all big cities to define the black ghetto, and this expansion produced intense conflicts with adjoining white districts that accelerated the patterns of white flight and de-industrialization that were already draining the central cities.[71] As Arnold R. Hirsch, author of Chapter 8, has shown in his classic study of postwar Chicago, idealistic planners in the 1940s attempted to breach the color line by building small "scatter-site" integrated housing projects in all-white neighborhoods. But the white reaction to this policy was invariably so negative—often violently negative—that planners were forced by city governments back into policies that not only accepted de facto segregation but actually reinforced the pattern.[72] But what Hirsch calls "making the second ghetto" was only one of the profoundly negative consequences of the principal urban planning strategy of the postwar period, "urban renewal."

Unwilling and unable to deal with the deeper aspects of the urban crisis, American planning turned to "urban renewal" as the answer to the city's problems. This set of programs enacted in the Federal Housing Acts of 1949 and 1954 appeared to be based on the most idealistic elements of the American planning tradition and on the most progressive elements of European modernism. In fact it combined a poorly understood caricature of modern design with a top-down authoritarianism rarely seen in American planning. Far from saving the cities, urban renewal became a potent symbol for misguided public policy and plunged American planning into a crisis of confidence from which it is only now recovering.[73]

Urban renewal started from the premise that the major cause of the urban crisis was the physical deterioration of cities—both in the "blighted" areas of the downtown and in the slums that disfigured urban neighborhoods. Planners believed that it was useless to try to renovate individual structures in these deteriorated areas, because small-scale improvements would be lost in the larger pattern of decay. Perhaps more important, renovation could at best prolong the older "horse-and-buggy" fabric of the city at a time when that fabric was hopelessly out of date because of the impact of the automobile. The point, according to urban-renewal theory, was to completely rebuild whole sections of the city using the best of modern technology and modern design.[74]

Planning theory further stated that the main barrier to this fundamental renewal of the American city was that urban land was overpriced compared to undeveloped land at the suburban fringe; moreover, urban land was invariably parceled out among hundreds of owners. The government must therefore use its power of eminent domain to condemn whole tracts of blighted or slum property. These tracts would be completely cleared and sold to developers who could rebuild using modern design. The federal government would subsidize these cleared tracts so that their cost would be competitive with suburban land. For the downtown, this meant replacing old-fashioned "blight" with high-rise office towers, stores linked to parking garages, and high-rise middle-class apartment towers. For the slums, the "developer" would be the city housing agency that could erect subsidized, affordable apartments to replace the demolished tenements.[75]

With its unrelenting focus on the total replacement of large tracts of the urban built environment, urban renewal implicitly rejected the American planning tradition's legacy of pragmatic compromise.[76] Ironically, the total power that urban renewal gave planners over the buildings, businesses, and people in a designated renewal tract was countered by the total impotence that physical planning displayed when facing the real social and economic crises of the city. Even in the most narrow design terms, the problems with urban renewal were quickly apparent—but not quickly enough to stop disastrous projects that continued through the 1960s. Downtown, the areas identified as "blighted" invariably contained a wonderful range of historic buildings and small businesses that gave the downtown its character. The renewal process of total demolition generally destroyed the businesses along with the buildings. Their replacements—if indeed developers could be found to build on cleared land—usually consisted of towers in a plaza, if not towers in a parking lot, dispersed structures oriented toward automobile users that failed to generate any genuine urbanity or street life.[77]

Moreover, as Hirsch has shown, urban renewal was from its origins fatally compromised by its role in maintaining racial segregation. The "blighted" areas were frequently chosen precisely to remove black neighborhoods located too close to the downtown and to replace them with expensive apartment towers and other facilities for whites. As for public housing projects for the black poor, they were strategically placed deep within the ghetto to create (along with the expressways that often ran beside them) an impenetrable barrier between the black and the white city.[78] For his chapter, Hirsch has turned to New Orleans to contribute an important variation on this theme. Precisely when the Supreme Court ruled that "separate but equal" was unconstitutional for education, the New Orleans "moderate" establishment turned to urban renewal projects as a way of reinforcing segregation by creating a few tokens of "separate but equal" facilities for blacks. But these projects were defeated, not by black activists or by white liberals, but by a reactionary-populist coalition that opposed even token projects for blacks funded by the federal government.

The failure of urban renewal undermined a basic element in the ideology of planning: that large-scale public enterprises based on modern design were necessarily superior to the piecemeal process that had built up the fabric of the old cities. A similar crisis of confidence struck almost simultaneously at planners who were primarily concerned with suburban and regional issues. Here again American planning was stymied by a destructive combination of power and impotence. The federal government's investments in regional infrastructure went far beyond what the regionalists of the 1920s or 1930s could have hoped. But, as Thomas observes in Chapter 2, the sprawling, corporate-sponsored growth that resulted was the opposite of the human-scaled community-building that the regionalists had hoped to promote. With power over land use fragmented among the hundreds of counties and municipalities at the edge of most regions, no means were available to limit or direct the destructive force of large-scale speculation fueled by government subsidies. Regionalists had argued in the 1920s that the cities must decentralize to the regions. Now this tide of decentralization was a reality, but it was simultaneously devastating the central cities and overrunning the regionalists' cherished "middle ground."[79]

Responding to this new situation required a drastic rethinking of both the metropolitan and the regionalist traditions, as well as building new coalitions between the cities and suburbs. In Chapter 7, Margaret Weir shows how difficult it was for planners to overcome the intellectual and physical fragmentation that worked against coalition-building. Her subject is the fate of Senator Henry Jackson's National Land Use Planning Act, first introduced in 1970. Despite its sweeping title, the Jackson bill was a procedural measure that attempted only to use federal incentives and sanctions to encourage the states to regulate land use. The states, it was hoped, could regulate regional growth in ways that neither the federal government nor local governments could manage. Even this modest bill was opposed by conservatives, and, to overcome their resistance, the bill needed the united support of both the cities and the nascent environmental movement. Unfortunately, the cities had little interest in any policy not directly aimed at federal subsidies for them and the environmental movement was so narrowly focused on passing new federal regulations that neither group saw any real benefit in a coalition.[80] The Jackson bill was finally defeated in 1974.

The folly of this fragmentation was soon evident during the Reagan administration, when the federal government cut back drastically on both subsidies to the cities and on environmental regulations. Such failures at the federal level continue to undermine national planning, but, as we shall see, these failures also had an unexpected benefit. They drove the American planning tradition back to its historic strength: coalition-building at the local and regional levels.

The Death and Life of the American Planning Tradition

The most powerful intellectual stimulus to the revival of the American planning tradition came from a book that was perhaps the most powerful attack on the idea of planning ever written. Jane Jacobs's *The Death and Life of Great American Cities* concentrated on the recent failures of urban renewal, but Jacobs also criticized virtually all the icons of American planning from City Beautiful to New Towns. The problem in all these design strategies, she charged, was that planners responded to what they saw as the "disorder" of the city by imposing their own designs, but they completely failed to understand and to respect the far more complex order that healthy cities already embodied. This complex order—what she calls "close-grained diversity"—was the result not of big plans but of all the little plans of ordinary people that alone can generate the diversity that is the true glory of a great city.[81]

Jacobs brilliantly supported these critiques with an abundance of detailed observations that contrasted the bleak and dangerous terrain of the planned public housing project with the vibrancy of traditional "unplanned" urban streets like Hudson Street in Manhattan's West Village, where she then lived. Although Jacobs's demolition of bureaucratic urban-renewal theory was the most brilliant and the most necessary part of her book, there were other aspects of her work that ironically proved highly useful to a planning revival. By drastically devaluing theoretical expertise, Jacobs was in a sense returning to the eclectic, pragmatic roots of American planning. By trusting the evidence of her own eyes, she countered the academicization of planning and helped to restore the "urban conversation" that had traditionally been at the core of the American planning tradition. Perhaps most important, Jacobs provided what urban planning needed most in an era of decentralization when almost all urban functions were rapidly suburbanizing. She provided a justification for the city.

In her analysis, urban density serves a positive function because it provides the rich, complex setting in which individuals and small businesses can best pursue their own plans. A big corporate bureaucracy could function in isolation, but a small business needs a multitude of complementary enterprises close at hand to succeed. The diversity of small urban enterprises sustains and is sustained by a dense and diverse urban population with highly varied tastes and needs.[82] As Jacobs emphasizes, this special urbanity is manifested in the street life of a great city. For Jacobs, what happens on the sidewalks is just as important as what happens in the buildings. A successful urban street is a complex blend of neighbors and strangers, a constantly changing "urban ballet" of familiarity and chance encounters that both defines a neighborhood and welcomes the outsider. These streets are safe not because they are constantly policed but because the citizens watch out for each other. Safe, lively, diverse streets are the essence of true urbanity.[83]

In ways that Jacobs herself never foresaw, her analysis of the city became the starting point for a redefinition of the goals and methods of urban planning. She not only indicated the new aim of urbanism—the preservation of the older urban fabric, with its precious legacy of human-scaled streets and other public spaces—but, equally important, she identified the limitations of planning. Where urban renewal had sought total control, post-Jacobs planning returned to Tocqueville's perception that the American style of governance is most powerful when it steps back and leaves room for the initiative and creativity of citizens. The areas that urban renewal had targeted for demolition were now identified as the areas to be lovingly protected, and the prime movers for this historic-preservation movement were now individuals willing to buy and renovate older structures. But planners soon won a more important role for themselves than such minimal tasks as providing brick sidewalks and fancy streetlights in historic districts. Successful historic preservation often involved the adaptive reuse of historic structures, which required the imagination to conceive effective new uses and the ability to recruit private developers who could carry out the transformation. Downtown planning became increasingly a kind of public entrepreneurship, in which the planners brokered deals to attract new investment. The model for this public-private partnership was the 1976 alliance of the city of Boston and the developer James Rouse to transform the 1826 Quincy Market into a contemporary shopping arcade that would soon prove to be one of the liveliest public spaces in the city. Downtown planning today aims at an eclectic mixture of preservation and adaptive reuse, with new office towers, atrium hotels, convention centers, and sports stadiums.[84]

Downtown planning's most notable recent success has been the transformation of what is perhaps the best-known public space in America, New York's Times Square. Beleaguered by crime and "blight," Times Square had been slated in the 1980s to be "renewed" into a sanitized collection of postmodern office towers. After widespread protests, a new plan—strongly backed by major investments from the Disney Corporation—was implemented that not only restored many of the derelict theaters but respected and recreated the Square's historic role as a lively, chaotic, raucous assemblage of every kind of urban entertainment. Although some commentators have deplored the "Disneyfication" of Times Square and other now-flourishing downtown sites, this approach to planning at least recognizes that it was crowds and commercialism that originally created the American downtown.[85]

The application of Jacobs's ideas to the depressed inner cities has proved far more difficult. After the Nixon administration stopped funding new publicly built housing projects in 1974, urban policy in the inner city has largely resolved itself into the frustrating search for the kind of public subsidies that will lure private developers and industries back to devastated neighborhoods. After fruitless debate under the Reagan administration, Congress during the Clinton administration in 1993 passed legislation for eleven urban "empowerment zones" that would combine federal aid for job training and other services, tax credits for businesses within the zones, and tax-exempt bond financing for businesses or renovation.[86] Perhaps the most successful inner-city enterprises have been a revival of the old Progressive tradition in housing called the "Community Development Corporations." These nonprofit organizations, many affiliated with church groups, seek private and public money to renovate ghetto housing and build new "infill" houses.[87] Finally, in a belated acknowledgment of the truth of Jacobs's ideas, the Department of Housing and Urban Development (HUD) has begun to demolish the worst of the high-rise housing projects. To replace the lost units, HUD now favors rebuilding the old, narrow streets that had been swallowed up in the project "superblocks" and lining them with low-rise townhouses that resemble Jacobs's beloved urban fabric before urban renewal.[88]

If the urban crisis had impelled Jacobs and her successors to rethink and reaffirm the meaning and importance of cities, the explosion of suburban sprawl similarly impelled the regionalists to rethink and reaffirm their commitment to human settlements in harmony with nature. As Thomas points out in chapter 2, the single figure whose importance for the regionalist tradition comes closest to Jane Jacobs's importance for the metropolitanists is Ian McHarg, the Scottish-born landscape architect and author of *Design with Nature*.[89] Like Jacobs, McHarg understood the fundamental problem to be combating a way of thinking and building that imposed a destructive simplicity on a complex system. For Jacobs, this complexity was the diverse city itself, imperiled by planners seeking to impose a simple pseudo-order. For McHarg, the complexity was the wonderfully varied ecological structure of the region, which was being destroyed by sprawling suburban building patterns that imposed the same destructively simple pattern of subdivisions and highways from the lowlands to the ridge tops. McHarg's solution was to "design with nature," i.e., to allow the ecology of the region to guide building. Only after a profound examination of the land—both scientific and aesthetic—can one identify the right sites for new construction and the form it must take. And this "ecological view" would similarly define the areas that would best be used for varied types of agriculture and the areas that must be preserved as wilderness. McHarg thus re-expressed the

fundamental ideals of MacKaye and the earlier regionalists in terms the growing environmental movement could understand. *Design with Nature* never attained the canonical status of *The Death and Life of Great American Cities,* but its ideas underlay the powerful upsurge of environmental activism on the regional periphery. Just as important, *Design with Nature* provided a language that acknowledged the place of human settlements in nature, a language that could accommodate the new coalitions between urbanists and environmentalists that began to emerge in the 1980s.

Perhaps the best sign of this revitalization of both the metropolitan and the regionalist wings of the American planning tradition is that no new orthodoxy has arisen that promises to solve all problems. Instead, we have a rebirth of "the urban conversation," now broadened into a truly regional conversation that seeks to overcome the barriers between disciplines and to see common interests among cities, suburbs, and rural areas.[90] At the annual meetings of the Congress for the New Urbanism, a voluntary organization that perhaps best captures the range of the conversation, one encounters planners; architects; landscape architects; local, state, and federal officials and elected representatives; developers; mortgage bankers; real estate consultants; historic preservationists; highway engineers; mass-transit operators; ecologists; farmland preservationists; housing advocates; social activists; journalists; academics; and yes, a few concerned citizens. From this plethora of voices I would single out two who perhaps best represent the creative encounter of contemporary planners with the American tradition: the team of Andres Duany and Elizabeth Plater-Zyberk, and Peter Calthorpe.[91]

Andres Duany and Elizabeth Plater-Zyberk have very consciously based their innovative urban designs on the practices of the

American planning tradition at its height in the early twentieth century. They have learned most, however, not from the "grand designs" of the City Beautiful movement but from the more modest American neighborhoods and their "intricate weave of small patterns." Their first major project, Seaside, a resort on the Florida panhandle, has been the most influential and controversial project of its time because Duany and Plater-Zyberk refused to consign the design principles that had once formed the best American neighborhoods and towns to a dead past. Instead, they tried to understand and adopt the complex "codes" that made these neighborhoods into communities: narrow streets with ample sidewalks; houses close to each other and close to the street line; porches that created a protected semipublic space between home and street; a walkable town center that served as a genuine social and civic focus. In Seaside and in subsequent projects, they then applied these codes—not as quaint historical curiosities, but as the best contemporary wisdom for American planning today. Their "neotraditional towns" on peripheral greenfield sites seek to limit sprawl and automobile use and thus to fit new building into an ecological framework. Their "infill" projects for cities attempt to respect and to reinvigorate the older urban patterns.

Peter Calthorpe—like Duany and Plater-Zyberk a cofounder of the Congress for the New Urbanism—has emphasized in his work another neglected legacy of American planning: the positive relationship between public transit and community. Calthorpe has revisited the era of the "streetcar suburb," when the transit line provided an outlet for growth but also a way of disciplining growth: people needed to live within a fifteen-minute walk of a transit stop. In his transit-oriented development, Calthorpe sees the transit line—perhaps an abandoned freight line in an Eastern city or a new light-rail line in the West—as

again an instrument of good planning. By limiting new building in a region to the area within walking distance of a transit line, transit-oriented development would ensure that all new residents would have the opportunity to use transit; the transit stop would also be the mixed-use, pedestrian-oriented community center. Calthorpe further emphasizes another legacy of the streetcar era: that busy transit lines keep their hub—the downtown—alive. So a transit-oriented regional policy would both limit sprawl at the edge and promote a true regional center (figs. 20, 21).[92]

The American region that comes closest to embodying not only Calthorpe's "transit-oriented development" but the full range of contemporary American planning is Portland, Oregon. For this volume Carl Abbott has attempted to explain why Portland has emerged as "the capital of good planning" (chapter 9). As he emphasizes, Portland's success stems from a "careful balance between environmentalism and urbanism." On the environmental side, Portland created a successful farmland protection program in 1973 and instituted an "urban growth boundary" to limit sprawl in 1979; on the urbanism side, Portland has succeeded in maintaining a "user-friendly," pedestrian-oriented downtown that is a true regional hub. Tying both together has been the region's commitment to mass transit and new light-rail lines in the spirit of "transit-oriented development." But, as Abbott observes, Portland's unique history and culture make it a difficult model for others to follow. Portland grew relatively slowly during the years 1945–70, when sprawl engulfed other regions; the region never experienced a "great migration" of blacks or serious racial polarization; and Portland's political culture makes it possible for leaders to use phrases like "moral obligation" without embarrassment. Portland is, as Abbott puts it, "a civic community [that] clearly lies toward one extreme of American political styles."

What, then, will be the fate of American regions that lie closer to the uncivic norms of polarization between the central cities and their suburbs?[93] Perhaps fortunately, the American federal system ensures that there cannot and need not be a single standard model of regional organization. Instead, we are in the midst of an era characterized by what the Minnesota legislator and political scientist Myron Orfield has called "metropolitics."[94] These are the difficult politics of creating regional cooperation in a historic and political context that has always encouraged selfish fragmentation. It is clear that the federal government cannot mandate cooperation by imposing its own planning. On the contrary, the most innovative recent federal approaches to these issues, most notably the Intermodal Surface Transportation Efficiency Act (ISTEA) process of transportation planning, have required the regions to create their own planning councils to take the responsibility for regional policy decisions. As Tocqueville rightly observed, "however enlightened and skillful a central power might be, it cannot of itself embrace all the details of the life of a great nation."[95]

Indeed, this devolution of power from the central government to the regions, which is now happening in all the industrialized nations, has led Neal R. Peirce and Curtis W. Johnson to predict that the future lies not with the nation-states but with what they call "citistates."[96] In a global economy, the true units are these regional economies that flourish or fail independently of their nation-states. The "citistates" that achieve a high degree of cooperation among their diverse "stakeholders" will flourish; those that do not will fail. In many ways the American regions are entering a situation similar to that of the American cities 150 years ago: they are being allowed and forced to take responsibility for their futures. Spurred by global competition, the regions have begun to respond with a range of adaptations and improvisations that Tocqueville would have understood: expanded regional authorities like the Minneapolis–St. Paul Metropolitan Council; public-private partnerships; the emergence of states like Florida or New Jersey as planners and intermediaries between city and suburb (figs. 22–24).[97]

In Chapter 10, Judith A. Martin and Sam Bass Warner, Jr., address this very theme of the challenges and difficulties of "metropolitics," or, as they term it, "urban federalism," in the Chicago metropolitan area. Their chapter is built on the contrast between two challenges: the social challenge of overcoming racial division in this deeply segregated region, and the environmental challenge of water management for this rapidly decentralizing region. As they show, the contrast demonstrates what they call "both the creativity and the inertia of American urban federalism." For creativity, they analyze the attempt of the suburb of Oak Park to initiate a policy of racial openness in contrast to the segregation around it. Here, Oak Park's municipal independence enabled concerned citizens to take advantage of the positive aspects of urban federalism to devise their own flexible programs to promote racial balance. For inertia, by contrast, they analyze the attempt of the Metropolitan Sanitary District to deal with the frequent flooding and pollution that accompanied postwar suburbanization. Instead of "designing with nature"—i.e., seeking out solutions responsive to the local ecology and utilizing natural techniques of flood control—the Sanitary District imposed a vast tunnel and treatment system on all the localities in the district. Not only was this "heroic engineering" ruinously expensive, but designed *against* nature, it has never worked effectively.

In our final chapter, Anne Whiston Spirn presents a vision for a future metropolitan Boston firmly grounded in the planning achievements of its past. She recognizes that some of the best-loved parts of the city—the Back Bay, Olmsted's Fens, and "Emerald Necklace" of parks—were results of an intense nineteenth-century public dialogue that generated "collective vision and sustained public energy." This shared respect for the public realm inspired Olmsted to achieve in Boston his greatest syntheses of environmental engineering and aesthetics. But in the twentieth century the dialogue has withered, and with it a respect for and a vision of the public realm. Like Martin and Warner, Spirn regards the twin issues of racial justice and environmental health as the crucial tests of a renewed planning tradition. She brings the special skills and perspectives of a landscape architect to the vital task of understanding the ecology under the inner city, and she uses that ecology as a vital guide to the reconstruction of parks, gardens, and other "common ground" for ghetto neighborhoods. Finally, she seeks a return to Olmsted's visionary synthesis of engineering and aesthetics. Her vision of a reclaimed metropolitan Boston, no longer polluting the rivers and ocean but in harmony with them—"a fragile, human construct, supported by the earth, permeated by air and water"—unites the past and the future of the American planning tradition.

Notes

1. Joseph Rykwerk, *The Idea of a Town: The Anthropology of Urban Form in Rome, Italy, and the Ancient World* (Princeton: Princeton University Press, 1976).

2. Richard Sennett, "American Cities: The Grid Plan and the Protestant Ethic," *International Social Sciences Journal* 42 (August 1990), pp. 269–85. The argument is expanded in Sennett, *The Conscience of the Eye: The Design and Social Life of Cities* (New York: Norton, 1992).

3. John W. Reps, *The Making of Urban America: A History of City Planning in the United States*

(Princeton: Princeton University Press, 1965). This book remains the canonical collection of the most important American planning maps, documents, and texts from the Law of the Indies to Burnham's *Plan of Chicago*.

4. Witold Rybczynski, *City Life: Urban Expectations in the New World* (New York: Scribner, 1995), chaps. 2 and 3.

5. Reps, *The Making of Urban America,* p. 297.

6. Two magnificent but contrasting books chart the full sweep of at least Western urbanism: Sir Peter Hall, *Cities in Civilization* (New York: Pantheon, 1998), emphasizing "the city as innovative milieu," contrasts with Lewis Mumford's profound and pessimistic *The City in History: Its Origins, Its Transformations, and Its Prospects* (New York: Harcourt, Brace, 1961).

7. William Cronon, *Nature's Metropolis: Chicago and the Great West* (New York: Norton, 1991). Cronon's very important book can be compared to four other important "city biographies" that show the scale of American urban growth: Sam Bass Warner, Jr., *The Private City: Philadelphia in Three Periods of Its Growth* (Philadelphia: University of Pennsylvania Press, 1968); Robert M. Fogelson, *The Fragmented Metropolis: Los Angeles, 1850–1930* (Cambridge, Mass.: Harvard University Press, 1967); Edward G. Burrows and Mike Wallace, *Gotham: A History of New York City to 1898* (New York: Oxford University Press, 1998); and Donald L. Miller, *City of the Century: The Epic of Chicago and the Making of America* (New York: Simon and Schuster, 1996).

8. Anthony Sutcliffe, *Towards the Planned City: Germany, Britain, the United States, and France, 1780–1914* (New York: St. Martin's, 1981), chap. 5.

9. Ibid., chap. 3.

10. Sam Bass Warner, Jr., *The Urban Wilderness: A History of the American City* (Berkeley: University of California Press, 1995), p. 16.

11. Richard Hofstadter, *The Age of Reform* (New York: Vintage, 1955), p. 41.

12. Richard C. Wade, *The Urban Frontier: The Rise of Western Cities, 1790–1830* (Cambridge, Mass.: Harvard University Press, 1959), p. 1.

13. Herman Melville, *The Confidence-Man: His Masquerade* (1857), chap. 9.

14. Alexis de Tocqueville, *Democracy in America,* ed. Richard D. Heffner (New York: New American Library, 1956; orig. published in 1835 and 1840), p. 108.

15. Ibid.

16. Ibid., p. 110.

17. Ibid., p. 70.

18. Ibid., p. 71.

19. Robert A. Caro, *Robert Moses and the Fall of New York* (New York: Knopf, 1974).

20. For a critical account of American city planning, see M. Christine Boyer, *Dreaming the Rational City: The Myth of American City Planning* (Cambridge, Mass.: MIT Press, 1983). A more balanced view is presented in two collections: Daniel Schaffer, ed., *Two Centuries of American Planning* (Baltimore: Johns Hopkins University Press, 1988), and Mary Corbin Sies and Christopher Silver, eds., *Planning the Twentieth-Century City* (Baltimore: Johns Hopkins University Press, 1996); especially valuable in the latter are the introduction and conclusion by Sies and Silver, "The History of Planning History," pp. 1–34, and "Planning History and the New American Metropolis," pp. 449–73. For the best survey of American urban history, see David Goldfield and Blaine Brownell, *Urban America: From Downtown to No Town* (Boston: Houghton Mifflin, 1979).

21. Morton and Lucia White, *The Intellectual Versus the City: From Thomas Jefferson to Frank Lloyd Wright* (New York: Oxford University Press, 1977).

22. Carl Bridenbaugh, *Cities in the Wilderness: Urban Life in America, 1625–1742* (New York: Capricorn, 1955).

23. Thomas Bender, *Toward an Urban Vision: Ideas and Institutions in Nineteenth-Century America* (Lexington: University Press of Kentucky, 1975).

24. Oscar and Mary Handlin, *Commonwealth, A Study of the Role of Government in the American Economy: Massachusetts, 1774–1861* (Cambridge, Mass.: Harvard University Press, 1947).

25. George Rogers Taylor, *The Transportation Revolution, 1815–1860* (New York: Holt, Rinehart and Winston, 1951), chap. 3; Michael Conzen, "The Maturing Urban System in the United States, 1840–1910," *Annals of the Association of American Geographers* 67 (March 1977), pp. 88–108.

26. Lewis Mumford, *The Golden Day* (New York: Harcourt, Brace, 1926).

27. James W. Livingood, *The Philadelphia-Baltimore Trade Rivalry, 1780–1860* (Harrisburg: Pennsylvania Historical and Museum Commission, 1947).

28. James Vance, *The North American Railroad: Its Origin, Evolution, and Geography* (Baltimore: Johns Hopkins University Press, 1995), chap. 1.

29. Benjamin Horace Hibbard, *A History of the Public Land Policies* (New York: Macmillan, 1924), chap. 12.

30. Hendrik Hartog, *Public Property and Private Power: The Corporation of the City of New York in American Law, 1730–1870* (Chapel Hill: University of North Carolina Press, 1983).

31. Eric H. Monkkonen, *America Becomes Urban: The Development of U.S. Cities and Towns 1780–1980* (Berkeley: University of California Press, 1988), chaps. 4–6; Terrence J. McDonald, *The Parameters of Urban Fiscal Policy: Socio-economic Change, Political Culture, and Fiscal Policy in San Francisco, 1860–1906* (Berkeley: University of California Press, 1986); Terrence J. McDonald and Sally K. Ward, eds., *The Politics of Urban Fiscal Policy* (Beverly Hills: Sage, 1984).

32. Frederick Law Olmsted, "Observations on the Progress of Improvement in Street Plans" (1868), reprinted in *Civilizing American Cities: A Selection of Frederick Law Olmsted's Writings on City Landscapes,* ed. S. B. Sutton (Cambridge, Mass.: MIT Press, 1971), p. 34.

33. Frederick Law Olmsted, "Notes on Franklin Park and Related Matters" (1886), reprinted in *Civilizing American Cities,* ed. Sutton, p. 252.

34. Ann Durkin Keating, *Building Chicago: Suburban Development and the Creation of a Divided Metropolis* (Columbus: Ohio University Press, 1988).

35. Steven P. Erie, *Rainbow's End: Irish-Americans and the Dilemmas of Urban Machine Politics, 1840–1985* (Berkeley: University of California Press, 1988), is the best general treatment of the machine era. Seymour Mandelbaum, *Boss Tweed's New York* (New York: John Wiley, 1966) remains valuable, as well.

36. Jon C. Teaford, *The Unheralded Triumph: City Government in America, 1870–1900* (Baltimore: Johns Hopkins University Press, 1984), part I: "The Structure of Urban Rule."

37. Ibid., chap. 9.

38. Anyone interested in the American planning tradition is forever indebted to the scholars who have produced the *Papers of Frederick Law Olmsted* (Baltimore: Johns Hopkins University Press, 1977–): vol. 1, "The Formative Years, 1822–1852," ed. Charles Capen McLaughlin, assoc. ed. Charles E. Beveridge (1977); vol. 2, "Slavery and the South," eds. Charles E. Beveridge and Charles Capen McLaughlin (1981); vol. 3, "Creating Central Park," eds. Charles E. Beveridge and David Schuyler (1983); vol. 4, "Defending the Union," ed.

Jane Turner Censer (1986), vol. 5, "The California Frontier, 1863–1865," ed. Victoria Post Ranney (1990); vol. 6, "The Years of Olmsted, Vaux & Company, 1865–1874," eds. David Schuyler and Jane Turner Censer (1992); and supplementary series, vol. 1, "Writings on Public Parks, Parkways, and Park Systems," eds. Charles E. Beveridge and Carolyn F. Hoffman (1997).

39. David Schuyler, *The New American Landscape: The Redefinition of City Form in Nineteenth-Century America* (Baltimore: Johns Hopkins University Press, 1986). Schuyler's more recent work, *Apostle of Taste: Andrew Jackson Downing, 1815–1852* (Baltimore: Johns Hopkins University Press, 1996), is especially valuable for showing Downing's role in beginning the "urban conversation" on parks that made Olmsted's achievement possible.

40. Bender, *Toward an Urban Vision.*

41. Geoffrey Blodgett, "Frederick Law Olmsted: Landscape Architecture as Conservative Reform," *Journal of American History* (1976), reprinted in Bruce Kelly, Gail Travis Guillet, and Mary Ellen Hern, eds., *Art of the Olmsted Landscape* (New York: New York City Landmarks Preservation Commission, 1981), pp. 111–24.

42. Roy Rosenzweig and Elizabeth Blackmar, *The Park and the People: A History of Central Park* (Ithaca: Cornell University Press, 1992), parts II and III.

43. Olmsted in Sutton, "Notes on Franklin Park and Related Matters" (1886), p. 255.

44. Frederick Law Olmsted, "Public Parks and the Enlargement of Towns" (1870), reprinted in *Civilizing American Cities,* ed. Sutton, p. 75.

45. Ibid., p. 89.

46. Mel Scott, *American City Planning since 1890* (Berkeley: University of California Press, 1971), chap. 1.

47. Peter Hall, *Cities of Tomorrow: An Intellectual History of Urban Planning and Design in the Twentieth Century,* updated ed. (Oxford: Blackwell, 1996), places American City Beautiful in its international context in chap. 6, "City of Monuments." Daniel T. Rogers, *Atlantic Crossings: Social Politics in a Progressive Age* (Cambridge, Mass.: Harvard University Press, 1998), chaps. 4–5 provides the international context for the politics of planning.

48. William H. Wilson, *The City Beautiful Movement* (Baltimore: Johns Hopkins University Press, 1989). See also two important articles by Jon A. Peterson, "The City Beautiful Movement: For-
gotten Origins and Lost Meanings," *Journal of Urban History* 2 (August 1976), pp. 415–34, and "The Nation's First Comprehensive City Plan: A Political Analysis of the McMillan Plan for Washington, D.C., 1900–1902," *Journal of the American Planning Association* 51 (Spring 1985), pp. 131–88.

49. Eugenie Birch, "Woman-Made America: The Case of Early Public Housing Policy," *Journal of the American Institute of Planners* 44: 2 (April 1978), pp. 130–44; Roy Lubove, *The Progressives and the Slums: Tenement House Reform in New York City 1890–1917* (Westport, Conn.: Greenwood, 1974).

50. Olivier Zunz, *The Changing Face of Inequality: Urbanization, Industrialization, and Immigrants in Detroit, 1880–1920* (Chicago: University of Chicago Press, 1982).

51. For these changes in the model American metropolis, see Daniel Bluestone, *Constructing Chicago* (New Haven: Yale University Press, 1991); and Mansel G. Blackford, *The Lost Dream: Businessmen and City Planning on the Pacific Coast, 1890–1920* (Columbus: Ohio University Press, 1993).

52. William R. Taylor, *In Pursuit of Gotham: Culture and Commerce in New York* (New York: Oxford University Press, 1992).

53. Carol Willis, *Form Follows Finance: Skyscrapers and Skylines in New York and Chicago* (Princeton: Princeton Architectural Press, 1995), is especially illuminating for the way the author demonstrates the emergence of "vernaculars of capitalism" in the two cities that provided a framework for profitable building while reflecting each city's distinctive identity.

54. Rem Koolhaas, *Delirious New York: A Retroactive Manifesto for Manhattan* (New York: Rizzoli, 1983.)

55. A dramatic and scholarly account of the heroic scale of these enterprises can be found in Clifton Hood, *722 Miles: The Building of the Subways and How They Transformed New York* (New York: Simon & Schuster, 1993); see also Joel A. Tarr and Gabriel Dupuy, eds., *Technology and the Rise of the Networked City in Europe and America* (Philadelphia: Temple University Press, 1988).

56. Mary Corbin Sies, *The Suburban Ideal: A Cultural Strategy for Modern American Living* (Philadelphia: Temple University Press, 2000), is an outstanding account of the upper-middle-class suburban ideal. Other notable work on suburban planning includes Henry Binford, *The First Suburbs: Residential Communities on the Boston Periphery,*

1815–1860 (Chicago: University of Chicago Press, 1985); Michael H. Ebner, *Creating Chicago's North Shore: A Suburban History* (Chicago: University of Chicago Press, 1988); Robert Fishman, *Bourgeois Utopias: The Rise and Fall of Suburbia* (New York: Basic Books, 1987); Kenneth T. Jackson, *Crabgrass Frontier: The Suburbanization of the United States* (New York: Oxford University Press, 1985); Margaret Marsh, *Suburban Lives* (New Brunswick, N.J.: Rutgers University Press, 1990); and John Stilgoe, *Borderland* (New Haven: Yale University Press, 1988). Richard Harris, *Unplanned Suburbs: Toronto's American Tragedy, 1900–1950* (Baltimore: Johns Hopkins University Press, 1996), not only provides an important comparative element, but also emphasizes working-class self-built suburban housing usually overlooked in suburban histories.

57. Sam Bass Warner, Jr., *Streetcar Suburbs: The Process of Growth in Boston, 1870–1900* (Cambridge, Mass.: Harvard University Press, 1962).

58. Alexander von Hoffman, *Local Attachments: The Making of an Urban Neighborhood, 1850–1920* (Baltimore: Johns Hopkins University Press, 1994). For an account of the survival of urban neighborhoods into the postwar period, see Alan Ehrenhalt, *The Lost City: The Forgotten Virtues of Community in America* (New York: Basic Books, 1995).

59. Scott, *American City Planning*, pp. 17–26.

60. For detailed references, see my "Metropolitan Tradition in American Planning," Chapter 3 in this volume.

61. For the international context of both metropolitanists and regionalists, see Hall, *Cities of Tomorrow,* chaps. 4 and 5.

62. Robert L. Dorman, *Revolt of the Provinces: The Regionalist Movement in America, 1920–1945* (Chapel Hill: University of North Carolina Press, 1993).

63. Marc A. Weiss, *The Rise of the Community Builders: The American Real Estate Industry and Urban Land Planning* (New York: Columbia University Press, 1987), gives a dramatic picture of the 1920s boom years especially in Los Angeles, followed by the devastating impact of the Depression.

64. Zoning was a major concern for the "metropolitanist" school of planning. The first citywide zoning ordinance was passed in Los Angeles in 1908; New York City's 1916 ordinance was perhaps the most influential. The 1926 Supreme Court decision in *Euclid v. Ambler* established the legality of zoning, which was conveniently codified by Herbert Hoover's Commerce Department in *A Standard City Planning Enabling Act* (1928). The zoning process, with its related "master plans" showing the various zoning districts, has often dominated both the professional activities of planners and the concerns of their critics. For the latter see James Kunstler, *The Geography of Nowhere: The Rise and Decline of America's Man-Made Landscape* (New York: Simon & Schuster, 1993). Yet zoning as a technique has always been subordinate to larger issues of planning, and has rarely been implemented with the rigor that either its proponents or its critics suppose. For a realistic view of zoning in practice, see Patricia Burgess, *Planning for the Private Interest: Land-Use Controls and Residential Patterns in Columbus, Ohio, 1900–1970* (Columbus: Ohio State University Press, 1994).

65. Gail Radford, *Modern Housing for America: Policy Struggles in the New Deal Era* (Chicago: University of Chicago Press, 1996).

66. Two important books on Los Angeles are especially relevant for understanding this era of what Greg Hise calls "suburbanization as urbanization": Greg Hise, *Magnetic Los Angeles: Planning the Twentieth-Century Metropolis* (Baltimore: Johns Hopkins University Press, 1997); and Richard Longstreth, *City Center to Regional Mall: Architecture, the Automobile, and Retailing in Los Angeles, 1920–1950* (Cambridge, Mass.: MIT Press, 1997).

67. Mark H. Rose, *Interstate: Express-Highway Politics, 1939–1989*, rev. ed. (Knoxville: University of Tennessee Press, 1990).

68. Jon C. Teaford, *The Rough Road to Renaissance: Urban Revitalization in America, 1940–1985* (Baltimore: Johns Hopkins University Press, 1990), chap. 2.

69. Thomas J. Sugrue, *The Origins of the Urban Crisis: Race and Inequality in Postwar Detroit* (Princeton: Princeton University Press, 1996).

70. Nicholas Lemann, *The Promised Land: The Great Black Migration and How It Changed America* (New York: Random House, 1991).

71. Sugrue, *The Origins of the Urban Crisis*.

72. Arnold R. Hirsch, *Making the Second Ghetto: Race and Housing in Chicago, 1940–1960* (New York: Cambridge University Press, 1983).

73. James Q. Wilson, ed., *Urban Renewal: The Record and the Controversy* (Cambridge, Mass.: MIT Press, 1966). In addition to Herbert Gans's influential article in the Wilson volume, "The Failure of Urban Renewal" (pp. 537–57), see also Gans's *The Urban Villagers: Life and Class in the Life of Italian Americans* (New York: Free Press, 1962).

74. Jose Luis Sert, *Can Our Cities Survive? An ABC of Urban Problems, Their Analysis, Their Solutions* (Cambridge, Mass.: Harvard University Press, 1942), gives the modernist case for urban renewal at the height of its confidence. Richard Plunz, *A History of Housing in New York City: Dwelling Type and Social Change in the American Metropolis* (New York: Columbia University Press, 1990), chaps. 6–8, gives perhaps the strongest design rebuttal.

75. Carl Abbott, "Five Strategies for Downtown: Policy and Planning since 1943," in Sies and Silver, eds., *Planning the Twentieth-Century American City,* pp. 404–27.

76. Howard Gillette, Jr., *Between Justice and Beauty: Race, Planning, and the Failure of Urban Policy in Washington, D.C.* (Baltimore: Johns Hopkins University Press, 1995), is an especially thoughtful and well-researched account of the failure of urban renewal in the context of Washington's long planning tradition.

77. June Manning Thomas, *Redevelopment and Race: Planning a Finer City in Postwar Detroit* (Baltimore: Johns Hopkins University Press, 1997).

78. To both visualize and comprehend these areas, see Camilo Jose Vergara, *The New American Ghetto* (New Brunswick, N.J.: Rutgers University Press, 1995).

79. John M. Findlay, *Magic Lands: Western Cityscapes and American Culture after 1940* (Berkeley: University of California Press, 1992); Joel Garreau, *Edge City: Life on the New Frontier* (New York: Doubleday, 1991).

80. For a telling account of the failures of urban politics and policy from the 1960s to the 1990s, see Fred Siegel, *The Future Once Happened Here: New York, D.C., L.A., and the Fate of America's Big Cities* (New York: Free Press, 1997).

81. Jane Jacobs, *The Death and Life of Great American Cities* (New York: Random House, 1961).

82. Jane Jacobs, *The Economy of Cities* (New York: Random House, 1969).

83. My view of Jacobs is indebted to Marshall Berman's brilliant discussion in *All That Is Solid Melts into Air* (New York: Simon & Schuster, 1982), chap. 5.

84. Bernard J. Frieden and Lynne B. Sagalyn, *Downtown, Inc.: How America Builds Cities* (Cambridge, Mass.: MIT Press, 1989). A more critical (and comparative) view of "planners as developers" is presented in Susan S. Fainstein, *The City Builders: Property, Politics, and Planning in London and New York* (Oxford: Blackwell, 1994); see also Hall, *Cities of Tomorrow,* chap. 11.

85. William R. Taylor, ed., *Inventing Times Square: Commerce and Culture at the Crossroads of the World* (New York: Russell Sage Foundation, 1991), addresses the cultural significance of Times Square when the square was still threatened by destructive redevelopment. Perhaps the most perceptive assessment of the redevelopment that actually took place is Marshall Berman, "Signs of the Times," *Dissent* 44 (Fall 1997), pp. 76–83.

86. *Neighborhood Works* 20: 1 (Jan./Feb. 1997), a special issue on empowerment zones.

87. Avis Carlotta Vidal, *Rebuilding Communities: A National Study of Urban Community-Development Corporations* (New York: New School for Social Research, 1992).

88. Andrea Oppenheimer Dean, "New Hope for Failed Housing," *Historic Preservation,* March/April 1998, pp. 52–9.

89. Ian L. McHarg, *Design with Nature* (Garden City, N.Y.: Doubleday/Natural History Press, 1969).

90. A book that captures the contemporary "urban conversation" at its best is Alexander Garvin, *The American City: What Works, What Doesn't* (New York: McGraw-Hill, 1996).

91. For the New Urbanism, see Peter Katz, *The New Urbanism: Toward an Architecture of Community* (New York: McGraw-Hill, 1994); Douglas Kelbaugh, *Common Place: Toward Neighborhood and Regional Design* (Seattle: University of Washington Press, 1997); and Alex Krieger, ed., with William Lennertz, *Andres Duany and Elizabeth Plater-Zyberk: Towns and Townmaking Principles* (New York: Rizzoli, 1991). For the debate surrounding the New Urbanism, see especially the articles in *Harvard Design Magazine,* Winter/Spring 1997, pp. 46–69.

92. Peter Calthorpe, *The Next American Metropolis: Ecology, Community, and the American Dream* (Princeton: Princeton Architectural Press, 1993).

93. For the crucial test case of the Los Angeles region, see William Fulton, *The Reluctant Metropolis: The Politics of Urban Growth in Los Angeles* (Point Arena, Calif.: Solano Press, 1997), especially impressive for Fulton's realistic grasp of the politics of regionalism. Two important collections of more theoretical work are Allan J. Scott and Edward J. Soja, eds., *The City: Los Angeles and Urban Theory at the End of the Twentieth Century* (Berkeley: University of California Press, 1996); and Rob Kling,

Spencer Olin, and Mark Poster, eds., *Postsuburban California: The Transformation of Orange County since World War II* (Berkeley: University of California Press, 1991).

94. Myron Orfield, *Metropolitics: A Regional Agenda for Community and Stability* (Washington, D.C.: Brookings Institution Press, 1997). This topic was forcefully raised by David Rusk in *Cities without Suburbs* (Washington, D.C.: Woodrow Wilson Center Press, 1993).

95. Tocqueville, *Democracy in America*, p. 66.

96. Neal R. Peirce, with Curtis W. Johnson and John Stuart Hall, *Citistates: How Urban America Can Prosper in a Competitive World* (Washington, D.C.: Seven Locks Press, 1993).

97. See, for example, New Jersey State Planning Commission, *State Development and Redevelopment Plan: Communities of Place* (1992) and its companion document, *Designing New Jersey* (1998).

PART ONE

TWO TRADITIONS

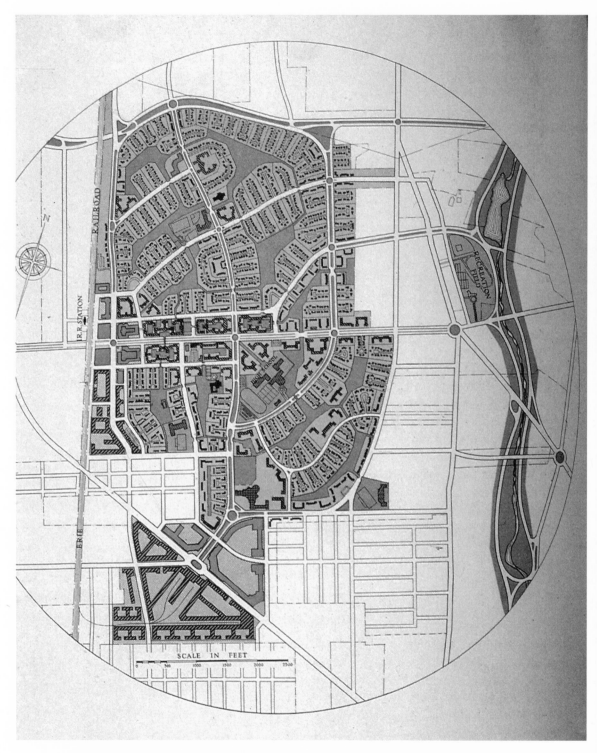

Radburn, Bergen County, New Jersey, 1929, designed by Clarence Stein and Henry Wright to be a prototype for the self-contained "New Towns" of 25,000 people with housing and industry, surrounded by a greenbelt, that would be the setting for a decentralized regionalist civilization. The only fragment of Radburn actually built is now engulfed in the sprawl of northern New Jersey. (From *Regional Plan of New York and Its Environs, vol. 2, Building the City,* 1931)

CHAPTER TWO

Holding the Middle Ground

■■
■■

JOHN L. THOMAS

One of the clarifying moments in the history of regionalism and regional planning in the United States in the twentieth century came early in the summer of 1932 in an acrimonious exchange in the pages of the *New Republic* between the regional theorist and critic Lewis Mumford and Thomas Adams, director of the monumental *Regional Plan of New York and Environs,* the tenth and final volume of which had recently appeared and whose recommendations Mumford dismissed as "a badly conceived pudding." Funded by the Russell Sage Foundation, the collaborative effort of dozens of city planners, economists, statisticians, and engineers, Adams's massive report had been a decade in the making. Adams himself was a widely known and highly respected urban planner with credentials acquired in England in the garden-city movement and, more recently, as town-planning adviser to Canada's Commission of Conservation. Adams's was an instrumentalist vision wedded to a sanguine political pragmatism, and it dominated the work of his collaborators. "There is nothing to be gained by conceiving the impossible," he warned as though to deflect the thrusts of critics like Mumford. In defending his monumental plan he declared the basic issue a simple one: "whether we stand still and talk ideals or move forward and get as much realization of our ideals as possible in a necessarily imperfect society, capable of only imperfect solutions of its problems."

From the outset Adams's philosophy of half-a-loaf had dictated a series of working assumptions, the first of which was the director's insistence that "we cannot overcome the economic forces that make cities as large as New York." Entirely reliable projections, Adams and his metropolitanists argued, placed the population of New York City in 1965 at the twenty-million mark, and this estimate necessitated some kind of "recentralization" of the metropolis, which would provide "concentration without congestion" and at the same time encourage controlled expansion into a carefully delineated metropolitan middle ground. The inner urban core would be connected to the city's suburban hinterland with lines of highway routes running like spokes on a wheel out to successive beltways along a receding periphery from Bridgeport to Newburgh to Far Hills and Asbury Park. Here in a neatly executed diagrammatic scheme was *one* representation of the region as a specifically delimited area of metropolitan influence and economic and cultural reach (figs. 16, 17).

The second major assumption that Adams and his staff made rested on their reading of the history of New York and similar large cities of the nation. "In the American city," the metropolitanists pointed out, "the disposal of lots to individuals with liberty to make the best use of them for private purposes was the governing factor in development." It would remain so in the future. Some restrictions on individual property rights, of course, were wholly desirable but "no further than it is reasonable to expect public opinion to go, or government to authorize in the future." To dream of massive alterations in the American political and economic structure was romantic folly. Mumford's alternative, outlined in his attack on the *Plan of New York,* was a pipe dream, Adams scoffed, which "would require the combined power of the President, Congress and state legislatures to bring about." Better to accept the limitations imposed by the real world.

Adams's chief adversary and the self-appointed custodian of an alternative definition of the regional middle ground was Mumford, who undertook in the pages of the *New Republic* to demolish the foundations of the *Plan of New York.* Mumford had served as leader of the "Barbarian Invaders"—as his colleague the land planner Benton MacKaye styled the regionalist insurgents—who throughout the 1920s had launched attacks

on the metropolitanists from their conceptual fastnesses up the Hudson. Now Mumford proceeded to repeat his warning: a genuine regional plan was not merely a technique or the property of a particular profession but instead "a mode of thinking and a method of procedure" which pointed toward "the reinvigoration and rehabilitation" of whole regions extending from the metropolis itself out through the rising countryside to wilderness at the top of valley sections. To illustrate their "visualization" (as MacKaye called it in distinguishing their plan from the geometrical precision of the metropolitanists' myriad maps) Mumford and his fellow members of the tiny Regional Planning Association of America (RPAA) had countered with their own relief model of the state of New York with L-shaped *plains* stretching up the Hudson and out across the Mohawk Valley filled with market gardens and orchards, small factories and medium-sized cities; *plateaus* as table-land for dairy and subsistence farming; and *highlands* with forest and water reserves up in the Adirondacks. At the bottom of the valley-section region and inextricably joined to it lay New York City in dire need, not of Adams's "reconcentration," but of a planned and orderly dispersal and diversification in a "fourth migration" out of the metropolis and into the regional middle ground (fig. 19).

Mumford's "fourth migration" was the culminating act in his capsule history of the wanderings of generations of Americans across their land. The first great migration in his saga involved the conquest of the continent, beginning in the seventeenth century and sweeping westward through successive frontiers. The symbolic vehicle of this initial migration was the covered wagon, carrying restless and wasteful pioneers across the continent in the course of three centuries. The second great migration, set in motion by the Industrial Revolution and overlapping with its predecessor, proceeded out of the now-settled countryside along canals and railroad lines into factory towns, mill cities, and railhead centers filled with ramshackle housing, crowded factories, polluted rivers, and cultural poverty. The motive behind a succeeding third migration into the metropolis, according to Mumford, was financial power concentrated in banks, the stock market, and insurance companies, and comprising altogether an empire of paper values. This exodus out of the provinces and across the middle ground into cities had drained natural regions of both people and money and was accompanied by growing inequality and deepening cultural impoverishment. By the 1920s, however, Mumford could discern the makings of a fourth migration out of the imperial city—*tyrannopolis*—made possible by the automobile and other technological innovations that functioned as distributing agencies in dispersing urban families into outlying suburbia in search of the good life.

The onset of the fourth migration provided Mumford with his primary objection to Adams's *Plan of New York*. The irreversible momentum provided by the automobile and the rapid electrification of the American hinterland meant, first of all, that to plan for reconcentrating city centers with skyscrapers, speculative housing, overcrowding, and pollution was an act of supreme foolishness. Nor were suburban bedroom towns randomly distributed along the rim of the burgeoning metropolis a workable or desirable solution to urban congestion. "Transitory suburban dormitories which we wistfully call garden cities are no substitute. . . ." Finally, Mumford pointed to the principal fallacy of the metropolitan regionalists: their insistence that the spatial suburban ring was a limited and bounded area waiting to be filled up at the whim of metropolitan planners. Such geometrically defined areas, Mumford argued, were abstractions unknown to nature: "geography wipes away the notion of defi-

nite boundary lines as anything but a coarse practical expedient." Real regions, he added, rested on a "natural basis."

Mumford extended his conceptual grasp of regional planning in a talk before the Roundtable on Regionalism held at the University of Virginia the same week that Adams's testy reply to his two-part article appeared in the *New Republic*. Here Mumford was even more adamant in insisting on the distinction between truly regional and merely metropolitan planning. "The first different factor in regional planning," he told an audience that included Nashville Agrarians and Howard Odum's regionalist contingent from Chapel Hill, "is that it includes cities, villages, and permanent rural areas, considered as part of the regional complex. While metropolitan planning regards the surrounding open country as doomed to be swallowed up in the inevitable spread and increase of population, the regional planner seeks to preserve the balance between the agricultural and the primeval background and the urban environment." Precisely here, he continued, was where metropolitanism, a fancy word for land-skinning, went wrong. "In the interests of urban growth, rising land values, opportunities for financial killings, it ignores the natural capacities of site and soil, and continues to spread a uniform urban layer over the countryside." True regional planning, on the other hand, began not arbitrarily with the city as a unit in itself, but naturally with the region viewed as a whole.

The clash between Mumford and Adams signaled a turning point in the history of American regionalism—a conceptual parting of the ways with Adams and a whole cadre of younger planners and theorists moving steadily toward a theoretical and technocratic approach to planning that stressed structure and function, systems and models as the tools of a universal science transcending specific regions. They would come to dominate regional planning in the half-century following World War II. Mumford's route carried him back into the nineteenth century and concerns about particular places and specific regions that encouraged what one might call a "diversitarian" method for dealing with the modern world. Adams angrily dismissed Mumford as an "esthete-sociologist who has a religion that is based on high ideals but is unworkable." Mumford scored Adams and his colleagues for just this disregard for a civic religion based on "the life-needs and spiritual impulses that bring men together in groups." That civic religion, Mumford was convinced, originated and now could only be nurtured in a middle ground that was the precise opposite of a metropolitan wasteland.[1]

Visualizing the Middle Ground

The middle ground, as Lewis Mumford's generation of regionalist critics and planners understood it, was first of all a specific place, an actual locale on the pathway to modernization halfway between the provinces and the metropolis. Patrick Geddes, Mumford's mentor and one of the great urban planners of the early twentieth century, defined the middle ground with autobiographical precision in recalling his own Mount Tabor Cottage on Kinnoul Hill above Perth in Scotland, halfway between civilization below and wilderness above. Downhill the River Tay wound through rich farmland, pointing south to the old kingdom of Fife and open water beyond. Upstream beneath Geddes's hill lay the Fair City of Perth with steeples, factory chimneys, winding streets, and the academy where the boy went to school. Above the cottage stood the summit of the 1700-foot Kinnoul Hill beyond the quarry and across the wild moor up through stands of beech, birch, and fir to the summit and the

sheer drop to the river. Here was an entire geological system that Geddes would call the "valley section"—the elemental unit of ecological study with high mountain tracts, pastoral hillsides, hamlets and villages dotting the descending terrain, farmland surrounding the market towns, and finally the great city where the river meets the sea.[2]

Three-quarters of a century later the Scottish regional planner and landscape architect Ian McHarg described his own middle ground above Glasgow on the west coast of Scotland. In his *Design with Nature* (1969), which he dedicated to Lewis Mumford, McHarg recounts a childhood and adolescence lived "squarely between two diametrically different environments," strung between the poles of man and nature. Ten miles below his home on the middle ground lay Glasgow, "one of the most implacable testaments to the city of toil in all of Christendom, a memorial to an inordinate capacity to create ugliness, a sandstone excretion cemented in smoke and grime." Lit by the perpetual flames of the blast furnaces here was a Turner fantasy made real. Glasgow was a no-place, an endless road leading through miles of dreary tenements to the mills—"despondent, dreary beyond description, grimy, gritty, squalid, enduringly ugly and dispiriting."

The young McHarg's alternate route, "learned incrementally," led upward through wheat fields and pastures filled with Clydesdales and Ayrshire cows to the Black Woods and clay drumlins, meadows and marshes. "Further yet was Craigallion Loch and the Firepot where hikers and climbers met, the Devil's Pulpit and the Pots of Gartness where salmon leapt, as far from my home as Glasgow was. Beyond lay Balmaha and Loch Lomond and then, much later in adolescence, Glencoe and Loch Rannoch, Lismore and Mull, Staffa and Iona, the Western Isles." In the middle ground places owned names.

Benton MacKaye, the American cousin in

this Scottish connection, completes the transplantation of the spatial concept of the middle ground. MacKaye, a forester turned ecological planner, was a follower of Patrick Geddes, a colleague of Lewis Mumford, and a forerunner of Ian McHarg. MacKaye grew up at the turn of the nineteenth century in the hill-country town of Shirley Center, Massachusetts. The center of village life was the nearby commons, a triangular green dominated by the meetinghouse with its belfry, which the young man likened to the sun at the center of the solar system, an adjoining cemetery filled with headstones dating back to the early eighteenth century, a town hall and clapboarded schoolhouse.[3] Over a nearby ridge and through thick alder growths ran the Nashua River in a setting Thoreau had revealed a half-century earlier. "A town is saved," wrote Thoreau, "not more by the righteous men in it than by the woods and swamps that surround it." MacKaye agreed: "The basic geographic unit of organic human society is the single town of definite physical limits and integrity." Shirley Center was one of those units, a pastoral waystation between Boston and the Berkshires and a staging area for the young man's frequent "expeditions" undertaken with notebook in hand. The vantage point for his many "visualizations" was nearby Hunting Hill, which he properly named a drumlin, pointing across Mulpas Brook in the foreground out to wilderness at the end of the state and, in the other direction, to the already encroaching suburban blight.

All of the first-generation American regionalists were similar postfrontier children for whom the example of Scotland extending back to the mid-nineteenth century and the widely read geologist-ethnographer Hugh Miller was particularly instructive. Howard Odum grew up in the Georgia hamlet of Bethlehem, many of whose customs and "folkways," as he would call them, he carried to Chapel Hill and applied to his project in Southern regionalism. Odum's early students were likewise products of the American middle ground: Rupert Vance from a cotton-crop crossroads in Arkansas, Arthur Raper from a similar tobacco town in Davidson County, North Carolina. The list follows the frontier west. Nashville Agrarian Donald Davidson from transplanted Highland stock to the mountains of eastern Tennessee lovingly recalled in poetry and prose. Herman Clarence Nixon, whose evocative *Possum Trot* was drawn from memories of an Alabama village boyhood. Walter Prescott Webb out of hardscrabble Texas hill country via the University of Chicago to Austin. Mari Sandoz leaving Sandhill country in Nebraska for Lincoln with vivid memories of Plains Indians, blinding snowstorms, and greedy land sharks. Bernard DeVoto, who discovered Sandoz's *Old Jules,* growing up "in-between" the grimy railhead town of Ogden and the towering Wasatch range above. Displaced persons all, out of the provinces and into the metropolis carrying recollections of place and inherited ways.

Thus the middle ground was also a temporal construct for the early regionalists. Miller originally defined it as comprising "districts peopled by men who have not reached the medium line" dividing premodern and modern worlds. From one perspective the middle ground appears to hold for its inhabitants all of the traditions and continuities of localism and provincialism, what D. H. Lawrence called the "spirit of place." This was the way Geddes memorialized Perth—as the scene of ancient conflicts between Highlanders and Lowlanders, and then between Scottish defenders of the Stuarts and Cromwellian invaders. Here along the dividing line myth abounds: stories of the thirty champions of Clan Chattan, of Sir Walter Scott's Fair Maid of Perth, of the outlaw Highland chief hiding yet in the forest. Viewed from the other side of the developmental line, however, middle-ground people appear to be displaced persons, "the solitary fast-sinking remnants of a traditional provincial culture" now confronting modern, energetic, mobile bourgeois invaders.

The idea of a median line between "primitivism" and "civilization" dated from the Scottish Enlightenment and the theorists Adam Smith, Dugald Stewart, and Adam Ferguson, who toyed with conjectural history—speculative comparisons designed to explain uneven rates of economic and cultural development in European "cultures" and non-European "primitive" societies and then possibly to account for Europe's own progression from "barbarism" to modernity. The conjectural historians sought to construct a "mechanics of transition" with a temporal map that would locate and perpetuate the middle ground as that point lying between under-development and over-refinement. The American variant of this utopian concept was the myth of the garden, the fervent hope that as a chosen people Americans might "stop time" at the precise meeting place of the two stages of development, preserving the innocence and simplicity of the pastoral stage yet enjoying all the amenities supplied by the industrial.[4]

Most important, therefore, was the notion of the middle ground as a source of alternative values with which regionalists on both sides of the Atlantic fashioned their reform program. Here again, Geddes pointed out the path and led the way in calling for the preservation of "the remains of hills and moorlands between rapidly growing cities and conurbations of modern industrial regions" so as to provide access to nature, recreation, and a means of escape from the urban wasteland. Geddes bypassed traditionally designed urban parks, "each with its ring-fence jealously keeping it apart from the vulgar world" and called for linear greenways and vest-pocket neighborhood enclaves as escapes from "super-Slums." "Some

day . . . ," he prophesied, "when its residents have become disenchanted with their isolated gentility, from their obsession with private property in these pitiable back-yard catwalks, and are again becoming citizens, these paltry little greens will be cheaply and simply thrown together into one worthy garden, with walks for the elders, flower borders, grass spaces and playcourts for the children, and with one central or lateral building, if need be, for a washing-house and drying-room together; with the tenement-backs orielled, balconied, ivied, embowered; with mews and garages concentrated at a few strategic centers." Such urban renovation along middle-ground lines should be the work of all classes cooperating in the spirit of civic responsibility that would prevent recourse to strikes and lockouts, fights over wages and profits. Civic education would thus foster a public movement crossing class lines and linking urban environments with their surrounding regions. While politicians continued to play with abstractions ("abstract politics has long raised them far above sharing the petty local interests of us city improvers or town planners, who occupy our minds with concrete trifles like homes and gardens, [and] pleasanter streets," Geddes commented with elaborate irony), field surveys, neighborhood committees, and energetic volunteers would do the actual work of renovating the cities. "We have got beyond the abstract sociology of the schools—Positivist, Socialist, or other—with their vague discussions of 'Society' and its 'Members' since we have reached the definite conception in which all these schools have been lacking—that of Cities and Citizens."[5]

MacKaye applied the same philosophy of communal responsibility and local voluntarism in the creation of the Appalachian Trail as he urged small groups of local citizens to put through a section of trail in their own neighborhoods. MacKaye called his new bar-

barians to come build "Utopia" and hold it against the incursions of the metropolitanists. "It matters little," he insisted, "whether the various sections be State lands, Federal, or whether you spell them 'Park' or 'Forest,'" just so long as all the lands were designated "public" and managed by the people acting together to protect their indigenous environment.

And in explaining the benefits accruing from his own ecological view of urban and regional planning, McHarg echoed these pleas for middle-ground values. Calling for the use of "we" as a substitute for the "I-it" pairing, McHarg urged the expunging of the biblical injunction to go forth and conquer nature. Instead, "the economic value system must be expanded into a relative system encompassing all biophysical processes and human aspirations." Law must be adapted to ecological imperatives, and science must concentrate less on therapy and more on health. Industry and commerce should be held strictly accountable. "But it is in education that the greatest benefits lie. Here separatism rules, yet integration is the quest. This ecology offers: the science of the relations of organism and the environment, integrative of science, humanities and the arts—a context for studies of man and the environment."[6]

Thus the American middle ground came to be marked by a distinct political economy and cultural outlook consisting of beliefs in a balanced society of small producers, an artisanal lifestyle, folk culture, the indigenous landscape, "natural" cooperation and communalism, and the powers of civic education. This complex of values mandated a response to capitalist consolidation that rejected Marxism and the premise of class warfare for the essentially counterrevolutionary strategy of diffusion and diversification combined in what regionalists tended to think of as a "natural socialism."

The two intellectual godfathers of Mum-ford's generation of regionalists, sometimes acknowledged, sometimes not, were the Harvard colleagues philosopher Josiah Royce and historian Frederick Jackson Turner. Royce employed a postfrontier California upbringing in fashioning his doctrine of provincialism as a defense against the homogenizing and leveling tendencies of modern mass society. The strength of the American province, in his view, rested on a tradition of localism and voluntary association in small communities of independent but naturally cooperative citizens marshaled against the invading forces of an unreflective mass mind. In this sense Royce was reinvigorating the Jeffersonian ideal of the republican community and civic virtue as the creed with which to join locality, province, and nation together in a network of mutually sustaining loyalties. Such an informed provincialism, Royce was convinced, could adjudicate and hopefully moderate the increasing claims of the national state, and at the same time foster an appreciation of ecological as well as cultural diversity with an ethic that would require the intelligent use of the American land and its resources.

With his colleague's assessment, which he quoted, Turner agreed. Turner drew on his own postfrontier heritage in Portage, Wisconsin, in providing Royce's philosophy of provincialism with a historical dimension and a national meaning. American history, Turner explained in an ongoing series of interpretive essays, begins with unfenced land, a vast unsettled tract lying beyond the immediate reach of successive settlements as they move across the continent. This open quarter, however, is rapidly filled with an inpouring of sequential waves of explorers, trappers, settlers, and developers—agents all of "continental conquest," acquiring in the process those individualist, democratic, self-reliant ways that, Turner argued, "powerfully affect" the settled East and Europe.

Out of this revitalizing contact with new land and the opportunities it offers to adventurous Americans, according to Turner, comes a second phase in his linear model of national development—the rise of the self-conscious section. Turner identified his regions—New England, the Middle States, Southeast, Southwest, Great Plains, Mountain States, and Pacific Coast—by discovering in each "its own rival interests" that foster a "sectionalism of material interest" but also an aggressive cultural sectionalism, "a real consciousness of sectional solidarity" setting it at odds with other, more settled parts of the country. The Civil War Turner considered simply the most "drastic" and "tragic" of sectional struggles between North and South for control of the West in "a contest for empire." Appomattox closes this second chapter in Turner's saga of American development, and with the end of Reconstruction a decade later the direction of new developmental forces are already clear: toward a powerful national state, a vigorous corporate capitalism, the growth of the metropolis, and the emergence of a consolidating consumer culture. The age of defensive sectionalism is over.

The twentieth century, Turner agreed with Royce, could replace a shattered sectionalism with a vibrant regional society and culture. Turner continued to use the word "section," which he employed interchangeably with Royce's "province," in explaining its cultural significance. "There is a sense in which sectionalism is inevitable and desirable," he insisted in calling for a new "sectional geography" based on "geographic regions," a science that would take into account political behavior, social opinion, and cultural grammar, as well as material interests. He admitted that there was some slight disposition on the part of various regions to consider themselves as synonymous with the whole nation, but even more threat-ening was the encroaching power of an imperial industrial culture. This could be thwarted only by "the vigorous development of a highly organized provincial life to serve as a check upon the mob psychology on a national scale, and to furnish that variety which is essential to vital growth and originality."

With an apprehension that Mumford and his regionalist collaborators quickly came to share Turner formulated a program of preservation that was ecological as well as cultural. "Now we are told by high authority," he warned early in the century, "that we shall feel the pinch of timber shortage in less than fifteen years. The free lands are no longer free; the boundless resources are no longer boundless." Here precisely lay the challenge to twentieth-century regionalists: to discover and perfect the techniques for conserving and stabilizing American life. Diversification and dispersal in order to build "restraints upon a deadly uniformity . . . breakwaters against overwhelming surges of national emotion . . . fields for experiment in the growth of different types of society, political institutions, and ideals."[7]

This was the legacy that Mumford and his regionalist cohort received from Geddes, Royce, and Turner and that informed all their efforts in the years between the two world wars—from Radburn and Sunnyside to the Greenbelt communities; from Lewis Gray's soil-conservation schemes to attempts at tenant-farmer cooperatives; from the "demonstrations" of the TVA to documentation by the FSA; from collections of folklore and folksay to Paul Robeson's rendition of "Ballad for Americans." Lewis Mumford's critical eye remained fixed on New York City and the schemes of Thomas Adams and his metropolitan cadre for expanding its reach. Insisting that the hope of New York and all major cities lay outside themselves, Mumford asked readers to "lift [their] eyes for a moment" and look beyond Broadway and 42nd Street and put the city into proper focus. "Forests in the hill-counties, water-power in the mid-state valleys, farmland in Connecticut, cran-berry bogs in New Jersey": the real challenge to regional planners, he repeated, was not to bring the middle landscape under deadening metropolitan influence and control, but to show "how the population and civic facilities can be distributed so as to promote and stim-ulate a vivid, creative life throughout the whole region." The American impulse for this fuller life propelling city-dwellers out into suburbia was understandable, perhaps commendable, but it was also uninformed and uncomprehending. People must be taught that their urge for a better life is pro-ceeding apace with an industrial counterrev-olution. Ever since the onset of the original Industrial Revolution American business has been piling up plants and factories in cities, concentrating wealth at the top of the hierar-chy while packing urban centers with badly paid workers. But now another industrial revolution promises to spread income as it decentralizes the economy. "Regional plan-ning is an attempt to turn industrial decen-tralization—the effort to make the industrial mechanism work better—to permanent so-cial uses" in a "New Conservation." End waste, he urged, save energy, and recover for the people all of that middle ground lying be-tween the junctions and terminal points of the nation's railroads and highways.

In pointing to the "land-in-between" the interurban highway interchanges and by-passes that connected cities to their sur-rounding regions Mumford touched directly on the central issue dividing his alternative scheme from that of Adams and a succeeding generation of metropolitan regionalists with whom the immediate future of planning would lie.

It was not Mumford but his friend and colleague MacKaye who provided the clear-est picture and made the most sweeping pro-posals for managing the regions of America. MacKaye's regional model was his native New England, with Shirley Center his point of departure for what in a book by that title he called "the new exploration." The crusty MacKaye—"old Benton," Mumford called him in likening him to a storybook Yankee—had received a degree in forestry from Har-vard in 1905 and joined Gifford Pinchot's Forest Service, serving his apprenticeship sur-veying and mapping the forest cover of New Hampshire's White Mountains. During a decade of government service in Washington as well as in the field MacKaye came to in-terpret the new concept of "conservation" as managing land for people as well as for tim-ber companies and profits. Forests and wa-tersheds linked individuals with primal na-ture, he realized, but they also concerned their communities and the kind of life and culture they enjoyed collectively. The quality of American life thus involved more than cut-capacities and timber-yields. Accordingly, in the early 1920s MacKaye turned to perfect-ing the project that would occupy him for the rest of his life—the plan for a "folkland" wilderness trail running the Appalachian ridge from Maine to Georgia. From the out-set he envisioned his Appalachian Trail as a complete network of interrelated natural sys-tems—"a thing to grow and be developed apart from our more *commercial* develop-ment." In a widely read article, "An Ap-palachian Trail: Project in Regional Plan-ning" (1921), he proposed the creation of a series of linked "neutral zones" comprising a "Backbone Openway" and offering all Americans an "equal opportunity for real life" as well as a way of visualizing the inter-connectedness of all natural phenomena. Be-neath the Appalachian ridge lay footlands ready for communal farms and recreation camps. Above them loomed the trail itself, "a path of exploration," he wrote, "leading to the mysteries of the land and sky inhabited by primal life dating from the verdant slime of the first pools of water." Here along the top was the climax of MacKaye's ecological drama—"the primal story of Planet Earth—its life, its structure, and its oneness" (fig. 19).

But it was in his own personal "realm of the living" in his dilapidated cottage looking out on Shirley Center that MacKaye began to assemble his various "visualizations" into a coherent regional plan. "I have carved out a little region in that realm," he reported to Mumford. "It consists of the territory around about Shirley Center. This little region embraces the fundamental environments (as I conceive them) which are necessary for man's full development. These are the primeval, the rural (the "colonial" in New England), and the urban. The primeval is represented by a little range of mountains—the Wapack Range. The colonial is represented by several "hill villages," among which is Shirley Center. The urban is represented by Fitchburg (of 40,000), and Boston is near by. Each environment, I point out, would be kept intact, developed as a basic human resource in itself." Yet each of these three environments, MacKaye warns, is threatened by the spread of a fourth "diseased environment"—the "metropolitan" oozing out of the center city and flooding the middle ground. The task of the regional planner, he now saw clearly, was to maintain the integrity of each segment of the New England (and by extension the American) landscape. As he weighed his options MacKaye saw his plan as consisting of three discrete but complementary tasks: "the *preservation* of the primeval; the *restoration* of the colonial; and the salvaging (some day) of the true urban."[8]

MacKaye's *The New Exploration: A Philosophy of Regional Planning* (1928) is a planner's *enchiridion,* a manual that elaborates on the sketch he offered to Mumford. The argument of the book is straightforward and simple: the old explorers were freeboot-ers and adventurers out for themselves; the new explorers are engineers, economists, landscape designers, all taking their cues from the regional planner who, in the spirit of Geddes, serves as a "composite mind." Primeval America of the pre-Columbian epoch still lies within the reach of the ecological imagination, MacKaye argues, and is still there to be preserved. Monadnock, Aroostook, Katahdin—"we spell these names and place them on our maps. We cleave to them as symbols. . . . We visualize the *name.* Our job now, in the new exploration, is to visualize the *thing.*" To look out across New England is to see in the distance rocky pastures, occasional outcroppings, and stands of fir and spruce, all reminding us of an "indefinite past" imaged in the campfire.

The iconographic center of the nearer rural environment is the village common, the nucleus of the vernacular community arranged "in all the structural symmetry of a starfish." The middle ground encircling the hill village boasts its own artisanal political economy with cultivated fields, sheep and cattle pastures, grist and saw mills supporting a participatory culture with "deeply embedded roots."

The genuine *cosmopolitan* environment—as distinguished from the pseudo*metropolitan*—is also essential to a healthy regional culture, for it is in essence simply the "village grown up," its institutions expanded and intensified—the town hall to domed state house, the schoolhouse to university, the country store to urban mart.

All three of these natural communities—the primeval, the rural, and the urban—are threatened by a metropolitan flood that has already swamped the city center and is now overflowing the middle ground with a kind of commercial sewage. This metropolitan sludge, the leavings of countless developers, will soon level both rural and primeval landscapes. "The invasion would take its start from the central community. Its movement here as elsewhere we may liken to a glacier. It is spreading, unthinking, ruthless. Its substance consists of tenements, bungalows, stores, factories, billboards, filling-stations, eating stands, and other structures whose individual hideousness and collective haphazardness present that unmistakable environment which we class the 'slum.' Not the slum of poverty, but the slum of commerce." With the coming triumph of the metropolitan invaders, MacKaye predicts, New England and then the United States will have become "a world without a country."

The urgent task of the regional planner, accordingly, is to devise a strategy for first checking and then, hopefully, reversing and mopping up the metropolitan flow. MacKaye's scheme, though quickly distorted and misapplied by developers, was an ingenious one. Since metropolitanism advances along the several highways radiating out from the metropolis, he insisted, it is precisely here on its outskirts that it must be checked by what he first called the "intertown" and then in an improvement, the "townless highway" encircling the city and serving at the same time as a barrier, "dike," or "levee" to hold back the spillage from suburbia. The central feature of MacKaye's containment strategy, then, was a mobile dam plugging the "thousand ruptured reservoirs" of suburban development and turning the flood of people back into the center city where a genuine cosmopolitan culture could be had. All along these throughways, MacKaye's maps indicated, lay wide strips of undeveloped public land to serve as free zones for the people, closed to development and reserved for parks. These "open ways," as he termed them, together with the public land that flanked and cut across them provide the barricades. At these and other crucial points the regional planner simply helps nature recover and hold the middle ground and primeval territory by first surveying and then

securing havens from commercial and industrial expansion: "Mountain crestline and summits (such as the Mt. Holyoke range). Escarpment, or steep slope from a lowland to upland (as the west side of Hoosac Mountain). Canyon, or steep valley along a stream (the Deerfield River). River Bottom, or level valley along a stream (Ipswich River). Swamp (the Great Cedar Swamp and others), Beach (wherever sufficiently unsettled)."[9] Despite the violence done to his ideas and the damage to his regional plan by metropolitan developers who turned his "townless highway" into Massachusetts's Route 128, MacKaye left an ecological inheritance for late-twentieth-century environmentalists who are busy picking up where he left off.

The Transformation of America's Middle Ground

If the alternative regionalists, following Mumford's directives, searched the nineteenth century for a usable past, so too did the metropolitan planners who discovered the empirical data and a rudimentary piece of theory to explain the rapid growth of what they now called "Standard Metropolitan Areas." The basic concept of metropolitan regionalism, complete with diagram, was presented early in the nineteenth century in a theory of agricultural markets by the Prussian economist J. H. von Thünen, whose formulations in *The Isolated State* (1825) provided would-be planners with the first abstract model of the regional city based on location theory. Von Thünen measured the regional reach of the metropolitan center in terms of agricultural markets and the process of exchange of goods between city and country, by drawing a series of concentric circles radiating out from the core and delineating zones of dwindling influence out to the periphery where transportation costs exceeded hopes of profit. The beauty of this early ex- ample of what came to be called "location theory" lay in the geometric starkness with which von Thünen mapped the middle ground surrounding his urban model. An- other notable feature of his model was the dy- namism inherent in it, which predicted change and suggested ways to accommodate the shifting forces of trade and the two-way passage of people across the middle ground between metropolis and periphery. Turner's account of American development was linear and sequential, proceeding in time, direction, intensity, and democratic effect from un- fenced land inward toward settled areas in a predictable pattern of revitalizing activity. Von Thünen's model, acquiring statistics and system as the century wore on, and employ- ing new combinations of demography, com- munications theory, and commercial data, would eventually turn Turner's exceptionalist theory of American development inside out.

In fact, entrepreneurially minded Ameri- cans in the Age of Jackson scarcely needed theoretical justification for their wheeling and dealing in a rapidly expanding inland trade. The shape and social composition of New England's middle ground, for example, began to change immediately following the American Revolution, as its native sons quickly discovered the possibilities of a lu- crative internal trade. Concord, Massachu- setts, is a case in point: fathers soon ran out of land to leave to their sons, and many of the young generation picked up and headed west, first out to the Berkshires, then on to New York's "Burned-Over District," and ulti- mately into the Ohio Valley and Old North- west. Meanwhile a brisk trade sprang up and fingered out along new turnpikes and canals as mercantile houses in seaboard cities like Boston, Providence, New London, and Ports- mouth dispatched commission agents and set up crossroads emporiums. Even before the cotton-mill towns began to mushroom along

the Merrimack, Blackstone, and Kennebec Rivers, there began a flow of goods and peo- ple back and forth, up and down inland wa- terways and turnpikes, changing the social contours of the middle ground irrevocably. By the middle of the fifth decade of the nine- teenth century the railroad had announced it- self as the common carrier of the future, as Thoreau noted apprehensively, emptying out many an inland town and filling it up again with new arrivals. Watching this unsettling process from his temporary haven at Walden Pond, Thoreau packed the meaning of this demographic shift into a compact image: "The whistle of the locomotive penetrates my woods summer and winter, sounding like the scream of a hawk sailing over some farmer's yard, informing me that many restless city merchants are arriving within the circle of this town."

By the third quarter of the nineteenth century all of the major cities of the United States were establishing tributary areas. Chicago affords a prime example, competing with and ultimately besting St. Louis, Kansas City, Milwaukee, and Minneapolis with ad- vertising, mammoth commercial houses, rate wars, board-of-trade battles, and bids for cheap immigrant labor, and quickly acquir- ing national recognition as the Midwest's gateway city. Other cities soon followed Chicago's lead. "By every peaceful means," reported the economic historian N. S. B. Gras in the early 1920s, "each of these cities had endeavored to outdo its rivals, by construct- ing highways, canals, and railroads . . . by es- tablishing transatlantic lines for freight and passengers and by setting as low land and wa- ter rates . . . as could be secured."[10]

By the end of the century all of the major American cities were busy widening their tributaries and extending their zones of influence. Gathering momentum in the three decades after 1900, the urbanization of America proceeded rapidly, drawing newcomers off the land and across the water and at the same time sending middle-class migrants out into new suburban areas. By 1950 the category "urban" was in need of redefinition as all places with more than 2,500 inhabitants but also the densely settled fringes of cities over 50,000 in population. A comparison of what were now called "Standard Metropolitan Areas" (SMAs) in 1900 and 1950 tells the story: a total of 52 in 1900 had tripled to some 168 half a century later. In 1950, 56 percent of the American people lived in SMAs, which covered 7.1 percent of the national land area. It was precisely the expansion of these new metropolitan domains that was the concern of Lewis Mumford and Adams as cities ballooned and perimeters expanded.

Just as Adams was undertaking his survey of New York City and its environs, another community of scholars, the so-called ecological school at the University of Chicago under the direction of sociologist Robert Park, was busy examining the city of Chicago. The Chicago school of regional analysis sought to comprehend and then describe with greater precision both the spatial and the social factors in regionalization. Park in particular was concerned with what he termed the "theoretical aspect of regionalism" with the hope of discovering the underlying principle of balance and ecological order inside an economic system of competitive individualism. Park and Adams thus made similar assumptions as to the future of American capitalism, assumptions Mumford and the regionalist cadre were determined to challenge and perhaps overturn.

It was Park's colleague at the University of Chicago, R. D. McKenzie, in *The Metropolitan Community* (1933), published a year after the completion of Adams's report, who provided the clearest description of metropolitan regionalism in action and predicted its future course with startling accuracy. "The population of the United States," McKenzie declared at the outset, "is tending to concentrate more and more in large regional aggregates. In every such aggregate, the population tends to subdivide and become multinucleated in a complex of centers that are economically integrated into a larger unity." Pointing out, as Adams had before him, that these metropolitan regions cut across local, county, and state lines, McKenzie dismissed all normative factors in treating the region, as he said, primarily as a "functional entity" that extends "geographically as far as the city exerts a dominant influence." Here was the Americanization of European location theory: the modern metropolitan region is the product of the transformative effects of capitalist consolidation and urban marketing along with the transportation-communication network that commerce engenders. The new region, unlike the inherited one, consists of centers, routes, and rims as in von Thünen's original circular diagram or is hexagonal as in Walter Cristaller's intricate geometry. As McKenzie put it, "smaller cities and towns tend to group themselves around larger ones somewhat as planets group themselves around a sun." McKenzie proceeded to describe this new solar system as the creation of the gravitational force of financial services, merchandizing, and light manufacturing pulling the American middle classes out of the central city and into the new middle ground.

Projecting his findings into the future, McKenzie predicted the disappearance of the old middle ground filled with places, local people, and their history as metropolitanism continued to erase the indigenous landscape and cancel ethno-cultural differences. As intensive suburbanization sweeps westward from its Eastern and Midwestern bases, "the various indices of maturation presented . . . definitely support the hypothesis that the different regions of the country are tending to become more nearly uniform in economic and cultural characteristics." With newly built zones of suburban settlement in the South and Southwest, McKenzie concluded, future regional supercommunities would come to look more and more alike in economic and social structure.

Thus viewed from the perspective of the twentieth-century metropolis, the old middle ground appeared less like Turner's seedbed of democracy and more like the captive colony of an imperial power moving in on neighboring rivals and vying for control of larger and larger amounts of territory. With the ongoing homogenization of the United States, McKenzie concluded, inherited regional distinctions—vernacular culture and folk memory—would continue to fade. New and tighter intraregional "bonds of common interests," primarily financial, would continue to redefine the region as essentially a "commercial province" with colonizing ambitions. Already, McKenzie noted in the early 1930s, "We can in fact draw a map tentatively allotting the entire territory of the continental United States to a comparatively small number of larger cities."

Employing McKenzie's findings and predictions, a student of metropolitan regionalism could foresee a much less appealing set of consequences of undirected decentralization: unregulated land use all along the city's peripheries; strip malls and scraggly commercial centers; sprawling spec-built suburban subdivisions; underuse of central city land; increased municipal taxes for fewer and poorer services; revenue shortfalls exacerbating urban poverty—all of the problems that Mumford identified in his epochal quarrel with the developmentalist Adams. But all would-be regional reformers—traditional and metropolitan alike—agreed that cooperation between politically independent and economically competing communities would prove very difficult to achieve. "It is highly improbable, within the near future at any rate, that any revolutionary changes will occur in population patterning," McKenzie concluded. "In all probability our great cities will continue to decentralize in the sense that population and economic functions will become more widely dispersed throughout the metropolitan region."

Within twenty years statistics had borne out all of McKenzie's predictions as the flow of people to the new metropolitan middle ground suddenly became a flood drowning the landscape. The population of SMAs, in the years immediately following World War II, skyrocketed from 89 million in 1950 to 113 million a decade later. Meanwhile central cities, increasing at a rate well below that of the national average, began to fill with the underprivileged and new ethnics whose needs strained the obsolescent plant and dwindling resources left behind by an increasingly affluent middle class.

By 1960 what was left of the old middle ground was itself filling with new arrivals buying up farmland and flattening the pastoral landscape with earth-movers. Soon the middle landscape became "interurbia," that district, Christopher Tunnard observed in 1958, "where a housewife's remark that she is just going to step out to take the children over to a neighbor's house means she is going to drive them five miles down a country road. Or if she says she's just running down to the store, she may drive fifteen miles to a shopping centre or a supermarket or an upholsterer."[11] By 1960 traditional distinctions between urban and rural had ceased to have any meaning as the middle ground filled with what census-takers now termed "rural-non-farm" settlers.

The Decline of Regionalism

Following the logic imposed by modernization, romantic regionalist hopes for a recast-

46

ing of America flared in the early years of the New Deal, flickered as the nation geared for war, and were seemingly extinguished in the war's aftermath. Yet while it lasted, the original regionalist "cultural motive," as Mumford called it, made transformative contributions to American life. Measured by any standards, regionalism was an impressive cultural achievement, an extended burst of creativity lasting a decade and covering the country. Consult a partial listing: Twelve Southerners' *I'll Take My Stand* (1930), the Nashville Agrarians' indictment of industrialism and modernism; Walter Prescott Webb's massive regional survey, *The Great Plains* (1931) and in the same year Benjamin Botkin's *The Southwest Scene,* the first volume in his folk history of American regions; Sandoz's prize-winning *Old Jules* (1935), her autobiographical account of the end of the High Plains frontier, and two years later William Faulkner's *Absolom! Absolom!* his great epic of the making of the Black Belt; Odum's huge compendium, *American Regionalism* (1938) together with Mumford's magisterial *The Culture of Cities;* John Steinbeck's mythic rendering of regional uprooting, *The Grapes of Wrath* (1940), and James Agee's and Walker Evans's transcendent documentary, *Let Us Now Praise Famous Men* (1941). Add to the list Willa Cather's evocation of the empty New Mexico landscape and Farm Security Administration photographer Russell Lee's sharp-edged portraits of the Spanish-American families of Chamisal and Peñasco. And Dorothea Lange's images of Okie migrants camped along Route 66. And Margaret Bourke-White's glimpses of Southern tenants forced off the land by mechanized cotton harvesters and hitting the road to nowhere. Or, in another medium, the Iowa landscapes and peoples of Grant Wood and the murals of Thomas Hart Benton covering public walls and spanning the whole of the middle ground. Or the regional documentaries *The River* and *The Plow That Broke the Plains.* In explaining the workings of the regional "cultural motive," Mumford pointed out the process of selective assimilation of the past and its transformation under modernizing pressures into new forms and icons. Culture, he insisted, is rooted in iconographic landscapes fashioned by memory, and in this sense *all* culture is indigenous to a place. And when a particular culture first bends and then fractures under the strain of rapid development and economic change, it undergoes a renaissance that yokes inherited impressions to new means of expression, making for just that jagged-edged perceptual disjunction that characterizes the lives of the generation experiencing it. The 1930s, caught in the vise of economic depression and political consolidation, was such a renaissance.

There were those regionalists unable or unwilling to cross the watershed between past and present, who remained on the far side with their inherited prejudices and racial and ethnic biases. Donald Davidson hymned the marvels of Tennessee's Tall Men but resolutely excluded those black Americans who didn't belong. The historian Frank Owsley, compiling his folk history of the South, dismissed antebellum African Americans as only a step away from the jungle. At Friday Mountain Ranch outside Austin, Webb, J. Frank Dobie, and their cronies conducted their closed fraternity meetings and swapped tall tales of Texas Rangers. The regionalist expatriate Bernard DeVoto summarized for his readers the Mountain West's creed in the command "Get out and send more money!" For every lingering prejudice, however, there were shocks of recognition and conceptual breakthroughs like Arthur Raper's discovery with Lillian Smith of the hypocrisy of "separate but equal," or Angie Debo's exposure of the plundering of Oklahoma's Cherokee Nation by greedy speculators and uncaring officials. Exclusivism was challenged if not always overthrown by the pluralism of investigators like Botkin and critics like Constance Rourke, who broadened the notion of the folk to include urban types and industrial workers, their class-based songs and ceremonies.

The regionalists' quandary lay elsewhere as they approached the question of what to do. Just how did they propose to defend the middle ground and repel the metropolitan invaders? Here there was little agreement on an agenda, and regionalism stood exposed as a movement guided by a persuasion rather than a party supplied with a program. There were a few regionalists like the sometime Nashville Agrarian William Yandell Elliot who proposed a wholesale political reordering of the country in actual regional units, and the National Resources Planning Board suggested piecemeal regionalization as a way around congressional gridlock and a means of strengthening the executive branch in a third New Deal. Implementing actual reforms, however, was another matter for what was after all a community of discourse rather than an organization seeking a national mandate. Regionalism maintained outposts in intellectual communities across the country from Chapel Hill and Nashville to Iowa City and Norman, Santa Fe, Taos, and Missoula, cultural collecting-points, many of them clustered around land-grant colleges and universities. Regionalism thus consisted of colonies of the like-minded who attended conferences and read each other's publications (*Prairie Schooner*, published in Lincoln, Nebraska, or *Midland*, issuing from Iowa City), but who constituted a loose confederation of local activists, fellow travelers, and summer soldiers unequipped with the weapons of partisan political warfare.

Regionalist critics and commentators, as distinct from the planners, tended to draw on a long tradition of expressive rather than instrumental politics, an approach to reform as old as the antebellum abolitionists who initi-

ated it. Expressive politics involved the evangelical techniques of preaching and conversion. Its style was the jeremiad, and its practitioners aimed to spread the gospel of civic republicanism formulated by Geddes and Mumford by making converts with a genuinely nonpartisan appeal to conscience, reaching into localities and neighborhoods for recruits. In this sense regionalism approximated a civic religion for the middle ground, a faith in what Willa Cather in a Virgilian allusion called her "country." But their emphasis on decentralization and dispersal made these true believers leery of formal organizations and programs while their hatred of corporate capitalism and consumer culture limited their options and cut off connections.[12]

It soon became apparent as the Depression deepened and the New Deal responded with proposals and programs that the future of regional planning rested with an increasingly energetic national government and one, moreover, that was *not* disposed to relinquish its recently acquired powers or to distribute decision-making to the provinces. Regionalism, as Washington politicians and bureaucrats understood it, was regional resource development to be managed from the center. Despite nods to a participatory politics at the local level as in the Tennessee Valley Authority's touting of "grass-roots democracy," the drift of regional development schemes was steadily toward centralized direction in rebuilding the infrastructure of South and West with agencies like the Reconstruction Finance Corporation, the Rural Electrification Administration, and the Public Works Administration. Even where there was the appearance of power-sharing with states and regions as in the Works Progress Administration and Agricultural Adjustment Administration reforms, the results favored organized interests—big business and agribusiness—that caught and held the ear of the federal government (fig. 18).

The Second World War only strength-ened the alliance between regional resource development and a state capitalism now fully recovered from economic hard times—pre-cisely the reverse of the decentralized partici-patory culture envisioned by the romantic re-gionalists. Corporate America, set back by the Depression, advanced and captured the very middle ground on which regionalists proposed to build their utopia. The history of the Tennessee Valley Authority (TVA) pro-vides a classic example. In its beginnings the TVA appeared to promise fulfillment of re-gionalist dreams of a small-scale cooperative alternative to the domination of big business in league with big government. There were brief glimpses of inexpensive vernacular housing, test-demonstration programs to im-prove crops, small industry and market-gar-den farming, greenbelts as hedges against speculative development, mobile libraries, and educational extension services—all tai-lored to the needs of an impoverished rural population in the valley. Arthur E. Morgan, the perennially embattled chairman of the TVA, pinned his faith on the future of small communities like the town of Norris next to the dam site twenty miles outside of TVA headquarters in Knoxville. Morgan saw his town as a prototype of a series of construc-tion communities planted along the banks of the Tennessee, and he included in his plans a cooperative barn for livestock, woodworking and electrical shops, and a folk museum filled with country crafts. His planners provided sketches for an encircling "town wood" and satellite villages in the garden-city mode. Norris was designed and for a brief time sur-vived as a "demonstration"—a key word in the regionalists' lexicon and a substitute for more controlling theory—a working model of an open-ended, self-correcting approach to problem-solving.

The Second World War changed the Ten-nessee Valley irrevocably, lining the banks of the Tennessee River with giant war indus-tries, chemical plants, and corporate con-cerns. Norris was quickly abandoned to the mercies of the state in 1948 and chartered as a regular municipality a year later. From an ecologically sound regional development ef-fort, the TVA, by 1960, had become one of the nation's largest polluters, home to atomic-energy waste and coal-fired electric plants, big business and a standardized com-mercial culture. Elsewhere throughout the country results of a postwar economic boom were similar. "Out where Frank Lloyd Wright once saw the beginnings of Broadacre City," writes historian Robert Fishman, "there one can see now a landscape domi-nated by an army base; the branch plant of a large corporation; by agribusiness, K-Mart and Wal-Mart, and network television."[13]

In what appeared to be a last look at American regions and regionalism in 1968 Rupert Vance, once a student of Odum and now a distinguished sociologist and demog-rapher at the University of North Carolina, seemingly discerned the end of the road. "In-dustrialization, social mobility—the shift from agricultural to mechanical and white collar occupation," Vance concluded, "mean that more people live in proximity to each other at focal points where transportation, communication, and mass services converge." Here was capitulation to metropolitans: "As other interests, such as those of social class or occupational group, gain importance, the re-gional may recede." Once upon a time South-erners, like Vermonters, were rustics—"somewhat cross-grained at times"—but "today we have mass culture and minds."

Vance's own career traced the declining curve of romantic regionalism that in a ret-rospective judgment he pronounced vague and too easy. As a corrective he offered a final clarification that incorporated the recent con-tributions of the metropolitan regionalists. There were in reality two kinds of region, he now argued, *uniform* and *nodal*. Uniform regions are homogeneous throughout, whereas nodal regions are homogeneous only with respect to internal structure and organization. Nodal regions center on a "focal point" with surrounding areas more or less tightly connected to it by "lines of circulation." Traditional uniform regions survived only so long as the middle ground was home to agriculture as the dominant mode of production. But now all is changed. "Nodal regions appear with increased technology and the growth of large-scale transportation, wholesale distribution, finance and manufacturing; in such regions, metropolises perform the central work of the economy." Here was a capsule history of romantic regionalism, a transition Vance himself had lived through—from normative to functional, from descriptive to predictive, from middle-ground hinterland to megalopolis. Vance closed his summary on a note of wistfulness characteristic of the lapsed disciple and reluctant recruit to regional science. "Because of the high population density of the megalopolis, its components stand in need of regional-urban planning of a type as yet undeveloped."[14]

Megalopolis and Science
Overtake Planning

By the time Rupert Vance called attention to the growing need to plan for "megalopolis," Geddes's original coinage had already been reintroduced by the sociologist Jean Gottman as the title of his massive survey. *Megalopolis* (1961) effectively completed the analysis of metropolitan regionalization originally undertaken by R. D. McKenzie three decades earlier. Gottman's study described vividly the fusing of once-distinct metropolitan regions encircling major eastern seaboard cities into one gigantic corridor running from north of Boston to Baltimore-Washington and be-

yond. What as recently as 1950 had been a string of separate urban regions, each with its own discernible boundaries dividing one metropolitan middle ground from another, had now melted into a single agglomeration itself denoted a giant region. Subtitled "The Urbanized Northeastern Seaboard of the United States," Gottman's survey, compiled for the Twentieth Century Fund, was a 782-page analysis of what he called "the Main Street of the Nation" that traced the growth of "an almost continuous system of deeply interwoven urban and suburban areas" that "straddles state boundaries, stretches across wide estuaries and bays, and encompasses many regional differences."

Gottman's megalopolitan drift is the reverse of Turner's democratic current, moving inexorably from east to west. By 1960, he pointed out, this developmental thrust had moved beyond Chicago to Los Angeles and the San Francisco Bay area, but nowhere as yet had it acquired the density of the corridor running from Boston to Washington. "None of them is yet comparable to megalopolis in size of population, density of population, or density of activities, be these expressed in terms of transportation, communications, banking operations, or political conferences." But the outward flow from the central city across the middle ground of expanding suburban centers, Gottman agreed with his predecessor McKenzie, will inevitably sweep westward. "As this tide reaches more and more cities they will burst out of old bounds to expand and scatter all over the landscape, taking new forms like those already observable throughout Megalopolis." By 1960, he admitted, the changes had become so enormous that "an analysis of this region's problems often gives one the feeling of looking at the dawn of a new stage in human civilization."

The "tidal movement" of people, goods, and services, in, out, and across the new middle landscape, Gottman warned, necessitated a wholesale redesigning and reshaping of land use, as agricultural land continued to surrender to industrial and residential use, and reforestation only partially compensated for an initial loss of trees. More significant still, the effects on city "downtowns" by 1960 had already become disastrous: city cores continued to crumble under the hammering of so-called "renewal" projects, while suburbia and increasingly exurbia flourished as they extended the widening band of megalopolis. Then too, the growing inequity in the distribution of amenities, Gottman warned in echoing McKenzie, required a whole new system of regional management because "the old system of local, state, and national authorities and jurisdictions, which has changed little, is poorly suited to present needs." Gottman's conclusion was an admonitory one: "In some ways this suburban sprawl may have alleviated a crowding [in central cities] that had threatened to become unbearable, for residential densities of population per square mile have decreased. But new problems have arisen because of activity and of traffic in the central cities and because the formerly rural areas or small towns have been unprepared to cope with the new demands on the resources. New programs are needed to conserve the natural beauty of the landscape and to assure the health, prosperity, and freedom of the people." Here Gottman threw down the ecological gauntlet to a new generation of regional planners and regional scientists who were busy equipping themselves with a new approach based on systems analysis, a seemingly revolutionary method which was to yield surprisingly meager results.

By the end of the World War II urban and regional planning was becoming more and more closely tied to and dependent on systems theory applied by social scientists who exchanged the normative for the techno-

cratic. The old romantic regional planning espoused by Mumford, MacKaye, Odum, and their followers had been based on quite simple notions of prediction and control—a linear two-phase process involving a preliminary survey and the resultant design and implementation of an essentially static arrangement. The new computer-driven systems analysis, by contrast, was dynamic and seemingly flexible, complete with "feedback" mechanisms that made the planning procedure infinitely adjustable, at least in theory. The first-generation regionalists were intimately concerned with specific areas and particular places, and they drew up their plans with concrete and irreversible changes in mind. The new regional theory inverted this procedure, working from universally applicable ideal types derived from models. In this sense the older progressive method of survey and data-gathering employed by Odum and his students at Chapel Hill and the new nomothetic approach of a regional scientist like Walter Isard were light-years apart. Odum worried lest he miss that last piece of specific evidence before risking a generalization; Isard dreamed of an ultimate "true set" of regions into which every conceivable variable could be fitted. Isard explained it this way: "imagine for each particular problem a specific best set of regions. From one problem or another this set would differ. However, as one proceeds from one order of problem to a higher order, these sets of regions tend more and more to coincide. Certainly, ultimately (in the millennium) whenever we attack the general problems of societal welfare and growth with a general theory of society, it would seem logical that there can be only one best set (the true set) of regions."[15]

The new systems-driven regional analysis bypassed normative assumptions about social behavior and design and concentrated instead on the structural and functional aspects of planning derived from spatial analysis and mathematical modeling. Cities were still seen as the determinants of the shape and workings of their surrounding regions, but the way they actually functioned was considered too complex and complicated as yet for social scientists to fathom fully. It was generally agreed, however, that normative prescriptions of what the metropolitan region *ought to be*—socially, economically, aesthetically—were personal, premature, and presumptuous.

In illustrating just how systems analysis aids the regional and urban planner in developing useful theory, Jay W. Forrester at the Massachusetts Institute of Technology built a computer model to form a bridge between engineering and social science, more specifically to show how "the feedback-loop structure of a system produces the dynamic behavior of that system." Forrester outlined a multistage design process: first, identify the symptoms of trouble; next search for the feedback structures that produce that trouble; then identify and describe the level and rate variables in the equations of a computer simulation model; fourth, use the computer model to simulate in the laboratory the dynamic behavior in the identified structure; fifth, modify the structure until its components and behavior agree with the observed conditions in the actual system; and, finally, introduce modified policies into the simulation model and see what happens. Forrester adds, seemingly as an afterthought, "This design process brings the essential substance of a social system into the laboratory where the system can be studied."

In applying the theory of feedback-system modeling to the interaction of the central city and what its practitioners called its "limitless environment," the new urban and regional science effectively obliterated the middle ground by defining the environment surrounding any urban area as quite literally the rest of the universe. Then too, they dismissed the traditional linear thinking of ear-

lier planners as totally inadequate. "The linearized models that have been used in much of engineering and in the social sciences," Forrester announced, "cannot even approximate the important modes of behavior in our social systems." Systems analysis alone makes useful prediction possible: "Again, if the influences can be discussed and described, they can be inserted in the policy structure of a model." It then followed for feedback system modellers that, as Forrester once more explained, "the same principles of structure and the same relationships between structure and behavior apply to a simple swinging pendulum, a chemical plant, the processes of management, internal medicine, economics, power politics, and psychiatry." Which in turn means that the individual's mastery of the method ensures access to universality. "The same person can clarify the dynamic of how a transistor functions, organize the process of a public health epidemic, design new management policies to avoid stagnation in product growths, discover the sensitive factors in ecological change, and show how government policies affect the growth and decline of a city." For particular cities and their outlying regions computer-based analysis meant the elaboration of a model that "with proper changes in parameters is good for New York, Calcutta, a gold-rush camp, or West Berlin. . . . The general model can strip away the multitude of detail that confuses any one specific situation."[16]

For all their confident pronouncements a number of the new social scientists—Forrester among them—agreed that the possibility of making radical changes in a complex urban system recedes in proportion to the number of complications. First of all, a complex system like megalopolis in all likelihood is "counterintuitive," that is, it tends to behave in ways that are precisely the opposite of what people expect. Then, too, it may be "highly resistant" to most policy changes and thus "tend to counteract most active programs aimed at alleviating symptoms." In other words, as systems cities fight back! In addition, short-term responses by a system to policy changes are apt to be the opposite of long-term effects. Thus when the would-be urban or regional reformer is apprised of Forrester's final caveat—that social systems like cities have evolved to "a very stable configuration"—they have received their marching orders: "*Festina lente!*" [Make haste slowly!]

Edge City

One sign of caution in the work of urban and regional planners as America entered the 1960s was the appearance of the open-ended design. Increasingly, regional planners and theorists began to construct multiple-choice plans for community consideration in place of the old normative schemes of Mumford and MacKaye's generation. Now they offered a range of alternatives tailored to the shifting needs of mobile citizens. One example of this new type of planning, *A Policies Plan for the Year 2000,* compiled for Washington, D.C., by the National Capital Planning Commission in 1961, was a hydra-headed report that presented seven different models. "A metropolis can now choose to grow in any one of a variety of ways," the regional planners announced boldly. "New tools are being created continually. . . . Used in concert, the means within our reach can shape the region and each of its parts into the form we desire." The planners' options ranged from a draconian "restricted growth" plan, rejected as politically unrealistic, to a design for a series of distanced new towns out on the far metropolitan rim, an idea quickly jettisoned as too expensive. More practical, apparently, was a model of "Planned Sprawl," providing much encouragement but little guidance in ushering would-be suburbanites to their proper

places in the middle landscape. The planning commission's final nod went to the "Radial Corridor Plan" with "controlled open space" —wedges of open land separating high-density corridors running out to the countryside. All of these alternatives, however, seemed superfluous once speculators convinced farmers to sell their land to builders and developers. Wedge boundaries proved unenforceable. Government agencies at all levels hesitated to use eminent domain as a device for placing the wedges into public ownership. And Americans—if their nation's capital was representative—were just not interested in regional planning.

Another example of the broad-gauged regional plan was the Comprehensive General Plan for the Development of the Northeastern Illinois Counties Area in 1968, which, like its Washington progenitor, proffered a variety of land-use and transportation options including satellite cities, peripheral expansion, and what its authors called a "finger plan" with digits poking out from a central-city palm pointing toward the middle ground and beyond. Once more the result was not what the planners had hoped for, but instead a mishmash of elements borrowed from competing visions.

In the central cities of the nation, however, calls for deliberation and warnings against haste fell on the deaf ears of urban planners and developers who tackled the job of urban renewal. Urban renewal and its proponents sought to recapture retailing for the inner city, fill its hotels, rebuild the tax base, and, above all, draw affluent middle-class suburbanites back into the inner fold. By 1960, as the urban historian Jon Teaford points out, the central city had become the poor relation of the larger metropolitan community. Median income discrepancies told the story: income averaged between eight and ten percentage points lower in most of the major cities of the nation than in suburbia. With the arrival of African Americans, Hispanics, and Asian Americans during and after World War II, whole city neighborhoods changed complexion, seemingly overnight. By 1960 one-quarter of the central-city population was nonwhite. While the demand for downtown office space remained high—at least for the moment—surrounding "gray areas" showed signs of deepening decay. Hopes rested with the return of the prodigal suburbanite.

By 1963 federal urban renewal programs were impacting on American cities large and small. Planning boards and boosters were enjoying a financial field day as urban renewal grants coming out of Washington reached hundreds of millions of dollars. Soon city planners turned away from the less remunerative task of building low-cost housing to commercial development, luxury housing, Gateway Centers (Minneapolis), Erieviews (Cleveland), and Government Centers (Boston). This shift from people to corporate projects was characterized by certain common features. First to feel the wrecker's ball, almost everywhere, were rundown waterfronts, skid rows, warehouse districts, and dingy neighborhoods no matter how lively and cohesive. All to make way for planned multi-use districts featuring luxury housing designed to draw the middle classes back to town cheek-by-jowl with office-apartment-shopping complexes. Urban renewal's casualties—poor families displaced by the bulldozer—mounted as patches of vacant land spread. "Hiroshima Flats" was what one dispossessed victim of a development project called Saint Louis's Mill Creek Valley, while another of the inner city's uprooted complained of having to move out to make room for "wealthy poodled people" lounging in luxury apartments.

The most articulate critic and energetic activist in the debate over urban renewal was Jane Jacobs, whose widely read *The Death and Life of Great American Cities* appeared in 1961. The target of Jacob's barbs was the arrogant assertions of profit-hungry developers and their planning colleagues that they were about to eliminate poverty once and for all—their "wistful myth that if only we had enough money to spend . . . we could wipe out all slums in ten years, reverse decay in the great, dull, gray belts . . . , anchor the wandering middle class and its wandering tax money, and perhaps even solve the traffic problem." No amount of projected increase in tax revenues, she scoffed, could compensate for the destruction of closely knit ethnic neighborhoods, a bit shabby, perhaps, but vital and varied, with their narrow crowded streets and outdoor culture. Urban renewal betokened a new American placelessness.

In any case, it failed to work. Urban renewal did not bring the middle class back into the fold but instead drove young "mobiles," as they were beginning to be called, deeper into the middle landscape. The planners of urban renewal, Teaford concludes, "were defying the social, cultural, and economic trends of the period and attempting to impose on American society a new way of life that few actually wanted. . . . Despite prophecies to the contrary, affluent suburbanites would not vie for downtown apartments, but remained largely in suburbia."[17] The exodus would continue into the 1970s and 1980s, as middle-class Americans followed their social fantasy into Edge City.

As Americans entered the last decade of the twentieth century, engineers and planners working in concert with blue-sky developers were planting the old middle ground with commercial strips, condominium clusters, industrial parks, hierarchical corporate offices—headquarters for a mushrooming "technoburbia" or "Edge City," as Joel Garreau calls it in a recent book by that title—outlying industrial villages encircling moribund central cities, the destination of young Americans seeking "life on the new frontier."

The transformation of the middle ground by unchecked decentralization was dramatic, if not drastic. The key to this spread was probably the national Highway Act of 1956, which pledged the federal government to build 41,000 miles of limited-access highways constructed in the beginning as links between growing suburban complexes but soon, with the creation of megalopolis, providing it with a motorized backbone. Public transportation both within and between cities declined accordingly as suburban family automobiles crowded these new throughways that sliced the middle landscape into new configurations and grids. A study of the growth of shopping centers found that nationally in 1960 there were almost sixty mammoth malls each with a floor area in excess of half a million square feet. Massachusetts's Route 128 girdling Boston, the bastard offspring of MacKaye's "townless highway" scheme, boasted ninety-nine available new industrial and commercial spaces.

Edge City, like the old central city before it, evolved over the decades, as the architect and planner Peter G. Rowe makes clear in his recent *Making a Middle Landscape* (1991). The old middle ground changed constantly as architects, planners, and builders discovered new forms and figures to sit on it. Uniform Levittowns providing cheap housing for veterans and escapees from city slums quickly gave way to an increasing variety of suburban housing types ranging from colonial revival to ranch style, bungalow to contemporary. Similarly, the old taxpayer blocks dating from earlier in the century were being replaced, first by strip commercial centers and then by shopping villages and giant pedestrian malls. Business followed the same routes out of downtowns, and soon industrial plants surrounded by acres of grim blacktopped parking areas were supplanted by carefully planned and landscaped "corporate estates" with enclosed atriums and green winter gardens proclaiming the new arrivals' respect for nature and philanthropic intentions surpassing the urge for profits.

The resultant Edge City is at once the endpoint of metropolitan regionalism, the negation of the civic spirit of the original regionalist reformers, and the beckoning future for legions of commercial expansionists and developers who continue to invade the middle ground, seize natural preserves, and use them up. Frank Lloyd Wright, in a plea for civic republicanism, urged Americans to "try to live deep in nature" so as to nurture the "democratic spirit of man" and foster a sense of commonality. Today, as Garreau points out, Edge City—"the workplace of the Information Age"—consists of any area of pristine land that can promise five million square feet of office space, half a million feet of leasable retail space, mammoth plots of upscale housing and eager young professionals to fill it, and a canopied shopping mall complete with entertainment module—altogether a consumer paradise that "has it all."

As an example of the postmodern American region flourishing in the Southwest and West, Garreau presents the "Sixty-Mile Circle" surrounding downtown Los Angeles and containing some twenty-six actual or potential Edge Cities. The old Los Angeles downtown, including East L.A. and Central, now holds less than 5 percent of the region's jobs—the rest have accompanied middle-class flight from the city. The Sixty-Mile Circle as a region boasts 139 colleges and universities, an intricate and badly overloaded transportation system, acres of agribusiness farmland, and hundreds of corporate headquarters complete with artificial lake and mandatory waterfall. What this particular Edge City and others like it lack are two critical components: an integrated public planning instrumentality and the will to use it, and the communitarian ethic and civic religion with which to construct a regional planning agenda for direct citizen participation. The first shortcoming leaves the door open to private developers practicing a new form of slash and burn. And the second leaves an ideological (some would say spiritual) vacuum that is quickly filled with speculative building, highway cloverleaves, drained wetlands, and a burgeoning service industry catering to jaded consumer appetites.[18]

There are dry-eyed observers of Edge City who happily discern there a new "placelessness" and characterize this zone as a "nonplace urban realm," as Melvin M. Webber describes it, where traditional notions of location and proximity defining community and civic interest are no longer operative. The future citizens of Edge City will no longer be *place*-bound, they predict, no longer confined either by their immediate surroundings or by neighbors. Postmodern placelessness makes Edge City a system of events rather than an arrangement of locations, an affectless society in which people consume not things but experience. "The modern metropolis," writes Andrea Branzi, a purveyor of new-wave urban design, "has ceased to be place and has become a condition . . . a state of being, uniformly articulated throughout society by consumer goods." Archizoom Associati designed a pop fantasy city of affectlessness to make its point in the form of a throw-away society of abundance where citizens, like Edward Bellamy's future inhabitants of Boston in the year 2000, once assured of an endless supply of disposable goods, no longer define themselves by their surroundings or their possessions and at long last are truly free. In this brave new world no one counts either the psychological or the ecological costs.[19]

A Resurgence of Regionalism

With precise Hegelian logic, however, the Edge City thesis has generated its antithesis in the form of resurgent ecological regionalism challenging the developmental agenda at every turn. Arrayed in a defensive posture against the builders of "technoburbia" in the last decade of the twentieth century stand the still thin but growing ranks of a new generation of ecological regionalists armed with the communitarian values of the early reformers but equipped as well with recently acquired scientific data on the state of the environment and the training with which to apply it. Unlike the old regionalism, which was largely anticipatory and preventive, the new ecology-based regionalism specializes in reclamation and repair. These new practitioners, moreover, have replaced the discrete and sharply demarcated land areas described by MacKaye with a concept of linkage. "Linkage," writes William H. Whyte, the veteran observer and critic of urban and regional planning, "is the key. Most of the big tracts in our metropolitan areas have already been saved, or they have already been lost. The most pressing need now [1968] is to weave together a host of seemingly disparate elements—an experimental farm, a private golf course, a local park, the spaces of a cluster subdivision, the edge of a new freeway right-of-way."[20]

The new regionalists have been busy reclaiming all three segments of Benton MacKaye's original region—wilderness, middle landscape, and city center—and applying similar scientific principles all along the route in order to regain the common ground. Best known, perhaps, is the work of innumerable wilderness advocates gathered in hundreds of organizations—local, state, and federal—to save what is left of pristine American wilderness. Their means and methods vary widely, ranging from privately funded land purchase to confrontational battles in the courts. A growing number of activists, additionally, are reaching across class and race barriers in both small and large communities, seeking to activate and politicize less articulate working-class and ethnic victims of toxic waste and environmental mismanagement.

Equally well known and boasting a history even longer than that of the conservation societies are the efforts of thousands of citizens' groups and government officials to create greenways running out from city centers through the middle landscape to open country and wilderness. The American lineage of the greenways movement originates with the pioneer work of Frederick Law Olmsted who designed the first linear parkway for his Prospect Park in Brooklyn in 1868—a "shaded pleasure drive," he called it, stretching from the park's southern end out through countryside to Coney Island. Olmsted's best-known and in some ways greatest achievement is Boston's "Emerald Necklace" (1887), a 4.5-mile linear park and greenway linking the downtown Boston Common with Franklin Park via the Back Bay Fens and the Muddy River. Now, more than a century later, the greenways idea has swept across the country, from Atlanta to Portland, Oregon; Redding, Connecticut, to Monterey, California. Rail-trail projects, flood-plains parks, scenic drives, nature corridors, land trusts singly and in combination are beginning to link middle ground and wilderness to the edges of the metropolis in an admittedly incomplete and haphazard way. An example of such partial linkage comes in the form of a specific answer to a practical question posed by Charles E. Little, author of *Greenways for America,* who asked a fellow planner just how far he could walk on connected trails from his home two blocks from Rock Creek Park in Washington, D.C. The directions: follow Rock Creek Park south to Georgetown and then on to the Washington & Old Dominion Trail through Bluemont, Virginia, and on up the Blue Ridge Mountains to join the Appalachian Trail. Or, he was told, you could follow the Chesapeake & Ohio Trail

out through Cumberland, Maryland, to Connelsville, Pennsylvania, and (in a piece of projection worthy of Benton MacKaye himself) soon on to Pittsburgh, across Ohio and Michigan, the Upper Midwest to the North Country Trail in North Dakota, which one day will connect with the national Lewis and Clark Trail, and that will take you all the way to Oregon.[21]

Ecological regionalists today take many of their cues from planner and pioneer redesigner of American landscapes, Ian McHarg of the Department of Landscape Architecture and Regional Planning at the University of Pennsylvania, who discovered the basic materials for regional reconstruction ready at hand in the shape and substructure of the land itself. Studying suburban expansion, McHarg singled out for condemnation those developers who, heedless of ultimate environmental costs, plunge joyfully into the work of destroying the land. McHarg marks our arrival at the edge of countryside by pointing to the "emblems" of development. "The cadavers of old trees piled in untidy heaps at the edge of razed deserts, the magnificent machines for land despoliation, for felling forests, filling marshes, culverting streams, and sterilizing farmland, making thick brown sediments of the creeks." Here at the edges of Edge City where public powers are weak or nonexistent and greed goes unchecked, the loss of values keeps pace with the erosion of the landscape. "Here are the meek mulcted, and the refugees thwarted."

Out in the middle ground the costs of development can be lowered if not eliminated, McHarg insists, through the simple process of identifying the natural design of a region or subregion—that system of streams and valleys, aquifers, and bedrock, wetlands and wooded slopes—which supplies all the needed directives. In 1965 McHarg, together with colleague David Wallace, drew up a plan for adapting settlement to regional imperatives for a group of large landowners in the Spring Green and Worthington Valleys northwest of Baltimore. Their "Plan for the Valleys *vs.* Spectre of Uncontrolled Growth" embraced some seventy square miles consisting of three valleys, several plateaus, and large farms whose owners had formed a council and hired planners. "Uncontrolled growth," McHarg warned in the prophetic mode of a Geddes or a MacKaye, "occurring sporadically, spreading without discrimination, will surely obliterate the valleys, inexorably cover the landscape with its smear, irrevocably destroy all that is beautiful or memorable. No matter how well-designed each individual sub-division may be, no matter if small parks are interfused with housing, the great landscape will be expunged and remain only as receding memory." Following nature's directives, instead, down the watercourses and along the forest cover on their sides leads to the solution: build cluster housing if you must, but selectively on the plateaus, and leave the valleys and their slopes alone.

In the nation's capital McHarg put similar principles to work in responding to an official request for advice in beautifying the city by planting Japanese cherry trees, petunias, zinnias, and begonias, "flowers that try hardest to look like colored paper." "Now this is a splendid impulse," he commented with a mordancy matching that of Geddes, "and much can be accomplished within its view, but it is clear that there are limits." Taking the call for help as providing a wider mandate, McHarg attempted to define for his clients the form of their city and, subsequently, to explain how its inevitable expansion should be managed. He began with a concept: "The image of Washington is of a great city meeting a great river."

The uniqueness of Washington lies in its morphology—more precisely in the Potomac River Basin and its surrounding geology.

"The Potomac enters the District through crystalline rock into which it has cut a deep and narrow channel; it is contained by the Palisades. As it crosses the Little Falls it encounters sedimentary material and cuts this deeply, revealing the exposed rock face. Beyond the Fall Line, it is no longer constrained and expands into the broad aspect of the estuarine river. In this lower Potomac there are wide floodplains and marshes; these are conspicuous in the Anacostia too."[22] As the nation's capital, Washington has been twice blessed, once by the landscape identity given it by nature, and again by the Renaissance vision of Pierre Charles L'Enfant, whose imperial inclination and axial arrangement may have been derived from the Age of Louis XIV but whose sense of the structure and the shape of the land he beheld was impeccable. Uniting the Capitol and the Potomac with the Mall and connecting it, in turn, with a cross-axis leading to the White House, L'Enfant paid particular attention to the natural characteristics of the site and proposed diagonal avenues radiating out to the surrounding hills, explaining to the president that his plan would "afford a greater variety of seats with pleasant prospects which can be obtained from the advantageous ground over which these avenues are chiefly directed." McHarg comments, "When cities are built upon beautiful, dramatic or rich sites, their excellence often results from the preservation, exploitation, and enhancement, rather than the obliteration of the genius of the site." "Historic Washington is, in essence, a neo-classical composition set in a half bowl, defined by two confluent rivers and an escarpment, with a backdrop of low hills. The entire city is like an inclined fan with the symbolic city at the base and the ribs revealed in the valleys of the Potomac, Glover Archbold, Rock Creek, Goose Valley and the Anacostia."

Washington's problems as of 1966 McHarg attributed to the unmanaged transformation from city to metropolitan area where followers of the American dream of better schools, clean government, and a safe environment are cruelly disillusioned. "The hucksters made the dream into a cheap thing, subdivided we fell, and the instinct to find more natural environments became the impulse that destroyed nature, an important ingredient in the social objective of this greatest of all population migrations." The chief reason for this reversal of expectations, McHarg argues, lies in the more fundamental failure to study the land, its formations, soils, and vegetations. McHarg restates the rule that he applies to all landscapes: "certain lands are unsuitable for urbanization and others . . . are intrinsically suitable." The trick is to distinguish between the two types, which he accuses the designers of the Year 2000 Plan of failing to do. McHarg applies his standard method: "if one selects eight natural features and ranks them in order of value to the operation of the natural process, then that group reversed will constitute a gross order of suitability for urbanization." The eight factors are surface water, flood plains, marshes, aquifer recharge areas, aquifers, steep slopes, forests and woodlands, and unforested land. An overlay of maps indicating the geology, physiography, hydrology, and other natural processes of the region gives the ecological planner his answer as to which lands are unsuitable for urbanization—"row-cropland, cropland and flood plains, slopes in excess of fifteen per cent, areas which (for reasons of erosion due to slope or soils) should be in forest cover, major aquifer recharges, forests and noise zones." Admitting that inevitably some agricultural land will be absorbed by suburbanization, McHarg nevertheless draws two conclusions: there was a striking amount of suitable land available as of 1966, and most of it lay in the northwestern quadrant of the land encircling the city. McHarg prefaced his study of Washington with a reproval—and here one hears echoes of Geddes, Mumford, and MacKaye's earlier reproaches. Would-be suburbanites should understand that a subdivision is not a community, nor is the sum of subdivisions along the metropolitan fringe. His own task, however, he concluded ruefully, was much more moderate: "The adoption of the ecological method could at least produce the negative value of a structure of open space wherein nature performed her work for man, or where development was dangerous."

Subsequently, younger, ecologically trained regional and urban planners have added both an aesthetic and an explicitly social and ethical dimension to the more strictly scientific method of McHarg. McHarg made innovative use of maps, plotting all the relevant factors—woodland, marshes, ridges, streams, and cropland—on separate sheets of Mylar and then laying one upon the other so that the resulting composite showed dark patches indicating areas suitable for development and lighter tracts where development was undesirable. Philip Lewis, the director of the University of Wisconsin's Environmental Awareness Center in Madison, uses maps differently in an approach that is more elaborate and aesthetically subjective then McHarg's. Lewis focuses his attention on the environmental corridor, which is a naturalized second-cousin-twice-removed of Geddes's "valley section." Environmental corridors, according to Lewis, tend to follow streams and riverbeds, a conclusion reached by plotting some 220 environmental values on a regional map with symbols denoting both natural values and human improvements ranging from waterfalls and wetlands to nature trails, archeological sites, and a highly personal category, the "visual quality of space." Such a loose and even impressionistic method suits Lewis's own preferences: "The flat, rolling farmlands and expansive forests," he admits, "have their share of beauty. But it is the stream valleys, the bluffs and ridges, the roaring and quiet waters, mellow wetlands, and sandy soils that combine in elongated designs, tying the land together in regional and statewide corridors of outstanding landscape qualities."[23] It is scarcely surprising then, that Lewis finds most of his symbolized values clustered along flowing water (figs. 22–24).

Anne Whiston Spirn, a colleague of McHarg at the University of Pennsylvania and a contributor to this volume goes even further than McHarg or Lewis in combining the natural and social worlds in a coherent vision of the regional public realm. "Neither the arcadian nor the imperialist view of nature," she writes, adapting Mumford's terms to her own purposes, "will serve to advance the field of urban and regional reform and reclamation." What is needed is a methodological "middle ground that aspires to a beneficial meshing of the cultural processes of society and the physical and biological processes of the natural world." Spirn's present experimental laboratory is West Philadelphia, a multiracial, low-income neighborhood filled with abandoned properties and vacant lands—a modern version with ethnic and racial variations of Geddes's slums of Edinburgh or McHarg's dismal working-class Glasgow. "I'm interested in the gardens as a vehicle for reshaping entire neighborhoods," she explains in pointing to the urban community garden as a key component of any landscape plan for a city. "For me, a community garden is a wedge into a neighborhood." *The West Philadelphia Landscape Plan: A Framework for Action* (1991), for which Spirn served as chief investigator and coordinator, consists of six reports that bound the area and shape its concerns. Like other landscape planners working in cities, she defines the urban landscape as a totality that includes hills, valleys, rock croppings, and underground streams but also streets and sidewalks, playgrounds, sewers, and vacant lots.

This is the terrain into which she seeks to drive a social as well as an environmental wedge.

Spirn's *West Philadelphia Plan* "is based upon the conviction that individuals, small groups, and local organizations all have a role in shaping the landscape of a city . . . [and] incremental improvements to the urban landscape made by individuals and small groups can have an enormous cumulative effect on the city and how it looks and functions." The success of any block plan for recovering vacant land and planting it so as to give form to the neighborhood must grow out of the particular place and the people who live in it. Popular participation activates and educates. "The projects have afforded people the opportunity to shape the place they live in, to give form to common needs and shared aspirations, to share and care for the common ground."[24]

What neighborhood participants generally lack, Spirn explains, are the means to acquire a more comprehensive regional vision, which it is the job of the planner to provide. "A plan should combine the overview with the local view." Spirn performs this task by examining such factors as air and water quality, energy efficiency, sewage disposal, and plant and wildlife habitat in the metropolis, acting as MacKaye's "composite mind," synthesizing these variables in a coherent scheme. For this larger task Boston serves Spirn as a natural laboratory. Boston's problems, according to her, are three: first and most important, the sewage crisis and the pollution of Boston Harbor; then the deterioration of inner-city neighborhoods; and finally the declining aesthetic quality of central city streets, plazas, and open spaces. Some small advances toward solutions to these problems have been made in the decade since Spirn pointed them out, but there is even today a good distance to go.

"Water is Boston's greatest problem and

its greatest resource," Spirn asserts in calling for a regional approach. Boston's second major problem, Spirn discovered (she would later recognize it in Philadelphia as well), involves the deterioration of *place,* specifically the inner-city neighborhoods filled with poor people, run-down housing and vacant lots. Here the planner with an overview can begin to coordinate the specifically local and the larger regional views by building playgrounds and linear parks, planting community gardens, and experimenting with natural meadows and orchards, bringing into the city all of those middle-ground devices and remedies once suggested by Geddes.

Solutions to the third of Boston's major problems—"the declining aesthetic quality of downtown streets and places"—also involves the middle ground but this time constructed *temporally* as the *history* of a place and the collective *memory* of the public realm. "It is a paradox," Spirn told the Boston Society of Architects in 1985, "that we are not creating for the future what we value from the past. What we now value about historic districts like Back Bay was achieved through a coherent vision of the public realm, not through fragmented assembly of private development projects, with the city trying to make the best of leftover space from the public realm." Here, like Lewis Mumford before her, Spirn reaches back into the nineteenth century for Boston's legacy: to the frame supplied by the Public Garden, the tree-lined mall that is Commonwealth Avenue, the parkway through the Fens, Riverway, and lands beyond. Cumulatively and across time nineteenth-century Bostonians built an integrated public infrastructure consisting of open space, a sewer system, transportation routes, and continuous parkway, providing altogether an integrated and comprehensive vision of the city linked to its hinterland.[25]

Vision—or "visualizing," as Benton MacKaye called it—involves first of all a vantage point. Patrick Geddes's vantage was his Outlook Tower in Edinburgh, nearly 100 feet off the ground. From this height the entire city unfolds in a panoramic sweep—Castle Hill immediately below, then out to the Firth of Forth eight miles distant, and beyond on a clear day to Ben Lodi and Ben Lomond fifty miles away. Ninety degrees to the northeast stands Calton Hill and the broad inlet fringed with coastal towns looking out to the North Sea. Closer in lie the great Castle on one side, and eastward, looking down the Royal Mile, Holyrood Palace. To the south the barren Pentland Hills and the wide valley of the Esk funneling out beyond the Old Town. Together these several views define Geddes's "valley section."

Lewis Mumford's vantage point was high on the piers of Brooklyn Bridge on a windy March morning in 1915, behind him the still low-profiled borough of Brooklyn, ahead the soaring towers of Manhattan, an emblem, he suddenly realized, of the possibilities of his own life. "Here was my city, immense, overpowering, flooded with energy and light . . . challenging me, beckoning me, demanding something of me that it would take a lifetime to give, but raising all my energies by its own vivid promise to a high pitch."[26]

Benton MacKaye's imagined vantage point came on top of his projected Appalachian Trail in the form of a conceit. "Let us assume," he wrote, "the existence of a giant standing high on the skyline along these mountain ridges, his head just scraping the skyline as he strode along its length from north to south." Before setting out, the giant stands on the summit of Mount Washington and points north to heavily forested hunting-grounds of the Indian; then west to the Berkshires and the Adirondacks; next to the "crowded east"—a chain of smoky beehive cities extending from Boston to Washington, and finally due south to the Southern Appalachians and a primal environment little changed since the time of Daniel Boone.[27]

Invoking the same privilege as her predecessors, Spirn sets her vista inside another venerable conceit—approaching utopia by water. "The place is Boston, the time is somewhere early in the next century." "From this vantage, the city is a silent silhouette, clearly seen for what it is, a fragile human construct, supported by the earth, permeated by air and water. . . ." Boston Harbor is now a vast state park. Of the city's three rivers the Charles and the Mystic have been thoroughly cleaned, and the Neponset is still a tidal river, its lower reaches lined with marshes. With decentralized purification plants in the southwestern part of the Boston region the hydrologic cycle is closed: "The presence of water is pervasive: by harbor and riverbank, permeating public places in the neighborhoods and downtown." And with the return of clean water in all its forms comes a new civic vitality and a genuine renewal of the inner city linked to its outlying region," a product of concerted, sustained, and visionary public effort."[28]

Now at the end of the century something approximating these visions together with other ideas for reclaiming and repairing the damage done by unplanned metropolitan expansion guides the activities of hundreds of nature conservancies, land trusts, shoreline commissions, park planners, housing agencies, and landowner compacts across the nation. Dimly discernible in all these efforts is the re-emerging philosophy of the commons—land set aside for all the people—which admittedly will be a hard sell to a national citizenry increasingly divided into high-mobile "haves" and low-mobile "have-nots." Lacking so far is the engagement of the federal government in promoting the idea of that national commons as it extends from revitalized inner cities out along natural corridors in the middle ground to regional parks and wilderness areas. Without this federal commitment the struggle between the ecological regionalists and their powerful enemies is bound to remain an unequal one. If the victories of the regional reformers to date have necessarily been partial and quite literally piecemeal, it can nevertheless be said that the communitarian vision of the original regionalists has not yet been lost nor their legacy spent.

Notes

1. The original exchange between Thomas Adams and Lewis Mumford together with other material on the RPAA including the *Report of the New York Commission of Housing and Regional Planning* is collected in Carl Sussman, ed., *Planning the Fourth Migration: The Neglected Vision of the Regional Planning Association of America* (Cambridge, Mass.: MIT Press, 1976). Mumford and Adams's debate is found on pp. 221–67.

2. There are two indispensable works on Patrick Geddes, his life and ideas: Marshall Stalley, ed., *Patrick Geddes: Spokesman for Man and the Environment* (New Brunswick, N.J.: Rutgers University Press, 1972), with a biography of Geddes by Abbie Ziffren together with selections from *Cities in Evolution. Talks from Outlook Tower,* and *Town Planning in Lahore;* and Philip Boardman, *The Worlds of Patrick Geddes: Biologist, Town Planner, Re-educator, Peace-Warrior* (London: Routledge & Kegan Paul, 1978), from which the material on Geddes's home and boyhood is taken. See especially ch. 1.

3. MacKaye's boyhood in Shirley Center is lovingly recalled in Percy MacKaye, *Epoch: The Life of Steele MacKaye, Genius of the Theatre, in Relation to His Time & Contemporaries* (2 vols.) (New York: Boni and Liveright, 1927), 2: 195–289.

4. For an enlightening discussion of the thought of Hugh Miller, regional differences in eighteenth- and nineteenth-century Scotland, and the Scottish Enlightenment see Bruce Evan Levy, "From Here to Modernity: Nation Building, the Writing of Place, and the Provincial Ideal in Hugh Miller and Edward Eggleston" doctoral dissertation, Brown University, 1993, ch. 1.

5. Geddes, *Cities in Evolution,* ch. 12, in Stalley, *Patrick Geddes,* p. 223.

6. Ian L. McHarg, *Design with Nature* (Garden City, N.Y.: Natural History Press, 1969), p. 197.

7. Turner's essays on section and region are available in two readily accessible volumes: Max Farrand, ed., *The Significance of Sections in American History* (New York: Peter Smith, 1950), and Ray Allen Billington, ed., *Selected Essays of Frederick Jackson Turner: Frontier and Section* (Englewood Cliffs, N.J.: Prentice-Hall, 1961).

8. Benton MacKaye to Lewis Mumford, December 3, 1926, MacKaye Papers, Baker Library, Dartmouth College, Hanover, N.H. Quoted with permission.

9. Benton MacKaye, *The New Exploration: A Philosophy of Regional Planning* (New York: Harcourt Brace, 1928), p. 195. MacKaye discusses the controls and their effects on metropolitanism in ch. 12, "Controlling the Metropolitan Invasion," pp. 168–200.

10. N. S. B. Gras, *An Introduction to Economic History* (New York: Harper, 1922), pp. 286–7, as quoted in Robert E. Dickinson, *City and Region: A Geographical Interpretation* (London: Routledge & Kegan Paul, 1964), p. 287.

11. Christopher Tunnard, "America's Super-Cities," *Harper's*, August 1958, pp. 59–65, as quoted in Dickinson, *City and Region*, p. 300.

12. Robert Dorman, *Revolt of the Provinces: The Regionalist Movement in America, 1920–1945* (Chapel Hill, N.C.: University of North Carolina Press, 1993) is a brilliant analysis of this regionalist movement.

13. Robert Fishman in comments to the author. See also Fishman's chapter in this volume (Chapter 3).

14. Rupert Vance, "Regions [1968]," in *Regionalism and the South: Selected Papers of Rupert Vance*, edited with an introduction by John Shelton Reed and Daniel Joseph Singal (Chapel Hill: University of North Carolina Press, 1982), pp. 311–2.

15. Walter Isard, "Regional Science, The Concept of Region and Regional Structure," *Papers and Proceedings, The Regional Science Association,* vol. 2 (1956), pp. 13–26, as quoted in J. Nicholas Entrikin, *The Betweenness of Place: Towards a Geography of Modernity* (Baltimore: Johns Hopkins University Press, 1991), pp. 81–2.

16. Jay W. Forrester, "Systems Analysis as a Tool for Urban Planning," in Nathaniel J. Mass, ed., *Readings in Urban Dynamics* (Cambridge, Mass.: Wright-Allen Press, 1974), vol. 1, pp. 15–28.

17. Jon C. Teaford, *The Rough Road to Renaissance: Urban Revitalization, 1940–1985* (Baltimore: Johns Hopkins University Press, 1990), pp. 161–2.

18. Joel Garreau, *Edge City: Life on the New Frontier* (New York: Doubleday, 1991), pp. 6–7.

19. For a full account of the changing American middle ground in the second half of the twentieth century see Peter G. Rowe, *Making a Middle Landscape* (Cambridge, Mass.: MIT Press, 1991). The material on Archizoom Associati and the quotation from Andrea Branzi is taken from pp. 238–9.

20. William H. Whyte, *The Last Landscape* (New York: Doubleday, 1968). See in particular chs. 9, 10, and 11.

21. Charles E. Little, *Greenways for America* (Baltimore: Johns Hopkins University Press, 1990), p. 104.

22. McHarg, *Design with Nature*, p. 177. McHarg discusses the region in the chapter entitled "The Metropolitan Region" and the city of Washington itself in the later chapter, "The City: Process and Form."

23. Lewis, quoted in Little, *Greenways*, p. 22.

24. *The West Philadelphia Landscape Plan: A Framework for Action* (Philadelphia: University of Pennsylvania Department of Landscape Architecture and Regional Planning, 1991), p. v.

25. Anne Winston Spirn, "Reclaiming Common Ground," lecture delivered at the Boston Public Library, April 1985. A revised version of this lecture is the basis for Chapter 11 in this volume.

26. Lewis Mumford, *Sketches from Life: The Autobiography of Lewis Mumford* (New York: Dial, 1982), pp. 128–30.

27. Benton MacKaye, "An Appalachian Trail: A Project in Regional Planning," *Journal of the American Institute of Architects,* October 1921. See also Benton MacKaye, *From Geography to Geotechnics* (Urbana: University of Illinois Press, 1968), a collection of MacKaye's essays edited by Paul Bryant.

28. Spirn, "Reclaiming Common Ground," p. 30.

State Street, Chicago, ca. 1910. The metropolitan tradition gloried above all in vital, crowded, prosperous downtown public spaces. "The busy crowd," as this postcard view is captioned, embodies both the commercial and the monumental visions of downtown. (Library of Congress Prints and Photographs Division, Detroit Publishing Company Photograph Collection)

CHAPTER THREE

The Metropolitan Tradition in American Planning

■■
■■

ROBERT FISHMAN

The outstanding fact of modern society is the growth of great cities.

—Ernest W. Burgess, *The City,* 1925.[1]

If, as Walter Benjamin has asserted, we can best grasp an intellectual tradition at the moment when it is most imperiled,[2] then now is surely the time to reassess the metropolitan tradition in twentieth-century American thought. In contrast to the intellectual confusion and political paralysis that mark the permanent urban crisis of our own era, the metropolitan tradition confidently proclaimed that the greatness of American life would be realized most completely in our largest cities. The exponents of this tradition not only discarded the Jeffersonian conception that the farm and the small town embodied the true America, they also were undeterred by the manifest ugliness, chaos, poverty, and corruption that pervaded the actual turn-of-the-century metropolis. For they believed that the unprecedented scale of the great city generated unprecedented diversity, and diversity was the key to the economic and cultural promise of twentieth-century life.

Only the metropolitan region, they argued, could generate the complex division of labor that was required to drive technological innovations to their limits and thus to achieve maximum economic growth. At the same time, the intense cultural mix of the metropolis—reinforced by millions of immigrants—meant the end of small-town conformities and the opportunity to create a genuinely cosmopolitan American culture. The combined economic and cultural diversity of the metropolis would liberate individuals to pursue their own paths through the thicket of urban life. Thus, the metropolitan tradition saw the great city as the true home of prosperity, pluralism, and individuality—the very values on which American democracy must be based.

Moreover, the metropolitan tradition asserted that the inhuman overcrowding and wasteful congestion of the existing metropolis were remediable by the intelligent and coordinated application of more advanced forms of the same technologies that had created the centralized industrial city. They were especially creative in their understanding of the potential of electric traction to relieve overcrowding at the core by distributing population and industry throughout the region. They saw the American industrial metropolis achieving not only an unprecedented metropolitan scale but also a "classic" form that would maximize efficiency and also rival the great cities of the Old World in beauty and order.

In this vision of the modern metropolitan region, "downtown" would not only be the commercial capital of the region, the bustling skyscraper hub of business, consumption, and entertainment, it would also be the civic center of the region where noble structures grouped around spacious public spaces would proclaim the importance of culture and the common good. Surrounding the center would be the "industrial zone" where most of the region's population would both live and work. Unlike the slums that had disfigured cities in the past, the industrial zone would be an open and efficiently planned area where the most modern factories could coexist with quiet neighborhoods of comfortable houses. But the industrial zone would also be sufficiently dense to prevent the metropolis from sprawling out into the surrounding countryside. The edge of the region would be reserved partly for elite suburbs but mostly for agricultural land and extensive parklands that would forever guarantee access to nature for the urban dweller.

As its advocates fully understood, this new metropolis required unprecedented planning and coordination. Competing transportation systems would have to be combined into unified systems; the sites for civic centers, parks, parkways, and other improvements located, coordinated, and secured. Most important, the fragmentation of political authority and economic power within the region had to be united behind a single overarching plan. Yet this seemingly impossible task did not deter the planners and activists. Creating the new metropolitan region was precisely the challenge that would finally demonstrate that, in Walter Lippmann's terms, mastery had overcome drift in American life.[3]

The metropolitan tradition emerged in the late nineteenth century from two distinct sources. The first was the long disputation of "metropolitan" thinkers with Jeffersonian antiurbanism, a disputation that would give rise to an extensive dialogue with the regionalist movement in the twentieth century. The second came out of the experience of architects, engineers, landscape architects, social workers, and other planners striving to cope with the overwhelming problems of exploding cities. By the 1920s these sources had merged to underpin those two great collective enterprises that are also the two great intellectual monuments of the metropolitan tradition: the Chicago School of Sociology and the *Regional Plan of New York and Its Environs*. If the metropolitan tradition as embodied in these works sometimes seems overoptimistic or even complacent about the costs of big-city life, the tradition at its best shares something of the confident grandeur of the great railroad terminals that are the most important architectural monuments of American metropolitanism.

And, like the great railroad terminals, the metropolitan tradition proved to be surprisingly vulnerable. If the 1920s saw the zenith of American metropolitanism, the 1930s set in motion fundamental changes that undermined its basic assumptions. By the end of the 1930s the metropolitan tradition was in crisis, unable to comprehend or to master the forces in regional form and national political economy that were hollowing out the supposedly "classic" form of the industrial metropolis, directing growth from the center to the periphery of urbanized regions or to newer areas in the South and the West. At the same time, the hopeful expectations of pluralism and assimilation began to founder on the racial conflicts that greeted the great black migration from the South.

Yet the metropolitan tradition in its heyday—like the large American city itself in the period from 1890 to 1930—was a phenomenon that still commands our interest and our respect. For the metropolitan tradition marks a key moment in what is arguably the most fundamental global transformation in our century: the change from a world still centered on the rural village to a world dominated by the "mega-city."

In the early twentieth century, the American metropolis was the crucial locus for this global transformation. First, the American city was the organizing point for the intensive exploitation of the North American continent that flooded the world with cheap food and other commodities and thus undermined the village economies throughout the world. This process vastly expanded the modern migration from countryside to metropolis that began with eighteenth-century England and that was now engulfing the world. The American metropolis was also the most important locus in the world for the innovations of "the second industrial revolution" in steel, electricity, chemicals, and the internal combustion engine that together created the products that fueled the twentieth-century "consumer society." Indeed, it was in the American city that consumption was democratized and the

promise of "high mass consumption" revealed to the world.

Perhaps most important, the American city in the era of mass immigration was open to the rest of the world. It was not only a distant source of the disturbances that were destroying traditional life but a destination where even the most humble could hope to share in the new life. The Italian writer Carlo Levi, exiled by the fascist regime to a remote village in the hills outside Naples, discovered that what he called the "true capital" of these seemingly isolated peasants was not Naples or Rome but New York. For those who had journeyed there, New York was the city where "a man goes to work, where he toils and sweats for his daily bread, where he lays aside a little money only at the cost of endless hardship, where he can die and no one will remember him. At the same time and with no contradiction, it is an earthly paradise and the promised land."[4]

The American metropolis was the capital of the world's poor precisely because it was a both a place of labor and a place of hope. Indeed, as the most perceptive members of the metropolitan tradition recognized, the true "monument" of the American city was not the dramatic skylines or even the civic centers they hoped to build, but the crowded, mundane streets of the ethnic neighborhoods in the industrial zone. There one could find people beginning to attain their material dreams, and other more fundamental transformations as well.

Never before in human history had so many groups of people from such diverse racial and national backgrounds lived so close to each other as in the American metropolis of the first half of the twentieth century. Yet the result was not escalating conflict and violence—Sam Bass Warner, Jr., aptly describes the American metropolis in 1930 as "an extraordinarily peaceable kingdom."[5] At a time when so many of the countries the immigrants had left were enmeshed in murderous hatreds, the American city offered the world a dramatic symbol of a secular, pluralistic, tolerant society.

Now, in our time, the American city has once again become a bewilderingly diverse capital for the world's poor, but instead of work and peace there is too often violence, despair, isolation, and abandonment. We might perhaps learn from the metropolitan tradition in its era of confidence and hope.

Origins of the Metropolitan Tradition

Like the early regionalists, the founders of the metropolitan tradition felt compelled to respond to the frightening scale, exploding population, and pervasive disorder of the largest American cities at the end of the nineteenth century. Their solution, however, was diametrically opposed to regionalist decentralization. The trouble with big cities, the metropolitanists declared, was that they were not big enough.

"Make no little plans," Daniel Burnham famously advised, and he and his colleagues followed this advice faithfully. One of the architects who presided over Chicago's great age of skyscraper design, Burnham was commissioned in 1906 by a Chicago businessmen's organization, the Commercial Club, to produce a unified plan that would address the major problems the region faced.[6] Published in 1909, the *Plan of Chicago* was to American urbanism what Burnham's Union Station in Washington, D.C., was to the American railroad station: an enduring monument. In the *Plan of Chicago,* Burnham asserted that if the American metropolis was to realize its true potential, it must transform itself into a true metropolitan region, a unified area stretching sixty miles or more in all directions from the core with a population double or triple that of any existing city. Within this vast area covering scores of large and small municipalities, a single unified set of plans must prevail. These plans would provide for a civic center and other public spaces at the core that would rival the grandest ensembles of Vienna or Berlin; parks more splendid than Hyde Park or the Bois de Boulogne; boulevards and parkways that would astonish the successors of Baron Haussmann. In addition, the metropolitan tradition advocated the rationalization and unification of the immense complex of competing railroad and transit lines that entangled every great city. And these were only their major concerns (figs. 11–15).[7]

Behind these brave pronouncements it was easy to hear the voice of urban boosterism, the conviction that bigger is always better. The metropolitanists never scrupled to hide their conviction that the implementation of their plans would mean windfall profits for downtown landowners and comfortable gains even for the smallest property owner. Perhaps most disturbing, their plans often betray a love of immensity for its own sake perhaps best symbolized by Burnham's megalomaniacal dome for his projected Chicago City Hall and tellingly expressed in his assertion that for boulevards, "there is a glory in mere length, in vistas longer than the eye can reach."[8]

But Burnham and his colleagues did not invent the scale of the metropolitan region out of some strange aesthetic impulse. The new metropolis they imagined was taking shape all around them as cities overflowed all previous bounds, annexed surrounding territory or transformed it into functional adjuncts of the central city, and the urban economy penetrated deep into the rural hinterland. The metropolitanists regarded this process as not only inevitable but desirable. The scale of their metropolitan visions reflected a deep conviction that the size and density of the giant city were necessary conditions to achieve the maximum dynamism in modern life. The metropolitanists not only saw how the vast new urban market could stimulate and reward innovation and thus be a major impetus to growth, they also saw how the resources created by urban growth could be mobilized to overcome the worst deficiencies of urban life and to provide for the health, safety, education, and recreation of every citizen.

The metropolitan tradition, therefore, stands firmly on the basic intuition that *metropolitan scale worked*. Burnham once observed that no diamond mine or gold rush ever generated the wealth that is produced by urban growth. But what precisely was the mechanism whereby the crowding together of unprecedented masses of people produced wealth instead of destroying it? In *Nature's Metropolis: Chicago and the Great West,* William Cronon gives one explanation that applies not only to Chicago but to other large American cities. As Cronon shows, the exploitation of North America's natural resources on thousands of scattered farms, forests, and other sites required central places where products could be gathered to form efficient commodity markets. By handling material in bulk, the largest centers were inevitably the most efficient, so traders, merchants, and bankers gathered there. So too did lumbermen, meatpackers, wholesalers, and others whose operations depended on an ample supply of commodities at favorable prices along with superior transportation facilities.[9]

A complementary explanation to Cronon's takes as its focus the great city as a manufacturing center. Here, paradoxically, the largest cities thrived because they offered the most opportunities to the thousands of small workshops that were the real heart of the urban manufacturing economy.[10] The nineteenth-century economy depended on artisan skills that were still practiced largely in small shops headed by an entrepreneur who

worked alongside his employees. These shops occupied very specialized niches in a dense urban economy where each small unit complemented the others. An urban district—the garment district of New York, the textile districts of Philadelphia—functioned like a single great enterprise where competing units nevertheless cooperated in producing goods of higher quality than could be produced outside the cities. As Philip Scranton has shown for the textile districts of Philadelphia, a specialized weaver depended on the equally specialized yarn spinners and dyers for the precise yarns he required, on skilled loom makers and repairers for the right looms, and on scores of other specialized craftsmen in his neighborhood for the skills and products necessary for his high-quality cloth.[11] Only the largest cities could sustain the optimum size and variety of these urban manufacturing districts, so the largest cities dominated the most profitable areas of production.

Thus increasing size brought increasing economic advantage. But this economic benefit would have been useless if the cities had been unable to cope with the costs of growth—if, for example, the costs of supplying the city rose even faster than the city grew, or if the cities began to poison their water supplies, perish in fires, or self-destruct in criminal violence. But these and other catastrophes were avoided by a crucial technique for turning urban wealth into public investment: borrowing against future growth.

Cities continually "leveraged" their tax base to finance the massive public works that kept the metropolis running. Jordan Schwarz has recently called attention to the importance of "state capitalism" in the New Deal era—public investment to promote economic development.[12] As I have argued in the introduction to this volume, cities in the nineteenth century had already mastered this form of investment. Cities borrowed heavily to create the infrastructure for business in harbor, rail, and other transport improvements. But they also used their borrowing power for measures that preserved public health and extended public welfare.[13]

Thus, the visionary scale of the metropolitan tradition becomes comprehensible when one measures it against the scale of urban growth and the magnitude of the public-works projects that had already transformed the American city in the nineteenth century. The most prominent exponents of metropolitanism were close students of or actual participants in those massive projects that had enabled the American city to cope with unprecedented increases in population through even more massive increases in public investment. Jon Teaford, who has particularly emphasized this aspect of urban history in *The Unheralded Triumph,* observes that in the 1830s Burnham's own Chicago was "a frontier trading post with a few log structures, a few muddy paths, and a few dozen inhabitants. Seventy years later it was a city of 1.5 million people, with a waterworks pumping 500 million gallons of water to its residents each day and a drainage system of over 1,500 miles of sewers. More than 1,400 miles of paved streets lighted by 38,000 streetlights crisscrossed the prairies, and 925 miles of streetcar lines carried hundreds of millions of passengers each year. A fleet of 129 fire engines protected lives and property, and over 2,200 acres of city parkland and a public library of 300,000 volumes offered recreation and a means for self-improvement."[14] Teaford adds that in June 1889 Chicago annexed 125 square miles to its former 43-square-mile territory, gaining 225,000 residents in a single day; that in the nine years between 1890 and 1899 the enrollment in Chicago public schools increased 78 percent from 136,000 to 242,000; and that during this period the city excavated 30 million cubic yards of earth for a sanitary and ship canal to reverse the flow of the Chicago River.[15]

In this context, the grand ambitions of the metropolitan tradition in the twentieth century seem to be reasonable extrapolations from the achievements of the nineteenth. The first generation of metropolitan planners did not invent the scale of metropolitan improvements. Rather, they added the conviction that the time had come for a general ordering of these improvements. Metropolitanism embodied a vision of a magnificent urban civilization that was firmly based on a detailed understanding of the complex infrastructure necessary to secure efficiency, a vision of urbanity that called for the intricate coordination of public and private interests, and a corresponding disdain for shortsighted politicians and backward-looking private enterprises that stood in the way of cooperation—the promise of a truly regional order based on the common good.

Urbanism as a Way of Life: The Chicago School of Sociology

The remarkable group of sociologists who gathered at the University of Chicago in the two decades after the *Plan of Chicago* had little interest in the grand tradition of physical planning exemplified by Burnham. Their contribution to the metropolitan tradition was to give a coherent explanation for the social, economic, and cultural vitality they experienced all around them. For, by the criteria of earlier social science, Chicago and cities like it were necessarily sites of personal anomie, social disorganization, and cultural conflict. Just as Burnham and his generation of planners had seen the potential for order and grandeur within the chaos of the American metropolis, so Robert Park, Ernest Burgess, R. D. McKenzie, W. I. Thomas, Louis Wirth, E. Franklin Frazier, and their students reconceived the monster city as the heartland of democracy.[16]

When Robert Park began teaching at the University of Chicago in 1914, the sociological analysis of the American city was still dominated by European social science, especially Ferdinand Tönnies's famous distinction between *Gemeinschaft* (community) and *Gesellschaft* (society). The great city was the essence of Gesellschaft: rational, contractual, impersonal relationships leading to isolation, stress, and disorganization. This dismal picture was further darkened by a long series of statistical studies that claimed to prove that the large city was as biologically destructive to health as it was culturally destructive to morals.[17]

This European critique was reinforced by the ruralist and small-town bias in American social thought. Anti-urbanism took on a particularly shrill and ugly tone among those Social Darwinists who saw the American city dominated by immigrants who were both culturally and physically inferior to older American stock. In their eyes the metropolis had become a breeding ground for "inferior protoplasm" that might eventually overwhelm the virtues of the true Americans.[18]

The Chicago sociologists also claimed to follow Darwin, but theirs was a very different Darwin from that of Herbert Spencer and his American acolytes. Park in his essay on "Human Ecology" emphasizes Darwin's understanding of "the 'web of life,' in which all living organisms, plants and animals alike, are bound together in a vast system of interlinked and interdependent lives."[19] For Park, human ecology does not, as one might expect, deal with the relationship of human beings to the natural world. It means rather the study of all those cultural interlinkings that bind human beings to each other. In analogy with natural ecological systems, the more complex these interdependencies are, the richer is human life. And of all the human ecologies, the richest and most complex is the great city.

As Louis Wirth elaborated the concept in his "Urbanism as a Way of Life," the largest cities support and indeed demand the greatest division of labor. This in turn supports and compels the most complex differentiations of individual skills and heterogeneity of human types. The city provides a constantly widening stream of choices through which its residents can attain ever-increasing individuality.

Thus, the immense scale of the great city does not reduce its inhabitants to a common denominator of mass culture, but density instead produces the most favorable conditions for diversity and individuality. In economics, the diversity of skills gives the city its great advantage over the small town. Culturally, the constant buffeting of choices and information gives the urbanite an "acceptance of insecurity and instability" that frees him from traditional conformities and encourages "sophistication and cosmopolitanism."[20]

To be sure, these insecurities can lead to the stress, loneliness, and anomie emphasized in the European literature on cities. But for the Chicago sociologists, the city had its remedy in its division into "natural areas." Just as plants and animals tend to cluster where conditions are most favorable to them, so the diverse urban types tend to find each other and create supportive communities. These might be based on ethnicity, or class, or even culture. Thus, Park noted the existence of a "kind of Latin Quarter" on Chicago's North Side where the little theaters, bookstores, and radical clubs clustered and together helped to alleviate the loneliness of the mostly young women who lived in the rooming houses of the district. He compared this "bohemia" to Chicago's skid-row "hobohemia," which offered its own form of mutual support for its residents. The more varied and interdependent were the natural areas of the city, the greater the urban culture.[21]

Given the social ecology of Chicago in the 1920s, the most important natural areas were the ethnic neighborhoods. Here the members of the Chicago School showed their superior understanding of the immigrant experience and its relationship to the American city. The work of the Chicago School had begun in the wake of the overheated patriotism of World War I and the consequent demands for the "Americanization" of immigrants. As one Americanizer put it, "Broadly speaking, we mean [by Americanization] an appreciation of the institutions of this country, absolute forgetfulness of all obligations or connections with other countries by descent or birth."[22]

But, as W. I. Thomas, co-author of the classic *The Polish Peasant in Europe and America,* asserted, "absolute forgetfulness" was absolutely destructive to the immigrant. Thomas observes that when Polish immigrants referred to a fellow immigrant as "completely Americanized," they meant someone who was completely demoralized.[23] The Chicago School constantly emphasized the value of immigrant groups holding onto as much of their heritage as they wish to. For the immigrants themselves, the "natural area" of the ethnic neighborhood with its shared language and culture was a crucial resource in preventing anomie and making possible a productive transition to American life. For the American city, the immigrant neighborhoods constituted a highly valuable element of diversity that enriched the complexity of the metropolis.

How, then, do the different "natural areas" of the city relate to each other? Once again borrowing an idea from plant and animal ecology, the Chicago School held that the metropolis as a whole had a natural and necessary form that reflected the outcome of the constant competition of "dominance, invasion, and succession" among the different groups. As rendered in Ernest Burgess's famous diagram, this metropolitan form looked remarkably like the concept advanced

by Burnham more than a decade earlier. Burgess's diagram shows the city as a series of concentric circles: downtown or "the Loop" at the core; surrounded by the "zone of workingmen's homes," the "residential zone," and finally the suburban "commuter's zone" (fig. 13).[24]

But implicit in Burgess's diagram is something very different from Burnham: not only a static depiction of the metropolis, but also a dynamic narrative of the immigrant's progress based on the key concepts of "mobility" and "assimilation." In Burgess's diagram one can see a small circle labeled "zone in transition" sandwiched between the Loop and the zone of workingmen's homes. The "transition" in this area refers partly to the buildings themselves, which, located just outside the fashionable core, are often the run-down remnants of once-desirable houses that have been subdivided into tiny apartments.

But this was a zone in transition in another sense: this was the area where immigrants settled first, the crowded slum or ghetto, that most intense of natural areas, the entry point of the metropolis. But the zone of transition also brought the immigrant into close proximity with the many job opportunities in the nearby factory zone and in the Loop itself. It also brought the immigrant into close proximity with others of his group, who both isolated and shielded him from the full force of Americanization.

The dynamic narrative implicit in the Burgess diagram is the story of the immigrant's progress from the zone in transition into the relative stability and prosperity of the ethnic neighborhoods in the zone of workingmen's homes and even beyond. This progress is summed up by the term "assimilation," the Chicago School's answer to Americanization. For assimilation meant not the stripping of one's former identity but the gradual self-creation within the metropolis. It meant learning the skills for productive employment, but also learning to choose among the many different identities that the metropolis offered. Assimilation meant attaining the freedom of the city.

Thus the "human ecology" of the metropolis functions as a great machine not so much for the accumulation of wealth as for the growing assimilation of its population. In this context it is notable that the Chicago School paid little attention either to the commercial life of the Loop or to the suburban life at the outer fringe. They concentrated instead on the seemingly mundane intermediate zones as the great theaters of assimilation, the places where the urban drama was most intense and meaningful. These dense mixtures of houses and workshops are not only the most productive areas of the city; they constantly introduce a dynamism that stems from their diversity.

This special dynamism in turn gives the great city its ascendancy over its hinterland; indeed, it creates its hinterland. Park characteristically attempted to define the "metropolitan region" not in terms of physical geography (Patrick Geddes's "valley section," for example) or history, but by tracing the circulation areas of the major metropolitan newspapers.[25] Newspaper circulation was a convenient source of data, but the big-city daily was above all an apt symbol for all that the Chicago School meant by "the metropolis."

With an irreverence and sophistication immortalized by Ben Hecht and Charles MacArthur's 1928 play *The Front Page*, the metropolitan newspaper juxtaposed the latest news of urban markets and industries with urban criminals and politicians (sometimes one and the same); big-city fashions, entertainment, and sports teams; the full range of downtown commercial culture from honky-tonk to the Chicago Lyric Opera. Far more than any civic center (real or imagined), the daily newspaper embodied the promise of "urbanism as a way of life."

Metropolitanism at Its Zenith: The *Regional Plan of New York and Its Environs* (1929–31)

The *Regional Plan of New York* was not only the culmination of the metropolitan tradition in American planning, it was also perhaps the most comprehensive analysis of a great industrial region ever published. Funded by more than one million 1920s dollars from the Russell Sage Foundation, the plan was truly a collective effort. Its two volumes of plans published in 1929 and 1931 were supplemented by eight massive volumes of "surveys" that investigated in exhaustive detail the region's geography, history, population, industries, transportation, and social services.[26] The researchers, for example, mapped the locations of more than four thousand garment workshops then located in Manhattan south of 59th Street; they mapped the home address of each child using Tompkins Square Park on the Lower East Side on a summer morning; they mapped the location of each of the forty-four legitimate theaters (total seating capacity 56,000) located within a thousand-foot radius of the 42nd Street subway station (figs. 16, 17).[27]

Yet out of this incredible mass of information came a genuinely comprehensive plan in the tradition of Burnham. Indeed, two former associates of Burnham headed the plan committee: Charles Dyer Norton and, after Norton's death in 1923, Frederic Delano, FDR's uncle and later head of the National Resources Planning Board. Norton had begun the plan's work in 1915 with a burst of Burnhamesque fervor: "From [New York] City Hall a circle must be swung which will include the Atlantic Highlands and Princeton; the lovely Jersey Hills back of Morristown and Tuxedo; the incomparable Hudson as far as Newburgh; the Westchester lakes and ridges, to Bridgeport and beyond, and all of Long Island."[28] This area was large enough to make even a Burnham pause: three states, twenty-two counties, over ten million people: the most important commercial and manufacturing region in the world. But the New York plan's strategy was essentially the same as Burnham's. Prepared by an independent body, the plan would embody the consensus of the best planning wisdom. With Thomas Adams as the executive director, the plan employed such notable figures as Harlan Batholomew, Edward H. Bennett, George B. Ford, John Nolen, and Frederick Law Olmsted, Jr. Backed by both planning expertise and the New York civic and business elite, the plan would thus set the agenda for all the governmental units in the region.

Moreover, the plan accepted the basic concept of the industrial metropolis as outlined in the Burnham *Plan of Chicago*. The region would be tightly centralized around its core—Manhattan south of 59th Street. Surrounding the core was a "20-mile industrial zone" where most of the region's population would live and work. The remaining territory—the "outer zone"—would be reserved for the elite suburbs, agriculture, and parks and other recreation areas.

Nevertheless, the New York plan went far beyond its Chicago counterpart in detailing the complex strategies necessary for maintaining the well-being of so vast a region. Adams summed up the basic strategy with the phrase "diffuse recentralization," a reference to the coordinated resettlement of industry and population out of Manhattan to more spacious and efficient locations within the industrial zone.

As the planners discovered, New York in the 1920s was intensely concentrated at its core. A survey taken in 1924 found that 2.2 million people entered Manhattan on a typical business day—23 percent of the population of the whole region. When, on such a typical day, one combined those residing in Manhattan south of 59th Street with those

who worked or visited there, the total came to 2.9 million people, or 30 percent of the region's total population.[29] These staggering numbers included points of especially intense congestion, such as the 175,000 people who worked in the garment center.[30]

Far from challenging this degree of concentration, the plan argued that such numbers would at least double by 1965 as the population of the region doubled. But they argued that, for the good of the whole region, Manhattan must change its character. Manhattan south of 59th Street was still a bustling manufacturing area; in addition to the garment center itself, there were scores of trades still centered in the lofts and other crowded spaces of the island. And, though depopulating, Manhattan from the Lower East Side to the West Fifties was still one of the most crowded "zones of transition" in the world, as tenements surrounded the skyscraper districts of Wall Street and Midtown.

The plan foresaw the organized movement of both manufacturing employment and of workers out of Manhattan. Where tenements or lofts once stood, new office towers or residences for the elite would rise to dominate formerly depressed areas like the East Side docks and even the Lower East Side. Manhattan would emerge as the world's ultimate downtown: the world financial center and the national corporate, cultural, and consumption capital.

Some recent critics of the plan have charged that in seeking to remove manufacturing and workers from the core, the planners showed their subservience to real estate interests and, worse, helped to initiate the deindustrialization of the region.[31] This is close to the opposite of the truth. To be sure, the plan very consciously wished to "gentrify"— as we would say now—the core, and its proposals for the derelict sectors of the waterfront anticipate similar projects of the 1970s and 1980s.

But, far from neglecting the manufacturing sector or its workers, the plan took as its primary goal the maintenance of the New York region as the world's premier industrial center. In particular, the plan committee understood the special importance of small businesses such as the ones located in Manhattan lofts for the region's prosperity. As one of the plan's economists put it, "the area is the paradise of the small manufacturer. The average number of employees per factory in the United States is 43, here it is a little over two-thirds of that number. In many lines of industry a small firm may conduct a national business without the owner traveling more than a few blocks in any direction. Supplies, related industries, financing, space in lofts or old buildings, labor at the door, styles or ideas, all in the very locality, and buyers who come regularly from all over the country at not distant hotels, all make it possible for the small fellow to exist."[32] To preserve the advantages that New York offered to small business, the plan accepted the logic of Burnham's view that the intense crowding of manufacturers at the center belongs to the pre-subway and pre-trolley era of urbanism. The place for most people and most manufacturing is in the more spacious industrial zone.

As the planners saw it, small manufacturers in Manhattan were forced to pay high rents for cramped space in congested streets in the older manufacturing districts or move to the outskirts where access to wholesale markets, transportation, and labor was slow and uncertain. Under these circumstances many manufacturers were tempted to leave the region entirely. Solving this problem required "diffused recentralization": a coordinated effort to "diffuse" manufacturing out of Manhattan and then to "re-centralize" it in specially planned districts in Brooklyn, Queens, the Bronx, and New Jersey. Although these districts would be miles rather than blocks away from Manhattan's whole-sale markets, the rail links to Manhattan would be so efficient that little convenience would be lost. Moreover, the new districts would have room for expansion and far better freight connections to national and world markets. These factory sites would be the most favored industrial sites in the world.

With careful planning, moreover, the "industrial zone" could also be a quiet and beautiful residential zone for most inhabitants of the region. Lower densities would mean lower land costs, lower rents for better housing, and even the possibility of home ownership. The plan had documented that the Lower East Side and Little Italy were already spontaneously depopulating as families moved out along the subway lines into more spacious quarters in the outer boroughs. But this move usually required a long and grueling commute back to a Manhattan workshop. The plan would locate both workers and jobs in the industrial zone, and both would benefit from the new quarters.[33]

The key to this new regional form was improved freight and mass rail transportation. The plan was fortunate to have the services of a visionary engineer, William J. Wilgus, who dramatically extended the possibilities of electric traction to shape a region over what Burnham had proposed for Chicago. But Wilgus essentially followed Burnham's lead in emphasizing the unification of competing lines into a single cooperative system (fig. 17).

The waterways that gave New York the greatest natural harbor in the world had long hampered freight transportation in the region. In the 1920s most freight from the rest of the country still had to be unloaded on New Jersey docks and be carried by barges over to Manhattan or Long Island. Competing carriers made the system even more chaotic. Wilgus proposed a cooperative belt railway running through the industrial zones of New Jersey and the outer boroughs that would both serve manufacturing there and coordinate the movement of freight into Manhattan through a series of new tunnels.

These tunnels would also serve the new regional passenger rail system that Wilgus envisioned. In addition to extending the New York City subway system, Wilgus proposed to unify the city subways with regional commuter lines and thus create a regional express-rail system. For example, he envisioned a loop line from New Jersey that would cross the Hudson at a new tunnel at 57th Street and then go underground beneath the city subways to stop at a few express stops between Midtown and Wall Street and then loop back under the Hudson to New Jersey. His ideas anticipate the "Regional Express Rail" system built for Paris in the 1970s and 1980s.

The plan also proposed an elaborate network of automobile roads, but they were clearly subordinate to the rail-based regional transit system. Whereas rail would handle the major work of transportation within the region—connecting the industrial zone to Manhattan—automobile parkways would fan out to the open space in the "outer zone." Thus the region would possess a transportation system balanced between rail and roads.

In general, Adams and the other consultants to the plan were suspicious of the early attempts at lower-middle-class automobile suburbs that pushed out toward the region's periphery. In part this attitude reflected their bias that these areas be reserved for elite suburbs. But, in a tradition going back to Charles W. Eliot and his plan for the Boston region, the planners primarily envisaged the "outer zone" as a permanent nature reserve for the region's population: the source of clean water, open space, and unspoiled parkland. To blur the edge of the industrial zone with what Adams called "premature subdivisions" would both destroy the beauty of the outer zone and also dissipate the efficiency of the

industrial zone itself as it scattered at the edge into chaotic development.

What unifies the plan's extensive discussions of the edge, intermediate zone, and center of the region is a remarkable confidence that *the proper form of the modern metropolis* is now known. Armored with this knowledge, the planners could sweep aside the contrary evidence that was accumulating even as they elaborated their projections for forty years into the future. The Port of New York Authority, which had been set up to implement a reform of rail transport in the region along the lines of the plan, discovered that the railroad companies refused to agree to the consolidations that Wilgus had proposed.[34] The wonderful new sites envisioned in the industrial zones failed to materialize, and small businesses either stubbornly clung to their urban lofts or they utilized the truck—a new form of freight transport—to move farther into the periphery than the planners had imagined. Meanwhile, suburban subdivisions continued to expand into the outer zone, despite Adams's warning that they were premature. These and other signs pointed to a more radical decentralization than the plan's concepts allowed. But these warning signs, though clearly visible in the data collected by the researchers, failed to shake the planners' belief that the New York region they envisioned embodied modernity itself: the form that every great city must take if it is to realize the promise of modern life.

The plan's elaborate depiction of the New York region in 1965 constitutes a kind of utopia for metropolitanism. The tenements of the East Side are replaced by Art Deco towers; spotless glass-and-brick factories in such industrial-zone showplaces as the South Bronx and Newark give New York world leadership in manufacturing; moderne-style apartment houses on broad boulevards house the factory workers of Brooklyn and Jersey

City; magnificent new rail terminals linked to a dizzying complex of new rail lines unite the region; and landscaped parkways rapidly transport the city dweller into the outer zone's still-unspoiled bucolic world of beaches, farms, and forests. The very elaborateness of vision was perhaps an unconscious premonition that metropolitanism had passed its zenith and was turning into fantasy.

The Crisis of the Metropolitan Tradition

The second volume of the *Regional Plan of New York, Building the City,* was published in 1931, a bad year both for building and for cities. Not only had the Great Depression virtually stopped both residential and commercial construction, ending the vision of an Art Deco Manhattan and much more, but the whole urban economy was under deep strain. Nevertheless, the metropolis with its multifaceted economy seemed far stronger than rural America, which had been in its own depression since the collapse of commodity prices in 1921. Moreover, the central cities seemed stronger than their suburbs, where speculative overbuilding had led to massive foreclosures, savings-and-loan bankruptcies, and thousands of acres of "ghost subdivisions."

With the coming of the New Deal many metropolitan planners saw an opportunity to advance their agenda in such key areas as housing and transportation. Under the auspices of the Public Works Administration (PWA) or the Works Progress Administration (WPA), the urban unemployed could be set to work on mass transit, freight rail and consolidation, parks, public buildings, and all the other elements for the metropolitan infrastructure that had been envisioned since Burnham's time. Some of these projects were indeed carried out, but, I would argue, the real impact of the New Deal years would prove to be far more negative.

The 1930s would mark the crisis of the metropolitan tradition, a severing of the metropolitan vision from reality that has never been remedied. In part this crisis reflected profound changes in technology, whose impact had been building since the turn of the century. But the New Deal itself introduced a crucial set of policies that deflected growth and investment away from the older cities and left these cities without the resources to compete effectively either with their own suburbs or with newer regions in the South and the West.[35]

Both the Chicago School of Sociology and the *Regional Plan of New York* had identified the industrial zone as the key locale for the health of the metropolis, and, inevitably, the crisis emerged first there. The prosperity of the industrial zone depended ultimately on its status as the best place for American manufacturers to do business, but in the 1920s profound forces in technology and in the economy has been eroding this advantage. Where the industrial zone had thrived through the multiplicity of small, interdependent firms, the large corporation strove to create systems of production based on manufacturing plants that were self-contained and thus no longer needed to be immersed in the fabric of urban life. Henry Ford's construction of the River Rouge plant outside Detroit symbolized this growing separation of production from the city.

Beyond these changes in corporate structure, new technologies were creating networks of movement and communication that no longer centered on a great hub—the metropolis—giving maximum advantage to facilities located near the center. Instead, these new networks—the emerging highway grid, electrical grids, the telephone system—permitted direct communication without going through an urban center, and gave equal access to the grid at all points. Just as trucks could now connect different manufacturing plants on the suburban periphery without going through a core distribution point, so telephone communication could put any two customers in a region in direct communication. The advantages once tightly held by a few great metropolitan centers where rail and water systems converged were now being distributed more evenly over whole regions.[36]

Moreover, just when the metropolitan industrial zones were losing their overwhelming locational advantages, their factories and infrastructure were also beginning to suffer from obsolescence. Where the most advanced techniques in mass production called for assembly to take shape as an unbroken flow along a single level, the typical industrial-zone plant was a multistoried structure in a crowded manufacturing-residential district that offered no scope to implement the new methods. Urban railroad yards and warehouses stranded shipments in limbo, while trucks were permanently stalled in urban traffic.

Housing in the industrial zone was also under stress, especially older multifamily units that dated back to the late nineteenth century. The ethnic neighborhoods that were once viewed as a major step upward out of the slums seemed inadequate compared to the automobile-based mass suburbia taking shape in the 1920s. The 1920s had seen a shift of investment capital away from rental housing—especially low-income rental housing—toward producing single-family houses for sale. Although these suburban houses remained too expensive for most working-class or lower-middle-class families—hence the collapse of the suburban housing market even before the stock market crash—there could be no doubt that housing in the industrial zone required substantial new investment to counter deterioration. The older

parts of the zone were filled with dwellings that still lacked indoor plumbing, hot water, or adequate light and air. The newer structures at the edge of the industrial zone were far better built, but such housing remained an uneasy compromise between urban land costs that mandated relatively high densities and families seeking greater room and privacy. Caught in the real estate collapse, these newer neighborhoods were often a strange hodgepodge of apartments, bungalows, and vacant lots.[37]

For the metropolitan planners of the 1930s, these deficiencies constituted a call to action. To restore the industrial zone to health—and therefore to safeguard the whole metropolis—they called for immediate action to upgrade urban manufacturing infrastructure along the lines proposed by the *Regional Plan of New York* in the 1920s: rail consolidation as part of a larger national reform of freight transport; harbor, bridge and road projects; and planned manufacturing sites within the industrial zone that could accommodate both small and large businesses.

Urban housing became a focus of particularly intense concern. Housing reformers influenced by European modernists had argued in the 1920s that American housing was crippled by relying on small speculative builders who built outmoded designs using inefficient techniques. The collapse of the private housing industry was seen as an opportunity to move toward large-scale projects that broke with the pattern set by small lots and achieved light and open space previously impossible. One important model was the Carl Mackley Houses in North Philadelphia, designed in 1933 by the Swiss modernist Oscar Stonorov as cooperative dwellings for the American Federation of Hosiery Workers. These bright and airy three-story garden apartments grouped around generous green spaces stood in a struggling neighborhood of older row houses and hosiery works, and seemed to announce the new housing forms that were coming to the American industrial zone.[38]

One important aspect of this new housing movement was that it was not seen as housing for poor people only. The reformers were confident that modern design would prove so clearly superior to the work of the speculative builders that people with a wide range of incomes would want to live there. The PWA, which had provided the loan for the Mackley Houses, was at this time interested in developing the new housing for a mix of classes. Soon after the completion of the Mackley Houses in Philadelphia, a group of planners and modernist architects proposed redeveloping a 484-acre site in Astoria, Queens. This area had been partially built up and was now occupied by scattered structures, almost all of which had been foreclosed. The project was supported by the Regional Plan Association, which saw it as the harbinger of the rebirth of the industrial zone.[39]

Taken together, the housing and other proposals put forward by planners constitute a program that one might call "metropolitan social democracy." It aimed to redevelop the cities for a coalition of working-class and lower-middle-class residents, who would benefit from the publicly supported housing, transportation, health care, libraries, school, parks, and other social programs.

But to implement metropolitan social democracy, the cities had to turn to Washington for funding, and this signalled a crucial change. In the past cities had funded massive improvements by borrowing against future growth, and they thus had the power to shape the future for themselves and the rest of their regions. In the 1930s, with many cities in literal default and none able to rely on optimistic projections of future growth, the power of the purse had moved to the federal government. On the basis of their population and their importance to the New Deal

political coalition, the largest cities should have been able to determine federal policy. But in fact the power of metropolitan interests was limited.

In contrast to the policies I have called "metropolitan social democracy," another set of policies arose, which I shall call "corporate regionalism." Corporate regionalism found its power base within the federal government in three interrelated "industrial policies," that is, close partnerships between the federal government and private industry that substantially reorganized those industries. These industrial policies I shall designate as (1) the suburban housing policy, (2) the automobile policy, and (3) the regional infrastructure policy.[40]

Like the planners and social critics grouped in such regionalist organizations as the Regional Planning Association of America (RPAA), corporate regionalism saw the central cities of the Northeast and Midwest as overpopulated. They aimed first at a movement of population and industry from the center to the periphery in the metropolitan regions, and also a movement from the "overdeveloped" Northeast and Midwest to the "underdeveloped" South and West.

But, as John Thomas emphasized in chapter 2 of this volume, the regionalist planners of the RPAA had seen decentralization in terms of preserving and creating small communities in balance with nature, advancing the values of variety and individuality, and opposing "the monolithic, corporate, industrial state." This "communitarian regionalism" found expression in the early Tennessee Valley Authority and in the Greenbelt towns, but it was in fact marginal to the New Deal and completely antithetical to the real meaning of corporate regionalism. Corporate regionalism was above all a technique for rapid economic development, the resuscitation of demand by creating vast new areas of growth to be transformed by corporate America.

The crucial housing policy emerged from a series of desperate improvisations in the face of the crash in middle-class housing. To save middle-class homeowners from mass foreclosure and to save the thrift industry from total collapse, the Roosevelt administration in 1933 created the Home Owners' Loan Corporation (HOLC) to refinance mortgages in arrears and thus also to "bail out" the thrift industry from its speculative orgy of the 1920s. To lower monthly payments to the minimum, the HOLC took a lesson from Populist agrarianism and instituted long-term, self-amortizing mortgages in place of the rickety, expensive system of short-term first and second mortgages that had been the rule. From this improvised base a remarkably strong suburban housing policy emerged, whose charter was the National Housing Act of 1934 and whose base was the Federal Housing Administration (FHA). The basic principle was to lower the cost of a suburban house by creating an efficient, low-cost system of housing finance and construction. This would widen the market for suburban houses, and the increased demand from this market would help to revive the whole economy.

Not only did this suburban industrial policy lower the value of urban real estate by creating cheap competition at the periphery, but the housing policy was designed to operate only at the suburban fringe of the region. Only there could one find cheap land for large-scale operations, and only on the edge could one find "stable" areas—as the FHA defined them—suitable for FHA mortgage insurance. The very maps that metropolitan planners drew up in the early 1930s to document the need for rebuilding were used by the FHA to "redline" virtually the whole industrial zone. As a result, the suburban edge of the region was the beneficiary of a federally insured flow of capital, while the industrial zones were subjected to systematic disinvestment.[41]

The "automobile policy" complemented the suburban industrial policy by creating at federal expense a decentralized network to serve the new houses and other facilities being constructed at the edge of the region. The crucial infrastructure for growth came directly from the federal government, enabling the suburbs to equip themselves even before they had developed a minimal tax base. Between 1933 and 1942 the federal government spent four billion dollars on roads—largely under the auspices of unemployment relief.[42]

Finally, the regional infrastructure policy—operating through such agencies as the Reconstruction Finance Corporation, the Rural Electrification Administration, the PWA, and the WPA—equipped the South and the West to compete with the urban industrial zone for jobs. Since these areas had not only lower wage costs but also a "better business climate" than the big city, the way to metropolitan de-industrialization was cleared.

The anti-urban implications of "corporate regionalism" were quickly grasped by the metropolitan planners. Their concerns were focused by the census of 1940, which clearly indicated the incipient crisis of the central cities. In the 140 "metropolitan districts" as defined by the Census Bureau, the central cities gained 6.1 percent but their suburbs gained 16.9 percent; more than a quarter of the central cities had actually lost population in the 1930s.[43] Planners observed the deterioration and abandonment of large portions of the inner industrial zone, prompting increasingly desperate recommendations of massive slum clearances for housing projects. In 1942, addressing the Commercial Club of Chicago (the same organization that had sponsored Burnham's 1909 plan), Louis Wirth asserted that 51 square miles out of Chicago's 212 square miles "need overhauling," including "11 square miles of housing so utterly unfit for human habitation it ought to be torn down immediately." Wirth spoke prophetically when he remarked, "Until our planning goes beyond the stage of projecting some more superhighways—which, incidentally, will take more of our people out into the suburbs and devastate the center even more dismally—until we really begin to rebuild the 51 square miles near the center of the city . . . we cannot have minimum standards of human decency and public services; and that means we will have an inordinate amount of crime, disorder, human wastage."[44] But metropolitan planning could hardly cope with the force of corporate regionalism, nor was Wirth's own remedy of massive slum clearances to build massive housing projects very convincing.

The Second World War revived the urban economies but, on balance, accelerated the agenda of corporate regionalism. The Defense Plant Corporation alone virtually changed the industrial map of the nation, directing growth almost exclusively to the suburban peripheries or to the developing Sunbelt. Perhaps more important, the war also precipitated the great black migration to the metropolis.

If the policies of corporate regionalism doomed the *Regional Plan of New York*'s hopes for the metropolis as an industrial center, the black migration tested the Chicago School of Sociology's hopes for the metropolis as the center of tolerance and assimilation. One can hardly accuse the Chicago School of ignoring blacks. Robert Park himself had been a close associate of Booker T. Washington; Franklin Frazier, whose first book was *The Negro Family in Chicago* (1932), was perhaps Park's most important student; and St. Clair Drake and Horace Cayton's *Black Metropolis* was perhaps the Chicago School's most important single volume.[45] Nevertheless, the Chicago School's theory of the metropolis was based finally on the experiences of white ethnics, and could never come to terms with the force of a black ghettoization

that shut down the possibilities of assimilation. Drake and Cayton emphasized that, for black assimilation to take place, white society must give up the "job ceiling" and the "color line" that limited blacks to low-paying jobs in segregated neighborhoods. But the job ceiling and color line held; indeed, Chicago as late as 1980 exhibited a 90 percent index of racial segregation, higher than any other major metropolitan area in either the North or the South.[46] Instead of the metropolis as an environment for learning and choice, the metropolis became the center of isolation and race conflict, the long war along the borders of the "zone of transition" so well documented by Hirsch.[47]

Unable to respond coherently to these changes, the metropolitan tradition split into a number of partial and contradictory fragments. One of the most important was the emergence of a "downtown" coalition dedicated to maintaining the downtown as regional core without regard to the fate of the rest of the central city. Burnham and the other metropolitan thinkers had never doubted that the downtown and its industrial zone would share the same basic interests. But the corporate elites that emerged in the era of corporate regionalism saw the downtown as a headquarters for regional restructuring where decisions would be made to move production from center to periphery or out of the region entirely.

Perhaps the strongest example of the intellectual fragmentation of the metropolitan tradition can be found in the work of Jane Jacobs. In many respects her work constitutes our most impressive restatement of that tradition. The Chicago School of Sociology at its best never equalled Jacobs's tribute to metropolitan diversity in her lyrical and closely observed account of the "intricate sidewalk ballet" on the streets of her own "natural area" of Greenwich Village.[48] Nor did the *Regional Plan of New York* provide so impressive and coherent an analysis of the strengths of an urban economy as Jacobs achieves in *The Economy of Cities*.[49]

But Jacobs is also deeply hostile to almost all the planning doctrines that come out of the metropolitan tradition. Not only is she the most devastating critic of modernist public housing, but she also criticizes virtually the whole vocabulary of metropolitan planning: civic centers, large public spaces, broad boulevards, the quest for visual order.

Most important, she criticizes the very attempt to conceive of metropolitan form and to plan at a regional level. The idea of a coherent order that would unite beauty and efficiency seems to her either a delusion or a tool for elites to impose their will on the neighborhoods that are the only real source of urban vitality. As she remarks, "'A Region,' someone has wryly said, 'is an area safely larger than the last one to whose problems we found no solution.' [At the metropolitan level] the mazes are too labyrinthine even to be kept mapped and open. . . . Citizens and officials both can wander indefinitely in these labyrinths, passing here and there the bones of many an old hope, dead of exhaustion."[50]

From the straight, unlimited vistas of Daniel Burnham's monumental boulevards to the mazes and labyrinths of Jane Jacobs: this symbolizes the trajectory of the metropolitan idea in twentieth-century America.

Epilogue: Metropolitanism and Regionalism

John L. Thomas's examination of the regional tradition in chapter 2 begins with the 1932 debate between Lewis Mumford and Thomas Adams over the *Regional Plan of New York*. This chapter ends with another perspective on the debate that Thomas rightly calls "one of the clarifying moments in the history of re-

gionalism and regional planning in the United States." Mumford had charged that the plan's intention of retaining the bulk of the region's population within the "20-mile industrial zone" reflected a capitulation to banking and real estate interests who wanted to maintain speculative land values within the metropolitan core. He called for the decentralization of both population and industry into self-contained "New Towns" in the region's "Outer Zone," for which Radburn, New Jersey, would be a model. Adams replied that the plan represented realism over Mumford's utopianism.[51]

Today that debate appears in a painfully ironic light. The sites that Adams and his colleagues "realistically" marked for growth and renovation—the South Bronx, Bedford-Stuyvesant in Brooklyn, Jersey City, Newark, and other industrial-zone sites—have become areas where depopulation, de-industrialization, and abandonment are at their worst. But this form of urban decentralization did not fulfill Mumford's hopes. Instead of planned decentralization into small-scale communities that would respect the natural landscape, a wave of low-density mass suburbanization and other forms of "corporate regional development" has now engulfed virtually all of the outer zone. Precisely the terrain that Mumford in the 1930s had envisaged for the locale of the new, human-scaled democratic civilization has become instead the sprawling "anti-city" he deplored at the end of his life.

We can now see that Mumford's communitarian regionalism and the metropolitanism of the *Regional Plan of New York* and the Chicago School of Sociology have more in common than was apparent to Mumford or Adams. Both were seeking a coherent and lasting relationship with nature, whether the New Town with its permanent Greenbelt or the metropolis with its permanent outer zone; both were seeking an environment where diversity and individuality could thrive. In 1937 Wirth pointed to some possible intellectual convergences between the two traditions: "There is a liberty of development in isolation and wide spaces, but there is also freedom in the many-sided life of the city where each may find his own kind. There is democracy in the scattered few, but there is also democracy in the thick crowd with its vital impulse and its insistent demand for a just participation in the gains of our civilization. There is fertility and creativeness in the rich soil of the broad countryside, but there is also fertility and creativeness in forms of industry, art, personality, emerging even from city streets and reaching toward the sky."[52] But these convergences never materialized in a common program that would have seen the rebuilding of the industrial zone and the creation of New Towns as mutually supporting objectives. Instead, both communitarian regionalism and metropolitanism proved vulnerable to a program of rapid economic development on the standardized corporate model.

But this model is itself reaching the point of bankruptcy and self-contradiction, and the urban and environmental devastation it has produced has led us to look again at the ideas it supplanted. The metropolitan tradition is important to us now not only because it speaks to our need to address the urban crisis, but because it preserves options, alternatives, *choices* that are not easily apparent in our culture today. It contains a rich legacy of possibilities for the economic and cultural revitalization of the inner city, for a balanced transportation system, the limitation of sprawl and other policies, but above all it encourages us to try to understand the great city as a whole and to imagine the metropolis as a coherent organism with a center and an edge and an irreplaceable role to play in the creation of American democracy. Such thinking is difficult in an era like our own, which constantly seeks to "de-center" and is more comfortable with fragments and subgroups than with attempts at unity. But perhaps now is the time to begin to reassemble the fragments.

Notes

1. Ernest W. Burgess, "The Growth of the City," in Robert E. Park, Ernest W. Burgess, and Roderick D. McKenzie, eds., *The City* (Chicago: University of Chicago Press, 1925).

2. Walter Benjamin, *Illuminations* (New York: Schocken, 1969), p. 255. The observation comes from his "Theses on the Philosophy of History," written in 1940.

3. Walter Lippmann, *Drift and Mastery: An Attempt to Diagnose the Current Unrest* (orig. ed. 1914), new edition with introduction and notes by William E. Leuchtenberg (Englewood Cliffs, N.J.: Prentice-Hall, 1961).

4. Carlo Levi, *Christ Stopped at Eboli,* trans. Frances Frenaye (New York: Farrar Strauss, 1947), pp. 124–5.

5. Sam Bass Warner, Jr., *The Private City: Philadelphia in Three Periods of Growth* (Philadelphia: University of Pennsylvania Press, 1968), p. 201.

6. Thomas S. Hines, *Burnham of Chicago: Architect and Planner,* rev. ed., (Chicago: University of Chicago Press, 1979).

7. Daniel H. Burnham and Edward H. Bennett, *Plan of Chicago* (Chicago: Commercial Club, 1909). In addition to the acknowledged assistance of Bennett, the "Burnham Plan" was in fact the work of a whole team of architects and planners. See especially the essays by Robert Bruegmann, Sally Chapell, and John Zukowsky in the exhibition catalogue, *Plan of Chicago 1909–1979* (Chicago: Art Institute of Chicago, 1979).

8. Burnham and Bennett, *Plan of Chicago,* p. 18.

9. William Cronon, *Nature's Metropolis: Chicago and the Great West* (New York: Norton, 1991). See also Donald L. Miller, *City of the Century: The Epic of Chicago and the Making of America* (New York: Simon and Schuster, 1996).

10. Jane Jacobs, *The Economy of Cities* (New York: Random House, 1969).

11. Philip Scranton, *Proprietary Capitalism: The Textile Manufacture at Philadelphia, 1800–1885* (New York: Cambridge University Press, 1983).

12. Jordan A. Schwarz, *The New Dealers: Power Politics in the Age of Roosevelt* (New York: Knopf, 1993).

13. Eric H. Monkkonen, *America Becomes Urban: The Development of U.S. Cities and Towns, 1780–1980* (Berkeley: University of California Press, 1988), chaps. 4–6.

14. Jon C. Teaford, *The Unheralded Triumph: City Government in America, 1870–1900* (Baltimore: Johns Hopkins University Press, 1984), p. 217.

15. Ibid., p. 220.

16. For general studies of the Chicago School, see Martin Bulmer, *The Chicago School of Sociology: Institutionalization, Diversity, and the Rise of Sociological Research* (Chicago: University of Chicago Press, 1984); Lee Harvey, *Myths of the Chicago School of Sociology* (Brookfield, Vt.: Gower, 1987); Fred H. Matthews, *Quest for an American Sociology: Robert E. Park and the Chicago School* (Montreal: McGill, Queen's University Press, 1977); Stow Persons, *Ethnic Studies at Chicago, 1905–45* (Urbana: University of Illinois Press, 1987); Dennis Smith, *The Chicago School: A Liberal Critique of Capitalism* (New York: St. Martin's, 1988); and Luigi Tomasi, ed., *The Tradition of the Chicago School of Sociology* (Brookfield, Vt.: Ashgate, 1998).

17. Andrew Lees, *Cities Perceived: Urban Society in Urban and American Thought, 1820–1940* (New York: Columbia University Press, 1985), part 3.

18. Richard Hofstadter, *Social Darwinism in American Thought* (Philadelphia: University of Pennsylvania Press, 1944).

19. Robert E. Park, *Human Communities: The City and Human Ecology* (New York: Free Press, 1952), p. 145.

20. Louis Wirth, "Urbanism as a Way of Life" (1938), in *Community Life and Social Policy: Selected Papers by Louis Wirth,* ed. Elizabeth Wirth Marvick and Albert Reiss, Jr. (Chicago: University of Chicago Press, 1956), p. 124.

21. Park, *Human Communities,* p. 89.

22. Quoted in Robert E. Park and Herbert A. Miller, *Old World Traits Transplanted* (New York: Harper, 1921), p. 281. The speaker is identified as "Superintendent of the New York Public Schools." The book itself was in fact written by W. I. Thomas. See Persons, *Ethnic Studies at Chicago,* p. 54.

23. Persons, *Ethnic Studies at Chicago,* p. 173.

24. Burgess, "The Growth of the City," p. 211.

25. Robert Park, in Roderick D. McKenzie, *The Metropolitan Community,* (New York: Russell and Russell, 1967 [1933]).

26. The best account of the plan is David A. Johnson, *Planning the Great Metropolis: The 1929 Regional Plan of New York and Its Environs* (London: E & FN Spon, 1996).

27. Committee on Regional Plan, *The Regional Plan and Surveys of New York and Its Environs* (New York: Committee on Regional Plan, 1924–31), 10 vols. See also my "The Regional Plan of New York and the Transformation of the Industrial Metropolis," in David Ward and Olivier Zunz, eds., *The Landscape of Modernity: Essays on New York City, 1900–1940* (New York: Russell Sage Foundation, 1992).

28. Norton memorandum of November 27, 1915, quoted in Johnson, *Planning the Great Metropolis,* p. 118.

29. *Regional Plan of New York,* vol. 4, pp. 36–9.

30. *Regional Plan of New York,* vol. 1b, "Clothing and Textile Industries," p. 12.

31. Robert Fitch, *The Assassination of New York* (London: Verso, 1993), provides an unwitting demonstration that conspiracy theorists are not limited to the Kennedy assassination.

32. *Regional Plan of New York,* vol. 6, p. 188.

33. Johnson, *Planning the Great Metropolis,* chap. 7.

34. Jameson Doig, "Joining New York City to the Greater Metropolis: The Port Authority as Visionary, Target of Opportunity and Opportunist," in Ward and Zunz, eds., *The Landscape of Modernity,* pp. 85–92. Doig tells the full story of the Port Authority's involvement with rail transport in his forthcoming definitive history of the Port Authority, *Empire on the Hudson.*

35. My thinking on the New Deal has been most strongly influenced by the work of a contributor to this volume: Alan Brinkley, *The End of Reform: New Deal Liberalism in Recession and War* (New York: Knopf, 1995). In addition, I am indebted to the perspective in Schwarz, *The New Dealers.* Finally, my thinking reflects many conversations with Gail Radford, whose work on New Deal housing, cited below, opens up the most important issues of New Deal policy.

36. I expand on this argument in "America's New City," *Wilson Quarterly,* Winter 1990, pp. 24–55.

37. Gail Radford, *Modern Housing for America: Policy Struggles in the New Deal Era* (Chicago: University of Chicago Press, 1996).

38. Ibid., chap. 5.

39. Clarence Perry, *The Rebuilding of Blighted*

Areas: A Study of the Neighborhood Unit in Re-planning and Plot Assemblage (New York: Regional Plan Association, Inc., 1933).

40. For a personification of "corporate regionalism," see the aptly titled memoir of Jesse H. Jones, a wealthy Houston businessman and head of Roosevelt's Reconstruction Finance Corporation: *Fifty Billion Dollars: My Thirteen Years with the RFC, 1932–1945* (New York: Macmillan, 1951).

41. The classic description of the impact of the FHA on American cities and suburbs is in Kenneth T. Jackson, *Crabgrass Frontier: The Suburbanization of the United States* (New York: Oxford University Press, 1985), chap. 11.

42. Jan Holtz Kay, *Asphalt Nation: How the Automobile Took over America, and How We Can Take It Back* (New York: Crown Publishers, 1997), chap. 9.

43. Jon C. Teaford, *The Rough Road to Renaissance: Urban Revitalization in America, 1940–1985* (Baltimore: Johns Hopkins University Press, 1990), pp. 10–18.

44. Louis Wirth, "Chicago: Where Now?" (1944), in *Community Life and Social Policy,* ed. Marvick and Reiss, pp. 323–4.

45. E. Franklin Frazier, *The Negro Family in Chicago* (Chicago: University of Chicago Press, 1932); material from this now-rare book was incorporated in Frazier's better-known *The Negro Family in the United States* (Chicago: University of Chicago Press, 1939). St. Clair Drake and Horace R. Cayton, *Black Metropolis: A Study of Negro Life in a Northern City* (New York: Harcourt, Brace, 1945).

46. Reynolds Farley, "Residential Segregation of Social and Economic Groups among Blacks, 1970–1980," in *The Urban Underclass,* ed. Christopher Jencks and Paul E. Peterson (Washington, D.C.: Brookings Institution Press, 1991), p. 277.

47. Arnold R. Hirsch, *Making the Second Ghetto: Race and Housing in Chicago, 1940–1960* (New York: Cambridge University Press, 1983).

48. Jane Jacobs, *The Death and Life of Great American Cities* (New York: Random House, 1961).

49. Jacobs, *The Economy of Cities.*

50. Jacobs, *The Death and Life of Great American Cities,* p. 410.

51. The debate is reprinted in Carl Sussman, ed., *Planning the Fourth Migration* (Cambridge, Mass. MIT Press, 1976), pp. 245–78.

52. Report of the Urbanism Committee to the National Resources Committee, *Our Cities: Their Role in the National Economy* (Washington, D.C., 1937), reprinted in Charles N. Glaab, ed., *The American City: A Documentary History* (Homewood, Ill.: Dorsey Press, 1963), p. 450.

PART TWO

THE QUEST FOR
NATIONAL PLANNING

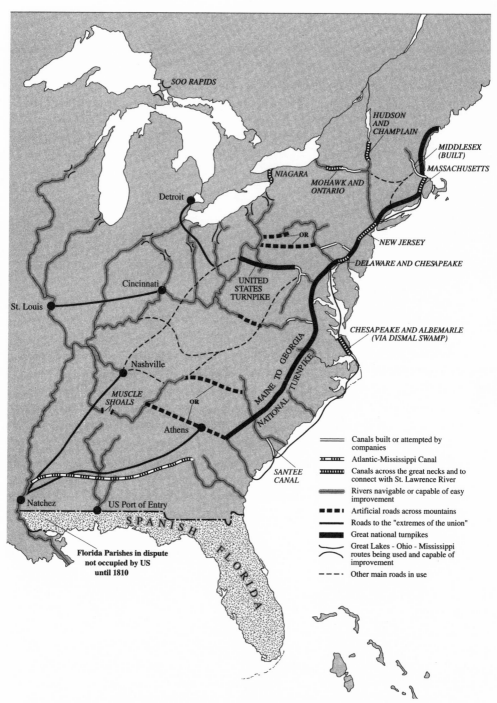

The Gallatin Plan, 1808. Secretary of the Treasury Albert Gallatin's comprehensive plan to use the resources of the federal government to build a system of canals and roadways linking the Atlantic port cities and the navigable rivers of the interior. He hoped his plan would knit together the separate states into a genuine nation. (From D.W. Meinig, *The Shaping of America: A Geographical Perspective on 500 Years of History, vol. 2* [New Haven: Yale University Press, 1993])

CHAPTER FOUR

Federalism and National Planning
The Nineteenth-Century Legacy

::

MICHAEL J. LACEY

Running a constitution, as Woodrow Wilson once remarked, is more difficult than writing one, and the observation might well be taken to heart by planners for whom the boisterousness and volatility of politics stand in such sharp contrast to the foresight and constancy their own work calls for.[1] Of the defining features of the U.S. Constitution, none has been more troublesome from the standpoint of foresight and constancy than its federal design, which retains the states as authentic polities in their own right, constitutional entities and not merely administrative ones. In this sense, decentralization is constitutionally mandated in America, and centralization seems often to violate its fundamental law. Measures favoring centralization, called "measures of consolidation" in the nineteenth century and vigorously opposed by many in the tradition of Thomas Jefferson and Andrew Jackson as the usurpation of states' rights, have long been focal points for political struggle. Rooting such measures in the practice of government has required over time a good deal of ingenuity and indirection.

Yet national planning, taken simply in its least controversial sense as farsighted and responsible government, requires some degree of consolidation, as is clear to those today who look to Washington to "do something" to secure the conditions for social and economic justice and environmental conservation and improvement, and to counter the negative effects of America's integration into increasingly global systems of production and exchange. Doing something, however, takes political and administrative capacity. Thus the old arguments over consolidation are important: they concerned building up the capacity of the federal system, so that it might be up to the level of the times.

This chapter will look at two episodes in that long struggle to develop capacity.

It will compare the first proposed national plan, Treasury Secretary Albert Gallatin's scheme for internal improvements submitted to the 10th Congress in 1808 with a second national plan submitted a century later to the 60th Congress in the form of Theodore Roosevelt's proposals for a nationwide program of conservation and development. The first was intended through a system of roads and canals to secure the Union and establish the physical and institutional infrastructure for a dynamic, interdependent national economy and culture. The second had the same basic goals; it was to be spearheaded by the new ideas of multipurpose river-basin development laid out in the report of Roosevelt's Inland Waterways Commission of 1908, a document that looked backward as well as forward in time and claimed Gallatin's work as its root and precedent.[2]

Both plans failed to secure congressional support. From the standpoint of many well-informed contemporaries, however, both were arguably on the right track, and the reasons for their failure point to deep-seated, enduring constraints in the American political tradition that continue to shape the possibilities of the future. Thus the hope of this chapter is that something valuable can be learned by recalling these episodes and the context in which they were argued. As will become clear, the most important aspect of context was the fact that both plans edged into a grey area of constitutional jurisdiction, where the legitimacy of action on the part of the national government was open to challenge.

The account that follows will emphasize the influence of uncertainties of jurisdiction within America's federal culture in retarding the development of relations between the national government and the states during the nineteenth century. It will focus on the sharply conflicting interpretations of what was needed to make federalism actually work that marked the public philosophy of the pe-

riod and continue into our own. The history of both theory and practice in this field is complicated and resists simplifying generalities. Despite its length, therefore, what follows is a selective sketch intended only to highlight the most important points that would have to be elaborated in detail in a thorough history of planning in the United States.

The ability of governments to cooperate is the key to the historical problem. Just how the operations of the national government were to fit together with those of the state and local governments on matters of common interest and responsibility has from the beginning been unclear. Indeed, from the start, with few exceptions, the very notion that there *were* matters of common interest and responsibility has been hotly contested, until well into the twentieth century usually successfully, by those who espoused a "dual federalism" reading of the Constitution—one that held that the governments in question had separate and distinct duties that should not be confounded for fear of corrupting one side or the other, or both. By insisting on keeping separate the spheres of authority, this perspective precluded as a matter of principle the development of habits of cooperation and the institutions required to facilitate common public enterprise.[3] This is one of the reasons why effective central public bureaucracy was slow to develop in America, while large-scale private enterprise was generally welcomed as it emerged in the course of the nineteenth century, first in transportation but then in other sectors of the economy, since to many it seemed so capable and efficient as compared to the hesitancy and impotence of government in dealing with big problems.

This retardant effect of the doctrine of dual federalism is a fact of some consequence for planning history. With the development of modern public policy in the fields of environment and social welfare, urban reconstruction and economic development, increasingly it has become clear that for planning to work in America, federalism of a cooperative kind must be devised and made to work. Much *has been* devised in piecemeal and haphazard fashion, particularly since the 1930s and thanks in large part to the rippling crises of depression, war, and cold war, which made vigorous national action a pragmatic necessity, no matter what the traditional prerogatives of state governments were. A vast and in some respects still uncharted world of intergovernmental relations has arisen, through which enormous sums of public funding circulate. In 1997 federal aid to state and local governments totaled over $234 billion. In the aggregate these relations comprise much of the substance of public or governmental planning in the United States—the cumulated, institutionalized answers to long-term policy problems formulated by Washington and all of the state capitals of the nation.[4]

As to the *quality* of the workings of these relations, however, or their deeper logic and effectiveness, little can be said with confidence. Few would claim much for them along these lines, since even after the barriers to cooperation were lowered, the problems of accountability grew apace. In fact, many of the environmentally and socially destructive effects of the growth machine that was turned loose after the Second World War by government initiatives in many fields—fiscal and monetary policies, for example, together with those in transportation, housing, urban renewal, and agriculture—are attributable to the lack of overall coherence among the many merely pragmatic, but piecemeal and fragmented, constitutional adaptations, each with its own mobilized clientele. It was in response to some of the pervasive problems generated by this way of governing that today's national apparatus of environmental regulation began to take shape.[5]

The growth of intergovernmental relations, in other words, cannot be taken to mean that the root problems of cooperative federalism have been satisfactorily addressed and resolved. They have never been frontally and systematically addressed by the appropriate constitutional authorities. There are no cooperative federalism amendments to the Constitution spelling out the principles of subsidiarity on which ideal intergovernmental relations ought to turn. Innumerable problems for both theory and practice remain, and since they constrain the political possibilities of the future, they are problems for those interested in the prospects of the American planning tradition.[6]

The Ambiguity of Federalism

The roots of the problem of establishing a satisfactory cooperative federalism go deep into the history of American thought and practice. Whether the Constitution represents the expression of a fundamentally unworkable compromise cobbled together by the founders, or a sophisticated theory of a complex national community that we are still trying to grow into, remains a matter of scholarly dispute. Interpretation is all, and so the history of interpretation as it changes over time comes into play. Whatever the intention of the founders, a glance into the history of the national government makes it plain that the federal design was an ideal arrangement of governmental powers for a people unable to make up its mind whether to be one community or many, and apparently determined to be both.[7]

Offering as it does so many arenas for public action, large and small, separate and overlapping (there are today roughly eighty-five thousand units of local government alone in the United States), America's extraordinarily fragmented federal culture is rich in opportunities to lead or follow, cooperate or obstruct, attend to inherited duties or revise them.[8] Merely by *being there,* the federal design encourages a good measure of social differentiation, but for the same reason it provides obstacles to such tendencies toward social and moral integration as may exist, and thus it links up with recurrent questions of national identity and purpose. The political culture set up by the federal design is accordingly complex. The actual workings and central tendencies of public authority within it are confusing and difficult to discern.

Martin Diamond, the political theorist and historian, has outlined the reasons why a federal society is likely to be shot through with ambiguities concerning the proper exercise of public authority, and why we should expect to find some ambiguity in its accumulating historical record. In an observation that fits public life at the municipal and state levels as well as the national, Diamond makes the following points:

> The distinguishing characteristic of federalism is the peculiar ambivalence of the ends men seek to make it serve. The ambivalence is quite literal: federalism is always an arrangement pointed in two contrary directions or aimed at securing two contrary ends. One end is always found in the reason why the member units do not simply consolidate themselves into one large, unitary country; the other end is always found in the reason why the member units do not choose to remain simply small, wholly autonomous countries. The natural tendency of any political community, whether large or small, is to completeness, to the perfection of its autonomy. Federalism is the effort deliberately to modify that tendency. Hence any given federal structure is always the institutional expression of the contradiction or tension between the particular reasons the member units have for remaining small and autonomous but not wholly, and large and consolidated but not quite.[9]

Not wholly and not quite, indeed! The contradictions and tensions that Diamond points to are profoundly consequential for fixing political responsibility in American affairs. At stake are fundamental issues of politics and administration, jurisdiction and competence, chief among them the meaning of the national domain and the role of the national government in its management and enhancement.

Here the central question is the *geography of jurisdiction* and changes within it from separate to mixed over time. Under the strict conditions of dual federalism that held sway from the founding through the Civil War, with the exception of its post offices and its few customs- and courthouses, the personnel and agencies of the national government were confined mainly to coasts and borders, to the moving margins of the American map—the portion that had, as yet, no states within it.

Of course the importance of those duties in foreign policy, the administration of public lands, currency matters, and military affairs that were clearly assigned by the Constitution to the national government are not to be gainsaid. Indeed, recent research has shown that the postal service, which was rooted in an enumerated power of the Constitution that permitted Congress "to establish post offices and post roads," quickly grew into the most sophisticated, energetic, efficient public enterprise in the nation, supplying a communications infrastructure that quickened the social and economic development of the early republic.[10] Despite the exceptions, however, from early on it was apparent to many among the founders that a government confined mainly to these areas and bereft of any more vital internal responsibilities was likely to remain at the periphery of the peoples' consciousness and to command only notional loyalty from them. Nation building itself *required* vital internal responsibilities for central government, so that in performing them the respect and attachments of the people might be secured. This insight was at the heart of the Federalists' vision and program. Alexander Hamilton in Federalist 27 laid out the core of the issue:

Man is very much a creature of habit. A thing that rarely strikes his senses will generally have but a transient influence upon his mind. *A government continually at a distance and out of sight can hardly be expected to interest the sensations of the people. The inference is that the authority of the Union and the affections of the citizens toward it will be strengthened, rather than weakened, by the extension to what are called matters of internal concern;* and that it will have less occasion to recur to force, in proportion to the familiarity and comprehensiveness of its agency. The more it circulates through those channels and currents in which the passions of mankind naturally flow, the less it will require the aid of the violent and perilous expedients of compulsion (emphasis added).[11]

For its own good the national government had to find a place within the dynamism of a developing culture, and that dynamism was concentrated where the people and their projects were, within the boundaries of the original thirteen states. But how to find a place here, out of what was already under the jurisdiction of state legislatures that existed prior to the establishment of national government? A mingling or mixing of jurisdictions was required, partnerships of some kind, and any opportunities that opened up along this line would have to be pursued. The ideal of cooperative federalism, in other words, is an implicit but nonetheless integral part of what has been called the *national theory* of federalism.[12] Again, Hamilton makes the point:

I will, in this place, hazard an observation which will not be the less just because to some

it may appear new; which is, *that the more the operations of national authority are intermingled in the ordinary exercise of government,* the more the citizens are accustomed to meet with it in the common occurrences of their political life, the more it is familiarized to their sight and to their feelings, the further it enters into those objects which touch the most sensible chords and put in motion the most active springs of the human heart, *the greater will be the probability that it will conciliate the respect and attachment of the community* [emphasis added].[13]

Cooperative Federalism and Public Philosophy

Needless to say, to assert an open-ended "intermingling" of governments as an ideal essential to nation building was not a consensus position in the 1790s. Establishing a rationale for cooperative federalism against the background of a newly ratified Constitution that could be read to prohibit cooperation—as it was to varying degrees by Jefferson, James Madison, James Monroe, and other architects of the emerging Republican Party (or Democratic Republicans, for they were called both)—was among the first problems encountered in organizing the national government. Although the Federalists' vision of an activist, planning and development–oriented national government (rooted in the mercantilist thought of the eighteenth century) was built upon the premise that such cooperation could be secured, and although the fortunes of American nationalism as anything more complex, culturally speaking, than xenophobia and chauvinism seemed to rest on the degree to which the purported link between intermingled levels of government and sentiments of national solidarity held true, cooperative federalism had very formidable opponents. In fact, the basic competitive two-party pattern that has marked the American political tradition from the 1790s on can be seen to issue from the different responses to the idea of national planning: attempting to elaborate or build on it through cooperative federalism, or to counter and ridicule the idea.

One stream of the tradition was sympathetic to the national theory of federalism and to government planning; indeed, it called for the creation of the theory's ideas and institutions and is incoherent without that theory. As a constitutional perspective this theory held that the states, despite the peculiar autonomy they enjoyed, were nonetheless subordinate to the nation and the needs of *its* government, since they had no genuine sovereignty except as members of the Union. The Union, in this view, was not created by the states or even by the people of the states, but by the people of the nation as a whole. It was the Union that won the war for independence, with the result, as Abraham Lincoln eventually put it, that "the Union is older than any of the states, and in fact it created them as States."[14]

This affinity for a broad reading of the powers and duties of the national government under the Constitution runs from the Federalists through some in the nationalist wing of their adversaries and successors in power, Jefferson's Democratic Republicans (source of the modern Democratic Party), to the newly founded Whig Party of the 1830s and finally to the party that grew out of the Whigs, the nation-building Republicans of Lincoln and Theodore Roosevelt. After the political realignment that emerged from the struggles within the Republican Party between Roosevelt's progressives and William Howard Taft's "stalwarts" in 1912, gradually the philosophy of a powerful national government found a home in the Democratic Party of Franklin Delano Roosevelt. The core of this tradition in public philosophy is commitment to a strong central government capable of defining the national interest and implementing it through patterns of cooperative federalism and large-scale public investments in internal improvements. From the start its key feature as an outlook on government has been its predisposition toward the creation of new public institutions (or mixed public-private ones) and experimentation with them in pursuit of national prosperity. It is a cosmopolitan vision, highly favorable to urbanism, that seeks to encourage and make use of social and economic diversity.[15]

To achieve these aims of fostered prosperity and general welfare, advocates of this tradition argued that it was necessary through law and regulation to *shape the circumstances* that give rise to a dynamic national community. In eighteenth-century thought, particularly that of the Scottish Enlightenment, which was so influential in America, these are the conditions associated with the rise of a distinctively modern civilization, and the notion that they could be artificially induced or at least encouraged is at the heart of Enlightenment theories of government. According to Hamilton,

these circumstances are: 1) The division of labor. 2) An extension of the use of machinery. 3) Additional employment to classes of the community not ordinarily engaged in the business. 4) The promoting of emigration from foreign countries. 5) The furnishing of greater scope for the diversity of talents and dispositions, which discriminate men from one another. 6) The affording of a more ample and various field for enterprise. 7) The creating in some instances a new, and securing, in all, a more certain and steady demand for the surplus produce of the soil. Each of these circumstances has a considerable influence upon the total mass of industrious effort in a community; together they add to it a degree of energy and effect which is not easily conceived.[16]

Modern governmental planning everywhere would arise out of the effort through politics to come to grips with the circumstances Hamilton identified. Attempts to encourage development of these conditions in American affairs during the early national period led eventually to the "American system" of interlocking national development policies and the Gallatin Plan for a national transportation and communications network.

The other stream in the tradition of American public philosophy was unsympathetic to the national theory of federalism and all that it implied for fostered prosperity. It held to a "compact" or "states-rights" theory of federalism, espoused by Jefferson, Monroe, John C. Calhoun, Andrew Jackson, Jefferson Davis, and others, in which the Union was conceived on the model of a treaty organization, a set of institutions created by the states, which ratified it, and granted by them only limited and specified duties. This view of the meaning of the Constitution has a literalist or "original-intent" orientation, and will not countenance broad readings of the text to justify "encroachment" by a consolidating national government. It is closely bound up with sectionalism and the defense of slavery, which provided continuing impetus for its elaboration. Extreme versions of the theory issue in the doctrine of nullification and the right of the states to secession.

It is important to note that the compact view is not necessarily opposed to governmental activism and intervention in the economy, so long as the initiative and responsibility for action are confined within the states themselves. It is not in principle a libertarian or laissez-faire view, though with the passage of time its adherents lean increasingly toward that position. Whereas the national theory implies a program of public policies sufficient to bring into being a sense of *national community,* supporters of the compact theory are suspicious of the whole idea of national

community as anything more than a figure of speech, a politically necessary figure of speech, perhaps, but still of only nominal weight. As Calhoun put it, "The very idea of an *American People* as constituting a single community is a mere chimera. Such a community never for a single moment existed—neither before nor since the Declaration of Independence." In this tradition, even to our own time, the only authentic community is the local one.[17]

While those who championed the national theory were ready to institutionalize their ideas and values through bureaucracy and regulation, as evidenced by the many and varied proposals contained in Hamilton's great reports on credit, the national bank, and manufactures, Jefferson's Republicans from the start were ambivalent about the whole idea of institutionalizing policy and public-sector innovation. At first they shared many of the neomercantilist objectives of the Federalists' program, but increasingly from the early 1790s on they stepped back from the policy implications of such innovations. In the end the Republicans typically came to deny the need for institutional experimenting and building up the capacity of the central government, sometimes even in matters of military preparedness.[18] It was this institutional dimension of their thought—more precisely the *want* of any genuine institutional dimension of their thought—that most set them apart from their adversaries. The possibility that deliberately designed institutions beyond those laid out in the Constitution itself might be enablers and enhancers of democracy made no sense to them. They leaned toward the view that political duty required them to keep open such opportunities for action as might be foreclosed by the schemes of the Federalists.

The Republicans represented the American branch of an adversarial tradition of "country-party" thought in the English political heritage, whose adherents saw themselves as the intended victims of the royal court's intrigues and the "corruptions" wrought by the king and his advisers in performance of the executive functions of government. From these beginnings a powerful antibureaucratic ethos grew up, one that confounded the idea of executive functions with royal autocracy. With it there arose an enduring antiplanning bias whose supporters were suspicious of all schemes of institutional innovation as *necessarily inviting political corruption* through patronage, favoritism, and the cultivation of dependent clienteles, no matter how lofty the stated aims of the proposals in question.[19]

In keeping with their adversarial mentality and rhetoric, Jeffersonian Republicans pioneered in the development of the antigovernment vocabulary and style of American politics. Strictly speaking the Jeffersonians had no program of their own for fostered prosperity. Nations happened; they were not developed by government policies. It was not a question of getting the details of institutional design *right,* for example, because the country party acknowledged no models of executive agency in which the virtues of democracy could be identified; all models were *aristocratical* in tendency. With the exception of their occasional gestures of deference to state legislatures, which were engaged in various interventions into social and economic life, Jeffersonians said little to indicate that they thought of the issue of what makes for legitimate executive agency as a problem.

Their political rhetoric favored the simple over the complex, the parochial and rural as the setting of natural virtue as opposed to the luxury and corruptions of the city. Rhetorically, although not always in practice, they preferred agriculture to manufacturing, associating the former with independence and the latter with the threat of servility due to the unequal relationship of employer and employee. In this sense they looked backward for inspiration, fashioning an image of the early modern countryside of small towns and thriving gentry as the ideal, and attempted to resist those social and economic trends that were undermining it. They were more sensitive to the risks of modernity than to its opportunities.

The differences between these broad outlooks on modernity meant different understandings of politics and interest-group conflict. Should such conflicts be acknowledged and used by governments as a kind of natural resource to build up a broader, common interest, or should they be overlooked and kept out of government policy to the extent possible? Here Jefferson, a man of variable opinion on the question, generally refused to relinquish what Hamilton refused to accept, the notion that agricultural interests and manufacturing interests were opposed to one another. "This idea of an opposition between those two interests is the common error of the early periods of every country," Hamilton insisted, "but experience gradually dissipates it." He conceded there might be cases where the notion of opposition made sense, but argued that it was "generally acknowledged, where there has been sufficient experience, that the aggregate prosperity of manufactures and the aggregate prosperity of agriculture are intimately connected." The fateful conclusion he drew from this point was that "ideas of a contrariety of interests between the Northern and Southern regions of the Union are, in the main, as unfounded as they are mischievous. The diversity of circumstances, on which such a contrariety is usually predicated, authorizes a directly contrary conclusion. Mutual wants constitute one of the strongest links of political connection; and the extent of these bears a natural proportion to the diversity in the means of mutual supply."[20]

It is hard to state exactly what the policy

contents of "pure republicanism," as espoused by the Jeffersonians, was. It developed more as a mood and attitude than a body of policy thought. Certainly any list of the core principles from which its policies are derived would include state sovereignty in domestic affairs (meaning rigid boundaries between the separate spheres of dual federalism), a preference for small government over large (the closer to "the people" the better), a commitment to low taxes and tax cutting (Jefferson was the first president to make tax cuts a priority of his administration), and a conviction that the liberties of the people, if unimpeded by the "artificial" regulations of government, would tend naturally toward the improvement of social conditions. Developments in *civil society* were not problematic, the growth of government was.

As Jefferson put it in his first inaugural address, "It is proper you should understand what I deem the essential principles of our Government, and consequently those which ought to shape its Administration." He made it clear that he did not intend to dismantle what had been put together by the Federalists, most importantly the National Bank (which had been attacked by many as unconstitutional because it was not based on an enumerated power of the Constitution, but rather on the doctrine of implied powers), but would not permit any further development of their ideas, either. His aim was to preside over "a wise and frugal government, which shall restrain men from injuring one another, and which shall leave them free to regulate their pursuits of industry and improvement, and shall not take from the mouth of labor the bread which it has earned." This minimalist perspective on national government was sufficient. "This is the sum of good government," Jefferson said, "and this is necessary to close the circle of our felicities."[21] He meant that this was *all* that was necessary, and the important note here is that the peo-

ple are to be free to regulate their own pursuits. The regulation in question is apparently to proceed voluntarily and without resort to governments. When pushed to its extremes, in this Jeffersonian ideal a properly functioning America is nothing *but* civil society, and civil society is not expected to change in its fundamentals over time.

Democratic Republicans were leery of "intermingling" governments, believing that such mixtures would result finally in a kind of imperial federalism through which the national government reduced the others to subservience. Where their adversaries sought measures tending toward "consolidation" (the nineteenth-century term) or "centralization" (the twentieth-century variant), the Republicans stood in opposition. So far as the continuity of party ideology is concerned, the carriers of this tradition of argument in public philosophy run from the Jeffersonian Democratic Republicans through the Democratic Party of Jackson and, after the realignments of the Progressive period, into the antigovernment politics of the modern Republican Party.

The strongest point in the Jeffersonian tradition is its democratic feeling and its high estimate of the potential of ordinary people. This is what saves its antimodern, adversarial cast from lapsing into mere stubbornness and complacency. Its oppositions are always justified in the name of protecting the people and their liberties from the machinations of government officials and their allies—predatory elites in commerce, manufacturing, and finance. The tradition tends to see all relations of social, economic, and political interdependence not in terms of developing community but in terms of exploitation, subordination, and subservience. Its weakest point accompanied this tendency: the difficulty it had in *thinking institutionally*, for if the liberties of the people and their prospects required new institutional and policy frameworks to flourish, the Jeffersonians and those who followed them were typically at a loss. Experimentation along this line was not in their nature, and they looked back to the purity of 1776 as a contrast to the slippery slopes constructed in the 1790s. In the circumstances of opposition through which they fashioned themselves in that decade and gave birth to the rudiments of the American party system, they became the champions of the democratic idea.[22]

Hamiltonian Federalists, on the other hand, championed the national idea, as did a minority in the leadership of the nationalist wing of the Republicans, and as did the Whigs, who arose as a party out of that minority and championed its aims. The strength of those who stressed the national idea was in the cogency and fecundity of their policy notions, their ability to think institutionally in ways that promised actually to advance the general welfare. Their achievement was to lay the basic foundations in both theory and practice for a powerful national government, though that power would develop very slowly in a stealthy, piecemeal fashion and only after the trial of civil war. The weakness in this tradition, as its commentators have long recognized, was the complacent elitism that marked its Federalist beginnings and lingered afterward, its suspicion of the people as naturally virtuous if left to their own devices, its fear that without leadership of an enlightened kind, specially qualified by education and social background, democracy would lapse into demagoguery and mob rule. Surely the Hamiltonian Federalists *were* elitists, but as Samuel Beer has pointed out, their elitism was at the service of their nationalism. It led them to recognize that in America the nation would *not* just happen. It had to be built. Loyalty to its institutions had to be earned by policies that gave some concrete meaning to such constitutional abstractions as a "more perfect Union" and the "general welfare."[23]

A useful shorthand way of contrasting these two streams in the tradition of American public philosophy was suggested by the historian Major L. Wilson in his *Space, Time, and Freedom: The Quest for Nationality and the Irrepressible Conflict, 1815–1861*. Wilson develops the comparison between those pursuing the national idea, who are devoted to the persistent cultivation of the American land through time via scientifically informed, government-aided projects, and those pursuing the democratic idea, who do not believe that one generation has the right to burden its successors, even with an inheritance of improvements, and emphasizes instead the rapid expansion of an agricultural homesteading culture through space.[24]

The American System and Internal Improvements

In his study of utopias Lewis Mumford observed, "one does not have to plan for chaos and dissolution, for this is what happens when the spirit ceases to be in command." With Thomas Jefferson's rise to power in the "revolution of 1800," the Federalists's nation-building spirit was put on the defensive and went into a decline from which it never returned. In the 1830s it reappeared in the program of the Whigs, and once again its ideas were put front and center. In between, the fate of the national theory of federalism and the related scheme of national planning was in the hands of Jefferson's Democratic Republicans, who dominated national politics and held the White House for an entire generation. Here what mattered most was a growing split within the party, which had its old antifederalist base on one wing and its guardedly "nationalist" wing at the other. Some in the leadership of this nationalist wing, chief among them Gallatin, John Quincy Adams, Henry Clay, and for a time,

Calhoun, kept alive the hope of a national planning policy.

Aside from the question of war and peace, the most significant issue at the national level throughout this generation was the issue of "internal improvements"—the need for an infrastructure of transportation and communication, and the role, if any, of the federal government in devising it. Repeatedly this question rose to the top of the congressional agenda and began to take programmatic form, only to be stymied repeatedly by last-minute constitutional scruples and unexpected presidential vetoes. After repeated failures in the Jefferson, Madison, and Monroe administrations (for each of these party leaders wavered at the crucial moment), the last major push for national planning in the antebellum period would come during the administration of John Quincy Adams. Adams's career traces the trajectory of the nation-building idea. He was in turn a Federalist senator, a leader of the nationalist wing of the Republicans (having broken with the Federalists over the Hartford Convention, which threatened the secession of New England in response to Jefferson's embargo policy in 1807), and finally, after his presidency, a Whig congressman who spent his last years as a thorn in the side of Jacksonian Democrats, flailing their policies of devolution and privatization. It was Adams as president who articulated in its strongest form the national planning idea.

With the rise of Jackson in 1828, however, the issue of cooperative federalism and a federal role in planning public enterprise and infrastructure would be settled decisively in the negative. An application of Jeffersonian principles would take place that Jefferson himself did not have the nerve to undertake. Jackson's Democratic Party ushered in America's first hard-hitting decentralization movement. They dismantled what remained of the old Federalist policy structure, killed the na-

tional bank, brought to a dead stop support for the few piecemeal odds and ends of federal aid for a system of roads and canals that had emerged out of the gridlock and wavering of the preceding decades, and encouraged the states to stop looking to Washington for help and get on with their own responsibilities. Most states were already doing so, in a vigorously competitive, uncoordinated fashion that would before long bring them to ruin, leaving them the empty husks of American constitutional government.

At no other time in the nation's history were the separate spheres of dual federalism so adamantly insisted on as during the Jacksonian era. Clearly Jackson was a unionist of a certain kind; he refused to countenance any talk of nullification and threatened to send federal troops into South Carolina when provoked along this line. But that was about the sum of Jackson's nationalism, too, and the idea that the central government had any legitimate business in trying to orchestrate national development was one he refused to entertain. To appreciate the significance for planning history of the sweeping repudiations of the Jacksonians, it is helpful to recover the logic of what was repudiated. Contemporaries in public life understood it as "the American system."

Though historians generally associate the phrase with the developmental policies advocated by Henry Clay as a leader of the Whig Party in the 1830s, both the phrase itself and the policy ideas it connotes rose out of the neomercantilist thinking of Hamilton and the Federalists. Its origin was in the effort to think through what was required after the Revolution for the new nation gradually to free itself from continuing economic dependency on England. The problem was to break out of the circular economic pattern of colonies devoted mainly to the export of agricultural goods to pay for the import of finished goods from the more developed countries and construct a modern mixed economy and culture with an internal dynamism of its own. This colonial dependence was established and held in place by the British-dominated European mercantilist system of international trade, and the American system was invented to cope with it. In Federalist no. 11 Hamilton exhorts his readers along these lines: "Let Americans disdain to be the instruments of European greatness! Let the thirteen States, bound together in a strict and indissoluble Union, concur in erecting one great American system superior to the control of all transatlantic force or influence and able to dictate the terms of the connection between the old and the new world!"[25]

In his lifetime the states would not fully concur in erecting the system he seems to have had in mind, but with the Constitution an important start was made. As it developed in the thinking of the Federalists, the American system was a theory of nation-building and public finance, a set of interlocking policies intended to place the federal government at the center of things, where it could preside over the development of a progressive, planned American civilization. Debate over the components of the American system was the debate over national planning in the early republic. The recurrent problem faced by its advocates was how to put the system of interlocking policies together with the federal design of the Constitution.

As it matured, the American system included seven components. First, it was a *foreign policy of American commercial imperialism* intended to counter the imperialism of the European powers and reduce or eliminate European influence in the Americas while at the same time extending the influence of the United States, all symbolized and codified by what came to be called the Monroe Doctrine, one of the main achievements, together with the Louisiana Purchase, of the nationalist Republicans. Second, it was a *national industrial policy,* intended through tariff protections, bounties, and subsidies to nurse "infant industries" and build up American manufacturing. Third, it was a *national banking policy,* intended to concentrate capital, secure the safety of public funds, provide a nationwide credit structure, facilitate commercial interchange, and prevent abuses by state-chartered banks. Fourth, it was a *public lands policy,* intended to encourage complex, mixed urban-rural development in the already settled original states by "hemming in" the pace of expansion into the territories. It was an antisprawl policy for the continent. The public lands were the principal asset in the nationalists' inventory of resources. They wanted them scientifically surveyed before being released, policed against squatters, and as pressure for new land mounted, sold at a price that would generate significant federal revenues. Fifth, it was a policy of *federal internal improvements,* intended to put the resources of the Union to work on the development of the national domain by funding, in whole or in part, an integrated system of transport and communication, a system beyond the competence of the states to conceive and arrange. Sixth, it was a *revenue policy,* intended to ensure that the Union had resources to invest in projects of internal improvement from the sale of public lands, from tariffs, customs, and excise duties, from profits accruing to the national bank, and eventually from the returns from the internal improvements, since the canals and turnpikes in question were not simply the objects of throw-away subsidies: they were remunerative public works, ongoing concerns of public enterprise, requiring long-term maintenance and management. Finally, it was a *policy of cooperative federalism,* intended to link national and state governments together in a common enterprise of planned development.

Had these policy schemes ever been brought into unity and put to work, American development would have taken a different shape. But the American system was never actually assembled legislatively and given a trial run. Parts of it—notably protective tariffs, the national bank, and for a time and fitfully (though never scientifically surveyed and policed), a revenue-oriented public-lands policy—were set up and became organizing points in political controversy. Hamilton's ideas for the encouragement of manufacturing by the central government were never taken up; the drive for federally supported internal improvements, as we shall see, produced little. For decades the Republicans flirted with the idea of cooperative federalism for internal improvements, but finally they could not bring themselves to act on it, and the notion was effectively quashed by the Jacksonians. The result, as Hamilton had predicted, was that up until the Civil War the national government was largely out of sight and out of mind so far as the great bulk of the American people were concerned.

The pivotal failure of the American system was in the debates over internal improvements, because there was to be no *system* unless federal revenues could be plowed back into infrastructure investments. Improvements closed the loop in the logic of the plan. Unless that link could be established through legislative enactment, federal surpluses, which arose from time to time throughout the century, were embarrassments to the Congress, symbols of the inability to make federalism work sensibly. Surpluses were also a source of irritation and complaint in the states. And it was the anxiety of the Republicans about confounding the separate spheres of dual federalism, no matter how compelling the argument in favor of doing so via voluntary, government-to-government cooperation, that scuttled federal internal improvements. The story of that failure and its impact thereafter on the role of government in American life begins with the Gallatin Plan.

The Gallatin Plan

The Gallatin Plan was the response to a Senate resolution introduced in February 1807 by Senator John Quincy Adams of Massachusetts calling for the secretary of the treasury to prepare "a plan for the application of such means as are within the power of Congress, to the purposes of opening roads, and making canals; together with a statement of the undertakings of that nature, which, as objects of public improvement, may require and deserve the aid of government; and also a statement of works of the nature mentioned, which have been commenced, the progress which has been made in them, and the means and prospect of their being completed." The result, Albert Gallatin's *Report on the Subject of Roads and Canals,* was submitted to the Senate in April of 1808. It provided an inventory—the first and only inventory until well into the twentieth century—of all the projects underway or planned within the states, together with a recommended plan for selecting among and complementing them so as to fuse together a national transport and communications infrastructure.[26]

Even by the standards of a later time the Gallatin Plan was a remarkable achievement of intellect and imagination. Conceived before the coming of the railroad, it would have bound together the Union with roads and waterways linking the entire national domain as of 1808, tying into a whole the Northwest and Louisiana Territories under federal jurisdiction with the most advanced projects that were underway within the jurisdictions of the states and localities. As geographer Donald Meinig has pointed out, the plan was fitted to both the natural and technological circumstances of the early republic, to what Mumford would later call the "eotechnic age" of wood, wind, and water characterized by clipper ships and keelboats, canals, waterwheels, windmills, and before long, paddlewheel steamers.[27]

Gallatin was suggesting an institutional framework for the way of life that Mumford later idealized in his *Golden Day,* in which he reviews appreciatively the culture of the time and sings the praises of those communities planted on the seaboard and up the river valleys in the seventeenth and eighteenth centuries that in antebellum days achieved their optimum development. "They had worked out a well rounded industrial and agricultural life," Mumford said of them elsewhere, "based on the fullest use of their regional resources through the waterwheel, mill, and farm, and they had created a fine provincial culture, humbly represented in the schools, universities, lyceums, and churches, which came to full efflorescence in the scholarship of Motley, Prescott, Parkman, and Marsh, and the literature of Emerson, Thoreau, Melville, Whitman and Poe."[28] This world was undermined by the forces of uncontrolled development and began to vanish in the late nineteenth century. Whether controlled development, along the lines laid out by Gallatin, might have sustained and elaborated it, cultivated it through time, and provided for its orderly expansion is an open question. The intention was there, and the logic of the plan pointed in that direction.

The design of the plan was one of circumferential waterways with the Ohio River as a central axis, augmented by a series of man-made connections—either roads or canals—that linked the several great hydrographic basins included within it to form an intricate interconnected system of transport and communication that bound together every state and territory east of the Mississippi (see Figure 4.1). Along the Atlantic coast, where the population density was greatest, there were parallel land and water pathways connecting north and south. Canals completed and unified the intercoastal waterway so that seagoing vessels could go all the way from Massachusetts to North Carolina,

while a great turnpike road extended from Maine to Georgia. Along the east-west dimension of the plan there were links between the major Atlantic river systems and the western waters of the Great Lakes system. On the perimeter the Great Lakes–St. Lawrence system was connected to the vast Mississippi watershed, promising a waterway from the Great Lakes to the Gulf that would close the great loop. The entire design of water routes was supplemented by connective roads crossing the mountains leading into the undeveloped and unexplored interior.

It was in its political and policy aspects, however, that the plan was most impressive. Infrastructure decisions are place and locality decisions. Once made, they benefit some places more than others, not only temporarily, but given the strong tendency in financial affairs to protect and augment large-scale investments, for the longer term as well. Gallatin's plan would benefit most directly what was then the urban core and its hinterlands of the Atlantic seaboard. This area, he conceded, "would receive greater local and immediate benefits than the eastern, and perhaps southern states." Since the expenses of the system would have to be defrayed in whole or in part from the general funds of the Union, it followed that "*justice, and perhaps policy not less than justice,* seem to require that a number of local improvements, sufficient to equalize the advantages, should be undertaken in those states, parts of states, or districts, which are less immediately interested in those inland communications" (emphasis added).[29] Here was the essence of the politics of cooperative federalism and the test for Hamilton's concert of interests vs. Jefferson's wary hesitation to work with them.

As presented in 1808, the estimated total cost for funding the improvements laid out by Gallatin (including compensatory local projects) was put at $20 million. He estimated further that under peacetime conditions the

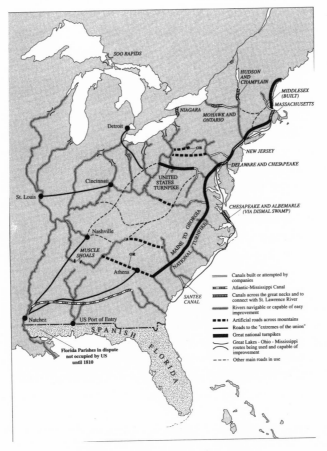

Figure 4.1   The Gallatin Plan, 1808

work could be accomplished within a decade, and recommended that the Congress appropriate $2 million annually for the purpose. What is perhaps most remarkable about the plan from the standpoint of national public ƒnance is Gallatin's argument that even after paying down the national debt, including the costs of the Louisiana Purchase of 1803, which doubled the size of the national domain, and meeting the annual operating costs of the general government, the improvements scheme would require only slightly more than one-third of projected *surplus* federal revenues. These proportions of the projected national budget underscore the need to come to terms with the requirement for institutions of cooperative federalism.

The report called attention to the fact that some of the works that had been undertaken in the states and localities had proven "unproƒtable; many more remain unattempted, because their ultimate productiveness depends on other improvements too expensive or too distant to be embraced by the same individuals." Obviously the national government alone was in a position to deal with obstacles of this kind, as it alone had the scope of responsibility and scale of resources required. "With these resources and embracing the whole Union," Gallatin insisted, "it will complete on any given line all the improvements, however distant, which may be necessary to render the whole productive, and eminently beneficial."[30] To ensure that the federal government would in the future be in a better position to know what it was doing in this field, Gallatin also requested the authority and the means to undertake the surveys and investigations required as the basis for more detailed planning.

As had Washington and Hamilton before him, Gallatin emphasized that, beyond practical revenue considerations, the improvements scheme had something more to recommend it. It would counter the tendencies toward disintegration inherent in the rapid expansion of both territory and population then underway, and bind the Union together. "Good roads and canals will shorten distances, facilitate commercial and personal intercourse, and unite by a still more intimate community of interests, the most remote quarters of the United States. No other single operation within the power of government can more effectually tend to strengthen and perpetuate that union, which secures external independence, domestic peace, and internal liberty."[31]

Though he was Hamilton's main adversary as a theorist of public finance and one of Jefferson's closest advisers, in making the claim that there was no other operation of government more important to securing the bonds of union than internal improvements along the lines of cooperative federalism, Gallatin saw eye to eye with Hamilton.[32] The Federalists in Congress would agree heartily, and if others among the nationalist wing of the Republicans could be brought along, how then might the federal government actually proceed? On the sensitive issue of the constitutionality of the proposed plan, Gallatin pointed out that the Jefferson administration had already recommended to Congress, which alone had the power to propose amendments to the Constitution, that it fashion an *internal improvements amendment* and send it to the states for approval. This amendment proposal was risky business, as all participants understood, since it would open up unpredictable possibilities, among them the chance that the old antifederalists might once again mount a campaign of opposition, or that the small states might hold the larger ones hostage by combining to urge new demands. Failure in the attempt to strengthen national government would weaken it, leaving everyone worse off.

Thus the report also made it clear that there was no need to wait for the outcome of a cumbersome amendment process, and perhaps as a practical matter, no *time* to wait for it. Of all the specific projects described in his plan, Gallatin observed, "there is hardly any which is not either already authorized by the States respectively, or so immediately beneficial to them, as to render it highly probable that no material difficulty will be experienced" in having the federal government pay for the work, either in whole or in part. As treasury secretary he read the dual federalism of the Constitution not to prohibit action by the national government but to require *"the consent of the State through which such road or canal must pass"* (emphasis added). This consent could be obtained on the basis of government-to-government negotiation, and Gallatin reasoned that case-by-case voluntary agreements obtained in this manner would amount to the equivalent of a constitutional amendment. By resorting to the principle of voluntary agreement as enabling cooperative federalism, he hit on the basic justification that would be used by the twentieth-century Supreme Court for the same reason.[33]

To stress still further the tractability of the internal improvements problem from the federal standpoint, Gallatin suggested a variety of techniques of public finance that might be developed if resort to the projected surpluses in general revenues was considered inappropriate. There was the possibility of a permanent revolving fund for internal improvements to come from the sales of the public lands, for example, so that the lands that belonged to all might be used to the benefit of all. There was the possibility of privatizing or devolving those turnpikes and canals that had generated enough revenue to repay the initial public investment in them by selling the government's stock in the enterprises to private companies or state corporations, then using the proceeds from the sales for still more improvements elsewhere. "And by persevering in that plan, a succession of improvements would be effected until every portion of the United States would enjoy all the advantages of inland navigation and improved roads of which it was susceptible." Whatever the technique employed, the underlying principle was the same: cooperative federalism was in the public interest and would benefit the people, state governments, and the national government as well. For the common good, a *national* plan was required, and decisions on specific projects would have to be taken. "The National Legislature alone," Gallatin concluded, "embracing every local interest and superior to every local consideration, is competent to the selection of such national objects."[34]

National Republicans and the Failure of the American Plan

Perhaps Congress embraced every local interest, but the hope that it might prove superior to every local consideration immediately was shown to be unfounded. No action of any kind was taken on the Gallatin Plan. No internal improvements amendment was introduced. Gallatin had been careful to stress that his was a *peacetime* proposal based on anticipated surplus revenues. Even before the ink was dry on his report, however, the fiscal effects of his president's failed embargo policy of 1807—Jefferson's "candid and liberal experiment" in "peaceful coercion" of the warring empires of Britain and France— would inspire thoughts of secession on the part of Federalist New England, shrink revenues, and light the fuse for the war of 1812. But these considerations alone do not account for the failure of the internal improvements plan, because immediately after the war the pressure to proceed with a national internal improvements policy arose again, this time with an added emphasis on its national defense benefits, which, some suggested, would have prevented the humiliations of the war in which the British had so easily taken the nation's capital.

In the two decades that spanned the submission of the Gallatin Plan and the election of Andrew Jackson, there were more attempts to revive the national planning idea, and it is worthwhile briefly to note them. What was occurring was a slow-motion failure of the national government under the leadership of the Democratic Republicans to get into the business of public enterprise and planning, a course of action many in the party, including from time to time its most influential leaders, thought necessary despite their constitutional qualms.

James Madison, the great architect of the Constitution and onetime ally of Hamilton in arguing for its adoption, had given a good deal of thought to the planning issue. In Federalist no. 14 he had argued that the central government needed the authority to work in this area and that it should be provided eventually through amendment. Earlier, during the Constitutional Convention of 1787, Benjamin Franklin had raised the internal improvements issue by moving that Article 1, section 8, which gave Congress the power to "establish Post offices and post roads," should be expanded to include "the power to provide for cutting canals where deemed necessary." Madison agreed and proposed that Franklin's motion be formulated in terms of a more general institutional capacity, one which would have given the central government all the constitutional warrant needed in this and other fields. He suggested that Congress should have the power "to grant charters of incorporation where the interest of the U.S. might require & the legislative provisions of the individual States may be incompetent."[35] Both proposals failed.

As president, Jefferson had called for an internal improvements amendment but had not exerted himself to get one. During his tenure in the White House Madison likewise supported the need for an amendment and likewise failed to exert himself on its behalf. Late in his second term, however, another opportunity for a national internal improvements plan arose. With the war settled and a surplus once again accumulating in the Treasury, naturally the question of what to do with it came up. Seemingly with the approval of the president, a "Bonus Bill" was fashioned and moved through the Congress under the leadership of the young Republican nationalists Henry Clay and John C. Calhoun. The bill was intended to direct the profits from the National Bank to the roads and canals first called for in Gallatin's *Report*. To the surprise of all, on his last day in office Madison vetoed the bill on constitutional grounds, declaring his support for its objectives but insisting that an amendment was necessary.[36]

Internal improvements schemes continued to bubble up during the Monroe administration. Like Jefferson and Madison before him, Monroe had been one of the creators of the new republicanism and the revolution of 1800. Like them he was conflicted about the internal improvements issue, acknowledging the need for a federal role but feeling power-less to do anything. Like Jefferson and Madison he called for an amendment. In the wake of the veto of the Bonus Bill in 1817 there was an extended effort in the Congress, particularly in the House of Representatives under the leadership of Henry Clay as Speaker, to overturn the effects of the veto, but it had garnered only limited success. Some individual projects advanced, but without linkage to any national plan.

After 1818 Congress in the normal course of business crept ever closer in piecemeal fashion—typically via land grants or discrete support for specific, local projects—to developing a de facto and uncoordinated internal improvements record. Disturbed by this legislative trend, in 1822 President Monroe vetoed a bill erecting tolls on the Cumberland Road, one of the national roads that had been begun. Like his predecessors, he insisted that he did so with regret and restated the need for an internal improvements amendment to the Constitution. In explaining the reasons for his veto, however, Monroe made a major effort to spell out the grounds on which he stood. His veto message, a lengthy essay of some twenty-five thousand words, is another important and neglected document in American planning history. It was intended to clear the air and examine the historical and constitutional roots of the issue once again. Its constitutionalism is that of the *compact theory of federalism,* a more systematic exposition of the dual federalism, separate spheres interpretation than any president, before or since, has provided.

Monroe's message is a kind of handbook summarizing what happens when a committed believer in dual federalism meets an admitted higher need for coordinating internal improvements. It reveals the deep fissures within the Republican mind, drawn to the obvious benefits of coordination on the one hand, but repelled by the institutional costs of coordination on the other. The message is aimed not simply at the Cumberland Road, but at the Gallatin Plan itself and its suggestion that federal action on improvements could be taken prior to a constitutional amendment. Gallatin's idea that voluntary government-to-government agreements were the next best thing to the legitimacy of an amendment is exactly what Monroe aimed to quash. The national government did not have the power to do this, he insisted, and "the States individually cannot grant it, for although they may assent to the appropriation of money within their limits for such purposes, *they can grant no power of jurisdiction or sovereignty by special compacts with the United States*" (emphasis added).[37]

Even voluntary agreements between two governments representing the same people are unconstitutional, in other words. All those who, like Gallatin, insisted that the national government *did* have the power to negotiate voluntary agreements with the states in the interest of coordinated planning rested their claims on a broad reading of the Constitution. "The advocates for the power derive it from the following sources," said Monroe. "First, the right to establish post-offices and post-roads; second, to declare war; third, to regulate commerce among the several States; fourth, from the power to pay the debts and provide for the common defense and general welfare of the United States; fifth, from the power to make all laws necessary and proper for carrying into execution all the powers vested by the Constitution in the Government of the United States or in any department or officer thereof; sixth and lastly, from the power to dispose of and make all needful rules and regulations respecting the territory and other property of the United States."[38] This was a catalogue of all the constitutional justifications cited by advocates of internal improvements in the previous generation. The bulk of Monroe's

message is devoted to rebutting each of them in turn.

There is more than narrow legalism in Monroe's text, however, for he recognized that the essence of the problem was one of *institutional design*. Beyond the need for grounds permitting cooperative federalism, there was the need for federal bureaucracy to make it work, a bureaucracy that would have to be equipped with powers of eminent domain. Derived powers would not do for the first need: "the great and essential power being deficient, consisting of a right to take up the subject on principle." And the second required institutional innovation of a kind not before attempted. It would be necessary, for example, "to cause our Union to be examined by men of science, with a view to such improvements; to authorize commissioners to lay off the roads and canals in all proper directions; to take the land at a valuation if necessary, and to construct the works; to pass laws with suitable penalties for their protection; and to raise revenue from them, to keep them in repair, and make further improvements by the establishment of turnpikes and tolls, with gates to be placed at the proper distances."[39] New worlds of government action and supervision would have to be brought into being.

One might think that after such an energetic display of obstacles to any federal internal improvements policy, Monroe would have concluded that the subject ought to be buried. To the contrary, however, at the end of his message he insisted that the advantages of lodging an internal improvements power within the national government "are almost incalculable, and that there was a general concurrence of opinion among our fellow citizens to that effect."[40] The only proper way to get that power, however, was through constitutional amendment. To make clear why such an amendment was urgently desirable, he laid out all the reasons favoring a coordinated system as preferable to any other alternative.

Gallatin's plan had shown that it was "practicable and easy" to lay out an interlocking national system, and Monroe reviewed with approval the utilitarian arguments on its behalf. These arguments, however, were "by no means the most important." What *was* most important, as Monroe plainly understood, was that American federalism itself would be improved, rather than destroyed, by the change: "Every power of the General Government and of the State governments connected with the strength and resources of the country would be made more efficient for the purposes intended by them."[41] Despite the fact that it appears in a veto message that undermined the possibility of a national internal improvements policy, that Monroe conceded this particular point— that both the national and state governments would be made more efficient for the purposes intended for them if the central government had jurisdiction in this area—shows how shallow were the ties that bound the Republicans to a rigid, dual-federalism doctrine. National planning was a live possibility in the early republic.

The Last Hurrah: John Quincy Adams and the Idea of Progressive Improvement

By going into such depth on the ins and outs of the problem, Monroe did more than Jefferson and Madison had done in wrestling with the issue. No action was taken on his amendment recommendation, however, and his veto brought to a stop one of the main building blocks in a haphazardly developing national system. This is how matters stood when John Quincy Adams, who had been secretary of state in the Monroe administration, entered the White House on March 4, 1825, determined to launch the third and, as

it happened, final attempt at a national planning policy in the antebellum period.

Adams had none of the ambivalence that hobbled his Virginia predecessors. He was not much impressed by the merits of the arguments against a federal internal improvements policy as laid out in Monroe's veto message, and did not believe that an amendment to the Constitution was necessary.[42] He was the strongest supporter of the national theory of federalism since Hamilton. "The organization of this Constitution is not of a confederacy," he wrote, "but of a national government complicated with a federation," perhaps the most concise and accurate statement of the problem confronting the theory ever penned. A shrewd political analyst as well, Adams understood precisely how the democratic and national ideas were bound up with the history of the developing party system, and he was critical of the merely tactical rhetoric of both sides.[43] From the beginning he had been a supporter of internal improvements, and it was he who had introduced the Senate resolution calling for Gallatin's report. When he put together his cabinet in 1824, Adams offered Gallatin his old post at the Treasury, in the hope that together they could succeed in one more push for a national plan. Unfortunately Gallatin declined, although it is not clear in retrospect that his presence in Washington would have made any difference to the outcome. The longer the government hesitated, the less likely anything could be done.

Adams was well aware of this, and so he made the philosophy of internal improvements the subject of his first annual message to Congress on December 6, 1825. His address is the culminating statement of a progressive, liberal nationalist political philosophy, and it is worth turning to it briefly for its bearing on the continuing problems of American planning. The purpose of government in Adams's view was not simply protection of individual rights, as Jefferson came near to asserting, with the people left to "regulate their own affairs" independent of government and law. Instead, "the great object of the institution of civil government is the improvement of the condition of those who are parties to the social compact, and no government, in whatever form constituted, can accomplish the lawful ends of its institution but in proportion as it improves the condition of those over whom it is established." What mattered was policy and results; help should go to where it was needed; thus roads and canals "are among the most important means of improvement."

But moral, political, and intellectual improvements are duties no less exigent than public works, and they apply "to social no less than to individual man." It followed for Adams that a ceaselessly active government was necessary as the medium through which this collective striving to perform God-given duties was expressed: "for the fulfillment of those duties governments are invested with power, and to the attainment of the end—the progressive improvement of the condition of the governed—the exercise of delegated powers is a duty as sacred and indispensable as the usurpation of powers not granted is criminal and odious."[44]

Of Monroe's veto message of the internal improvements bill, Adams remarked that "it contains whatever of argument the intellectual power of man can eviscerate from reason against the exercise, by Congress, of the contested power" but, like Gallatin and Clay before him, Adams concluded there were better arguments for simply *using* the contested power and letting precedent do the work of advance agreement.[45] He regretted bitterly all the laborious indecision and waste of time that had been permitted to go on, and he worried that a failed amendment (always possible given the mobilization of activist minorities like Virginia's neo-antifederalists)

would be a catastrophe for national government, reducing it to something like the feeble structure of the Articles of Confederation, which had proven so inadequate for national affairs.

Thus Adams saw himself as something of a last hope in the effort to secure a coordinating, shaping role for national government. It all came down, he believed, to the fundamental *purposes* of political power, and he regretted that the founders had not been more venturesome and candid in their arguments on this matter. Instead they showed an evasiveness about the ultimate aims of national power that made Jefferson's periodic condemnations of national authority possible. The founders, Adams insisted, "did not sufficiently foresee that this excessive caution to withhold beneficent power in the organic frame of government" was as important a defect as the failure to limit its powers would have been. Powers *not* delegated, he observed, deftly reversing a republican commonplace, "cannot be exercised for the common good," and it followed that denial of such powers amounted to an abdication of the pursuit of the common good by the people themselves. "All the impotence of government, therefore, thus becomes the impotence of the people who formed it; and in its results places the nation itself on a footing of inferiority compared with others in the community of independent nations."[46] This passage expressed the essence of the case against administrative nihilism at the national level, and the essence, also, of the national theory of federalism.

Better to assert the power to act, develop legislation, and let precedent nourish legitimacy. This was Adams's strategy, but he soon found that in the wake of Monroe's veto message the precedent-setting strategy was as unlikely of success as the idea of a constitutional amendment. He could not write the laws himself, nor could he organize and sustain within the Congress the majorities he needed to make the American system work at its vital points—tariffs, bank policy, and public lands, not to mention the organization of an inventory of public works keyed to Gallatin's plan, each with its own peculiarities. This was too much to ask from a Republican-dominated congressional government in the 1820s. Although a modest new start on internal improvements was made during the Adams administration—the General Survey Act of 1824 made possible the surveying work required as a preliminary to federal roads and canals (as Gallatin had proposed in 1808), a few land grants to western states were made for transportation, the beginnings of rivers and harbors appropriations by Congress came in 1826, and federal subscriptions to four canal construction projects were authorized—these were piecemeal initiatives and of small scale.

It soon became clear that Adams's program was politically unworkable, except for its function in providing a focus for the belligerent attention of Andrew Jackson and his followers. They began organizing Adams's overthrow the day he entered office. Like Jefferson and his allies in the 1790s, the Jacksonians were looking for mirror-image opposites of the American system and any rationale that assisted that end. The Federalist Party had long been in ruins, and the Democratic Republican Party, nearing the end of a full generation of one-party rule, was breaking up in conflicts between its nationalist and "old republican," states-rights wings. Out of this split eventually the Whig and Democratic Parties would emerge. Predictably Adams found the aims and the style of the Jacksonians contemptible. As he saw it, what Jackson's new democratic order of the common man amounted to was "land-jobbing, stock-jobbing, slave-jobbing, rights-of-man-jobbing, all were hand in hand, sweeping over the land like a hurricane."[47]

When Jackson entered the White House in 1829, he began energetically to dismantle what remained of the national development plan and the internal improvements strategy. Like Jefferson, Madison, and Monroe, he insisted that an internal improvements amendment was necessary to work in this area. Over the next few years with his veto of the Maysville Road bill, his withdrawal of deposits from the National Bank, his tariff changes, his installation of squatter-friendly, cost-reducing changes in public land policy, and still other initiatives, Jackson would bring the American system to a slow stop. Even the General Survey Act was abolished in 1831. Jackson saw all his targets as the embodiments of "class legislation" set up by the Federalists and sustained by the nationalist Republicans at the behest of rich men intent on making themselves richer at cost to the interests of ordinary people. "By attempting to gratify their desires," he argued in explaining his animus against the National Bank, "we have in the results of our legislation arrayed section against section, interest against interest, and man against man, in a fearful commotion which threatens to shake the foundations of our Union."[48]

From Adams's standpoint the new policies amounted to a systematic repudiation of the American system: "The total abandonment by President Jackson of all internal improvement by the authority of Congress, and of all national protection of domestic industry, was a part of the same system, which, in the message of December, 1832, openly recommended to give away gratuitously all the public lands, and renounce forever all idea of raising revenue from them. This was nullification in its most odious feature." Jackson had introduced a policy idea of devolution and privatization that none of the Republicans of the previous generation had been quite comfortable with—the idea, as Adams put it, "of giving away the national inheritance to private land jobbers, or to the states in which they lie," a fundamental challenge to the thinking of the progressive nationalists, and one that would bedevil the schemes of government planners ever after.[49]

Although there were many reasons for the setback, Adams attributed the failure of national planning ultimately to the underlying problem of race. The states-rights constitutionalism pioneered by Jefferson sank the American system to preserve slavery. For a long time there had been significant southern support for the idea of federally funded internal improvements, particularly in the South Carolina of John C. Calhoun, an Adams rival and the secretary of war in his cabinet. Once a reliable nationalist and supporter of an improvements policy despite his championship of sectional interests, Calhoun, who became Jackson's vice president, had begun during the Adams administration to turn to the states-rights constitutionalism for which he later became famous.

In an address to his congressional constituents in 1842, Adams laid out the linkage between national planning and slavery:

> The root of the doctrine of nullification is that if the internal improvement of the country should be left to the legislative management of the national government, and the proceeds of the sales of public lands should be applied as a perpetual and self accumulating fund for that purpose, the blessings unceasingly showered upon the people by this process would so grapple the affections of the people to the national authority that it would, in process of time, overshadow that of state governments, and settle the preponderancy of power in the free states; and then the undying worm of conscience twinges with terror for the fate of *the peculiar institution*. Slavery stands aghast at the prospective promotion of the general welfare, and flies to nullification for defense against the energies of freedom, and the inalienable rights of man.[50]

Life did not stop with the demolition of the American system. Bustling development went on, a point Adams well understood. Perhaps some rough equivalent for the Gallatin Plan "may still be done half a century later and with the limping gait of State legislature and private adventure," he conceded after leaving the White House, but "I would have done it in the administration of the affairs of the nation." Hamilton had been right. Consolidation was essential to the health of the national government, and without it, Adams reasoned, dissolution was inevitable. "My hopes for the long continuance of this Union are extinct," he would muse in 1834. "The people must go the way of all the world, and split up into an uncertain number of rival communities."[51]

Failure of State Enterprise and the Rise of Private Agency

Adams would turn out to be a better prophet than he knew. Twelve years after his death, the Civil War would come. And as it happens, it *did* take "the limping gait of State legislature and private adventure" about a half a century to accomplish what Gallatin had suggested might be the work of a decade. But neither Adams nor anyone else could foresee just how damaging the effects of the failure to establish a policy of cooperative federalism for internal improvements would be for the political dynamics of America's federal society. Identifying those effects and tracing those dynamics would fall to the first great modern student of American public finance since the time of Hamilton and Gallatin, Henry Carter Adams (1851–1921), no relation to the former president. In 1878 Adams was the first person to earn a doctorate in economics and political science from Johns Hopkins University. In the years that followed he became one of the most imaginative and influential policy thinkers in the United States, and played a central role in the development of the "democratic statist" form of the American new liberalism, that version of the nation's public philosophy out of which Theodore Roosevelt's progressivism would emerge.[52]

In addition to his scholarly work and teaching at the University of Michigan, Adams was deeply involved in the cutting-edge political issues of his day. He was a leading expert on the regulation of railroads, and from the founding of the Interstate Commerce Commission (ICC) in 1887 to his retirement from the post in 1911 he was the ICC's "first statistician," essentially the director of its research department. Adams did pioneering work on how corporations, particularly railroads, might be administratively regulated by government through monitoring the internal fiscal information on the basis of which they made their operating decisions. He was the country's best-known advocate of the need for "physical valuation" (requiring railroads to provide exact data on their assets for regulatory purposes) and of the threat of government publicity of corporate abuses as a means of controlling them—proposals of the sort Theodore Roosevelt took up in his "New Nationalism" speeches.

Adams laid out his analysis of what had happened in the wake of the failure to secure a national internal improvements policy in his *Public Debts: An Essay in the Science of Finance* (1887), the published version of his doctoral dissertation. At the time of his writing it was widely assumed that the nation had been *born* with a full-blown public philosophy of laissez faire, so common had its praises become in the 1870s and 1880s. Adams knew better. He had studied the policy and economic history of the early republic. He knew about the era's shortage of labor and capital, the lack of anything resembling the legal form of the modern industrial corporation, and the prevalence, early on, of

public enterprise via corporate charters granted by state legislatures. Laissez faire doctrine and the modern corporate form had come only with the waning of these, and in his research he looked into the reasons for the changes and their implications for politics and the common good.

Turning his attention to the age of the Democratic Republicans, he noted "the prevailing sentiment of the time did not deny to government agencies the right of assuming control over industrial enterprises. The doctrine of laissez faire, so far as matters of internal organization were concerned, had not then many converts in this country." That had come later, and only after the results of Jackson's devolution policies were registered in state legislatures. Adams's inquiry took him to what happened when state governments, without the prospect of any federal help, had embarked on internal improvement policies of public enterprise on their own. "This experiment by the States proved a failure," he concluded, "and because of the financial disasters which followed, the entire business of internal improvements was passed over to the control of corporations." Something new came into being in the Jackson era, perhaps unintentionally. "In our day private corporations compete with governmental agencies for the administration of great affairs," Adams noted, "but at that time private enterprise was not thought to be adequate to meet the demands of the public for internal improvement. The States were thus forced into a prominent position."[53]

The rise of private corporations competing with government for the administration of great affairs marked a momentous change in political culture, and the brilliance of Adams's thesis was in the way he brought the change into focus. He saw it as an element in the dynamic history of American federalism, and explained what the one had to do with the other. He also outlined the implications of the change for the politics of the future. "The American people deceive themselves in assuming to think their liberties endangered only by the encroachments of government," he noted, using the term previously reserved for complaints about national power invading the jurisdictions of the states. "The center from which power may be exercised is of slight importance; it is the fact of its irresponsible exercise which may justly occasion apprehension." Power was being exercised increasingly by a new *type* of institution, untested so far as its public responsibilities were concerned, and coming to terms with it would require building up the capacities of the federal system to bring them into adjustment with it. "The growth of private corporations is a step in the development of our social constitution," Adams noted. "They arose upon the ruins of the States as centers of industrial administration, and it is because the States have failed to retain a proper control over them that they now menace the permanency of our popular government."[54]

Adams's study revealed the operation of a vicious circle previously undetected in appraisals of America's federal society, all flowing from the politics of public debt. As Hamilton had seen at the beginning, public credit provides the engine of public enterprise; the loss of it brings on the impotence of government together with the land jobbers and stock jobbers that John Quincy Adams scorned. The gradual loss of public credit is what happened to most of the states as freestanding republican polities in mid-century. After the assumption in 1790 of the debts of the states by the new federal government, a tactic devised by Hamilton as the fulcrum of his plan to secure the support of the states for the national government, the states made no extensive use of public credit until the 1820s. Beginning slowly then in response to popular enthusiasm for growth and development policies, an enormous boom in grand projects

for internal improvement got underway in competitive and uncoordinated fashion, with New York's Erie Canal, begun in 1817 and finished in 1825, providing the prime example. With no organizing logic from above, of the kind called for in the Gallatin Plan, a great many bad bets were made by state legislatures.

By the mid-1840s the annual interest charges on state debts exceeded $12 million, and it was becoming clear that many projects were mistaken and unproductive. "It was then," Adams noted, "that the word 'repudiation' crept into the financial vocabulary of the American people." With the federal government standing aloof from all the enterprise and the exigent need to pay off on poor investments, the state governments became targets for popular animosity. "As the people had driven their representatives to enter upon internal improvements without caution," Adams reported, "so, when taxes began to press, they censured them without justice, and disowned the policy. The action was complete and irresistible, and one may discover now two facts that are traceable to it." Those were the enfeeblement of federalism, since the states were placed *hors de combat* in the field of public enterprise, and the emergence of the modern private corporation to fill the vacuum.

Adams's evidence pointed to a wave of political revulsion in the states during the 1840s and 1850s that led to radical changes in their constitutions. "Previous to 1830," he wrote, "no State in the Union was in any way restricted in the employment of its credit; at the present time, however, *there are but three States whose constitutions do not limit in some way the power to borrow money*" (emphasis added). Popular elections had forced changes in state constitutions and the result of the new limits on public debt was to render the state governments, like the federal government before them, effectively impotent with respect to the developmental functions of government. "Many constitutions," Adams pointed out, "by curtailing the power to contract a debt, render it impossible for States to incur those business obligations necessary for the economical prosecution of great works. It became the general cry that public works should be carried on by private enterprise, and to secure this, the States were prohibited from interference." No longer would they have anything to do as planners and investors, in whole or in part, via mixed corporations, with remunerative public works requiring capital and long-term management. This is how the era of state power ended.

The new mechanism that made it possible for private enterprise to enter the field and develop on a large scale was illustrated by the case of Illinois. It had undertaken both state banking and state-financed internal improvements, and had failed at both. "In her new constitution of 1848," Adams pointed out, "she retained the clause that internal improvements should be encouraged, *but with this significant modification—this was to be done 'by passing liberal laws of incorporation'*" (emphasis added).[55] Henceforth privately owned and operated corporations—railroads and canal companies, for example—would be more easily formed, and would not be tied into the same kinds of partnerships with government that earlier incorporations had required.

Although the national legislature did not have the power to grant charters of incorporation where the public good may require them, as Madison had recommended it *should* have during the Constitutional Convention, state legislatures *did* have this power. The power had driven the internal improvements boom. Through incorporation laws the states granted charters enabling private corporations to form for the purpose of

undertaking activities of specified kinds, sometimes with state participation in the ownership of stocks. It was through the specifications of the charter and sometimes through ownership participation via government investment in stocks that public enterprise was supervised and directed; these mechanisms provided the controls on public enterprise. Liberalizing laws of incorporation meant beginning to take governments out of the process of specifying terms and conditions and eliminating state participation in their administration. Under the press of interstate competition, liberal incorporation laws gradually became *general* incorporation laws, perfunctory arrangements having nothing necessarily to do with advancing a public interest. With this trend in the governmental practice of the states, a virtually unlimited field for private enterprise increasingly free of state participation, was opened up.

The states were abandoning the field, inviting in new forces in the hope that they would do better. But exercise is necessary for the organism of government, and in withdrawing from the field of enterprise, the states began to decay as polities, as had the Federal government before them. In the decades following the Civil War, many state governments became organizations that bordered on constitutional fraud. On paper they were imposing republican polities, but in practice they were underpowered, underfunded governments with very limited administrative capacity, presided over by underpaid, little-known members of part-time, rural-dominated legislatures. As governments, the states were about to enter a long period to be marked by what Justice Louis Brandeis would call a "competition in laxity," as they vied with one another to attract industry and employment opportunities by cutting regulations and offering tax subsidies and other incentives as lures for enterprises located elsewhere. Such was the long-term fallout of devolution and the dual federalism of the Jackson era.[56]

The ironic effect of these trends in federal governance was that the *governments of cities,* the least formally "constitutional" entities in the federal system in the sense that they are not mentioned at all in the Constitution but rather have the legal status merely of municipal corporations chartered by state governments, now became the most dynamic levels of government in the land. In his analysis of the history of public debts Adams traced the origins of widespread municipal corruption, such a central concern of Progressive Era politics, to the same failure to deal properly with internal improvements through some form of cooperative federalism. The cities were the really thriving American polities by mid-century and thereafter, and they were bound up in a process of rivalry and developmental competition that had been pioneered by the state legislatures before the breakdown of public enterprise.[57]

Adams pointed out that the most successful of state-financed internal improvements, the Erie Canal, had the effect of spurring city-led competition that ushered in the earliest form of metropolitan regionalism. "Previous to the completion of this highway of commerce," he observed, "the city of New York, like the cities of Boston, Philadelphia, and Baltimore, had been a local village, draining the country naturally dependent upon it; but, with the completion of the canal, it at once became a port of importance to the entire country west of the Allegheny Mountains and north of the Ohio River." With this development the local interests of Philadelphia and Baltimore were placed in jeopardy, and in response these cities and others undertook their own projects to leverage the patterns of inland commerce in their favor. "Then began that struggle between the seaboard cities for commercial supremacy over the West, which has become more and more intense even to the present time," Adams observed. "The point which I wish to make is this: About 1830, men in the East were for the first time coming to realize the great possibilities of the West, and the rivalry between the various sections of the East to secure to themselves the benefits of the trade which was sure to spring up, induced men in these sections to lend freely to such enterprises as would be of special advantage to themselves."

With the slow-motion collapse of public enterprise in the states the cities and towns were left to themselves. They were required to face the most pressing problems of governance in a turbulent period of growth and change. The result was inevitable, Adams suggested. "The main fact is well recognized. The States have ceased to employ largely their public credit, and the cities and minor divisions have come forward as the chief borrowers of money."[58] This, too, was a fateful turn in the history of America's federal society. Without the collapse of state enterprise under public electoral pressure, Adams believed, urban America would never have attained the gargantuan scale that it did. "One is warranted in suggesting, at least," he remarked, "that had the States been free from the legal restrictions imposed upon them by their constitutions, the inferior governments would never have been forced to respond to popular clamor for a collection of capital by government agency."[59]

The rise of urban America was bound up with this collection of capital by big-city government, and so was the rise of municipal corruption. Adams's work showed that public management at the urban level had been shaped by three facts in the boom period between the Civil War and the time of his writing in 1887: the rapid growth of population, which imposed new duties in the infrastructure and public health areas; the fade-out of state support in transportation planning, which forced private corporations to present their appeals for support to the cities; and what he called "the imperfect development of administrative methods under democratic rule," meaning the lack of any competent and effective civil service, which invited corruption on the part of local officials.[60]

In this postwar period the federal government had responded to new pressures for growth by making liberal but unplanned and uncoordinated appropriations of the ever receding public lands within its jurisdiction to railroad corporations to hasten the opening up of the West. Meanwhile state governments, despite their own diminishing powers, "yet discovered a way of granting material aid," Adams pointed out. They did so by enabling the cities to take all the risks in the public credit market. "The minor civil divisions were not included in the disabling acts of the new or amended constitutions. Being creatures of the legislatures, their powers were determined by the legislatures, and it was no difficult task to obtain for them authority to issue bonds in favor of private corporations." Thus it happened that the municipalities ended up with public credit as a resource. "It is not, then, an accident that the expansion of local credit took place almost immediately after the States had been shoved off the stage of industrial action."[61]

The net result of the interplay of these dynamics was an uncontrolled process of inter-urban and interregional competition for growth fueled by municipal bonds held by the capitalist urban elites who pioneered in the development of the modern corporation, a process led by the transportation sector and the railroads on which Adams had specialized as an economist. This evolving system did not fit the complexities of fragmented public authority in a federal society. The failure to acknowledge the importance of what had happened to state governments was resulting in a situation wherein the exercise of the new corporate powers provoked a threatened resort to *national* government as the only agency capable of curbing them. Adams was uneasy about this tendency, because it wrote off the states as genuine polities. He feared it would result in a gross simplification of the principles of federalism. It invited what he called "the Imperial idea," the prospect of a centralized and remote federal government that was federal in name only, administering the affairs of the nation directly, taking up the work that the states were no longer able to do.

That would be the end of the American experiment in federalism, and Adams wanted to make certain that it did not happen. The only alternative was reconstruction of the federal polity along lines not possible under stiff dual-federalism constraints. It required rebuilding the administrative capacities of state governments, something for which there was no popular constituency or even consciousness. It also called for developing the capacities of the national government to deal with national issues, cooperate with the states on common problems, and jointly to curb the powers of the corporations so as to make them accountable to a democratic society. Adams offered no specific recommendations on how to proceed with reconstruction, but he did suggest two "fundamental principles of republicanism" to be kept in mind in taking up this work. "First: All concentration of power, no matter by whom exercised, should be held to strict accountability. Second: The exercise of all responsible power should lie as closely as possible to the people over whom it is exercised."[62]

Adams knew that the corporations now engaged in interstate and international commerce were not held to strict accountability, and since the principle of subsidiarity, his second fundamental principle of republicanism, was plainly not intended by the founders to eventuate in municipal corruption and the impotence of state governments, it followed that the tasks of reconstructing a modern republican order and a federal society that *worked* were going to be difficult. The whole question boiled down to the need "to correlate public and private activity" throughout the federal system as a whole, a formidable problem in both theory and practice that resulted from "the imperfect development of administrative methods under democratic rule" in the middle years of the century. For American democracy to flourish, it was going to have to devise new administrative methods within the context of a newly fashioned cooperative federalism. The first attempt to address these problems was Theodore Roosevelt's.

Nationalism New and Old

The "new nationalism" that Theodore Roosevelt propounded in the run up to the election of 1912 was not chauvinism directed outward toward foreign competitors, but the reappearance of the old national theory of federalism updated and directed inward against the constraints of the old "dual sovereignty" federalism of the compact theory that had generated the disasters of Jacksonian devolution. The new nationalism, in other words, was a new attempt to establish cooperative federalism. Its target was the administrative impotence of the federal polity as a whole. The populist rhetoric of Roosevelt's progressivism was rooted in the national theory of federalism and its insistence that the people as a whole were the source of sovereignty for the national government, not the states or the people of the states considered singly.

As a political program the new nationalism was based upon a critique of inherited constitutional arrangements. It was aimed at what Roosevelt believed to be the near-sighted, obstructive behavior of the Supreme Court and the fragmentation of authority and responsibility in Congress, as well as the notion that the states had exclusive jurisdiction in what had plainly become areas of vital *national* policy. Whereas most nineteenth-century governance had been decentralized, confined to the separate spheres of dual federalism, and dominated by legislatures at both the state and national levels, the problems of the twentieth century called for a new emphasis in governance. "This New Nationalism regards the executive power as the steward of the public welfare. It demands of the judiciary that it shall be interested primarily in human welfare rather than property, just as it demands that the representative body shall represent all the people, rather than any one class or section of the people."[63]

As Roosevelt formulated it, the new nationalism was premised on the idea that the old federalism of separate spheres was no match for the organized forces of business and industry, led by the transportation sector, particularly the railroads, that emerged out of the ruin of the states, to use Henry Carter Adams's phrase. As a statement of public philosophy, the bedrock principle of the new nationalism was the assertion that "the citizens of the United States must effectively control the mighty commercial forces which they have themselves called into being," a task that would require a new politics and new capabilities for public management as well. Since "corporate expenditures for political purposes . . . have supplied one of the principal sources of corruption in our political affairs," a reference to the sorry record of elected officials at all levels of government since the Civil War to distance themselves from increasingly organized and manipulative private interests that were in the midst of forging a nationwide industrial economy, it followed that the "special interests" would have to be driven out of politics. The Constitution guaranteed protection to property, Roosevelt observed, "but it does not give the right of suffrage to any corporation." He recommended as a start campaign finance reform, the first appearance of the idea at the level of national politics: "all moneys received or expended for campaign purposes should be publically accounted for, not only after the election, but before the election as well."[64]

But this was only to start on the problem of cleaning up politics and building up the capabilities of the public sector. The private sector, as it came to be called, was demonstrating the increasingly impressive abilities of business and industry to master the practical problems of planning—to marshal and coordinate resources and deploy them strategically for the development of national and international markets. Here neither the academic community nor government took the lead. Rather it was the corporations that pioneered in planning and the development of American resources in the post–Civil War period. They experimented in new fields of technological innovation, hierarchical bureaucratic organization aimed to achieve concrete goals, and the orchestration of various kinds of expert knowledge into a unified framework. Whereas "consolidation" had once referred to the threat of federal domination of public enterprise, in the midst of the first great merger movement at the turn of the century it came to refer instead to corporate domination of American affairs through private enterprise.

Roosevelt was perplexed by the horse-and-buggy conservatism of political institutions that showed so little ability to comprehend the centralizing trends of the times and adapt to new conditions. He understood that the major obstacle to doing anything about it was the type of federalism that continued to valorize localism and private agency as fixed

and traditional, and hence made consolidating *public* power so as to match private power so difficult. The only counter to the regime of rising corporate pluralism and an ever more fragmented federalism of waning public power was nationalism. "I do not ask for over centralization," Roosevelt insisted, "but I do ask that we work in a spirit of broad and far reaching nationalism when we work for what concerns our people as a whole." State governments must be modernized and made "efficient for the work which concerns only the people of the state, and the nation for that which concerns all the people." The jumble of governmental jurisdictions incapable of effective action must no longer provide opportunities for the powers of commerce and industry to manipulate politics and elude public regulation: "There must remain no neutral ground to serve as a refuge for lawbreakers of great wealth, who can hire the vulpine legal cunning which teaches them how to avoid both jurisdictions."

There were proposed remedies as well as criticisms in the new nationalism. The "Roosevelt policies," as they were known, had matured slowly over the years of his presidency and had taken on a few new aspects since he left office in February 1909. As he pulled together his policy thought in the late summer of 1910, he called for a variety of measures, from a "scientific" tariff commission so designed as to reduce the irrationalities that all too predictably grew out of congressional logrolling, to a graduated income tax aimed at those who could well afford to pay it. But so far as his main object was concerned, the need to ensure that the forces of government kept abreast of the forces of commerce and industry, two of his proposals had a special strategic significance: his ideas for the national regulation of business and his conservation program.

With respect to the first of these, Roosevelt argued the need to learn something from the futilities of the government's experience in attempting to live with the shortcomings and contradictions of the Sherman Anti-Trust Act, passed nearly a generation earlier, which sought to deal with the rise of private power by declaring in essence that if such power tended to monopoly it should not be allowed to succeed, and letting it go at that. "The effort at prohibiting all combination has substantially failed," he insisted, and "the way out lies, not in attempting to prohibit such combinations, *but in completely controlling them in the interest of the public welfare*" (emphasis added). But how to control them? New controls were now possible because new administrative institutions, not on the horizon when the Sherman Act was written, were in position to do the job. "For that purpose the Federal Bureau of Corporations is an agency of the first importance. Its powers, and, therefore, its efficiency, as well as that of the Interstate Commerce Commission, should be largely increased."

What Roosevelt proposed to augment the capacity of national government was a modern substitute for providing the legislature with powers of general incorporation, as Madison had proposed in 1787. Madison's idea would have permitted the Congress to establish public corporations to undertake operations in congressionally warranted areas of policy, a Board or Commission on Internal Improvements, for example. Roosevelt's idea was to require all corporations engaged in interstate commerce to obtain a federal license as a condition for continuing to do so. Before the emergence of general incorporation laws, in granting corporate charters, state legislatures, when they wished to do so to advance the public interest in enterprise, had the power to insert specifications or provisions for participation by government in ownership rights in the charters themselves. Under Roosevelt's scheme the conditions attached to a corporation holding

a federal license would permit government to establish reporting requirements that would enable it to monitor the relevant internal conditions and administrative management of corporations.

"It has become entirely clear that we must have government supervision of the capitalization," Roosevelt insisted, "not only of public service corporations, including, particularly, railways, but of all corporations doing an interstate business." Here the basic regulatory principle of the new nationalism, intended to keep the capabilities of the institutions of government on a par with those of the world of finance, business, and industry, was clear enough: the only responsible alternative to government impotence which carried with it the risk of antimodern blundering of the sort threatened by the Sherman Act was "thoroughgoing and effective regulation." This, in turn, was possible only if based "on a full knowledge of all the facts" that came into play in the strategic decision-making of corporations. Effective government would have to be knowledgeable government, and the knowledge required could not be simply summoned up as needed by Congress. It had to be cultivated over time by administrative agencies.

But getting access to the facts inside the corporations would not prove to be an easy matter. Many theorists insisted on constitutional grounds that the government did not have the power to act on the question. Just as Jefferson, Madison, and Monroe believed that an amendment was required to permit participation in the field of internal improvements, so some in the Progressive Era argued that an amendment would be required to permit national government's regulation and supervision of corporations involved in interstate commerce. "It would obviously be unwise to endeavor to secure such an amendment until it is certain that the result cannot be obtained under the Constitution as it now is," Roosevelt remarked, echoing the position John Quincy Adams had taken on an internal improvements amendment, but "I believe that this regulation and supervision can be obtained by the enactment of law by the Congress."[65]

Even thoroughgoing regulation was merely reactive, however, intended, as the Sherman Act had been, primarily to prevent abuse. But preventing abuse was not the be all and end all of the new nationalism. It was a public philosophy of nation-building and governmentally fostered prosperity. As such it aimed to overcome the weaknesses of government that had marked so many areas of policy in the previous century and to make the national capital a significant center in the social, economic, and environmental development of the national domain. To begin to move in this future-oriented direction, the chosen vehicle was the package of conservation policies that together with his subordinates Roosevelt had devised. Taken as a package, these proposals marked the reappearance of the planning orientation in the affairs of national government. It was the internal improvements movement updated and adapted to new conditions.

Roosevelt and the Second National Plan

The second national plan appeared in the form of the interlocking conservation policies Roosevelt advocated. Considered as a set of policy proposals, it was reminiscent of the American system of the early republic. It was grounded in the same theory of national federalism, and premised on the same insight that loyalty to the national government had to be earned by good works, without which government might succumb to impotence and go to seed. But just as the American system and the Gallatin Plan had suffered from their complexities, particularly the need to

link administrative methods with democratic rule in the framework of cooperative federalism, when they were confronted by the strong currents of localism and sectionalism that coursed through the Congress, so Roosevelt's conservation plan would suffer, and for the same reasons. A new terminology, suited to the claims of the new nationalism and the introduction of a new policy area in national affairs, was devised to make the attempt, however, and it would prove to be an important contribution to modern thought about government. It was the vocabulary of scientific conservation.

Until the spring of 1907 the term "conservation" had no special resonance in the political vocabulary of Americans, but within a few years it had acquired the status of a serious, worthy word. Prominent persons were expected to have views about it, and a good deal of bombast resulted. For some conservation was "the greatest economic movement ever organized by any age or nation." For others it was merely "the unreal fabric of a bureaucratic dream," the result of the efforts of "a few well meaning zealots to install themselves as official prophets and saviors of the future, and from that exalted position to regulate the course of evolution." Despite the elusiveness and ambiguity of the term, it soon claimed a measure of popular appeal. As President Taft remarked in 1910, the year in which Roosevelt would decide to come out of retirement and oppose him, his handpicked successor, for the next Republican presidential nomination, purely out of anger over the significance of their growing differences in this new area of national policy, "a great many people are in favor of conservation, no matter what it means."[66]

Roosevelt's critics frequently charged that the conservation proposals he espoused were half-baked and did not make economic or constitutional sense. During the second meeting of the National Conservation Congress, a private association begun and organized by Gifford Pinchot and other Roosevelt disciples in St. Paul, Minnesota, in September 1910, heated debate about the meanings of the term for governance took place. President Taft, who before long would end up on the Supreme Court, preferred narrow canons of constitutional interpretation on this matter rather than the broad ones Roosevelt preferred ("if it is not prohibited, it is permitted" had been Roosevelt's rule). Taft had opened the meeting with a major address, his most comprehensive on the subject, and had closed his talk with the call for a "halt to general rhapsodies over Conservation, making the word mean every good thing in the world." The criticism that the rhetoric of conservation was vague and uncertain of its aims, or perhaps deceptive with regard to them, was picked up by others and runs beneath the surface of discussions that took place over the following two days.

On the closing day of the conference, Pinchot, Roosevelt's friend, principal aide, and adviser on conservation policies (who had been fired from his post as chief of the Forest Service by Taft a year earlier for his role in a policy dispute with Richard Ballinger, Taft's secretary of the interior) took his opportunity to respond to this current of criticism:

> Among the things which have been charged against the conservation movement is this, that Conservation does not know what it wants—that the Conservation movement is an indefinite striving after no one knows exactly what. I want to tell you, on the other hand, that the Conservation program is now, and has been for at least two years, a definite concrete attempt to get certain specific things; and that the impression which has been made, or which has been sought to be made, that we didn't know what we were after, is wholly misleading. The conservation program may be found, most of it, in the following reports— the report of the Public Lands Commission of

1905; the report of the Inland Waterways Commission, March, 1908; the great Declaration of Principles adopted by the Governors at the White House in May, 1908—one of the great documents of our history; the report of the Commission on Country Life, January, 1909; and the Declaration of the North American Conservation Conference, February, 1909. By the close of the last Administration, the Conservation program had grown into a well defined platform.[67]

These are the documentary sources for Roosevelt's version of the second national plan, his attempt to establish something like the American system of the antebellum period and repair the damage inflicted on America's federal society by the policies of the Jackson era. Pinchot's remark that the program had been a "definite concrete attempt to get certain specific things" for "at least two years" is a reference to the centrality of the inland waterways plan of 1908, which, for complex reasons, had dawned on Roosevelt's people only in the spring of 1907, when there were less than two years remaining in the life of the administration and Roosevelt was effectively a "lame duck."[68]

Before looking briefly at the individual components of the proposed program and searching out the institutional logic of the package as a whole, it is important to make again the general point that the process of institution-building Roosevelt had in mind was intended not to displace the role of the states in American federalism but to reinvigorate that role by establishing the possibilities for new forms of cooperative relationships among the nation, the states, and the municipalities. The process of institution-building Roosevelt sought to initiate was conceived as extending downward in the political order through the establishment of state-level conservation commissions, recommended by Roosevelt at the Conference of Governors in 1908, and to penetrate deeper into the countryside via new federal programs aimed at modernizing and rebuilding rural society through the Department of Agriculture, which was the goal of the Country Life Commission.

At the same time the institution-building agenda extended outward to the international level through the North American Conservation Conference of February 1909, which occurred just days before Roosevelt left office. This was the first international meeting in which national governments acknowledged the existence and importance of environmental conservation. It was devoted to discussion of common resources problems with Canada and Mexico and resulted in the call for all nations to meet in a world conservation conference the following year.

To get some idea of how this second national plan was supposed to work as a system of interlocking policies, we must turn to the individual elements of it that Pinchot identified in his response to Taft's charge of vagueness and ambiguity.

The Public Lands Commission

The aim of Roosevelt's Public Lands Commissions (for there were two of them, reporting out in 1903 and 1905, respectively) was to lay the foundations for a reversal of the dominant privatization trend of disposal of the public lands that had been underway since the Jacksonian era. Throughout the nineteenth century the great issue of public lands policy had not been *land use*, as likely would have been the case under the American system if the national government had had responsibilities for overseeing internal improvements and the design of a national transportation and communications infrastructure, but rather land *ownership*. From the 1830s onward the overriding policy goal was privatization, as rapidly as possible, and the arguments of national policy were over

the terms and conditions under which federally owned lands would be turned over to individuals and corporations before being bundled up with new boundaries and granted new political jurisdiction as semisovereign states. Roosevelt sought to stem the privatization trend, to secure (with minor exceptions) the remaining public lands in permanent public ownership, and to establish new "lease and fee principles" of public management—as opposed to sales in fee simple—for the resources that remained on the public lands.

At the time the first commission was established, the public domain included over a billion acres, roughly a third of the American land mass. Located mainly in the public land states of the West and Alaska, it represented from 5 to 95 percent of the land area in the jurisdictions within which it was located. Little of it was prime agricultural land. Most of it was inaccessible, arid, mountainous, or heavily forested. Such lands as were suitable for the needs of still more yeoman farmers, so strongly featured in public lands debates of the previous seventy years, would be available to them, but beyond that the commissions sought replacement of disposal policies by public ownership and management.

The main emphasis of the commission's work in 1905 was summarized with the remark that "the fundamental fact that characterizes the situation under the present public land law is this, *that the number of patents issued is increasingly out of all proportion to the number of new homes*" (emphasis added).[69] This was a lightly stated criticism of the trend of privatization policy that had been obvious since the time John Quincy Adams had expressed his contempt for "land jobbers, stock jobbers, and rights-of-man jobbers." The patents referred to were documents that granted deeds of ownership to previously public lands. If they were not being used for new farms, and farming had for long been known to be a declining occupation in terms of the numbers of workers involved in it, then what *were* they being used for? In keeping with its Jeffersonian-Jacksonian origins, the privatization policy had been intended rapidly and cheaply to extend the agricultural republic through space, thus helping to realize the democratic idea. It was premised on the notion that land was a simple thing, an undifferentiated resource useful mainly for growing things on. Some land was better, and better located, than other land, but still for disposal purposes it was *just land,* and that was that. There was no need from the governmental standpoint to tarry over these transactions; let the land office pinpoint locations, measure it up, move it out, and get on to the next section.

In the other national planning tradition of public philosophy, however, land was a *complex resource,* one of the keys to realizing the national idea, and there was nothing simple about it. The public domain was part of the treasury to be drawn upon in nation-building. It was to be scientifically surveyed and studied so that it could be properly assessed and differentiated. The mineral resources underneath the land, for example, or the water adjacent to it, might be far more important than the land itself, a point that had been quite clear to Hamilton. In the *Report on Manufactures* he had argued that with the development of a mixed agricultural-manufacturing culture, "the bowels as well as the surface of the earth are ransacked for articles which were before neglected. Animals, plants, and minerals acquire a utility and a value which were before unexplored."[70] As a complex resource, the public lands called for complex administration. The land should be disposed of slowly and in light of its value and utility with respect to all that was going on inside the lands it bordered.

Thus the criticism being developed by Roosevelt's commissioners was that under

the guise of an expanding agricultural republic, no matter how well intentioned the egalitarian land disposal policies had been, what was actually occurring whether by accident or design was that industrial resources of timber, water power sites, minerals, and other commodities were finding their way into the new corporate hierarchies. Because the lands had not been scientifically surveyed until late in the nineteenth century, and even then the legislature had refused to link disposal policies to what the surveys suggested the best use of the lands might be, there had been no significant changes in the trend of policy since the Jackson era. Roosevelt's commissioners reasoned that the inertial momentum of past policy had to be slowed down. Careful provision should be made to ascertain how much really useful agricultural land remained, and in the meantime the lands should be taken out of play and held under government control.

The group reported on the operation of what they considered the most offensive and wrongheaded of the particular land laws that together made up a badly fragmented public lands policy: the desert lands act, the timber and stone act (which made possible direct purchase in fee simple of forest tracts), and the commutation clause of the Homestead Act (which made it possible to sell and exchange relatively worthless lands for valuable ones). They recommended corrections or repeals. The commission also suggested that the president be given the authority to set aside grazing districts by proclamation (as Roosevelt had done with enormous tracts of forest lands until Congress put a stop to the practice) and that the secretary of agriculture be given the authority to appraise the grazing values of these lands and establish an appropriate system of fees for grazing permits, the rationale of the system that would finally be established only a generation later in the 1930s. None of the recommendations of the commissions were taken up by Congress during the Theodore Roosevelt administration.[71]

The Inland Waterways Commission

The February 26, 1908, report of the Inland Waterways Commission is an important document in the history of American planning. The work of a nine-person group appointed by Roosevelt less than a year previous and serving without congressional authorization (or, as it happened, approval), the report introduced into the discourse of American policymaking the notion of integrated, multipurpose river-basin planning and management. The idea was new to public affairs, and was not actually taken up until the Tennessee Valley Authority (TVA) of the 1930s, which represents a pilot project version, on a smaller scale, of what the new nationalists of the Progressive Era had in mind. The 1908 plan was ambitious, complex, and daring, far too much so for the politics of the day. It combined ecological and engineering ideas with those of productive, revenue-generating public enterprise in a waterways plan that appealed strongly to Roosevelt because it promised to provide some of the links he needed to get the national government into the domain of the state governments, and to get both of them back into the business of public enterprise. Not the least of its virtues, as Roosevelt said of the plan, was that "it affords a most promising field for cooperation between the states and the nation."[72]

Roosevelt's hope was that through the plan the federal government might put itself in a position to participate in American land-use planning and development on a scale never before possible. He was seeking a measure of nationalization through the government's previously undeveloped jurisdiction over interstate waterways. The basic notion was that the central government, by asserting its primacy of jurisdiction in matters of water resources policy and interstate commerce, would take the lead in vast multipurpose river-basin development schemes in the major hydrographic basins of the nation. The hydroelectric facilities that made up the central components of the plan would be permanent public assets, which, after paying for the cost of their construction and upkeep, would generate revenues that would go into a revolving fund sufficient to finance other public works and infrastructure, and so on indefinitely. To make the scheme work, federal jurisdiction had to be primary in the large, interstate drainage basins, and to secure this control wherever it was doubtful Roosevelt argued that if necessary lands under state jurisdiction should be deeded back to the federal government.[73]

In his message accompanying the commission's report, Roosevelt pounded home the argument that the inland waterways "of no other civilized country are so poorly developed, so little used, or play so small a part in the industrial life of the nation" as was the case in America, and he asked why this should be so. The answer was a historical one. It had to do with the neglected costs of leaving so important a function as the planning of the nation's transportation infrastructure to urban rivalry, competitive private enterprise and the catch-as-catch-can subsidies that had been available at various points in the federal system. The commission found that "it was unregulated railroad competition which prevented or destroyed the development of commerce on our inland waterways."

The report cited the example of traffic on the Mississippi, made famous by the writings of Mark Twain. Once without rival in any country, by 1908 traffic on the river was negligible. As the railroads had grown in capacity and influence, Roosevelt pointed out, "they prevented the restoration of river traffic by keeping down their rates along the rivers, recouping themselves with higher charges elsewhere. They also acquired water fronts and terminals to an extent which made water competition impossible." Rather than blending with it, a new technology had killed off an old one. This was a phenomenon that would recur again and again in the transportation policy area, as the advocates for the newly successful technological systems—the highway lobby of the automobile age, for example—worked to squeeze out support for the older ones. After holding down the waterways, the railroads would become victims in turn.

Roosevelt noted that hitherto the national policy of inland waterways development "has been largely negative," and he spoke with contempt of what had been the prevailing "policy of repression and procrastination." He had in mind here the world of logrolling in rivers and harbors bills in Congress, which had never been linked up to any national plan. In those limited areas where Congress felt it had the jurisdiction to commit resources, "there had been frequent changes of plan and piecemeal execution of projects." The overall result, he observed, was that "in spite of large appropriations for their improvement, our rivers are less serviceable for interstate commerce today than they were half a century ago, and in spite of the vast increases of our population and commerce, they are on the whole less used."[74] To make the point forcefully that things might have been otherwise, and to reinforce the bona fides of his own proposals, the Roosevelt commission's report carried as an appendix the full text of the Gallatin Plan of a century earlier.

The secretary of the Inland Waterways Commission and the person responsible for coming up with the new policy ideas was W J McGee (who insisted on using his initials without punctuation), a veteran of Washington's scientific civil-service community that had grown up in the 1880s and 1890s. McGee believed that if properly institutionalized a National Waterways Commission of the kind recommended in the report would be able to accomplish four things of fundamental importance to American development in the twentieth century. First, there was the improvement of the physical environment through integrated, multipurpose, river-basin planning, the omnibus "conservation idea" that promised ultimately to be able to provide simultaneously for power development and navigation, flood control, irrigation, wildlife preservation, and the upgrading of water quality. Second was the generation of long-term persistent demand for public works and employment, together with the means for meeting the demand. Third there was the development of what McGee believed would become the strategic energy resource of the future, clean and renewable hydroelectric power. Finally and most important, there was the chance to get American government back into the business of public enterprise, giving it the capacity to take up the work of internal improvement in a modern, high-technology context.

While the federal government's claim to any direct jurisdiction over land use within the states was shaky, its claim to responsibility for the quality and uses of interstate waters was much stronger. Water is a fundamentally different *kind* of resource than land. Like the air, it is inherently a commons resource, "a prime necessary of life" as McGee liked to put it, and its legal bearings with respect to ownership, use, and the public interest were accordingly different from land, a point that McGee saw early on. He had done some of the federal government's earliest work on the hydrological cycle, and was the first scientist to estimate the total water resources of the United States.

Water *moves,* and it moves in a cycle. This simple fact has long-term implications for governmental jurisdiction and responsibility. McGee spoke of America's water resources as "essentially a grand physical unit made up of interdependent parts, and each stream, despite its essential unity and the interrelation of all its parts, is but an integer within the larger unit." The inference he drew from this line of reasoning was that ultimately, with further industrialization and the advance of scientific knowledge, the federal government's claim to jurisdiction over water policy would prove to be stronger than the claims of the states and localities. New relationships of governance would have to be set up to reflect this condition.[75]

Though he spoke of developing the major rivers and streams of the nation, McGee was careful to point out that "picturesque streams and cataracts should be saved as scenic features, for natural beauty is a national asset beyond material measure, but the ignoble wild should be harnessed to the plow of progress." He spoke also of the need, seen as urgent as early as 1908, to purify the waters of the continent, and he meant the term quite literally. McGee was the first in Washington scientific circles to call for what would later become known as a "no discharge" policy as applied to waterways: "Refuse from household, farm, factory, mine, and city should be prevented from polluting streams, or extending needlessly into the ground water or contaminating the air," he insisted, and it should be used for modern purposes. "In rural households and communities refuse should be so treated as to yield high grade fertilizer; urban sewage should be converted and utilized as a source of municipal revenue; and mine refuse should be treated as a by product."[76]

McGee reasoned that if the waters could be purified via new legal regulations of the no discharge type, then it would be possible to expand, rather than reduce, the kinds of uses

to which water was put with the growth of industrial civilization. Recreation might become a major use, along with certain kinds of wildlife preservation, and fisheries might be restored. "Fish could be propagated and protected in streams and lakes," he pointed out, "and necessary fishways should be provided in connection with dams and other works; and State and federal laws relating to fish and fisheries in inland and coast waters should be unified."[77]

Just as Gallatin's plan had been "high tech" by the standards of 1808, so the waterways plan was high-tech in character by the standards of 1908. McGee was given to tracing the history of progressive advances in science and technology, and he noted that in the 1890s the technology of electric power transmission over long distances had begun reconstructing industries, the internal combustion engine had been developed, irrigation had opened up a new era in standards of agricultural productivity, and steel-concrete construction had revolutionized the possibilities for earthworks on a scale never before imagined. It was these new construction techniques that made feasible the enormous dams and reservoirs that were to come, though not before the New Deal. The conclusion that McGee drew from this conjuncture of long-term water use requirements on the one hand and new technical abilities on the other was the need for a new kind of federal agency, a "presumptively temporary federal administrative agency, created or empowered to make investigations and take actions looking toward the progressive control and regulation of the water of the country with respect to all its uses, both directly and in cooperation with the states and when needful with individuals, corporations, communities, and municipalities."[78]

From the standpoint of planning history, the most significant features of the inland waterways plan were its jurisdictional and public finance aspects. The power generating facilities were to be set up as remunerative public works. After meeting construction and operating costs, these facilities would continue, through the imposition of a "conservation charge" levied on companies transmitting the hydroelectric power, to provide a revolving fund that would be used for other public works throughout the county, just as Gallatin would have intended. As in the Gallatin Plan, the works would be constructed and operated through a complicated set of cooperative arrangements with states, municipalities, and private corporations. The federal government would have the upper hand in determining the direction of these relations, since it had the fundamental claim to responsibility for the quality and uses of the water itself.

Finally, with regard to the areal aspects of the waterways plan, in his covering message to Congress accompanying the report Roosevelt pointed out that, although no specific plans or recommendations for particular projects had been made, nonetheless the first of these works would of course concern "the Mississippi and its tributaries, whose commercial development will directly affect half of our people. The Mississippi should be made a loop of the sea and work upon it should be begun at the earliest possible moment." There was mention also of California's possibilities and those of the Northwest, which could not be overlooked: "The need for the developing of the Pacific coast rivers is not less pressing." And though it was not singled out for discussion as a separate river-basin system, the report included data on those sections of the Ohio, Mississippi, and Tennessee Rivers that would actually become the first ones developed along the proposed lines by the TVA a generation later.

The major legislative recommendation of the commission was that Congress authorize the president to appoint a National Waterways Commission, which would be given the task of bringing into coordination the work of the four federal departments that then dealt with water resources, that the new commission have the power to direct these agencies to conduct whatever studies it deemed necessary in connection with the idea of multipurpose river-basin development, and that the commission be empowered to frame specific plans, and, as authorized by Congress, to carry them out. There was immediate opposition to the recommendations from one of these agencies, the Army's Corps of Engineers, which did not wish to be coordinated. Congress took no immediate action on any of the recommendations. Twelve years later, however, in 1920, the Federal Water Power Act was passed, which set up the Federal Power Commission and clarified the matter of public supervision of hydroelectric power on both the navigable streams and the public lands. This was a single-purpose bill, however, and no ideas of linkage to modern forms of internal improvements and multipurpose planning were taken up.

The White House Conference of Governors

The third element in the conservation strategy mentioned by Pinchot in his response to President Taft was the Conference of Governors held in the White House in May 1908, the first meeting of its kind in American history. The aim of this gathering was to look into possibilities for new forms of cooperative federalism and to encourage building up both the administrative capacity and the information base of government—at the national level and the state level as well—so as to lay the foundations for subsequent regulation and planning. In October of 1907 McGee and Senator Theodore Burton of the Inland Waterways Commission had written to Roosevelt suggesting that he convene the conference.

Among the reasons given was the following: "We are of the opinion that the time has come for considering the policy of reserving these material resources on which the permanent prosperity of our country and the equal opportunity of all our People must depend; we are also of the opinion that the policy of conservation is so marked an advance on that policy adopted at the outset of our National career as to demand the consideration of both Federal and State sponsors for the welfare of the people." The conference was intended, in other words, to be the next best thing to a constitutional convention.

The immediate purpose of the conference was to get into the same room as many as possible of those officials collectively responsible for the operations of America's federal society as a whole and have them discuss the interdependencies of resources policy in the hope that they might be inspired to think new thoughts about the need for intergovernmental cooperation. The conference included not only the governors, but also members of Congress, justices of the Supreme Court, members of the Cabinet, and some prominent private citizens. McGee served as secretary of the conference, drafted Roosevelt's opening speech, and drafted the "Declaration of Principles" resulting from the meeting.

There were dozens of speeches given during the two-day event, and the only formal item to emerge from its deliberations was the "Declaration of Principles." These principles expressed the "conviction that the use of the natural resources of our independent states are interdependent and bound together by ties of mutual benefits, responsibilities and duties." It expressed the hope that the beauty, health, and habitability of the nation would be preserved and increased. It recognized that private ownership of forest lands entailed responsibilities to all the people, and favored "the enactment of laws looking to the protection and replacement of privately owned

forests." It strongly endorsed the waterways plan: "We especially urge on the Federal Congress the immediate adoption of a wise, active, and thorough waterway policy, providing for the prompt improvement of our streams and the conservation of their watersheds required for the uses of commerce and the protection of the interests of our People." Finally it called for the appointment by each state of a commission on the conservation of natural resources, and suggested that the federal government do likewise.[79]

Almost immediately after the governors' conference, in June 1908, Roosevelt appointed a National Conservation Commission, the task of which was to compile the first comprehensive inventory of American natural resources. Pinchot was chairman of the commission, and McGee the secretary of its section on water resources. The commission produced a three-volume study within nine months of its establishment, operating as quickly as it did by drawing on the data developed in the research bureaus of the Interior and Agriculture Departments in the preceding decades. The report restated the need to link up the ideas of the public lands commission, the waterways commission, and the governors conference. Its most important plea, however, was for the establishment of a permanent National Conservation Commission itself, since Pinchot's had only the status of a presidentially appointed group and enjoyed no congressional sanction.

The report recommended that such a permanent National Conservation Commission be empowered by Congress to cooperate with such state commissions as had been or would be established in the effort to refine and coordinate knowledge on the distribution, abundance, and rates of use of American natural resources. The premise here was that in the long-term future, with detailed information on trends in both renewable and nonrenewable resources use in place, the basis would be provided for anticipatory or corrective legislation within the federal system. These commissions were to accumulate the data and the experience necessary for ecologically sophisticated planning along the lines of voluntarily cooperative federalism. Congress did not budge. No federal commission was established, and few of the states had conservation commissions or agencies until well after the New Deal period, when the problem of creating governmental structure and capacity in this field was taken up again by the National Resources Planning Board.

The Commission on Country Life

The fourth element in the national conservation plan cited by Pinchot was the report of the Country Life Commission, established by Roosevelt in August 1908, just six months before the close of his administration. The purpose of this commission was to deal with what Roosevelt's advisers viewed as a lack of balance and adjustment between rural and urban life in America, and the work of the group marks the first appearance of this concern at the level of the national government. Chaired by Liberty Hyde Bailey, an agronomist from Cornell University, it included Pinchot, Henry Wallace, and Walter Hines Page, editor of *The World's Work*. The theme of the commission's report, which appeared in February of 1909 just as Roosevelt left office, was the need for reconstruction of the open countryside, and it issued a call for the development of rural sociology and economics as fields of policy-relevant knowledge to assist in the work. The commission insisted that the improvement of country life was not a matter simply of raising more and better crops, but rather a matter of establishing better forms of social organization and community life in the rural areas, as a number of Euro-

pean governments were attempting to do via cooperative associations of various kinds. Among other things, the commission wanted to slow down migration into the cities and encourage people to live in the countryside by making it more attractive.

The Country Life Commission developed the argument that there was a need to put farmers on a par with other occupational groups in society, and that one of the chief difficulties in attempting to do so was a *cultural* problem, the need to satisfy the higher social and intellectual aspirations that induced people to leave the country for the greater variety and stimulus of the cities. Speaking of the farmer in this connection, for example, the commission pointed out, "If he wishes to educate his children, he avails himself of the schools of the city. He does not as a rule dream of a rural organization that can supply as completely as the city the four great requirements of man—health, education, occupation, society." The cities enjoyed a higher quality of life, in other words, and that quality was higher not simply because of the diversity of occupations that Hamilton and his successors had spoken of, but because they had the money to provide for the basic needs of physical and cultural infrastructure. On the other hand, the rural areas, which should have been a Jeffersonian paradise if the theory that government is best which governs least held true, were institutionally starved by their antitax county and state governments.

They could not provide the level of public services in education and health that a proper republican order called for. There was no need for things to remain this way, the commission insisted. "While his brother in the city is striving by moving out of the business section into the suburbs to get as much as possible of the country in the city, he does not dream that it is possible to have most [of what] is best in the city in the country. The time has come when we must give as much constructive attention to the development of the open country as we have given to other affairs."[80] Since rural government became enfeebled after the incentives for high competence in it were removed by the withdrawal of the states from public enterprise, federalism would have to be fixed to do so.

Among the major deficiencies of country life, the commission cited speculative holding of lands, monopolistic control of streams, and the wastage of forests, all of which tied its work into the thrust of the other elements in the national conservation plan. Together they promised to be able to cushion and control the inroads into the hinterlands of uncontrolled corporate capitalism, for which rural governments were simply no match. The Country Life Commission also argued the aesthetic importance of the countryside. In a remarkably prescient way it suggested how the countryside might be put together with the expanding urban areas for the benefit of both:

> We must not forget the value of scenery. This is a distinct asset, and it will be more recognized as time goes on. It will be impossible to develop a satisfactory country life without conserving the beauty of the landscape and developing the people to the point of appreciating it. In parts of the East a regular system of parking the open country of the entire State has already begun, constructing the roads, preserving the natural features, and developing the latent beauty in such a way that the whole country becomes part of one continuing landscape treatment. This in no way interferes with the agricultural utilization of the land, but rather increases it. The scenery is, in fact, capitalized, so that it adds to the property values and contributes to local patriotism and to the thrift of the commonwealth.[81]

The commission's chairman, Bailey, in his 1911 book on the country life movement, made the point that as an adjunct to the Roosevelt conservation movement the commission was trying not simply to shore up an old way of life, but instead to suggest the possibilities of the countryside as a setting for new ways of life that were becoming feasible by the development of science and technology. Rather than allowing the rural areas to empty out and become derelict, the commissioners wanted to devise opportunities for the kind of town life in the prosperous countryside that so appealed to the young Mumford. "The country life movement does not imply that all young persons who hereafter shall remain in the country are to be actual farmers. The practice of customary professions and occupations will take on more importance in country districts. The country physician, veterinary, pastor, lawyer, and teacher are to extend greatly in influence and opportunity," Bailey insisted. "But aside from all this, entirely new occupations and professions are to arise, even the names of which are not yet known to us. Some of them are already underway. There will be established out in the open country plant doctors, plant breeders, soil experts, forest experts, farm machinery experts, drainage and irrigation experts, recreation experts, market experts, and many others."[82]

Like the other Roosevelt conservation commissions, the Country Life Commission inspired no enthusiasm in the nation's legislature. As a preliminary to planning and policymaking it called for the government to make thoroughgoing surveys of the population, infrastructure, and cultural resources of all agricultural regions in the United States. It encouraged the Congress to develop and expand a system of extension work in rural communities through the land grant colleges with the people at their homes and on their farms. It called for an investigation by experts of the middleman system in handling farm products, an inquiry into the control and use of streams in the United States "with the object of protecting the people in their ownership and reserving to agricultural uses such benefits as should be reserved for those purposes," the establishment of a highway engineering service or organization, "to be at the call of the States in working out effective and economical highway systems." It sought the establishment of a system of parcel post and postal savings banks for the countryside, and finally the "providing of some means or agency for the guidance of public opinion toward the development of a real rural society that shall rest directly on the land."[83] As opposed to the myth of simple agrarian virtue, the *real* rural society could not be institution-free. It was going to have to be modernized, mixed, and balanced. To bring it into being would require help from federally coordinated governments. Programs in this field would not be taken up in earnest until the New Deal.

Worldwide Conservation

The final element in the Roosevelt conservation plan was its foreign policy component, the attempt to internationalize the movement and put the problems of environmental conservation on the agenda of the world's governments. This, too, was a remarkably forward-looking idea to entertain at a time when there was no institutional forum for discussion of global problems, indeed when there was little official consciousness of global problems of any kind beyond the economics of empire and the threats of war.

The North American Conservation Conference was held in the White House in February, 1909, just weeks before Roosevelt left office. The conference was the first international meeting of governments ever to address any of the problems of environmental resources and conservation. It included the United States, Mexico, Canada, and the then-colony of Newfoundland. Delegates produced a "Declaration of Principles" very much like the one produced by the governor's conference ten months earlier. The declaration included the principle that "natural resources are not confined by the boundary lines that separate Nations. We agree that no Nation acting alone can adequately conserve them, and we recommend the adoption of concurrent measures for conserving the material foundations of the welfare of all the Nations concerned, and for ascertaining their location and extent."

Delegates recommended that the first thing to be done was the establishment of National Conservation Commissions by each of the participating governments. The purpose of the commissions would be to develop and exchange the kinds of scientific information necessary to identify and understand changing environmental conditions and the possibilities for improving them through new techniques and technologies. This was the international side of cooperative federalism, the recognition that for the common good other sovereign states would have to participate in global public policy. Necessarily such participation would have to be voluntary, and delegates to the conference outlined the way in which a kind of voluntary "leveling up" of best practices in conservation might proceed. The declaration noted that "when such Conservation Commissions have been established, a system of intercommunication should be inaugurated, whereby, at stated intervals, all discoveries, inventions, processes, inventories of natural resources, information of a new and specially important character, and seeds, seedlings, new or improved varieties, and other productions which are of value in conserving or improving any natural resource shall be transmitted by each commission to all of the others, to the end that they may be adopted and utilized as widely as possible."

The delegates from Mexico and Canada adopted some of the principles Roosevelt and his aides had been trying to establish nationally, particularly those bearing on the principle of public control over or influence on patterns of resources development: "We agree that those resources which are necessaries of life should be regarded as public utilities, that their ownership entails specific duties to the public, and that as far as possible effective measures should be adopted to guard against monopoly." Ownership of forests and water resources were singled out in this connection, and the argument was again endorsed, here in an international context, that surface rights and underground mineral rights should be separately dealt with so as to permit use of the surface while retaining government control over mineral and oil development.

There were two recommendations made which applied specifically to relations among the nations of the continent, one dealing with pollution control and the other with wildlife conservation. On the pollution issue, the conference concluded "that immediate action is necessary to prevent further pollution, mainly through sewage, of the lakes, rivers, and streams throughout North America. Such pollution, aside from the enormous loss in fertilizing elements entailed thereby, is an immediate and continuous danger to public health, to the health of animals, and, when caused by certain chemical agents, to agriculture. Therefore we recommend that preventive legislation be enacted." On the question of wildlife conservation, conferees recognized formally the principle that game preservation and bird life are related to the principles of forest conservation, water development, and other issues: "We therefore favor game protection under regulation, the creation of extensive game preserves, and special protection for such birds as are useful to agriculture."[84]

The most prescient recommendation of the conferees, however, was their call for a world congress of conservation modeled on the Conference of Governors of 1908. Here delegates suggested that the president of the United States take the initiative in convening a world conference on the subject of global resources and their inventory, conservation, and development. Immediately Roosevelt did so. With concurrence of the government of the Netherlands, invitations were extended to fifty-eight nations to gather in the Hague the following year.

The State Department's circular of instruction to its diplomats, who were to brief foreign governments and officially extend the invitations, stressed the need to make it clear that this new area of policy involved more than advocating a conservative approach to the use of nonrenewable resources, "that reparatory agencies should be invoked to aid the processes of beneficent nature, and that the means of restoration and increase should be sought whenever practicable."

In keeping with the basic maxim of planning in any field—survey first, then plan—the aim of Roosevelt's proposed world conference was to get together representatives of the world's governments "with a view to considering a general plan for an inventory of the natural resources of the world and to devising a uniform scheme for the expression of the results of such inventory to the end that there may be a general understanding of the world's supply of the material elements which underlie the development of civilization and the welfare of the peoples of the earth." This was a job likely to require decades of work on the part of scientific communities throughout the world, but it was not an end in itself. "It would be appropriate also," the circular stated, "for the conference to consider the general phases of the correlated problem of checking, and, when possible, repairing the injuries caused by waste and destruction of natural resources and utilities and make recommendations in the interest of their conservation, development, and replenishment."[85] The proposed conference sought, in other words, to lay the groundwork for what is today called "sustainable development," based on international agreements made against the background of economic and ecological knowledge. Nothing came of this Roosevelt idea either, as President Taft, shortly after entering office, withdrew the Roosevelt invitations to governments and brought an end to the conference plan.

Conclusion

Like the nationalists of old in the early republic, the new nationalists failed, at least at the beginning. But they gave expression to a new way of thinking about the possibilities of American governance that showed a respect for the difficult problems of a poorly functioning federalism that had been bequeathed to them by history. This way of thinking about the overall requirements for cooperation within the federal system remains as pertinent to the problems of today as it was nearly a century ago.

Presidents are not emperors, but imagine that magically Roosevelt had been able to install the requirements of the second national plan simply by presidential proclamation. What might the results have been? If we give the benefit of the doubt to the Roosevelt proposals, it might have been something like this. A prosperous and ecologically healthy American civilization, balanced in its makeup of urban, rural, and wilderness zones, would be sustained and cultivated in "one continuous landscape treatment," as the Country Life Commission put it, by the ceaselessly active and intelligent governments that made up its federal structure. The national domain would be supervised by the coordinated agencies of cooperative federalism, and metaphors of gardening rather than reinvention

and mechanical disassembly would dominate theories of politics.

America's airsheds and waterways would have been rescued from pollution and abuse, and once again its waters would be "fishable and swimmable," to use the legislative language of a later day. The wilderness of civilization created by uncoordinated enterprise would be gradually reclaimed by nature, with roadless areas of nature reserves linking up nationwide for the good of humans and other species and as an enhancement for the cultural life of those who lived in the cities and towns. Gradual but persistent improvement of the American environment, upgrading "the foundations of our prosperity," as the conservationists put it, would be a prime task of government, and "design with nature" its motto. A stable federal revenue system would produce the money to do the job, and resources would be fed into the new forms of internal improvements that accompany the continuing development of science and technology.[86]

Coordinated governance would be the order of the day. No longer would the weaknesses of the federal system as a system provide opportunities for evading the responsibilities of corporate power. Government would have enough control over its own activities to ensure that it did not do more harm than good. It would be responsive to genuine democratic complaint, but would not capitulate to narrow private interests or the passing, short-term pressures exerted by Congress. Government's relations with private corporations would be ordered with the needs of its long-term improvement responsibilities in mind, making certain that private enterprise, on which the prosperity of all depends, was encouraged to flourish but not permitted to take on the trappings of sovereignty or define its own as the public's interest.

The national government would house the chief steward of the public interest, as

Roosevelt suggested it should, but he (or she) would not be the only steward, for the obligations of stewardship would be widely diffused. The principles of federalism require that the national government not overextend itself, both for its own good and the good of those over whom it holds jurisdiction. The integrity of state and local governments would be respected, provided that they *had* integrity and the capacity to do their jobs. If not, both would have to be carefully built up. Reciprocity and voluntary agreements would prevail in relations of cooperative federalism, but such necessarily fragile relations would be monitored by all parties and when cooperation broke down, the reasons for the breakdown and the parties responsible for it would be public knowledge. The national government would be especially concerned with organizing and updating social, economic, and ecological knowledge regarding what was happening in the federal system as a whole, so that the health and vitality of the whole, and of the parts in relation to the whole, could be monitored by all. It would be responsible for the nation's foreign relations, and these, too, would be designed not to beggar the neighbors but patiently to secure a gradual upgrading, *a leveling up,* of social and environmental conditions around the world through international law, regulation, and commerce.

But to go on this way reminds us just how far over the horizon the ideal of a properly functioning national democracy "complicated by federalism" remains, how remote from the real world of politics and government. Roosevelt was thwarted by democratic politics, as was John Quincy Adams before him and the Federalists before that. All of them understood that any solution to the problems of inconstancy, willfulness, and shortsightedness that accompany democratic politics lies in the creation of democratic methods of administration, knowledgeable

bureaucracies, as a mechanism to counterbalance the incessant changes of legislators and provide the traction necessary for collective organization and achievement. And these institutions must be capable of orchestrating their work not only with the legislature that directs them but with the duties of bureaucracies at all other levels of government as well, not in organizationally self-serving fashion, but so as actually to get the job done.

In ordinary speech to plan is to think ahead, to have some sense of what your responsibilities are and how you are going to fulfill them. Infants are not planners; they live in a world of immediacy. Adults, however, are by nature planners, more or less successfully, and do not expect any special praise for engaging in the act. To do so is a part of growing up; to refuse is to attempt to prolong infancy beyond its natural term. Those on the national planning side of the American tradition of public philosophy understood that this observation applied to governments as well as to individuals. They did not conceive planning as something exotic to be grafted onto the sinews of American government, but as something natural that came from the inside out in the actual experience of governing as part of a process of maturation. It was an aspect of American government's growing up, and was to be expressed by the emergence of new relations of cooperative federalism.

By Roosevelt's time they understood, too, the irony of the fact that the "private sector" had emerged out of the failures of early government properly to grow up and take on its responsibilities for planning the workings of the public sector. This feature of the actual social and economic constitution of American life had come to command the loyalty and respect and hopes of multitudes for its abilities in "the administration of great affairs," as Henry Carter Adams had put it. It was an attachment to the cornucopia of the modern consumer culture generated by private enterprise that had become a mighty force in American culture.

The power of these attachments threatened the ideals of the American experiment with a federal republic root and branch. To their credit Roosevelt and his disciples understood the need to limit these attachments. They refused to accept the notion that corporate elites were the de facto higher civil servants of the United States. They knew that a consumer culture was not necessarily a worthy democratic one, that the latter required all private enterprise ultimately to be accountable politically for its exercise of power. They saw, too, that for politics to exert directive force over the turbulent, organized energies of private life, it was necessary to rebuild American federalism, not simply to build up the powers of national government. Finally they sensed the possibilities for good in an entirely new field of national government activity: environmental conservation and development. In bringing these questions to the surface of public life, they were the first to identify the essential and recurrent problems of government planning in the twentieth century, and for that they deserve a generous measure of respect.

Notes

1. Woodrow Wilson, "The Study of Administration," *Political Science Quarterly,* June 1887, pp. 197–222. This article is focused on the importance of previously neglected problems of *administration,* rather than politics, and for that reason is said to mark the emergence of public administration as a professional field of study in America. From the beginning, issues of planning have been bound up with those of national public administration.

2. United States Inland Waterways Commission, *Preliminary Report of the Inland Waterways Commission* (Washington, D.C.: U.S. Government Printing Office (GPO), 1908). The Gallatin report is reprinted as an appendix, and introduced with the observation that "Gallatin's work . . . may be said to have inaugurated the waterway policy of the United States."

3. For a carefully argued, wide-ranging review of the literature of scholarly dispute over the meanings, appropriate chronology, and criteria for thinking about the course of American federalism, see Harry N. Scheiber, "Federalism and Legal Process: Historical and Contemporary Analysis of the American System," *Law and Society Review* 14, No. 3 (Spring 1980), pp. 663–722. See also his "The Condition of American Federalism: An Historian's View: A Study Submitted by the Subcommittee on Intergovernmental Relations to the Committee on Government Operations of the United States Senate," Committee Print, 89th Congress, 2nd Sess. (Washington, D.C.: GPO, 1966). This study contains Scheiber's own rendering of the historical stages of development within federalism. His first stage, which he calls the era of "rivalistic state mercantilism," runs from the founding to the Civil War. It is marked by effective separation of national and state powers and by *public enterprise competition* among the states themselves in pursuit of state-led economic growth. Finally, note should be taken of Scheiber's "Federalism and the States," in Stanley Kutler, ed., *Encyclopedia of the United States in the Twentieth Century* (New York: Charles Scribner's Sons, 1996), vol. 1, pp. 427–50. The article provides an especially rich account of twentieth-century relations between the states and the nation.

4. On the growth in scale and importance of intergovernmental relations, see W. Brooke Graves, *American Intergovernmental Relations: Their Origins, Historical Development, and Current Status* (New York: Scribners, 1964). On the current level of aid to the states, see United States Office of Management and Budget, *Analytical Perspectives, Budget of the United States Government, Fiscal Year 1999,* 105th Congress, 2nd Sess., H. Doc. 105-177, Vol. III (Washington, D.C.: GPO, 1999), pp. 213–17. For an analysis of recent attempts to comprehend and reform intergovernmental relations, see Timothy Conlan, *From New Federalism to Devolution: Twenty-Five Years of Intergovernmental Reform* (Washington, D.C.: Brookings Institution Press, 1998). An important collection of scholarly articles with commentary on the development and present functioning of the system is provided in Laurence J. O'Toole, Jr., ed., *American Intergovernmental Relations: Foundations, Perspectives, and Issues,* Third Edition (Washington, D.C.: CQ Press, a division of Congressional Quarterly Inc., 2000).

5. The National Environmental Policy Act (NEPA) of 1969, for example, which marks the coming of age of modern environmentalism at the level of the federal government, was the statutory response that began to deal with the harmful effects of these uncoordinated governmental energies. NEPA requires all federal agencies to give full consideration to environmental effects in planning and carrying out their programs. The "action forcing" mechanism chosen to bring about the desired reforms in government's decision-making processes was the requirement that for each major action an "environmental impact statement" be prepared and circulated to other federal agencies, to state and local governments, and to the general public. For detailed discussion of NEPA and its provisions, see Frederick R. Anderson, Jr., "The National Environmental Policy Act," in Erica Dolgin and Thomas Guilbert, eds., *Federal Environmental Law* (St. Paul, Minn: Environmental Law Institute, 1974), pp. 238–419. For a review of responses at the federal level to the environmental problems generated by the extraordinary growth of the postwar economy, see Michael J. Lacey, ed., *Government and Environmental Politics: Essays on Historical Developments since World War Two* (Baltimore: Johns Hopkins University Press, 1991). For a concise review of early postwar developments in all fields of domestic policy at the national level, which also examines the pervasive influence of organized interest groups in the process, see Robert Griffith, "Forging America's Postwar Order: Domestic Politics and Political Economy in the Age of Truman," in Michael J. Lacey, ed., *The Truman Presidency* (New York: Cambridge University Press, 1989), pp. 57–88.

6. Samuel Beer suggests how the problems of relations between the states and national government link up. In his article "The Modernization of American Federalism," *Publius: The Journal of Federalism* 3, No. 2 (Fall 1973), pp. 49–95, Beer sets out a model for the understanding of the historical development of American intergovernmental relations. In his chronology the post–World War Two period is marked by the emergence on a very large scale of what he calls "the professional-bureaucratic complex," a new political force in its own right that generates some problems while it solves others. "The system has not yet taken a stable form," Beer notes, "so one must talk about pressures, opportunities, and tendencies." Beer spells out the emerging new functions of state governments in this era, which continues to the present day: 1) planning and control,

and 2) the mobilizing of consent. Both tasks are appropriate to an intermediate level of decision-making. "So much that is bogus has been written on the topic of planning," says Beer, "that one must blush to mention the word. Yet it is the best term available to indicate the direction of certain new pressures and opportunities that have arisen at the level of state governments" (p. 81). Of the system of intergovernmental relations as a whole, Beer observes, "the problem of planning and control is severe and the need for new tools—for analysis, evaluation, reorganization—is as great as even students of administration say it is. The trouble is that these themes have little political appeal. In the political marketplace they cannot compete with demands for greater equality, redistribution of income, and new and larger social programs. As a consequence, attempts to strengthen planning and control lack any political thrust that would come from having the support of a large and broad-based coalition. This central problem of the technocratic welfare state awaits a political solution" (p. 91).

Another important and neglected contribution of Beer's work is the notion of "public-sector politics," which is the phrase he uses in contrast to private-sector politics (essentially the familiar world of interest-group pressures on government) to call attention to pressures exerted *inside the public sector itself,* typically within the world of intergovernmental relations. Such pressures were the driving force behind general revenue-sharing in the Nixon administration. On this idea, see Beer's "The Adoption of General Revenue Sharing: A Case Study in Public Sector Politics," *Public Policy* 24, No. 2 (Spring 1976), pp. 127–42. Finally, on the importance of contemporary moral and social theory in relation to federalist thought, see Philip Selznick, "Afterword: Federalism and Community," in Martha Derthick, ed.,, *Dilemmas of Scale in America's Federal Democracy* (Cambridge and Washington, D.C.: Cambridge University Press and the Woodrow Wilson Center Press, 1999), pp. 355–67.

7. For an account of the dynamics of development within federalism and an assessment of the costs to local communities occasioned by the rise of ideas and policies of national community in the Progressive, New Deal, and civil rights eras, see Martha Derthick, "How Many Communities? The Evolution of American Federalism," in Derthick, ed., *Dilemmas of Scale.*

8. Data on the number of governmental entities is taken from U.S. Bureau of the Census, *Census of Governments* (Washington, D.C.: USGPO,

1992). For an up-to-date review of the problems and practices of today's local governments in America, see Kathryn M. Doherty and Clarence N. Stone, "Local Practice in Transition: From Government to Governance," in Derthick, ed., *Dilemmas of Scale,* pp. 154–86.

9. "The Ends of Federalism," in William A. Schambra, ed., *As Far as Republican Principles Will Admit: Essays by Martin Diamond* (Washington, D.C.: American Enterprise Institute, 1992), p. 145.

10. On the importance of the postal system as a public enterprise at the core of American development, see Richard R. John, *Spreading the News: The American Postal System from Franklin to Morse* (Cambridge, Mass.: Harvard University Press, 1995).

11. Clinton Rossiter, ed., *The Federalist Papers* (New York: Mentor Books, 1961), p. 176.

12. Samuel H. Beer, *To Make a Nation: The Rediscovery of American Federalism* (Cambridge, Mass.: Harvard University Press, 1993). The author of seminal work on both the theory and practice of American federalism, this is Beer's culminating statement, via the history of ideas, of the origins and development of what he calls the "national theory of federalism." Beer shows how the theory has faced three great historical trials: the trial of sectionalism, culminating in civil war; the trial of industrialism, beginning in the Progressive era and culminating in the Depression and the New Deal; and finally, the trial of racism, taken up by the national government in the civil rights era of the 1960s and thereafter.

13. Rossiter, ed., *The Federalist Papers,* p. 76.

14. Cited in Beer, *To Make a Nation,* p. 13.

15. For a discussion of the Federalist program and its sources in intellectual history, see Stanley Elkins and Eric McKitrick, *The Age of Federalism: The Early American Republic, 1788–1800* (New York: Oxford University Press, 1993). See also Leonard D. White, *The Federalists: A Study in Administrative History* (New York: Macmillan, 1948). For recent scholarly reappraisals, see Doron Ben-Atar and Barbara Oberg, eds., *Federalists Reconsidered* (Charlottesville, Va.: University Press of Virginia, 1998). Richard R. John provides an overview of the historiography on government and public policy in his "Government Institutions as Agents of Change: Rethinking American Political Development in the Early Republic, 1787–1835," *Studies in American Political Development,* Summer 1997, pp. 347–80. For an influential study that continues to provoke a reappraisal of the ways in which the

history of American political ideology is organized and evaluated, see Daniel Walker Howe, *The Political Culture of the American Whigs* (Chicago: University of Chicago Press, 1979). The Whigs were the carriers of the national planning impulse in their own day. "The chief reason for remembering the Whig party today," Howe notes, "is that it advanced a particular program of national development," one which turned on "providing centralized direction to social policy" (p. 9). In their social and moral thought, and in their theological reasoning, the Whigs were committed to the notion that they were under an obligation to seek "improvement," both individually and collectively, and Whig political culture—Howe defines political culture as "an evolving system of beliefs, attitudes and techniques for solving problems"—reflects this view. The relation between Whig ideology and the ideology of the Federalists is a matter of scholarly dispute. Whigs shared many of the policy goals that were laid out in Federalist writings, but no doubt saw themselves as more democratic and less given to centralization of power than the Federalists were accused of being.

Howe concludes on this question that "the closest ideological predecessors of the Whigs seem to have been not the Federalists but the 'moderate' or 'nationalistic' wing of the Republicans. This group combined . . . a country party respect for constitutional balance, legal tradition, and executive restraint with a belief in federally sponsored economic development and government 'for' rather than 'by' the people" (pp. 90–91).

For a study of public policy and political leadership from roughly 1812 to 1852 via a collective biography of three American statesmen who came from the ranks of the national republicans, see Merrill D. Peterson, *The Great Triumvirate: Webster, Clay, and Calhoun* (New York: Oxford University Press, 1987), particularly chapter 2, "Dimensions of Nationalism," pp. 47–112. On the continuation of bipolarity after the Whigs, see J. David Greenstone, *The Lincoln Persuasion: Remaking American Liberalism* (Princeton: Princeton University Press, 1993). The classic study of the bipolarity of the tradition, of course, is Herbert Croly's *The Promise of American Life* (1909), which sets up the contrast between Hamiltonian and Jeffersonian views as expressing the national idea vs. the democratic idea. Croly's second chapter, on federalism and republicanism, remains an outstanding critique and appraisal of both orientations. To get some view of the nationalist tradition in debates over contemporary public philosophy, see Michael Lind's introductory essay in his edited collection *Hamilton's Republic: Readings in the American Democratic Nationalist Tradition* (New York: Free Press, 1997).

16. Saul Padover, ed., *The Mind of Alexander Hamilton* (New York: Harper and Brothers, 1958), p. 310 (a selection of Hamilton's writings). The passage is from Hamilton's *Report on Manufactures.*

17. The Calhoun quotation is cited in Beer, *To Make a Nation,* p. 8. Beer also points out that Ronald Reagan's "new federalism," which was intended to "restore the balance between levels of government," was based on the old compact theory of federalism. As Reagan put it in his inaugural address of January 20, 1981, "The Federal government did not create the states; the states created the Federal government," the opposite of the position Lincoln had taken. An important element in contemporary American conservatism is the assault on the idea of national community as the justification for intrusive bureaucratic giantism that destroys localism and self-reliance. Joyce and Schambra, for example, argue that "beneath the variety of intellectual currents of revolt during the 1960s lay this central truth: progressive liberalism's intent to eradicate 'parochial' loyalties and allegiances on behalf of the great national community had failed miserably. The failure became ever more conspicuous during the 1970s and 1980s, when the nation's political landscape reshaped itself to accomodate this truth, along with the groups that had been roused to an angry political revolt over the assault on their 'organic networks.' The often overlooked fact is that after 1964, *no one* would again win the presidency by boasting about building a Great Society, a great national community, in America." Joyce and Schambra, "A New Citizenship, A New Life" in Lamar Alexander and Chester E. Finn, Jr., eds., *The New Promise of American Life* (Indianapolis: Hudson Institute, 1995), p. 149. For contemporary conservative approaches to the complexities of today's intergovernmental relations, see Michael S. Greve, *Real Federalism: Why It Matters, How It Could Happen* (Washington, D.C.: The AEI Press, 1999) and Adam D. Thierer, *The Delicate Balance: Federalism, Interstate Commerce, and Economic Freedom in the Technological Age* (Washington, D.C.: The Heritage Foundation, 1998).

18. Federalists and Jeffersonian Republicans were at odds on institutionalizing national defense. The Federalists, under the leadership of Washington and Hamilton, sought a professional army and navy. Though Jefferson sponsored the establishment of the U.S. Military Academy, founded in 1802, he and Albert Gallatin and others in the leadership of his party were especially leery of the growth of a professional military, fearing it would be used for the repression of legitimate dissent. They preferred to rely as far as possible on the tradition of citizen militias operating at the state level as constituting a reserve that could be called upon by a modest national force in times of emergency. Only gradually did they ease their fears of a standing army and accept the need for professionalization in the military field. They could not make this same move with respect to the civilian side of national affairs.

19. The rediscovery in the past generation of republicanism and country party ideology with all of its nuances and variations has spawned an enormous scholarly literature. A useful recent point of entry is Isaac Kramnick, *Republicanism and Bourgeois Radicalism: Political Ideology in Late-Eighteenth-Century England and America* (Ithaca: Cornell University Press, 1990). Of the range of ideological "languages" in evidence during the founding period, Kramnick identifies four: republicanism, Lockean liberalism, work-ethic Protestantism, and state-centered theories of power and sovereignty. These viewpoints converge and separate in complex ways, blurring the boundaries that distinguish one from another. Kramnick would not dispute the sense in which Jeffersonian Republicans, with their emphasis on the defense of the local community from the forces of cosmopolitan modernity, were in the country party tradition. He points out, however, "that an equally strong case can be made for the Federalists as republican theorists, and here we see full blown the confusion of idioms, the overlapping of political languages, in 1787" (p. 270). It is not clear that this case is, in fact, equally strong, but what Kramnick has in mind is the sense in which "republican" stands in contrast both to monarchy and to direct democracy, thus the association between republican thought and the function of legislative representation, rather than direct, unmediated democracy. Kramnick associates this sensibility with the Federalists' concern about the "filtering" rather than "mirroring" emphasis in their remarks about legislative representation at the national level—i.e., their hope that Congress would be made up of enlightened officeholders, capable of transcending mere self-interest and local interest in pursuit of the public good, along the lines Madison laid out in *Federalist* no. 10, rather than simply reflecting the interests of those who elected them. Perhaps so. There are no traces of the country party

mentality of suspicion about policy in Hamilton, however, and as Kramnick points out, the fateful differences between these two seminal figures was over giving positive, directive power to the executive agency of central government, which Madison could never bring himself to endorse. While Hamilton spoke of heroic state-building and the orchestration of private interests in the planned development of a national culture, Madison preferred instead to describe the central government's role as that of an "umpire" regulating private interests.

20. Alexander Hamilton, *Report on Manufactures,* reprinted in Padover, ed., *The Mind of Alexander Hamilton,* p. 341.

21. James D. Richardson, *A Compilation of the Messages and Papers of the Presidents, 1789–1902* (Washington, D.C.: Bureau of National Literature and Art, 1907), Vol. 1, p. 323. In keeping with the tone of his address, Jefferson's top domestic priority became eliminating the national debt (which had been ingeniously assembled and used by Hamilton to justify his activist schemes), a task that Jefferson assigned to his Treasury secretary, Albert Gallatin. To reduce the debt, Jefferson embarked on a policy of retrenchment, cutting appropriations of the fledgling executive departments, severely so in the case of the Navy. He also got through the legislature a major tax cut, American history's first.

22. Croly's *Promise of American Life,* a classic formulation of the developing political thought of the Progressive era based on a critical reappraisal of the shortcomings of the public philosophy of the past, works out the contrast between the national and democratic ideas and makes the case for merging them through changes in the operations of federalism. On the ideology and program of the Jeffersonian Republicans, see Elkins and McKitrick, *The Age of Federalism,* particularly chapter seven, "The Emergence of Partisan Politics: The 'Republican Interest.'" See also Joseph J. Ellis, *The American Sphinx: The Character of Thomas Jefferson* (New York: Knopf, 1998), a meticulously researched reappraisal of Jefferson's life and thought, together with the trajectory of the Jefferson legend. Another recent and very critical scholarly reappraisal is Peter S. Onuf, ed., *Jeffersonian Legacies* (Charlottesville: University Press of Virginia, 1993), a collection of essays by distinguished scholars of the period. One that is especially important in connection with the argument of this chapter is by the leading contemporary student of internal improvements issues: John Lauritz Larson, "Jefferson's Union and the Problem of Internal Improvements," analyzes Jeffer-

son's inconsistent positions on these issues over time, a story that ended up with the elderly Jeffersonian using libertarian rhetoric that opposed government action even on behalf of majorities.

Other important accounts of the ideas of the Republicans include Richard Buel, Jr., *Securing the Revolution: Ideology in American Politics, 1789–1815* (Ithaca, N.Y.: Cornell University Press, 1972); John R. Nelson, Jr., *Liberty and Property: Political Economy and Policymaking in the New Nation, 1789–1812* (Baltimore: Johns Hopkins University Press, 1987); Lance Banning, *The Jeffersonian Persuasion: The Evolution of a Party Ideology* (Ithaca: Cornell University Press, 1978); and Drew R. McCoy, *The Elusive Republic: Political Economy in Jeffersonian America* (Chapel Hill: University of North Carolina Press, 1980). For a discussion of the administrative context and fallout of the split between Hamilton and Jefferson, the leading members of George Washington's cabinet, see White, *The Federalists.* Also important in this connection is Noble E. Cunningham, Jr., *The Process of Government under Jefferson* (Princeton: Princeton University Press, 1978).

23. Following Croly, whose work was a source of inspiration for him, Beer looks for a merging of the national and democratic ideas as the ultimate goal toward which the national theory of federalism points. Of Hamilton's elitism he says, "Hamilton promoted capitalism, not because he was a lackey to the capitalist class—indeed, as he once wrote to a close friend, 'I hate moneying men'— but just the opposite: his elitism was subservient to his nationalism. In the same cause he was not only an elitist, but also an integrationist. I use that term expressly because of its current overtones, wishing to suggest Hamilton's perception of how diversity need not be divisive but may lead to mutual dependence and union." Beer, *To Make a Nation,* p. 6. In his classic study *The Liberal Tradition in America* (New York: Harcourt, Brace and World, 1955), Louis Hartz argued that the want of any genuine democratic feeling and the need to overcome its elitism represented the Whig dilemma. They had to come up with log-cabin candidates of their own, as they did most famously with Lincoln. Of Hamilton, Hartz said, "The idea of a national capitalist partnership in democratic terms was outside the path of his vision. His 'nationalism,' like Marshall's in *McCulloch v. Maryland,* was legal rather than social, defending a federal government but not embracing in any Rousseauean sense—as, ironically enough, Jefferson's 'anti-

nationalism' did—the American popular community" (p. 109).

24. Major L. Wilson, *Space, Time, and Freedom: The Quest for Nationality and the Irrepressible Conflict, 1815–1861* (Westport, Conn.: Greenwood Press, 1974). See especially chapter 3, "Time and the American System," pp. 49–72. Jefferson's anti-institutionalism is rooted in his view that one political generation cannot bind its successors, a radical position on the meaning and value of tradition which has perplexed those in the Jeffersonian heritage ever since. In what is perhaps the most famous of his letters, written to Madison on 6 September, 1789, he asserts "the earth belongs in usufruct to the living; that the dead have neither powers nor rights over it," a claim which Madison knew to be too sweeping. For a discussion of this idea and its place in Jefferson's political thought, see Herbert E. Sloan, *Principle and Interest: Thomas Jefferson and the Problem of Debt* (New York: Oxford University Press, 1995).

25. Rossiter, ed., *Federalist Papers*, p. 91. For a discussion of American neo-mercantilism as a widely shared view of political economy, featuring ideas of the need for state intervention in economic affairs in the early republic, see Harry N. Scheiber, "Economic Liberty and the Modern State," in Harry N. Scheiber, ed., *The State and Freedom of Contract* (Stanford: Stanford University Press, 1998), pp. 134–43. Peterson's *The Great Triumvirate* offers a careful account of the American system, focusing on Henry Clay's understanding of it, on pp. 68–83. The exact sources and contents of the American system—i.e., the number of its interlocking components—are matters of some scholarly disagreement. Some stress origins in the ideas of the Federalists, some place them in the thought of the National Republicans. Peterson's account acknowledges the plausibility of ties to the policy thought of the Federalists, but emphasizes the need of the Nationalist Republicans to distance themselves from their adversaries despite policy affinities: "whatever its policy debt to the Hamiltonian tradition," he notes, "the American system was the legitimate outcome of Jeffersonian experience at the helm of government since 1800. . . . [T]he Republicans had *become* the nation, and so could be inspired more by their hopes than by their fears of government. . . . It never occurred to Clay, or to Calhoun and many other Republicans, that in advocating an enlarged role for government in the promotion of economic development, he was surrendering Jeffersonian principles for Hamiltonian ones." It was on precisely this issue, however—i.e., how, exactly, to obtain an enlarged role for national government in economic affairs within the context of argument over enumerated vs. implied powers in the Constitution—that the Nationalist Republicans would prove themselves so ineffective, as indicated by their inability to resolve within their own party the cooperative-federalism aspects of the internal improvements problem. The Whigs picked up where the National Republicans left off. For another recent discussion of the American system, see Maurice G. Baxter, *Henry Clay and the American System* (Lexington: University Press of Kentucky, 1995).

26. U.S. Treasury Department, *Report of the Secretary of the Treasury on the Subject of Roads and Canals,* Reprints of Economic Classics (New York: Augustus M. Kelley, 1968). The text of the Senate resolution appears on p. 3.

27. D. W. Meinig, *The Shaping of America: A Geographical Perspective on 500 Years of History,* Volume 2, *Continental America, 1800–1867* (New Haven: Yale University Press, 1993), is a powerful synthesis of national development from the standpoint of historical geography deeply informed by Mumford's work. Meinig's discussion of the Gallatin plan is on pp. 313–23. For a comprehensive survey of the canal era, see Ronald E. Shaw, *Canals for a Nation: The Canal Era in the United States, 1790–1860* (Lexington: University Press of Kentucky, 1990). The best scholarship on the politics of internal improvements in this period is John Larson's. In addition to his "Jefferson's Union and the Problem of Internal Improvements," see his "Liberty by Design: Freedom, Planning, and John Quincy Adams's American System," in Mary O. Furner and Barry Supple, eds., *The State and Economic Knowledge: The American and British Experiences* (New York: Cambridge University Press, 1990), pp. 73–102; and his "'Bind the Republic Together': The National Union and the Struggle for a System of Internal Improvements," *Journal of American History* 74 (1987), pp. 363–87.

28. Lewis Mumford, *"The Fourth Migration"* (1925), reprinted in *The Urban Prospect* (London: Secker and Warburg, 1968), pp. ix–x.

29. Gallatin, p. 68.

30. Ibid., pp. 7–8.

31. Ibid., p. 8.

32. For a discussion of Gallatin's career and thought that makes the point that he and Hamilton agreed on this question, see L. B. Kuppenheimer, *Albert Gallatin's Vision of Democratic Stability: An Interpretive Profile* (Westport, Conn.: Praeger,

1996). For the argument that Gallatin's political economy differed significantly from Hamilton's, see John R. Nelson, *Liberty and Property: Political Economy and Policymaking in the New Nation, 1789–1812* (Baltimore: Johns Hopkins University Press, 1987). Nelson argues that despite what he said and wrote in official reports on the matter, Hamilton was indifferent to the development of American manufactures and content to live within the framework of British economic colonialism. He devotes a chapter to the career of Gallatin as a critic of the Federalists and another to Gallatin as a policy maker. Nelson's Gallatin is the heroic figure in early American policy thought: "He proved during his cabinet tenure to be a master of integrating interests, ideology and circumstances into a political economy that rivaled Hamilton's in its subtlety and surpassed Hamilton's in its vision." The differences between the two in this view relate to Gallatin's greater willingness to risk conflict with the British over trade policy and his purportedly greater concern with the expansion of the national market into the West. Whatever the merits of these arguments, it should be noted that Nelson does not suggest that the two great theorists of national development had any differences on the desirability of federally supported internal improvements.

33. The case in question was *Massachusetts v. Mellon* (1923), cited in Harry N. Scheiber's "Federalism and the States," in Stanley Kutler et al., eds., *Encyclopedia of the United States in the Twentieth Century* (New York: Scribner's, 1996), Vol. 1, p. 432, which, according to Scheiber, "drew a dictum from the Court to the effect that grants of aid did not constitute compulsion, hence could not be viewed as violative of federalism principles."

34. Gallatin, pp. 72–75 *passim.*

35. Max Ferrand, ed., *The Records of the Federal Convention of 1787,* rev. ed. (New Haven: Yale University Press, 1937), Vol. 2, p. 615. Cited in John Seelye, *Beautiful Machine: Rivers and the Republican Plan, 1755–1825* (New York: Oxford University Press, 1991), p. 257. Chapter 6 of Seelye's book, "Stately Decree," provides a richly detailed account of the origins and fate of the Gallatin plan.

36. Richardson, *A Compilation of the Messages and Papers of the Presidents,* Vol. 1, carries the text of the veto message. In it Madison says, "I am not unaware of the great importance of roads and canals and the improved navigation of water courses, and that a power in the National Legislature to provide for them might be exercised with

signal advantage to the general prosperity. But seeing that such a power is not expressly given by the Constitution, and believing that it cannot be deduced from any part of it without an inadmissible latitude of construction and reliance on insufficient precedents . . . I have no option but to withhold my signature" (p. 585).

37. Richardson, *A Compilation of the Messages and Papers of the Presidents,* Vol. 2, p. 143.

38. Ibid., p. 156–7. There is some evidence that a majority of the members of the Supreme Court disagreed on the need for an internal-improvements amendment and would have found central government participation constitutional on implied-powers grounds, as they had done with respect to the constitutionality of the national bank. Monroe sent a copy of his veto pamphlet to the members of the Court. Justice William Johnson consulted with other members of the Court and prepared a private response to the president, a very unusual procedure in relations between the White House and the Court. In it Johnson remarked, "The Judges are deeply sensible of the mark of confidence bestowed on them in this instance and should be unworthy of that confidence did they attempt to conceal their real opinion. Indeed, to conceal or disavow it would be impossible as they are all of the opinion that the decision on the Bank question completely commits them on the subject of internal improvement, as applied to Postroads and Military Roads. . . . The principle assumed in the case of the Bank is that the granting of the principal power carries with it the grant of all adequate and appropriate means of executing it. That the selection of these means must rest with the General Government, and as to that power and those means the Constitution makes the Government of the U.S. supreme." Reported in Charles Warren, *The Supreme Court in United States History* (Boston: Little, Brown, 1922). Quotation is taken from vol. 1, p. 596. This remarkable response to Monroe makes it plain that as a practical matter those, like Gallatin, who argued that no internal improvements amendment was necessary were correct, so far as the Court was concerned.

39. Ibid., p. 175.

40. Ibid., p. 175.

41. Ibid., p. 177.

42. A recent biography of Adams is Paul C. Nagel, *John Quincy Adams: A Public Life, A Private Life* (New York: Alfred A. Knopf, 1997). For a study of the Adams presidency, see Mary W.M. Hargreaves, *The Presidency of John Quincy Adams* (Lawrence: University Press of Kansas, 1985). The

most cogent and suggestive brief account of Adams's political and policy beliefs is Howe, *Political Culture of the American Whigs,* chapter 3, "John Quincy Adams: Nonpartisan Politician," pp. 43–68. The most useful discussion of Adams on national planning is John L. Larson, "Liberty by Design: Freedom, Planning, and John Quincy Adams' American System," in Furner and Supple, eds., *The State and Economic Knowledge,* pp. 73–102.

43. Adrienne Koch and William Peden, eds., *The Selected Writings of John and John Quincy Adams* (Westport, Conn.: Greenwood Press, 1981), p. 324. The quotation appears in a manuscript providing Adams's account of the growth of parties in the United States that was not published until 1941. In it he laid out the opposition between the democratic and the national ideas. Adams faulted the Federalists, of whom he was once a member, for being too narrow in their nationalism: "the purposes for which the exercise of power was necessary were principally the protection of property, and thereby the Federal Party became identified with the aristocratic part of the community." The Anti-Federalists, on the other hand, always had "the advantage of *numbers*. Their principles, being those of democracy, were always favored by the majority of people; and their cause, being more congenial to that of our Revolution, gave them the opportunity of making their adversaries obnoxious as Tories." Jefferson's Republican policies, however, had been in Adams's view nearly ruinous, strongly encouraging sectionalism by Jefferson's failure to have any constructive national plans. The embargo act had nearly precipitated "a Northern confederacy" under the leadership of New England Federalists ready to secede from the Union in protest. Adams's nationalism prevented him from going along with the Federalists, and led eventually to his joining the Republicans. He faulted Jefferson for playing a type of low, instrumental politics in setting up a party system mirrored on the oppositions of Whig and Tory in England. If the rhetoric of opposition Jefferson was devising was used in the United States "to turn back the progress of internal improvements in ghastly horror at the phantom of consolidation, it is devoutly to be hoped that it may not be nourished."

44. Ibid., p. 361.

45. Ibid., p. 374.

46. Ibid., p. 374.

47. Ibid., p. 391.

48. For a carefully balanced account of the differences between Jackson and his adversaries, to-gether with a collection of key documents and brief biographies of two of the principal combatants, see Harry L. Watson, *Andrew Jackson vs. Henry Clay: Democracy and Development in Antebellum America* (Boston: Bedford/St. Martin's, 1998). The Jackson quotation is on p. 187. Jackson's position on the need for an internal improvements amendment is found in his veto message regarding the Maysville Road bill. For reviews of Jacksonian thought and policy, see also Daniel Feller, *The Jacksonian Promise: America, 1815–1840* (Baltimore: Johns Hopkins University Press, 1995); Donald B. Cole, *The Presidency of Andrew Jackson* (Lawrence: University Press of Kansas, 1993); and Maurice G. Baxter, *Henry Clay and the American System* (Lexington: University Press of Kentucky, 1995). Though many of its details have not held up, the classic and still influential account of the era is Arthur M. Schlesinger, Jr., *The Age of Jackson* (Boston: Little, Brown, 1945), a brilliant book that manages the unlikely feat of making Jackson a forerunner of the New Deal. For a recent critical analysis of the rise of modern bureaucratic government in America from the standpoint of Jacksonian anti-institutionalism, see Robert Wiebe, *Self-Rule: A Cultural History of American Democracy* (Chicago: University of Chicago Press, 1995). Note especially chapter 9, "The State," in which all the institutional innovations that expanded national government from the New Deal onward and are the substance of today's cooperative federalism are interpreted as the work of "the compromise of the 1930s." This was an unsavory bargain, as Wiebe tells it, in which genuine democracy lost all around. The compromise built up the centralized bureaucratic hierarchies of big government. It brought together the representatives of a suspect "national class" of middle-class professionals without strong roots in local communities and "local class" elites bereft of any sentiments of national community and intent on protecting their own narrow interests. New Deal programs full of lofty democratic rhetoric thus linked the worst of both worlds. In terms of the actual workings of the federal system, the result was that "national government would increase its economic assistance for local America" in return for party loyalty, while "members of the local middle class would set the rules in their own localities, including many of the decisions about how federal monies would be allocated" (p. 211). So far as remedies are concerned, Wiebe's proposals are those of the Jeffersonian-Jacksonian tradition. He commends institution-free governance, increased demo-

cratic participation, the virtues of local (but not national) community, and a kind of "guerrilla politics" aimed at cutting down to size all centralized hierarchy, public and private.

49. Quoted in Henry Adams, *The Degradation of Democratic Dogma* (New York: Peter Smith, 1949), p. 27.

50. Koch and Peden, eds., *Selected Writings,* p. 392.

51. Ibid. The first quotation appears on p. 389, the second on p. 382.

52. On the transformation of American public philosophy in this period and Adams's role in it, see Mary O. Furner, "The Republican Tradition and the New Liberalism," in Michael J. Lacey and Mary O. Furner, eds., *The State and Social Investigation in Britain and the United States* (New York: Cambridge University Press, 1993), pp. 171–235. Note also by the same author "Knowing Capitalism: Public Investigation and the Labor Question in the Long Progressive Era," in Furner and Supple, eds., *The State and Economic Knowledge.* For a biographical synopsis and appraisal of Adams's career as a thinker and reformer, see Joseph Dorfman's introduction, "Henry Carter Adams: Harmonizer of Liberty and Reform," in Joseph Dorfman, ed., *The Relation of the State to Industrial Action and Economics and Jurisprudence: Two Essays by Henry Carter Adams* (New York: Columbia University Press, 1954), pp. 3–55.

53. Henry Carter Adams, *Public Debts: An Essay in the Science of Finance* (New York: D. Appleton and Company, 1887). The first two quoted passages appear on p. 342, the second on p. 321. Adams's scholarship on federalism was unfortunately neglected by those who came after him, and up until the World War II period there was little memory of what had happened to atrophy the organs of federalism in the nineteenth century. In the late 1940s, however, Adams's work was rediscovered by the economist Carter Goodrich, who thereafter wrote several important pieces on planning in the antebellum period, among them "The Revulsion Against Internal Improvements," *Journal of Economic History* 10, no. 2 (Nov. 1950), pp. 145–69; "National Planning of Internal Improvements," *Political Science Quarterly* 63, no. 1 (1948), pp. 16–44; "American Development Policy: The Case of Internal Improvements," *Journal of Economic History* 16, no. 4 (December 1956), pp. 449–60; and "The Gallatin Plan After One Hundred and Fifty Years," *Proceedings of the American Philosophical Society* 102, no. 5 (October 1958).

See too his *Government Promotion of American Canals and Railroads, 1800–1890* (New York: Columbia University Press, 1960). At just about the same time, a number of historians were rediscovering the importance of state-led public enterprise in the antebellum period. The most important of these studies are Louis Hartz, *Economic Policy and Democratic Thought: Pennsylvania, 1776–1860* (Cambridge: Harvard University Press, 1948); Oscar Handlin and Mary Flug Handlin, *Commonwealth: A Study of the Role of Government in the American Economy—Massachusetts, 1774–1861,* rev. ed. (Cambridge: Harvard University Press, 1969); and Harry N. Scheiber, *The Ohio Canal Era: A Case Study of Government and the Economy, 1820–1861* (Athens: Ohio University Press, 1969).

54. Adams, p. 393.

55. Ibid., pp. 340–1.

56. The remark of Justice Brandeis is cited in Scheiber, "Federalism and the States," p. 448.

57. Martha Derthick points out in this connection that "local governments became for most Americans most of the time the most important domestic governments. As the twentieth century began, they administered and overwhelmingly financed schools—the agents of socialization, the most important domestic public institutions. They predominated in the administration and finance of poor relief. They administered and overwhelmingly financed road construction. They financed and were responsible for police protection. At the opening of the twentieth century, local governments were raising more revenue and doing more spending than the federal and state governments combined. The bedrock of domestic government was local." See her "How Many Communities?" in Derthick, ed., *Dilemmas of Scale,* p. 130.

58. Ibid. The first lines quoted appear on p. 330, the last line on p. 346.

59. Ibid., pp. 356–7.

60. Ibid., p. 348.

61. Ibid., pp. 356–7. Adams was convinced that without the collapse of state enterprise under popular electoral pressure, urban America would never have attained the extraordinary scale that it did attain. "One is warranted in suggesting, at least," he remarked, "that had the States been free from the legal restrictions imposed upon them by their constitutions, the inferior governments would never have been forced to respond to the popular clamor for a collection of capital by government agency" (p. 357).

62. Ibid., p. 392.

63. Theodore Roosevelt, *The New Nationalism, with an Introduction by Ernest Hamlin Abbott* (New York: The Outlook Company, 1910). The volume is composed of the speeches Roosevelt gave as he journeyed around the country in August and September of 1910. The quotation appears on p. 28. Originally a steward was the manager of a large household estate, and in conceiving the president as "steward of the public welfare" Roosevelt is pointing to his role in managing the national domain, a role that was impossible to conceive under dual federalism, unless the national domain meant simply the federally owned public lands.

64. Ibid. Unless otherwise indicated, all the quotations attributed to Roosevelt in connection with the new nationalism are taken from his speech by that title given at Osawatomie, Kansas, and published in this volume on pp. 3–33.

65. Theodore Roosevelt, *The Roosevelt Policy: Speeches, Letters and State Papers, relating to Corporate Wealth and Closely Allied Topics* (New York: The Current Literature Publishing Company, 1908), Vol. 1, p. 325. The most cogent presentation and analysis of Roosevelt's plans for regulation is found in Martin J. Sklar, *The Corporate Reconstruction of American Capitalism, 1890–1916* (New York: Cambridge University Press, 1988), particularly pp. 333–64.

66. The first quotation is from *The Chautauquan,* June 1909, p. 20; the second is from George L. Knapp, "The Other Side of Conservation," *North American Review* 19 (April 1910), p. 479; the third is from *Outlook,* May 14, 1910, p. 57. This passage as a whole, and many that follow describing the details of Roosevelt's conservation reports, are taken from chapter 5, "The Conservation Movement and the Restoration of the Commons," in Michael J. Lacey, The Mysteries of Earth-Making Dissolve: A Study of Washington's Intellectual Community and the Origins of American Environmentalism in the Late Nineteenth Century" (Ph.D. diss., George Washington University, 1979). The standard study of the Roosevelt conservation program, which takes a different line of interpretation from this one, is Samuel P. Hays, *Conservation and the Gospel of Efficiency* (Cambridge, Mass.: Harvard University Press, 1959).

67. National Conservation Congress, *Proceedings of the Second National Conservation Congress* (Washington, D.C.: National Conservation Congress, 1911), p. 293. The breakup of the Republican Party in the election of 1912 was rooted in the disagreements between Roosevelt and Taft over the

conservation strategy. Roosevelt decided finally to oppose Taft, his handpicked successor, because of the latter's failure to continue the policies Roosevelt called for in his last year in office. Gifford Pinchot, in his autobiography *Breaking New Ground* (New York: Harcourt, Brace, 1947), suggests an element of duplicity and personal betrayal was involved. He reports a meeting between Roosevelt, Taft, and himself in the White House shortly after Taft got the party's nomination in 1908, a meeting intended to get an agreement from Taft to continue the policies Roosevelt was then advocating. "We went over essential Conservation questions in detail, and water power in particular," said Pinchot, and with reference to Taft he remarked, "and in general he bound himself, as completely as one man can to another, to stand by and go forward with the TR conservation policy" (pp. 375–6).

68. The short answer as to why such an ambitious set of proposals did not snap into focus much earlier in the life of the administration, when Roosevelt might have had a better opportunity to move them through Congress, is that at first there was only one man, W J McGee, who understood the connections among them and saw how to put them together, and he was not "in the loop" until late in 1906. It was McGee who devised the inland waterways plan and sold it to Roosevelt. He then served as secretary of the Inland Waterways Commission and wrote its report. In his autobiographical account of the beginnings of the conservation movement, Pinchot refers to McGee as "the scientific brains" behind the movement. For twenty-five years McGee had been a civil servant, a member of Washington's governmental scientific elite, a disciple of John Wesley Powell. For personal reasons he had been out of Washington between 1903 and late 1906. From the time of his return until the time of his death in 1912 he was closely associated with Pinchot, and through him, with Roosevelt. McGee's thinking and career are taken up in Lacey, "The Mysteries of Earth-Making Dissolve."

69. United States Public Lands Commission, *Report of the Public Lands Commission, with Appendix,* S. Doc. 189, 58th Congress, 3rd sess. (Washington, D.C.: GPO, 1905), p. xii.

70. Padover, *The Mind of Alexander Hamilton,* p. 317.

71. The history of public lands policy is extraordinarily complicated and difficult to unravel, and here the great scholarly achievement is Paul Gates's comprehensive and encyclopedic *History of Public*

Land Law Development, written for the United States Public Land Law Review Commission (Washington, D.C.: GPO, 1968).

72. Roosevelt, *The New Nationalism,* p. 84.

73. Ibid., p. 83.

74. United States Inland Waterways Commission, *Preliminary Report of the Inland Waterways Commission* (Washington, D.C.: GPO, 1908), pp. 3–7.

75. W. J. McGee, "Principles of Water Power Development," *Science* (December 1911), p. 816.

76. United States National Conservation Commission, *Report of the National Conservation Commission,* S. Doc. 676, 60th Congress, 2nd sess. (Washington, D.C.: GPO, 1909), p. 46.

77. Ibid., p. 47.

78. McGee, "Principles of Water Power Development," pp. 824–5.

79. Conference of Governors of the United States, *Proceedings of a Conference of Governors in the White House, Washington, D.C., May 13–15, 1908* (Washington, D.C.: GPO, 1909), pp. 192–4. The quotation from Burton and McGee to Roosevelt is taken from p. viii.

80. United States Commission on Country Life, *Report of the Country Life Commission. Special Message from the President of the United States Transmitting the Report of the Country Life Commission,* S. Doc. 705, 60th Congress, 2nd sess (Washington, D.C.: GPO, 1909), pp. 49–50.

81. Ibid., p. 53.

82. Liberty Hyde Bailey, *The Country Life Movement in the United States* (New York: Macmillan, 1911), p. 203.

83. United States Commission on Country Life, *Report of the Country Life Commission,* pp. 15–16.

84. North American Conservation Conference, "Declaration of Principles," Appendix 2 in Charles R. Van Hise, *The Conservation of Natural Resources in the United States* (New York: Macmillan, 1910). The declaration appears on pp. 385–93. Van Hise was president of the University of Wisconsin. His book is the first systematic statement of conservation doctrine, and it is based on the data of the National Conservation Commission.

85. United States Department of State, *Papers Relating to the Foreign Relations of the United States, with the Annual Message of the President Transmitted to Congress December 7, 1909* (Washington, D.C.: GPO, 1914), Correspondence, Circulars, pp. 1–2.

86. The possibilities of a reconquest by nature (under human guidance) of the wilderness of civilization is the theme of Benton MacKaye, *The New Exploration: A Philosophy of Regional Planning* (New York: Harcourt, Brace, 1928). MacKaye conceived the idea for the Appalachian Trail, an experiment in planning and cooperative federalism, and was a powerful advocate for its development. *Design with Nature* is the title of Ian McHarg's influential treatise on ecologically informed large-scale landscape planning, originally published in 1969 (New York: Wiley, 1992). The "design with nature" theme is applied to the urban environment by McHarg's student and colleague Ann Spirn, in her *The Granite Garden: Urban Nature and Human Design* (New York: Basic Books, 1984).

A model watershed. The Colorado River Basin encompassing territory in seven states and Mexico. The Colorado Basin was mapped by the U.S. Bureau of Reclamation in 1934 especially to locate potential dam sites for electric power and irrigation. (From National Resources Committee, *Regional Factors in National Planning* [Washington, D.C.: Government Printing Office, 1935])

CHAPTER FIVE

"Watersheds" in Regional Planning

■■
■■

JAMES L. WESCOAT, JR.

Water analysts and users have converged once again on "watersheds" as a context for regional planning.[1] Some assert that watersheds are "natural regions" for planning. Others remind us of the multiple aims and scope of watershed planning. Increasingly, watersheds are also portrayed as promising contexts for community- and place-based planning.

Ironically, as watershed initiatives proliferate, larger-scale river-basin organizations, including the flagship Tennessee Valley Authority (TVA), are faltering. Their legislative, political, and financial support erodes while watershed planning is rediscovered. On the one hand, this decline of river-basin planning may be viewed as the logical complement of watershed revitalization—federal water planning gives way as local, citizen-based initiatives advance. On the other hand, such simple oppositions between federal and local planning (or top-down and bottom-up approaches) ignore the basic continuities between watershed and river-basin planning.

The terms "watershed" and "river basin" both denote areas that drain to a common outlet—they refer to the same physiographic phenomena. Their usage in planning practice, however, diverged a half century ago as "watershed" came to connote small-scale upstream land and water management supported by the Soil Conservation Service, whereas "river basin" connoted large-scale multiple-purpose water-development programs of the Army Corps of Engineers and Bureau of Reclamation.

These distinctions between large and small ignore the continuing involvement of federal agencies in local watershed initiatives and of local interests in federal river-

This paper benefited greatly from the constructive criticism of Gilbert F. White, Michael J. Lacey, and graduate students in the Department of Geography at the University of Colorado at Boulder.

basin planning. They also ignore the fact that some large-scale problems, such as floods in the Mississippi River basin, cannot be resolved by local initiatives alone. There are deeply rooted divisions, and affinities, between watershed planning and other realms of planning in the United States today. Battles continue, for example, over the definition of "navigable waters of the United States."[2] For more than a century, these battles have reworked the administrative boundaries between land and water ecosystems—between river channels, headwaters, floodplains, wetlands, and watersheds. Although they sometimes reinforce the oversimplifying oppositions between upstream and downstream, watershed and river basin, federal and local, and large and small, at other times they reconfigure or break down those oppositions. The current generation of watershed organizers has yet to fathom these historical processes.

While recent watershed initiatives diffuse with lightning speed through clearinghouses and electronic media, their historical antecedents and analogues remain largely ignored. Watershed organizers rarely explore their historical connections with other planning fields. They have yet to acknowledge the repeated revival and eclipse of watershed planning over the past century.

In response to these criticisms, watershed activists might reasonably question whether practical lessons can be drawn from earlier watershed programs. To jump to one conclusion of this chapter, historical analysis can help identify potential coalitions between watershed planning and related fields of urban, regional, and resource planning. A century ago, for example, watershed planning provided a common focus for forest, urban, and soil conservation movements—and the government agencies that represented them. This early watershed coalition shaped major government programs and planning innovations, but it collapsed in less than twenty years. Other historical watershed initiatives were triggered by natural disasters, economic restructuring, technological change, or institutional reorganization—yet others were undermined by such events. Activists and planners can better understand the dynamics of watershed planning through historical analysis of this experimental record.

Few scholarly investigations of water planning have compared historical water development with current policy situations.[3] In keeping with the pragmatic tradition of American water planning, this chapter begins with a survey of current initiatives in watershed planning.[4] It retraces late-nineteenth-century antecedents through the Progressive, New Deal, and postwar eras. It then uses this historical-geographic perspective to redefine the current situation and prospects for regional water planning.

The Current Situation

In December 1992, a month after the election of President William Clinton, progressive water analysts urged that "watersheds should form the basic unit of analysis and activity in order to protect and sustain aquatic biological diversity, including instream, wetland, riparian, and related upland resources."[5] This recommendation reflected the revival of interest in watershed planning. Numerous local groups were organizing around watershed issues, ranging from riparian habitat restoration to non–point source pollution control. Some were citizen-based, whereas others had strong agency involvement. This diversity has led some to question over whether watershed planning is a "fad."[6] It is useful, therefore, to briefly survey these initiatives from the local to the international scale.

Several academic studies of local watershed activities have been carried out in the 1990s. The University of Colorado Natural Resources Law Center examined seventy-six watershed groups in the western United

States.[7] It found a common emphasis on collaborative citizen-based communication, maintaining a "sense of place" associated with watersheds, and balancing commitment to environmental protection and local economic development. By 1995, the "Know Your Watershed" clearinghouse at Purdue University identified more than six hundred local watershed initiatives.[8] However, the California Watershed Projects Inventory identified almost three hundred watershed initiatives in that state alone.[9] River Network, a nonprofit organization, identified thousands of river protection initiatives.[10] The Coalition for the Restoration of Urban Watersheds organized a network of urban stream-protection groups.[11] All of these surveys reported enormous "diversity" among watershed movements—in terms of their size, aims, and relations with state and federal government.

Some local initiatives, for example, are heavily supported by state river-basin and floodplain-management programs.[12] Oregon has an expansive program of statewide watershed planning.[13] Massachusetts, Minnesota, and West Virginia have considered reorganizing their natural resources departments along watershed lines. Decades ago, Texas adapted the TVA model for state purposes by establishing river authorities on the Colorado and Brazos Rivers.[14] These programs are regularly discussed and compared at state watershed conferences.[15]

There is a major institutional shift between the state and interstate scales of river-basin planning. The latter occurs, on a cooperative basis, only when there is either substantial federal funding for water development or substantial violation of federal law (e.g., the Endangered Species Act) that threatens existing water users. The latter situation has recently prompted interstate aquatic ecosystem recovery programs in the South Platte, upper Colorado, and Columbia River basins. Interstate compacts, negotiated with the permission and ratification of Congress, are the principal institutional vehicle for cooperative river-basin planning. Interstate conflicts, which are played out in the U.S. Supreme Court as the court of original jurisdiction, involve considerable river-basin analysis but do not yield plans as such. In every case, federal institutions become mandatory at the interstate scale.

Federal water planning operates at all scales, but some of its programs are more constitutionally secure than others, and all of them change in strength and impact over time. Federal water planning has once again entered a creative yet tenuous phase. "Reinvention" of government in 1992 included promising watershed proposals by the Environmental Protection Agency (EPA) and other agencies. A flood disaster in the upper Mississippi basin in 1993 prompted calls to re-establish river-basin commissions abolished in 1981—but as yet to no avail.[16] Although these proposals lost momentum with the election of a conservative Congress in 1994, some watershed programs endured, including the Soil Conservation Service's and Natural Resources Conservation Agency's small watershed programs for agricultural water management, fish and wildlife, recreation, and rural flood protection.[17] The EPA has increasingly advocated watershed planning for water-quality improvement.[18] It also hopes to coordinate watershed planning with its wetlands protection, pollution permitting, clean lakes, endangered species, habitat restoration, and state environmental support programs.

But federal water programs face escalating political constraints and budget cuts. The TVA, the oldest federal experiment in river-basin planning, faces massive debt and management controversies. The restructuring of the TVA has included reduction of its floodplain and watershed programs.[19] At the same time, the TVA is developing a highly sophisticated river-basin decision-support system, known as TERRA, to integrate planning considerations with real-time river operations.[20] The relations between these technological and institutional changes remain unclear.

Similar contrasts exist at the international level. The United States has been a leading exporter of river-basin planning around the world but has been unable to sustain those programs at home. Basin planning between the United States and Canada has advanced in institutional and scientific terms, especially on the Great Lakes, but planning on the U.S.-Mexico border has lagged.[21]

This overview of watershed planning at different institutional levels and geographic scales helps sort out some of the diversity in current trends. It does not explain that diversity or indicate why some watershed initiatives have advanced while others faltered, but it does point toward five historical factors and themes that can shed light on the current situation.

First, during each period, especially the Progressive Era, *coalitions* of political and scientific groups effected major advances in watershed planning. It is useful to analyze how those coalitions formed among water-user groups and government agencies, how they affected policy, and why they failed to endure.

Second, natural *disasters* have also shaped water resources policy. Although some floods or droughts have catalyzed watershed planning, others have led away from it. These contrary tendencies may be better understood by analyzing flood hazards policy during the relatively neglected transition period between the Progressive and New Deal eras.

Third, the economic disaster of the 1930s led to *economic recovery* programs that placed remarkable emphasis on regional water planning as a means of economic redevelopment. New institutional approaches were devised and tested. Some, like the TVA, had enormous influence—but they were never replicated in other regions. Other putatively "integrated" approaches fell prey to various forms of institutional fragmentation.[22] These New Deal concepts and experiments in integrated basin development and institutions, established in a context of economic recovery, persisted with variable effects in the different situations that followed.

Fourth, water policy during periods of *growth in wealth and technology* reflected quite different interests in macroregional river-basin planning at the national level. Primary concerns during periods of growth revolved around issues of federal spending, bureaucratic reorganization, and scientific innovations in river-basin modeling, as evidenced particularly in the 1950s.

Finally, another cross-cutting theme for each period, exemplified from the 1960s through the 1980s, has involved struggles over the *centralization and decentralization* of water planning authority. Then as now, most advocates have debated the *inherent* virtues or deficiencies of centralized approaches. A historical perspective on these debates leads to the conclusion that a far more practical task is to understand how watershed planning has or has not adjusted to changes in the relative authority of different levels of government and interest groups. Some programs adapt; others fold.

Although these five major themes in regional water planning are thematically associated with specific historical periods in this paper, it is important to acknowledge their presence in varying ways and degrees in each period. It is also important to follow their historical interactions with each other over time.

Coalitions: The Progressive Era and Its Antecedents, 1878–1912

Watershed planning is a modern science compared with the more established field of river engineering.[23] Public water law also rests on a constitutional foundation of rights to "navigable waterways" and not to watershed uses.[24] These constitutional and scientific foundations constrain public efforts to extend the scope of water planning from river channels to watersheds.[25] Notwithstanding these constraints, the lessons of European watershed-conservation experience were spread in the United States through the popular scientific writings of George Perkins Marsh, who stressed the importance of such efforts for forestry and floodplain protection.[26] Joseph Nicollet advanced ideas and methods of scientific river-basin surveys in the upper Mississippi River basin in the 1830s.[27]

Although these early ideas had little immediate effect, they were renewed by John Wesley Powell in his capacity as director of the Rocky Mountain Geographical and Geological Survey.[28] Powell observed that land survey and settlement in the western United States did not conform with the natural terrain or resources of the region. He drew attention to 1) the underutilization of large streams, 2) the inefficient use of tributaries for valley bottom irrigation, 3) underdeveloped reservoir storage, and 4) upstream-downstream and transboundary conflicts.[29] Powell's "physiographic" proposals combined watershed protection in forested uplands with large grazing allotments on hill slopes and smaller irrigated farmsteads in the valley bottoms. Although initially rejected by Congress, Powell's proposals foreshadowed coalitions that would later be forged between forestry and irrigation by his protégés Gifford Pinchot and Francis H. Newell.

Powell's recommendations resurfaced almost verbatim in an 1888 Senate resolution directing the Geological Survey to survey lands susceptible to irrigation in the arid West.[30] Newell directed the four-year Irrigation Survey. His initial report restated Powell's concerns about inefficient patterns of water development and speculated that upper-basin storage might even reduce lower-basin floods in the Missouri River:[31] "Catchment areas and farming areas are thus interdependent, though separate. The farming interests on the irrigable lands of the plains and valleys must, somehow or other, be able to protect the catchment areas on which their agriculture depends."[32] Topographic surveyors used river basins as the unit of analysis to determine "the total annual discharge from each catchment basin" beginning in the headwaters of the Missouri and Columbia basins.[33] But the practical connection between hydrologic measurement and regional water management remained slight as irrigators feverishly sought water supplies and dam sites inside and outside their local watersheds.[34]

Resource conservation movements coalesced in the Progressive era policies of Theodore Roosevelt. Roosevelt gathered an extraordinary group of Powell protégés (including W J McGee, Newell, Pinchot, and James Garfield) to advance his conservation agenda in government agencies. Roosevelt himself gave speeches on forest protection, flood control, and irrigation development: "I believe to the last point in the vital necessity of storing the floods and preserving the forests, especially throughout the plains and Rocky Mountains."[35] In his first presidential address on December 3, 1901, he added that "forests alone cannot conserve the waters of the arid region . . . [G]reat storage works are necessary to equalize the flow of streams and to save the flood waters. Nor by states alone, for there are interstate problems and resources [needed] beyond the capacity of the states."[36] Roosevelt thus envisioned a multiple-purpose approach to water development, and federal-state cooperation to achieve it.

The forest, irrigation, and waterways movements came together between 1900 and 1908. Foresters like Pinchot supported the irrigation movement, the new Reclamation Service, and its directors Newell and Arthur Davis. Newell's first Reclamation Service report likewise stressed the importance of headwaters forest protection and timber production, as well as irrigation development.[37] In 1902, the American Forestry Association joined forces with the National Irrigation Association, renaming its journal *American Forests* as *Forestry and Irrigation*.[38] The Forest Service and Weather Bureau established an "experimental watershed" in 1909 at Wagon Wheel Gap, Colorado, to study rainfall-runoff relations. Pinchot reached out to the urban-watershed protection interests of utilities, including the controversial Hetch Hetchy reservoir in California. City and state governments also passed urban-watershed protection acts.[39]

The most important coalition for water-resources planning, however, was led by McGee. In 1906, railway congestion had decreased waterway freight transport (the decrease was also attributable in part to discriminatory pricing by the railways) and, together with severe floods in Pittsburgh, led to the establishment of the Inland Waterways Commission (IWC). The IWC was chaired by Theodore Burton, a congressional representative from the flood-stricken state of Ohio, with Senator Francis Newlands, a reclamation advocate from Nevada, as vice chair. The commission included five federal-agency representatives: McGee (Bureau of Soils), Pinchot (Forest Service), Newell (Reclamation Service), Herbert Knox Smith (Bureau of Corporations), and Alexander Mackenzie (Army Corps of Engineers). McGee served as secretary.

The IWC issued a preliminary report in 1908 calling for greater cooperation and coordination among federal agencies, analysis of the local and national benefits of navigation projects, coordination of waterways and railroad transportation systems, and ap-pointment of a National Waterways Commission to accomplish these goals.[40] Roosevelt endorsed the idea of a "permanent commission authorized to coordinate the work of all the government departments relating to waterways, and to frame and supervise the execution of a comprehensive plan."[41] But the Army Corps of Engineers strongly opposed the idea of a permanent commission that might oversee its rivers and harbors activities.[42] This pattern of bureaucratic reform and opposition has had many subsequent incarnations up to the present day.

Michael Lacey argues persuasively that the IWC anticipated the spatial extension of waterways engineering to multiple-purpose river-basin planning.[43] Roosevelt had asserted that "each river system, from its headwaters in the forest to its mouth on the coast, is a single unit and should be treated as such."[44] Although this vision would not quickly be realized, the IWC sketched out the key principles and intergovernmental bridges necessary for its realization. While organizing a technical conference on conservation, for example, IWC commissioners learned of a conference of governors that was being organized by the Lakes-to-Gulf Deep Waterways Association, which led them to seek the involvement of governors to extend the coalition of federal agencies and conservation groups to state governments. They persuaded Roosevelt to convene the historic "Conference of Governors" at the White House in 1908, several sessions of which combined forestry, reclamation, and sanitation in integrative ways.[45] It was a time of great reports and conferences. The National Conservation Commission issued a three-volume report in 1909 that included chapters on water resources, floods, and catchment-area management.[46]

The end of the Roosevelt presidency signaled the end of these federal conservation coalitions. One of the last acts of Roosevelt's secretary of the interior, James Garfield, was to remove scores of potential hydropower sites on the public lands from private entry by electric-power utilities. When President Taft appointed Richard Ballinger as the new secretary of the interior, Ballinger immediately began to restore those sites, invoking the wrath of Pinchot and other Roosevelt conservationists. Pinchot's attacks cost him and Ballinger their jobs, and the coalitions among federal bureaus gave way to a compartmentalization of resource-management sectors in general, and of water-resources programs in particular.[47] The IWC never produced a final report. Although some of its recommendations were examined and tested at various times, including the proposal for a comprehensive water-planning commission, these water-policy experiments developed tentatively over a period of many decades.[48]

It is hard to imagine this extraordinary record of bridge-building among federal bureau chiefs, conservation groups, and resource users during the first decade of the twentieth century.[49] It is less difficult to imagine the pitfalls faced by those early water planners. But watershed organizers could profit from a close analysis of the accomplishments and failings of these Progressive Era coalitions.

Disasters: Regional Flooding and Watershed Planning, 1907–27

Although floods had secondary importance for the IWC, they received increasing attention from Congress in the early twentieth century. Flood losses escalated after the mid-nineteenth century due to rapid settlement of the Ohio, Mississippi, and Missouri River floodplains. These flood disasters influenced watershed planning and river engineering in divergent ways.

A series of flood disasters prompted the Pittsburgh Flood Commission to revisit the role of reservoirs and watershed management in flood control.[50] The Corps of Engineers and the Weather Bureau remained skeptical.[51] The debate intensified after the 1911 Mississippi River floods, which led to the passage of the Weeks Act authorizing states to cooperate on fire protection in forested watersheds and providing for federal land acquisition in the headwaters of navigable rivers.[52]

The science-policy stage was thus set for a watershed approach when disastrous floods ripped through the Miami and Ohio River valleys in 1913. Although Pinchot had been dismissed from the Forest Service, and Progressive coalitions had begun to unravel, a new maverick advocated watershed planning as the antidote to disaster: Arthur E. Morgan. Morgan was an imaginative, idealistic, and largely self-made drainage engineer who helped draft the Ohio Conservancy District Law after the 1913 floods. His firm prepared engineering plans for the new Miami River Conservancy District, which included a combination of reservoirs, levees, and land-management practices—i.e., a multiple-means approach to address the single flood-control objective.[53] The plan was accepted over criticisms by the Army Corps of Engineers and scientists opposed to reservoirs.[54]

Severe floods struck the Mississippi and Sacramento Rivers in 1916, prompting the first "official" federal flood-control act on March 1, 1917.[55] In one of its general provisions, the act stated, "All examinations and surveys of projects relating to flood control shall include a comprehensive study of the watershed or watersheds."[56] A National Waterways Commission, the dream of Roosevelt and McGee, was also created in 1917 to "secure the necessary data, and to formulate and report to Congress, as early as practicable, a comprehensive plan or plans for the development of waterways and water resources of the United States for the purposes of navigation *and for every useful purpose* [emphasis added]."[57]

In the 1920s, an accidental convergence occurred between hydropower and flood-control policies. The 1920 Federal Water Power Act established a commission to issue licenses for hydropower development on navigable rivers and public lands (the very issue that had divided Pinchot and Ballinger a decade earlier).[58] In the same year, partly in response to flood damages in the lower Colorado, Congress directed the secretary of the interior to report on water-development opportunities for the Imperial Valley.[59] The resulting Fall-Davis Report of 1922 became a model for "multiple-purpose" analysis, covering flood control, hydropower, sedimentation, and reclamation; it also linked these analyses with the proposed dam at Boulder Canyon and with the interstate compact negotiations facilitated by Secretary of Commerce Herbert Hoover.[60] Although focused on specific projects, the entire Colorado River basin was included within the scope of investigation.

Hoover's attitude toward multiple-purpose water planning deserves close attention.[61] Hoover supported federal involvement in commercial waterways development (e.g., the St. Lawrence, Great Lakes, and Mississippi River waterways) and multiple-purpose river-basin analysis. But he opposed other types of public water development for hydropower, irrigation, and industrial projects (e.g., at the Muscle Shoals facility). He regarded multiple-purpose planning as a rational basis for coordinating private water development and public water interests, and not as a means for public water development. Thus for Hoover, river-basin planning served limited regulatory and federal navigation purposes. Hoover also advocated reorganizing the federal natural-resources agencies to achieve these ends, including transfer of rivers and harbors responsibilities

from the military to a civilian public-works agency.[62]

Congress thought otherwise. Federal reclamation projects had financial problems, and without supplemental revenues new water projects were uncertain. For some in Congress, federal hydropower development offered a solution. In addition to combating the power utilities, revenues from public power could be applied to other water-development purposes. In 1925, Congress therefore requested the Army Corps of Engineers and the Federal Power Commission to estimate the cost of systematically appraising the feasibility of power development in combination with navigation improvements, flood control, and irrigation on the "navigable streams of the United States and their tributaries."[63]

Their estimate of $7,322,400 was presented in 1926 in House Document 308, which was a first step toward large-scale federally sponsored multiple-purpose water planning.[64] The last sentence of that document states, ". . . there is a very fair possibility that the investigations of power values and possibilities may in many cases be obtained without cost on the part of the United States by private interests interested in securing the power."[65] This concept would later be expanded to use power revenues to finance federal water projects.

Again, a flood disaster brought together disparate threads of federal water policy. Floods on the Mississippi River in 1927 had an enormous impact on the national consciousness.[66] Because the Corps of Engineers had already embarked on the multiple-purpose "308 reports," Congress found it expedient to shift the emphasis of those studies from hydropower to flood control.[67]

Forest fires also revived, on a more modest geographic and financial scale, Progressive concerns for forest, watershed, and soil conservation. The Clark-McNary Act of

1924, for example, authorized cooperation with states for "the continuous production of timber" and "the protection of watersheds of navigable streams."[68] A 1928 act provided modest funds for weather forecasting and scientific experimentation related to fire hazards and watershed protection.[69]

Thus, despite the collapse of Progressive water coalitions, the 1910s and 1920s witnessed an integrative trend in water planning prompted by natural disasters in the Ohio, Mississippi, and Sacramento basins. Not all major floods triggered policy change, though they did contribute to incremental policy development. In the interwar period, floods tended to have a major impact on policy (a) when they coincided with parallel planning efforts (e.g., the "308 reports"), (b) when they facilitated special water-district legislation (e.g., the Ohio Conservancy District act), and (c) when they helped justify river-basin planning for other purposes (e.g., the Boulder Canyon Project Act of 1928).

Recovery: Varieties of New Deal Water Planning (1933–1943)

Conflict over the federal role in water development yielded temporarily to the economic crises of the 1930s, which broadened federal response to disasters and enabled the first full flowering of large-scale river-basin planning. Although federal planning is often portrayed as "top-down," in contrast with local "bottom-up" approaches, neither category is homogeneous. The variety of New Deal river-basin planning initiatives aimed at national, regional, and local economic recovery illustrates this point. Four institutional approaches to river-basin planning emerged in the New Deal:

1. Single-purpose agency plans: Bureau of Reclamation; Army Corps of Engineers

2. Federal river-basin corporations: Tennessee Valley Authority
3. Special-purpose commissions created by executive order: Mississippi Valley Committee, National Resources Committee, National Resources Planning Board
4. Coalitions of resource agencies with rural resource constituencies: e.g., between the Soil Conservation Service, the Rural Electrification Agency, and the Forest Service.

Although these approaches shared some common assumptions about the aims and functions of water planning, they used different institutional structures and approaches to achieve those ends. They shared the rhetoric of "multiple-objective planning," for example, but as shown below they pursued it in ways that distinguished themselves from one another (e.g., in different regions, water sectors, and constituencies).

Single-Purpose Resource Agencies

Despite its early start with the "308 reports," the Corps of Engineers' ambivalence toward river-basin planning ensured that it would have a technically important but politically conservative or sometimes obstructive role.[70] Like Hoover, the Corps viewed basin planning as an analytical tool for navigation and flood control rather than as a vehicle for regional development.

Other agencies had grander visions. The Bureau of Reclamation won massive dam projects, such as the Grand Coulee and Fort Peck dams, which adapted the multiple-purpose dam concept to New Deal opportunities in 1933. Although nominally linked with basinwide development schemes, Gilbert White rightly describes such dams as "multiple-purpose/single-means" projects where reservoir construction was only tenuously linked with river-basin planning.

Federal Corporations:
The Tennessee Valley Authority

The Tennessee Valley Authority (TVA), created in 1933 by Franklin Roosevelt and Congress, is the only river-basin organization that is a federal corporation.[71] It is subject to limited congressional and executive oversight and is otherwise semi-autonomous in its financial and substantive operations. Creation of the TVA in 1933 exemplifies the expansive process of multiple-purpose planning. The TVA originated in the Muscle Shoals controversy over a World War I–vintage nitrate plant and dam near Florence, Alabama. Eclectic proposals for the facility, including some by Henry Ford, led to its eventual connection with hydropower, navigation, flood control, land, and water-management objectives. Concerns about a local facility grew to encompass the entire river basin and beyond.[72]

The focus on the river-basin context is attributable in large measure to Arthur E. Morgan, an unabashed utopian who sought to extend his earlier single-purpose experiments in watershed flood control to include more comprehensive water, land, and community planning. A second TVA director, David Lilienthal, pushed the TVA's public power agenda, bringing that Progressive idea to fruition. For Lilienthal, the basin was a hydropower region that could be used to challenge exploitative regional electric utilities. Harcourt Morgan, the third director, promoted soil conservation using the voluntaristic (putatively "grassroots") methods of the agricultural extension service.

Visionary directors and its semi-autonomous status gave the TVA room to experiment with innovative planning approaches. Its planning staff developed a multivariate land-use classification system using emerging aerial-photo interpretation techniques.[73] Another TVA group promoted floodplain management along the main stem and tributaries. A third initiative linked construction camps with new-town planning and innovative uses of building materials.

Franklin Roosevelt supported the directors' ideas but ironically could not lead them to cooperate with one another. With the exception of floodplain management, which persisted through the diligence of James Goddard and others at TVA (as well as additional legislative action), its land- and water-planning programs declined with the forced departure of their main advocate, Morgan, and the concomitant ascent of the TVA's electric-power role over all other functions.[74]

Special-Purpose Commissions Created
by Executive Order

Roosevelt used executive orders to create a series of special-purpose planning boards. The "President's Commission on Water Flow," established in 1934, made general policy recommendations and identified ten river basins for more detailed study.[75] The Mississippi Valley Committee surveyed flood-control alternatives in that basin.[76] "Joint investigations" were undertaken in selected basins (e.g., the Rio Grande) to guide water development and interstate compact negotiations.[77]

Influenced by his uncle, the planner Frederic A. Delano, Roosevelt appointed a spectrum of boards and committees to analyze New Deal policy options and guide the rapid growth of infrastructure investment. The genealogy of these committees—from the National Resources Board (1934) and National Resources Committee (1935) to the Natural Resources Planning Board—is not as important as their continuing efforts to advance regional planning through multiple-purpose river-basin development.[78] Between 1935 and 1938, the National Resources Committee applied river-basin planning methods to water problems in all of the drainage basins in the nation.[79] These basin reports invited and compiled the contributions of hundreds of public groups and experts in each basin. Like the Progressives, but unlike TVA, this committee also sought close linkages with state planning.[80] The National Resources Committee even invited criticisms of the role of river-basin planning as a tool for regional development, though it is not clear whether those criticisms affected its water-planning activities.[81]

Although analytically impressive, these commissions had little political support outside the White House. In 1943, the National Resources Planning Board, the last incarnation of Roosevelt's special-purpose planning organizations, was eliminated from the budget by Congress, but not before it and other presidential commissions demonstrated the value of high-quality investigations, maps, participatory methods, and judicious recommendations, which established new standards and methods for regional water planning.

Coalitions of Resource Agencies

A fourth institutional experiment in New Deal water planning involved a breakaway coalition of three new agencies charged with various aspects of rural well-being: the Rural Electrification Administration (REA), headed by Morris Cooke, a specialist in public utilities; the Soil Conservation Service (SES), directed by Hugh Hammond Bennett and Walter Clay Lowdermilk; and the Farm Security Administration, led by Rexford Tugwell, a New York planner who later went to the University of Chicago. In 1935 they commissioned a small manifesto titled *Little Waters: A Study of Headwater Streams & Other Little Waters, Their Use and Relations to the Land.*[82] Although criticized as simplistic by other water planners, *Little Waters* made a

clearly written appeal for rural people and places. It revived the Progressive Era coalition between watershed planning and forest protection, and extended it to encompass soil management, farmer-run cooperatives, and rural conservation districts.

As in Progressive times, the agency coalition did not endure, but the SCS did use it to launch a lasting program of rural watershed management. As a land resource agency, the SCS focused on linkages between land cover, runoff, erosion, and sedimentation. Catastrophic drought and erosion in the Great Plains in the 1930s reinforced these SCS watershed-protection efforts.[83] Not surprisingly, these local land-management programs developed separately and sometimes in conflict with the large-scale river basin engineering of the Army Corps of Engineers.

Summary

These four institutional paths inherited the coalition-building legacy of the Progressive Era, as well as its distinction between watershed planning and river-channel engineering.[84] As in the Progressive Era, the coalitions were transitory, and bureaucratic divisions became more deeply entrenched. Indeed, further distinctions emerged between watershed planning and river-basin planning that involved bureaucratic competition as well as competing scientific ideas.

Although the Flood Control Act of 1936 provided for watershed protection as well as larger river-basin works, institutional fissures blocked their integration.[85] Presidential planning commissions pursued these visions of integration but lacked the political authority to achieve them. The TVA had the authority but lacked the internal organization to sustain a balanced multiple-purpose planning. Of the four approaches, the "single-purpose agency" approach dominated water planning in the 1940s, driving out the competition, weathering the political opposition, and subsuming weaker coalition members during periods of restructuring.

Growth: Economic and Technological, 1944–1964

Postwar economic and technological growth posed new problems and tensions for regional water planning. As public infrastructure spending grew, so did criticisms of it. Numerous attempts were made to rationalize spending and reorganize and coordinate federal water agencies. At the same time, new analytical tools and technologies developed that promised advances in certain aspects of multiple-purpose planning while obscuring or compromising others.

In the postwar economy, large-scale infrastructure projects boomed across the country, fueled by congressional spending. Water agencies grew larger; small watershed programs expanded in number and extent. The Pick-Sloan Plan on the Missouri River, prepared in December 1944 months after the war but years after the plan's initial conception, exemplified this new era of "gigantism" that eclipsed even the TVA and Bureau of Reclamation projects of earlier decades.[86]

Walter Prescott Webb referred to rivers like the Missouri as "wrong way rivers" because they flow from semi-arid areas into more humid downstream environments.[87] They also marked the juncture of two federal water titans—the Bureau of Reclamation in their irrigable headwaters and the Army Corps of Engineers in their navigable mouths. The postwar challenge on such rivers was to forge agreements among states and agencies that enabled development and spending to proceed. River basins served as the regional context for this brand of cooperation aimed at the construction of dams, levees, and irrigation works for all who could muster the congressional support for them.

For a time, TVA enthusiasts envisioned a Missouri Valley Authority, but that idea was resisted by the states, the politically conservative Congress that represented them, and the dominant water agencies that served them. These groups preferred instead the approach developed on the Colorado River, which combined large-scale federal construction spending with weak river-basin organizations. Thus, a Missouri Inter-Agency River Basin Commission (MIARBC) was created in 1945 to facilitate implementation of the Pick-Sloan Plan as well as smaller water programs and concerns. Membership included federal water agencies and states. The MIARBC and similar basin organizations were criticized from beginning to end, however, for their lack of authority, of scientific water data, and of planning expertise—i.e., the opposite of the criticisms leveled at the "creeping socialism" of the TVA.

The TVA itself had shifted its emphasis from water to power development, where there were greater financial and technical opportunities. It added thermal and nuclear facilities to its hydroelectric portfolio. Although rejected as an institutional framework for river-basin planning in the United States, the TVA did advance several water-planning programs in the United States (e.g., floodplain management), and it exported its grander visions of "integrated river basin development" to the new nations of Africa and Asia.[88]

Dissatisfaction with both the strong and weak models of river-basin planning and concern about inefficient federal spending led to a series of elite study commissions on the reorganization of the executive branch. President Truman appointed a commission under Hoover that recommended in 1949 the creation of a "Board of Impartial Analysis of Engineering and Architectural Projects," whose name spoke volumes (literally) about federal water development, but which was not adopted.[89] Other commissions in the 1950s proposed reorganizing the executive water agencies and limiting their patronage relations with Congress, each one contributing to the scientific understanding of water policy issues but none of them to major bureaucratic reform.[90]

One of the most probing scientific appraisals was prepared by the president's Water Resources Policy Commission, chaired by Cooke, which assessed "the development, utilization, and conservation of water resources, including related lands uses and other public purposes."[91] This commission produced an impressive three-volume report in 1950. Volume one, entitled *A Water Policy for the American People,* undertook an extensive public as well as expert survey to identify national water problems, recommend policy adjustments, and rationalize government programs. The commission also recommended establishment of "river basin coordinating committees" to improve communication and planning among federal, state, and local agencies.[92] As noted, these interagency coordinating committees had little authority or resources and were often deemed ineffective.

Volume two, entitled *Ten Rivers in America's Future,* developed detailed case studies that built upon the earlier ten-basin study of the President's Commission on Water Flow. Not surprisingly, one of the basins selected was the Missouri River, which was undergoing rapid development under the Pick-Sloan Plan. The Missouri case study highlighted, among other things, the lack of scientific data available to guide engineering works, and it laid out standards for data collection, which led Truman to create a Missouri Basin Survey Commission for that purpose in 1952. The survey fulfilled some of its

water-data functions, but it had limited impact on broader planning decisions.[93]

Even the small watershed programs grew large in funding, bureaucratic apparatus, and aspirations. The SCS launched a pilot watershed program in 1953 that boomed with the passage of the Watershed Protection and Flood Prevention Act of 1954 (PL-566). That act revived the headwaters protection, upstream engineering, and *Little Waters* initiatives of earlier periods—and it situated them within a secure bureaucratic niche in the Department of Agriculture. No longer dependent on fragile coalitions, but rooted instead in a vast network of agricultural extension offices and soil conservation districts, the small watershed program spawned myriad storm-water detention reservoirs and soil conservation projects.

This simultaneous expansion of small watershed and large river-basin programs set the stage for conflict (as well as competition and divisions of the spoils) among federal water agencies. The half-century-old flood-control controversy about headwaters protection versus river-channel engineering resurfaced between the Army Corps of Engineers and the SCS.[94]

In the midst of these bureaucratic struggles, two scientific developments redefined water-planning problems and practice in the 1950s. The Harvard Water Project assembled an eminent team of hydrologists, engineers, mathematicians, economists, and political scientists. This multidisciplinary group sought to apply the new scientific methods of operations research, synthetic hydrology, and optimization modeling—and the new computer technologies that made them possible— to multiple-purpose river-basin planning.[95] These investigations marked a transition from descriptive river-basin surveys to quantitative evaluations of alternative river-basin plans. They represented a major advance in the logic and techniques of planning, but also an overconfidence about what such tools could encompass and accomplish.[96]

The second scientific advance involved floodplain-management research. Floodplains are the main locus of flood damages, but they had received limited attention in either river-channel or watershed engineering. Early studies in the 1930s by White and his colleagues linked increasing flood losses with intensified floodplain development. As floodplain development and losses increased in the postwar period, analysts began to focus on the social-scientific and behavioral factors that influenced floodplain occupance decisions.[97] These studies entered into the sensitive realm of local land-use planning, which water planners generally sought to avoid. But they showed that flood hazards could not be reduced by river engineering or watershed management alone and that floodplain management constituted a crucial link between watershed planning and river-channel engineering. In the 1950s, none of these contexts for regional water management were well coordinated with one another.

Fragmentation of federal water programs was nothing new, but it generated greater frustration and waste in the context of increased public water spending. Weak proposals for river-basin coordinating committees did little to reduce frustration or integrate plans. Finally, in 1959, the Senate established a select committee, chaired by Robert S. Kerr of Oklahoma, to review and chart a broad course for federal water policy. The select committee commissioned some ninety studies and published thirty-two reports that reviewed past water-policy initiatives, water quantity and quality issues, emerging technologies, and river-basin plans.[98] Old patterns of patronage persisted—Senator Kerr obtained the Arkansas–White–Red River Basin Commission and the massive McClellan-Kerr navigation and flood-control project for his region—and they undermined the credibility of multiple-purpose river-basin planning.

Nevertheless, the conjunction of scientific advance and federal policy formulation in the 1950s had two major consequences for regional water planning. First, it contributed to the centralization of water planning at the national level, which led to more systematic reviews of water plans and projects. The select committee investigations, for example, shaped the groundbreaking Water Resources Planning Act of 1965. Second, federal water-policy analysis expanded during this period to include the social and behavioral sciences, as well as the physical, engineering, and biological sciences.[99] These advances in river-basin planning did not fully anticipate the problems of centralization in water planning, nor did they fully address the growing social concerns and conflicts over water pollution and environmental protection.[100]

Centralization: Vicissitudes of Federal Water Planning, 1965–1981

The Water Resources Planning Act of 1965 marked the culmination of these trends toward centralization and coordination of multiple-purpose river-basin plans. The 1965 Act established three geographic levels of planning: the national level, the regional (i.e., river basin) level, and the project-planning level. It created the Water Resources Council to conduct the national water assessments, coordinate agency programs, and assist river-basin commissions. The river-basin commissions took a variety of geographic forms, from multiple-basin regions like New England to individual basins like the Colorado and partial basins like the upper Mississippi. They varied in the rigor and vigor with which they prepared water plans and weighed competing economic, environmental, and social interests.

This balancing of multiple objectives was guided by "Principles and Standards for Planning Water and Related Land Resources," prepared by the Water Resources Council in 1973. The "Principles and Standards" stipulated four planning criteria or "accounts": 1) national economic development, 2) regional economic development, 3) environmental quality, and 4) other social effects.[101] This multiple-criteria framework began to standardize and formalize planning practices across agencies and regions. The four objectives were weighted differently: national economic development was the primary planning criterion for all federal actions; environmental quality assessment could trump economically feasible plans; social and regional impacts were factors to be considered, justified, and mitigated.

These policies fueled the largest program of national and regional water planning in American history, building on the approaches developed in the New Deal. By the 1970s, individual river-basin plans were running five to fifteen volumes in length. They compiled masses of data on basin water use, issues, and trends, and they assessed alternative plans and policies. One pathbreaking report illustrated the alternatives-analysis approach in the Colorado River basin, even considering non-water-related alternatives (e.g., investment in education) for regional development.[102]

The Water Resources Council carried out national water assessments in 1968 and 1978.[103] These national water assessments coincided with new environmental-protection legislation that required environmental-impact assessments, air- and water-quality regulation, and endangered-species protection. The "Principles and Standards" sought to coordinate water-resources investigations with these related realms of environmental policy. In addition, a National Water Commission presented a major report to Congress and the president on *Water Policies for the Future* in 1973, which included recommendations for the organizations that plan and manage "river basins and other regions."[104]

These national trends were paralleled at the metropolitan level by renewed interest in urban watershed planning across multiple counties and municipalities. Comprehensive plans were prepared by the Northeastern Illinois Planning Commission to address problems of flooding, water supply, waste treatment, and land-use planning in regionally integrated ways.[105] Other experiments established special-purpose water organizations like the Urban Drainage and Flood Control District in metropolitan Denver.[106]

Not surprisingly, as these increasingly detailed policy studies were prepared, fewer large-scale water projects were built, and the tensions inherent in the centralized water-planning framework deepened. First, the historical role of federal basin planning in facilitating water development came into question. Previously, the aim had been to determine *which* projects should be built, not *whether* they should be built. Some regarded this increased analysis as a measure of declining productivity, others as a belated but inadequate brake on unsound federal water development. As the role of planning in water development became less clear, its political support eroded.

A second set of tensions involved the river-basin level of analysis. Some supported the strengthening of river-basin commissions as the most logical scientific context for analysis, while others continued to oppose it. Events from the late nineteenth century on indicate that political objections to river-basin organizations are very deeply rooted. In addition, water-construction agencies manipulated and competed with river-basin organizations.[107] Local water developers complained about the addition of another level of bureaucratic reviews, costs, and delays.

Third, some water experts criticized the multiple-objective and multiple-criteria framework. Some doubted that different values in water could be reconciled—e.g., that the intrinsic value of aquatic habitat could be traded off against the commercial value of water in urban or agricultural use. Others believed such tradeoffs *must* be made, but that the pluralistic framework of the "Principles and Standards" could not guide those decisions. Some economists insisted on a common metric for comparing alternatives: anything short of that had illusory value. For them, the national economic development criterion was sufficient; river basins were units of accounting and not contexts for regional development at the expense of the nation or for the furtherance of regionalist aims.

For a time, those who fashioned the national planning framework were allowed to proceed with their experiments. They persuaded others that the pluralistic multiple-objective framework that weighed economic, environmental, and social factors separately and in their own terms was appropriate. They managed tussles among water agencies and levels of government, maintaining support for collaborative national and river-basin planning.

But when President Carter suggested that the Water Resources Council should have greater regulatory and project-review authority, the political precariousness of the entire framework was exposed (as it was in the New Deal planning boards). Up to that point, even modest interventions by the Water Resources Council and river-basin commissions encountered fierce criticism from all levels and branches of government. Local groups and congressional representatives howled about project costs, delays, permits, and denials. Federal water agencies undermined actions that encroached on their administrative, regional, and regulatory turf. Business groups highlighted regulatory costs, contradictions,

and penalties. Scientific groups chimed in to criticize the quality of scientific data and, as noted above, the inherent difficulties of multiple-objective multiple-criteria analysis. Toward the end, even Water Resources Council's supporters had doubts.[108]

The apparatus of national water planning that had emerged after a century of effort did not withstand these pressures for long. The Reagan administration undid much of it during its first year of business. It repealed the 1965 Water Resources Planning Act. It abolished the Water Resources Council and river-basin commissions. It diluted the "Principles and Standards" into "Principles and Guidelines."[109] The SCS's small watershed programs were allowed to proceed quietly, and a few river-basin organizations continued to operate with local and state support. At the metropolitan scale, organizations like the Northeastern Illinois Planning Commission lost much of their authority through broader forces of urban political and economic restructuring. Interestingly, special-purpose water and drainage districts managed to avoid this fate when they could secure funding for water-pollution control and treatment from EPA policies that continued in the 1980s. By 1983, however, the centralizing trend in multiple-purpose water planning had collapsed, and its planning apparatus went into eclipse.

Conclusions

A decade later, in 1993, floods raged through the upper Mississippi and lower Missouri basins. Old river-basin studies were dusted off and new digital databases constructed. Bold floodplain, wetlands, and watershed management proposals were advanced—along with proposals for new river-basin commissions. In the interim, new technologies and tools had developed. Old-line agencies, faced with increased public criticism of their management abilities (e.g., the TVA and the Bureau of Reclamation) developed impressive "spatial decision support systems" that integrated operations, management, and geographic information systems.[110] Over the same decade, thousands of local watershed initiatives sprang up, billing themselves as bottom-up, citizen-run, place-based approaches—different from everything that had gone before.

Between 1993 and the present, however, new conjunctions of disasters, technologies, economic restructuring, and political coalitions have arisen. This historical review sheds light on the issues and prospects that these local, regional, and national water-planning groups face. Local watershed advocates display the enthusiasm of all pioneers. They perceive a situation that cries out for their watershed approach, and they build coalitions that would seem to succeed in that situation.

But these local organizations might profit by considering the following historical evidence. First, new watershed groups are filling a *temporary* institutional vacuum created by the dismantling of federal water-planning programs. They should expect, within the decade, another wave of legislation that may or may not support their initiatives. To adapt to that changing situation they should examine, through historical-geographic comparisons and analogies, how they resemble or differ from the accomplishments and failings of watershed coalitions and legislation of the past century.

Second, local watershed organizations will have to coordinate their activities with regional water-management issues and organizations, and they will have to create much more effective means of intergovernmental coordination. Although "watersheds" are small river basins, gaps endure between watershed and river-basin planning. Intergovernmental water organizations have lacked the power, resources, and coordination to influence water policy. Executive water-policy commissions have had greater resources but lacked broader political support. Public corporations like the TVA are a rare and endangered species, but meso-scale basins like that of the Tennessee River may be the most promising contexts for integrating watershed and river-basin planning.[111] A historical perspective indicates that regional organizations must have greater authority to determine regional water-policy questions and greater resources to coordinate local and regional concerns.

Third, some federal water agencies are now reaching out to emerging watershed groups. The EPA has assumed a supportive role, perhaps because it envisions a promising local means (perhaps its only means) to implement non-point-source water-quality regulations. But the EPA shows no sign of undertaking detailed historical or scientific analysis of the half-century of experience that the SCS has had with local conservation districts. If it did, it might better understand factors that shape the success and failure of local organizations, and the role of federal agencies in those results.

Some federal water agencies are responding to the current situation by developing new operations and management technologies that echo earlier scientific initiatives in water planning and investment modeling. The TVA TERRA model for water and power operations and the Bureau of Reclamation decision-support systems are good examples. Although these agencies and their modelers have learned from experience about the importance of behavioral factors, scientific visualization, and geographic information systems in developing these new tools, they have not, to my knowledge, undertaken detailed post-audits of previous river-basin modeling advances, such as the Harvard Water Project.[112]

Post-audits have been undertaken only for a limited number of flood-hazards projects and programs. Several studies consider the role of disasters in shaping regional water policy, such as how floods in the 1910s on the Ohio River and the 1920s on the Mississippi River influenced the Flood Control Act of 1936.[113] The historical relations between flood hazards and policy remain unclear. The 1993 floods on the upper Mississippi have not as yet yielded major policy changes in that river basin or in the nation. Federal planners have compiled massive databases and reports but seem at a loss to explain why this disaster has not yielded policy change outside of "politics."

These observations have particular relevance for local watershed groups that are established in the aftermath of other types of crises (e.g., a fish kill). They should analyze other organizations created in the wake of disaster, as well as those that fold or endure in subsequent disasters. Watershed groups at all levels can profit from long-term studies of the Ohio conservancy districts, Midwest drainage districts, and most recently, local floodplain-management programs.

Watershed planning has great promise in the twenty-first century, but it is important to remember that similar hopes arose in the 1900s, 1930s, and 1950s—as they did for river-basin planning in the 1930s, 1950s, and 1970s. These experiments of the past century offer valuable insights into current water-policy problems and potentially valuable analogies for future planning experiments—analogies that do not presume to predict the future but rather seek to identify creative alternatives and avoid common pitfalls.

Notes

1. See Bob Doppelt, et al., *Entering the Watershed: A New Approach to Save America's River Ecosystems* (Covella, Calif.: Island Press, 1993); Douglas Kenney, *The State Role in Western Watershed Initiatives* (Boulder, Co.: Natural Resources Law Center, University of Colorado, 1998); Peter M. Lavigne and Kevin J. Coyle, *The Watershed Innovators Workshop,* Proceedings from Cummington, Mass., June 4–5, 1995 (Portland, Or.: River Network, 1995); D. R. Montgomery; G. E. Grand; and K. Sullivan, "Watershed Analysis as a Framework for Implementing Ecosystem Management," *Water Resources Bulletin* 31 (1995): 369–86; National Research Council, Water Science and Technology Board, *New Strategies for America's Watersheds* (Washington, D.C.: National Academy Press, 1999); Natural Resources Law Center, *The Watershed Source Book: Watershed-Based Solutions to Natural Resource Problems* (Boulder: University of Colorado, 1996); Betsy Rieke and Doug Kenney, *Resource Management at the Watershed Level* (Denver: Western Policy Review Advisory Commission, 1997); U.S. Environmental Protection Agency (USEPA), *The Watershed Protection Approach: An Overview,* EPA 503/9-92-002 (Washington, D.C.: USEPA, 1991); and *River Voices,* 5:2 (Summer 1994) the issue of the quarterly publication of River Network on watershed activism. The USEPA also publishes two electronic newsletters, *Watershed Highlights* and *Watershed Update.*

2. See, for example, the National Research Council, Water Science and Technology Board, *Wetlands: Characteristics and Boundaries* (Washington, D.C.: National Academy of Sciences Press, 1995).

3. Exceptions include D. J. Allee, "River Basin Management," in *The Role of Social and Behavioral Sciences in Water Resources Planning and Management,* eds. Duane D. Baumann and Yacov Y. Haimes (New York: ASCE, 1988), pp. 294–312; Douglas Helms, "Small Watersheds and the USDA: Legacy of the Flood Control Act of 1936," in *The Flood Control Challenge: Past, Present and Future,* eds. H. Rosen and M. Reuss (Chicago: Public Works Historical Society, 1988), pp. 67–88; L. Teclaff, *The River Basin in History and Law* (The Hague: Martinus Nijhoff, 1967); Norman Wengert, "The Politics of River Basin Development," *Law and Contemporary Problems* 22 (1957): 258–75; James L. Wescoat, Jr., "Beyond the River Basin: The Changing Geography of International Water Problems and International Watercourse Law," *Colorado Journal of International Environmental Law* 3 (1992): 301–30; Gilbert F. White, "A Perspective of River Basin Development," *Journal of Law and*

Contemporary Problems 22 (1957): 155–87; Idem, "Contributions of Geographical Analysis to River Basin Development," *Geographical Journal* 129 (1963): 412–36; and Idem, "Watersheds and Streams of Thought," typescript presentation to Soil and Water Conservation Society, Des Moines, Iowa, 8 August 1995.

4. See James L. Wescoat, Jr., "Common Themes in the Work of Gilbert White and John Dewey: A Pragmatic Appraisal," *Annals of the Association of American Geographers* 92 (1992): 587–607.

5. Long's Peak Working Group on National Water Policy, *America's Waters: A New Era of Sustainability* (Boulder: Natural Resources Law Center, 1992, p. 5). Cf. Gregory J. Hobbs, Jr., "Ecological Integrity, New Western Myth: A Critique of the Long's Peak Report," *Environmental Law* 24 (1994): 157ff.

6. W. Goldfarb, "Watershed Management: Slogan or Solution?" *Boston College Environmental Affairs Law Review* 21 (1994): 483–509.

7. Natural Resources Law Center, *The Watershed Source Book: Watershed-Based Solutions to Natural Resource Problems* (Boulder: University of Colorado, 1996).

8. Conservation Technology Information Center, Purdue University, "Know Your Watershed Program," database diskette and newsletter, 1995.

9. California Watershed Projects Inventory, updated 24 July 1995, available on the World Wide Web at info@ice.ucdavis.edu.

10. *River Voices* 5:2 (Summer 1994). Many of these organizations are general environmental organizations and not watershed groups per se.

11. Personal communication with Gilbert F. White, professor emeritus, University of Colorado, 24 July 1995; cf. Ann L. Riley, *Restoring Streams in Cities: A Guide for Planners, Policymakers, and Citizens* (Covella, Calif.: Island Press, 1998).

12. For a review, see USEPA *Watershed Protection: A Statewide Approach*, EPA 841-R-95-004 (Washington, D.C.: Office of Wetlands, Oceans and Watersheds, 1995). For flood-plain management, see Association of State Floodplain Managers, *NANIA "All Together": Comprehensive Watershed Management*, Proceedings of the Eighteenth Annual Conference of the Association of State Floodplain Managers, 8–13 May 1994, Tulsa, Ok., Special Publication 30 (Boulder: Natural Hazards Research, Application, and Information Center, 1994).

13. M. L. Soscia, presentation on Oregon watershed programs at University of Colorado Law School, 1995; U.S. Congress, House of Representatives, Bill 961, "Clean Water Act Amendments of 1995. Section 321. State Watershed Management Programs." See also USEPA.

14. L. Koesters, presentation at the University of Colorado Law School, Boulder, 1995.

15. *Arizona Watershed Symposia,* Annual proceedings, 1973–1994. Phoenix: Arizona Water Commission: Biennial Watershed Management Conference, *Watersheds '94: Respect, Rethink, Restore* (Davis: Centers for Water and Wildland Resources, University of California, Davis, 1994); and *California Watershed Management Conference* (West Sacramento: Wildland Resources Center, University of California, 1986).

16. Interagency Floodplain Management Review Committee (IFMRC), *Sharing the Challenge: Floodplain Management into the 21st Century* (Washington, D.C.: IFMRC, 1994); Idem, Scientific Assessment and Strategy Team, *Science for Floodplain Management into the 21st Century: A Blueprint for Change, Part V* (Washington, D.C.: IAFMC, 1994); and Association of State Floodplain Managers, *NANIA "All Together."*

17. E. C. Buie, *A History of Water Resource Activities of the United States Department of Agriculture* (Washington, D.C.: U.S. Department of Agriculture, Soil Conservation Service, 1979); Melville H. Cohee, "Over 50 years—The Conservation Movement and SWCS," *Journal of Soil and Water Conservation* 50 (1995): 343–5; D. Helms, *Readings in the History of the Soil Conservation Service,* Economics and Social Sciences Division, NHQ, Historical Notes No. 1 (Washington, D.C.: United States Department of Agriculture, Soil Conservation Service, 1992); and U.S. Department of Agriculture, Soil Conservation Service, *National Watershed Manual,* 2d ed., 300-V-NWSM (Washington, D.C.: U.S. Department of Agriculture, 1992).

18. USEPA, Office of Wetlands, Oceans, and Watersheds newsletters: *Watershed Events,* which deals with thematic issues, and the more general *Watershed Highlights,* both available on the World Wide Web at http://www.epa.gov/OWOW/index.html.

19. Walter L. Creese, *TVA's Public Planning: The Vision, the Reality* (Knoxville: University of Tennessee Press, 1990); Erwin C. Hargrove, *Prisoners of Myth: The Leadership of the Tennessee Valley Authority, 1933–1990* (Princeton: Princeton University Press, 1994); Erwin C. Hargrove and Paul K. Conkin, eds., *TVA, Fifty Years of Grass-*

roots *Bureaucracy* (Urbana: University of Illinois Press, 1983); and Allan G. Pulsipher, "TVA's Debt Limit," *Public Utilities Fortnightly,* March 1, 1995, pp. 39–42.

20. R. Reitsma et al., "Geographically Distributed Decision Support: The Tennessee Valley Authority TERRA System," in D. G. Fontane and H. Tuvel, eds., *Water Policy and Management: Solving the Problems* (New York: American Society of Civil Engineers, 1994), pp. 311–4.

21. The National Research Council, for example, suspended research on U.S.-Mexico water issues due to insufficient support and funding. WSTB Newsletter 13:1 (1996). For a partial watershed-landscape plan, see Sandra Cleisz et al., *A Management Framework for the Tijuana River Valley* (Pomona: California State Polytechnic University, Department of Landscape Architecture, 1989).

22. Gilbert F. White, "Watersheds and Streams of Thought," presentation to Soil and Water Conservation Society, Des Moines, Iowa, 8 August 1995. White describes four known opportunities for integrated planning that were *not* pursued in the 1930s.

23. The antecedents of late-nineteenth-century watershed hydrology and river-channel engineering are not examined here, but see Frank D. Adams, "The Origins of Springs and Rivers," in *The Birth and Development of the Geological Sciences* (New York: Dover, 1938), pp. 426–60; Ellen C. Semple, "Anthro-geography of Rivers," in *Influences of Geographic Environment, on the Basis of Ratzel's System of Anthropo-Geography* (New York: H. Holt, 1911), pp. 336–79; and C. T. Smith, "The Drainage Basin as an Historical Basis for Human Activity," in *Water, Earth and Man: A Synthesis of Hydrology, Geomorphology, and Socio-Economic Geography* (London: Methuen, 1979), pp. 101–11.

24. *Gibbons v. Ogden,* U.S. 1, 6 L.Ed. 23 (1824).

25. An early debate between "levees only" and "multiple" approaches followed the Mississippi River floods of 1850 in such works as C. S. Ellet, Jr., *The Mississippi and Ohio Rivers: Containing Plans for the Protection of the Delta from Inundation* (Philadelphia: Lippincott, Grambo, 1853); and A. A. Humphreys and H. L. Abbot, *Report upon the Physics and Hydraulics of the Mississippi River: Upon the Protection of the Alluvial Region against Overflow* (Washington, D.C.: Professional Papers of the Corps of Topographical Engineers, U.S. Army, 1861).

26. See, for example, G. P. Marsh, *Man and Nature, or the Earth as Modified by Human Action,* ed. D. Lowenthal (Cambridge, Mass.: Belknap, 1965 [1864]), pp. 281–381.

27. Martha C. Bray, *Joseph Nicollet and His Map* (Philadelphia: American Philosophical Society, 1980); and J. N. Nicollet, *Report intended to illustrate a map of the hydrographical basin of the upper Mississippi River (List of fossils belonging to the several formations alluded to in the report, arranged according to localities),* 26th Cong., 2d sess., S. Doc. 237 (1843).

28. John Wesley Powell, *Report on the Lands of the Arid Region,* 45th Cong., 2d sess., Ex. Doc. 73 (1878); and Wallace Stegner, *Beyond the Hundredth Meridian: John Wesley Powell and the Second Opening of the West* (Lincoln: University of Nebraska Press, 1953).

29. Powell's explanations focused on "aggregate capital" and "co-operative labor," and reported favorably on the latter in Utah. Powell, *Report on the Lands of the Arid Region,* pp. 9–11.

30. U.S. Geological Survey (USGS), *10th Annual Report of the Geological Survey, part 2, Irrigation* [1st irrigation report], 51st Cong., 1st sess., Ex. Doc. 1, part 5 (1890 [1889]). Cf. Stegner, *Beyond the Hundredth Meridian,* pp. 301–4.

31. USGS, *10th Annual Report,* pp. 28 and 31; and USGS, *11th Annual Report of the Geological Survey, volume iv, part 3* 51st Cong., 2d sess., Ex. Doc. 1, part 5 (1890), p. 7.

32. USGS, *10th Annual Report,* p. 29.

33. USGS, *10th Annual Report,* p. 10. All four annual irrigation survey reports followed watershed boundaries in sections titled the "hydrography of drainage basins." After completing the irrigation survey authorized by Congress, the USGS continued its work in a series of scientific publications titled *Water Supply and Irrigation Papers,* beginning with a survey of "Irrigation on the Great Plains" by Newell. The series continued as the *Water Supply Papers* into the 1990s with over 2,340 issues.

34. *Coffin v. Left Hand Ditch Co.,* 6 Colo. 443 (1882), established the principle that the place of water use, even if outside the watershed, does not matter in states that follow the "prior appropriation" doctrine.

35. Albert Bushnell Hart and Herbert R. Ferleger, *Theodore Roosevelt Cyclopedia,* rev. 2d ed. (Oyster Bay, N.Y.: Theodore Roosevelt Association and Meckler, 1989), p. 103.

36. Ibid., p. 640.

37. Francis H. Newell, *First Annual Report of the Reclamation Service, from June 17 to December*

1, 1902, 57th Cong., 2d sess., H. Doc. 79 (Washington, D.C.), pp. 26 and 29. Unlike earlier irrigation surveys, the Reclamation Service reports were organized by state (i.e., client groups).

38. This name proved short-lived; in 1908 the journal received the broader title of *Conservation.*

39. William E. Sopper, "Watershed Management," in *Origins of American Conservation,* ed. Henry Clepper (New York: The Ronald Press Company), pp. 101—18; and Nelson Blake, *Water for the Cities: A History of the Urban Water Supply Problem in the United States* (Syracuse: Syracuse University Press, 1956).

40. Inland Waterways Commission (IWC), *Preliminary Report,* 60th Cong., 1st sess., S. Doc. 325, pp. 25–6.

41. Roosevelt, 8th Annual Message," December 8, 1908, reprinted in Hart and Ferleger, *Theodore Roosevelt Cyclopedia,* pp. 260–1.

42. Ibid., pp. 30–1.

43. Michael James Lacey, "The Mysteries of Earth-Making Dissolve: A Study of Washington's Intellectual Community and the Origins of American Environmentalism in the Late Nineteenth Century" (Ph.D. diss., George Washington University, 1979).

44. IWC, *Preliminary Report,* p. iv.

45. Conference of Governors, *Proceedings of a Conference of Governors in the White House, Washington, D.C., May 13–15, 1908,* 60th Cong., 2d sess., H. Doc. 1425 (1909). McGee again served as recording secretary.

46. National Conservation Commission, Report of the National Conservation Commission, 60th Cong., 2d sess., S.Doc. 676 (1909). An influential article on watershed-flood relations was M. O. Leighton's "Floods," in voume II, pp. 95–111.

47. See James Penick, Jr., *Progressive Politics and Conservation: The Ballinger-Pinchot Affair* (Chicago: University of Chicago Press, 1968).

48. U.S. Congress, *Final Report of the National Waterways Commission,* 62d Cong., 2d sess., S. Doc. 469 (1912).

49. For an example of remarkable collaboration between government and nongovernmental organizations—using a watershed approach—see U.S. Secretary of Agriculture, *A Report of the Secretary of Agriculture in Relation to the Forests, Rivers and Mountains of the Southern Appalachian Region,* 57th Cong., 1st sess., S. Doc. 84 (1902).

50. Pittsburgh Flood Commission, *Report* (Pittsburgh, 1912), and also M. O. Leighton, "The

Utility of Storage Reservoirs for Flood Prevention, Power and Navigation," pp. 133–74; and Raphael Zon, "Forests and Water in the Light of Scientific Investigation," pp. 205–302 (both app. to the National Waterways Commission, *Final Report,* 1912).

51. Sopper, "Watershed Management," pp. 108–9, cites critical papers by Chittenden of the Army Corps and Moore of the Weather Bureau.

52. "Weeks Act—Watershed Protection and Fire Protection," 61st Cong., 3d sess., ch. 186 (1911), pp. 961–3.

53. Arthur E. Morgan, *Dams and Other Disasters: A Century of the Army Corps of Engineers in Civil Works* (Boston: Porter Sargent, 1971); and idem, *The Miami Conservancy District* (New York: McGraw-Hill, 1951). Morgan opposed multipurpose dams in the Miami basin. Gilbert White examines the relations between "multiple-purposes" and "multiple-means" in *Strategies of American Water Management* (Ann Arbor: University of Michigan Press, 1969), pp. 34–56.

54. A critique by the corps appeared just months before the March 1913 floods: "Report on the Necessity and Practicability of Establishing a System of Impounding Reservoirs at the Headwaters of the Allegheny, Monongahela, and Ohio Rivers and Their Tributaries," 62d Cong., 3d sess., H. Doc. 1289 (1913).

55. 39 Stat. 948. This step toward multiple purposes also involved an explicit extension of federal jurisdiction from river channels to floodplains.

56. Ibid., sec. 3, p. 950.

57. "Act of August 8, 1917," 65th Cong., 1st sess., ch. 49 at p. 269. The "permanent commission" was abolished three years later.

58. Some members of Congress worried about the concentration of water-power sites in private hands. See U.S. Secretary of Agriculture, "Electric Power Development in the United States," 64th Cong., 1st sess., S. Doc. 316 (1916). But power companies exerted heavy influence on the drafting of the Federal Water Power Act ("Act of June 10, 1920," 66th Cong., 2d sess., ch. 273, p. 1063 *et seq.*), which also abolished the National Waterways Commission (at p. 1077).

59. "Report by the Director of the Reclamation Service on Problems of Imperial Valley and Vicinity with Respect to Irrigation from the Colorado River together with the Proceedings of the Conference on the Construction of the Boulder Canyon Dam held at San Diego, Calif.," also known as the "Fall-Davis Report," 67th Cong., 2d sess., S. Doc. 142 (1922).

60. Gilbert F. White, "A Perspective of River Basin Development," *Journal of Law and Contemporary Problems* 22 (1957): 155–87, describes this as an example of "multiple-purpose—single-means" planning.

61. The primary studies to date are Donald C. Swain, *Federal Conservation Policy, 1921–1933*, University of California Publications in History, vol. 76 (Berkeley: University of California Press, 1963); and Bruce A. Lohof, "Hoover and the Mississippi Valley Flood of 1927" (Ph.D. diss., Syracuse University, 1969).

62. Joint Committee on Reorganization of the Executive Branch of Government, "Reorganization of the Executive Departments," 68th Cong., 1st sess., H. Doc. 256, pp. 20–1. Cf. Hoover's executive orders that reorganized federal water agencies, including rivers and harbors, under an assistant secretary of the interior for public works, an action proposed too late in his presidency to be accepted. 72nd Cong., 2d sess., H. Doc. 493, pp. 2–3.

63. "Rivers and Harbors Act of March 3, 1925," 43 Stat. 1186 section 3. The Colorado River, which was under the jurisdiction of the Bureau of Reclamation, was excluded.

64. The resulting plans, authorized and prepared on the basis of that document, were known as "308 reports."

65. "Estimate of Cost of Examinations, etc., of Streams Where Power Development Appears Feasible," 69th Cong., 1st. sess., H. Doc. 308 (1926).

66. Pete Daniel, *Deep'n as It Come: The 1927 Mississippi River Flood* (New York: Oxford University Press, 1977); and Joseph L. Arnold, *The Evolution of the 1936 Flood Control Act* (Fort Belvoir: Office of History, United States Army Corps of Engineers, 1988).

67. The upper Mississippi River flood of 1993 also catalyzed data collection and policy analysis, but these activities were not sustained, in part because, unlike the 1927 disaster, they were not followed by a national economic crisis.

68. 43 Stat. 653, at sec. 1–2.

69. 70th Cong., 1st sess., ch. 678 (1928), pp. 699–701.

70. Arthur Maass, *Muddy Waters: The Army Engineers and the Nation's Rivers* (Cambridge, Mass.: Harvard University Press, 1951).

71. "Act of May 18, 1933," 48 Stat. 69, sec. 23.

72. Creese, *TVA's Public Planning;* T. K. McCraw, *Morgan vs. Lilienthal: The Feud within the TVA* (Chicago: Loyola University Press, 1970);

Muscle Shoals Commission, *Muscle Shoals: A Plan for the Use of the United States Properties on the Tennessee River by Private Industry for "the Manufacture of Fertilizers and Other Useful Products"* (Washington, D.C.: U.S. Government Printing Office (USGPO), 1931); Tennessee Valley Authority, *Annual Report* [1st annual report] (Washington, D.C.: USGPO, 1935).

73. These experiments were led by G. Donald Hudson of the Land Classification Section of the TVA. See his "The Unit Area Method of Land Classification," *Annals of the Association of American Geographers* 26 (1936): 99–112; and Charles C. Colby, "Changing Currents of Geographic Thought in America, Phases of the Planning Process," *Annals of the Association of American Geographers* 26 (1936): 1–38.

74. For an early sociological critique of the TVA that stimulated subsequent organizational assessments, see Philip Selznick, *TVA and the Grass Roots: A Study in the Sociology of Formal Organizations* (New York: Harper & Row, 1964 [1949]). For more recent institutional critiques, see Erwin C. Hargrove, *Prisoners of Myth: The Leadership of the Tennessee Valley Authority, 1933–1990* (Princeton: Princeton University Press, 1994); and Erwin C. Hargrove and Paul K. Conkin, eds., *TVA: Fifty Years of Grass-roots Bureaucracy* (Urbana: University of Illinois Press, 1983). On Goddard's contribution, see Association of State Floodplain Managers, *NANIA "All Together,"* pp. 407–12.

75. President's Commission on Water Flow, "Development of the Rivers of the United States," 73rd Cong., 2d sess., H. Doc. 395.

76. U.S. Public Works Administration, *Report of the Mississippi Valley Committee* (Washington, D.C.: USGPO, 1934).

77. U.S. Natural Resources Committee, *Regional Planning. Part VI—The Rio Grande Joint Investigation in the Upper Rio Grand Basin in Colorado, New Mexico, and Texas, 1936–1937* (Washington, D.C.: USGPO, 1938); and U.S. Bureau of Reclamation, *Character and Scope of the Columbia Basin Project Joint Investigations* (Washington, D.C.: USGPO, 1941).

78. Marion Clawson, *New Deal Planning: The National Resources Planning Board* (Baltimore: Johns Hopkins University Press for Resources for the Future, 1981). Cf. also Chapter 6, by Alan Brinkley, which indicates the broader economic and social policy contexts of these resource committees.

79. United States National Resources Committee, Water Resources Committee, *Drainage Basin Problems and Programs* (Washington, D.C.: USGPO, 1936).

80. U.S. National Resources Committee, *Land Classification in the United States* (Washington, D.C.: USGPO, 1941); idem, *State Planning, A Review of Activities and Progress* (Washington, D.C.: USGPO, 1935); idem, *State Planning Programs and Accomplishments* (Washington, D.C.: USGPO, 1937); idem, *The Future of State Planning* (Washington, D.C.: USGPO, 1938); Clifford J. Hynning, *State Conservation of Resources* (Washington, D.C.: USGPO, 1939); and USNRC, "Report on Water Pollution by the Special Advisory Committee on Water Pollution," Washington, D.C., 1935.

81. Some geographers and planners argued against using river basins as a "natural context" for anything but hydrologic science. They emphasized the lack of spatial conformity between watersheds, economic regions, ecological communities, and political boundaries. U.S. National Resources Committee, *Regional Factors in National Planning and Development* (Washington, D.C.: USGPO, 1935).

82. H. S. Person, *Little Waters: A Study of Headwater Streams & Other Little Waters, Their Use and Relations to the Land* (Washington, D.C.: U.S. Rural Electrification Administration, Soil Conservation Service, and Farm Security Administration, 1935 [revised April 1936]). Person was a member of the Mississippi Valley Committee and the National Resources Board's Water Resources Committee before following Cooke to the REA. A more scientific conference organized in response was the Upstream Engineering Conference, *Headwaters Control and Use* (Washington, D.C.: USGPO, 1937).

83. E. C. Buie, *A History of Water Resource Activities of the United States Department of Agriculture* (Washington, D.C.: U.S. Department of Agriculture, Soil Conservation Service, 1979); D. Helms, "Small Watersheds and the USDA: Legacy of the Flood Control Act of 1936," in *The Flood Control Challenge: Past, Present and Future,* ed. H. Rosen and M. Reuss (Chicago: Public Works Historical Society, 1988), pp. 67–88; and D. Helms, *Readings in the History of the Soil Conservation Service,* Economics and Social Sciences Division, NHQ, Historical Notes no. 1 (Washington, D.C.: United States Department of Agriculture, Soil Conservation Service, 1992).

84. Luna B. Leopold and Thomas Maddock, Jr., *The Flood Control Controversy: Big Dams, Little Dams and Land Management* (New York: Ronald Press Company, 1954).

85. Disasters continued to play a role, in some situations, in policy formulation. See, for example, Joseph L. Arnold, *The Evolution of the 1936 Flood Control Act* (Fort Belvoir: Office of History, United States Army Corps of Engineers, 1988).

86. For two views of the Missouri River development program, see John Ferrell, *Big Dam Era: A Legislative and Institutional History of the Pick-Sloan Missouri Basin Program* (Omaha: Missouri River Division, U.S. Army Corps of Engineers, 1993); and Henry C. Hart, *The Dark Missouri* (Madison: University of Wisconsin Press, 1957).

87. Walter Prescott Web, *More Water for Texas* (Austin: University of Texas Press, 1954).

88. United Nations, Department of Economic and Social Affairs, *Integrated River Basin Development,* rev. ed. E.70.II.A.4 (New York: United Nations, 1970 [1958]). See also Gilbert F. White, "A Perspective of River Basin Development," *Journal of Law and Contemporary Problems* 22 (1957): 155–87.

89. Commission on the Reorganization of the Executive Branch of Government [First Hoover Commission], "Report," 81st Cong., 1st sess., H. Doc. 122, pp. 2–4 (1949).

90. See Senate Select Committee "Report no. 2, Reviews of National Water Resources During the Past Fifty Years," *Water Resources Activities in the United States* (Washington, D.C.: USGPO, 1960) for a brief inventory and overview of these commissions. There had also been exposés of unsound federal water development, most notably Arthur Maass, *Muddy Waters: The Army Engineers and the Nation's Rivers* (Cambridge, Mass.: Harvard University Press, 1951).

91. Executive Order no. 10095, January 3, 1950.

92. U.S. President's Water Resources Policy Commission, *A Water Policy for the American People* (Volume 1); and idem, *Ten Rivers in America's Future* (Volume 2) (Washington, D.C.: USGPO, 1950).

93. Senate Select Committee, "report no. 2," p. 37. Interestingly, the report did predict the subsequent decline of large river-basin projects as choice dam sites were taken.

94. Analyzed in Leopold and Maddock, *The Flood Control Controversy.*

95. The results are presented in a highly

influential work: Arthur Maass, *Design of Water Resource Systems* (Cambridge, Mass.: Harvard University Press, 1962).

96. There has been little retrospective analysis of this project, though archives and participants are available, such as K. Alan Snyder, *Register of the Arthur Maass Papers* (Fort Belvoir: Office of History, U.S. Army Corps of Engineers, 1990); and personal communications with Gilbert F. White, 1 April 1996, David Major, 20 January 1996, and Rene Reitsma, 5 April 1996.

97. Rutherford Platt, "Floods and Man: A Geographer's Agenda," in *Geography, Resources and Environment: Volume 2, Themes from the Work of Gilbert F. White,* eds. R. W. Kates and I. Burton (Chicago: University of Chicago Press, 1986), pp. 28–68; and Francis G. Murphy, "Regulating Flood Plain Development," Research paper no. 56 (Chicago: University of Chicago, Department of Geography, 1958). For a compendium of influential papers on floods and other topics by White, see Robert Kates and Ian Burton, *Geography Resources and Environment: Volume I, Selected Writings of Gilbert F. White* (Chicago: University of Chicago Press, 1986).

98. U.S. Congress, Senate Select Committee on National Water Resources, *Water Resources Activities in the United States,* 32 reports (Washington, D.C.: USGPO, 1958–61).

99. The Water Resources Research Act of 1964 funded water resources research institutes in state land-grant universities.

100. Beatrice Holmes, *History of Federal Water Programs and Policies, 1961–1970,* Department of Agriculture, Economics, Statistics, and Cooperatives Service, Misc. Publication no. 1379 (Washington, D.C.: USGPO, 1972); and Jamie W. Moore and Dorothy P. Moore, *The Army Corps of Engineers and the Evolution of Federal Flood Plain Management,* Special Publication 20 (Boulder: Institute of Behavioral Science, University of Colorado, 1989), pp. 55–76.

101. U.S. Water Resources Council, "Principles and Standards for Planning Water and Related Land Resources," *Federal Register* 38:174, pp. 24778–869 (September 10, 1973).

102. National Research Council, *Water and Choice in the Colorado River Basin* (Washington, D.C.: National Academy of Sciences, 1968); and idem, *Alternatives in Water Management* (Washington, D.C.: National Academy of Sciences, 1966).

103. U.S. Water Resources Council, *The Nation's Water Resources: The First National Assessment* (Washington, D.C.: The Council, 1968); and idem, *The Nation's Water Resources: The First National Assessment,* 6 vols. multiple parts (Washington, D.C.: The Council, 1978).

104. National Water Commission, *Water Policies for the Future* (Washington, D.C.: USGPO, 1973), pp. 414–32.

105. John R. Sheaffer and Leonard Stevens, *Future Water* (New York: William Morrow, 1983); Northeastern Illinois Planning Commission (NIPC), *The Water Resource in Northeastern Illinois: Planning Its Use,* prepared by John R. Sheaffer and Arthur J. Zeizel (Chicago: NIPC, 1966).

106. See discussion of this and similar experiments in Anne Whiston Spirn, *The Granite Garden: Urban Nature and Human Design* (New York: Basic Books, 1984), pp. 129–70.

107. David Major and Harry Schwarz, *Large-Scale Regional Water Resources Planning: The North Atlantic Regional Study* (Boston: Kluwer Academic Publishers, 1990), and interview with Frank Gregg, 1995.

108. Henry Caulfield, "Let's Dismantle (Largely but Not Fully) the Federal Water Resource Development Establishment: The Apostasy of a Longstanding Water Development Federalist," in *Water Needs for the Future,* ed. Ved P. Nanda (Boulder: Westview Press, 1977), pp. 171–8.

109. U.S. Water Resources Council, "Economic and Environmental Principles and Guidelines for Water and Related Land Resources Implementation Studies," 48 CFR 10249–10258, March 10, 1983.

110. See, for example, R. F. Reitsma et al., "Construction Kit for Visual Programming of River Basin Models," *Journal of Computing in Civil Engineering* 8 (1994): 378–84; idem, "Experiment with Simulation Models in Water Resources Negotiations," *Journal of Water Resources Planning and Management* 122 (1996): 64–70; and idem, "Geographically Distributed Decision Support: The Tennessee Valley Authority TERRA System," in D. G. Fontane and H. Tuvel, eds., *Water Policy and Management: Solving the Problems* (New York: American Society of Civil Engineers, 1994), pp. 311–14.

111. Other precedents for meso-scale experiments include the Connecticut, Susquehanna, Wabash, Willamette, and Yellowstone River basins. See Ronald R. Boyce, *Regional Development and the Wabash Basin* (Urbana: University of Illinois Press, 1964); and Constance Boris and John V. Krutilla, *Water Rights and Energy Development in the*

Yellowstone River Basin: An Integrated Analysis (Baltimore: Johns Hopkins University Press, 1980).

112. See Howard Rosen and Michael C. Robinson, "Post Audits in Public Works: The Role of History," in *Post-Audits of Environmental Programs and Projects,* ed. C. G. Gunnerson (New York: American Society of Civil Engineers, 1989), pp. 5–16.

113. Joseph L. Arnold, *The Evolution of the 1936 Flood Control Act* (Fort Belvoir: Office of History, United States Army Corps of Engineers, 1988); and Gilbert F. White, "When May a Post-audit Teach Lessons?" in *The Flood Control Challenge: Past, Present and Future* (Washington, D.C.: Public Works Historical Society, 1988).

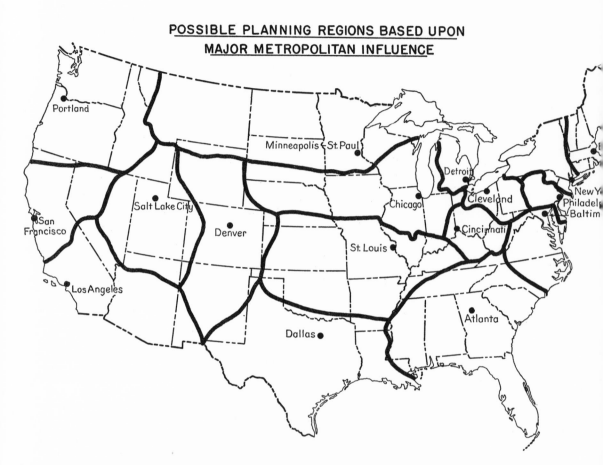

POSSIBLE PLANNING REGIONS BASED UPON
MAJOR METROPOLITAN INFLUENCE

Portland

Minneapolis · St. Paul

Detroit

New York

Cleveland

Philadel

Baltim

Chicago

Salt Lake City

Cincinnati

San Francisco

Denver

St. Louis

Los Angeles

Dallas

Atlanta

Prepared in Office of The National Resources Board

The United Regions of America, as mapped by the National Resources Board in 1935. The board identified 16 metropolitan regions that it believed would be more rational and effective units for national planning than the 48 states. (From National Resources Committee, *Regional Factors in National Planning* [Washington, D.C.: Government Printing Office, 1935])

CHAPTER SIX

The National Resources Planning Board and the Reconstruction of Planning

ALAN BRINKLEY

The idea of planning in modern America—an idea that has enchanted, and frustrated, generations of scholars, intellectuals, and policymakers—has moved along two parallel tracks. One track, the dominant one through most of the twentieth century, includes a range of efforts to plan the nation's physical landscape and its relationship to its natural resources. It has included city planning, regional planning, planning for resource development, and (more recently) planning for the preservation of the environment. It has experienced successes and failures, has seen its power to influence public affairs ebb and flow. But whatever its fortunes, it has long remained an important part of the policy world.

The second track, in many ways more expansive than the first, has consisted of plans for the larger social and economic development of the nation. It has included a range of efforts to impose some kind of central planning on the industrial economy and to create a web of social programs intended to bring order or justice or both to American society and culture. Perhaps because of the boldness and diffuseness of its aims, it has been consistently weaker than city, regional, and resource planning. At times, it has seemed almost to vanish as a significant element of public life.

These two forms of planning have shared a belief in the capacity of purposeful social intelligence to shape a better world. They have shared, too, a belief that trained, enlightened elites, acting through the state, are capable of ordering society in ways not likely to emerge naturally through the workings of the market. But despite their common intellectual roots, they have intersected relatively rarely. City and regional planners and national social and economic planners have tended to sympathize with and support one another, but on the whole they have inhabited separate worlds.

For a moment before and during World War II, however, these dual planning traditions seemed briefly to converge in an agency of the federal government that promised to make the idea of planning a permanent part of the national state for the first time in American history. The success of this agency in articulating a vision of America's future that combined some of the ideas of regional planners with those of national planners suggests the potential for fusion of the two approaches. Its demise reveals the obstacles that continue to obstruct an effective planning mechanism at the national level.

The Founding of the NRPB

The National Resources Planning Board began its life in the shadows of one of the first great New Deal bureaucracies. When Congress created the Public Works Administration (PWA) under the National Industrial Recovery Act in 1933, Harold Ickes, the director of the new agency, created an office to help coordinate its work: the National Planning Board.[1] He did so at the behest of Charles W. Eliot II, the young scion of a distinguished Massachusetts family (and the grandson of a celebrated Harvard president). Eliot came out of a well-established tradition of city and regional planners; a landscape architect by training, he had worked previously as a city planner in Massachusetts and with the National Capital Park and Planning Commission.

The planning board Ickes created in response to Eliot's suggestion had the clear stamp of that background. Its chair, Frederic A. Delano (Franklin Roosevelt's uncle), had directed the National Capital Park and Planning Commission, on which Eliot had served; Eliot was the staff director. In its statement of purpose, the board set for itself the goal of preparing "comprehensive and coordinated plans for regional areas," to help the PWA decide which public works projects to finance.

It considered its mission an enlarged version of the same kind of resources and development planning that Eliot, Delano, and many others had grown accustomed to considering for cities and regions. *The American City,* an urban planning journal, excitedly described the members of the board in 1933 in explicit city-planning terms, as "architects building a habitation for a new social order" engaged in "the most worthwhile and inspiring job in the United States today."[2]

But the new board embodied another, broader planning impulse as well. It embraced an ambitious program of research into "the distribution and trends of population, land uses, industry, housing, and natural resources" and the "social and economic habits, trends, and values involved in development projects and plans." Out of that research would come planning on a genuinely national scale, planning for the structure and performance of the economy and the society as a whole. Charles E. Merriam, who was (along with Delano and the economist Wesley Mitchell) one of the three original "citizen members" of the board, described this second purpose as the creation of "a plan for national planning."

Merriam, in fact, was the most influential figure in the new agency almost from the beginning. An eminent political scientist at the University of Chicago, he had a social scientist's faith in the value of surveys and research. He had been one of the founders of President Hoover's Social Science Research Council, which had prepared a series of reports in the early 1930s on broad social trends. He was accustomed to thinking of planning in national terms. Indeed, he spent his life trying to fit his deep faith in planning into the structure of democratic politics. The new board, he came to believe, could become a mechanism by which planners would have a permanent voice in government, through

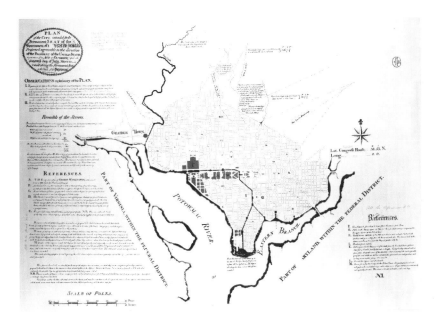

Figure 1 The Grid and the Diagonal. Pierre Charles L'Enfant's Plan for Washington, D.C. (1791), which superimposes diagonal baroque avenues and round-points over a rectangular grid of streets. Source: The Library of Congress, Map Collection.

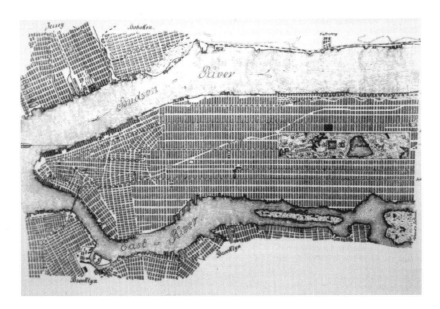

Figure 2 The Grid Triumphant. The Commissioners' Plan of New York City (1811), showing Frederick Law Olmsted's and Calvert Vaux's masterly insertion of Central Park (1858) within the grid. Source: The Library of Congress, Map Collection.

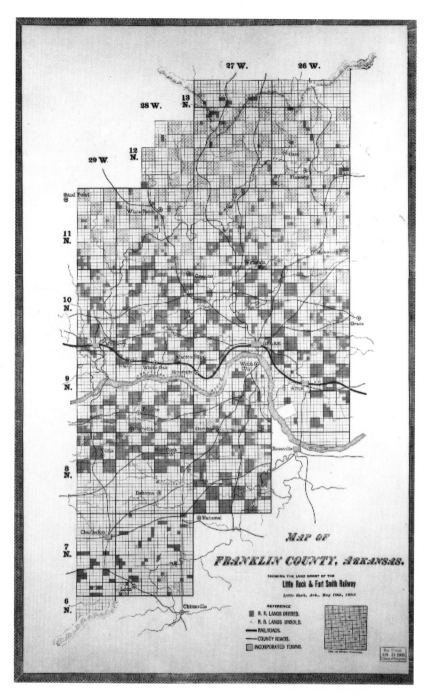

Figure 3 The Grid and Land Speculation. This map of Franklin County, Arkansas (1893) encapsulates a whole system of 19th century rural settlement and land speculation. The railroad opens access to the land and makes it valuable; the survey grid subdivides the land for sale and settlement; and the sale of railroad land grants, shown on the map as the darkened squares, repays the cost of the railroad. Source: Library of Congress, Railroad Maps.

Figure 4 The Grid and the Frontier City. Topeka, Kansas (1869), showing the rural grid as the template for the urban street system. Source: Library of Congress, Panoramic Maps Collection.

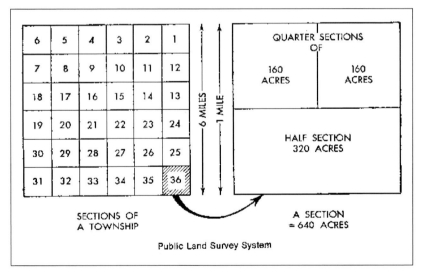

Figure 5 The Grid on the Land. As established by the Land Ordinance of 1785 and the Land Act of 1796, the Public Land Survey System mapped land owned by the federal government for sale in gridded units of a township (6 square miles); a section (1 square mile), half and quarter sections. This system sub-divided a continent. Source: *Encyclopedia of American History* (1976).

Figure 6 Metropolitan Industrialization. Illinois Steel Works, South Chicago, Illinois, 1905. The grand scale of early twentieth-century urban industry made the metropolis the dominant locale of American industry and provided the resources to transform the city. Source: Library of Congress, Detroit Publishing Company Photograph Collection.

Figure 7 Metropolitan Amenities. Lake Shore Drive, Chicago, 1905. The raw waterfront on Lake Michigan is here transformed into a civilized park and parkway. Source: Library of Congress, Detroit Publishing Company Photograph Collection.

Figure 8 Metropolitan Culture. Boston Public Library, Copley Square, built 1887-98. Architects McKim, Mead &White here give the Public Library an appropriately monumental form as an ideal of a civic culture that is solid, symmetrical, harmonious, and classical. Source: Frances Loeb Library, Harvard University Graduate School of Design.

Figure 9 The Metropolitan Experience. Imaginary New York City Street, 1898. This imaginary street scene encapsulates the very real bustle and variety that constituted the urban experience at the turn of the century. Source: Frances Loeb Library, Harvard University Graduate School of Design.

Figure 10 Metropolitan Technics. The Brooklyn Bridge (1883) seen from the Manhattan side, 1901, exemplifies the technical sophistication and grand scale of major metropolitan public works projects. Source: Library of Congress, Detroit Publishing Company Photograph Collection.

Figure 11 Metropolitan Regionalism. Chicago as a metropolitan region focused on its downtown core as depicted in the Burnham and Bennett's Plan of Chicago.
Source: Plan of Chicago (1909).

Figure 12 Metropolitan Complexity and Efficiency. The Chicago River with projected multi-level facilities for river freight, avenues along the river, and river crossings. Source: Plan of Chicago (1909).

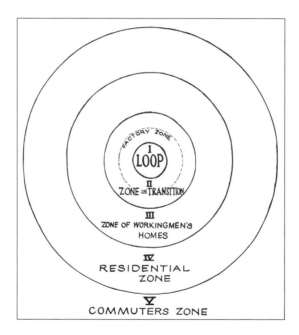

Figure 13 Metropolitan Structure. *The Growth of the City:* "The Chicago School's vision of a centralized metropolis organized around Chicago's downtown hub or *loop*" surrounded by the slum or "zone in transition;" factories and finally zones of increasing residential prosperity and assimilation. Source: Ernest Burgess, *The Growth of the City,* in Park, Burgess, and McKenzie, editors, *The City* (1925).

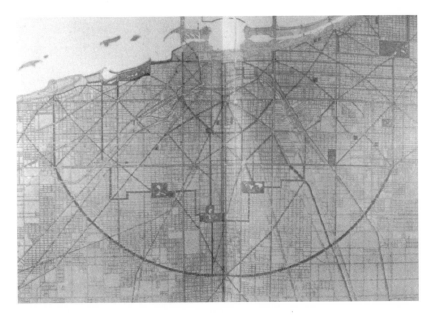

Figure 14 Metropolitan Planning. The synthetic vision of the Plan of Chicago: "A Complete System of Street Circulation and System of Parks and Playgrounds," as the caption to this drawing asserts, "Presenting the City as an Organism In Which All Functions Are Related One to Another." Source: Plan of Chicago (1909)

Figure 15 Metropolitan Civics. The monumental Chicago Civic Center proposed by the Plan of Chicago as the focus of the metropolis with the domed City Hall or "Central Administration Building" shown, as the caption puts it, "as the center of the system of arteries of communication and of the surrounding country." Source: Plan of Chicago (1909).

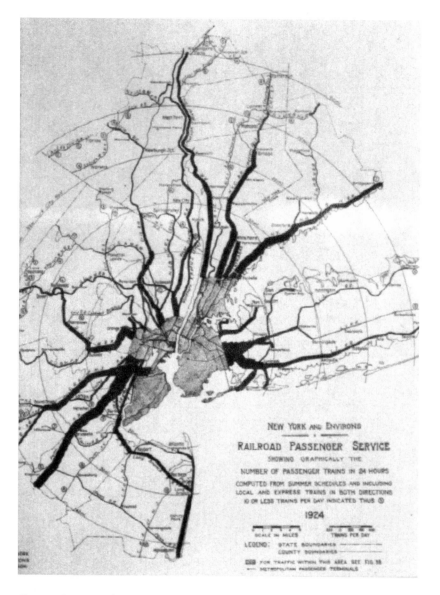

Figure 16 Metropolitan Transportation. The classic hub-and-spoke pattern of rail lines converging on a major urban center and deep-water port, in this case the Port of New York. Source: *Regional Survey of New York and Its Environs, Vol. IV, Transit and Transportation* (1928).

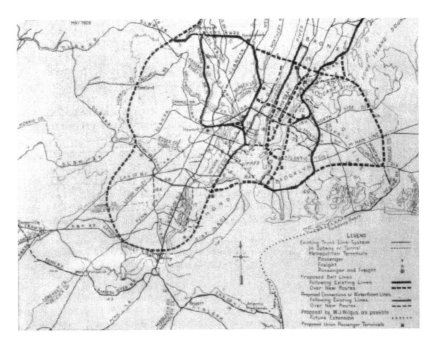

Figure 17 A Metropolitan Transit System. William J. Wilgus's plan for an integrated regional rail system prepared for the *Regional Plan of New York and its Environs* (1929) that would move freight efficiently and people rapidly. Source: *Regional Survey of New York and Its Environs, vol. IV, Transit and Transportation* (1928).

Figure 18 The Regional City. Replacing both the overcrowded city and the sprawling suburb, the regionalist New Town is a compact, human-scaled community set within an unspoiled rural landscape. This drawing shows a 1936 sketch of "Green Brook: A proposed New Deal AGreenbelt Town" for the rural outskirts of Bound Brook, New Jersey. Source: Library of Congress, Farm Security Administration Collection.

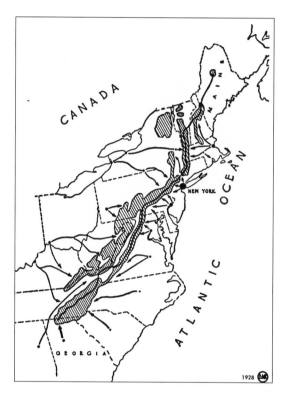

Figure 19 The Regional Wilderness. Benton MacKaye's original diagram for the Appalachian Trail that would put city dwellers back in touch with the mountain ridges that defined the geology and ecology of the Eastern United States. Source: Benton MacKaye, *The New Exploration* (1928).

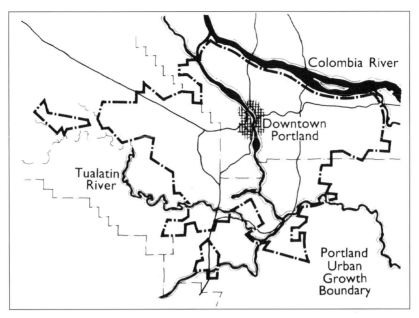

Figure 20 The New Regionalism: Portland, Oregon's Urban Growth Boundary maintains a stable border for the region, promoting clustered development within the boundary and preserving the rural landscape and economy outside it. Source: Peter Calthorpe, *The Next American Metropolis* (1993).

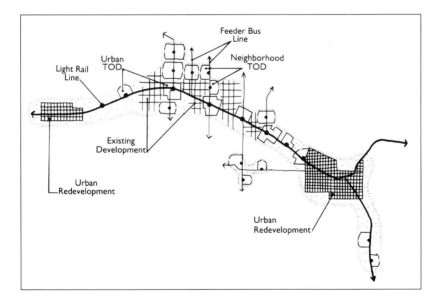

Figure 21 The New Regionalism: "Transit-oriented development" (TOD) as conceived by architect Peter Calthorpe, who rediscovers the basic principles of turn-of-the-century streetcar suburbs, using the light-rail line to organize development and limit sprawl. Source: Peter Calthorpe, *The Next American Metropolis* (1993).

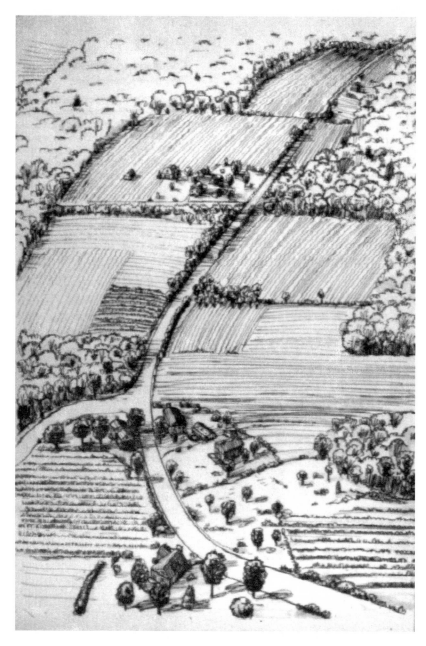

Figure 22 A New Regionalist Triptych, I: "Existing Conditions," the still-unspoiled edge of a metropolitan region. Source: New Jersey State Planning Commission, *Communities of Place: The New Jersey Preliminary State Development and Redevelopment Plan, vol. 1* (1988).

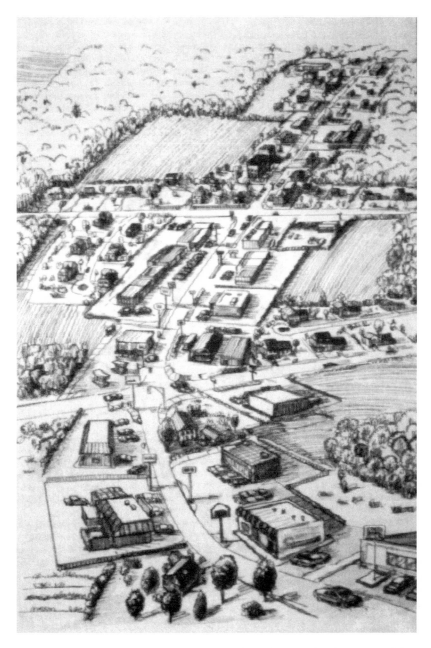

Figure 23 A New Regionalist Triptych, II: "Trend Conditions." The destruction of the landscape as sprawl and strip development overwhelm a rural road. Source: New Jersey State Planning Commission, *Communities of Place: The New Jersey Preliminary State Development and Redevelopment Plan, vol. 1* (1988).

Figure 24 A New Regionalist Triptych, III: "Plan Conditions." The successful application of "smart growth" techniques to cluster growth at the edge and thus combine development with the preservation of a rural landscape. Source: New Jersey State Planning Commission, *Communities of Place: The New Jersey Preliminary State Development and Redevelopment Plan, vol. 1* (1988).

which they could persuade the public—and the political system—to make rational choices about the future.[3]

In its early years, the board devoted most of its energies to "resource planning": crafting proposals for the regulation and development of land, water, forests, and other natural resources. But the broader planning agenda was never far from the surface. "There is need for government economic planning," Merriam wrote in 1935, in a discussion of the agency's early work, "not to replace business planning, but to render services to the general public, and to business itself, which business cannot render. . . . Business cannot protect itself effectively against the business cycle hazard."[4]

In the course of the 1930s, the planning board moved through several incarnations. Each of them helped move it closer to Merriam's vision of an agency committed to broad concepts of research and planning with influence at the highest levels of government. And each of them increased the strains between Merriam and Eliot, whose interest in planning was always more project-oriented. In 1934, the president folded the National Planning Board into a new National Resources Board, an independent agency indirectly responsible to the president; no longer was it just an adjunct of a public-works program. A year later he renamed it the National Resources Committee (NRC), in a largely technical effort to detach it from the National Industrial Recovery Act after the Supreme Court struck that legislation down. And in 1939, as part of a larger reorganization of the executive branch (which Merriam and the NRC had helped initiate), it became the National Resources Planning Board (NRPB)—a formal part of the Executive Office of the President, reporting directly to Roosevelt.[5]

The NRPB was in many respects simply a continuation under a different name of the three planning boards that had preceded it.

Delano was still the chair; Merriam, now vice chair, continued to dominate the substantive work of the agency; Eliot remained the staff director. (George Yantis, an economist from Washington state with a background in natural-resource issues, replaced Wesley Mitchell as the third citizen member; his impact on the board was never great.) But there were important differences. Unlike its predecessors, the NRPB needed direct congressional appropriations to survive; as a result it no longer had the relative protection from partisan politics it had enjoyed in its earlier incarnations. At the same time, the board was accelerating its already significant movement away from choosing sites for dams and public buildings and toward broader questions of industrial production, consumer expenditures, and employment levels—the kinds of questions Merriam had been pressing the board to consider from the beginning.[6]

One indication of this changing focus was the increasing involvement of economist Alvin Hansen in the board's deliberations. Eliot and others wrote him frequently asking advice on economic questions. Hansen used his relationship with the board to promote his own ideas on full employment and fiscal policy. He was the author or co-author of many of its most important reports.[7]

Another indication was the close relationship between the NRPB and the Fiscal and Monetary Advisory Board, which had been created in 1938 (at the urging of Delano and Merriam) to advise the president on "government spending, taxation and monetary activities in such a way as to smooth out so far as possible the upswings and downswings of the business cycle." Its principal members were Delano, Henry Morgenthau (secretary of the treasury), Marriner Eccles (Chairman of the Federal Reserve Board), and Harold Smith (director of the Bureau of the Budget); its "basic purpose," according to the original proposal, was "to develop studies and plans for high living standards." (It, too, frequently consulted with Hansen.)[8]

But the Fiscal and Monetary Advisory Board was an unsatisfactory answer to Merriam's call for a planning body to shape the structure and performance of the economy. It was an informal group, and it met only occasionally. Its work suffered, moreover, from a lack of sympathy for its central task by its highest-ranking member, Morgenthau. The committee issued a few reports promoting increased government spending to spur full employment, and it had a few meetings with the president (who talked with the members mostly about the political obstacles in the way of their proposals). It soon lapsed into obscurity. As the inadequacy of the Fiscal and Monetary Advisory Board became clear, some members of the NRPB grew increasingly interested in taking over its functions.[9]

Discussions of how to achieve full employment had been well underway within the NRC as early as 1938. At a meeting on industrial policy that year, members and staff had agreed that "government policy should include both direct efforts to place more funds in the hands of consumers and direct efforts to influence the nature of production and price policies." Most participants had agreed that both efforts were important. But the question remained (as Thomas Blaisdell put it in 1938) "whether the orientation of intervention should be toward the producer or toward the consumer." Over the next several years, the most influential members of the committee had come to favor the latter.[10]

In June 1940, the newly reorganized NRPB issued one of its first major publications, *The Structure of the American Economy, Part II*. Part I, published in 1939 by the NRC; had described "basic characteristics" of the economy; part II outlined an ambitious agenda for making "full use of resources"

and raising the "general standard of living." It referred in passing to other work of the board (reflected in such publications of 1940 as *Deficiencies in Hydrologic Research, Land Classification in the United States,* or *Housing: The Continuing Problem*) as useful complements to "this broad purpose"—a reference that no doubt annoyed Eliot and others, who still considered such projects the NRPB's primary mission. But the document had little time for the details of public works and regional planning; it attempted, rather, to explain the importance of a firm commitment to the idea of full employment through increased consumption: "The development and adoption of techniques for bringing about and maintaining reasonably full employment of men and machines is not only a major problem, but is today the Nation's most pressing economic problem, relegating all other economic problems to a secondary position so long as it remains unsolved."[11]

The five economists who contributed essays to the "symposium" (as the NRPB called it) were not in full agreement. But all of them emphasized the degree to which the ostensible subject of their publication—the "structure" of the economy—was, in fact, less important than what one called its "operating characteristics." There was nothing wrong, they conceded, in considering structural changes—in challenging excessive economic concentration, for example. But such efforts would always be inadequate to the task of achieving full employment, which had more to do with changing the way consumers and producers alike behaved in their daily lives than in changing the structure of institutions. More important than reforming or regulating production, then, would be policies designed to encourage consumers to spend more and producers to produce and invest more, as well as policies to discourage everyone from excessive, unproductive saving. Over the next two years, the NRPB would elaborate on those ideas and make them the basis of several extraordinary documents.[12]

Plans for an Expanding Economy

American involvement in World War II changed the NRPB's mission substantially. No longer was the board part of the effort to produce economic recovery; war production had ended the Depression quickly and decisively. No longer was it making plans for New Deal public-works programs; most such programs quickly ceased operations as the government shifted resources and energies to war production. Instead, the NRPB began to plan for the world after the war. How could the United States ensure that the Depression would not return once the fighting ended? What policies would guarantee the continuation of full production and full employment in peacetime? The board addressed these questions in most of the dozens of pamphlets and reports it issued in 1942 and 1943.[13]

The NRPB continued during the war to outline public works projects and to insist on their importance, but even more than in 1940, it now portrayed such projects less as vehicles for remaking the environment than as tools for countercyclical government spending. Its mission was to create a "shelf" of potential public undertakings, from which the government could, "at a moment's notice," draw projects "as insurance against industrial collapse and unemployment." The intrinsic value of the projects themselves in terms of older notions of urban or regional planning had become decidedly secondary.[14]

The NRPB's principal mission had become devising policies that would create a high-production, full-employment economy. Its wartime reports called explicitly and re-

peatedly for government programs to maintain a "dynamic expanding economy on the order of 100 to 125 billions in national income," a figure that only a few years earlier would have seemed preposterously high. "We must plan for full employment," members of the board wrote in a 1942 article explaining their proposals. "We shall plan to balance our national production-consumption budget at a high level with full employment, not at a low level with mass unemployment."[15]

Of the many things the NRPB published in its ten-year life, nothing had as great an impact as *Security, Work, and Relief Policies,* a prosaically titled report released in March 1943 (after Roosevelt, skittish about its political impact, had held it for over a year). The report attempted to lay out a coherent plan for a postwar social order. To many liberals, the document became something close to a programmatic bible; to conservatives, it was evidence of the dangerously statist designs of the NRPB and the New Deal as a whole. It simultaneously ensured the NRPB's centrality to liberal thinking, and guaranteed its demise.[16]

Security, Work, and Relief Policies outlined a program of "social security" of such breadth and ambition that it was widely dubbed the "American Beveridge Plan," a counterpart to the contemporaneous report in Great Britain (the product of a planning commission chaired by Sir William Beveridge), which outlined the framework of what became the postwar British welfare state. There was, in fact, some modest communication between the two planning efforts (and considerable mutual admiration and congratulation when their reports appeared). Beveridge himself made a well-publicized visit to the United States in May 1943, during which he met with most of the members of the NRPB and many other American full-employment enthusiasts.[17] But the NRPB report was fundamentally a product of the emerging American liberalism of the war years—particularly in its ebullience. The Beveridge plan tempered its proposals with a sense of economic and fiscal limits; not until 1945, in a second report, did Beveridge become a real convert to the full-employment idea. The NRPB's proposals were wholly rooted in the concept of full-employment planning from the start, and they reflected the newly strengthened confidence of American liberals in the potentially limitless resources of the American economy.[18]

For most of its more than 600 pages, *Security, Work, and Relief Policies* laid out a broad and ambitious plan to make "adequate provision for those who have no means of livelihood or only inadequate means"—a plan that accepted, but greatly expanded on, the outlines of the social insurance and social provision systems the New Deal had created in the 1930s. Even sixty years later, its proposals are striking for their sweep—and for the generosity of spirit (so seldom evident in discussions of public assistance in America) that surrounded them. The report spoke of the "millions of cases where deep anxiety, haunting fear of want, acute suffering and distress blight and sear the lives of men and women, and children, too. Most of the drifting souls are those on whom the door of hope has been closed either by nature's equipment or by the unfortunate circumstances of unkind social experience." And it rejected outright the idea that a "complete system of social security" would destroy incentives and encourage people to avoid work: "We must and do assume that the bulk of mankind who are able to work are willing to work, and that they will strive for something more than a doghouse subsistence on a dole."[19]

The report called for extensive federal work programs, administered through a new Federal Work Agency (modeled vaguely on the New Deal's Works Progress Administra-

tion), to provide jobs for "all who are able and willing to work." It outlined a greatly expanded program of social insurance for the unemployed, the disabled, and the elderly, based on the Social Security system the New Deal had created in 1935. It called for significant increases in "general public assistance" for those whom the work programs and the social insurance failed to help—again an extension of programs the Roosevelt administration had launched in the 1930s. And it endorsed generous new programs of public services in health and education, even if it provided few details about how such programs would work. Together, its proposals embraced much of what became the liberal social agenda for decades after World War II.[20]

But the NRPB plan reflected more than social generosity. It was a product, too, of a firm commitment to the goal of a "high-income, full-employment" economy and of a belief that programs of public aid would help create it. "Full economic activity and full employment are our first need," the authors of the report claimed. A full-employment economy would create the resources necessary to support the ambitious NRPB agenda. ("Financial problems need be no hindrance," they confidently declared.) But an extensive program of public aid would also help create and maintain full employment. "All the various elements in the public-aid programs have a common quality in that they put money into the hands of individuals in the low-income brackets," the authors explained. The experience of the 1930s made clear that such programs "substantially contributed to the consumers' expenditures of these years," and it was equally clear that such programs, if "coordinated with the broader economic and monetary policies of government," would contribute to maintaining high levels of employment consumption. For example, "if an expansionist [fiscal] program is desired, the unemployment compensation systems, suitably amended, offer a speedy and almost automatically operating mechanism for distributing funds to those who will spend them."[21]

The report did not wholly ignore other, more traditional approaches to economic and social reform. Improved labor relations, it said, could play an important role in creating the new economic order. So could effective use of antitrust laws. But what was striking about the discussion of these issues was, first, the exceptionally small role they played in the fabric of the report as a whole; and second, the modest, even tentative character of the NRPB's embrace of them. The report talked of the need for "statesmanlike union leaders and managers" to refashion labor relations to serve the demands of the new full-employment, high-consumption economy; building that economy, it suggested, would do more than any reform of the workplace in improving the lives of workers and capitalists alike. It conceded the value of using the antitrust laws in situations where "monopolistic power restricts employment opportunity and the expansion of national income." But it said nothing of the value of the laws in increasing opportunities for producers, and it noted the ways in which antimonopoly efforts could actually harm the prospects for full employment, could "become destructive of labor standards and produce poverty and wage slavery instead of full employment and high incomes." Structural reform of the economy was clearly secondary: "Full economic activity and full employment are our first need," the authors stated bluntly. And the best vehicles for achieving those goals were fiscal and monetary policies—and the systems of public aid the NRPB was proposing.[22]

Security, Work, and Relief Policies was a product of the Committee on Long-Range Work and Relief Policies, which the NRPB had created late in 1939. William Haber, a liberal economist at the University of Michigan, chaired the committee; Eveline Burns, an economist from Columbia University who had once studied at the London School of Economics (where Beveridge taught), was the director of research. They did their work in relative isolation from the other parts of the NRPB. And in transmitting their report to the president, Delano was careful to indicate that its proposals—welcome as they may have been—did not embrace all the board's aims. It had a "strategic place" in the NRPB's plans for the economy, but it was not the whole of those plans. As if to make that clear, the board published (almost simultaneously with the security report) Hansen's *After the War—Full Employment*, a bold summary of his already well-known views on the importance of using fiscal policy and, if necessary, deficit spending to raise consumption, stimulate economic growth, and achieve full employment. "It is the responsibility of Government to do its part to insure a sustained demand," he wrote. "We know from past experience that private enterprise has done this for limited periods only." Programs of social insurance and public aid would be useful complements to this goal, but they were clearly secondary to it.[23]

The Demise of the NRPB

The simultaneous release in early 1943 of *Security, Work, and Relief Policies* and *After the War—Full Employment* made the NRPB, for the first time in its history, the focus of considerable public attention. The breadth of the reports, and perhaps equally important, the boldness of their language, excited many full-employment liberals and alarmed many of their more conservative critics. In the short term, at least, the critics prevailed.

But that was not for lack of effort among those who admired the reports and embraced their recommendations. The American Federation of Labor, the Congress of Industrial Organizations (CIO), the National Farmers Union, and others gave immediate, fulsome endorsements. Liberals in Congress called them, as one put it, "nothing short of magnificent." The *Security* report, a *Nation* editorial proclaimed, "has given the American people a dramatic reply to question: 'What are we fighting for?' . . . It epitomizes, as no other statement has done, the contrast between the way of life of free men and the way of life in the dictatorships. It is a natural supplement to the Atlantic Charter, but it is . . . far more inspiring to the average man." A special issue of the *New Republic* called the NRPB plan "a revolutionary answer to the needs of a revolutionary age," and a potentially powerful weapon in "demoralizing the enemy," "heartening our friends," and "winning the war." There were complaints about the vagueness of the reports and about their neglect of some issues (most notably the failure to endorse a comprehensive national health care system). But there was widespread enthusiasm for the NRPB's larger aims.[24]

But if the reaction to the reports revealed the outlines of a new liberal agenda for the postwar era, it also revealed the strength of the obstacles to that agenda. Within days of their release, the reports were engulfed in a storm of conservative attacks—in the press, in Congress, and among New Deal critics everywhere. The NRPB proposals were "nonsense," Senator Robert Taft claimed; if the United States were to embrace them, "we will be ruined long before the war is over." A Republican congressman from Ohio called the reports a plan for "nothing less than the absorption by the state of all economic functions and the complete demolition of free enterprise." A Georgia Democrat complained of more practical problems: the NRPB program, he said, "looks like a $50,000,000-a-year proposition. I don't see where we could get that kind of money." Others dismissed the reports as nothing more than the president's

"opening gun for a fourth term." The *New York Times* compared them, preposterously, to "Bismarck's state insurance systems, which laid the foundation for the German welfare state that ended in naziism." The head of the American Chamber of Commerce denounced them as a "totalitarian scheme." Such extravagant rhetoric was not uncommon among the NRPB's foes.[25]

Within weeks, critics were consigning the NRPB reports to the dustheap. It was the "flop of the year," *Time* magazine crowed. "Seldom has so important a report disappeared from public debate so quickly," *Newsweek* claimed.[26] The NRPB itself was already a target of conservatives in Congress even before the release of the reports. In the first half of 1943 the abuse escalated dramatically, and hostile members began working to destroy the agency altogether. Members of the board flailed about, arguing first for the importance of their work, then considering a mass resignation—in hopes of saving the agency itself, even if not their own jobs. The president enlisted Donald Nelson, Chairman of the War Production Board, and others to make the case for the NRPB's importance to the war effort, and he wrote privately to several crucial senators and representatives urging the survival of the board. But as on other issues not directly related to the war, he made no strenuous efforts. In the end, Congress authorized no funds for the board in the budget it approved in June. Ten years after its creation in the first heady days of the New Deal, and little more than ten weeks after the release of its two most important reports, the National Resources Planning Board was dead.[27]

In part, the NRPB fell victim to the frenzied efforts by conservatives in Congress—Democrats and Republicans alike—to dismantle as much of the New Deal as possible under the mantle of a wartime economy. In part, too, it was a casualty of its own political failings: the passivity of the aging Delano; the ineffectiveness and unpopularity of Eliot; the fuzzy, abstract character of many of the NRPB's proposals; the insistence of Merriam that the board should (as a critical observer at the time wrote) "merely offer the elder statesmen a kind of counsel and shun the tough battles that would be necessary to perform the essential functions of planning."[28] But the most important reason for the board's demise were two larger fears.

One was a concern, primarily within Congress, about the growing power of the executive branch at the expense of the legislature. Merriam's association with the executive reorganization bills of 1938 and 1939, which had crystallized that concern, made the NRPB particularly vulnerable to such criticisms. But so did its reports, which did indeed propose a series of measures that would have centralized considerable new authority in the White House. The NRPB's call in some earlier documents for the creation of new regional-planning authorities, what some called "Seven Little TVAs," was particularly alarming to members of Congress who saw it, correctly, as an effort to circumvent local political leaders and reduce opportunities for patronage. But even more disturbing was the very existence of the board, which served as a symbol to many members of Congress of their increasing irrelevance to basic policymaking. Legislators had been aware for years of the contempt with which many New Deal liberals viewed Congress and their thirst for vehicles of governance independent of legislative authority. That had been one of the reasons for the intense hostility to the president's executive reorganization plans. Now the war was producing a plethora of new agencies, many exercising unprecedented power, over which Congress had scant control. The NRPB, many members feared, would give the executive new tools to erode the authority of Congress further in peacetime.[29]

The other, greater fear extended well beyond Congress. It was the broad popular fear of bureaucracy and state power—a central element of American political culture throughout the nation's history. Even at the height of its popularity, the New Deal had aroused considerable misgivings on this score. Many Americans had liked the benefits the Roosevelt administration was providing them and, indeed, quickly came to think of them as basic rights (or "entitlements"). But many of those same people remained uneasy about expanding the power of the state, even as they called for the expansion of services that benefited them. Farmers, for example, were indefatigable in fighting for federal controls and subsidies to stabilize their economy, and yet the leading farm organization (the American Farm Bureau Federation) and many, perhaps most, of the farmers it represented were continually critical of the New Deal for extending the reach of bureaucracy and eroding individual freedom. The unprecedented government intrusiveness into everyday life during the war greatly inflamed such concerns. And the NRPB, with its expansive vision of planning and social provision and its blithe indifference to the political climate in which it was operating, became a natural target of those in Congress attempting to exploit and inflame those popular resentments.[30]

Whatever the reasons, the demise of the NRPB struck many liberals as a heavy blow to their hopes for full employment after the war. For the government to play its proper role in creating and sustaining economic growth in peacetime, it would need (in Bruce Bliven's words) a new "postwar layer" of administrative capacity. The NRPB did not have to be that layer; but the hostility to bureaucracy that the battle against it had revealed made clear how difficult it would be to create it elsewhere. "It is one of the besetting evils of an irresponsible press and a partisan-minded Congress," Bliven complained, "that all advances in the administrative arts must be made under the hail of the most virulent abuse." Even more important, others argued, was the impact of the NRPB's institutional collapse on the proposals it had made in its last reports—its efforts to tie the concept of full employment to a broad expansion of social insurance and social welfare. Congress was, it seemed, killing more than the messenger: it was killing the message itself. "And so without fanfare or lament," the editors of *Commonweal* concluded at the close of the battle, "dies the present hope of an intelligent, self-disciplined America based on an economy of abundance."[31]

The NRPB reports captured more fully than any other documents of their time the contours of what would soon become the heart of postwar American liberalism. They outlined an active role for the federal government in stabilizing the economy and planning for economic growth—a role related to, but also significantly different from, earlier Progressive and New Deal notions of economic policy. The reports did not advocate substantial state intrusions into the affairs of capitalist institutions. They called instead for the federal government to make aggressive use of its fiscal powers—spending and taxation—to prevent future depressions and ensure full employment. They outlined, too, an expansive role for the state in protecting American citizens from the vicissitudes of the industrial economy. They proposed a substantial expansion of the social insurance and social welfare mechanisms the New Deal had created in the 1930s.

Both those ideas survived to shape the liberal agenda for at least a generation after World War II. But another part of the NRPB vision did not survive nearly so successfully. The 1943 reports—indeed virtually the entire wartime record of the board—represented an effort to link the commitment to full employment with the commitment to a generous welfare state. The two efforts would complement one another: economic growth would make a generous welfare state possible; a generous welfare state would help stimulate economic growth. But even before the end of the war, it became clear that the linkage between the two ideas was a frail one. By early 1946, the two commitments had begun to move along quite separate paths—with important consequences for both. Two pieces of legislation—the Serviceman's Readjustment Act of 1944 (better known as the G.I. Bill) and the Employment Act of 1946—revealed both the extent of and the substantial obstacles to the new liberal agenda.

The G.I. Bill

Although Congress passed the G.I. Bill well after the NRPB had ceased to exist, the planning board was centrally involved in shaping it. In July 1942, the NRPB convened a Conference on Post-War Readjustment of Civilian and Military Personnel in response to a vague directive from the president, who was already feeling pressures from within his administration to begin planning for demobilization.[32] A year later, it presented Roosevelt with a report outlining a series of measures to ensure that returning veterans had access to jobs, education, and—when necessary—financial assistance. Similar recommendations were coming simultaneously from a War Department committee the president had established late in 1943 to study the same questions, and from the American Legion, the nation's most powerful veterans' organization, which offered proposals of its own.[33]

Roosevelt endorsed the idea of special benefits for veterans in a fireside chat in July 1943, following the advice of several members of the administration that making provisions for returning soldiers "is not only the right thing to advocate, but it also has enormous appeal." "Among many other things," the president told his radio audience, "we are, today, laying plans for the return to civilian life of our gallant men and women in the armed services. They must not be demobilized into an environment of inflation and unemployment, to a place on the bread line or on a corner selling apples. We must, this time, have plans ready—instead of waiting to do a hasty, inefficient, and ill-considered job at the last moment." In October, he sent a formal message to Congress (although no specific legislation) proposing a broad range of veterans' benefits.[34]

Early in 1944, the American Legion presented Congress with a single, comprehensive veterans' bill that became, after modest amendments, the Servicemen's Readjustment Act of 1944. (It was the Legion that coined the title "G.I. Bill of Rights.") Roosevelt allowed the Legion's bill to supersede his own, less well-developed proposals. It passed through Congress with relative ease. The Senate approved it unanimously, after a perfunctory, forty-minute debate. In the House, deliberation took longer—in part because the Mississippi segregationist John Rankin insisted on amendments diluting some of the education and unemployment benefits, which, he claimed, would encourage "50,000 Negroes" from his state to "remain unemployed for at least a year." In the end, however, the House unanimously passed a bill only slightly less generous than the Senate's version. The president signed it in June.[35]

The G.I. Bill provided veterans with many of the benefits the NRPB, and other liberals, had hoped to provide all Americans after the war. It gave them enhanced unemployment and pension benefits, significant help in finding new jobs, generous economic assistance for all levels of education, and low-interest loans for buying homes, farms, and businesses. Later legislation added a comprehensive national health care system centered in an expanded network of Veterans Administration hospitals. It won the support of liberals because they hoped it would become the basis of a broader network of social programs aimed at the entire population. But it won the support of conservatives precisely because it was limited to veterans and because many elements of it would, presumably, wither away as the veterans re-established themselves in society, aged, and ceased to need public assistance.[36]

Like the elaborate pension system established for Civil War veterans in the 1860s, the G.I. Bill could generate broad support only because it aimed its benefits at a specific population, whom most Americans (and thus most politicians) believed had a special claim to public generosity. And like the Civil War pensions, the G.I. Bill failed to become what some liberals had hoped it would be: the opening wedge in the battle for more universal social-assistance programs. It placed administration of its programs within the Veterans Administration, which reduced the chances of their expanding to serve a larger constituency. It reinforced invidious distinctions between "deserving" and "undeserving" citizens and sustained the popular belief that public generosity should be reserved for those with a special claim to public attention. (Men in uniform, the president argued, had "been compelled to make greater economic sacrifice and every other kind of sacrifice than the rest of us.") The framers and promoters of the G.I. Bill did nothing to link it to the larger vision of a full-employment economy sustained by an elaborate welfare and social insurance system.[37]

Setting the Stage for Postwar Planning

At almost the same time that Congress was embracing the G.I. Bill, it was agonizing over another legacy of the NRPB: legislation that would have committed the federal government to ensure full employment in the postwar era. The Full-Employment Bill, as it was widely known, emerged from many sources. The president's 1944 "State of the Union" address, plainly influenced by the NRPB reports, seemed to endorse a full-employment strategy with its call for an "economic bill of rights"—among them "the right to a useful and remunerative job" and "the right to earn enough to provide adequate food and clothing and recreation." Political rights alone, Roosevelt said, were "inadequate to assure us equality in the pursuit of happiness." Individual freedom could not exist "without economic security and independence." The speech emboldened liberals in Washington and elsewhere to press for legislative action.[38]

Progressives in the labor movement (most notably the CIO's new Political Action Committee) lobbied vigorously and effectively for full-employment policies as part of any reconversion legislation.[39] Agrarian progressives, mobilized through the National Farmers Union, were at the center of the battle as well. Keynesian economists, who saw the transition to peace as their best opportunity to entrench their ideas in public policy, promoted guarantees of full employment as the best vehicles for ensuring postwar prosperity. Alvin Hansen, in particular, produced a flurry of articles in popular magazines in support of the bill.[40] The Union for Democratic Action (later reconstituted as Americans for Democratic Action) was a liberal organization founded in 1941 to unite antifascist groups in support of the war. By 1944, it was fighting for a progressive postwar agenda, and it made the battle for full-employment legislation its principal commitment. Liberal members of Congress, convinced that the public expected protection from a peacetime economic slump, considered full employment a politically attractive cause.[41]

By the time James E. Murray of Montana introduced the Full-Employment Bill to the Senate on January 22, 1945, many of its provisions had already bounced around the legislative process for months. Much of the early initiative came from the National Farmers Union (NFU), which represented mostly small farmers and which embraced a much more progressive economic agenda than its more powerful counterpart (closely linked to commercial farmers), the American Farm Bureau Federation. The NFU's energetic president, James Patton, helped persuade the sponsors of a bill expanding postwar unemployment benefits (the Kilgore Reconversion Bill) to attach an amendment mandating the federal government to guarantee full employment after the war through aggressive fiscal policies. Both the amendment and the bill died in the Senate. But the concept of government-guaranteed full employment generated considerable popular support, both in opinion polls and—indirectly, at least—in the 1944 presidential election. Despite the forced removal from the Democratic ticket of Henry Wallace, one of the leading proponents of full employment, most liberals interpreted Roosevelt's substantial fourth-term victory as an endorsement of the economic bill of rights he had presented earlier in the year.[42]

The bill Murray introduced early in 1945 included a defensive endorsement of "free competitive enterprise," one of a number of largely cosmetic changes to the NFU proposal designed to make the law politically palatable to moderates. But the heart of the bill was the statement that "all Americans able to work and seeking work have the right to a useful and remunerative job. . . . [I]t is essential that continuing full employment be maintained in the United States." The legislation called for the president to prepare each year a National Production and Employment Budget. It would estimate the "number of jobs needed during the ensuing fiscal year or years to assure continuing full employment," and it would calculate "the estimated dollar value of the gross national product . . . required to provide such a number of jobs." If it seemed likely that private-sector spending and investment would not create the necessary jobs, the government would be expected to step in with a program of loans, expenditures, and public investments to bring the economy up to full-employment levels.[43]

The Full-Employment Bill did not specify what kind of spending the government should use to create the necessary jobs. Nor did it contain any explicit call for expanded programs of social insurance and public assistance, as the NRPB reports had done. But the full-employment liberals who had embraced the NRPB ideas in 1943 considered the bill a vehicle capable of sustaining their highest hopes. It was the "most imaginative [proposal] yet made for postwar America," and "a beginning of a far-reaching program for progressives"; it would "create the conditions for greater enjoyment of traditional as well as new liberties"; it would "provide a framework for an economy at once sufficiently planned to maintain full employment and sufficiently flexible to give ample scope to . . . free enterprise"; it would be "a firm assurance that unemployment never again will be permitted to become a national problem"; it was "probably our only alternative to an otherwise irresistible drift toward real socialism."[44]

Perhaps most important, the bill made possible the linkage that had been so important to the NRPB reports: the connection between a generous program of social insurance and an aggressive program of government spending to ensure economic growth. It called for the kind of sustained economic planning that the NRPB had hoped to provide, and it gave the government tools with which to convert its plans into policy. The bill did nothing, its supporters conceded, to attack the "problems of monopoly." But it would solve through other means the prob-

lems monopoly helped cause without creating a "creeping bureaucracy all of us want to avoid."[45]

Supporters of the Full-Employment Bill—among them the new president, Harry S Truman—considered it an effective "middle way" between a heavily statist solution to the problems of the economy and a return to the kind of unmediated private enterprise that had produced the Great Depression. But opponents in Congress and elsewhere had no such faith. Although virtually no one openly challenged the goal of reducing unemployment, there was considerable debate about the desirability (and the meaning) of the idea of full employment. Even the most fervent champions of full employment had never proposed a literal "right to a job" for every individual; they envisioned, rather, an economy that would produce enough jobs to employ everyone, conceding that there would nevertheless always be some people—whether because of geography, training, or preference—who would be unable to find work. But opponents in Congress and elsewhere seized on the phrase and warned demagogically of a vast state bureaucracy that would compel everyone to work and determine what jobs they could have. Ultimately, the bill's sponsors agreed to a new phrase—"maximum employment"—which they hoped would seem less threatening.[46]

Some of the conservative opposition, however, was based on a more rational calculation of the likely economic effects of the bill. Employers (mobilized through the Chambers of Commerce and the National Association of Manufacturers) and commercial farmers (mobilized through the American Farm Bureau Federation) feared that a high-employment economy would raise their labor costs and make it difficult to find workers for menial jobs such as seasonal farm work. Fiscal conservatives recoiled at the idea of using deficit spending as a normal tool of economic planning and sought to remove from the bill any suggestion that government spending would be the preferred route to economic growth. Skeptical economists called attention to the difficulty of preparing accurate economic forecasts, as the Murray bill required; that the debate on the bill occurred at the same time that widespread predictions of a postwar depression were proving inaccurate only increased the skepticism. Most of all, perhaps, conservative members of Congress of both parties, who had spent a decade chafing against what they considered a dangerous concentration of power in the executive branch (and who had killed the NRPB in 1943 to express their unhappiness with that trend), saw the Full-Employment Bill as another vehicle for inflating the president's power at the expense of their own.[47]

In the end, the strength of conservatives in Congress was too much for the uneasy coalition of liberals who were supporting the Full-Employment Bill. Having lost 50 seats in the House in 1942 (reducing their majority to 10), Democrats gained only 22 in the 1944 elections. They lost a seat in the Senate. The coalition of Republicans and conservative Southern Democrats continued to dominate Congress, and that coalition, although not powerful enough to kill the bill altogether, voted a series of amendments that substantially, some believed fundamentally, changed its character. By the time both houses of Congress finally approved a bill in early 1946—after considering it intermittently for more than a year—it was no longer the *"Full-*Employment Bill"; it was the Employment Act of 1946. Gone was the ringing mandate for the president and Congress to ensure "full employment" (a term that appeared nowhere in the final version of the law). In its place was a statement of purpose so filled with qualifications and ambiguities that it was almost meaningless:

The Congress hereby declares that it is the continuing policy and responsibility of the Federal Government to use all practicable means consistent with its needs and obligations and other essential considerations of national policy with the assistance and cooperation of industry, agriculture, labor, and State and local governments, to coordinate and utilize all its plans, functions, and resources for the purpose of creating and maintaining, in a manner calculated to foster and promote free competitive enterprise and the general welfare, conditions under which there will be afforded useful employment, for those able, willing, and seeking to work, and to promote maximum employment, production, and purchasing power.

The law created a Council of Economic Advisers, to be located in the White House and appointed by the president, "to formulate and recommend national economic policy to promote employment, production, and purchasing power under free competitive enterprise." Nothing in the law required either the president or Congress to respond to the council's recommendations in any particular way.[48]

Reaction to the Employment Act among its original supporters was mixed. Some were relieved to have salvaged anything from the brutal legislative process, and they comforted themselves with the thought that, as Eccles put it, "Congress has gone a long way . . . in recognizing that the Government has definite economic responsibilities and in stating as a mandate the objectives toward which public policy and action should be directed. This is a tremendous step." The Council of Economic Advisers, Eccles and other believed, could, if staffed with progressives and supported by the president, become a potent force within the federal bureaucracy for a full-employment agenda.[49] But others saw in the "badly watered down" bill of 1946 a symbol of liberal impotence. Having adjusted their goals to an increasingly conservative, antistatist climate, having taken care to avoid politically explosive efforts to regulate corporate power and attack monopoly, liberals had been unable to salvage more than a few rhetorical gestures even from their revised and, they believed, modest agenda.[50] Both evaluations contained elements of truth.

The fight for the Full-Employment Bill, and its ambiguous conclusion, was in one sense an ending. It was the last great legislative battle of the Roosevelt presidency (even though most of it occurred after Roosevelt's death), and as such, it was, in effect, the last great battle for the New Deal. It was also the climactic battle to establish some form of social and economic planning at the heart of the federal government, and the bill's effective demise was a significant defeat for planners as well. But it was also a beginning. For it revealed much of what in early 1946 had already become the postwar agenda of most American liberals. It revealed, too, the many obstacles that agenda would encounter over the next quarter century. Its supporters did not say so, and perhaps were not even aware of it, but in struggling to win passage of the bill, and in compromising on a pale but still recognizable version of their real hopes, they were sketching the outlines of the postwar liberal world.

Notes

1. In a 1933 speech about the National Planning Board, Ickes expressed the hope that "long after the necessity for stimulating industry and creating new buying power by a comprehensive system of public works shall be a thing of the past, national planning will go on as a permanent Government institution." See "City Planning Merges into National Planning," *The American City,* November 1933, p. 65.

2. "City Planning Merges into National Planning," p. 65; National Planning Board, *Final Re-*

port, *1933–1934* (Washington: U.S. Government Printing Office [USGPO], 1934), p. 1. On the NRPB, see Alan Brinkley, *The End of Reform: New Deal Liberalism in Recession and War* (New York: Knopf, 1995); Philip W. Warken, *A History of the National Resources Planning Board, 1933–1943* (New York: Garland Publishing, 1979), p. 47; Frederic Delano, "Statement for National Planning Conference," May 1939, Delano MSS 24 Frederic A. Delano Papers, Franklin D. Roosevelt Library, Hyde Park, New York; Patrick D. Reagan, "The Architects of Modern American National Planning" (Ph.D. diss., Ohio State University, 1982), pp. 39–67.

3. Barry D. Karl, *Charles E. Merriam and the Study of Politics* (Chicago: University of Chicago Press, 1974), pp. 255–7; Charles E. Merriam, "The National Resources Planning Board," *Public Administration Review* 1 (Winter 1941), 116–21; Merriam, "The National Resources Planning Board: A Chapter in American Planning Experience," *American Political Science Review* 38 (December 1944), 1075–88.

4. Charles E. Merriam, "Planning Agencies in America," *American Political Science Review* 29 (April 1935), 202–7.

5. George T. Renner, "NRC—The National Planning Agency," *Social Forces,* December 1935, pp. 301–2; Warken, *History of the National Resources Planning Board,* pp. 55–105; David Cushman Coyle, "The American National Planning Board," *Political Quarterly* 16 (July/September 1945), 246–7.

6. Frederic A. Delano, "New National Resources Planning Board," *Planning and Civic Comment* 5 (July/September 1939), 1; John D. Millett, *The Process and Organization of Government Planning* (New York: Columbia University Press, 1947), pp. 85–93, 145–6; Warken, *History of the National Resources Planning Board,* pp. 108–9.

7. Delano to FDR, December 31, 1940, OF 1092, FDR Library (FDRL), Hyde Park, N.Y.; Charles W. Eliot II to Alvin Hansen, March 8, 1939, Hansen MSS 3.10 Alvin Henry Hansen Papers, Harvard University Archives, Pusey Library, Harvard University, Cambridge, Mass.; Minutes of Industrial Committee meeting, January 13, 1939, Means MSS 7, Gardner Means Papers, FDRL.

8. *Washington Post,* November 19, 1938; "A Fiscal and Monetary Advisory Board," August 10, 1938, Eccles MSS 38–7 Marriner S. Eccles Papers, Marriott Library, University of Utah, Salt Lake

City; Morgenthau to Harold D. Smith, June 23, 1939, Fiscal and Monetary Advisory Board, Records of Daniel W. Bell (Bell records), Bureau of the Budget, Record Group (RG) 51, Series 38.3, National Archives and Records Administration (NARA), Washington, D.C.

9. Fiscal and Monetary Advisory Board statement, May 25, 1939; Ruml to Daniel W. Bell, November 2, 1938; and Minutes of Conference with the President, December 19, 1938, all in Bell records, NARA; Harold Smith diary, May 12, 1939, Smith MSS 1 Harold S. Smith Papers, FDRL; Millett, *Process and Organization of Government Planning*, pp. 142–3.

10. Corwin Edwards, Summary of NRC Meeting on Industrial Policy, June 5, 1938, Interior Archives, RG 48, Box 10 ("Cohen"), NARA; Thomas Blaisdell to Thomas Eliot, July 9, 1938, ibid.

11. National Resources Planning Board, *The Structure of the American Economy: Part II. Toward Full Use of Resources* (Washington, D.C.: US-GPO, 1940), pp. 1–2, 6; National Resources Committee, *The Structure of the American Economy: Part I. Basic Characteristics* (Washington, D.C.: US-GPO, 1939). The three other NRPB reports mentioned here were all published by the USGPO in 1940. For a summary of the NRPB's work in 1940, see Frederic A. Delano to FDR, November 12, 1940, OF 1092, FDRL.

12. NRPB, *The Structure of the American Economy: Part II*, pp. 3–4, 10, 16–9, 26, 33–4, 45. Implicit and on occasion explicit in this discussion was a rejection of part I of *The Structure of the American Economy* for its unreflective preoccupation with older, structural ideas of reform and its lack of attention to newer, compensatory approaches. The writers of part II referred diplomatically to the first document as a useful reference work. Harold Smith, describing an NRPB meeting in Charlottesville in the fall of 1939 to discuss part I, referred to part I as "a very tedious performance." Smith diary, September 17–20, 1939, Smith MSS 1. See also Delano to FDR, December 31, 1940, OF 1092, FDRL.

13. Frederic C. Delano et al., "National Resources Planning Board," *Free World,* November 1942, pp. 175–8; Delano to FDR, March 14, 1941, and "Proposed Messages to Congress on Post War Security," October 1, 1941, both in OF 1092, FDRL; Millett, *Process and Organization of Government Planning*, pp. 118–9, 142.

14. Delano to Eccles, June 16, 1939, Eccles MSS 6-1; Delano to FDR, January 30, 1941, March 14, 1941, OF 1092, FDRL; "Plan for the Future,"

Time, August 25, 1941, p. 18; George Soule, "The Bogey of Excess Capacity," *New Republic,* April 7, 1941, p. 460.

15. NRPB, "Full Employment Now and Tomorrow: An Approach to Post-Defense Planning," July 1941, OF 1092, FDRL; NRPB, "The NRPB in Wartime," *Frontiers of Democracy* 8 (February 15, 1942), 143. See also memorandum to Stephen Early (telephone summaries), February 4, 1943, OF 1092 (5), FDRL; L. B. Parker to Rep. Harry Sheppard, March 11, 1943, OF 4351 (2), FDRL; Bruce Bliven, Max Lerner, and George Soule, "Charter for America," *New Republic,* April 19, 1943, p. 528; J. Raymond Walsh, "Action for Postwar Planning," *Antioch Review* 3 (1943), 153–61; Frederic Delano et al. to FDR, August 24, 1943, OF 1092, FDRL; NRPB, "Post-War Plan and Program," February 1943, Senatorial File 43, Harry S Truman Library (HSTL), Independence, Mo.

16. The NRPB presented the report to the president a few days before Pearl Harbor, and Delano remained reluctant to push for its release for many months after America entered the war. Only late in 1942 did he and other NRPB members begin gently prodding the president to send the report to Congress; he finally did so in March 1943, in part because the release of the Beveridge report in Britain a few months before had increased the pressure on him to act. Keith W. Olson, "The American Beveridge Plan," *Mid-America* 68 (1983), 90–2; Marion Clawson, *New Deal Planning: The National Resources Planning Board* (Baltimore: Johns Hopkins University Press, 1981), pp. 136–43; Warken, *History of the National Resources Planning Board,* pp. 215–6, 224–6.

17. *New York Times,* January 20, 1943; Mordecai Ezekiel, "Full Employment—Beveridge Model," *Nation,* March 3, 1945, p. 253; "A New Bill of Rights," *Nation,* March 20, 1943, p. 401; Alvin Hansen, "Beveridge," *New Republic,* February 19, 1945, p. 251–2; Richard L. Strout, "The Beveridge Report," *New Republic,* December 14, 1942, p. 785; Memorandum, Political and Economic Planning (PEP) Committee, June 4, 1942, CAB.87—80, Public Records Office (PRO), Kew, London; William Beveridge, memorandum to PEP Committee, "The Scale of Social Insurance Benefits and Allied Services," January 16, 1942, CAB.87—80, PRO, 79; British Press Service, "American Survey," December 4, 1942, and Office of War Information, "U.S. Newspaper Comment on Beveridge Report," December 27, 1942, both in Beveridge MSS XI, William H. Beveridge Papers, British Li-

brary of Political and Economic Science, London School of Economics 32.

18. Eveline Burns, "Comparison of the NRPB Report with the Beveridge Report," December 26, 1942, PIN.8—167, PRO; Marriner Eccles to FDR, December 17, 1942, Eccles MSS 5-11; Louis Bean to Milo Perkins, December 21, 1942, Bean MSS 34, Louis H. Bean Papers, FDRL; G. E. Millard to T. Daish, February 18, 1943, and Dash to Millard, February 27, 1943, PIN.8—167, PRO; Edwin E. Witte, "American Post-War Social Security Proposals," *American Economic Review* 33 (December 1943), 830; Alvin Hansen to Beveridge, July 3, 1943, Beveridge MSS XI, 31.

19. National Resources Planning Board, *Security, Work, and Relief Policies* (Washington, D.C.: USGPO, 1942), p. 1.

20. Ibid., pp. 1, 546–9.

21. Ibid., pp. 325–338, 341, 495, 502.

22. Ibid., pp. 2–3.

23. Alvin H. Hansen, *After the War—Full Employment* (Washington, D.C.: USGPO, 1942); Olson, "The American Beveridge Plan," pp. 87–8; Clawson, *New Deal Planning,* pp. 137, 182–3; Warken, *History of the National Resources Planning Board,* p. 216.

24. "A New Bill of Rights," *Nation,* March 20, 1943, p. 401; Bruce Bliven, Max Lerner, and George Soule, "Charter for America," *New Republic,* April 19, 1943, pp. 523–4; I. F. Stone, "Planning and Politics," *Nation,* March 20, 1943, p. 405; "America's Beveridge Plan," *Nation,* December 19, 1942, pp. 669–70; "A Beveridge Plan for America," *New Republic,* December 21, 1942, pp. 810–1; "Cradle to the Grave," *Christian Century,* March 24, 1943, pp. 350–1; Max Lerner, "Problems of a Postwar World," *Proceedings of the National Council of Social Work, 1943* (New York: National Council of Social Work, 1943), p. 404; "The NRPB in War-Time," *Frontiers of Democracy,* February 15, 1942, p. 143; L. B. Parker to Harry Sheppard, March 11, 1943, OF 4351 (2), FDRL; "Postwar Portent" and "Promised Land," *Newsweek,* March 22, 1943, pp. 27, 30–34; "Cradle to Grave," *Time,* March 22, 1943; Ernest K. Lindley, "How the Postwar Reports Came to Be," *Time,* March 22, 1943; Edwin E. Witte, "American Post-War Social Security Proposals," *American Economic Review* 33 (December 1943), 825–38; Richard Chapman, *Contours of Public Policy 1939–1945* (New York: Garland Publishing, 1981), pp. 255–7.

25. *New York Times,* March 14, 1943; Ralph Robey, "Postwar Bureaucratic Utopia: Part II,"

Newsweek, May 10, 1943, p. 62; "New Deal Plans Industry Council," *Business Week,* March 20, 1943, pp. 16–7; Chapman, *Contours of Public Policy,* pp. 252–4; Warken, *History of the National Resources Planning Board,* p. 227.

26. "Cradle to Grave," p. 13; "Promised Land," pp. 30–1; Witte, "American Post-War Social Security Proposals," p. 832; John C. Cort, "Design for Planning," *Commonweal,* July 2, 1943, p. 270.

27. Wayne Coy, report on conference with the president, April 9, 1943, and Harold Smith, memorandum on conference with the president, June 3, 1943, both in Smith MSS 3; "To Save the Planning Board," *Business Week,* April 17, 1943, p. 8; Warken, *History of the National Resources Planning Board,* pp. 240–5; Clawson, *New Deal Planning,* pp. 238–341; Reagan, "Architects of Modern American National Planning," pp. 370–5.

28. Memorandum accompanying NRPB reports, from British Embassy, Washington, to Economic Reconstruction Department, Foreign Office, London, March 27, 1943, FO371—35367, PRO (hereafter cited as British Embassy memorandum).

29. Frederic A. Delano to FDR, November 4, 1942, OF 1092, FDRL; George Soule, "Planning Wins," *New Republic,* March 8, 1943, p. 309; British Embassy memorandum.

30. Helen Fuller, "Look Who's Planning," *New Republic,* July 26, 1943, p. 104; Donald Worster, *Dust Bowl: The Southern Plains in the 1930s* (New York: Oxford University Press, 1979), pp. 149–63; Grant McConnell, *The Decline of Agrarian Democracy* (Berkeley: University of California Press, 1953), pp. 97–126.

31. Bruce Bliven, "Charter for America," *New Republic,* April 19, 1943, pp. 541–2; "Canning the Planners," *Commonweal,* June 11, 1943, p. 192; Charles E. Merriam, "The National Resources Planning Board: A Chapter in American Planning Experience," *American Political Science Review* 38 (December 1944), 1083–4.

32. Roosevelt issued a statement when he signed a bill reducing the draft age in 1942 in which he called for "planning in advance" to "enable the young men whose education has been interrupted to resume their schooling and afford equal opportunity for the training and education of other young men of ability after their service in the armed forces has come to an end." "Statement on Signing the Bill Reducing the Draft Age," November 13, 1942, in *The Public Papers and Addresses of Franklin D. Roosevelt,* ed. Samuel I. Rosenman, 4 vols. (New York: Harper and Brothers, 1938–1950), 1942 vol-

ume, p. 470. Nine earlier volumes of the *Public Papers* were published at various times by several publishers under several editors.

33. Warken, *History of the National Resources Planning Board,* pp. 193–8; Davis R.B. Ross, *Preparing for Ulysses: Politics and Veterans during World War II* (New York: Columbia University Press, 1969), pp. 52–64; NRPB, "The Demobilization of Men (Program for Training, Counselling, Rehabilitating, Readjustment and Placement)," June 1942, and "Preliminary Readjustment of Civilian and Military Personnel," March 1943, both in RG 187, NARA.

34. "Fireside Chat on the Progress of the War and Plans for Peace," July 28, 1943, *Public Papers and Addresses,* 1943 volume, p. 333; Oscar Cox to Harry Hopkins, January 2, 1943, February 4, 1943, June 5, 1943, Hopkins MSS 329, Harry L. Hopkins Papers, FDRL; Draft of Address on Veterans' Readjustment, June 9, 1943, Hopkins MSS 329; Ross, *Preparing for Ulysses,* p. 64.

35. Richard Polenberg, *War and Society: The United States, 1941–1945* (Philadelphia: J. B. Lippincott, 1972), pp. 76–96; Roland Young, *Congressional Politics during the Second World War* (New York: Columbia University Press, 1956), pp. 213–7.

36. Ross, *Preparing for Ulysses,* pp. 102–21; Chapman, *Contours of Public Policy,* p. 260.

37. *Public Papers and Addresses,* 1942 volume, p. 470; Edwin Amenta and Theda Skocpol, "Redefining the New Deal: World War II and the Development of Social Provision in the United States," in *The Politics of Social Policy in the United States,* ed. Margaret Weir, Ann Shola Orloff, and Theda Skocpol (Princeton: Princeton University Press, 1988), pp. 82, 108; Ross, *Preparing for Ulysses,* p. 57. For discussion of the Civil War pensions system, see Theda Skocpol, *Protecting Soldiers and Mothers: The Political Origins of Social Policy in the United States* (Cambridge, Mass.: Harvard University Press, 1992), ch. 2.

38. "Message on the State of the Union," January 11, 1944, *Public Papers and Addresses,* 1944–1945 volume, pp. 41–2.

39. Stephen K. Bailey, *Congress Makes a Law: The Story Behind the Employment Act of 1946* (New York: Columbia University Press, 1950), pp. 92–6; Nelson W. Polsby, *Political Innovation in America: The Politics of Policy Initiation* (New Haven: Yale University Press, 1984), pp. 104–6; Steve Fraser, *Labor Will Rule: Sidney Hillman and the Rise of American Labor* (New York: Free Press, 1991), pp. 507–9.

40. Alvin H. Hansen, "Planning Full Employment," *Nation,* October 21, 1944, p. 492; Hansen, "Beveridge on Full Employment," *New Republic,* February 19, 1945, pp. 250–4; Hansen, "For a Stable Market Economy," *Atlantic,* August 1945, pp. 78–81; Hansen, "Wages and Prices: The Basic Issue," *New York Times Magazine,* January 6, 1946, pp. 9, 36; Hansen, "Social Planning for Tomorrow," in Hansen et al., *The United States after War* (Ithaca: Cornell University Press, 1945), pp. 15–34.

41. Bailey, *Congress Makes a Law,* pp. 81–92; John D. Millett, *Process and Organization of Government Planning,* pp. 129–30; Steven Gillon, *Politics and Vision: The ADA and American Liberalism, 1947–1985* (New York: Oxford University Press, 1987), pp. 9–19, 64.

42. "For Full Employment," *Nation,* December 23, 1944, p. 761; James G. Patton and James Loeb, Jr., "The Challenge to Progressives," *New Republic,* February 5, 1945, pp. 187–206. Michael W. Flamm, "The National Farmers Union and the Evolution of Agrarian Liberalism" (M.A. essay, Columbia University, 1992), pp. 55–71, describes the NFU role in the battle for the full-employment bill.

43. Alvin H. Hansen, "Suggested Revision of Full Employment Bill," July 28, 1945, Hansen MSS 3.10.

44. James G. Patton and James Loeb, Jr., "The Challenge to Progressives," *New Republic,* February 5, 1945, p. 188; Heinz Eulau, Mordecai Ezekiel, Alvin H. Hansen, James Loeb, Jr., and George Soule, "The Road to Freedom—Full Employment," *New Republic,* September 24, 1945, p. 414; "For Full Employment," pp. 761–2; Stanley Lebergott, "Shall We *Guarantee* Full Employment?" *Harper's,* February 1945, p. 200.

45. I. F. Stone, "Capitalism and Full Employment," *Nation,* September 1, 1945, pp. 198–9; Patton and Loeb, "Challenge to Progressives," p. 188; Flamm, "The National Farmers Union," p. 68.

46. Herbert Stein, *The Fiscal Revolution in America* (Chicago: University of Chicago Press, 1969), pp. 200–1.

47. Margaret Weir, "The Federal Government and Unemployment: The Frustration of Policy Innovation from the New Deal to the Great Society," in *The Politics of Social Policy in the United States,* ed. Weir, Orloff, and Skocpol, p. 160; Robert M. Collins, *The Business Response to Keynes, 1929–1964* (New York: Columbia University Press, 1981), pp. 102–9; Bailey, *Congress Makes a Law,* pp. 129–49; Stein, *Fiscal Revolution,* pp. 202–4.

48. Bailey, *Congress Makes a Law,* pp. 228–32; John Morton Blum, *V Was for Victory: Politics and American Culture during World War II* (New York: Harcourt, Brace, Jovanovich, 1976), pp. 329–32.

49. Eccles to Truman, March 15, 1946, Eccles to Harold Smith, February 15, 1946, both in Eccles MSS 5-12; Robert Lekachman, *The Age of Keynes* (New York: Random House, 1966), pp. 174–5; Millett, *Process and Organization of Government Planning,* pp. 27–8, 103–4, 133.

50. Chester Bowles, "Speech to New York Chapter of Americans for Democratic Action," November 12, 1947, Lerner MSS 1, May Lerner Papers, Yale University Library, New Haven, Conn.; "Is It Full Employment?" *New Republic,* February 18, 1946, p. 240; Guy Greer, "More Work Than Workers," *Social Forces,* October 1946, pp. 49–51; Lekachman, *The Age of Keynes,* pp. 170–1; Theodore Rosenof, *Patterns of Political Economy in America: The Failure to Develop a Democratic Left Synthesis, 1933–1950* (New York: Garland Publishing, 1983), pp. 205–6.

"Brownfields" in Camden, New Jersey, 1991. The divisons in the 1970s between environmentalists and urban activists not only doomed national land use planning legislation, these divisions forestalled a coalition that might have combated sprawl in the suburbs and helped to rebuild devastated urban neighborhoods like this one. (Photograph by Robert Fishman)

CHAPTER SEVEN

Planning, Environmentalism, and Urban Poverty

The Political Failure of National Land-Use Planning Legislation, 1970–1975

MARGARET WEIR

I n the two decades after World War II, Democrats and Republicans alike embraced economic growth as the cornerstone of federal domestic policymaking. The postwar growth machine tempered the political divisions that had stalled the New Deal: conflicting regional interests and opponents from organized labor and management could all agree on the desirability of growth. But the political success of the growth strategy rested on its sharply limited scope: the federal government did not impinge on the prerogatives of state and local governments by attempting to direct the pattern or tempo of growth.

By the 1960s, two new concerns challenged this federal hands-off approach to growth: the first was declining cities, the second was the environment. Deteriorating urban cores, increasingly populated by poor minorities, together with "white flight" to the suburbs, renewed interest in the metropolitan tradition, lending the older vision of planning and coordination new purpose and urgency. At the same time, voices from the emerging environmental movement lamented the negative consequences of growth, drawing national attention to air and water pollution and to the destruction of natural beauty by development. Together, these concerns posed anew the question of whether the federal government should step in to guide growth, and if so, how? What tools did it have or could it develop to address these new concerns?

This chapter examines an effort in the first half of the 1970s to create new governmental capacities to shape growth patterns through land-use planning. Because such powers were constitutionally lodged in the states and because the federal government had limited capacity to engage in physical planning, planning advocates in the 1970s sought to use federal power to build new capacities in the states. First introduced in 1970 by Senator Henry Jackson (D-Wash.), the National Land-Use Planning Act relied on federal incentives and sanctions to encourage the states to manage land-use planning. Focused on procedure rather than substance, the act aimed to create a new forum for planning in which states would oversee a more deliberate consideration of competing environmental and developmental objectives within a broader spatial and temporal framework than was characteristic of local land-use decisions. The bill did not guarantee any particular outcome; it was essentially an institution-building measure. After five years of congressional consideration, Jackson abandoned the effort in 1975.

This chapter considers why the land-use planning act remained simply an elite-backed proposal, failing to attract strong support from potential allies among urban advocates and environmentalists but engendering energetic opposition from pro-development interests. It argues that this configuration of disinterest and opposition stemmed from a politics of federalism in which each cluster of interests sought to institutionalize powers at the level of government where it believed it could most easily and effectively exercise influence. Urban and environmental interests both focused on the federal government, although in separate spheres: urban advocates sought guaranteed federal subsidies, whereas environmentalists pursued federal regulation. Development interests, particularly those from the South and the West, who would become especially significant in Congress, preferred the existing practice of local control over land use. Neither set of interests was eager to build a new arena in the states, where their power was less certain. Thus, the state capacity–building approach of the bill,

in which new planning procedures would help balance objectives and compromise interests, held little appeal and found few fervent supporters outside the elite network of lawyers and planners who initially devised it.

The story of land-use planning in the 1970s highlights the enduring effects that weak state governments and sharply limited federal planning capacities have had on American politics, not least by channeling the strategies of new social interests toward some kinds of capacity-building and not others, and toward some kinds of alliances and not others. Political scientist Stephen Skowronek has called nineteenth-century American government a state of "courts and parties," and his account of the Progressive Era recounted the limited success of efforts to build federal administrative capacities.[1] The paths taken by environmental and urban movements in the 1960s and 1970s reflected the enduring attraction of these well-worn routes of legal action and party patronage.

The story of the land-use act has broader implications than simply a piece of failed legislation because it reveals much about the development of urban and environmental interests and about the relationship between them. The availability of separate federal channels of assistance helped shape the organizational form these groups took and in so doing reinforced narrow and "pure" interpretations of their interests. Both the organizational forms and the ideas animating urban and environmental interests discouraged them from finding common ground. Although these approaches succeeded in the short term, they produced narrowly focused urban and environmental policies, with limited effectiveness and fragile political support.

In the 1980s and '90s, conservatives reduced urban subsidies and sought to roll back environmental regulation. Yet their case against "big government" missed the point. Federal subsidies and regulatory strategies reflected long-standing governmental weakness: the inability of the states and the federal government to shape the broad patterns of development and growth in ways that weighed competing concerns in an effort to discern the public interest.

Federalism and the Problem of Land-Use Planning

Problems of suburban sprawl, urban decline, and environmental pollution in the late 1960s revived interest in land-use planning. Lawyers and policymakers concerned with land-use issues converged on a critique of the system of local control put into place during the Progressive Era. Proposing that the federal government provide incentives and sanctions to induce the states to plan, both groups acknowledged that the states were the appropriate constitutional location for such planning but expressed doubt about whether states would undertake such action of their own accord.

The "Growth Machine" and the Limits of the Progressive Land-Use Planning System

The federal government emerged from the political and economic upheaval created by the Great Depression and World War II with unprecedented financial resources and considerable new powers to influence national life. With the passage of the Employment Act of 1946, the federal government assumed responsibility for monitoring national economic conditions, and the American public now looked to the federal government to ensure economic well-being. Accompanying these new expectations were a range of new federal expenditures, devoted first and foremost to the national defense—a rubric that came to encompass a vast range of infrastructural and social expenditures—but also including a variety of social expenditures unconnected to defense. Each of these developments pointed in the same direction: henceforth, the federal government would be the steward of national economic growth.

But the political compromise that underlay the New Deal coalition circumscribed federal capacities in distinct ways. As Alan Brinkley shows in chapter six of this volume, political struggles over the National Resources Planning Board, the Full-Employment Bill, and the development of Keynesian economic tools made the federal government responsible for growth but stripped it of the ability to engage in planning of either the economic or the physical variety.[2] Postwar federal initiatives to promote economic growth and national prosperity, accordingly, proceeded with little deliberate evaluation of their physical and spatial consequences. Instead, spending programs reflected the logic of congressional logrolling, which tended to spread money across congressional districts. Major national spending programs, such as the Interstate Highway Act, were inaugurated with little consideration for the spatial consequences. The federal role was to promote growth, using its new financial capabilities to underwrite infrastructural development and ease postwar housing needs. Physical planning was the province of states and localities.

The flaw in this single-minded pursuit of growth was that the states, in fact, engaged in little planning. During the Progressive Era, states had ceded a variety of powers, including that of land-use planning, to their localities. Progressive social and political reform was first and foremost municipal reform. But if localities were to be freed from corruption and supplied with new tools of governance, they needed to become more independent of their states. Many reformers traced municipal corruption to the alliances and maneuvering of state political factions. Among the reforms they championed were home-rule charters designed to limit the ability of state politicians to interfere in local issues for their own political ends. To promote orderly urban development, Progressive reformers not only urged states to delegate their land-use planning authority to localities but drew up model statutes to guide them. As secretary of commerce in the 1920s, Herbert Hoover oversaw the development of two model statutes. Through the Standard State Zoning Enabling Act and the Standard City Planning Enabling Act, the states would empower their localities to plan, zone, and subdivide land. State legislatures across the country quickly adopted the zoning statute and, to a lesser extent, the city-planning provisions.[3]

The delegation of land-use powers to local governments provoked little opposition and initially contributed to orderly urban development. But as early as the 1930s, urban planners noted the limits of this system. In its 1937 report entitled *Our Cities,* the National Resources Committee (a precursor to the National Resources Planning Board) recommended changes to the Standard City Planning Enabling Act that would create regional- and city-planning agencies with the power to determine land use in the unincorporated areas on the city's periphery. The report contended that "the greatest obstacle to the full emergence of a metropolitan community is the great number of conflicting and overlapping political and administrative units into which the area is divided." It noted that in 1930, there were 272 separate incorporated places in the New York–Northeastern New Jersey metropolitan area, 135 in the Pittsburgh area, and 115 in the Chicago area.[4]

Postwar federal growth policies greatly exacerbated such metropolitan fragmentation because the system of local land-use control provided no overarching authority to assess the broader spatial impact of development. As postwar suburban development took off, metropolitan fragmentation increased expo-nentially.[5] Although the regulations governing federal initiatives in housing and highway building had no specific consideration of spatial issues, they were in fact profoundly anti-urban, favoring new development over rehabilitation of older areas. They were also discriminatory, denying assistance to racially heterogeneous areas.[6] The pattern of suburban sprawl and unchecked development also depleted farmland, encroached on areas of natural beauty, and transformed landscapes.

By the 1960s, mounting evidence showed the negative consequences of relying on a system of local land-use planning in an era of rapid development.[7] Critics pointed to four types of problems. First, local planning authorities typically failed to consider how their decisions would affect adjacent jurisdictions. Second, local planners had little incentive and few tools for addressing problems that crossed local boundaries, such as traffic congestion and pollution. Third, economic competition encouraged localities to engage in fiscal zoning in order to attract the most favorable kinds of development and residents. It also encouraged the obverse: exclusionary zoning to discourage development or residents that would have an unfavorable effect on the tax base. Finally, in many states, and in rural areas in particular, there was little interest or experience in using the local land-use planning tools, such as zoning, that did exist.[8]

During the 1950s and 1960s, as criticism by elite networks of professional planners, urban advocates, and land-use lawyers mounted, states took few steps to reclaim their land-use planning powers from localities. The failure of states to take action stemmed from political factors as well as administrative incapacities. Most state legislatures were dominated by rural interests, which enjoyed a lock on state legislative power thanks to the gross malapportionment of legislative districts. To preserve rural power, some states had not redrawn legislative districts in over fifty years.

Not surprisingly, state legislatures had little interest in urban problems and rural-urban antagonism was a persistent theme in many state politics. With weak governors and little in the way of professional administrative capacity, state politics were imbued with cronyism, patronage, and particularism. Increasingly, state governments had become irrelevant to domestic policymaking.

By the late 1960s, however, it was possible to envision stronger states. In response to the Supreme Court's decisions in *Baker v. Carr* (1962) and *Reynolds v. Sims* (1964) declaring "one person, one vote," states had begun to reapportion their legislatures, giving metropolitan areas a voice equal to that of rural areas for the first time. Moreover, state administrative capacities were growing, in part, because the federal government had relied on the states to implement a range of New Deal and Great Society programs. These changes—combined with growing disillusion about the federal government's ability to address urban problems—prompted a rethinking of the role that states might play in the federal system and in the area of land-use planning in particular.

Arguments for Planning

The earliest efforts to impose some order on postwar metropolitan development used federal incentives to promote regional cooperation. Section 701 of the Housing Act of 1954 promoted metropolitan planning by providing grants for small cities and metropolitan areas to draw up development plans. By the late 1960s, the Department of Housing and Urban Development (HUD) was dispensing $50 million annually to metropolitan, state, and local governments for such planning. Metropolitan planning was strengthened in 1966, when the act establishing the Model Cities program also called for regional agencies to review applications for a wide variety

of federal programs with a regional impact, such as transportation. This so-called A-95 process spurred the development of regional councils of government (COGs), charged with reviewing applications. But the councils had no authority and their review was only advisory. Moreover, because their main membership was local elected officials, the COGs had trouble articulating alternatives that went beyond the localism of their members' views.[9]

In the late 1960s and early 1970s, planning proponents came at the issue from a new direction. A remarkable range of influential public and quasi-public reports condemned the Progressive system of local land-use planning obsolete. These reports reflected the growing consensus of a professional elite about the need for states to take a more assertive role in the organization of localities and in the course of local development. Initially impelled by concern about urban problems and metropolitan development, by the 1970s they also became attentive to environmental issues, such as open space and agricultural land preservation.[10]

One of the first and most comprehensive of these reports was *Building the American City,* issued in 1968 by the National Commission on Urban Problems. The commission was created by a presidential request to Congress in 1965, and approved in the Housing and Urban Development Act of that year. Chaired by Senator Paul Douglas (D-Ill.), the commission was charged with examining "building codes, housing codes, zoning, local and federal tax policies and development standards" with the aim of providing knowledge that would "be useful in dealing with slums, urban growth, sprawl and blight, and to ensure decent and durable housing."[11] Reform of existing land-use planning practices was central to the commission's recommendations. Rather than strip localities of these functions, however, the commission recommended altering local government structure and finance arrangements so that localities could exercise their powers more effectively. The aim was to create localities of a size and economic mix that would provide a strong private economic base and to equip them with the means for using that base for broad public purposes. In this recommendation, the commission joined a chorus of voices criticizing metropolitan political fragmentation and the irrationality of creating many small jurisdictions.[12]

Although the commission continued to view local governments as the proper place for most land-use planning, it called on state governments to take a much more vigorous role in shaping local government and setting the terms for local planning. Most important was the state's responsibility for reforming local government structure. The commission urged states to facilitate annexation, set higher standards for municipal incorporation, reduce limitations on local taxing and borrowing, and decrease local dependency on the property tax. States would also take the lead in promoting regional planning where local governments were too small. In addition, the commission stressed the need for state leadership to ensure that adequate low- and moderate-income housing was available throughout the metropolitan area. Toward this end it urged that state planning and zoning enabling acts be amended to include provision of adequate sites for housing for persons of all income levels.[13] The federal government's role in this new system was to provide financial incentives for the states to oversee planning and to ease local finance through revenue sharing. The Douglas Commission's recommendations thus envisioned a substantially different federalism, at the center of which were reinvigorated states.

Similar concerns lay behind a proposed new "Model Land Development Code" in the early 1970s. With a grant from the Ford Foundation, the American Bar Foundation's research arm, the American Law Institute, re-examined land-use laws with an eye to addressing problems of racial discrimination and urban poverty.[14] The institute circulated several tentative drafts of the code before the final version was published in 1974. The code called on states to override local land-use decisions in areas that the states deemed of statewide concern due to natural-resource considerations or the existence of key developments, such as highway intersections. In addition, the code called on the states to formulate rules related to developments with impact beyond localities, such as airports.[15]

A research report commissioned by President Nixon's Council on Environmental Quality, *The Quiet Revolution in Land Use Control,* published in 1972, suggested that hopes for a greater state role in land-use planning were increasingly plausible. Surveying the development of state activity in land-use planning, the report maintained that "a quiet revolution" was underway in which the system of local land-use planning was being overthrown as states began to reassert their authority over land-use planning. Reflecting the growing interest in environmental issues, the report placed a strong emphasis on planning as a means for protecting the environment as well as for addressing urban problems. Included in the study were analyses of nine innovative state programs, including the extensive state land-use controls put into place in Hawaii in order to protect agricultural land; controls on development in Vermont; the areawide coordination powers of the Metropolitan Council in Minneapolis–St. Paul; and the "anti-snob" zoning ordinance in Massachusetts, designed to ensure adequate low- and moderate-income housing throughout the state.

The report applauded these state initiatives, noting that state activity and experimentation were the best way to accommodate the need for national variation in land-use planning. But the report took a more narrow focus than the Douglas Commission. It did not call for major reform of local government structure and had little to say about the effects of intergovernmental finance on land-use practices. The report did, however, note that many of the states were engaged in regulation aimed at limiting or prohibiting development, instead of planning. It expressed concern that states also develop planning processes that would better permit balancing among conflicting goals, such as those of development versus conservation.[16]

This same concern about the need to create processes to balance growth and conservation objectives was evident in the 1973 report of the Task Force on Land Use and Urban Growth, entitled *The Use of Land*. This private task force, funded by the Rockefeller Brothers Fund, drew its executive director, William K. Reilly, from the Council on Environmental Quality and reported to a presidentially created Citizens' Advisory Committee on Environmental Quality. Its report reflected the increasingly common view that improved land-use planning could help achieve goals related to environmental preservation as well as to urban development and social problems. Similar to earlier reports, it called for states to take a greater role in land-use planning in order to "correct the limited view and property tax preoccupations of local governments."[17] It noted that federal efforts to promote areawide planning through the A-95 process, which created metropolitan COGs, had failed to promote meaningful regional planning. Because the COGs and other regional bodies formed in the 1960s were largely advisory agencies, they remained, in the report's words, "agencies with more responsibility than authority."[18] It argued that, given their authority to tax, regulate, and condemn land, the states were the proper level of government from

which to promote a regional approach to metropolitan development and preservation of open space.

Thus, in five years, a strong and well-publicized elite consensus had emerged around the need for land-use planning. Such planning would address the two great social concerns that preoccupied Americans in the late 1960s and early 1970s: environmentalism and urban decay. Relying on newly activated state capacities, it would take some of the burden off Washington in both areas. Building state planning capacities would allow for more variation in development patterns across the country and would provide a more effective way to balance competing demands for development and preservation than would local planning or federal regulation.

Designing the National Land-Use Planning Act

Many of the ideas in these reports found their way into the various versions of the National Land-Use Planning Act considered in Congress between 1970 and 1975. Senator Henry Jackson was the initial champion and major congressional proponent of the bills. Long allied with conservation forces in his native Washington, Jackson had been a proponent of federal dams and development in the Northwest as well. He generally supported multiple-use approaches to public lands, seeking to strike a balance between development and conservation objectives.[19]

Although Jackson's 1970 bill was never reported out of the Senate Interior Committee, the White House drew up and championed subsequent versions of the legislation. In 1972, the Senate Interior Committee approved a bill that embodied a compromise between Jackson and the administration. This bill passed the full Senate in 1972 and again in 1973. The going was considerably rougher in the House. Initially, the unfriendly chair of the House Interior and Insular Affairs Committee, Wayne Aspinall (D-Colo.), sunk the bill's chances by packaging it with controversial provisions for public lands. In 1973, prospects in the House brightened when Morris Udall (D-Ariz.) took over the committee in the wake of Aspinall's defeat in the 1972 elections. But by then the bill's opponents had begun to mobilize and concentrate their energies on killing it in the House. After considerable maneuvering the bill was defeated on a procedural vote on the House floor in 1974.

As land-use planning supporters in the administration and the Congress drafted their bills, they confronted four basic issues. First, they had to make the case that it was appropriate for the federal government to promote land-use planning capacities in the states. Second, they had to determine the scope of planning and distinguish between planning and regulation. Third, they had to manage the tension between creating a planning process and achieving substantive goals. Finally, they had to decide whether to employ federal sanctions as well as incentives to promote land-use planning in the states.

In the five years of congressional maneuvering over these issues, it became clear that the ambitious versions of the bill with federal sanctions would not pass. Throughout, the bill remained somewhat vague in its intentions and expectations. Yet even the less stringent versions of the bill would have created processes and resources for state land-use planning, potentially altering the dynamics of development and preservation.

The Federal Role The bill that Jackson first introduced in 1970 provided federal funds to the states as incentives to plan. States would draw up plans identifying how land should be classified in broad categories such as housing, recreation, and industry. The funds would allow them to undertake extensive analysis of land and develop a database that would provide critical information for resolving future disputes about land use. Moreover, the information would allow the federal government to implement its policies in accordance with the state plan. This latter aim was a central impetus for the Jackson bill. Earlier, Jackson had presided over hearings on a proposed jetport to be built near Florida's Everglades National Park. Opposed by environmentalists, the project involved four different federal agencies, none of which knew what the others were doing. A state plan, in Jackson's eyes, would have provided guidance and coordination for federal activity.[20]

Within the Nixon administration, opinion about Jackson's bill was divided. On the one hand, administration political strategists realized that environmentalist sentiment was broad-based and wished to appeal politically to the growing number of voters who sympathized with the movement. Toward this end, the president had signed Jackson's earlier bill, the National Environmental Policy Act (NEPA), setting up the Council on Environmental Quality (CEQ) and requiring environmental-impact statements for federal activities. On the other hand, the administration was seeking to break the Democratic version of "creative federalism" based on categorical grants to states and localities. In its place, Nixon aimed to create a "New Federalism" characterized by block grants with less federal direction than in the past. Grants to support planning effectively created a new categorical grant at the very time the administration was consolidating existing programs into block grants.

Opposition to the bill centered in the Office of Management and Budget (OMB), which was leading the charge for the New Federalism. Supporters came from the CEQ and most significantly from John Ehrlichman, assistant to the president for domestic affairs and a former land-use lawyer in Seattle. Ehrlichman's strategic position in the administration and his expertise tipped the scales in favor of support. The president, far more concerned with international affairs but attuned to the growing political appeal of environmentalism, simply deferred to Ehrlichman's judgment.[21]

Comprehensive Planning or Regulating Critical Areas?

The administration changed the bill's focus. The drafters of the administration bill, CEQ staffers Boyd Gibbons and Reilly, rejected the idea of comprehensive planning. This decision reflected disappointment with planning processes initiated in cities and regions during the 1960s, and it embodied the latest thinking of professional land-use lawyers who were drawing up a new Model Land Development Code for the American Law Institute. Instead of a statewide plan, they proposed that the states act only in areas of "critical environmental concern," and instead of a plan, they sought state regulation.

The administration bill defined four critical areas: regions of environmental concern, such as wetlands, historical areas, and ecosystems; large-scale developments, such as subdivisions and industrial parks; key facilities, such as airports and highway interchanges; and developments of regional benefit, such as low- and middle-income housing and landfills. In each of these areas, the state would be responsible for ensuring that a viewpoint broader than that of localities was represented and that states would override local decisions when necessary.

The bills introduced from 1971 on adopted the administration's focus on state regulation of critical areas rather than comprehensive planning. Persuaded that this strategy was more feasible and sophisticated, Jackson dropped the comprehensive planning approach. States were still charged with developing plans for the critical areas and with collecting data relevant to land-use decisions. Thus, the land-use bills considered after 1970 were a hybrid between planning and regulation.

Process or Substance?

Throughout the five years of debate, Jackson steadfastly maintained that his bill was process-oriented, not associated with any substantive mission. He called it a measure that would "require the states to exercise states' rights."[22] An early CEQ memorandum stated that "land use policy is a start at institution-building, and is designed to cause states to develop their own programs without much substantive federal direction."[23]

Yet there was an inherent tension between substance and process in the bill. This issue was joined as Gibbons and Reilly prepared the administration's bill in 1970–71. As members of the CEQ, they were clearly identified with environmental concerns. Reilly, moreover, had previously been on the staff of the National Urban Coalition, a liberal Washington-based group formed to advocate on behalf of cities in the aftermath of several major urban riots. As such, he was closely attuned to metropolitan issues affecting cities and the urban poor, including open housing. From these different perspectives, they agreed that the key problem in land use was the failure of states to override local decisions that by their very nature could not adequately take metropolitan or environmental concerns into account. Their initial bill required states to regulate in these "critical areas."

But the issue of how the federal government would decide if the states were engaging in the desired planning and whether it should issue guidelines for state planning remained hazy. Jackson's original bill provided for a federal interagency review process that would simply approve funding if the state engaged in a planning process. But pressure to enunciate some federal guidelines mounted from different directions. Jackson's Senate rival for leadership on environmental issues, Edmund Muskie (D-Maine), pressed hard for substantive guidelines defending environmental-preservation goals. His proposals for guidelines were voted down on the Senate floor in 1972. The following year in Senate hearings on the bill, representatives from industry as well as conservation groups argued in favor of some sort of national guidelines. Still reluctant to embrace guidelines, Jackson ultimately accepted an amendment that provided for a three-year study period to consider whether guidelines were desirable. The CEQ was charged with overseeing the study with the participation of the Interagency Advisory Board and state and local governments.[24]

One substantive amendment, however, did slip through the Senate committee and was in the bill the Senate approved in 1973. This was a provision requiring the states to regulate the second-home industry, imposing stiff conditions on the construction of vacation-home developments. A recent explosion in such developments, combined with widely publicized fraud in the industry, accounted for the amendment's broad support.[25]

This exception aside, the bill's sponsors sought strenuously to avoid formally associating the bill with any particular substantive outcomes. Their goal was to create state-level processes in which competing objectives could be aired and outcomes decided in accordance with the evidence and interests particular to each case.

Sanctions or Incentives? Another recurrent issue was whether the federal government should use only incentives to encourage the states to plan or whether it should also impose sanctions if they failed to plan. Jackson's initial bill provided only for grants to assist in planning. Early drafts of the first administration bill and Jackson's initial bill contained grants as well as strong penalties if states failed to create planning processes. Noting that a state decision to preempt local land-use

planning authority was a "major political decision," an internal memorandum declared that it would "require more than a new grant to assure its implementation."[26] Proposed penalties included a cutoff of federal funds for airport and highway construction and land and water conservation programs (not including interstate highway funds) at a rate of 7 percent a year up to 35 percent. This proposal did not survive to the final draft. Officials at the OMB objected to legislation that would cut off funds to states at the very time they were enacting revenue-sharing that would give the states more discretion over federal grants. CEQ Chair Russell E. Train expressed regret at losing sanctions, telling a news briefing, "We need some levers and we'd like to have more than we've got."[27]

Sanctions supporters managed to reinsert these provisions (with the cutoff at 21 percent of funds) in the bill reported out of the Senate Interior Committee in 1972. Their impact would have been significant: according to the Interior Department 7 percent of the funds states received under the three programs amounted to $123 million annually. The carrots were small by comparison: the planning grants in the committee report amounted to $100 million a year for eight years.[28] The sanctions did not survive the floor debate and the bill that passed the Senate in 1972 authorized $40 million annually for the first two years and $30 million for the next three years.

Undeterred, the Senate Interior Committee's 1973 bill once again revived the debate over sanctions. The Nixon administration supported sanctions, acknowledging that states were going to need more prodding if they were to take back some of their planning functions from local governments. In Undersecretary of the Interior John C. Whitaker's words, sanctions were needed "because of a tremendous political crunch that has to take place between the state level and local level officials within the government."[29] Despite the strong support of Jackson and the administration for sanctions, an amendment to include sanctions was defeated by eight votes on the Senate floor during the 1973 consideration of the bill. The bill's advocates failed to reinsert sanctions in the House bill.

The Failed Coalition

Neither urban advocates nor environmentalists forcefully supported the bill. To understand the failure of such a coalition to coalesce around the land-use planning legislation requires analyzing how the bill fit into the organizational strategies of urban and environmental interests and the ideas that animated these groups. Both the organizational forms and the policy strategies of these groups were themselves affected by existing institutional levers that made some paths easier and more rewarding than others. For urban interests linked to the Democratic Party, increasing direct federal subsidies was the paramount goal; for antigovernment environmentalists, litigation and building a new set of federal regulations came first. Neither camp ranked Jackson's bill as essential and, at times, each viewed it with suspicion. The availability of the party-subsidy and court-regulation channels meant that these groups had no need to cooperate and few institutional channels through which to explore common interests. Instead, each embraced policy routes that emphasized differences rather than points of commonality.

Land-Use Planning and Urban Interests

As the land-use planning bills were being considered, there were three distinct sources of urban political and policy influence: officials at HUD, mayors and their congressional allies, and African-American community-based ac-

tivists. In the 1960s, the federal government launched its first full-scale urban policy, with substantial federal grants directly available to cities. Organized urban interests, whether in HUD, among mayors, or among black community activists, aimed to preserve and extend such federal assistance as their first priority. All three groups viewed environmentalists as potential competitors for federal resources. Moreover, these groups shared progovernment, prodevelopment ideas that were at odds with those of the environmentalists. In addition, racial divisions distinguished urban advocates from environmentalists, as urban problems became increasingly identified as a "black" issue and the environment a "white" concern.

HUD HUD officials might have been expected to be most sympathetic to the aims of the bills. Since the 1950s, federal housing officials had been experimenting with a variety of initiatives to promote metropolitan solutions to urban problems. In addition to the planning grants that created the metropolitan COGs, HUD officials supported open-housing measures and an urban-growth policy.

Open housing aimed to distribute poor households throughout metropolitan areas. The specter of decaying cities with large minority populations surrounded by a "white noose" of suburbs was persistent in the late 1960s. To forestall its famous prediction of "two societies, one white, one black," the Kerner Commission, which was set up to investigate the urban riots of the 1960s, urged that policy provide both "ghetto enrichment" and integration of metropolitan areas.[30] The Nixon administration initially pursued this agenda. In 1970, HUD Secretary George Romney proposed legislation that would give the federal government power to override local zoning ordinances that excluded federally subsidized low-income housing projects. Although the bill was defeated in subcommittee deliberations, HUD continued to press for open communities by withholding federal funds to induce suburbs to accept subsidized housing. Confronted with charges of "forced integration" and bitter local protests, the administration quickly backed down. Although it continued to profess a strong commitment to countering racial discrimination, the administration reconfirmed its deference to local control over land use and housing and disavowed any effort to promote economic mixing.[31]

In the early 1970s a number of bills proposing some version of a national growth policy were introduced in Congress. The idea of a national growth policy was in some ways a competitor to the land-use planning bill and was more associated with liberal urban interests. These bills aimed to provide grants to city and state agencies to plan how growth should occur. These ideas lay behind a provision in the Urban Growth and New Community Development Act of 1970, which called on the federal government to work with state and local governments and the private sector to establish a national urban-growth policy. However, the language was mainly exhortatory. Its one mandate required a biennial presidential report on urban growth.[32]

Given the limited results of voluntary metropolitan planning and the failure of open communities and the urban-growth policy, the National Land Use Planning Act offered a possible alternative route to achieve similar objectives. This goal was certainly on the minds of the initial drafters of the legislation, particularly Reilly. Reilly's concern for open housing and dissatisfaction with voluntary regional planning were key to his interest in state land-use planning. Aware of the possible social uses of the act, Reilly notified Ehrlichman early on that the bill could be used to attack exclusionary zoning.[33]

But a combination of bureaucratic competition and suspicion considerably dampened the support of HUD officials. To HUD, the key role of Senator Jackson, who chaired the Senate Interior Committee, signaled an early identification of the bill with environmental issues. Jackson had earlier sponsored the charter legislation of the environmental movement, the National Environmental Policy Act. The sense that land-use planning was an environmental bill, not an urban bill, intensified when the administration decided to make Interior, not HUD, the lead department administering the act. HUD Secretary Romney made it clear to Senator Jackson and to the administration that his agency's experience with the 701 metropolitan-planning program made it the natural choice to oversee any new planning initiatives. He also expressed fears that the act would simply duplicate the planning sponsored by HUD's 701 funds. Aware of HUD's experience in promoting planning, the administration initially intended to give it authority over the new program. But faced with arguments that HUD had no experience with nonurban planning and that its close ties to development interests would alienate environmentalists, Nixon officials turned to Interior. HUD was instead given veto power over plans with a significant metropolitan impact.[34]

The decision to make Interior the lead agency confirmed the fears of some urban advocates that urban issues were losing ground to environmental concerns. Former HUD undersecretary Robert Wood disparaged what he called "environmental escapism" and warned of a "disturbing tendency to replace national goals rather than fulfill them."[35] This sentiment was widespread among urban advocates in Congress, who felt that social and economic goals related to planning would be shortchanged in the bill. In the words of one urban consultant, "The Interior guys are basically land classifiers. . . . They're used to dealing with farmers and ranchers and sheep herders."[36]

HUD officials supported the bill during the first years it was considered, but by 1975 the department's position had shifted. Changes in personnel had weakened the supporters of metropolitan planning within HUD and in a new climate of budgetary stringency, top HUD officials feared that the land-use planning bill would simply disrupt existing grants that the department controlled.[37]

Mayors Throughout the life of the land-use planning act, the major organizations of local officials, including the U.S. Conference of Mayors, expressed qualified support. The bill never threatened their control over land use since it exempted land within incorporated cities that had populations over 250,000 and had an established planning authority.[38] But the National League of Cities and the Conference of Mayors did express concern that state land-use regulation could reduce local government tax revenues. Efforts to address this issue with amendments to compensate local governments for lost revenue were defeated in 1973. But the bill's sponsors did make other concessions to retain the support of local government. In 1974, when the bill's House supporters were attempting to stave off growing opposition, they sought to hold on to the local government lobby with amendments that guaranteed local authorities rights vis-à-vis state land-use planning commissions.[39]

Even though the bill managed to retain the support of local governments, mayors were never strong advocates of land-use planning. Throughout the 1950s and '60s, as suburbanization depleted urban populations, mayors responded by physically renewing their downtowns to make them attractive shopping and business centers. Federal funds were a key part of this strategy. The major interest of most mayors during the Nixon presidency was to secure the flow of federal funds that had begun in the previous decade. In this they were successful, backing Nixon's block grants in the areas of community development, employment and training, and social services and securing new no-strings-attached funding through general revenue-sharing.[40] Moreover, mayors had always been somewhat suspicious of metropolitan housing strategies, fearing that they could end up reducing federal grants for housing in cities.

In the numerous hearings on the bills, there was little evidence that mayors feared the consequences of strengthening state governments. The explicit protections for large cities were clear from the outset. Nonetheless, in 1974 when the bill had passed the Senate and was being considered in the House, Chicago Mayor Richard J. Daley withdrew his support. Engaged in a struggle with Governor Daniel Walker to control the Illinois Democratic Party, the mayor feared that a state planning commission would be used against the city. In fact, through its political organization, Chicago dominated its six-county metropolitan region, controlling most regional facilities, including airports. The new act would have defined Lake Michigan as an area of critical environmental concern, inviting a hostile state government to poke about in what the mayor viewed as Chicago's business. Four of the seven members of Chicago's congressional delegation, which answered to Daley, voted against the rule to consider the bill on the House floor in 1974. Those four votes represented the margin by which the bill was defeated—the last time it received serious consideration.[41]

African-American Community Activists A third group of urban interests, mobilized in the 1960s, was the African-American community. In many cities, minority activists, concerned about urban poverty and the lack of minority influence in city governments, mobilized in the 1960s. For this group, land-use planning was a remote good-government measure that had little immediate appeal. And in some respects, the social implications of the land-use bill—facilitating open housing and movement of African Americans out of the city—cut against the grain of what minority urban activists were trying to do. In the late 1960s, the idea of community control and the quest to secure federal funds that went to cities, and ultimately to win political power in cities, were at the forefront of the African-American urban political agenda.[42]

There were also deep-seated tensions between environmentalists and civil rights groups that made coalition-building difficult. Many mainline civil rights organizations, such as the National Association for the Advancement of Colored People, saw economic growth and jobs as key to black advancement; environmentalists' notions about limiting growth did not sit well with these groups. In the late 1970s, the Sierra Club sought to bridge this divide with its Urban Environment Task Force and later a "City Care" program, an initiative concerned with urban parks and other environmental issues. Together with the Urban League, the Sierra Club sponsored a conference in Detroit for environmentalists and black urban advocates to meet, both to address the initiative and for more general purposes of coalition-building. It was difficult to build an enduring alliance out of the meeting. Reflecting the tensions between environmentalism and many mainstream urban interests, Detroit Mayor Coleman Young refused to support the conference and dissuaded Vice President Mondale from speaking at it. Dedicated to urban economic development, Young held close ties to the automobile industry, which had frowned on the effort to unite urban and environmental interests. Unique among environmental groups for its attention to cities, the Sierra Club's main urban focus in the late 1970s was public works

to rebuild infrastructure—an approach that fit well into the subsidy approach favored by most urban interests.[43]

Land-Use Planning and Environmentalists

In the early 1970s, as Congress considered the land-use planning legislation, the environmental movement was in a period of tremendous growth. Traditional conservation organizations like the Sierra Club and the Audubon Society experienced dramatic increases in membership and new organizations, such as Friends of the Earth and Environmental Action, formed as enthusiasm for environmental issues swept the country.[44] Much of Senator Jackson's interest in the bill stemmed from environmental concerns and the decision to make Interior the lead department should have made the bill particularly attractive to environmental organizations. For the most part, however, these groups did not evince much interest in Jackson's bill. Instead, they pursued a federal regulatory strategy that resonated more closely with the organizational bases and the animating ideas of the movement.

Planning, Regulation, and the Organizational Bases of the Environmental Movement The institution-building goal of the land-use acts held little appeal for environmental groups. It did not tap into or augment the movement's resources in terms of expertise or mobilization capabilities. Far more amenable to environmental organizations were substantive fights over particular dangers, which could rouse grassroots participation or federal regulatory strategies that required a small, legally trained, Washington-based staff.

Substantive fights over particular threats were especially attractive to some of the newer groups, such as Environmental Action and Friends of the Earth. These groups consisted of Washington offices linked to a loosely organized network of unaffiliated locals that had sprung up after the first Earth Day in 1970. The immediacy of fights over particular issues—such as the effort to kill the supersonic aircraft—was far more likely to mobilize the membership base of such organizations than were procedural issues. As Senate Interior Committee Counsel William Van Ness complained of the environmental groups, "They're either unaware of or uninterested in some of the really important issues like . . . Senator Jackson's land use policy bill, which offers great promise to really deal with the critical environmental problems facing the nation. When it's not glamorous, like saving the redwoods or being against the jetport, they just aren't around to help."[45]

It wasn't just the glamour but the direct-action orientation of these groups that made substantive fights so attractive. As historian Samuel P. Hays has noted, it was difficult for environmental groups to mobilize the sustained interest required for planning because planning was far less crisis- or project-oriented than fights over substantive issues.[46] The details and complexities of planning were not suited to the organizational strengths of direct-action groups, which relied on immediate threats to mobilize their base.

The second kind of environmental group that sprung up in the early 1970s was also unlikely to embrace the state-level planning strategy embodied in the land-use planning bills. These groups, which included the Environmental Defense Fund and the Natural Resources Defense Council, were small Washington-based organizations financed by foundation grants. They were staffed by lawyers, who saw their main aim as influencing federal policy and creating environmental regulation through the legal system. And indeed, they were extremely skilled in both endeavors. Their strategy was facilitated by the growing decentralization of power in Congress, which made it easier for environmental lobbyists with little grassroots support to gain a hearing with sympathetic subcommittee and committee staffers.[47] This enabled them to "insert specific phrases in the record that could then serve as "hooks" on which to hang future litigation."[48] Through such litigation, environmental lawyers and judges essentially wrote a new body of regulation designed to achieve environmental objectives.

In the early 1970s, the possibilities for using the courts in this way expanded considerably. In several key decisions, the Supreme Court broadened the rules of standing. In the past, the courts required that plaintiffs show economic or direct physical harm—not something less tangible, such as the destruction of natural beauty—and they restricted the class of interests that could sue. When the Court relaxed both requirements in the early 1970s, it opened the door for public-interest environmental groups to initiate a wide range of legal cases, challenging development on the grounds that it harmed the environment. Together with the new environmental laws passed in the early 1970s, the changed rules governing legal standing made federal regulation and litigation powerful tools for environmental groups. For example, the environmental-impact statement required of all federally funded projects by the National Environmental Policy Act provided one of the major hooks that environmental groups repeatedly used to challenge development.[49]

The substantial success of this federal regulatory/litigation strategy and the lack of state-level organization or expertise on the part of most environmental groups meant that the land-use planning bill held little interest for them. One exception was the Sierra Club, with chapters organized initially in the West but whose local base grew in the East as well during the 1960s. Although the club's chief priority was wilderness preservation, it supported the land-use act. When the act finally died in Congress, the club embraced a "back door approach" to land use, relying on more targeted efforts toward agricultural lands, coastal zones, and public works for cities. Thus, the club continued to be concerned with land-use issues but within a regulatory/subsidy framework, rather than one that would promote planning.[50]

Development or Preservation These organizational features of the environmental movement both complemented and reinforced the preservationist ideology that animated it. Hays contrasts the ideas of wise use of natural resources that animated an earlier generation of conservationists with the more staunchly antidevelopment views that characterized the new wave of environmentalists that emerged in the 1960s and 1970s.[51] These ideas made the new environmentalists inherently less interested in notions of balanced development; their ability to enact detailed regulations in Congress and to enforce and extend them in the courts meant that they did not have to compromise their goals.

The ideas underlying Jackson's land-use act were fundamentally at odds with the approach that environmentalists were developing. Senator Jackson came out of the older school of conservationists, sympathetic to many of the goals of environmentalists but also deeply concerned with establishing procedures that would allow for development. The emergence of local antigrowth and antidevelopment movements had raised concerns that purely local land-use controls could block needed development. Some issues, such as the siting of power plants and other major projects, were particularly thorny. Proper procedures, in this view, would help ensure an appropriate balance. But, as advocates for

preservation, environmental organizations were far more interested in opposing development than in establishing procedures for how it should proceed. The land-use act's effort to make state-level planning a tool for balancing preservation and development goals was thus fundamentally at odds with the ideas that energized the new environmental movement.

In some cases, the environmentalists' antidevelopment bias coincided with positions of the administration and Senator Jackson. In 1972, environmentalists opposed the House version of the Land-use Planning Act. Drawn up by House Interior and Insular Affairs Committee Chair Aspinall, who was close to Western land interests, the bill included "multiple use" provisions regarding public lands. Environmentalists opposed these provisions, fearing that they would turn public lands over to private mining and grazing interests.[52] They were not the only opponents: the administration also wanted to decouple the public-lands provisions from the land-use planning bill. The 1972 bill died in the House after Aspinall refused to detach the provisions for public lands.

Environmentalists also monitored the debate over land-use planning to make sure that it contained no provisions that would tilt the scales toward development. Several times, they were able to eliminate provisions that they believed would facilitate power-plant siting by giving the state special authority in issues involving energy development.[53]

But the bill always remained secondary to the much more clearly pro-environmental measures that had passed beginning with the National Environmental Policy Act. The regulatory/legal approach that became the cornerstone of environmental activist strategy allowed these groups to sustain a more "pure" version of the preservationist ideology than planning processes would: by its very nature, planning would have forced environmentalists to justify compromises with development. Planning would also have entailed a permanent expansion of bureaucracy and state government authority. As political scientist David Vogel has noted, the environmental movement of the 1970s was strongly anti-institutional, preferring to use private power through the courts to achieve its goals rather than to create new permanent government capabilities.[54] The availability of these legal channels allowed the movement to go further in this direction and away from the compromises among interests that accompany the exercise of public authority.

The Opposition

Little opposition emerged during the first years that Congress considered Jackson's bill. It was considered "innocuous good government legislation."[55] Large corporate interests, concerned about growing local opposition to siting large developments, believed that the bill would reduce such local barriers to development or at least make sitting processes more rational.

But early qualms expressed by smaller businesses, real estate, and rural interests foreshadowed later opposition. Small businesses and developers in the South and West, in particular, benefited from the existing system of local land-use controls.[56] In most Sunbelt areas, fragmented political institutions and low levels of political participation ensured these business interests considerable influence over local development decisions.[57] These interests repeatedly challenged the land-use act for granting too much authority to higher levels of government. For Sunbelt agricultural and development interests, state-level planning institutions posed a threat to their influence over land use, especially if planning operated in accordance with federal guidelines. Their opposition—mobilized and

magnified in the mid-1970s—ultimately defeated the bill.

Federal vs. State Authority

Supporters of land-use planning took pains to emphasize that their bill would not abrogate state responsibilities. Instead, it would simply encourage states to exercise their authority over land use. But congressional opponents and business interests had expressed doubt on this account from the beginning. Testifying in 1971, a Chamber of Commerce representative did not take a stand on the bill but noted that some of his members might fear that the policy would eventually lead to greater federal control over land use.[58] Concern about states' rights and excessive federal intervention lay behind the failure to attach sanctions to the bill. As Senator Dewey F. Bartlett (R-Okla.) saw it, the purpose of sanctions was "not to prod or to encourage the states; it is to force them to do something that the sponsors of the bill know the lawmakers in the states do not want. Its advocates want to force lawmakers to do something that the people in the local communities are not asking for and do not want—and that is federal interference."[59]

Senator Bennett Johnston, Jr. (D-La.), aligned with oil interests in his home state and a strong supporter of states' rights, sought to reduce the federal role with an amendment that would allow the states to determine what constituted an area of "critical environmental concern." The bill defined such areas as nonfederal lands "where uncontrolled or incompatible development could result in damage to the environment, life or property, or the long-term public interest which is more than local significance."[60] Vigorously opposed by Jackson as a way to gut the bill, Johnston's amendment was defeated.

But as opposition mobilized, the arguments about "federal overkill" were heard with increasing frequency. One of the main opponents of the bill in the House, Sam Steiger (R-Ariz.) a cattle rancher, began offering substitute bills in the 1974 committee deliberations. These substitute bills would establish land-use planning grants for states that wished to receive them, with virtually no federal role. Although Steiger's bills did not pass, Steiger played a key role in the House opposition that derailed the land-use planning bill when it first reached the Rules Committee and in defeating it later on the House floor.

Substance vs. Procedure

The lack of substance in the bill initially muted potential opposition. In early testimony, the Chamber of Commerce, the National Association of Home Builders, and the National Association of Manufacturers (NAM) simply counseled caution. Home Builders worried that the bill would preserve undeveloped areas and stymie the development of low-cost suburban housing. NAM noted the long history of local control over land use and was not enthusiastic about increasing state authority. Later testimony emphasized the need for a balanced approach to land use.[61]

Although Senator Jackson believed that his bill provided just such a balance, business interests grew suspicious as they watched the implementation of air- and water-pollution laws. Using these laws, environmentalists had delayed construction of the trans-Alaskan pipeline, power plants, and refineries. By 1973, Chamber of Commerce lobbyist Dan Denning became convinced that the land-use bill would be one more arrow in the quiver of environmentalists. As such, he believed, it contained a profound antidevelopment bias. In 1973, Denning wrote an analysis of the bill, arguing that it would have an impact similar to that of the recently passed air- and water-pollution laws. Equating the bill with these measures, he cautioned, "The

effects of these three measures on growth come via not only the provisions of the actual legislation, but also through their judicial and regulatory offspring."[62] Recognizing that the bill had strong support in the Senate (where it passed twice), Denning sought to fight the bill in the House, which was inherently more amenable to local interests and interests that benefited from local control of land use. To mobilize support he formed a Coordinating Committee on Land-Use Control that brought potential opponents in the business and agricultural world together.

The Takings Issue

The linchpin of Denning's argument against the bill centered on its purported threat to private-property rights. This issue did not come into focus until 1973 with the publication of the Rockefeller Brothers Fund's report on *The Use of Land* and a CEQ report entitled *The Taking Issue*. Both reports made it clear that supporters of land-use planning also believed that the public interest in land use would entail restrictions on the private use of land. Moreover, both documents were reticent about whether and to what degree private-property owners would be compensated for the diminished value of their land that would occur as a result of such restrictions.[63]

Portraying the bill as an assault on private-property rights helped to galvanize a much broader and more fervent opposition. Denning hammered on this issue, writing analyses and circulating scenarios in which small property owners could be prevented from developing their land and would not be compensated for the loss.[64] Congressional mail ran 10-1 against land-use planning. One member of Congress reported getting "letters from people who said the government was going to take their house and garden away."[65] Although the bill's sponsors sought to allay these fears with amendments stipulating that the bill would not affect property rights defined by the Constitution and state laws, they could not mollify their opponents.

The White House and the Defeat of Land-Use Planning

From the start, land-use planning split congressional Republicans. Many conservative Republicans from the West and from rural areas had repeatedly opposed Jackson's bill. President Nixon's decision to support the bill was consistent with his efforts to respond to the broad public sympathy for the environmental goals within the limits of what he viewed as realistic and financially feasible. Land-use planning, he was assured by Ehrlichman, was such a measure. Support for land-use planning legislation also fit with the liberal Republican cast of the first Nixon administration. Big-business interests were not opposed to government, they wanted more rational and predictable government.[66]

By 1974, the political world looked quite different to the president. Ehrlichman had left the White House as the Watergate scandal mounted and Nixon now faced possible impeachment. The president's political vulnerability drew him closer to the conservative wing of his party, whose strong support was vital if he was to resist impeachment. The bastions of conservative Republican strength were in the West and the rural areas that had opposed the land-use act from the beginning. In this setting, the White House withdrew its backing from Jackson's bill. Administration officials explained the switch in terms of the broader program of New Federalism: "The President desires legislation which would maximize the responsibilities of the states and local governments and minimize the role of the federal government in this area and that, of course, is in accordance with his strong principles of New Federalism."[67] Indicative of the switch, the president praised Representative Steiger, the chief opponent of land-use

planning in the House, calling Steiger his "top adviser in the field of land use." In the 1974 House debate over land-use planning, the president reversed four years of support for Jackson's bill and gave his endorsement to Rep. Steiger's substitute, which provided grants to the states but no federal role.[68]

An analysis of the final House vote that killed the bill showed that Republicans and rural members of Congress were the most consistent opponents. Republicans voted against the rule to consider the bill 136 to 46; more than half the Republicans that voted to consider the bill were from suburban areas. Southern Democrats voted heavily against the rule.

Defeated after five years of consideration, the bill was never revived. Both Senator Jackson and Representative Udall were running for president, and neither was inclined to reintroduce the bill.

Subsidizing and Regulating Localism

Although the National Land-Use Planning Act failed, the environmental and urban concerns that had originally sparked interest in land-use policy stimulated the passage of numerous other federal measures and new state laws during the 1970s. Cities got federal revenue-sharing and block-grant assistance; environmentalists got a variety of federal regulatory statutes aimed at specific problems. Despite this flurry of activity, these measures largely failed to challenge the narrow localism in land-use decisions that had fostered many urban and environmental problems in the first place. Instead, the federal government sought to compensate for the effects of localism with regulations and subsidies. By the 1990s, the limited effectiveness of these strategies and their negative political consequences for urban and environmental interests revealed the flaws of this approach.

In the 1970s, cities used their political power to secure relatively high levels of subsidy from the federal government. Block grants plus no-strings-attached revenue-sharing constituted new place-based entitlements. But this assistance could not remedy the underlying arrangements in local government structure and finance that were draining cities of businesses and taxpaying residents. Moreover, the subsidies themselves were politically vulnerable. Cities, which were once at the center of Democratic political power, began to lose their pivotal political role.[69] After the 1980 census, urban advocates lost power in Congress as redistricting reflected the population loss in northern cities. During the 1980s, at the urging of President Reagan, Congress slashed federal assistance to cities. By one estimate, aid to big cities fell by some 50 percent.[70]

Environmentalists were more successful. Federal regulations helped to clean up and preserve critical environmental areas, and the broad popularity of environmental goals made opponents reluctant to organize open opposition. But the regulatory strategy had negative consequences over time. For one thing, it demobilized much of the grassroots environmental movement, as environmental organizations focused their energies on Congress and the courts. This strategy also had limited effectiveness: the tough comprehensive regulations that guided environmental policy proved difficult to enforce.[71] Moreover, individual regulations created a piecemeal approach to environmental protection that overregulated some areas and left gaps in others; it also offered few tools for more proactive planning approaches to pollution prevention.[72] The proliferation of detailed regulations made environmental laws a vulnerable political target. By the 1990s, an increasingly vocal opposition, which now included a revived private-property-rights movement, sought to limit regulation. Although broad support for environmental goals caused the Republican-led 104th Congress to back off from its early efforts to reduce environmental regulations, increased regulation is not politically promising nor is it likely to result in greater environmental protection.

In addition to these federal policies, a handful of states have enacted a mixture of planning requirements and regulations to manage growth. The most expansive of these, such as Oregon's, effectively address both environmental and suburban sprawl/urban disinvestment problems. But there are important limitations to this state movement. For the most part, the states have focused on environmental, not urban, problems.[73] Moreover, in many states, planning processes are only weakly enforced; in others, strong prodevelopment pressures undermine existing planning procedures or prevent them from being put into place at all.[74]

Conclusion

It is hard to predict what impact the National Land-use Planning Act would have had on contemporary urban and environmental problems. Over the course of its history, the bill took many different forms, some of which were unlikely to have much effect on existing development practices. The act's impact would also have depended on how strongly and in what directions the federal government pushed state planning processes.

But the act would have had an impact on the politics of urban and environmental issues by creating an alternative institutional setting where advocates from both groups could interact. In so doing, it would have created new possibilities for compromise and prompted a search for common ground among these interests. Given the institutional configuration of American politics, it is likely that the state planning process would have constituted a secondary track for both urban and environmental interests. Nonetheless, such arenas are often critical for reconceptualizing interests and creating new models for action.

Twenty years after the defeat of the land-use planning bills, there is renewed interest in such planning. Urban advocates, resigned to much-reduced assistance from the federal government, are turning to the idea of metropolitanism as a solution to the isolation of central cities.[75] Many environmentalists, disillusioned by the consequences of and prospects for regulation, have embraced the idea of "sustainable development," which seeks to find a balance between the goals of preservation and economic development. The environmental justice movement has made the case that environmental issues greatly affect minority communities. Yet, as in the past, these alternatives are hampered by the absence of metropolitan-level political authority and the reluctance of most states to interfere with local land-use decisions and to take a directive role in jurisdictional arrangements.

Contemporary enthusiasts of devolution assume that the states are capable of taking the lead in a variety of domestic policy domains. Yet the states have been reluctant to intervene in matters that impinge on local autonomy. Until they exercise their extensive powers over land use, local political organization, and public finance, public solutions to a range of urban and environmental concerns will remain elusive.

Notes

1. Stephen Skowronek, *Building a New American State* (New York: Cambridge University Press, 1982).

2. See Robert Collins, *The Business Response to Keynes: 1929–1964* (New York: Columbia University Press, 1981).

3. National Commission on Urban Problems (NCUP), *Building the American City* (Washington, D.C.: U.S. Government Printing Office [USGPO], 1968), p. 205; Frank J. Popper, *The Politics of Land-Use Reform* (Madison: University of Wisconsin Press, 1981), p. 47. For data outlining the adoption of these programs see Nelson Rosenbaum, *Land Use and the Legislatures: The Politics of State Innovation* (Washington, D.C.: Urban Institute, 1976), pp. 6–7.

4. United States National Resources Committee, Research Committee on Urbanism, *Our Cities: Their Role in the National Economy*, June 1937 (New York: Arno Press, 1974), p. 67.

5. See, for example, Robert C. Wood, *1,400 Governments* (Cambridge, Mass.: Harvard University Press, 1961).

6. Kenneth T. Jackson, *Crabgrass Frontier: The Suburbanization of the United States* (New York: Oxford University Press, 1985).

7. Richard F. Babcock, *The Zoning Game: Municipal Practices and Policies* (Madison: University of Wisconsin Press, 1966); Committee on Economic Development, *Reshaping Governments in Metropolitan Areas* (New York: Committee for Economic Development, 1970).

8. Frank J. Popper, *The Politics of Land-Use Reform* (Madison: University of Wisconsin Press, 1981).

9. Michael N. Danielson, *The Politics of Exclusion* (New York: Columbia University Press, 1976), pp. 243–78.

10. In addition to the three reports discussed here see the Advisory Commission on Intergovernmental Relations (ACIR), *Urban America and the Federal System* (Washington, D.C.: ACIR, 1969); and President's Task Force on Suburban Problems, *Final Report*, ed. Charles M. Haar (Cambridge, Mass.: Ballinger Publishing, 1974). This report was transmitted to the president in 1968; see also Donald M. McAllister, ed., *Environment: A New Focus for Land-use Planning* (Washington, D.C.: National Science Foundation, 1973).

11. NCUP, *Building the American City*, p. vii.

12. See, for example, Committee for Economic Development, "Modernizing Local Government," statement on National Policy by the Research and Policy Committee of the Committee for Economic Development (New York: Committee for Economic Development, 1966).

13. NCUP, *Building the American City*, pp. 240–2.

14. Sidney Plotkin, *Keep Out: The Struggle for*

Land Use (Berkeley: University of California Press, 1987), pp. 160–1.

15. See A Model Land Development Code (Philadelphia: American Law Institute, April 15, 1974).

16. Fred Bosselman and David Callies, The Quiet Revolution in Land Use Control Summary Report (Washington, D.C.: USGPO, 1972), pp. 28–30.

17. Task Force on Land Use and Urban Growth, The Use of Land: A Citizen's Policy Guide to Urban Growth (New York: Thomas Y. Crowell, 1973), p. 6.

18. Ibid., p. 237.

19. See William W. Prochanu and Richard W. Larsen, A Certain Democrat: Senator Henry Jackson (Englewood Cliffs, N.J.: Prentice-Hall, 1972), ch. 12.

20. Noreen Lyday, The Law of the Land: Debating National Land Use Legislation, 1970–75 (Washington, D.C.: Urban Institute, 1976), p. 10.

21. John C. Whitaker, Striking a Balance: Environment and Natural Resources Policy in the Nixon-Ford Years (Washington, D.C.: American Enterprise Institute, 1976), p. 158.

22. James A. Noone, "Environment Report: Congress Considers Bills Increasing State, Federal Role in Land-Use Decisions," National Journal, May 5, 1973.

23. Richard Corrigan, "Environment Report: Interior Department Finesses HUD in Scramble Over Land Use Program," National Journal, March 20, 1971, p. 598.

24. Noone, "Congress Considers Bills," p. 638; Lyday, The Law of the Land, pp. 35–7.

25. Lyday, The Law of the Land; Judy Gardner, "Consumer Report: Land-sales Industry Braces for Tighter Federal, State Regulation," National Journal, January 20, 1973, pp. 90–8.

26. Corrigan, "Interior Department Finesses HUD," p. 601.

27. Ibid., pp. 601–2; Whitaker, Striking a Balance, p. 158.

28. James A. Noone, "Resources Report: Senate, House Differ on Approaches to Reform of Nation's Land-Use Laws," National Journal, July 22, 1972, p. 1193.

29. Noone, "Congress Considers Bills," p. 640.

30. United States, Kerner Commission, Report of the National Advisory Commission on Civil Disorders (Washington, D.C.: U.S. Government Printing Office, July 1968), pp. 220–6.

31. Danielson, The Politics of Exclusion; Corrigan, "Interior Department Finesses HUD," p. 605.

32. William G. Colman, Cities, Suburbs, and States (New York: Free Press, 1975), pp. 96–8; on other congressional initiatives, see Noone, "Congress Considers Bills," p. 641.

33. Lyday, The Law of the Land, p. 22.

34. Corrigan, "Interior Department Finesses HUD."

35. Robert Wood, Journal of the American Institute of Planners, November 1970.

36. Corrigan, "Interior Department Finesses HUD," p. 607.

37. "Land Use Legislation: A Precarious Future," Congressional Quarterly Weekly Report, March 1, 1975, p. 429.

38. Lyday, The Law of the Land, p. 6.

39. On the 1973 amendments, see Noone, "Congress Considers Bills," p. 642; "Land Use Legislation: A Precarious Future," p. 432. See also the testimony of Jack Barnes on behalf of the National League of Cities and the Conference of Mayors in U.S. House of Representatives, Hearings Before the Subcommittee on Interior and Insular Affairs 93rd Cong., 1st sess., (March 26, 27; April 2, 3, 4, 1973).

40. On the growth of urban aid in the 1970s, see Carol O'Cleireacain, "Cities' Role in the Metropolitan Economy and the Federal Structure," Interwoven Destinies: Cities and the Nation, ed. Henry G. Cisneros (New York: Norton, 1993), p. 174.

41. "Land Use Legislation: A Precarious Future," p. 432; "Land Bill Dies with a Whimper—This Year," Planning, July 4, 1974, p. x.

42. On community control see Alan A. Altshuler, Community Control (New York: Pegasus, 1970).

43. On the Sierra Club's urban initiatives see J. William Futrell, "'Love for the Land and Justice for Its People': Sierra Club National and Southern Leaders, 1968–1982," an oral history conducted in 1982 by Ann Lage, in Sierra Club Leaders II, 1960s–1970s, Regional Oral History Office, Bancroft Library, University of California, Berkeley, 1984, chs. 5–6.

44. For a description of the growth of these groups see Robert Cameron Mitchell, "From Conservation to Environmental Movement: The Development of the Modern Environmental Lobbies," Government and Environmental Politics, ed. Michael J. Lacey (Washington, D.C. and Baltimore: Woodrow Wilson Center Press and Johns Hopkins University Press, 1989), ch. 2.

45. Jamie Heard, "Washington Pressures/ Friends of the Earth Give Environmental Interests

an Activist Voice," *National Journal* August 8, 1970, p. 1718.

46. Samuel P. Hays, *Beauty, Health, and Permanence: Environmental Politics in the United States, 1955–1985* (New York: Cambridge University Press, 1987), p. 475.

47. On the decentralization of power in Congress, see, for example, Lawrence C. Dodd and Bruce I. Oppenheimer, "Maintaining Order in the House: The Struggle for Institutional Equilibrium," *Congress Reconsidered* 5th ed., ed. Lawrence C. Dodd and Bruce I. Oppenheimer (Washington, D.C.: Congressional Quarterly Press, 1993), ch. 2.

48. Marc K. Landy, Marc J. Roberts, and Stephen R. Thomas, *The Environmental Protection Agency: Asking the Wrong Questions* (New York: Oxford University Press, 1990), p. 26.

49. See Mitchell, "From Conservation to Environmental Movement," pp. 100–2; on the issue of courts and standing see Karen Orren, "Standing to Sue: Interest Group Conflict in the Federal Courts," *American Political Science Review* 70 (September 1976): 723–41.

50. See Futrell, "Love for the Land," pp. 123–4; 128–30; William Futrell, "Taking the Lead on Land Use," *Sierra Club Bulletin* (March 1977).

51. See Hays, *Beauty, Health, and Permanence,* ch. 1, for an elaboration of this distinction.

52. Noone, "Senate, House Differ," pp. 1192–201.

53. Lyday, *The Law of the Land,* p. 44; Noone, "Congress Considers Bills," p. 643.

54. David Vogel, "The Public Interest Movement and the American Reform Tradition," *Political Science Quarterly* 95 (Winter 1980–81): 607–27.

55. Lyday, *The Law of the Land,* p. 33.

56. Plotkin, *Keep Out,* p. 200.

57. Amy Bridges, *Morning Glories* (Princeton: Princeton University Press, 1997).

58. Richard Corrigan, "Interior Department Finesses HUD," p. 607.

59. "Senate Approves Land-Use Planning Bill, 64–21," *Congressional Quarterly Weekly Report,* June 23, 1973, p. 1597.

60. Ibid.

61. Corrigan, "Interior Department Finesses HUD," p. 607.

62. Lyday, *The Law of the Land,* p. 46.

63. See the critique of the ALI Code in Peter G. Brown, *The American Law Institute Model Land Development Code, the Taking Issue and Private Property Rights* (Washington, D.C.: Urban Institute, 1975).

64. Lyday, in *The Law of the Land,* quotes from a Chamber of Commerce newsletter written by Denning entitled "Without Just Compensation," which received wide circulation (p. 47).

65. "Land Use Legislation: A Precarious Future," p. 431.

66. Plotkin, *Keep Out,* pp. 176–8.

67. James A. Noone, "Environment Report: Land Use Bill Derailed after White House Ends Support," *National Journal,* March 9, 1974, p. 369.

68. James A. Noone, "Environment Report: House Deals Fatal Blow to 1974 Land Use Legislation," *National Journal,* June 22, 1974, p. 929.

69. For an elaboration of this argument see Margaret Weir, "Poverty, Social Rights and the Politics of Place in the United States," *European Social Policy: Between Fragmentation and Integration,* ed. Stephan Leibfried and Paul Pierson (Washington, D.C.: Brookings Institution Press, 1995), ch. 10.

70. Demetrios Caraley, "Washington Abandons the Cities," *Political Science Quarterly* 107 (1992): 1–30.

71. See David Vogel, *National Styles of Regulation: Environmental Policy in Great Britain and the United States* (Ithaca, N.Y.: Cornell University Press, 1986), ch. 4.

72. This argument is developed in J. William Futrell, "Law of Sustainable Development," *Environmental Forum* 2 (March 1994): 16–21.

73. One important exception has been Minnesota, which instituted a limited form of regional tax-base sharing. See John J. Harrigan, "The Politics of Regionalism in the Twin Cities," paper presented at Roundtables on Regionalism, Social Science Research Council and HUD, Washington, D.C., January 1995.

74. For an overview of the accomplishments and limits of these state planning processes, see Sarah Hughes Sigel, "Statewide Growth Management Planning," *Land Development* (Fall 1992): 14–19; David L. Callies, "The Quiet Revolution Revisited," *Journal of the American Planning Association* 46 (April 1980): 135–44; David L. Callies, "The Quiet Revolution Revisited: A Quarter Century of Progress," *The Urban Lawyer* 26 (Spring 1994): 197–213.

75. See Todd Swanstrom, "Ideas Matter: Reflections on the New Regionalism," paper presented at Roundtables on Regionalism, December 1994; see also David Rusk, *Cities without Suburbs* (Washington, D.C. and Baltimore: Woodrow Wilson Center Press and Johns Hopkins University Press, 1993).

PART THREE

RECREATING THE "COMMONS"
THE LOCAL EXPERIENCE

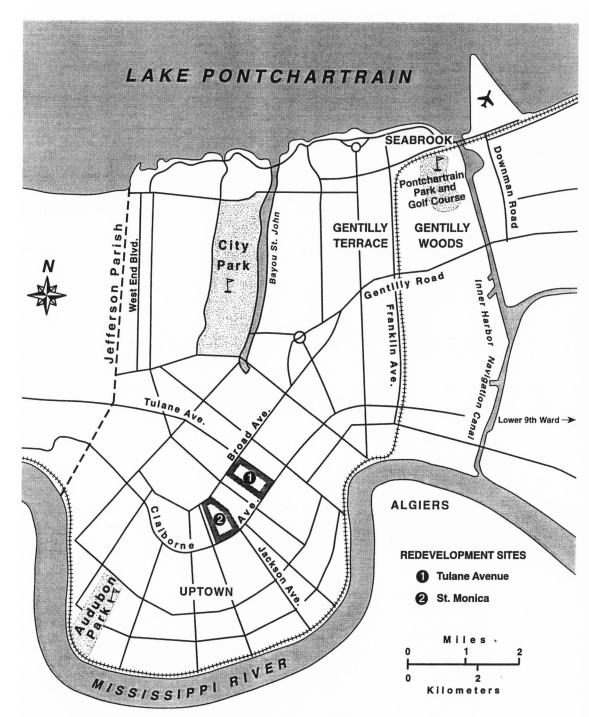

New Orleans in the 1950s (the historic Vieux Carre is at the bend of the Mississippi River opposite the Algiers district) showing areas of racial conflict discussed in this chapter: Seabrook, a beach on Lake Pontchartrain used by blacks despite the protests of whites in nearby Gentilly; Pontchartrain Park and Golf Course, a housing development and golf-course for middle-class blacks developed by the city in order to preserve the white-only status of City and Audubon Park golf courses; and redevelopment sites at Tulane Avenue and St. Monica. (Cartography by Jeanie Taliancich)

CHAPTER EIGHT

Race and Renewal in the Cold War South: New Orleans, 1947–1968

■■
■■

ARNOLD R. HIRSCH

The headlines in American newspapers brought momentous and alarming news of all kinds in the spring of 1954. Over a period of days and weeks, the U.S. Supreme Court's desegregation ruling in *Brown v. Board of Education of Topeka, Kansas*—and the reaction to it—vied for top billing with Senator Joseph McCarthy's showdown with the Army in congressional hearings and the fall of Dien Bien Phu in northern Vietnam. Crawling in beneath the bolder headlines, news of President Dwight D. Eisenhower's urban-renewal initiative, the Housing Act of 1954, earned less immediate attention but promised a fundamental restructuring of American society. Academic specialists may hold such events in suspension, picking them up one at a time for analysis, but people live their lives whole. For individuals experiencing an era of demographic and racial change, of urban growth and decay, and of federal government expansion and influence, such cataclysmic events took meaning from each other, illuminating and, perhaps, enhancing (or distorting) perspective.

Southern cities could perhaps be excused for feeling themselves at the center of such swirling change. The coincidence of the civil rights revolution with the era of urban redevelopment and renewal brought the inhabitants of a region long suspicious of federal authority into a new relationship with the national government at a time when that government was itself perceived to be in crisis and susceptible to the most insidious influences. If Southern business and civic elites had eagerly experimented with locally funded and controlled urban planning in the 1920s, their post–World War II experience unfolded in a greatly altered political, social, and economic setting.

New Orleans is less an archetype of Southern cities in this period than it is an exemplar of certain themes. It is clear that Northern cities, no less than Southern ones, seized this malleable historical moment to redefine racial relationships and reshape their physical configurations to meet a rising tide of African American migration and obdurate white demands for segregation. New Orleans and its Southern counterparts, however, had the added burden of doing so at a time when their traditional attitudes, institutions, and values came under direct, frontal assault. Lacking the cover and comfort provided by a system of de facto segregation and nominally open, participatory local democracies, the Crescent City had to confront postwar realities armed with little more than atavistic slogans and archaic shibboleths. It displayed, in short, a regionalism that was less ecological or geographic than socio-historical and intellectual.

The task of converting traditional impulses into a modern idiom fell (it was hardly sought out) to a local political and civic elite that embarrassingly revealed its limits. What passed for urban planning in post–World War II New Orleans was both race-based and politically driven. It reprised, in some ways, the dawning of the age of segregation, when Southern "progressives" fashioned the Jim Crow system.[1] Now the metaphorical descendants of those architects, the postwar "moderates," made a last-ditch effort to salvage that framework with new tools. Attempting to head off black protests and federal reprisals, New Orleans leaders tried to resuscitate the principle of "separate but equal" through redevelopment, even as the Supreme Court rendered that principle a nullity. In the end, however, a highly mobilized hard-line opposition, fueled by a reflexive distaste for federal authority and a deeply rooted local populism, exploited the perennial factionalism of Louisiana politics to kill all subsequent efforts at urban renewal for a decade and a half. A cowed and directionless business elite, paralyzed by the prospect of racial change, proved no match for the reac-

tionary wave generated by that challenge. From the *Brown* edict to the assassination of Martin Luther King, Jr., the most significant residential initiative successfully implemented in New Orleans was a middle-class complex and park for black homeowners that was designed to forestall a decision that had already been made.

The Creation of Pontchartrain Park

Pontchartrain Park, a subdivision constructed for middle-class African Americans in the Gentilly section of New Orleans, found itself by 1956 nestled among the finest recreational facilities, including a golf course, tennis courts, baseball diamonds, picnic grounds, and not-too-distant bathing facilities, on the shores of Lake Pontchartrain. Conceived in the immediate postwar era, the development represented the intersection of three distinct but overlapping racial crises that fortuitously met in Gentilly. The first was a dispute, going back at least to the Great Depression, over black access to swimming facilities along the lakeshore. In a subtropical climate and in an era before air conditioning, such access was no small matter—it could make life tolerable in New Orleans for six months or more each year. Second, as was the case in most cities at the time, there was a general housing shortage, one that was worse for blacks than for whites, and one that particularly pinched a growing African American middle class whose augmented resources placed it beyond the help of public housing. Finally, there was a rising tide of black protest, a restlessness that challenged Jim Crow and forced the city's political and civic leadership to respond, even before *Brown*.

The confrontation over the Seabrook area, a stretch of lakefront and seawall between Franklin Avenue and the Industrial Canal, went back at least to the late 1930s, when city police began chasing off blacks who attempted to swim there. Daniel E. Byrd of the New Orleans branch of the National Association for the Advancement of Colored People (NAACP) contended that "by custom, if not by law, our people have used the Seabrook Area over a long period of time and we feel we are entitled to a sanitary beach."[2] But as whites settled more densely in the previously sparsely populated Gentilly neighborhood nearby, complaints mounted. Finally, in 1943, the city simply closed the area as a wartime necessity (Army camps and industrial plants were in close proximity) and urged—with the Board of Levee Commissioners—that African Americans trek out to Lincoln Beach, another five to six miles beyond Seabrook and more than twice that distance from centers of black populations.[3]

The Levee Board had already spent some $200,000 of its own money and Works Progress Administration (WPA) funds, it noted, "to erect a modern bathhouse for the pleasure and convenience of the colored people" at the Lincoln Beach site. Located on land donated by United Fruit Company president Samuel Zemurray, Lincoln Beach nonetheless remained an expensive destination for those needing the two buses required to reach it from the city and was grossly polluted by the septic-tank toilets that emptied into the lake from nearby homes and "camps" that extended out from the shore on pilings.[4] Even the city's business leaders had to admit that fecal contamination fouled the water at the site and that the attempt to force black patronage there amounted to little more than a "subterfuge" to head off "the assignment of a more conveniently located beach."[5]

After the war, both black protest and white resistance increased. African Americans petitioned to repeal the wartime ordinance that banned civilian access to Seabrook and, more important, simply reclaimed their turf. Black New Orleanians flocked to the

lakefront at the Industrial Canal and, lacking bathhouse facilities, changed their clothes in their cars or behind available foliage. Mrs. W. H. Maddox typified the white correspondents who wrote the recently elected young mayor, DeLesseps S. (Chep) Morrison, in the spring of 1947 to complain about the black presence on "our beautiful Lakefront." "It is the most horrible, disgraceful thing I have ever seen," she lamented. "Sunday afternoons they look like a lot of naked savages out of Darkest Africa. . . . During the war they chased the negros [sic] out. Please do this again."[6]

For his part, the mayor recognized the "impracticability of removing Negroes from this neighborhood" and pushed an agreement with the Levee Board and the Army to "permit the use of the area in question as a bathing area for Negroes." Providing both lifeguards and regular police patrols, Morrison facilitated the black occupation of Seabrook and suggested in writing to one African American correspondent "that your people continue to use these facilities on the lakefront." To Mrs. Maddox, he contended that it would be "practically impossible" to exclude blacks from the area and that "any fair policy would have to permit them some use." He disingenuously added that this arrangement would last only "until better transportation facilities could be provided for colored persons to use Lincoln Beach."[7]

Not only were Gentilly's whites unable to recover a section of the lakefront from customary black usage, the remaining vacant land in the surrounding area also proved attractive as a potential solution to mounting housing problems. That the Crescent City's African American population required more and better housing could hardly be doubted. In 1940, the city's population stood at 494,537, of which 149,762 (30.3 percent) were black. Ten years later the population had increased to 570,445, with African

Americans numbering 182,631 (32.0 percent). Estimates in late 1952 counted 593,000 New Orleanians, among them 208,600 (35.1 percent) blacks.[8]

Among nonwhites, overcrowding increased between 1940 and 1950, and waiting lists for public housing lengthened; where 20,000 queued up for such units in 1947, some 30,000 were waiting within months of the *Brown* decision. The quality of housing similarly deteriorated—28,750 dwelling units occupied by African Americans lacked indoor baths or running water in 1950 as opposed to 26,919 ten years earlier—and vacancy rates in the private sector improved for whites even as they plummeted for blacks; already a paltry 0.8 percent in 1951, the vacancy rate of units "available for Negro occupancy" dropped to 0.3 percent a year later. In 1953, the New Orleans Home Builders Association estimated that 48,000 new homes had been built since V-J Day, but that "probably less than 500 and certainly not more than 1,000 of these homes were built for Negro occupancy." The Chamber of Commerce acknowledged that something other than economic competence accounted for that discrepancy: "many negroes with money would like to build substantial homes," it noted, "but [they] are restricted from building in white neighborhoods and did not want to construct them in ramshackle colored sections." The local Urban League agreed, concluding in the early 1950s that "the Negroes' plight has worsened almost unbelievably" since the end of the war and that the most pressing concern was "with the dearth of private sale and rental housing for the Negro market." "While the situation in the low rent housing field is perhaps even more pitiable at the moment," the league's executive director wrote, "much more has been done in that field through the Housing Authority of New Orleans."[9]

The provision of private middle-class housing for New Orleans's African American community subsequently became a priority for the Morrison administration, but such interest stemmed less from humanitarian concerns than from a sudden threat to the finest public amenities the Crescent City had to offer its traditional white elite. Nothing mobilized the city's civic, business, and political leadership more quickly than growing and persistent postwar black demands for access to previously denied facilities in fashionable Audubon and City Parks. A planned community for middle-class blacks consequently resulted from the demands of a handful of African Americans to play golf.[10]

The dearth of such recreational facilities for blacks in New Orleans had been well documented by Harland Bartholomew and Associates in the studies that accompanied their master plan for the city in the 1920s. In 1929, Bartholomew reported that there "are at present no parks exclusively for the colored people." Black children played in the streets and on the city's railroad tracks and levees; adults were "forced to go out of the city for their diversions." "Audubon Park, City Park, and West End Park," he noted, "now exist for the exclusive use of white persons." He advised that "it would be the best policy to provide [blacks] with their own parks in their own districts." Tentative plans included the possibility "of a colored park near the Industrial Canal." This isolated locale "would seem to be a logical place for a colored lakefront park," Bartholomew concluded. The Great Depression and World War II forestalled any such development, however, and even as late as 1947, city and civic leaders remained noncommittal on the provision of recreational facilities for blacks.[11]

Things changed quickly thereafter. By the spring of 1949, the managers of both Audubon Park and City Park informed business and civic leaders of "the rapid infiltration of Negroes into the two parks [and] their demands for the use of the golf courses, swimming pools, tennis courts, as well as use of the picnic grounds." Indeed, it became clear to the civic affairs committee of the Chamber of Commerce that "unless facilities are provided for the Colored shortly, demands will be made for the joint use of the two parks" and that such an eventuality will "probably result in a riot."[12]

Equally alarming was the prospect of legal action to compel black access to City and Audubon Park golf courses and the tone of the protests lodged by increasingly assertive members of the black elite. Hippolyte Dabezies, vice president of the National Bank of Commerce and member of the City Park Board, wrote Mayor Morrison directly to complain about the black attorney, A. P. Tureaud, who filed suit to desegregate the public links in November 1949. Tureaud, Dabezies wrote, "practically served notice on me that he was going to have negroes use City Park." When Dabezies responded that such action would "probably lead to trouble," Tureaud replied that "they were willing to take their chances, and were tired of being given the run-around by the City, and that he was not asking for advice." The political point was made. The governing boards of the white parks placed their planning units at the city's disposal to facilitate the creation of a park for the exclusive use of African Americans, and the mayor's advisers began speaking of "the crying need for Negro recreation facilities." The "only real solution," the mayor's Advisory Committee concluded, "will be the construction of a proper Negro park with golf course and other facilities."[13]

The most immediate obstacles standing in the way of such plans involved the location of a proper site and the availability of funds. Brief consideration of one city-owned (and hence affordable) site revealed the planning criteria employed by the mayor. He suggested a public dump deemed an "eye sore" on the

less-developed west bank of the Mississippi River that had fallen on hard times since its rehabilitation as a park by the WPA. "It has water hazzards [sic], roadways, arched overpasses of concrete, . . . everything necessary to make it an ideal course for the jiggerboos," Morrison wrote. Furthermore, it was isolated enough in a "corner of Orleans Parish over in Algiers," he went on, so that it would not "cause a big howl from the gentry because of colored encroachments." If the "jiggs" complained about having to cross the river to play a round of golf, moreover, it could be pointed out that west bank whites had to endure the same indignity.[14]

The site eventually chosen, however, first came to the city's attention in 1947 as a private offering of 366 acres situated between the white-occupied Gentilly Woods subdivision and the Seabrook beach. The realtor recommending the site to the city advised that "this tract of ground offers the best solution to the present problem of finding a suitable place with sufficient acreages and readily accessible at the same time, being so isolated by natural barriers . . . that it would not interfere or be detrimental to any of the surrounding properties." Morrison, well aware "of the constant pressure upon the park authorities, and also the constant pressure of the Negroes wishing to have an adequate beach area," seized the opportunity to resolve both issues. Moving quickly to head off a threatened Levee Board lease of the Seabrook area for military use that would have ended its status as a black beach, the administration conceived of a "restricted housing development" in conjunction with the golf course and park that would have an "outlet to the Lakefront" and, most important of all, solve the difficult problem of financing.[15]

Not only were there problems with the cost of the land, but the expense of extending city utilities, particularly sewerage and drainage, proved daunting. Indeed, this was doubly so after Earl Long's election as governor in 1948 and his subsequent political assault on archrival Morrison. Determined to crush the New Orleans's anti-Longs, the governor and a compliant legislature halved the city's sales-tax revenue while compounding municipal expenses. In the spring of 1949, the financial squeeze proved so tight that Morrison embarked on a "retrenchment program" that "made it folly even to consider" acquiring land for a massive and, as yet, unfunded park development. Blaming the "punitive legislation by the Governor and his colleagues in Baton Rouge" for his plight, Morrison sought salvation in the redevelopment program embodied in the federal Housing Act of 1949.[16]

Just three months after nearly abandoning his plans due to state-induced financial exigencies, the mayor announced that it would be possible to "finance a Negro public park in connection with new housing units" under the recently passed federal "slum clearance" act. By devoting 140 of the site's vacant acres to housing, the project became eligible for federal assistance because, as Morrison observed, the act did not require the actual clearance of slums and it permitted construction anywhere in the city. Although it appears the administration first contemplated a public housing project in connection with the park, the mayor soon appealed directly to the Federal Housing Administration (FHA) to help meet "a vital need for single family type homes for colored." It was, Morrison informed the FHA, "our fervent belief that homes built in the area, adjacent to Lake Pontchartrain and bordering a full scale Negro city park can be marketed rapidly, and with everyone's cooperation, properly financed." His administration was "vitally interested" in the development, he emphasized, and would "bend every effort to make this badly needed project a reality."[17]

The shift to more upscale black housing proved successful, and in 1954 some 1,000 homes priced between $9,500 and $25,000 went on the market in a $15,000,000 subdivision in the Seabrook area. Edgar B. Stern, philanthropist, mayoral adviser, and president of Pontchartrain Park Homes, Inc., announced the sale along with fellow investor Charles Keller, developer W. Hamilton Crawford, and FHA representative Dr. George Snowden. The investors' reimbursement of advances made by the federal government and the developer facilitated construction, as did contributions by city agencies such as the Sewerage and Water Board. Revealing perhaps more than he intended, Morrison exuberantly declared that the project offered "Negroes in New Orleans, for the first time, an opportunity to buy a home in a community that provides hard-surfaced streets, sewerage, water, gas, electricity and other facilities second to none." Another city official also commented tellingly that "our long range plan for a fine public park along 'country club recreational lines' rather than 'Lincoln Beach lines' was proper." For his part, Edgar Stern simply asserted that the homes in Pontchartrain Park would "equal or surpass homes in [the] adjoining Gentilly Woods Subdivision."[18]

If there was any hope that the status of their new neighbors would dampen the protest of Gentilly whites, it proved ill-founded. They perceived that the administration now approved "the movement of an element into a section of the city where that element does not at present exist except in infinitesimal quantity." Borrowing language successfully employed by the politically connected "gentry" in other areas, they bemoaned the "infiltration into our most highly valued section" and believed that a black subdivision developed in conjunction "with Lincoln Beach would be better."[19] As a fallback, those resigned to the construction of the Pontchartrain Homes tried to change elements of the project's design. Whites complained that the entrances to the park, as originally conceived, would "bring thousands of Negroes through their property at all times of the day and night throughout the year," devaluing their property and increasing the "danger and fights which have arisen in similar situations." If developers could place one entrance on the lakefront and another "at some location other than the back of Gentilly Woods," one resident wrote, "we will have no problem."[20]

Given his earlier support for so many of the physical improvements that had made the white occupation of Gentilly possible, Morrison felt put upon by such protests, but he tried to placate the disturbed citizens, nonetheless. At a raucous April 28, 1950, Commission Council meeting held to approve several needed ordinances prior to construction, the mayor assured Gentilly residents that the new black homes would be separated from them by a "Chinese Wall," a railroad embankment through which no safe passageway existed or was planned between Gentilly Highway and Downman Road; he also made mention of the City Park golf suit and the possibility of losing it without the development of Pontchartrain Park. Privately, he told one constituent that the new subdivision would be of "less annoyance to you . . . than the present Seabrook-Lakefront beach use." To another, he explained, "My own feeling is that regardless of whether this will satisfy the group or not, at least it is the best that we can do in view of the shortage of large land areas in the built up part of New Orleans. This is our last chance to give the Negroes a full scale park within our pocket books. We have just got to make up our minds that if we are going to preserve traditions and habits in our city (which includes segregation) that we are going to have to provide facilities to meet the demands of the Negro group."[21]

In the end, the courts moved more quickly than the bulldozers. In 1952, three years after the suit to desegregate New Orleans's white golf courses had been filed, an arrangement between African Americans and City Park granted blacks access to one City Park course on Tuesdays and Fridays as "a temporary expedient" that would be "revoked when the Seabrook Park is ready." Though several Southern cities removed racial barriers from their municipal links in the wake of *Brown*—Houston, Dallas, and Louisville among them—New Orleans contemplated no further change, and a year later Morrison aides corresponded with mayor William B. Hartsfield of Atlanta after the U.S. Supreme Court voided restrictions there. The decision, Morrison aide W. Ray Scheuering wrote, "created considerable anxiety in and around New Orleans." The Crescent City apparently still intended to reimpose the old system when the Pontchartrain Park course was completed. By the time the first nine holes of the new course opened in 1956, however, court rulings made it a municipal park open to all.[22]

Perhaps the most remarkable aspect of the whole affair was the unity and alacrity with which the political, civic, and business elite moved when faced with the threat of racial change. Indeed, when the board of directors of the Chamber of Commerce, in a near panic following the appearance of blacks in City and Audubon Parks, urged the mayor to "expedite . . . the work of providing a park for the colored people with all necessary facilities," the city leapt into action. The political and economic obstacles that had to be overcome were not insubstantial, and the exploitation of federal resources showed no small measure of creativity. Following the diversion of WPA funds that aided the development of Lincoln Beach, it simply confirmed that locals quickly discovered the usefulness of federal authority and money in reinforcing parochial patterns.

More than a determined defense of Jim Crow, the construction of the Pontchartrain Park development represented its apotheosis in New Orleans. In a land-starved city whose congested neighborhoods had—for more than two hundred years—sheltered diverse congeries of people, Pontchartrain Park achieved a standard of racial homogeneity and isolation rarely seen before. Only the Housing Authority of New Orleans (HANO), in its federally supported, locally administered public-housing program for low-income residents, could challenge Pontchartrain Park in "set[ting] a pattern of segregation," according to local NAACP president Arthur J. Chapital.[23] No prior regime, no matter how reactionary, had been able to accomplish such results, though some, especially in the 1920s, had tried. It was the progressive Morrison administration, backed by the city's most prominent racial moderates, and federal assistance that had both literally and figuratively broken this new ground.

The Battle for Urban Renewal

Even more striking than the determined action that produced Pontchartrain Park was its contrast with the halting, timid, and ineffectual response on the part of the same authorities when faced with the broader task of urban renewal. Threats to the established social order evoked consensus (only those whites directly affected by the sitting of the new black development broke ranks), but once the defense of racial hierarchy became blurred, or bore no compelling relation to future proposals, that consensus evaporated. Indeed, the "progressive" Morrison administration moved quickly to capitalize further on the Housing Act of 1949, and that of 1954 as well, only to fail to realize its plans for slum clearance and renewal. Moreover, the mayor's very actions provoked a reaction

among white Louisianians that, in the context of the budding civil rights era, prohibited New Orleans's and the state's participation in such federally supported programs for nearly fifteen years. Only after the assassination of Martin Luther King, Jr., and in conjunction with a host of novel pressures, did the state repeal its restrictive legislation and permit its cities to engage in such activity.

Other Southern cities such as Memphis, Atlanta, Richmond, and Miami moved much more aggressively in the postwar period to take advantage of augmented public powers and resources to stabilize and reinforce, or, when necessary, reconfigure racial accommodations to suit segregationist impulses. Racial zoning, segregation ordinances, restrictive covenants, and "gentleman's agreements" among private realtors were now supplanted or supplemented in those cities by public housing, slum clearance, urban renewal, urban planning, and highway construction. Public policy, in short, began to replace de jure segregation even before the latter was struck down. New Orleans's development of Pontchartrain Park and its public-housing program fit that pattern. But there was, at least in some of the less progressive bastions of the Old South, or those cities where whites exhibited deep class or other internal divisions, some reticence as well. Richmond, for example, resisted for years the impulse to create a public housing authority to assist in redevelopment before it succumbed to what one mayor called a violation of "every principle of sound business, democracy, Americanism, and individualism." New Orleans may have moved with more resolve to create its new agencies, but it quickly fell behind the others, as a unique blend of Southern conservatism and its own peculiarities combined to slow its march to modernity.[24]

Such did not at first appear to be the case. In the decade between the end of the war and the Montgomery bus boycott, New Orleans not only developed Pontchartrain Park, but built a new civic center complex that necessitated some slum clearance, and made numerous street improvements as well. A cooperative state legislature and a seemingly anxious business elite appeared poised to push further. In 1948, the state approved urban redevelopment acts that empowered municipalities to seize private property for slum clearance via eminent domain and to pass such parcels over to private housing corporations for development. A companion measure enlarged HANO so that the agency entrusted with overseeing redevelopment (in addition to public housing) in New Orleans would be up to the task.

Though many in the business community and among the civic elite continued to display an almost reflexive hostility toward public housing, these measures attracted warm support. Members of the Home Development Committee of the Chamber of Commerce recommended approval of the redevelopment bills to the chamber's board because of the manifest need "to clean up unsanitary and deteriorated or otherwise blighted areas." The board, recognizing the impossibility of acquiring such properties through "ordinary channels" and "feeling that the safeguards as provided by the act were sufficient," approved its committee's recommendations unanimously.[25]

Passage of the federal Housing Act of 1949 seemed to add momentum to the redevelopment movement. Not only did Chep Morrison contemplate its use in Pontchartrain Park, but HANO's general counsel, William Guste, believed it brought more grandiose plans within reach. Expecting the Crescent City's share of the largesse to include some 5,500 public housing units, Guste asserted that "we will be able to renovate the entire city."[26] HANO's chairman, Olin Linn, also explicitly linked public housing with contemplated slum-clearance/redevelopment

plans when he called them "spearheads of modern progress that will elevate the condition of thousands of underprivileged families . . . and clean up large segments of the city's worst slum districts."[27] Even more significant, the city brought back Harland Bartholomew to "update" his 1926–31 master plan for New Orleans in light of the new possibilities. Bartholomew, in conjunction with HANO, ultimately produced a twenty-five-year, $100 million slum-clearance program to be completed under the aegis of the Housing Act of 1949.

The first site recommended by Bartholomew included some one hundred acres bounded by Tulane Avenue, Poydras, Broad, and Claiborne. Estimates pegged the project's net loss after acquisition, clearance, and resale at $6 million; the federal government could be expected to pick up two-thirds of that cost. HANO had to admit that the area was "not the city's worst slum" even though its 1,477 resident families (446 white and 1,031 black) lived in units that were overwhelmingly substandard: more than half were classed as "dilapidated" and 27 percent still had outdoor toilets (another 28 percent shared toilets with other units). The area was selected primarily because its central location was attractive to potential commercial and industrial tenants, and because already completed or approved street improvements in the area could be applied to the city's share of the project's overall cost.[28]

There was, however, one drawback to the site that escaped immediate attention. Indeed, years later mayoral adviser David R. McGuire acknowledged that the proposed project "was so located that it became politically controversial." It fell within the bailiwick of assessor James E. Comiskey, a staunch Morrison adversary and a major cog in the Regular Democratic Organization (RDO), the "machine" turned out of office by the young mayor in 1946. Representing constituents who were the antithesis of the genteel, uptown, reform element that made up Morrison's political base, Comiskey helped organize an Owners-Tenants Association (OTA) specifically to oppose slum clearance and orchestrated a massive letter-writing campaign against the proposal. Indulging personal and political grievances while responding to cries from local slum owners (only 21 percent of the whites and only 11 percent of the blacks in the target area owned their own homes), Comiskey also shrewdly played on populist, anticorporate themes that still resonated in precincts that had deep and fond memories of Huey and Earl Long. Comiskey, McGuire admitted, proved "successful in stirring up a substantial portion of the community against urban renewal on the basis that it would make displaced persons out of a substantial part of the population. He was successful in presenting a case on the rights of the small individual property owner opposed to big government and big business."[29]

Additional opposition rallied around traditional conservative slogans and represented an ideological or philosophical attack on the premises of the program itself. The New Orleans Homestead and Savings and Loan League urged the defeat of the Tulane project because it believed that "acquiring property through expropriation proceedings and reselling the property to other private owners ... constitutes a departure from the generally accepted rights of eminent domain." OTA attorney Albert J. Flettrich condemned the potentially "dangerous concentration of power" in municipal and federal housing agencies, and Representative F. Edward Hebert (another Morrison adversary) heatedly extended the critique to include "increased governmental regimentation by the centralized socialistic government in Washington." Even the *Times-Picayune,* at this point still friendly to the notion of redevelopment, concluded

that the program was opposed "mostly on the ground that it was inconsistent with the American system to expropriate property" for anything other than a direct public use.[30]

Most telling, perhaps, was the tepid support, if not outright opposition, furnished by those constituencies usually deemed most friendly to the Morrison administration. Neither New Orleans's blacks nor its white business community embraced the Tulane slum-clearance plan. African Americans, for example, were already feeling the pinch associated with the slum clearance that preceded the construction of the civic center complex and new HANO developments. Outspoken black journalist John E. Rousseau complained to Morrison in the midst of the debate over the Tulane project that "hundreds of Negro families are being rendered homeless by the expropriation of their properties by the City of New Orleans in its modernization program and by the Housing Authority of New Orleans in its expansion program." Those forced to sell homes and uprooted by HANO faced particular difficulty as they, in many cases, possessed resources that made them ineligible for the new public housing. Rousseau pleaded with Morrison "to refrain from being a party to a system, which, in addition to having deprived many Negro families of their homes, would render them the helpless prey of scheming landlords and profiteering realtors."[31] The prospect of additional Tulane-site refugees seeking housing on the private market could not have been comforting, and many redevelopment-area residents undoubtedly found assessor Comiskey's frightening blandishments convincing in light of such circumstances.

As for the commercial and civic elite, it remained somewhat divided and largely on the sidelines during the Tulane redevelopment controversy. Although some still spoke of using HANO to "pave the way for rehabilitation" and private redevelopment, most now expressed misgivings at what F. Poche Waguespack, realtor and chair of the Chamber of Commerce's Subcommittee for Rehabilitation of Slum Housing, called "creeping socialism." The "bug" in the plan, according to Waguespack, was public housing. Though he believed "a certain amount" might be necessary for the relocation of site residents, he remained convinced that public housing was "not the answer to the slum problem" and feared HANO's expansive agenda.[32]

The Chamber of Commerce, in fact, had already begun a search for a more ideologically acceptable alternative. Chamber executive vice president W. F. Riggs, Jr., believed the situation to be "psychologically right to undertake a program to rehabilitate slum housing . . . along the lines of the Baltimore Plan"—a program of slum rehabilitation through strict code and law enforcement. The chamber not only brought G. Yates Cook, the "father" of the Baltimore Plan, to New Orleans to pitch his program but dispatched a "small, informal investigative group" to Baltimore and Charlotte, North Carolina, to see it in operation. The businessmen subsequently concluded that the redevelopment of slum areas could be handled three ways: through public housing; through some combination of federal and city action to purchase, raze, and resell such sites to private developers; or through revitalization by individual property owners who would meet minimum living and sanitary standards. The chamber now voiced interest only in "the third type. "Communicating and working closely with the mayor, the Chamber of Commerce noted in its executive committee minutes that Morrison was "willing to go along with [the] plan."[33]

Given the lack of committed support and, according to the *Times-Picayune*, the "bitter opposition [of] property owners and many real estate men," Morrison abandoned the redevelopment plan. In so doing, he noted

that the project "has been distorted and misrepresented continuously by some opponents who have selfish interests to serve," although he also had to admit that the city, indeed, lacked "available residential units in which to relocate the citizens who would be displaced." In a letter to HANO's Olin Linn, Morrison endorsed the notion of an alternative revitalization campaign modeled on the Baltimore Plan and the belief that 80 percent of the slum conditions could be corrected through neighborhood and individual action. The city would not, he said, make any further attempts at redevelopment under the Housing Act of 1949; the Bartholomew twenty-five-year program was permanently shelved.[34]

The final indignity, however, did not come until two years later. In 1954, in the wake of the *Brown* decision, a series of state legislative acts repealed the enabling legislation of 1948 that permitted the city to participate in the federal program and stripped HANO of the power to acquire slum property for clearance and resale to private interests. Drafted and lobbied through the legislature by the OTA, the prohibition on the municipal exercise of eminent domain for all but direct public uses effectively locked New Orleans out of prospective renewal and rehabilitation projects facilitated by the new federal Housing Act of 1954. New Orleans's Council of Social Agencies offered only ineffective and token opposition, arguing that the bills were intended to "make slum clearance and redevelopment programs impossible."[35]

Chep Morrison, however, thought the Eisenhower administration's initiative provided a ray of hope in spite of the restrictive state action. If New Orleanians feared mass demolition and clearance, he could now offer them rehabilitation and spot removals. Pushing ahead, his administration offered an urban-renewal program for the St. Monica area, an uptown site encompassing 162 acres between Toledano, Broad, Melpomene, Claiborne, and Jackson. Plans called for the bull-dozing of only half the homes in the area, and the construction of at least one new school and several playgrounds, along with massive street and utility improvements. Given federal cost-sharing formulas and the extensive city improvements already planned for the site, officials believed no more than $142,000 in new municipal funds were needed in order to realize the $1.5–$1.8 million development.[36]

It was not to be. The same political opposition manifested itself, this time in the context of a heated gubernatorial campaign that pitted Morrison against Earl Long. District councilman Paul Burke, an occasional Morrison ally, opposed the project and denounced what he called the "harassment" of local residents by officious city representatives. "That gave the people who fought the Tulane Ave. redevelopment plan the chance to go in there," Burke exclaimed, "and say 'this is the same deal; only instead of redevelopment, Morrison's people are now calling it renewal—but they are going to confiscate your homes just the same.'" Scare stories abounded in the campaign, and consultant David McGuire told Morrison point-blank that James Comiskey and the "Long people" will "get St. Monica killed." They "effectively alarmed all of the Negro families in this area that the Mayor planned to demolish the homes they live in and throw them out on the streets," McGuire wrote Morrison. Comiskey in particular, he noted, "exerted more effective [pressure] against it than you have for it." Ultimately, McGuire advised Morrison to cut his losses. "Sometimes you can lead so greatly that you are marching alone in front of the crowd. . . . Now is the time to listen to public opinion."[37]

This time there was little for Morrison to do. The federal government insisted, without success, that Louisiana repeal its restrictions on expropriation, and, in April 1956, the City Council rejected the plan outright. Councilman (and later mayor) Victor H. Schiro, summed up much of the opposition's sentiment when he called the whole scheme "un-American." Venting some of the feeling that became evident in the post-*Brown* South, Schiro asked rhetorically, "Why don't we turn over to the federal government the entire city? You might as well resign yourself that you are not living in a democracy anymore when you depend so much on Uncle Sam."[38]

Supporters or potential advocates of urban renewal barely raised a finger. The Chamber of Commerce remained committed to its program of rehabilitation through private enterprise, and its board members had to be reminded a month before the City Council killed the St. Monica project that they "had taken no official position with regard to the Urban Redevelopment Program." The *New Orleans Item* registered the strongest protest in a sarcastic editorial that attacked St. Monica's antagonists as well as those who believed that individual initiative leavened by civic pride could eradicate slums. "Since only 18% of the St. Monica property is resident-owned," the editors wrote, "here is a fine chance for humanitarianism and altruism as well as civic pride to have a field day." The city's major daily, the *Times-Picayune*, simply thought it a "shame to pass up the benefits." Offering more analysis than regret, the paper concluded that the project got caught in the "expropriation nutcracker" and "involved in the ugliest sort of politics, in which confusion and misinformation ran rampant."[39]

Attempts to repeal the 1954 legislative restrictions on urban renewal failed in 1958 and 1960; even the city's own delegation in Baton Rouge had "mixed feelings" on the matter, according to McGuire, or, in the case of Morrison's opposition, "were politically opposed to the bill on a factional basis."

Having sent it down to defeat, the Louisiana legislature refused to budge on the issue for nearly a decade more. Populist arguments regarding the impropriety of expropriation for private development and the thought that developers earned unconscionable profits after squeezing the "little guy" still resonated in the post-*Brown* era, but other themes quickly achieved greater stature. Increasingly, the claim that urban renewal was socialistic or communistic and "usurp[ed] states rights" began to be heard. These allegations had, of course, been present earlier. But with the race issue placed squarely on the table now, with the "Southern way of life" at stake, such charges achieved dominance.[40]

Indeed, Southern congressional Democrats linked renewal and race within days of the *Brown* decision when they tried, unsuccessfully, to strip provisions for public housing from the Housing Act of 1954; the *Item* reported that their action "stemmed from fears growing out of a Supreme Court anti-segregation ruling." The linkage became even more explicit when James J. Kilpatrick, editor of the Richmond *News Leader* and leading critic of federally sponsored redevelopment (it cast the "Shadow of Marx" over his city, he claimed), dusted off the doctrine of interposition and became a leading spokesman and guiding intellectual light for the segregationists.[41] New Orleans boasted no theorist of Kilpatrick's mettle, but the antirenewal arguments became more vitriolic, and fears of federal intervention on the local level deepened accordingly. Where the postwar racial moderates found federal assistance helpful in shoring up segregation and, indeed, even in extending it, the post-*Brown* racial hard-liners viewed the national government as an enemy bent on undermining traditional values and society.

Rev. William A. Miller, a Redemptorist priest from the city's Irish channel, a working-class neighborhood deeply affected by HANO's construction program, stood among New Orleans's most vehement critics. For him, the proponents of urban renewal were "communistic termites" who tried to "undermine our American form of government" and "invite[d] all the evils of open housing and racial discord." Segregationist and sometime political candidate A. Roswell Thompson displayed even more vehemence in rejecting one of the proposed urban-renewal bills as "the most dastardly unchristianlike law that could be put into effect by a legislature." Urban renewal, Thompson fumed, would drive blacks out of the slums to "infiltrate the neighborhoods of our people."[42]

Such critics and the tension palpably manifest in the age of massive resistance made dissent difficult and, for politicians, dangerous. Chep Morrison, for one, still entertained hopes of becoming governor in the campaign of 1959–60 and thus stayed out of the urban-renewal debate, as McGuire put it, for "tactical" reasons. Moreover, the "moderate" Morrison accommodated himself to the racial frenzy then sweeping the state by denying that he was "soft" on segregation and touting himself as the state's leading defendant in NAACP lawsuits. Defeated nonetheless by a rabidly racist reaction, those in the Morrison camp trembled for the future. "I think we have some rough times ahead in this race situation in the South," McGuire wrote Atlanta's William Hartsfield, "and I wish there was some way to convince the majority of the white people who are normally level-headed that they should think with their heads instead of their emotions on this subject."[43]

In this climate, New Orleans's commercial elite ran for cover, unlike its counterparts in other cities who led the way on planning and renewal initiatives. Indeed, one of the reasons Morrison refused to touch the issue at this time, a mayoral confidant concluded, was because the "business and civic leadership of this City ha[d] not made known to the public its support of redevelopment and/or urban renewal legislation."[44] Moreover, on the key question of segregation, the Chamber of Commerce remained divided and could agree only that the organization should take no formal or public position. The only exception to that policy came in reaction to the Eisenhower administration's proposal to establish a commission on civil rights and a civil rights division within the Department of Justice. On that question, the chamber's board of directors found the gumption to stand unanimously in opposition on the grounds that it "would constitute an invasion or attempted invasion of . . . State's rights."[45]

The first hints of change did not come until the mid-1960s. In 1964, Louis D. Brown of the Chamber of Commerce admitted that New Orleans's business community spent a good deal of effort "trying to develop . . . an effective urban . . . redevelopment program . . . without the use of expropriation powers or federal funds." After "years of soul searching," however, they finally determined that "no large scale slum clearance . . . program can be accomplished without the use of eminent domain for the assembly of land." They also had to have known by then that their program of slum eradication through inspection and code enforcement held little promise. Indeed, consultant Howard W. Hallman, brought to the city in early January 1966 by the Stern Family Fund, reported that New Orleans had "an appallingly low number of housing inspectors." A city of New Orleans's size should have seventy such inspectors, Hallman noted; instead, the city authorized the hiring of only ten, and no more than five were "now actively engaged."[46]

Second, even though they disliked "running to Washington for money," local elites now believed, according to Brown, that the

cash poured into competing cities by such national programs "work[ed] to the serious disadvantage of . . . New Orleans." Indeed, protesting Louisiana's status as the only state to prohibit its cities from participating in urban renewal, Rev. Eugene McManus, S.S.J., the director of the Archdiocesan Commission on Housing and Community Life, complained that it seemed "grossly unfair that we should be financing urban renewal in 49 other states and yet are prevented by our state legislature from using such funds for our own needs."[47]

Even Chep Morrison's successor, former councilman Vic Schiro (who became mayor following Morrison's resignation in 1961), backpedaled on the issue. Earlier, Schiro had eagerly sought and won the political (and financial) support of one of New Orleans's leading anti–urban renewal polemicists, Col. Bluford H.J. Balter, by proclaiming his opposition to urban renewal "via Eminent Domain" and his allegiance to the "free enterprise system." He had contributed in no small part to the fact that, in the eyes of the black-owned *Louisiana Weekly,* the state had "distinguished itself as the nation's last bastion of ultra-conservatism and backwardness" for "fear of offending the advocates of states' rights." By the mid-1960s, however, Schiro asserted that "We are tired of being better patriots, better states righters than our fellow Southerners in Mississippi or Alabama. . . . We are tired of Louisiana being the only state . . . that can't get what's rightfully hers." It was time, he said, to stop treating Washington, D.C., as though it were the capital of an alien nation.[48]

Obvious need, the inadequacy of private efforts, and financial pressure, though, were not sufficient to overcome deeply entrenched political resistance. The turning point came only in 1965 when two key events—the passage of the Voting Rights Act and the arrival of Hurricane Betsy—finally tipped the balance in favor of accepting federal assistance.

There is no question that the augmentation and mobilization of black political strength in New Orleans got Vic Schiro's attention. Running to be elected mayor in his own right in 1962, Schiro capitalized on the tensions still flowing out of the previous year's disorderly brush with school desegregation, ran a viciously racist campaign, and stumped gladly with the endorsement of the White Citizens' Council. Four years later, however, he campaigned feverishly for black votes, won a substantial minority, and earned a second full term. Even the subsequent polling done to sample attitudes toward urban renewal in New Orleans tested blacks now and revealed that this most rapidly growing segment of the Crescent City's electorate favored it even more strongly than did whites, though both groups—by the late 1960s—voiced strong support.[49]

Perhaps even more significant, however, was the emergence of a nascent black political elite and the possibility of its cultivation through a rich new source of patronage. Such considerations had never been too distant from the process of urban reconstruction and, in fact, Chep Morrison had offered parcels of land in Pontchartrain Park to his political favorites. He also made certain that the concessions in the park were funneled through A. L. Davis, founder of the Orleans Parish Progressive Voters League and Morrison's chief lieutenant in the African American community. As for Vic Schiro, he now promised black leaders that at least 50 percent of the staff in the city's first development project would be black, including at least one slot at a policy-making level—and this from a mayor who had only recently closed the city's swimming pools rather than see them integrated.[50]

The project that Schiro had in mind encompassed the lower Ninth Ward of New Or-

leans, an area devastated by Hurricane Betsy on the night of September 9, 1965. Overwhelming levees in eastern Orleans Parish, the hurricane inundated much undeveloped land but also submerged a poor and poorly served district largely inhabited by African Americans below the Industrial Canal. Housing in some blighted areas, according to Schiro, remained "under flood waters long after the Hurricane." Much of the district still lacked paved streets and subsurface drainage, and it became clear the city could not afford—and would not undertake—a rebuilding program on its own. The "city alone cannot do the job in this area," Schiro declared. "We need outside federal help and we need it now." The city subsequently prepared a proposal for a survey and planning assistance preparatory to a renewal project.[51]

The problem, as always, was the city's lack of legal standing to undertake a federally supported renewal project. In a letter initially rejecting the city's application, Jack D. Herrington, regional director of the Urban Renewal Division of the Department of Housing and Urban Development, declared that the proposed project appeared "ineligible for Federal financial assistance" because New Orleans had "no urban renewal powers." "State legislation," he advised, "is the only means by which cities in Louisiana may obtain the legal means of undertaking activities such as those proposed." A city delegation pursued a follow-up meeting in Washington, D.C., to plead its case, but got little comfort from HUD secretary Robert Weaver. "The history of your state legislators and legislation is the problem," he told them.[52]

New Orleanians hardly had to be reminded of the state's legislative restrictions. They had, in fact, finally reintroduced a new urban-renewal bill in the legislature in 1966, less than a year after Hurricane Betsy and six years since their last serious effort. New Orleans's state senator Laurance Eustis sponsored a "local option" urban-renewal bill that permitted voluntary municipal participation. To those still squeamish about accepting federal assistance, Eustis said simply, "it's our money." For those raising the standard of states' rights, he pointed to the $82 million in urban-renewal funding that had gone to George Wallace's Alabama and asserted that the safeguards built into the legislation made it "the very essence of home rule." Though it did not pass, the issue now remained on the state's agenda.[53]

Another effort the next year produced a new wrinkle and a new problem. Mayor Schiro, who, complained the *States-Item,* "didn't exactly knock down the doors of legislative committees . . . on behalf of local option urban renewal," fully committed himself to the rehabilitation of the still-devastated Ninth Ward by early 1967. To cover himself—and perhaps to placate those still suspicious of outside assistance—he added a call for a citywide referendum to approve New Orleans's creation of an urban-renewal agency. Despite solid backing in New Orleans and growing support from other Louisiana cities, however, the rurally dominated state legislature remained recalcitrant. "The boys from upstate, with arguments as narrow as a country lane, fell on the New Orleans urban renewal proposal with obvious relish," wrote *States-Item* columnist David Snyder. It was a "monumental example of short-sightedness and political pettiness," his paper editorialized, and did nothing but enable Louisiana to preserve "the dubious honor of being the only state in the nation without authority to embark on urban renewal projects."[54]

Finally, a third consecutive effort produced the elusive victory in 1968. The key to success proved to be a new reapportionment plan that altered the political balance of power. Previously, the 105-member Louisiana House of Representatives had at least one rep-

resentative from each of the state's sixty-four parishes; consequently, those from but fifty-three of the state's overwhelmingly rural parishes could defeat any action. Under the new reapportionment plan, parish lines no longer served as mandatory district boundaries, and the cities gained proportionately. Less than two months after the assassination of Martin Luther King, Jr., the Louisiana Senate passed an urban-renewal bill, and the state House followed by early July. Four Louisiana cities—New Orleans, Lake Charles, Shreveport, and Monroe—now had the power to participate in federal renewal projects after conducting local referenda. Arousing much less acrimonious debate than in years past, the new law seemed almost an anticlimax.[55]

Conclusion

Ironies abounded in this situation. It was, first of all, the Southern "moderates," individuals such as Chep Morrison, who were dogged by the charge of being "soft" on segregation even as they used the tools of urban redevelopment to separate the races to a greater extent than ever before. Left to their own devices before the *Brown* decision, Morrison and his cohort imparted a flexibility and resiliency to Jim Crow that they hoped would save it. After *Brown,* a whirlwind of reaction cut the ground from beneath the moderates, thwarting Morrison's ambitions and effectively ending his political career. The racial hard-liners that emerged ascendant in the mid-1950s not only provided a more inviting target for civil rights forces but consciously rejected the devices being used in Northern and more "progressive" Southern cities to redraw and reinforce racial boundaries. It was those on the left of this skewed political spectrum that fought to make "separate but equal" a reality; those on the right choked at the thought of "equality" in any form and were not as interested in "separation" as much as hierarchy and subordination.

Second, the long-awaited embrace of urban renewal in Louisiana came virtually as the practice was discredited everywhere else. In retrospect, those who charged it was a developer's land grab that endangered working-class homes and neighborhoods and would do the poor no service had a compelling argument. In any event, the program had largely run its course and would not transform the face of New Orleans. The somnolent Crescent City had earlier dozed through the age of industrialization; it missed urban renewal in much the same way. More dynamic cities with more vibrant economies ripped their cores, bulldozed their neighborhoods, and sent thousands on an urban trail of tears looking for new accommodations. For better or worse (and either case could be made), New Orleans opted out.

Ultimately, the coincidence of the cold war, the civil rights revolution, and the era of urban redevelopment and renewal emphasized the contingency of what passed for urban planning in post–World War II New Orleans. The craft proved to be neither art nor science, but a bare-knuckle brawl fueled by changing demographics and the agency of African Americans. Politically driven, New Orleans demonstrated that the process could dispense with the best-laid plans of the most prestigious consultants if they interfered with electoral considerations, or if they raised the specter of the threat *du jour*. In the end, the virtual absence of anticommunist rhetoric in 1968, even in the midst of a hot war in Vietnam, shows the distance traveled between *Brown* and the emergence of mainstream black politics in the wake of the Voting Rights Act. If the civil rights movement had triumphed over Jim Crow, it seemed equally certain by the time the Louisiana legislature accepted the principle of urban renewal that neither the physical city nor its social structure would be transformed. Both the threat and the promise of the age dwarfed the reality.

Notes

1. John W. Cell, *The Highest Stage of White Supremacy: The Origins of Segregation in South Africa and the American South* (Cambridge: Cambridge University Press, 1982), pp. 171–91.

2. Daniel E. Byrd to DeLesseps S. Morrison, March 17, 1949, box 28, folder: NAACP, 1948–1949, DeLesseps S. Morrison Papers, Howard-Tilton Memorial Library, Tulane University (TU), New Orleans, La. The Works Progress Administration (WPA) noted in 1938 that the section of seawall near the Industrial Canal was "reserved for Negroes." See *The WPA Guide to New Orleans* (New York: Pantheon, 1983 [1938]), p. 296.

3. *Pittsburgh Courier,* January 14, 1950, clipping found in Scrapbook 40, Morrison Papers, TU.

4. New Orleans Association of Commerce, minutes of the regular monthly meeting of the Civic Affairs Committee, April 20, 1949, in New Orleans Association of Commerce, *Minutes, December 1948–December 1949, Vol. 2,* Chamber of Commerce Papers, Earl K. Long Library, University of New Orleans (UNO); Robert B. Delahoussaye to Office of the Director, City Board of Health, April 27, 1949, box 28, folder: NAACP, 1948–1949, Morrison Papers, TU.

5. Delahoussaye to the Director, April 27, 1949; New Orleans Association of Commerce, minutes of the regular monthly meeting of the Civic Affairs Committee, May 18, 1949, in New Orleans Association of Commerce, *Minutes, December 1948–December 1949, Vol. 2.*

6. New Orleans Chamber of Commerce, minutes of the meeting of the Civic Affairs Committee, March 7, 1950, in New Orleans Chamber of Commerce, *Minutes, December 1949–December 1950, Vol. 2,* Chamber of Commerce Papers, UNO; Mrs. W. H. Maddox to Morrison, May 13, 1947, box 3, folder 14, Morrison Papers, TU.

7. Morrison to Ray Scheuering, June 10, 1949, box 3, folder 15, Morrison Papers, TU; Morrison to Lucious L. Jones, June 2, 1949, box 3, folder 15, Morrison Papers, TU; Morrison to Mrs. W. H. Maddox, September 11, 1947, box 3, folder 14, Morrison Papers, TU.

8. J. Westbrook McPherson, "The Problem of Housing for Negroes in New Orleans," March 30, 1953, box 2, folder: Board of Directors Minutes, 1953, Council of Social Agencies Papers, Earl K. Long Library, UNO; Robert F. Morrow to Morrison, September 12, 1947, box 10, folder 33, Morrison Papers, TU.

9. Morrow to Hale Boggs, May 21, 1947, box 10, folder 34, Morrison Papers, TU; New Orleans Chamber of Commerce, minutes of the meeting of the Executive Committee, October 22, 1952, New Orleans Chamber of Commerce, *Minutes, 1952, Vol. 1,* New Orleans Chamber of Commerce Papers, UNO; McPherson, "Problem of Housing for Negroes in New Orleans."

10. This assessment differs sharply from that offered by Kim Lacy Rogers, who emphasizes the liberal and philanthropic impulses of Charles and Rosa Keller and Edgar and Edith Stern. The financing and leadership provided by the Kellers and the Sterns proved essential to the construction of Pontchartrain Park, but the impetus for the development had different roots. Rogers's account relies too heavily here on oral histories gathered from interested parties. See Kim Lacy Rogers, *Righteous Lives: Narratives of the New Orleans Civil Rights Movement* (New York: New York University Press, 1993), p. 28.

It is clear that Stern was deeply concerned by a possible legal challenge to the maintenance of white-only golf courses. After receiving a copy of a letter from the director of public welfare in Miami detailing a "mandamus court action" there, he wrote to close Morrison adviser David McGuire informing him that it was "quite likely" a similar action would be forthcoming in New Orleans, and that it was "absolutely essential" that the mayor "give further careful consideration to the possibility of purchasing the tract of land that has been offered for a Negro park." "I'll be glad to do anything I can to facilitate the consummation of this idea," he advised. Edgar B. Stern to Dave McGuire, July 21, 1949, box 3, folder 15, Morrison Papers, TU.

11. Harland Bartholomew and Associates, "Report on a System of Recreation Facilities, New Orleans, Louisiana" (mimeo., Louisiana Collection, Earl K. Long Library, UNO, October 31, 1929), pp. 69–70; *Louisiana Weekly,* August 2, 1947, p. 1.

12. New Orleans Chamber of Commerce, minutes of the regular monthly meeting of the Civic Affairs Committee, April 20, 1949, New Orleans Chamber of Commerce, *Minutes, December 1948–December 1949, Vol. 2.*

13. W. Ray Scheuering to H[ippolyte] Dabezies, June 1, 1949, box 3, folder 15, Morrison Papers, TU; Dabezies to Chep [Morrison], May 18, 1949, box 3, folder 15, Morrison Papers, TU; minutes of the Mayor's Advisory Committee meeting, June 9, 1949, Scott Wilson Papers, Howard-Tilton Memorial Library, TU. Four months before the suit was filed, the city attorney advised Dabezies that "there was no way of keeping the colored players from using the municipal links." The "solution to the problem," he suggested, "is the building of a golf course for negroes only." See Knox Eldridge to Dabezies, July 14, 1949, box S56-25, folder: Negro Park, DeLesseps S. Morrison Papers, New Orleans Public Library (NOPL).

14. Handwritten note attached to W. Ray Scheuering to Morrison, March 23, 1949, box 3, folder 14, Morrison Papers, TU. In his outstanding work on Louisiana in the civil rights era, Adam Fairclough misidentifies the author of the "jigger-boo" comments as mayoral aide Scheuering; it is clear, though, that the handwritten addendum to Scheuering's memo is addressed to "Ray" and is Morrison's response. See Adam Fairclough, *Race and Democracy: The Civil Rights Struggle in Louisiana, 1915–1972* (Athens: University of Georgia Press, 1995), pp. 508–9.

The mayor's top political consultant, Scott Wilson, also made explicit the key criterion for site selection. "The difficulty will arise," Wilson wrote, "over the problem of finding a park area in a negro section so that the aggravating necessity of them moving through white sections will be forestalled." He believed the park issue was "bound to have some nasty repercussions politically," although he urged action, believing "the issues are more important than such considerations." Scott Wilson to Dave R. McGuire, May 28, 1949, box 3, folder 14, Morrison Papers, TU.

15. Gerald O. Pratt to Brooke Duncan, October 17, 1947, box S56-25, folder: Negro Park, Morrison Papers, NOPL; minutes of the Mayor's Advisory Committee meeting, July 28, 1949, box 2, Wilson Papers, TU; minutes of the Mayor's Negro Advisory Committee meeting, August 11, 1949, box 3, folder 16, Morrison Papers, TU.

16. Edward F. Haas, *DeLesseps S. Morrison and the Image of Reform: New Orleans Politics, 1946–1961* (Baton Rouge, Louisiana State University Press, 1974), pp. 119–39.

17. Minutes of the Mayor's Advisory Committee, July 28, 1949, box 2, Wilson Papers, TU; minutes of the Mayor's Negro Advisory Committee

meeting, August 11, 1949, box 3, folder 16, Morrison Papers, TU; New Orleans Association of Commerce, minutes of the regular meeting of the Civic Affairs Committee, November 16, 1949, and minutes of postponed (August) meeting of the Civic Affairs Committee, September 7, 1949, New Orleans Association of Commerce, *Minutes, December 1948–December 1949, Vol. 2*; Morrison to Ralph Agate, September 20, 1954, box S56-25, folder: Negro Park, Morrison Papers, NOPL.

18. *Louisiana Weekly*, November 27, 1954, clipping in Scrapbook 40, Morrison Papers, TU; *Pittsburgh Courier*, January 14, 1950, clipping in Scrapbook 40, Morrison Papers, TU; Morrison to Pontchartrain Park Homes, Inc., February 13, 1954, box S56-25, folder: Negro Housing, Morrison Papers, NOPL; Lester J. Lautenschlaeger to Lester E. Kabacoff, April 26, 1956, box S56-25, folder: Negro Park, Morrison Papers, NOPL.

19. Dr. Andrew Macaluso and E. J. Fontan to Lionel G. Ott, May 31, 1950, box S56-25, folder: Negro Park, Morrison Papers, NOPL.

20. Robert E. Wood to Morrison, May 11, 1953, box S56-25, folder: Negro Park, Morrison Papers, NOPL.

21. *New Orleans Times-Picayune*, April 29, 1950, p. 1; *Pittsburgh Courier*, May 6, 1950, clipping in Scrapbook 40, Morrison Papers, TU; Morrison to Louis Reicke, May 3, 1950, box S56-25, folder: Negro Park, Morrison Papers, NOPL; Morrison to Andre Couturie, May 30, 1950, box S56-25, folder: Negro Park, Morrison Papers, NOPL.

22. *New Orleans Times-Picayune*, May 6, 1952, p. 1; Warren O. Coleman to Allen H. Generes, March 12, 1952, box S56-25, folder: Negro Park, Morrison Papers, NOPL; William B. Hartsfield to Morrison, November 12, 1955, box S56-25, folder: Negro Park, Morrison Papers, NOPL; W. Ray Scheuering to Hartsfield, November 16, 1955, box S56-25, folder: Negro Park, Morrison Papers, NOPL; *Louisiana Weekly*, June 19, 1954, and May 2, 1956, clippings in Scrapbook 40, Morrison Papers, TU.

23. Text of remarks by Arthur J. Chapital at the Conference of the Housing and Home Finance Agency, October 7, 1953, New Orleans, Louisiana, in box 28-210, folder: President's Reports, 1951–55, in the New Orleans Branch NAACP Papers, Earl K. Long Library, UNO.

24. Ronald H. Bayor, "Roads to Racial Segregation: Atlanta in the Twentieth Century," *Journal of Urban History* 15 (November 1988): 3–21; Raymond A. Mohl, "Making the Second Ghetto in Metropolitan Miami, 1940–1960," *Journal of Urban History* 21 (March 1995): 395–427, and "Race and Space in the Modern City: Interstate-95 and the Black Community in Miami," in Arnold R. Hirsch and Raymond A. Mohl, eds., *Urban Policy in Twentieth Century America* (New Brunswick, N.J.: Rutgers University Press, 1993), pp. 100–158; Christopher Silver and John V. Moeser, *The Separate City: Black Communities in the Urban South, 1940–1968* (Lexington: University Press of Kentucky, 1995); Christopher Silver, *Twentieth-Century Richmond: Planning, Politics, and Race* (Knoxville: University of Tennessee Press, 1984), p. 147.

25. New Orleans Association of Commerce, minutes of the meeting of the Board of Directors, May 25, 1948, New Orleans Association of Commerce, *Minutes, 1948, Vol. 1*, New Orleans Chamber of Commerce Papers, UNO; Home Development Committee, "Annual Report for 1948," November 24, 1948, in New Orleans Association of Commerce, *Minutes, December 1947–December 1948, Vol. 2*, New Orleans Chamber of Commerce Papers, UNO; *New Orleans Times-Picayune*, January 15, 1948, p. 1.

26. *New Orleans States*, July 15, 1949, p. 3; *New Orleans Item*, August 2, 1949, p. 3.

27. *New Orleans Item*, March 26, 1950, p. 8.

28. New Orleans Association of Commerce, minutes of the regular monthly meeting of the Civic Affairs Committee, July 20, 1949, New Orleans Association of Commerce, *Minutes, December 1948–December 1949, Vol. 2*; HANO and City Planning and Zoning Commission, "Progress in Slum Clearance and Urban Redevelopment—Report to Honorable Mayor and Commission Council" (mimeo., November 1952), box 41, folder: Urban Renewal and Redevelopment Programs, Council of Social Agencies Papers, Earl K. Long Library, UNO.

29. David R. McGuire to L. H. Lewis, July 24, 1957, box 6, folder 4, David R. McGuire Papers, Howard-Tilton Memorial Library, TU; Haas, *DeLesseps S. Morrison and the Image of Reform*, pp. 173–74; James Roch Andre, "Urban Renewal and Housing in New Orleans: 1949–1962" (M.A. thesis, Louisiana State University, 1963), 40–43; HANO and City Planning and Zoning Commission, "Progress in Slum Clearance and Urban Redevelopment," pp. 6–7.

30. Report of the Housing Committee, New Orleans Homestead and Savings and Loan League, on Proposed Tulane Urban Redevelopment (mimeo., February 1, 1953), box 523, folder 7, Chamber of Commerce Papers, UNO; Haas, *DeLesseps S. Mor-*

rison and the Image of Reform, pp. 173–74; Andre, "Urban Renewal and Housing in New Orleans," 41; *New Orleans Times-Picayune,* May 6, 1953, p. 1.

31. John E. Rousseau to Morrison, July 10, 1952, box 28-67, NAACP Papers, UNO.

32. New Orleans Chamber of Commerce, minutes of the meeting of the Executive Committee, October 22, 1952, New Orlean's Chamber of Commerce, *Minutes, 1952, Vol. 1,* Chamber of Commerce Papers, UNO.

33. New Orleans Chamber of Commerce, minutes of the meeting of the Board of Directors, December 23, 1952, New Orleans Chamber of Commerce, *Minutes, 1953, Vol. 2,* Chamber of Commerce Papers, UNO; New Orleans Chamber of Commerce, minutes of the meeting of the Executive Committee, March 6, 1953, New Orleans Chamber of Commerce, *Minutes, 1953, Vol. 2;* New Orleans Chamber of Commerce, minutes of the Executive Committee, August 3, 1953, New Orleans Chamber of Commerce, *Minutes, 1953, Vol. 1,* Chamber of Commerce Papers, UNO.

34. *New Orleans Times-Picayune,* May 5, 1953, p. 1; *New Orleans States,* May 8, 1953, p. 9.

35. William H. Forman, Jr., "The Conflict over Federal Urban Renewal Legislation in Louisiana," *Louisiana Studies* 8 (Fall 1969), 256; Andre, "Urban Renewal and Housing in New Orleans," 27; Harland Bartholomew and Associates, "Preliminary Report on Administrative and Legislative Needs and Resources" (mimeo., April 1968), p. 21; Council of Social Agencies (CSA), press release, June 18, 1954, box 10, folder: Legislative Committee, 1949–1958, CSA Papers, Earl K. Long Library, UNO.

36. *New Orleans States,* February 15, 1955, p. 1; *New Orleans Item,* February 8, 1956, p. 36, and May 15, 1956, p. 1.

37. *New Orleans Item,* May 15, 1956, p. 1, and May 16, 1956 p. 1; David R. McGuire to Mayor Morrison, January 30, 1956, box 5, folder 1, McGuire Papers, TU; McGuire to Mayor Morrison, n.d., box 3, folder 38, McGuire Papers, TU.

38. *New Orleans Times-Picayune,* April 27, 1956, p. 60; *New Orleans Item,* April 30, 1956, p. 12.

39. New Orleans Chamber of Commerce, minutes of the regular semimonthly meeting of the Board of Directors, March 27, 1956, New Orleans Chamber of Commerce, *Minutes, 1956, Vol. 1,* New Orleans Chamber of Commerce Papers, UNO; *New Orleans Item,* April 30, 1956, p. 12; *New Orleans Times-Picayune,* April 28, 1956, p. 8.

40. Ralph N. Jackson to Louis D. Brown, May 19, 1960, box 115, folder 1, Chamber of Commerce Papers, UNO; "Talk on Urban Renewal delivered by Mr. Favrot on June 21, 1961 at panel discussion sponsored by Home Improvement Council" (typescript), box 115, folder 1, Chamber of Commerce Papers, UNO, p. 6; Michael J. Klarman, "How *Brown* Changed Race Relations: The Backlash Thesis," *Journal of American History* 81 (June 1994): 81–118.

41. *New Orleans Item,* June 4, 1954, p. 2; Silver and Moeser, *The Separate City,* p. 148.

42. Rev. William A. Miller, "Urban Renewal and the Wages of Sin" (typescript, n.d.), and "Urban Renewal Weighed and Found Wanting" (typescript, n.d.), both in Community Service Series, box 13, folder: Urban Renewal, 1967–68, CSA Papers, UNO; *New Orleans Times-Picayune,* May 16, 1967, clipping in Community Service Series, box 13, folder: Urban Renewal, 1967–68, CSA Papers, UNO.

43. Fairclough, *Race and Democracy,* 231–32; Haas, *DeLesseps S. Morrison and the Image of Reform,* 245–48; David R. McGuire, Jr., to Mayor William B. Hartsfield, January 25, 1960, box 9, folder 18, McGuire Papers, TU.

44. David McGuire to Admiral Whitaker F. Riggs, Jr., May 6, 1960, box 9, folder 5, McGuire Papers, TU; McGuire to L. H. Lewis, July 24, 1957, McGuire Papers, TU.

45. New Orleans Chamber of Commerce, minutes of the special meeting of the Board of Directors, October 18, 1954, New Orleans Chamber of Commerce, *Board Minutes, 1954, Vol. 2,* Chamber of Commerce Papers, UNO; New Orleans Chamber of Commerce, minutes of the meeting of the Board of Directors, May 22, 1956, New Orleans Chamber of Commerce, *Minutes, 1956, Vol. 1,* Chamber of Commerce Papers, UNO.

46. Louis D. Brown to Andrew V. Santangini, January 14, 1964, box 115, folder 4, Chamber of Commerce Papers, UNO; Howard W. Hallman to Victor H. Schiro, Walter M. Barnett, and Thomas P. Godchaux, January 11, 1966, Community Service Series, box 13, folder: Urban Renewal, 1954–66, CSA Papers, UNO.

47. Brown to Santangini, January 14, 1964; Rev. Eugene McManus, S.S.J., "A Developing Community Needs Urban Renewal" (typescript, n.d.), Community Service Series, box 13, folder: Urban Renewal, 1954–66, CSA Papers, UNO.

48. Victor H. Schiro to Col. Bluford H.J. Balter, February 2, 1962, Schiro correspondence file, box

2, Wilson Papers, TU; Schiro to Balter, February 5, 1962, box S62-3, folder: Campaign, Victor H. Schiro Papers, NOPL; *Louisiana Weekly,* May 13, 1967, p. 4; *New Orleans States-Item,* May 6, 1967, clipping in box 6, folder 1, Moon Landrieu Papers, Loyola University (LU) Library, New Orleans.

49. Arnold R. Hirsch, "Simply a Matter of Black and White: The Transformation of Race and Politics in Twentieth-Century New Orleans," in Hirsch and Joseph Logsdon, eds., *Creole New Orleans: Race and Americanization* (Baton Rouge: Louisiana State University Press, 1992), 283–84, 289; Louis, Bowles, and Grace, Inc., "Orleans Parish Attitudes toward Federal Urban Renewal" (mimeo., March 1968), box 184-92, folder 646, Bureau of Governmental Research (BGR) Papers, UNO.

50. Kim Lacy Rogers, "Humanity and Desire: Civil Rights Leaders and the Desegregation of New Orleans, 1954–1966" (Ph.D. diss., University of Minnesota, 1982), p. 42; Morrison to Lester Lautenschlaeger, March 16, 1955, box S56-25, folder: Negro Park, Morrison Papers, NOPL; *Louisiana Weekly,* March 9, 1968, clipping in box 5, folder 2, Landrieu Papers, LU; Hirsch, "Simply a Matter of Black and White," p. 288.

51. *New Orleans Times-Picayune,* January 19, 1967, clipping in Community Service Series, box 13, folder: Urban Renewal, 1967–68, CSA Papers, UNO.

52. Jack D. Herrington to Victor H. Schiro, December 8, 1966 and Sherman N. Copelin, Jr., Report of the Meeting in Washington, D.C., January 18, 1967, (mimeo., n.d.), both in Community Service File, box 13, folder: Urban Renewal, 1954–66, CSA Papers, UNO.

53. *New Orleans States-Item,* June 15, 1966, clipping in box 15, folder 14, Landrieu Papers, LU.

54. *New Orleans States-Item,* January 7, 1967, clipping in box 15, folder 14, Landrieu Papers, LU; Victor H. Schiro to Friend, May 11, 1967, box SPR-35, folder: Urban Renewal Legislation, Schiro Papers, NOPL; *New Orleans States-Item,* clipping in box 51, folder 9, Landrieu Papers, LU; *New Orleans States-Item,* clipping in box 39, folder 2, Landrieu Papers, LU.

55. Forman, "The Conflict over Federal Urban Renewal Enabling Legislation," 262–63; *New Orleans States-Item,* July 10, 1968, clipping in box 39, folder 3, Landrieu Papers, LU.

Portland, Oregon, Region 2040 "Growth Concept," 1994. The visual representation of Portland's planning process. The map emphasizes downtown development (the large circle in the middle); an urban growth boundary (dark areas at the edge); and development in-between tied to light-rail lines that connect to downtown. (Portland Metro Council)

CHAPTER NINE

The Capital of Good Planning
Metropolitan Portland since 1970

■■
■■

CARL J. ABBOTT

n 1970, the city of Portland, Oregon, completed the Forecourt Fountain to local applause and national acclaim. Located in an urban-renewal district near the southern edge of downtown, the fountain was a carefully crafted landscape that covered an entire city block. Although themselves outsiders to the city, designers Lawrence Halprin and Angela Danadjieva created a distinctive place that is emblematic of Portland's approach to city-making, for it holds in tension the distinct values of environmentalism and urbanism.

Set between an office building and a parking garage, the fountain is an oasis and a refuge within the city, anchoring a series of open spaces that break the monotony of a high-rise urban-renewal district. The fountain's sloping contours transform a city block into an analog of a Cascade mountain stream. Shrubs and trees create tiny, cool glades. Water gathers in narrow channels at the top, tumbles across concrete lips and plates, sloshes around artificial boulders, and plunges into a pool. As viewers drift toward the surging waters, the fountain echoes the Olmstedian goal of urban parks that draw their users away from the city.

The same space is also designed for intense urban use, however. It serves as a plaza for the Civic Auditorium.[1] Especially in its early years, before growing vegetation began to block sight lines, it was a socially charged public space. Office workers walked out of their way to see the water turned on at 11:00 A.M. Families brought picnics on summer weekends. Hippies bathed in the pools, smoked pot, and drove the city's parks commissioner to distraction. The fountain has accommodated rock concerts, ballet performances, baptisms, and weddings.

Contemporary Portland offers other symbols of this creative cohabitation of country and city. Metropolitan-area voters in 1994 and 1995 taxed themselves both for the acquisition of stream corridors, parks, and other open spaces and for light-rail construction, with its promise to intensify land uses.[2] Both officially and unofficially, the city uses two very different emblems or mascots to epitomize its character as a community. One is the blue heron, a graceful bird that thrives in the riverside marshes that wend through the metropolitan fabric and appears on city letterhead and microbrewery labels. The other is a huge hammered-copper statue of "Portlandia" reaching down from a city office building toward the downtown bus mall. The statue represents civic life and commerce. Its installation occasioned a spontaneous community celebration as thousands of Portlanders turned out on a Sunday morning to watch the statue carried on a barge upriver like a red-orange Cleopatra and hoisted onto its niche in the heart of downtown.[3]

This careful balance between environmentalism and urbanism serves as an organizing theme for this chapter. Over the last quarter century, Portlanders have tried to redefine and bridge a fundamental divide in urban and regional planning. Builders of modern cities have long been torn between the preference for "going out" or "going up"—for lowering the overall density of metropolitan settlements or for increasing the intensity of land use. In terms of professional planning practice, we see this dichotomy in the differences between regionwide prescriptive "mapping" of urban form and detailed small-area planning for downtowns and neighborhoods. In the Portland case, environmentalism as an urban-planning goal draws explicitly on the thought of Frederick Law Olmsted and Lewis Mumford, with their visions of cities and towns interlacing with the natural and cultivated environments in a democratic regionalism. Portland's eclectic urbanists borrow the insights of urban design critics Jane Jacobs and William H. Whyte to assert the value of civic interaction in public spaces and the theory of philosopher John Stuart Mill to argue the creative and liberating effects of social and cultural diversity.[4]

These conceptual and practical choices are common to every American metropolis. They are central terms in our planning and policy vocabulary. Yet Portland may be one of the few cities that has actively reconciled their inherent tension. According to its press clippings, it is one of the few large cities in the United States "where it works."[5] Over the past twenty years, it has frequently appeared near the top of urban livability rankings. An informal poll of planning and design experts in 1988 rated Portland's efforts to deal with urban design issues among the best in the United States. The city makes regular appearances as well on lists of the nation's best-managed cities.[6]

Taken together, these positive assessments suggest that metropolitan Portland comes close to matching an emerging model of good urban form. Dominating discussion of metropolitan planning and policy in the 1990s, this model embraces a series of normative prescriptions about the characteristics of a balanced metropolis. In particular, it assigns high value to the maintenance of strong downtowns in order to nurture cultural vibrancy, promote social cohesion, and support nationally competitive advanced-service industries. Since the famous report on *The Costs of Sprawl* appeared in the early 1970s, advocates of the compact city have had practical justifications for their argument that the centered metropolis should also be a compact metropolis. The concentration of urbanized land within radial corridors and nodes presumably preserves green spaces and farmlands, reduces energy consumption, and keeps infrastructure affordable.[7]

Portland as both city and metropolitan region has earned a reputation as a capital of "good planning" for pioneering the actual implementation of this compact-city model.

In terms of cityscape and urban form, Portland has managed with some success to bring environmentalism and urbanism together in a coherent package of mutually supportive planning and development decisions. The result, in its simplest formulation, is a metropolis that is stronger at its center than at its edges, whether we measure that strength in political clout or the allocation of investment. In political perspective, metropolitan Portland in the last quarter of the twentieth century has been noteworthy for a political culture that treats land-use planning, with its restrictions on private actions, as a legitimate expression of the community interest.

Most observers see that strength in Portland's downtown. Visitors to the city nearly always start at the center. *Time,* the *Atlantic Monthly,* and *Architecture,* have all reported to their readers on the strength of downtown design, the careful conservation of a sense of place, and the enhancement of the downtown with public art. *The New Yorker* pointed to "closely controlled new building, the carefully monitored rehabilitation of worthy old buildings, [and] the vigorous creation of open space" as key factors creating a city of "individuality and distinction." Portland's downtown design earned a City Livability Award from the U.S. Conference of Mayors in 1988 and an Award for Urban Excellence from the Bruner Foundation in 1989.[8]

Beyond their attractions of place, Portland's central districts have retained economic and institutional dominance in the metropolitan area. Downtown had 105,000 jobs in 1993, up from 63,000 in 1970. Downtown and adjacent districts claim nearly all of the major metropolitan cultural institutions and gathering places: museums, performing arts center, stadium, convention center, new Blazerama basketball stadium, Pioneer Courthouse Square for political rallies, and Waterfront Park for community festivals.

Strong central districts are buttressed by the peculiarity of Portland's social geography. The city lacks the zones of abandonment that blight the image and weaken the political economy of many U.S. cities. There are no gaps between the downtown fringe and residential neighborhoods. Substantial public investment in housing rehabilitation has helped Portlanders recycle most of their 1885–1930 neighborhoods for late-twentieth-century residents and has preserved neighborhood commercial districts in the process.

Absent from most descriptions of Portland are suburban cities and counties. In the urban America of the 1990s, it is impossible to write comprehensively about Washington, D.C., without mentioning Tyson's Corner or about greater Los Angeles without Orange County. The situation is different in Portland. In contrast to the central business core and the older neighborhoods, there is nothing particularly *distinguished* or *distinguishing* about Portland's suburban zones. Portland suburbs have plenty of people (70 percent of the primary metropolitan statistical area, or PMSA; see Table 9.1) and plenty of jobs (45 percent of the PMSA), but they remain supplementary employment and consumption arenas with none of the area's essential public facilities or attractions—no John Wayne Airport or Cal-Irvine campus, no Mall of

Table 1

Portland Metropolitan Population
Since 1950

	City of Portland	Metropolitan area*
1950	374,000	705,000
1960	373,000	822,000
1970	382,000	1,007,000
1980	365,000	1,242,000
1990	437,000	1,515,000
1998 (est.)	504,000	2,149,000

*Metropolitan area comprises four counties in 1950–80, six counties in 1990 and 1994.

America or Disneyland to draw all eyes. Specialists on the multinodal city can identify only one "edge city" or "suburban activity center," and even that is only a flimsy example.[9] Washington County has a handful of major corporate headquarters, such as Tektronix and Nike, but even Nike boss Phil Knight entertains friends and clients at downtown restaurants as well as at his woodsy suburban corporate campus.

Portland's ability to "do it right" by developing in ways counter to powerful trends that are reshaping many other American metropolitan areas raises important questions. First, we might ask whether Portland has truly chosen an alternative development path toward an uncommon urban form, or whether it is simply engaged in a delaying action against the rise of the outer city. Second, we want to know which aspects of Portland's experience are rooted in the peculiarities of location and history, and which we might generalize or reproduce elsewhere.

The next section of this chapter examines the particular characteristics of Portland's economic and social development that have promoted or facilitated a tightly focused urban form. It then looks at the political institutions and processes that have linked these framing conditions to specific planning and policy decisions that actually moved Portland toward the *standard* model. This narrative section constitutes the heart of the interpretive argument, for it is the contingencies of politics and policy-making in city, region, and state that have effectively linked disparate interests and visions of the good community. It is equally vital to understand the regulations and bureaucratic procedures that link the urbanist and environmentalist agendas, for there are logical connection points but no logically *necessary* connections. Indeed, in the context of the late twentieth century United States, the central puzzle about Portland is understanding how and why urban

and regional planning have achieved their unusual prominence as tools of public policy and their unusual acceptance as expressions of the civic interest. The logic of this chapter is to move from context to text, from structure to agency, from unique local conditions and historical circumstances to the possibility of transferable institutional innovations and political actions.

The Portland Setting

A number of factors make it relatively easy for Portlanders to accept and act on the principles of the compact metropolis. These include the landscape and resulting sense of place, the evolution of metropolitan economic geography, and an unusual degree of social homogeneity.

Portlanders live with daily reminders that high-quality farmland and urbanizable land are limited commodities. Metropolitan Portland is already lapping against the natural barriers of the Coast Range and the Cascade foothills. Relatively little land remains to the east or the west between the suburban frontier and the edges of the forest. In purely visual terms, residents can stand on the hills west of the central business district and see forested mountains in three directions as distinct limits to metropolitan growth. On a slightly larger scale, the same sense of the larger Willamette Valley as a finite region helped to make a statewide land-use planning program acceptable in the 1970s.[10]

The sense of natural limits on horizontal expansion is softened by the presence of large amounts of very visible natural landscape within the core of the metropolis. The metropolitan area is bisected north-south by the Willamette River and east-west by the Columbia River. Green spaces within the urban fabric include the margins of the rivers, large semi-natural parks, and wildlife refuges within half an hour of downtown. These spaces quietly assure Portlanders that intensification does not threaten a totally built-up landscape.

Whereas Portland has a multitude of green spaces, it has few grey spaces. An important feature of the cityscape is the absence of discarded industrial districts. Sawmills and factories lined the nineteenth-century waterfront, but the city completed the transition from manufacturing to commerce and services by the 1950s. Having deindustrialized before anyone had coined the term, it was in good position to catch the rise of the information economy as a financial, wholesaling, and professional-service center. In the service city, outmoded industrial districts have been opportunities for high-density redevelopment, not blighting gaps in the urban fabric, because of their waterfront sites.[11]

Another peculiarity of the Portland scene is the lack of a complete suburban beltway. In the 1950s, highway engineers decided to bring the city's first limited-access freeways into the center of the city and connect them with a tight freeway loop that hugged the edges of the central business district. As an engineering decision, the route took advantage of available or easily acquired rights of way and avoided the steepest parts of the West Hills. The economic consequence was to maintain downtown Portland and its nearby neighborhoods as the most accessible parts of the metropolitan area after the demise of streetcars and interurban railways.[12] The eastern half of a suburban freeway bypass through the less fashionable side of the metropolitan area did not open until the 1980s. A southwestern quadrant is currently under intense debate and a northwestern quadrant that would violate parks and open spaces and require multiple bridges across the Columbia River is unlikely to be built.

One reason for the slow development of suburban freeways was Portland's failure to catch the postwar economic boom. From 1945 to 1965, Portland was stodgy in social tone, cautious in leadership, and stingy with public investments. The neoprogressive political reform movements that transformed cities such as Denver and Phoenix bypassed Portland. Within the Pacific Northwest, Seattle consolidated its economic lead by risking strategic investments in the University of Washington, in the Century 21 exposition, in facilities to handle containerized cargo, and in community infrastructure. Saving rather than risking public funds, Portland grew much more slowly as a regional wholesale and service center.[13] Limited economic development meant slow suburbanization, with consequently slow development of suburban political capacity and distinct suburban agendas.

The economic strength of the central city and the slow development of suburbs also dampened the class dimension of metropolitan politics. The income gap between the central city and the suburbs is relatively small. Median family and household income patterns in the Portland PMSA can be compared with those in twenty-four other metropolitan statistical areas (MSAs) or PMSAs with 1990 populations between 1 million and 2.5 million (see Figures 9.1 and 9.2). Portland's ratio of metrowide family income to central-city family income was 1.14, below the middle value for the whole set of metropolitan areas (1.20). Using households rather than families, the Portland metro:city ratio of 1.21 falls below the midpoint for the set (1.28). A statewide move toward equal levels of school funding in 1990s, instigated by rural legislators seeking resources from central city *and* suburbs, has further reduced the importance of the city-suburban boundary as a socioeconomic divide.

In a similar manner, Portland's racial history and racial geography have meant that city-suburban politics has not revolved around race. Although the city was a major

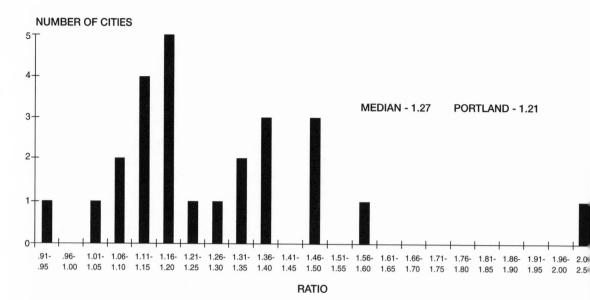

Figure 9.1 Household Median Income in the United States (PMSA/Central-city ratios)

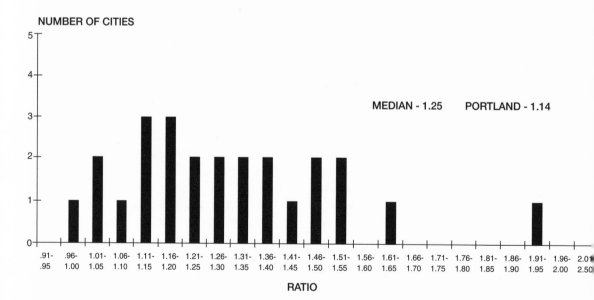

Figure 9.2 Household Median Income in the United States (PMSA/Central-city ratios)

destination for Asian immigrants in the nineteenth and early twentieth centuries, its distance from the South has made it one of the whitest cities in the United States today. An African American population of only 2,000 in 1940 grew to 20,000 during the shipbuilding boom of World War II and inched upward to 38,000 by 1990—8 percent of the central city and only 3 percent of the metropolitan area. Most of these newer Portlanders have replaced European immigrants in working-class neighborhoods on the east side of the Willamette River, where they have been physically isolated from downtown Portland. In part because of the same small numbers, racial groups are relatively well integrated on the neighborhood scale. Portland in 1990 had only six census tracts that were more than 50 percent African American.[14] The index of dissimilarity was .63 for black/non-black, .21 for Asian/non-Asian, and .18 for Hispanic/non-Hispanic.

As a result, racial avoidance has had *relatively* little impact on white residential choices and spatial politics. During the decades from 1910 to 1940, there was no racial pressure to prevent close-in locations for the first generation of middle-class automobile suburbs. Nor did many of these same neighborhoods, which dot the east side of the city, experience massive racial turnover after 1940. White Portlanders have still chosen suburban housing for a wide variety of reasons, but racial flight has not been prominent among them.

The peculiarities of Portland's history and social geography are perhaps most striking in the case of the set of neighborhoods grouped as the "West Hills." Here racial patterns have interacted with the attractions of place to preserve an extensive elite enclave in the heart of the city. Downtown Portland occupies an oval benchland that slopes gently up from the west bank of the Willamette River. Between .5 and 1.5 miles back from the

Willamette, this lozenge of easily developed land meets a ring of steep hills that rise 500 to 1,000 feet above the river. Initially opened to residential development by cable cars, the West Hills became Portland's upscale neighborhood with the advent of family automobiles in the 1910s and 1920s. For three generations, the affluent highlanders of King's Heights, Arlington Heights, Willamette Heights, Portland Heights, and Council Crest have enjoyed views of Mount Hood and ten-minute commutes to downtown offices. Protected by elevation from the lower-income residents and the mixed uses of the downtown fringe, successful businessmen, ambitious professionals, and heirs of monied families have been able to maintain social status and leafy living without needing to flee to suburbia. They have also found that downtown remains the most convenient place to work and shop.

Planning Metropolitan Growth

In themselves, these idiosyncrasies of Portland-area history have only set the stage for the politics of metropolitan planning. It has required deliberate public efforts to build on these preconditions in the interest of a compact and centered metropolis. Portland-area policies over the past two decades contain no single element that has not been discussed or tried in other cities. What may be different is the political will to link the elements together as a single strategy and to implement them as interlocking packages of city and metropolitan initiatives. Beginning in the 1970s, Portland experienced a startling transformation from laggard to leader—from a city that followed national planning trends to a city that developed and implemented new ideas. The emergence of the political environment for "good planning" is thus a distinct historical event that sets the puzzle of "why Portland?"

Within the city, the planning consensus was associated with a "revolutionary" transition of leadership from an older to a younger generation.[15] Between 1960 and 1970, the proportion of Portlanders aged 15–34 increased from 22 percent to 30 percent. In partial response, the average age of Portland City Council members dropped by fifteen years between 1969 and 1973. Voters made similar changes in other local governing bodies and in the city's legislative delegation. This generational turnover transformed many basic assumptions of civic debate. Ideas of the older leadership had been formed by the tumultuous years that stretched from the mid-1920s to the mid-1940s. Their goal for the postwar city was social and economic stability. The newer leaders, in contrast, came of age during the optimistic boom years of 1945–74.

This local revolution in public leadership coincided with changes in the national dialogue about city planning and politics. Portland's new politics was informed by the urban renewal and freeway critics of the 1960s, who emphasized the value of small-scale and vernacular urban environments and the excitement of large cities. City planners rediscovered that downtowns were complex collages of subdistricts rather than unitary wholes. Both quality-of-life liberals working in the growing information industries and members of minority communities reemphasized the values of place and sought to make neighborhoods effective instruments of resistance to large-scale changes in the urban fabric. Within this changing national discourse, Portland stood out not for the content of its vision but for its effectiveness in transforming the common vision into public policies.

The chief symbol and beneficiary of the political transition was Neil Goldschmidt, elected to the City Council in 1970 and elected mayor in 1972 at age thirty-two.[16] By the start of his first mayoral term, Gold-

schmidt and his staff had drawn on a ferment of political and planning ideas and sketched out an integrated strategy for the city that involved the coordination of land-use and transportation policies. They were strongly influenced by the 1970 census, which showed the effects of a declining proportion of middle-class families on neighborhood diversity and city tax base. During 1973, 1974, and 1975, Goldschmidt's team brought together a variety of ideas that were waiting for precise definition and articulated them as parts of a single political package that offered benefits for a wide range of citizens and groups.

This so-called population strategy emphasized public transportation, neighborhood revitalization, and downtown planning. Improved public transit would improve air quality, enhance the attractiveness of older neighborhoods, and focus activity on downtown. In turn, a vital business center would protect property values in surrounding districts and increase their attractiveness for residential reinvestment. Middle-class families who remained or moved into inner neighborhoods would patronize downtown businesses, and economic prosperity would support high levels of public services. Neighborhood planning would focus on housing rehabilitation and on visible amenities to keep older residential areas competitive with the suburbs.

One essential piece of the city strategy was preservation of a user-friendly downtown.[17] Business worries about suburban competition and parking problems coincided at the end of the 1960s with public disgust with a blighted riverfront. In 1970–72, an unusual alliance between city and state officials opened the opportunity to rethink downtown planning. Goldschmidt and other city leaders worked with Governor Tom McCall and with Glenn Jackson, an electric-utility executive who chaired the state Highway Commission, to remove a multilane expressway from the downtown waterfront. The action fired imaginations about radical responses to other downtown problems. A younger generation of technically sophisticated citizen-activists worked with city officials, downtown retailers, property owners, neighborhood groups, and civic organizations to treat previously isolated issues (parking, bus service, housing, retailing) as part of a single, comprehensive package. The resulting Downtown Plan offered integrated solutions to a long list of problems that Portlanders had approached piecemeal for two generations. It was technically sound because its proposals were based on improvements in access and transportation. It was politically viable because it prescribed trade-offs among different interests as part of a coherent strategy. Specific proposals ranged from a waterfront park and pedestrian-oriented design to high-density retail and office corridors crossing in the center of downtown. Sixteen years later, a new Central City Plan (1988) updated the design elements and called for the careful extension of a thriving business core into downtown fringe areas.[18]

A second piece of the strategy was to recycle older neighborhoods built from the 1880s through the 1930s. The city used Housing and Community Development funds and leveraged private capital with tax-free borrowing for an extensive housing rehabilitation program. Inflation of suburban housing costs in the 1970s also helped to retain families in older, affordable neighborhoods. Several neighborhoods between the downtown and the base of the West Hills experienced gradual gentrification by new residents looking for Portland's closest imitation of a sophisticated urban environment. The bungalow belt on the east side of the Willamette attracted a new generation of Portlanders looking for traditional city neighborhoods of 50 × 100 foot lots, trees, sidewalks, and stores within walking distance.

Direct investment policy was accompanied by a political bargain with neighborhood interests. After a series of confrontations between neighborhoods and city hall in the late 1960s, the Goldschmidt administration decided to legitimize and partially coopt neighborhood activists by incorporating independent neighborhood associations as secondary participants in public decision-making.[19] The acceptance and financial support of voluntary neighborhood groups has offered a *partial* alternative both to confrontational tactics from the grass roots and to top-down management of citizen participation from city hall.

The third element of the strategy was to shift investment from highways to public transit. The bankrupt private bus system had been absorbed into a new Tri-County Metropolitan Transit District (Tri-Met) in 1969. One of the key features of the Downtown Plan of 1972 was a transit mall that drew on the experience of Minneapolis. Completed in 1978, the mall increased the speed of bus service and facilitated transfers. The second major transit decision was the 1975 cancellation of the so-called Mount Hood Freeway, a five-mile connector that would have devastated half a dozen lower-middle-class neighborhoods in southeast Portland. Most of the federal money was transferred to build a successful fifteen-mile light-rail line from downtown to the eastern suburb of Gresham.

Public transit policy, of course, is regional as well as municipal. For nearly twenty years, Portland officials used their technical knowledge and political know-how to influence the decisions of regional planning and service agencies. Tri-Met operates a radial bus and rail system that carries 43 percent of the workers who commute into downtown Portland (compared to 20 percent in Phoenix, 17 percent in Salt Lake City, and 11 percent in Sacramento). Careful political deal-making under the aegis of the Metropolitan Service District (Metro), the area's regional-planning agency since 1978, has convinced the suburban counties to agree to a staged expansion of the light-rail system with several arms that will converge in downtown Portland and relieve congestion on key suburban highways. With the exception of weakly organized suburban manufacturers, who prefer cross-suburb road improvements, Portland's civic leadership now considers strong public transit to be one of the axioms of regional development (fig. 23).

In turn, regional planning takes place within the context of Oregon's twenty-year-old statewide land-use planning system. By the end of the 1960s, Willamette Valley residents from Portland to Eugene had begun to view low-density suburbanization as a serious environmental problem that wasted irreplaceable scenery, farmland, and energy. Much of the leadership came from farmers, who knew that scattershot subdivisions could create major problems for commercial agriculture. A key document for defining the problem was Lawrence Halprin's 1972 report, *The Willamette Valley: Choices for the Future*, which clearly described a future scenario of landscape sprawl and clutter in the absence of planning intervention. In the back of Oregonians' minds was a fear of the coming supercity—the megalopolis of Jean Gottman or the ecumenopolis of Constantinos Doxiados as filtered through layers of journalistic shorthand. Suburban sprawl and second-home subdivisions were explicitly associated with the painful example of California and roundly condemned by Governor McCall in 1972: "There is a shameless threat to our environment and to the whole quality of life—the unfettered despoiling of the land. Sagebrush subdivisions, coastal condomania, and the ravenous rampage of suburbia in the Willamette Valley all threaten to mock Oregon's status as the environmental model for the nation. . . . The interests of Oregon for to-

day and for the future must be protected from grasping wastrels of the land."[20]

Legislation in 1973 created a farmland protection program administered through a new Land Conservation and Development Commission (LCDC). The debates and votes on the legislation cut across political parties but were divided by region. Oregon is dominated by the Willamette Valley, the original goal of the Oregon Trail emigrants, which contains the state's richest agricultural land and its three largest cities in a corridor roughly 120 miles north-south and 50 miles east-west. Within the valley, suburban sprawl and farmland preservation seemed like pressing practical issues to both city Democrats and rural Republicans, especially given the prominence of Willamette Valley farming in the state's historically based sense of itself as a Jeffersonian community. In the much more sparsely populated ranching and logging communities of coastal and eastern Oregon, the same issues seemed irrelevant. It was Willamette Valley legislators who passed the land-use program in 1973 and Willamette Valley voters who subsequently defeated three anti-LCDC ballot measures. As recently as 1995, the Oregon Farm Bureau joined with big-city environmentalists and planning advocates to fight off "property rights" challenges to the state planning system.

The Oregon system is anchored by the LCDC's authority to define statewide planning goals (initially fourteen in number) and to require every Oregon city and county to prepare a comprehensive land-use plan that responds to the goals in light of local conditions. Local governments thus retain their customary responsibility for land-use planning, but within the constraints of an explicitly defined public interest. Although the legislators and lobbyists who framed the LCDC system were very much aware of the experiments in state and regional land-use and environmental planning that were summarized in Fred Bosselman and David Callies's *The Quiet Revolution in Land Use Control,* they explicitly chose not to expend political capital on establishing new regional-planning agencies.[21] Instead, regional solutions would have to emerge from the cooperation of existing general-purpose governments.

From the start, the statewide goals linked older urban-planning concerns to a newer environmentalism. The LCDC program rapidly evolved from a purely reactive effort to fend off erosion of the state's farm economy to a positive attempt to shape a particular urban form. Several goals have been of special importance for directing metropolitan growth: goal 3 on the preservation of farmland, goal 5 on the preservation of open space, goal 10 on access to affordable housing, goal 11 on the orderly development of public facilities and services, goal 13 on energy-efficient land use, and goal 14 on the definition of urban growth boundaries (UGBs) to separate urbanizable from rural lands. Although very different in origins from Portland's *city* planning initiatives, the state program thus ended up blending the interests and combining the votes of urbanists, agriculturalists, and environmental advocates in a way that has mirrored and supported the similar alliance at the metropolitan scale.[22]

The UGB for the Portland area was adopted in 1979. Supposedly embracing a twenty-year supply of developable land, the UGB is intended to prevent sprawl by providing for "an orderly and efficient transition from rural to urban use." Within the UGB, the burden of proof rests on opponents of land development. Outside the boundary, the burden rests on developers to show that their land is easily supplied with necessary services and not worth retention as open space or farmland. Studies indicate that UGBs around Portland and the other Willamette Valley cities have created a dual land market that

recognizes the different value of acreage inside and outside the boundary (fig. 20).[23]

The UGB is coupled with goal 10, which essentially mandates a "fair share" housing policy by requiring that every jurisdiction within the UGB provide "appropriate types and amounts of land . . . necessary and suitable for housing that meets the housing needs of households of all income levels." In other words, suburbs are not allowed to use the techniques of exclusionary zoning to block apartment construction or to isolate themselves as islands of large-lot zoning. By limiting the speculative development of large, distant residential tracts, the LCDC system has tended to level the playing field for suburban development and discourage the emergence of suburban "super developers" with overwhelming political clout.[24] In the Portland region, a housing rule adopted by the LCDC now requires that every jurisdiction zone at least half of its vacant residential land for attached single-family housing or apartments. In effect, the rule enacts a version of a fair-share program that hopes to reduce socioeconomic disparities between city and suburbs by manipulating density and urban form.

The LCDC has also adopted a transportation rule that requires local jurisdictions to plan land uses and facilities to achieve a 20 percent *reduction* in vehicle miles traveled per capita over the next twenty years.[25] This rule flies in the face of the explosive nationwide growth of automobile mileage; it requires a drastic rethinking of land-use patterns and transportation investment to encourage mixed uses, higher densities, public transit, and pedestrians. It makes local land-use planners and the Oregon Department of Transportation into allies at the same time that the federal Intermodal Surface Transportation Enhancement Act is forcing highway builders to rethink their jobs.

In the early 1990s, Portland found itself

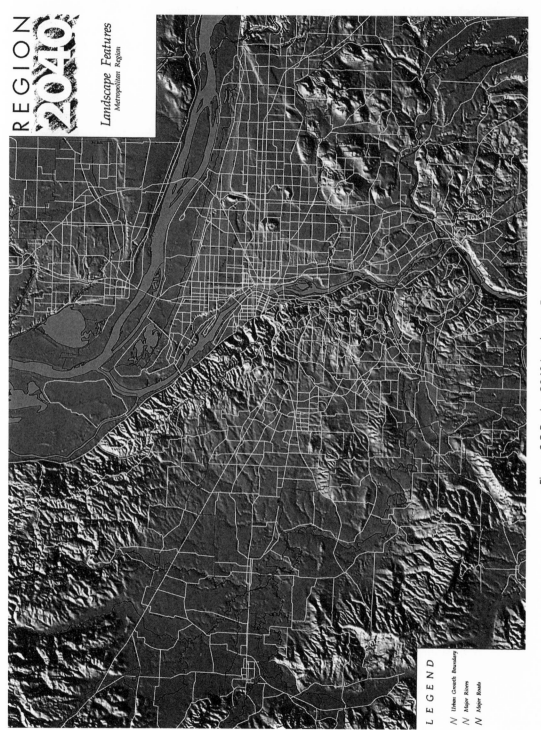

REGION
2040

Landscape Features
Metropolitan Region

LEGEND

N Urban Growth Boundary
N Major Rivers
N Major Roads

Figure 9.3 Region 2040 Landscape Features

in an prolonged and intelligent debate about metropolitan growth and form. Metro, the regional government with responsibility for regional planning and selected services, has been the lead agency for responding to predictions of a 30 percent increase in metropolitan population over the next two decades. Metro's staff in 1988 realized that there was no established process for amending the Portland-area UGB, even though the state requires periodic review and anticipates incremental UGB expansion. The agency therefore designed a classic planning process to develop a "Region 2040" plan to accommodate a projected 1.1 million more residents in the four core counties. National growth-management experts such as John DeGrove and Peter Calthorpe told Portlanders that the UGB has put the city on the right track but also challenge them to take the next vital steps for promoting compact settlement patterns.

The 2040 plan expresses a public consensus that spans environmental activists, homebuilders, commercial real estate interests, and advocates of city living. It matches the national professional belief in the standard model by calling for compact development focused on downtown Portland, urban and suburban centers, and transportation corridors; by identifying rural reserves to remain permanently outside the UGB (including farm and forest land and prominent natural features); by providing for additional open-space preservation within the UGB; and by adapting transportation improvements to the land-use goals (see fig. 9.3).[26]

The Culture of Metropolitan Planning

The preceding discussion has repeatedly suggested it has been Portland's civic consensus and political will that have pulled policy frag-

ments into a coherent and effective strategy for metropolitan development. It is clear that most American cities have access to the technical and policy tools they need in order to maintain centered metropolitan areas. The achievement of compact and efficient urban form is a solvable issue of the sort that James Q. Wilson wrote about twenty-five years ago: "These problems . . . fiscal imbalance, traffic congestion, air pollution, the movement of jobs away from minority groups . . . are susceptible to rather precise formulation and study; alternative ways of coping with them can be conceived and evaluated with a certain rigor; the obstacles to remedial action are primarily political (and to a certain degree economic) . . . what is most important, something *can* be done."[27]

The obvious question, then, is why Portland? Twenty-five years after Wilson's challenge, Portlanders have chosen to act where other metropolitan communities from Seattle to San Diego to Philadelphia have not. Beyond the physical and social context described earlier, what else has allowed this particular city to "do it right?" One possible answer starts with the realm of political culture and draws links to coalition-building as a political style and in turn to the institutions and regulations that make the coalitions meaningful and effective.

Portland as a civic community clearly lies toward one extreme of American political styles. For just one illustration, Oregonians find it perfectly reasonable when the CEO of one of the state's wealthiest real estate enterprises urges an audience to fulfill its "moral obligation to the idea of Oregon." This sort of value-laden discourse, with its invocation of abstract standards of judgment, is rooted in an Oregon style of politics and public policy. There is a reservoir of support for land-use planning and growth management because both the concepts and the tools for implementation fit an underlying political culture that views planning as a neutral arbiter of the public interest.

This interpretation draws on the argument of Daniel Elazar that American cities and states can be categorized according to the prominence of traditional, individualistic, or moralistic approaches to the public business. In particular, moralistic communities "conceive of politics as a public activity centered on some notion of the public good and properly devoted to the advancement of the public interest."[28] An examination of Oregon's history shows that moralistic politics has slowly squeezed out individualistic politics during the past fifty years.[29] Postwar Oregon has ranked high on indices of "general policy liberalism" and policy innovation.[30]

Policy innovation remains an important trait. Examples in the last two decades include the Oregon land-use planning system, statewide education reform, the Oregon Health Plan, and Oregon Benchmarks. The health plan is characteristic of the state, attempting to use rational procedures to prioritize medical conditions and treatments for Medicaid funding. Oregon Benchmarks is another rational effort to set hundreds of measurable long-term outcome goals for public programs and to allocate state budget increments to work toward those goals.

The conviction that public action can promote the public interest is interwoven with a substantial environmental ethic. In one aspect, environmentalism is part of a status quo conservatism that also values social stability. Oregonians like what they have and want to keep it. A recent survey asked residents what worried them most about the state's future. The most frequent answers were "overpopulation," "environmental destruction," and "becoming like California." Oregonians offer strong support for environmental conservation and for land-use planning as a tool for such conservation. They are equally reluctant to throw away perfectly good neighborhoods in favor of sprawling suburbs.

There is also a positive metropolitan vision embedded in environmentalism. As mentioned, the names most often invoked in Portland planning are Olmsted and Mumford, the advocates of middle landscapes and balanced regionalism. John Olmsted visited Portland in 1903 to design the site for the Lewis and Clark Centennial Exposition (1905) and to prepare a city parks plan, which remains a touchstone for open space and natural-areas planning. Lewis Mumford stopped for a brief visit and speech in 1938 and left a short but eloquent "memorandum" that advocates of regional planning still quote to good effect.[31]

As Portlanders have begun to take their downtown for granted, as a success that needs to be managed, they have turned their attention to issues of regional-growth management and protection of natural areas. Many have been working to "secure" the metropolitan borders with larger protected blocks of land such as the Columbia River Gorge National Scenic Area and a downtown-to-coast wildlife corridor. At a finer grain, watershed planning and restoration and urban wildlife conservation are issues of growing concern, local organizing, and public support.

One consequence of these civic values has been a willingness to accept the procedures of planning and growth management as everyday routines. The legislature followed the Progressive Era tactic of depoliticizing governmental decisions in the interest of good government when it placed the state planning system under an independent commission. The good government ethos also makes Portland a good place for bureaucrats. Examples of the bureaucratization of "good planning" include the regular participation of neighborhood associations in Portland planning decisions, the application of design review to downtown development, and the depoliticizing of metropolitan transportation decisions.[32] Planning bureaucracies have brought strong community movements into regular relationships with other interests. They have helped to channel high levels of public concern into accepted procedures designed to implement a community consensus. At best, the same procedures equalize access to public decision-making and tend to reduce the privileges of wealth.

A second consequence has been a willingness to support governments with a strong regional agenda. Portland since 1980 has annexed nearly one hundred thousand new residents. In 1978 voters merged a limited regional service agency and a council-of-governments-style planning agency into Metro, a regional government with a directly elected executive and council. They expanded its independence and purview by approving a home-rule charter in 1992. Not every voter who cast a ballot in favor of strong regional government may have known the implications, but the fact remains that Portland is one of the few metropolitan areas that has voluntarily established and enhanced such a metropolitan-level government.

In Portland, a strong central city and strong regional government are balanced against the historic weakness of suburban municipalities. Oregon law in the postwar decades facilitated the creation of special service districts to provide suburban services. In particular, most suburbanites used single-function districts for fire protection, water, sewers, and recreation and relied on counties for law enforcement. Between 1941 and 1967, the number of water districts in the three metropolitan counties grew from thirty-one to fifty-seven, fire districts from eight to forty-four, and sanitary districts from zero to thirty-three.[33] This fragmented system of suburban governance responded to private market pressures for residential and commercial growth but left the central city of Portland as the only entity interested in and capable of articulating a vision of regional development. Only in the last decade have powerful full-service suburban governments emerged to challenge central-city control of the regional agenda, a situation far different from those of Denver, Phoenix, Dallas, and other comparable cities, where competition between city and suburb emerged much earlier in the development process.[34]

A third consequence has been a willingness to search for common interests and to privilege political coalition-building. Perhaps the most important result of Portland's city-level planning initiatives, for example, has been an ability to avoid viewing downtown and neighborhoods as rivals in a zero-sum game. Urban politics nationwide has frequently pitted advocates of neighborhood needs against proponents of downtown development, with both sides fighting for the attention and resources of city hall. Examples of this polarization can be drawn from every part of the country—from Chicago to San Antonio to Seattle and Los Angeles.[35] Since the 1960s, in contrast, Portlanders have remained largely satisfied that the "Goldschmidt strategy" makes every district within five miles of the central business district into a winner.[36] In turn, a unified and consensual polity has enhanced Portland's ability to dominate metropolitan politics.

A similar consensus has developed about regional growth policy. The majority of *involved* citizens in both Portland and its suburbs share a basic vision of a metropolis that above all else is "not Los Angeles" and "not Seattle." They agree that the best way to avoid the gridlock and endless subdivisions that presumably characterize their West Coast neighbors is to support relatively compact land development within the constraints of the UGB. In effect, the recent neotraditional vision of compact development has been layered on the environmental regionalism of Lewis Mumford. The result is a potent alliance between the friends of city life and the friends of trees.

An example of coalition-building at the regional scale involves the so-called Westside Bypass—in effect, the southwestern quarter of an outer beltway. The bypass proposal was strongly favored by economic and political interests within Washington County. Environmentalists, however, opposed it for opening farmland to development, particularly because it would have swung outside the UGB. Urbanists opposed it for threatening suburban sprawl. The combined opposition raised the local political costs and allowed an outgoing governor to end state planning support for the project in 1994.

Conclusions

One lesson that other communities might draw from Portland is the continuing importance of leadership from the central city. The classic urban-renewal elite of downtown business and property owners, utilities, and metropolitan news media still have the biggest economic stake in a compact city. The strongest opponents will be elected and appointed representatives of suburban governments, whose own interests lie in the care and feeding of independent political units. The challenge for the advocates of the compact city is to appeal over the heads of suburban officials to suburban voters, who are already concerned about rising service costs and traffic congestion but whose normal political

arena of neighborhood and suburb is too limited for effective action. These suburban citizens (especially those in inner suburban rings) are potential recruits for the compact city if offered a clear vision and practical policies.[37]

Even more important is the necessity to incorporate all the pieces in a single strategy. Here is where the cultural and institutional factors come together, as well as the urban and environmental agendas. The recent history of Portland shows that core city revitalization, neighborhood conservation, and suburban growth management are not separable options. Growth management without acknowledgment of the importance of a strong center will not shape a metropolitan area according to the standard model; neither will investment in downtown office towers that ignores a city's close-in neighborhoods. The former will simply push growth back and forth from one side of a metropolitan area to the other like water sloshing in a shallow pan. The latter undercuts its own competitive edge with suburban development. A metropolis that works, in short, is one that has given equal attention to all of its pieces.

To repeat an earlier point, it is particularly through transportation plans and programs that Portland's environmental activists have been converted or won to the agenda of the urbanists. Given the American penchant for green space and natural landscapes, it is not really news that urban advocates can also favor environmental protection. More interesting is the "man bites dog" story that treehuggers can also be recruited to favor revitalized downtowns, expensive rail systems, and the like. Groups and individuals committed to preserving natural systems have been convinced that the way to accomplish this goal is through compact development around strong downtowns—a position that many larger developers are willing to live with. In other words, the environmental ethic has been tied to the option of going "up" with compact and higher-density development rather than the option of going "out" with low-density Broadacre Cities and virtual communities of upscale telecommuters.

One important issue that remains is how to construct and maintain an infrastructure of civic cooperation. As Robert Putnam has argued, a community's habits and institutions for constructive civic participation make a difference to policy outcomes.[38] Like Boston in the late nineteenth century and Chicago in the early twentieth century, Portland has benefited from wide public involvement in discussion of the metropolitan future. As with the earlier examples, Portland demonstrates the overall importance of broad involvement by the top ten thousand activists as well as the top ten corporate executives and landowners. It also shows the value of a dense network of civic action organizations, from neighborhood associations to environmental advocates, whose overlapping goals and memberships help to link the urban and environmental agendas.

However, Portland also shows troubling signs of erosion of the downtown-neighborhood alliance. Citizen participation is a fragile component of political systems. Compromises of coalition-building inevitably bury some concerns as they satisfy others. Because Portland's elite values politeness in civic discourse, well-mannered activists get invited to the committee meetings and the ill-mannered get locked out of the "club." The lack of the safety valve of vigorous electoral politics may be allowing a buildup of unsatisfied discontent.[39] For example, the citywide neighborhood association program, which emphasizes process over program, is beginning to unravel under cumbersome procedures. Neighborhoods are also starting to resist their part of the urbanism bargain by rejecting higher densities associated with row houses, accessory apartments, and other deviations from the single-family model.

Portland's public consensus is also vulnerable to the mobilization of new interests that have not agreed to the rules of the game. Newcomers to Oregon are most likely to be suburb-to-suburb migrants with no ties to the central city. They also lack any understanding of the metropolitan and statewide land-use compromises crafted two decades ago. More specifically, the metropolitan economy is increasingly dominated by branch electronics plants whose managers are interested only in suburban locations, labor force, and access. As they become the most powerful suburban employer group, they may be able to sway suburban governments against the urbanist coalition. In particular, there is the possibility that Washington County may decide to pick up its tax dollars and head off on its own, prodded by new residents and businesses that see no economic or personal interest in a strong center.

Some critics also argue that the Portland model is possible because Clark County, Washington, acts as a land-development safety valve. Clark County is a halfhearted participant in metropolitan planning schemes, despite recent growth-management legislation in the state of Washington, and its voters in February 1995 overwhelmingly declined to pay for a trans-Columbia light-rail link. Clark County's politics are sympathetic to sprawling residential and commercial development, while Washington's lack of a state income tax attracts many of the area's entrepreneurially minded residents. In short, persons unsympathetic to the Portland-area growth model can exit by moving across the Columbia River while still participating in the metropolitan economy.

In its broadest implications, the Portland experience is a reminder of the need to understand regions as systems that integrate centers and edges. In one sense, the essence of the urbanist-environmentalist alliance is the mutual support of central and peripheral conservation. In turn, some in the Portland area are starting to think about core and periphery on a larger scale and addressing the difficult question of how widely to draw the bounds of place. The entire metropolitan area, or at least its four largest counties, is the center of larger natural and economic regions—the Willamette Valley, the Columbia Basin, the northwestern rain-coast, the Cascadian economic region. However delineated, these are regions that have been shaped and organized by and around cities. Their history is inextricably linked with metropolitan growth and change, and their futures are likely to be equally shaped by the influence of their major cities.

Comprehensive planning on this scale of river basins, city-states, and multistate regions was last attempted in the 1930s by the Pacific Northwest Regional Planning Commission and state planning boards associated with the National Resources Planning Board. Since that time, regional planning has focused on single resource or development issues such as energy supply, forest management, the survival of salmon runs, or regional economic marketing.[40] In the process, the region may have ignored the Oregon land-use lesson that a basic strategy for conserving natural systems and rural communities is to protect and enhance the attractions and efficiency of focused metropolitan centers. The solution to the very real environmental problems of the greater Northwest, in other words, may be an expanded version of metropolitan Portland's promotion of urban values and its careful balancing of city and country. As projected on this broader canvas, such an approach to comprehensive regional planning may be the Portland area's most important contribution to the national discussion of land policies and environmental protection.

Notes

1. When the fountain was built, the Civic Auditorium was the only large city-owned assembly hall in the central business district. In the 1980s a new Performing Arts Center located several blocks closer to the retail center took away many of the Civic Auditorium's events and concerts.

2. In November 1994, voters in the three central metropolitan counties agreed to a $475 million bond measure for a north-south light-rail line. The measure passed by 66 percent in Multnomah County (containing the city of Portland), by 62 percent in suburban Clackamas County, and by 59 percent in suburban Washington County. In May 1995, a $136 million bond issues for open space and park acquisition and stream protection passed in all three counties with the support of 66 percent of voters in Multnomah County, 59 percent in Washington County, and 58 percent in Clackamas County. The light-rail situation has since grown more complicated because of failure of support in Clark County, Washington. Voters statewide rejected state aid in 1996. Voters in the tri-county area narrowly rejected local support for a reduced north-south line in 1998. As of mid-1999, a spur to the airport was beginning construction and a northside-only spur under serious discussion.

3. Tom Wolfe, "The Copper Goddess," *Newsweek*, July 14, 1986, pp. 34–35.

4. "Urbanism" as used in this chapter conveys many of the same values that Robert Fishman has summarized in his chapter as "metropolitanism."

5. *Economist*, September 1, 1990, pp. 24–25. The Portland metropolitan area in 1990 ranked ahead of Columbus and San Antonio in population but behind Kansas City and Milwaukee.

6. Joan Laatz, "Urban Experts Like Portland's Style," *Oregonian*, May 6, 1988; Tom McEnery, *The New City-State: Change and Renewal in America's Cities* (Niwot, Colo.: Roberts Rinehart, 1994).

7. Real Estate Research Corporation, *The Costs of Sprawl: Environmental and Economic Costs of Alternative Residential Development Patterns at the Urban Fringe* (Washington, D.C.: U.S.

Government Printing Office, 1974). Explications of aspects of the compact-city model are found in Anthony Downs, *New Visions for Metropolitan America* (Washington, D.C.: Brookings Institution Press, 1994); Philip Langdon, *A Better Place to Live* (Amherst: University of Massachusetts Press, 1994); Peter Calthorpe, *The Next American Metropolis: Ecology, Community, and the American Dream* (Princeton: Princeton University Press, 1993); David Rusk, *Cities without Suburbs* (Baltimore and Washington, D.C.: Johns Hopkins University Press and Woodrow Wilson Center Press, 1993); and James Howard Kunstler, *The Geography of Nowhere: The Rise and Decline of America's Man-Made Landscape* (New York: Simon and Schuster, 1993).

8. W. A. Henry III, "Portland Offers a Calling Card," *Time,* December 12, 1988, p. 88; Philip Langdon, "How Portland Does It," *Atlantic Monthly,* November 1992, pp. 134–41; Donald Canty, "Portland," *Architecture: The AIA Journal* 75 (July 1986): 32–47; Berton Roueche, "A New Kind of City," *New Yorker,* October 21, 1985, pp. 42–53; Neal R. Peirce and Robert Guskind, *Breakthroughs: Re-Creating the American City* (New Brunswick, N.J.: Center for Urban Policy Research, Rutgers University, 1993). A not-surprising reaction to all this good ink is a skeptical recharacterization of downtown Portland as a Disneylike theme park rather than a "real" place. See, for example, Robert Shibley in Peirce and Guskind, *Breakthroughs,* p. 80; Robert Bruegmann, "New Centers on the Periphery," *Center: A Journal for Architecture in America* 7 (1992): 25–43.

9. Discussions of the concepts of the "edge city" and the "suburban activity center" can be found in Joel Garreau, *Edge City: Life on the New Frontier* (New York: Doubleday, 1991); and Robert Cervero, *America's Suburban Centers: The Land-Use Transportation Link* (Boston: Unwin Hyman, 1989), respectively. Garreau identifies the Beaverton-Tigard-Tualatin triangle and Cervero the I-5 corridor from Tigard to Wilsonville.

10. Contrast this sense of a limited supply of farmland with the very different sense of unbounded land surrounding a city such as Indianapolis or Des Moines.

11. Westside riverfront sites have developed or are likely to develop with upscale mixed-use residential/commercial space. Eastside sites have been recycled for new generations of industrial use, especially in wholesaling and distribution.

12. Steve Dotterrer, "Cities and Towns," in *Space, Style, and Structure: Building in Northwest America,* ed. Thomas Vaughan and Virginia Ferriday (Portland: Oregon Historical Society, 1974).

13. Carl Abbott, "Regional City and Network City: Portland and Seattle in the Twentieth Century," *Western Historical Quarterly* 23, 3 (1992): 293–322.

14. Carl Abbott, *Ethnic Minorities in Portland: A 1990 Census Profile* (Portland: Center for Urban Studies, Portland State University, 1991).

15. Carl Abbott, *Portland: Planning, Politics, and Growth in a Twentieth-Century City* (Lincoln: University of Nebraska Press, 1983).

16. Goldschmidt served as mayor until 1979, when he became secretary of transportation in the Carter administration. He served as governor of Oregon from 1987 to 1990.

17. Carl Abbott, "Urban Design in Portland, Oregon, as Policy and Process, 1960–1989," *Planning Perspectives* 6, 1 (1991): 1–18; Peirce and Guskind, *Breakthroughs.*

18. Norman Krumholz and Pierre Clavel, *Reinventing Cities: Equity Planners Tell Their Stories* (Philadelphia: Temple University Press, 1994).

19. Howard Hallman, *The Organization and Operation of Neighborhood Councils* (New York: Praeger, 1977); William Cunningham and Milton Kotler, *Building Neighborhood Organizations* (Notre Dame: Notre Dame University Press, 1983); Bruce Clary, *A Framework for Citizen Participation: Portland's Office of Neighborhood Associations* (Washington, D.C.: International City Management Association, 1986); Jeffrey Berry et al., *The Rebirth of Urban Democracy* (Washington, D.C.: Brookings Institution Press, 1993).

20. Tom McCall and Steve Neal, *Tom McCall: Maverick* (Portland: Binford and Mort, 1979), p. 196.

21. Fred Bosselman and David Callies, *The Quiet Revolution in Land Use Control* (Washington, D.C.: U.S. Council on Environmental Quality, 1971); Carl Abbott and Deborah Howe, "The Politics of Land-Use Law in Oregon: Senate Bill 100, Twenty Years After," *Oregon Historical Quarterly* 94, 1 (1993): 5–35.

22. The politics of the Oregon land-use planning system are discussed in Gerrit Knapp, "Land Use Politics in Oregon," in *Planning the Oregon Way,* ed. Carl Abbott, Deborah Howe, and Sy Adler (Corvallis: Oregon State University Press, 1994); Brent Walth, *Fire at Eden's Gate: Tom Mc-*

Call and the Oregon Story (Portland: Oregon Historical Society, 1994); R. Jeffrey Leonard, *Managing Oregon's Growth* (Washington, D.C.: Conservative Foundation, 1983); and Abbott and Howe, "The Politics of Land-Use Law in Oregon." The system is evaluated in Gerrit Knapp and A.C. Nelson, *The Regulated Landscape: Lessons on State Land Use Planning from Oregon* (Cambridge, Mass.: Lincoln Institute of Land Policy, 1992). When the system came under attack in the 1995 legislative session, the pro-planning alliance included the Farm Bureau as well as metropolitan legislators and lobbyists.

23. Arthur C. Nelson, "Using Land Markets to Evaluate Urban Containment Programs," *Journal of the American Planning Association* 52, 2 (1986): 156–71.

24. Nohad A. Toulan, "Housing as a State Planning Goal," in *Planning the Oregon Way,* ed. Abbott, Howe, and Adler.

25. Sy Adler, "The Oregon Approach to Integrating Transportation and Land Use Planning," in *Planning the Oregon Way,* ed. Abbott, Howe, and Adler.

26. The 2040 Plan was followed in October 1996 with adoption of the Urban Growth Management Functional Plan and in December 1997 with adoption of the Regional Framework Plan. Mandated by Metro's charter, the Framework Plan integrates land use, transportation, parks, and open space plans. Local comprehensive plans must be compatible with the Framework Plan. Metro, *Region 2040: Concepts for Growth,* and *Region 2040: Recommended Alternative Decisions* (Portland: Metro, 1994).

27. James Q. Wilson, "Urban Problems in Perspective," in *The Metropolitan Enigma,* ed. James Q. Wilson (New York: Anchor Books, 1970), p. 398.

28. Daniel Elazar, *American Federalism: The View from the States* (New York: Thomas Crowell, 1972), p. 96.

29. Between 1950 and 1975, four self-confident politicians in the moralistic mode set the style for Oregon politics—Wayne Morse, Richard Neuberger, Mark Hatfield, and Tom McCall.

30. David Klingman and William Lammers, "The 'General Policy Liberalism' Factor in American State Politics," *American Journal of Political Science* 28, 3 (1984): 598–610; Jack Walker, "Diffusion of Innovation among the American States," *American Political Science Review* 63, 3 (1969): 880–89.

31. Olmsted Brothers, Landscape Architects, "Report to the Board of Park Commissioners, December 31, 1903," in Portland Board of Park Commissioners, *Report of the Park Board,* Portland, 1904; Lewis Mumford, *Regional Planning in the Pacific Northwest* (Portland: Northwest Regional Council, 1939); R. Bruce Stephenson, "A Vision of Green: Lewis Mumford's Legacy in Portland, Oregon," *Journal of the American Planning Association* 65, 3 (1999): 259–69.

32. Sy Adler and Gerald Blake, "The Effects of a Formal Citizen Participation Program on Involvement in the Planning Process: A Case Study of Portland, Oregon," *State and Local Government Review* 22, 1 (1990): 37–43; Abbott, "Urban Design in Portland, Oregon"; Sheldon Edner and Carl Adler, *Challenges Confronting Metropolitan Portland's Transportation Regime* (Washington, D.C.: National Academy Press, 1991).

33. Portland State University Urban Studies Center, *A Review of City/County/Special District Functional Relationships in the Portland Urban Area* (Portland: Portland State University, 1969).

34. Carl Abbott, "The Suburban Sunbelt," *Journal of Urban History* 13, 3 (1987): 275–301; Paul George Lewis, "Organizing Urban Regional Development: The Political Economy of the New Suburban Growth" (Ph.D. diss., Princeton University, 1994). The most active suburbs, with their 1990 populations, are Gresham (68,000), Beaverton (53,000), Hillsboro (38,000), Tigard (29,000), and Tualatin (15,000). Paul Lewis has recently argued that this institutional structure of Portland-area government should be viewed as a primary cause of the area's policy choices rather than an aspect of those choices.

35. Gerald Suttles, *The Man-Made City: The Land Use Confidence Game in Chicago* (Chicago: University of Chicago Press, 1990); Carl Abbott, *The New Urban America: Growth and Politics in Sunbelt Cities* (Chapel Hill: University of North Carolina Press, 1987); Mark Richard Bello, "Urban Regimes and Downtown Planning in Portland, Oregon, and Seattle, Washington, 1972–1992" (Ph.D. diss., Portland State University, 1993); Mike Davis, *City of Quartz: Excavating the Future in Los Angeles* (New York: Vintage, 1992).

36. In Paul Peterson's terminology, neighborhood and downtown interests unite around a carefully balanced developmental agenda rather than fighting over redistribution of resources. In the terms of John Logan and Harvey Molotch, down-

town and neighborhood interests come together as parts of a mild-mannered growth machine. Paul Peterson, *City Limits* (Chicago: University of Chicago Press, 1981); John R. Logan and Harvey Molotch, *Urban Fortunes: The Political Economy of Place* (Berkeley: University of California Press, 1987).

37. Rusk, *Cities without Suburbs*.

38. Robert Putnam et al., *Making Democracy Work: Civic Traditions in Modern Italy* (Princeton: Princeton University Press, 1993).

39. Bello, "Urban Regimes and Downtown Planning."

40. A federally mandated Pacific Northwest River Basins Commission in the 1970s never found a niche within the region's political ecology and disappeared during the Reagan administration.

Middle-class houses in Oak Park, Illinois, west of Chicago, 1990s. Oak Park unites a classic suburban landscape with a determined effort to achieve racial integration. (Photograph by Judith A. Martin)

CHAPTER TEN

Local Initiative and Metropolitan Repetition
Chicago, 1972–1990

■ ■
■ ■

JUDITH A. MARTIN AND SAM BASS WARNER, JR.

The research for this chapter was undertaken to discover how a modern metropolis might respond to two fresh goals for American planning—the goal of residential racial openness and the goal of employing natural systems for urban environmental management. Although we found vigorous and sustained activity around both goals within the Chicago metropolis, each has advanced only within the conµnes laid down by the structures of American urban federalism.

With respect to the racial challenges within the Chicago area, the residents and government of one suburb (Oak Park) long ago initiated a policy of racial openness. Despite the surrounding neighbors' and governments' policies of racial segregation, this goal has been continually sustained. Oak Park thus stands as a monument to Justice Louis Brandeis's hopes for the creativity of American federalism.

The environmental case, however, stands in contrast to this success. The Tunnel and Reservoir Plan of the Chicago Metropolitan Water Reclamation District reveals some of the obdurate problems of federalism. This massive construction project proved on investigation to be the prisoner of professional inertia—an example of the lag and drag imposed by the weight of accepted professional practice. An elected board of commissioners and an expert staff failed to adapt to unfolding environmental criticism and experiments or to citizen initiatives. Here, at a big state-created metropolitan agency, we met the governmental inertia that urban reformers more commonly identify as the hallmark of city halls and town ofµces.

Thus, what follows is an exploration of both the creativity and the inertia of American urban federalism.

The Setting

If we were to take the successes of the civil rights and the environmental movements of the past thirty years seriously, we would judge any urban-planning project according to two criteria. First, no project, large or small, ought to intensify the racial segregation of its metropolitan area. Ideally, a project should help open up the housing market to all comers. Second, every new building or reconstruction project should employ natural systems as much as possible for its energy and its management of water, wastes, and landscapes.[1]

Over the past hundred years city planners and architects have built a number of projects that were specifically designed to relieve class and racial segregation; these have incorporated some good site plans and landscapes. But the two post-1970 criteria have seldom been consciously embraced as the goals of good policy and good design. At present, however, the social and economic costs of American race relations and the burdens of our urban engineering and commonplace landscapes suggest that these two goals should be essential criteria for any future projects.

The injustice and destructive consequences of racial segregation have relentlessly torn America's cities. These conflicts have overwhelmed both the small communities that make up American metropolises and the metropolises themselves. As segregation conflicts acted in concert with urban deindustrialization, corporate restructuring, skill dilution, and overall job losses, they imposed staggering human and economic losses.

The consequences of environmental mismanagement are equally pervasive: poisoned urban land, toxic air and contaminated groundwater, wasteland parking lots, desert streets, and expensive remediation. The realization that we are creatures of nature whose well-being depends on our interactions with the air, water, soil, plants, and creatures that surround us has been slow to reach public consciousness. Our cities have been especially separated from this realization because our environmental tradition has stressed urban parks and remote forests and wildernesses as remedies for urban living. Yet the air, water, plants, and living things of the city and its suburbs are as vital to human survival and well-being as the conditions of prairies and forests.

Racism and Environmentalism

Contemporary issues of race and environmental management share many parallels. Both sets of issues depend on goals for individual rights, goals for community efficiency and well-being, and goals for cultural choice.

Racism and segregation attack the accepted American concepts and laws about citizens' rights—rights to move freely and safely throughout a metropolitan region, rights to equal access to public education and public services, rights to rent or purchase real property wherever one can afford it, and rights to be employed wherever one's talents, training, and experience match an employer's standards. These are rights established by federal and state constitutions and civil rights legislation. Together they define our current consensus about what constitutes racial justice.

Racism and segregation also attack goals for carrying out community tasks in an efficient manner. When children cannot get access to effective education, and when adults cannot get access to jobs for which they are qualified, the community is denied the energy and talent of its fellow citizens. Segregation in housing both inflates and deflates housing markets so that in some cases families must spend a disproportionate share of their income for housing. In other circumstances, resident families, and the community as a whole, lose the accumulated wealth embodied in standing structures through neglect and abandonment. Finally, racism and segregation foreclose the cultural choices of many Americans by denying those who wish to live in racially mixed communities the opportunity to do so.

Environmental practices carry with them similar consequences. Every American citizen has a right to clean air, clean water, wholesome food, decent shelter, and a safe sanitary environment. Such rights stem in part from legislation and regulation: clean-air laws, regulations for pure food and drugs, laws to control emissions of toxic matter, regulations of water supplies, building codes, and public health measures. These rights also flow from the essential qualities of human beings as organisms who require a satisfactory environment to flourish. In practice, the sum of all these laws and regulations falls short of guaranteeing these biological rights to all American citizens, just as civil rights legislation and regulations fail to protect all American citizens.

Environmental practices also have pronounced impacts on the efficiency of communities. American metropolises bear the burden of many high-cost and inefficient environments: air-conditioned skyscrapers and shopping malls, unmetered public water supplies, combined sanitary and storm sewer systems, and treeless streets and house lots. The private land use, the buildings, the public utilities and the infrastructure of any community should be examined for their short-term and long-term costs. Those environments that are the most efficient use natural resources as sources of energy, to process wastes, and to shelter buildings. They are less costly in the long run than those that depend on heavy use of fossil fuels and mechanical and chemical processing of wastes. Finally, the design of urban and

suburban environments can reinforce people's awareness of themselves as members of the universe of living organisms, or they can promote the denial of that consciousness.

These issues of rights and efficiencies are but the cold substrate of the opportunities that a democratic society and an environmentally conscious society can confer on its citizens. In communities not ruled by racial prejudice, conflict proceeds within the manners and rules of a democratic polity. Similarly, a nature-maximizing community allows its residents to understand and to experience themselves as creatures of nature. They can then manage the surrounding natural systems in ways that express their shared biological qualities with the creatures and plants that sustain human life.

The interactions of race relations and the dynamics of natural systems play themselves out at every scale from the national to the regional and local. Racism flows inevitably from American history and culture. It is fostered or checked by state governments and private institutions, and it reveals itself in neighborhood accommodation or violence. Acid rain drifts across the continent, produced by regional power plants and fostered by federal regulations, but in the end it kills the fish in a particular pond and erodes the stones on a particular building.

Our system of government partitions these interactions among federal, state, and local levels. Although there are essential tasks for the federal government in both race relations and environmental management, the possibilities for fresh ideas and new methods are best observed at the metropolitan and local level. Here, alternative institutions, policies, and outcomes can be observed close-up.

Accordingly, the metropolis of Chicago and its western suburbs will be used as the case study of this chapter. Chicago has been chosen because it is home to the second-largest concentration of African Americans

Table 10.1

Total Population of the Top Ten African American Metropolises

(Varying metropolitan definitions (CSAs), 1950, 1970, 1990)

	Total population		
	1950	1970	1990
New York	12,912,000	16,179,000	18,087,000
Chicago	5,495,000	7,612,000	8,066,000
Los Angeles	4,368,000	7,032,000	14,532,000
Philadelphia	3,671,000	4,818,000	5,899,000
Washington	1,464,000	2,861,000	3,924,000
Detroit	3,016,000	4,200,000	4,665,000
Atlanta	672,000	1,390,000	2,834,000
Houston	807,000	1,985,000	3,193,000
Miami	495,000	1,268,000	3,193,000
Dallas	615,000	1,556,000	3,885,000

Sources: U.S. Bureau of the Census, *Census of Population: 1950* vol. 2, *Characteristics of the Population*. United States Summary (Washington, D.C.: U.S. Government Printing Office [GPO], 1953). Table 86: *1970 Census of Population and Housing*. PHC(2) *General Demographic Trends for Metropolitan Areas, 1960 to 1970* (Washington, D.C.: GPO), June 1971), Tables 1 and 2: *Census of Population: 1990* (1990 CP-1-1) *General Population Characteristics, United States* (Washington, D.C. GPO, 1992). Table 266.

Table 10.2

African American Population as a Percentage of Total Population in the Top Ten

African-American Metropolises

	1950		1970		1990	
	African American population	Percentage of total population	African American population	Percentage of total population	African American population	Percentage of total population
New York	1,046,000	8.1	1,883,000	16.3	3,289,000	18.2
Chicago	605,000	11.0	1,343,000	17.6	1,548,000	19.2
Los Angeles	276,000	6.3	763,000	10.8	1,230,000	8.5
Philadelphia	484,000	13.2	844,000	17.5	1,100,000	18.6
Washington	342,000	23.4	704,000	24.6	1,042,000	26.6
Detroit	362,000	12.0	757,000	18.0	975,000	20.9
Atlanta	166,000	24.7	311,000	22.3	736,000	26.0
Houston	150,000	18.7	384,000	19.3	665,000	17.9
Miami	65,000	13.2	190,000	15.0	591,000	18.5
Dallas-Ft. Worth	83,000	13.6	249,000	16.0	555,000	14.3

Sources: U.S. Bureau of the Census, *Census of Population: 1950* vol. 2, *Characteristics of the Population*. United States Summary (Washington, D.C.: U.S. Government Printing Office [GPO], 1953). Table 86: *1970 Census of Population and Housing*. PHC(2) *General Demographic Trends for Metropolitan Areas, 1960 to 1970* (Washington, D.C.: GPO), June 1971), Tables 1 and 2: *Census of Population: 1990* (1990 CP-1-1) *General Population Characteristics, United States* (Washington, D.C. GPO, 1992). Table 266.

in the United States (see Tables 10.1 and 10.2).[2] The near western suburbs, including the adjacent Austin neighborhood of Chicago, have been selected because they demonstrate a wide range of racial practices and policies from the most difficult to the most promising. Likewise, the environmental management of metropolitan Chicago exemplifies American infrastructure engineering and landscaping over a range from the most costly to the most efficient. The low-lying and flat nature of Chicago's terrain presents a special set of challenges that have fostered practices that press the limits of conventional metropolitan engineering.

The Inheritance from the Past, 1880–1950

Ideas, behaviors, and constructions from the past century have shaped the recent history of all American metropolises. Perhaps none has felt this more forcibly than Chicago, a city first cast in a nineteenth-century mold and then thoroughly refashioned according to the principles of the early twentieth century.

The city-bound tides of rural Americans and Europeans brought the metropolises of the Northeast and Midwest into being. This late-nineteenth-century migration bequeathed a social inheritance that still influences contemporary settlement patterns. Three attitudes and practices stand out as our patrimony: first, the practice of separating activities by economic function throughout the metropolitan region; second, the separation of economic classes within the residential areas of the region; and third, the forcing of African American citizens into less-than-citizen roles. These three social legacies have driven the recent history of all American cities and suburbs, and they continue to dominate the geography, economy, politics, and social life of the Chicago metropolis. It is toward the possibilities for change in this tra-

dition that the new planning goal of inclusiveness addresses itself.

No less so than in social matters, the ideas, institutions, and constructions of the 1880–1950 era still direct interactions among metropolitan human settlements and their nonhuman natural systems. This era passed down the basic infrastructure of paved streets, unified metropolitan water and sewer systems, organized waste disposal, and municipal and metropolitan parks and forests. The character of this infrastructure and its use and placement in turn are derived from the unique technological mixture of the 1880–1950 era: steam railroads, electric street railways, ubiquitous electric power and telephone service, concrete and steel construction, the automobile, and the airplane.[3] These basic technologies and the attitudes that directed their use still provide the armature that holds together people and nature in the Chicago metropolis of the 1990s. The perceived design imperatives have long been oriented toward progress, as defined by engineering values. Consequently, the entire cycle and congregation of urban nature has to adapt to such values.

Since 1950, the tension between American citizens and their metropolitan environments has only increased, as city dwellers experienced the old metropolis being extended into its new, dispersed, automobile form. The multiple unforeseen and unwelcome social and environmental problems facing us today challenge most of the city-planning and environmental accomplishments of preceding generations.

The Racial Setting of the Chicago Suburbs

Extraordinary tides of migration, movements of the magnitude of the pre–Civil War westward conquest and the post–Civil War European immigration, have dominated the years since the outbreak of World War II. White Americans have moved in massive numbers from metropolis to metropolis, and within each they have carried their settlements outward from established center cities to a spread of peripheral cities and towns.[4] New superhighway networks facilitated this transformation and also refashioned earlier patterns of suburban travel. Formerly, quotidian movement flowed from outer residence to inner workplace. In the post-1950 decades the whole metropolitan traffic system came to resemble a tangled skein of multidirectional journeys for work, errands, business deliveries, visiting, and pleasure rides. This process has advanced so far that journeys to work are no longer the leading cause of automobile traffic.[5]

Such thoroughgoing transformations, rushing on during a few decades, were a sufficient challenge to test the goodwill of any community. Yet this white dispersal went forward amid an extraordinary northward and westward migration of rural African Americans. Until World War II the African American populations of northern big cities constituted about 6 percent of the whole, while their suburban populations were about 3 percent black. Such small concentrations in part account for black political powerlessness during this time.[6] The shortage of white labor during World War II, caused largely by the restriction of European migration during the 1920s and 1930s, re-ignited migration from the rural South, while the mechanization of the cotton farms pushed millions of African Americans toward the cities of the North and the West.[7] Chicago's 1930 black population of 234,000 doubled by 1950, and then doubled again during the twenty years from 1950 to 1970. Then, as the civil rights movement in the South bore fruit in opening up opportunities for African Americans, and as American and foreign firms sought nonunion labor, the black migration to the

North and Midwest slowed, and even reversed itself for a time in the late 1970s.[8] This shrinking northward migration then combined with a new suburban-bound black population, so Chicago's African American population actually declined from its 1970 peak (see Table 10.3).

Because of white prejudice and hostility, African American citizens of Chicago, old-timers and newcomers alike, came to live in clusters. No migrant groups, before or since, have dwelt in American cities under circumstances of such intense segregation.[9] In Chicago the ghetto boundaries had been established between 1910 and 1920. Thereafter, their expansion to the south and west proceeded through the addition of adjacent neighborhoods.[10]

During the 1960s black settlements in suburban towns and manufacturing cities began to grow rapidly, so that by 1980, 29 percent of African Americans who lived in American metropolises lived in some sort of suburb yet even here the pattern of intense segregation repeated itself.[11] These fringe black ghettos stand in shocking contrast to the much more diffused settlements of Hispanics and Asians.[12]

During the 1980s a few hopeful signs of progress toward full metropolitan citizenship for African Americans appeared. Many suburbs that had few or no blacks added to their black populations. Also, here and there, the intensity of segregation declined.[13]

The ghetto confinement of African Americans has also burdened the economies of American metropolitan regions by inflating their economic and social costs. The residential dispersal of metropolitan whites carried with it a parallel dispersal of stores, offices, warehouse, and factories. Such job migration left the growing ghetto populations to compete for jobs at the old establishments. When manufacturing fled the Northeast and Midwest after the Vietnam War, the

Table 10.3

African American Population in Chicago and the
Balance of Cook County 1930–90

	Chicago			Balance of Cook County		
	Total population	African American population	African American percentage of total	Total population	African American population	African American percentage of total
1930	3,376,000	234,000	6.9	606,000	13,000	2.1
1950	3,621,000	492,000	13.6	888,000	47,000	5.3
1970	3,367,000	1,103,000	32.8	2,125,000	80,000	3.8
1990	2,784,000	1,088,000	39.1	2,321,000	229,000	9.9

Notes: 1950 racial category is "non-white," 1930 and 1970 it is "Negro," 1990 it is "Black." Cook County represents a falling percentage of the Chicago CSA Metropolitan area from 1950 on: in 1950 Cook County is 82.1 percent of the metropolitan population; by 1990 it is 63.1 percent, as defined by the U.S. Census.

Sources: U.S. Bureau of the Census, Fifteenth Census of the United States: 1930, Population, vol. 3, Pt. 1 (Washington, D.C.: GPO, 1932), Table 21; U.S. Census of Population: 1950, Characteristics of the Population, Part 13, Illinois (Washington, D.C.: GPO, 1952), Tables 10, 12, 34, 41; U.S. Census of Population; 1970, Pt. 15, Illinois, Sec. 1 (Washington, D.C.: GPO, 1973), Tables 23, 24; U.S. Census of Population: 1990 (1990 CP-1-1) General Population Characteristics, United States (Washington, D.C.: GPO, 1992), Table 266.

African American ghetto became an island of unemployed and low-wage workers situated far from the new economic opportunities of the metropolis.[14] This concentration of poverty, in turn, withdrew tax resources from local governments at the very time when extra efforts were required to maintain and expand social and educational services. All the while, white and black conflict prevented the modernization of ghetto real estate and businesses except by the processes of all-white urban renewal and related subsidized programs. Such has been the level of conflict and distrust between the races that few whites would venture to invest in the black ghetto.

Case Study: Oak Park in Context

The western suburbs of Chicago provide a vibrant environment within which to consider these complex issues. As in many other U.S. metropolitan areas, the historic western border of the city has long been shared with other independent municipalities. These are communities that, for a variety of reasons (fiscal prudence, fear, hatred, a feeling of superiority, etc.), chose not to be annexed by Chicago back in the nineteenth century. They have a long heritage of independence in local political and social matters, but have been forced to cooperate with the city on environmental issues such as sewerage and waste treatment. They are also communities that are aging and facing the challenges of being left behind by newer, "better" places even further to the west. These communities are thoroughly in the middle: they lie somewhere near the center of the Chicago metropolitan area and they maintain a stubborn stance of independence, while necessarily functioning as part of a larger metropolitan system. To an uninformed eye, they are physically an extension of Chicago, an impression that would be strongly disputed by most local residents.

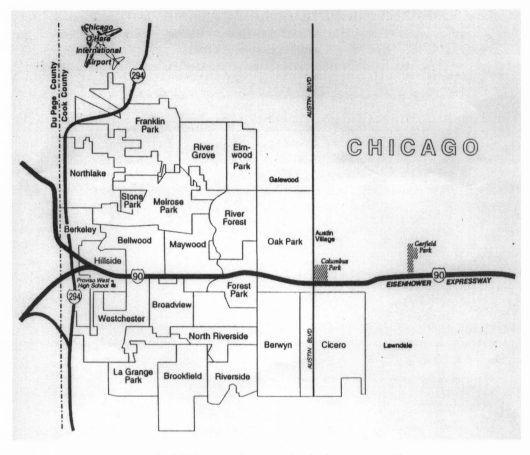

Figure 10.1 Chicago and near west suburban communities

The geographical context of Oak Park, likely the best known of this group of suburbs, is crucial to understanding the area's diversity efforts. Oak Park shares a border with Chicago's both to the east and to the north (see fig. 10.1). To Oak Park's south is Berwyn, and just east of Berwyn is Cicero (which also shares two borders with Chicago). Cicero has long been noted for stridently opposing racial diversity, having violently resisted the marches led by Martin Luther King, Jr., in the 1960s To the immediate west of Oak Park are the communities of River Forest and Forest Park. Further to the southwest is Riverside, the famed nineteenth-century garden suburb designed by Frederick Law Olmsted.

In this greater western suburban universe. Oak Park has sat squarely in the middle, both socially and economically. It has always been a more "upscale" community than blue-collar Cicero, Berwyn, or Forest Park. It was never quite the social equal of River Forest or Riverside, though few Oak Parkers would admit this even of this today. One example Oak Park's "middling" position can be seen in its efforts to control alcoholic beverages. Until the early 1980s, Oak Park was a "dry" community surrounded by other communities with bars, largely due to the efforts of a nineteenth-century temperance activist. Henry Austin, who founded the nearby community named after him, and then moved to Oak Park and bought out the existing saloons.[15] Today, although many Oak Park restaurants now have wine/beer licenses, there are no liquor stores in the community. River Forest and Riverside are even more limiting in this regard. These alcohol policies are just one example of the solidly middle-class values that have defined Oak Park for more than a century.

Oak Park's Situation

In 1970 Oak Park, Illinois, had a troubling sense of its future: a nice, older, suburban area transformed into a landscape of disinvestment and trouble. This frightening projection did not require a crystal ball; it merely required one to look across Austin Boulevard, the shared boundary between Oak Park and the far west side of Chicago. Between 1960 and 1970 the Austin community, quite similar to Oak Park in the age of its housing stock. its population composition, and its community values, quickly fell into the pattern of residential succession that had been driving the black ghetto from the near west side of Chicago toward the city limits since the 1940s.

From East Garfield Park through Austin the process was well understood: a few black families moved into a neighborhood, and within a few years the whole area resegregated from all-white to all-black. In the process, home-ownership rates dropped, absentee landlords proliferated, property values declined, retailers moved away, education suffered. The familiar and abysmal litany of urban woes was clearly evident throughout the greater west side, as was the blockbusting role played by unscrupulous real estate agents.[16] In neighborhood after neighborhood throughout the west side, this process was virtually continuous from the late 1950s

on. Central and south Austin were transformed in five years, becoming nearly all-black by 1970. North Austin, which had fewer apartment buildings, was slower to change, but change seemed inevitable, and was nearly complete by 1980. In 1970 Oak Park stood squarely in this path.

What was at stake for Oak Park in 1970 was literally the future of the community. Whether or not it could escape the experience of the west side of Chicago was on the minds of many. Oak Park had always considered itself "better" than nearby Chicago neighborhoods, and it possessed a treasure trove of Frank Lloyd Wright houses to underscore this sensibility. But apart from this architectural distinction, it had little that could not be found in literally hundreds of outer urban–inner suburban communities across the country.

Like many other Northeastern and Midwestern suburbs, Oak Park developed between the 1870s and 1920s. In classic suburban style, it had many neighborhoods of single-family houses ranging from bungalows to oversized Victorians. But because it was one of the first suburbs to be connected to the city by rail, it also had areas with dense concentrations of two- and three-story apartment buildings. Oak Park had (and still has) a good school system, a number of well-supported cultural institutions, an active civic life, and a large number of deeply attached residents. Interestingly, until the early 1960s. much the same could have been said of the Austin community.[17]

What Oak Park did have to clearly distinguished from Austin was political independence. It was not a part of Chicago, which meant that Oak Park could, at a minimum, define the terms and conditions under which changing real estate conditions might be played out. This independence stood in great contrast to the predicament of Austin, where efforts to maintain the community ran headlong into larger Chicago politics (over school desegregation, among other issues).[18] The difference in political situation between these two communities would ultimately prove to be critical in defining Oak Park's options and gave the community flexibility at a critical moment.

Pro-diversity Policies

The political context of Oak Park has played an important role in the community's diversity efforts. Though widely perceived as a Republican stronghold (like River Forest, unlike Austin), Oak Park took some decidedly liberal positions in the 1960s. The village created a community-relations commission in 1963. It also passed a fair-housing ordinance in 1968, which banned, among other things, housing discrimination as well as steering and blockbusting. This meant that what passed for business as usual in Chicago could be legally prosecuted in Oak Park.[19] Perhaps the most important decision that the village made in this period was the creation of the Oak Park Housing Center (OPHC) in 1972. This was a nonprofit agency whose stated mission was to promote the affirmative marketing of Oak Park housing and to ensure racial diversity, despite the almost invisible minority population at the time.[20]

In 1970, despite a general worry about the future, Oak Park's immediate concerns were quite specific: the southeastern corner of the village, with its numerous large apartment buildings, was viewed as vulnerable to the kind of rapid racial transition and declining property values then affecting Austin. Oak Park responded to the expected racial change in an unusual way: it chose to regard integration as a positive experience, defining the challenge as one of management rather than one of resistance. If the southeastern corner of Oak Park could escape wholesale

white flight, there was hope that the entire village could be spared Austin's fate.

The OPHC founded by Bobbie Raymond (who was its co-director until 1997), was a critical instrument in the village's effort to manage change. Among the center's goals were the following: to attract to Oak Park newcomers interested in a diverse community; to counsel prospective residents; to maintain files on the availability of housing and on the lending institutions and realtors active in the residential market; to run community-education programs and provide a forum for residents; and to aid in legal referrals.[21] The OPHC's housing-integration efforts have been focused primarily on the rental market, which comprises nearly 45 percent of the total housing stock. In its early years the OPHC also listed homes for sale, to help stimulate white housing demand in southeastern Oak Park. Within a few years this approach of intentionally seeking out white residents willing to live in south Oak Park was adopted by local realtors, as was a commitment to diversify the home-owning population of the rest of the village—something that was possible only because the village had an independent real estate board. Since the late 1970s the OPHC has devoted its efforts to the village's rental housing stock, with a primary focus on the many large apartment buildings rather than the smaller two- and three-flat structures.[22]

Perhaps the most controversial activity of the OPHC's more than twenty-five years of operation has been this process of what might be considered "reverse steering." This intentional effort to encourage prospective white residents to consider living in the southeastern sector of the community, while encouraging prospective black residents to look at other areas, although philosophically reasonable from the perspective of diversity, has been an ongoing challenge for the OPHC.

Over the past twenty-five years this practice has in fact effectively interspersed minorities throughout the entire village. This has happened even in the face of the relative concentration of apartment buildings in certain sectors of the community, and despite the fact that the OPHC has virtually no impact on the rental policies of the mostly owner-occupied small apartment buildings. Surprisingly for our litigious culture, and despite occasional threats, this practice has never been legally challenged.[23] More than anything else, this legal truce underscores the value that all Oak Park residents (and even some outsiders) place on the efforts that the village is making toward advancing the cause of diversity.

Oak Park's elected leadership supported the OPHC throughout the 1970s by adopting several challenging and proactive integration policies. These included housing audits to test for diversity, invoking the "exempt location" clause of the fair-housing ordinance (to aid in integration efforts), and banning redlining. A proposal to legislate racial quotas limiting each block to a maximum of 30 percent minority (widely perceived as a "tipping point") was discussed at one point but was never imposed. The village strictly enforced housing codes, licensed and inspected multifamily buildings, and initiated housing rehabilitation programs. In 1978 it went even further, by establishing an "equity assurance" program to assuage the fears of white homeowners that their property values would decline in the face of increasing diversity. To date no claims have been made against this fund.[24]

All of these official *policy* efforts were reinforced by the 1974 construction of a new village hall in southeastern Oak Park, a clear statement in bricks and mortar about the village's intent to maintain viability throughout the entire community. By the late 1980s the village had also established a "diversity assurance" program, an ongoing effort to actively market racial diversity, which the OPHC runs under contract. (An example of this program was described to us: a southeast Oak Park building with a 98 percent black residential profile was purchased by a new owner, who applied for assistance in the form of low-interest rehabilitation loans and employed a white building manager; some tenants moved to other parts of the village while rehabilitation occurred; the village paid a percentage of the rent while units were vacant and being remarketed; OPHC escorted prospective white renters to the building and actively solicited white tenants; two years later the building's racial profile was 70 percent white, 30 percent black, and rental increases have been held to $5 per year.)[25] Taken together, these policies appear to have succeeded. Oak Park has become a well-integrated community—by white standards, at least. It has, for the time being, escaped the Austin model.

The Regional Context

The effects of Oak Park's diversity efforts have been impressive. The area today remains an attractive community—one that people with other options chose to live in, though it still borders the problematic landscape of Austin. This result is partly due to the village's integration efforts, partly due to the cachet of Oak Park deriving from its international architectural reputation, partly due to the still highly regarded school system, and partly due to its highly accessible location with respect to both downtown Chicago and to the edge-city commercial core in western DuPage County. It has a well-integrated population and an extremely well-maintained housing stock. Property values are high enough to force some would-be Oak Parkers to search out other alternatives (northern Maywood, with its small number of comparable houses, for example). The minority population has increased to 20 percent (from less than 1 percent in 1970) and has not become geographically concentrated, as in Austin.

The foregoing describes Oak Park today but says little about the challenges still facing the community. Those responsible for its success to date know that they cannot simply relax and enjoy, for despite all the apparent good news about Oak Park, there is still the larger regional context to consider. Austin, for example, is widely viewed as a disaster: the commercial streets are decimated and many apartment buildings are burned out, boarded, and vacant. Although the South Shore Bank is attempting to replicate in Austin some of the community-revival success it has had on Chicago's South Side, and there is modest evidence of new single-family home construction on what were burned-out parcels seven years ago, much remains to be done to even approach stability.[26] There is the historic "Austin Village" area, which an integrated group of residents has worked to maintain and which has an annual home tour, started in part with the help of Oak Parkers. This area has been losing "pioneer" white residents who moved there for the Victorian houses but now find that their houses and neighbors cannot compensate for difficult school conditions, for the lack of recreational programs, and for the lack of a support system.[27] River Forest, which shares the northern portion of Oak Park's western boundary, is still expensive and nearly all-white. Forest Park is in transition, but without any of the formal programs that Oak Park has pioneered (see Table 10.4).

Further to the west is Maywood, historically an integrated community, now 84 percent black, and beyond that Broadview and Hillside, which seem to be following Maywood's path, though twenty years ago they were almost all-white. Galewood, the Chicago neighborhood to the north of Oak Park, is also losing white residents. To the south, Berwyn is maintaining its staunchly middle- and working-class white profile, though adjoining Cicero is now 25 percent Hispanic. (It is interesting to note that Hispanics, who are more likely to be in traditional family settings and to be Catholic, are on average poorer than blacks, who are still not welcome in Cicero). Thus, Oak Park finds itself alone in its immediate surroundings in promoting the positive value of integration, and black demand for the better housing and education offered by Oak Park continues unabated.

The OPHC has long recognized the inherent challenges in its situation. To be widely known as a community open to diversity offers the potential to be overwhelmed by success—to the point where increasing minority interest in Oak Park means that diversity (the original goal) becomes more difficult to achieve.[28] With this in mind, the OPHC since 1987 has been actively promoting its pro-integration program in fifty Cook County and DuPage County suburbs. In 1991 the OPHC established a regional outreach office in Westchester: the Near West Suburban Housing Center (more widely known as "New Directions"). The mission of this office is explicitly to help prospective black tenants find housing in suburbs other than Oak Park, oftentimes exactly the suburban locations to which clients already commute for work.[29] As in Oak Park, owners of rental housing are the focus of their work (though single-family homes form the bulk of the housing stock in their service area). This is not a program to disperse low-income residents or an effort to scatter Section 8 certificates. Clients of this service are people with good jobs who can afford good housing (from $900–$1,200 in monthly rent). They are people who want apartments with new

Table 10.4

Populations of Selected Western Chicago Suburbs, 1980 and 1990

	1980			
	Total	White	Black	Hispanic
Oak Park	54,887	46,738	5,929	1,364
Berwyn	46,849	46,155	13	1,128
Cicero	61,232	58,557	74	5,291
River Forest	12,392	11,967	106	188
Maywood	27,998	6,038	21,015	1,893
Forest Park	15,177	13,385	636	447

	1990					
	Total	White	Black	Hispanic	Asian	Median household income
Oak Park	53,648	41,313	9,804	1,915	1,785	$40,453
Berwyn	45,426	43,409	—	3,573	790	$31,326
Cicero	67,436	50,692	—	24,931	1,092	$27,170
River Forest	11,669	11,053	—	—	—	$62,469
Maywood	27,139	3,258	22,733	1,795	—	$30,780
Forest Park	14,918	11,421	1,942	734	1,260	$30,572

Source: U.S. Census, 1980/1990 (1990 Census of Population and Housing—Summary Tape, File 3A).

appliances, or with amenities like exercise rooms, which are scarce in Oak Park rentals. Most clients (90 percent) are referred by the OPHC, where staff ask all clients where they work and suggest that suburban commuters might find better options further out.[30] New Directions does much the same work as the OPHC: searches out available units, sets up appointments and escorts clients to prospective units, shares data on quality-of-life issues (e.g., school scores, crime statistics, and information about laundromats, car insurance, and beauty parlors), and speaks honestly about community responses to racial minorities. The primary difference seems to be that New Directions has to advocate a change in mindset in addition to offering housing assistance (the position of the black staffers is

"You should be able to live anywhere"). They also offer assistance with credit problems (a seminar, discouraging defaulting on student loans, etc.). Unlike the OPHC, New Directions staff do not have apartment keys on hand—they adjust their schedules to those of the building managers. They also cover a significantly more dispersed geographical area than Oak Park staffers do—on average, three hours are spent with each client per visit.[31]

Much of the work done at New Directions is genuine counseling. Despite the professional or financial standing of their clients, many have to be convinced that options other than Oak Park do exist. Few clients want to be "pioneers" or to have their children feel isolated. Fears about safety are also expressed, as are concerns about being too far away from culturally specific resources in the city. African American clients from out-of-state appear to be more amenable to moving beyond Oak Park, according to staffers—they typically come without preconceived ideas about where it is "OK" for them to live. African Americans who have long experience in Chicago are more likely to view Oak Park as a "safe" suburban location and to view other communities with suspicion. They may also have family in the city who discourage moves further out.[32] OPHC and New Directions staff frankly discuss the perception (from clients and others) that this effort is meant to "save Oak Park." It is that, but it is also the right of people to know fully what their options might be.

The Chicago metropolitan area also has a Leadership Council for Metropolitan Open Communities (LC), an advocacy group that searches out discrimination, does testing, and brings legal challenges when barriers to open housing are found. The LC produces what is called an "ABC" list of the suburbs, which rates communities according to the percentage of apartment buildings and percentage of minority residents. The bulk of New Directions' work occurs in "B" suburbs—nearly all-white areas with many large apartment complexes ("A" areas have few apartments, "C" areas already have a 5–10 percent minority population).[33] The LC also offers a home-buying seminar, to which New Directions staff direct appropriate clients.

The urgency of Oak Park's concerns about spreading the integration message were underscored in a 1994 *New York Times* article focused on the problems of Proviso West High School. This institution serves a number of communities to the west of Oak Park, most now identified as "C" areas by the LC. The issues highlighted by the *Times* would not be news to anyone who has paid attention to cities in recent decades: a

significant population decline (a township population loss of 152,000 in twenty years); a diminished school-age population, but massive increases in minority student numbers (98 percent white in 1974, 82 percent minority in 1994; although whites still dominate the township population, the children of the aging white population have long since left home); a declining tax base and correspondingly declining resources available to the school district; and students alleged to be unprepared for or uninterested in education.[34] Here was a tale of suburban change that contrasts dramatically (and in the article, explicitly) with Oak Park's efforts.

The Current Situation: Race, Class, and Culture in Oak Park

It is clear that Oak Park has thoughtfully and progressively tried to address issues that many communities ignore. Still, the community feels challenged, existing as it does within a larger society that is nervous about safety, education, and race. Concerns about education, public policy, and culture surface, as does the question of Oak Park's long-term future. Probably the most difficult reality for Oak Park is the absence of any supportive state or federal policy to help the community (and others like it) to succeed—a waiver of federal fair-housing regulations for communities trying to remain integrated is one avenue that might provide some relief to such places. Worse perhaps is the overall national apathy, and now also antagonism, toward integration efforts.[35]

Education is one cutting-edge issue for Oak Park. The village still has neighborhood schools at the elementary level (there is only a very modest amount of busing). Crosstown mixing begins at the junior-high level—a new wrinkle dating from the 1970s, when junior-high schools were first created. The normal path is for most teenagers to then go to the one high school (which, with 2,400 students, serves both Oak Park and River Forest).[36] As in the rest of the Chicago area, there are also private schools, predominantly Catholic, which include two large high schools (Fenwick, a formerly male academy in Oak Park, now co-ed; and Trinity, a River Forest female academy). Concerns about cutbacks in state funding for schools clearly affect Oak Park and other middle-class communities trying to preserve quality public education. This is a place where the goodwill, time, and efforts of parents are devoted to ensuring that supplementary music and theater programs are maintained.

As elsewhere across the country, worries about the uneven progress of kids through the school system are present in Oak Park, particularly since student progress appears to differ along racial lines. OPHC staff discussed the real and perceived problems in the schools, among them the fact that many black students do not succeed academically at the same rate as the white students. This contentious issue was in part the undercurrent of 1995 school-board elections. One recently elected board member said that race relations within the high school in particular are a major concern: "We need to try new strategies to get African American underachievers to become achievers." Another recent board addition pointed out the need to involve more African American parents in school activities at all levels.[37] A columnist for the Oak Park paper recently summed up the challenges facing the village in the educational area:

Our new school board has to be open in talking about the hard-to-talk-about matter of race in our school. No more chasing down odd paths using code words, no more fears of being labeled racist when important issues are discussed. Our high school needs to figure out where common middle class values, balanced

and effective discipline, and allowances for cultural differences puts us in the day-to-day functioning of the school. We need to acknowledge and dynamically address the segment of our black student body that is failing academically.[38]

African American students who do succeed academically are considered "hot," but have to contend with rejection by other black students. This problem was emphasized by a self-described African American parent who noted in a letter that "It's hard for the middle class and upper class African American kids in Oak Park. It's a struggle for them. There's much peer pressure for them not to succeed and the African American lower class is constantly trying to pull them down."[39] Although this is clearly only a single perspective, this view likely captures the sentiments of many minority parents in Oak Park. This mother was asking for what generations of Oak Park mothers have taken for granted—that her boys associate with people who had values and morals similar to hers. At the moment this long-held presumption is under siege. This parent's great fear was that Oak Park schools would soon come to mirror those in Chicago and no longer provide a viable education for either minority or white children.

For white parents, especially those who have moved to Oak Park "for the schools," the cultural divide among black students may be less important than the impacts that such situations have on their own children. Oak Park apparently has a group of parents actively promoting "excellence in education" who are unfazed by integrated schools except when standards appear to be lessening. Their concern is less racial than class-conscious—they want their children attending school with minority children who also have parents and home environments supportive of educational achievement, not with children they call "urban orphans."[40] In this, their concerns coincide with those of the mother cited above—she too identified Oak Park's educational problem as one of class rather than simply one of race.

This reality underscores how much a community like Oak Park is entwined within a larger social system, even though the local school district coincides with the village for the most part. All American children are surrounded by larger cultural messages that rarely advocate education but that ardently promote consumption and entertainment. There is much competition for the attention of school-age kids, regardless of income or cultural background. Viewed through this lens, the well-intentioned efforts of committed Oak Parkers to filling the educational gaps left by the larger society seem a daunting prospect indeed. A community may actively market educational programs to black parents and try to get kids of disparate races to mix together in lunchrooms, and yet not manage to overcome existing national cultural imbalances.

Cultural and class issues pervade almost every aspect of Oak Park life, as in the rest of middle-class America. These issues can surface in surprising ways, and they suffuse nearly any public discussion. Even an apparently objective issue such as parking restrictions comes freighted with racial implications, as a recent local commentator noted:

Overnight parking only seems simple on the surface. Scratch the surface and you find that overnight parking is really about Oak Park's efforts at racial and economic integration. These efforts are totally linked with the needs of landlords to attract middle class tenants. . . . Middle class people . . . expect a parking place, or two. . . . Tell them the nearest parking place is in a village lot three blocks away and that they'll get ticketed every night they leave their car on the street, and they tend to move to the near North where

they can park on the street. . . . Take a less affluent person, often a black person, whose primary goal is to get off the West Side and/or get their kids into Oak Park schools, and the bizarreness of our parking [regulations] is just another annoying thing you put up with in life.[41]

This observation highlights the fact that in Oak Park, as elsewhere, the white middle class has many more residential choices, which only heightens the importance of the diversity work that OPHC is pursuing in other communities to diminish this imbalance.

Oak Park is a thoroughly middle-class community, one in which middle-class activities like gardening, interest in the local symphony and in arts programs, and concern about environmental problems set a tone for the village, though perhaps less for black residents than for white Oak Parkers with longer connections to the village.[42] Such differences may be short-lived or may indicate deeper cultural splits. Longtime Oak Parkers strongly feel the need for continuity of village traditions and institutions—by this they mean attention to education, valuing high-level landscaping, and support for arts programs. The reality is that, because Oak Park housing (rental as well as owner-occupied) is relatively expensive,[43] the longtime, defining concerns of the village will likely last into the foreseeable future. But this will be the case only as long as Oak Park continues to attract white households, to maintain diversity and not slip into the Austin mode. In the larger context of Chicago and the western Chicago suburbs, there is no room for complacency.

Throughout the 1970s serious questions were raised about whether Oak Park could successfully function as an integrated community. Carole Goodwin's 1979 study concluded that Oak Park's aggressive use of local community control and acceptance of responsibility for the community's future were critical to its success in this endeavor. This still seems apt. In addition, as she noted, the fact that the larger metropolitan housing market was beginning to open up to minority households (and has since done so to a significant degree) has clearly aided Oak Park's goals.[44] Perhaps even more important to this effort has been the relatively slow pace of racial change in Oak Park, unlike in Austin and further-out suburbs like Bellwood and Hillside. Oak Park has been able to plan for and respond to any problems associated with integration, largely because it has not been overwhelmed by rapid change. It has also had the benefit of committed individuals advocating a pro-integration agenda, a critical element identified in other studies of suburban integration.[45]

Oak Park's twenty-plus years of commitment to diversity is an extraordinary example of traditional American social values being successfully challenged and altered, as in other well-known examples such as Shaker Heights, Ohio. The mid-1970s question ("Can it work?") has been answered in the affirmative. From today's vantage point, the question to answer instead may be "Does anyone care?" The number of communities nationwide following this path are small, and other Chicago suburbs seem much more likely to emulate Austin than Oak Park. The clearly unfortunate implication to be drawn from this is that at a time when our confusions about racial issues seem only to be increasing, our national turmoil about race keeps us from actively searching out and emulating the lessons that Oak Park and other communities have to teach.

Water Management in Chicago

Oak Park and the Deep Tunnel

The layers of past constructions weigh heavily on any strategy for urban environmental management. Too often the significance of a physical inheritance is overbalanced by traditions, professional conventions, and institutional structures. In Chicago these human factors have proven more powerful constraints on environmental management than has previous building. The shape of the land, of course, exerts a glacial force, and bricks and concrete are obdurate. But the attitude of each generation's builders ultimately determines how people make and remake their settlement. On Chicago's flatland, a proud tradition of heroic civil engineering, professional narrowness, and the weaknesses of the urban federal system have converged to maintain a costly and inefficient environmental adjustment.

Chicago is a city built on low flatlands and swamps next to Lake Michigan, a site that does not favor human comfort or well-being. As in New Orleans, Venice, or Amsterdam, commercial advantage dictated the city's location—a situation that called for unceasing attention and effort to make the place habitable. In Chicago a flat plain of clayey soil serves as the foundation on which all else must be built. The plain tilts slightly upward from east to west: it rises but thirty-five feet from the level of Michigan Avenue near the lake to Ridgeland Avenue, eight and a half miles inland in Oak Park.[46] This almost-level plain, subject to a thirty-two-inch annual rainfall, is drained by the Chicago River, which branches into two main north-south streams a few blocks inland from the lake. These branches originate in swamps within the plain: the North Branch in the Skokie marshes, the South Branch in a large slough called Mud Lake. Both of these marshes served as natural storage areas, soaking up water and mitigating the rush of spring floods, before they were paved with streets and built on.

A slight rise near Ridgeland Avenue marks the watershed between the Chicago

River and the Des Plaines River. It is the boundary between the Great Lakes and St. Lawrence River basin and the Mississippi River basin. The Des Plaines is the natural drainage for the near western suburbs of Chicago. It is a sluggish river originating near Racine, Wisconsin, which runs north to south about ten miles inland from Lake Michigan. It turns abruptly southwest at the Chicago suburb of Riverside, then parallels the old bed of Mud Lake, and finally joins the Kankakee River to form the Illinois River beyond Joliet, fifty-four miles from downtown Chicago.[47] Pioneer Chicago, a clapboard cluster near the mouth of the Chicago River, was a town of muddy streets, board sidewalks, and frequent floods. Although the dunes protected the city from lake storms, the banks on which the town had gathered stood only two feet above the level of the river.[48]

From hindsight it is not hard to imagine that a soggy city like Chicago might develop a system of house-building that would keep the rooms always dry. Perhaps Chicagoans could have imitated New Orleanians, their active trade partners, by developing a characteristic architecture of houses without cellars—something that at least stood a bit above the ground and thus would be safe from floods in most years. Another alternative might have been to adopt some variant of seventeenth-century London, the root of much of Yankee culture. The Londoners excavated their house lots to build up the streets. Had Chicagoans continued such a practice it would have lifted both the houses and the streets above the level of spring floods and summer rainstorms.[49] Right from the first years, however, the force of tradition weighed against an easy adaptation to Chicago's natural setting. The city's pioneers were predominantly from the Northeast, a region of cellars dug beneath the houses.

In the areas of first settlement the flooding and drainage problems soon grew so

acute that the City Council ordered sewers to be built down the middle of the existing streets and then added ten feet of fill to raise the street levels to a higher grade. In time, owners of abutting buildings and houses raised their structures to match the new street grades. This 1855 initiative later served as the precedent for the construction of downtown Chicago's famous two-level street system.[50]

Chicagoans were in a hurry. They were boosters, a merchant and speculator community gathered together to exploit the riches of the Michigan and Wisconsin forests, the Michigan and Minnesota mines, and the produce of the new prairie farms. The population of Chicago was 30,000 in 1850, 503,000 in 1880, 2,700,000 in 1920, and 3,621,000 in 1950, the city's population apogee.[51] The street-raisings of the center city, however, were not uniformly demanded elsewhere. New outer streets and suburbs went forward at grade, with builders digging conventional seven- and eight-foot cellars beneath their houses. Land speculators filled wetlands and marshes, so that as the city grew the intervals between flooding became shorter and shorter.[52] Instead of raising up the streets and houses, Chicago's ingenuity spent itself on building conventional houses ever faster. The city's immense growth fostered a new form of wooden framing and nailing: the balloon frame, a system that required less skilled labor than its heavy timber predecessors.[53]

The pioneer city street-raisings gave temporary relief to the town's desperate drainage problems, but they did nothing to ease the menacing disease environment of Chicago. The city's chief engineer, Ellis S. Chesbrough (1813–86), a railroad engineer who had achieved great success in constructing Boston's public-water system, elected to solve the drainage problem in the simplest and least expensive way: a combined sewer system. Under this method, the runoff and sanitary wastes from the houses and roofs join the runoff from the street to drain into a single combined sewer pipe underneath the street. These pipes discharged into the nearby Chicago River, where they mixed with the floating and dissolved effluent from the city's slaughterhouses, lumber mills, and tanneries. Together, butchers' offal, rubbish, toilet and sink wastes, manure, tannic acid, cyanides, and arsenic drifted toward the intake pipe of the water company, which drew its water from the lake, seven hundred feet offshore.

In the early years the private water company and its municipal successor served many fewer than half the inhabitants. Most people drew their water from shallow backyard wells that were often contaminated by nearby privies. The poorest residents, who lacked even wells, carried their water directly from the polluted Chicago River. Cholera arrived in 1849, and typhoid fever visited every summer. In fact, nineteenth-century Chicago soon developed a reputation as the nation's typhoid capital.[54]

In 1863 Chicago established a water-management program that would last through most of its boom years until the 1920s, when lawsuits forced it to turn to a sewage-purification strategy. The new Board of Public Works, led by its chief engineer Chesbrough, began an ambitious program to seek pure drinking water ever farther offshore in Lake Michigan. The sewer system, in turn, relied on clean water to dilute and thereby reduce the toxicity of the river. No measures to conserve the urban or regional natural systems were undertaken.

Chesbrough proposed a two-mile tunnel for the clean-water intake, and steam pumping stations to distribute water throughout the city. Unfortunately, the Board of Public Works, like other city boards at the time, initiated a rate schedule that encouraged waste. Every subscriber was to pay a yearly fee; there were to be no meters. Large establishments like hotels and factories were to pay at

most fifty times the householder's minimum. Later, only the largest users were metered, so that favorable rates for the big consumers and the absence of meters in the homes encouraged wasteful practices throughout the city.[55]

Every year after the 1863 waterworks extension, Chicago had to concentrate its efforts to separate its sewage from its lake intake. It was not an easy task, because the post–Civil War boom in food processing and manufacturing dumped more and more wastes into the Chicago River. The Union Stock Yards had set up on 375 acres at 39th and Halsted Streets, and across the South Branch Cyrus McCormick located his reaper works. Both discharged directly into the river, as did hundreds of smaller establishments. Soon the river became so foul that the Illinois and Michigan Canal was deepened in the hope of providing a current that might carry off some of the Chicago River's flow.[56]

Chesbrough's works won national recognition for their vigorous execution of the engineering wisdom of the day. Soon, however, storms revealed the Chicago River and Michigan Canal's limited power to dilute the city's wastes and to thereby render them harmless. Once again the city turned to massive civil engineering. Unlike the new skyscrapers, this new construction was not a novel technology, but a heroic exercise in canal building, and an important innovation in urban federalism.

In 1885 a spectacular flood on the South Branch of the Chicago River carried the stinking offal of the stockyards past the downtown and set it drifting out toward the nearby water-supply intake cribs. Fear of cholera prompted first a citizen's commission, then a mayor's commission, and next extended state legislative hearings. Finally, in 1889 a new state agency was created, the Chicago Sanitary District (its name was changed in 1955 to the Metropolitan Sanitary District of Greater Chicago and again in 1955 to the Metropolitan Water Reclamation District of Greater Chicago). The district's elected officers stood charged with gathering up all the sewage from the city and the suburbs throughout much of Cook County. To do this, they were instructed to build a massive eighty-mile canal-and-river system that would reverse the flow of the Chicago River and thereby carry all the runoff and sewage to the Illinois River. The legislative charge called for a triumphal piece of civil engineering: a giant Sanitary and Ship Canal that would extend twenty-eight miles east of Chicago to Lockport, where the river fell off thirty-five feet. Later generations of schoolchildren would be taught that this was the "eighth wonder of the world."

The Sanitary District met the challenge. The Sanitary and Ship Canal, a dig that moved more earth and stone than the Panama Canal, opened for service in 1900, thereby reversing the Chicago River's flow.[57] This massive physical presence, the great locks at the entrance to Lake Michigan, the many bridges, the ships and barges—all combined to celebrate the city's "think big" outlook. First came the giant waterworks and sewers; then Daniel Burnham's plan for streets, boulevards, and parks; later a metropolitan Forest Preserve, metropolitan transit, and a giant airport. Each of these constructions was the responsibility of a special agency whose managers looked out on the city through lenses that revealed a big metropolitan picture. Unfortunately big plans, big works, and big agencies carried with them no ways to observe the variations, local landscapes, and small human and natural systems that kept the metropolis alive. This limitation, this lack of feedback, made such agencies prisoners of oversimplified thinking.

The original 1889 Illinois Act contemplated diluting the sewage by adding water from Lake Michigan to the volume of the river system. Initially the Sanitary District diverted 8,500 cubic feet per second from the lake, a volume that exceeds the annual average flow of the Merrimack River (7,474 cu. ft./sec.), New England's second-largest river. Such a draw brought a succession of lawsuits by nearby states and Canada from 1913–61; their outcome limited Chicago's diversion to 3,200 cu. ft/sec.[58] Of this total, 1,500 cu. ft/sec. is currently allocated for Chicago's water supply.

As these lawsuits went forward a new technology of sewage treatment that had been developed in Germany and England became available, so the Sanitary District did not need to rely on dilution alone to purify its wastes. From 1921 to 1939 the district constructed the world's largest sewage-treatment system, capable of providing secondary treatment for 90 percent of the flow on days without precipitation. The Stickney Reclamation Plant, still the world's largest, handles a flow of 2,000 cu. ft./sec. Despite this enormous effort, on rainy days the combined sewers of Chicago and fifty-four nearby suburbs delivered more water than the system could treat. Only 6 percent of the extra storm flow could be processed.[59]

In addition to the new system's inability to clean storm wastes, conditions at the south end of Lake Michigan brought an unheeded early warning of the ultimate failure of the big-engineering approach. A sewer system that did not institute programs to contain and reduce wastes at their source could never keep up with the city's expansion. In this case, new houses, steel mills, oil refineries, and related industries near Lake Calumet in southern Cook County and neighboring Lake County, Indiana, were polluting Lake Michigan by dumping untreated wastes into the water. The Sanitary District had struggled mightily with the problems of the far south metropolitan area: sewers were extended, the flow of the Calumet rivers had been reversed by building the new Calumet-Sag Ship and Sanitary Canal, and a new South Side sewage treatment plant had been built. Still, hydrochloric acid, coal tar, phenols, and naphthalene ran freely into the lake. Such chemicals threatened the water intakes of the City of Chicago and its Indiana neighbors.[60]

In 1930 the State of Illinois forbade the construction of any new combined sewer systems. Thus when the post-Depression building boom came to Cook County's outer suburbs (totaling 387 sq. mi.), they delivered separate sanitary and storm waters to the Sanitary District. In these suburbs it was later possible to institute storm-water detention regulations and to build retention reservoirs to reduce both the storm floods and pollution loads on the centralized Sanitary District facilities.[61]

Oak Park's Water Situation

Water management in Oak Park mirrored that of Chicago: drinking water from Lake Michigan, and combined sanitary and drainage sewers. In 1883, while still a part of Cicero township, Oak Park had no paved streets, no water supply, no sewers, no public services of any kind. Its population of 2,500 drew its drinking water from private wells and dropped its wastes into backyard cesspools.

In 1872 James W. Scoville, a banker and owner of large property, built a reservoir to store water from his artesian well. He offered his water free to anyone who would connect their own pipes to his tank. In 1887, as the village's population surged when a second commuter railroad line and station were built, Scoville reconstituted his private works as a public utility, the Cicero Water, Gas, and Electric Light Co. In 1885 the Cicero trustees authorized the construction of a brick sewer down Oak Park Avenue, a north-south street that now runs the length of the village. Later, in 1891 a parallel main sewer was built down

Ridgeland Avenue. The two sewers were then extended south to 31st Street, where they emptied into the Ogden Ditch, an open drain that connected to the Chicago River.

These were boom times for Oak Park. Streetcar service began in 1891; by 1895 there were three lines running down the main east-west streets to Chicago, as well as frequent commuter-rail service.[62] By 1900 about ten thousand people lived in this section of Cicero, and two years later they established their own government as the incorporated village of Oak Park.[63]

Soon both the water supply and the drainage system were failing to keep pace with real estate development. In 1908, following controversies and complaints that the private water company could supply neither safe water nor enough pressure for fire protection, the village joined the City of Chicago's system. By 1910 Oak Park had grown to 19,000 inhabitants; as the population more than doubled to 40,000 by 1920, the sewer system was soon strained beyond its capacity.[64] Still, despite periodic flooding, the voters refused to authorize a bond issue to enlarge the system. Fortunately there were no major storms and floods between 1919 and 1936.[65]

By 1930, with a population of 64,000, Oak Park was practically built out. As the Great Depression brought the federal government for the first time into direct management of urban projects, local taxpayer reluctance could now be overcome with federal programs. In 1935 the village applied for and received a federal public-works grant, which supplemented a large bond issue to be paid by an annual $16 charge on every water bill. A new sewer main was constructed along East Avenue, twenty-seven feet below the surface, to connect with a new Sanitary District tunnel on the Berwyn border at Roosevelt Road. Despite these enlargements, storm flooding continued in parts of the village, especially at its north end. In 1940 Oak Park reached its population apogee of 66,000. Subsequently it declined slowly to 64,000 in 1950, 63,000 in 1970, and 54,000 in 1990. This 18 percent population loss echoes Chicago's 23 percent loss from 1950 to 1990.

Managing the New Environment

In 1950 it would have been reasonable to observe that the Chicago metropolis possessed some magnificent architecture and engineering, that it had dramatized its lakefront site, and that throughout the city and the suburbs it was managing its human and natural environments as well and as badly as other American cities. When, in 1946, Chicago embarked on a major postwar modernization of its sewers, conventional wisdom held that the cost of separation into a dual system "would be prohibitive." A 1949 overview by the U.S. Public Health Service called for improved maintenance, tightened enforcement, and more effort along well-established professional lines. No fresh departures in concept or execution were called for, even as rapid change overtook the city.[66]

Between 1950 and 1990 the Chicago metropolitan region added 2.5 million inhabitants. Most of them spread out over Cook County and DuPage County, its western neighbor. Cook County alone grew by 1.4 million—60 percent of the entire regional growth. During the same forty years, Chicago lost 837,000 residents. Such a dispersal required an enormous private and public investment to build houses, factories, offices, stores, parking lots, warehouses, highways, roads, schools, and infrastructure of all kinds.

The new dispersed settlements implied the possibility of new relationships with the natural environment. There could be more green spaces and more than just the squares of parks and playgrounds or the small yards of the city and its old suburbs. But the new green suburbs

carried with them some surprises. The roads, highways, parking lots, and the spread-out low commercial buildings and houses and garages covered so much land that 30 percent of it was impervious paving or roof. The new suburban Chicago thus would continue to be a place of much storm runoff.[67]

Worse still, during the first decades of decentralization, local planning boards were slow to recognize the consequences of exploitive lowland development, which placed new houses in jeopardy of frequent flooding. In 1958 the chief engineer of the Sanitary District, Horace P. Ramey, attacked the continuing suburban failure of local regulatory boards to protect the public. "In recent years a considerable amount of building has been permitted on low lands subject to overflow from the high floods of the Des Plaines River. Innocent purchasers of houses in such areas have suffered unexpected and unwarranted damages from high water. No public agency should approve such construction, regardless of pressure applied by subdividers and builders."[68]

It took some decades for local planning boards to establish regulations and practices that offset the new paving and builder inattention to flooding. Now suburban planning boards routinely require developers to set aside sufficient land in each subdivision to catch and store the runoff. Furthermore, the Sanitary District itself has begun to build retention reservoirs to stem the rush of storm waters into its system. These are the metropolis's first steps in a new awareness by public agencies that natural systems can be used to reduce public capital and operating costs.

The City of Chicago and its older neighboring suburbs did not participate in this learning process. The fifty-four cities and towns that had been built prior to the Illinois ban on combined sewers depended on the Sanitary District for collection and treatment of their sanitary and storm water. The Sanitary District, in turn, responded to new flooding problems and water-quality goals by falling back on its nineteenth-century pattern of heroic engineering. Instead of seeking fresh methods that work with natural systems, it built and continues to build a vastly expensive tunnel and treatment system that inevitably falls short of contemporary goals for clean-water maintenance.

The responsibility for this costly shortfall does not rest on the Sanitary District trustees and executives alone. Rather, it demonstrates the sluggishness of American urban federalism when faced with the need to adapt to new social circumstances and new popular goals. The responsibility for failure rests at every institutional level—from the national professional organizations and the federal government, to the Sanitary District and its coterie of private engineering firms, on down to the ignorance of the voters and the resulting helplessness of their local governments. Under the prevailing metropolitan-federal ethos, there is no timely or effective feedback system linked to the giant engineering projects of the national and state governments and their metropolitan agencies. The citizen veto, the NIMBY ("not in my backyard") response, inevitably comes too late and cannot address the substance of these giant proposals.

Chicago's problems began at the national level with the profession of sanitary engineering. During the 1950s, sanitary engineers became isolated from the excitement and innovations of contemporary science and engineering, which were focused on electronics. Academic science had not yet made the fresh connections to biology that it would in the 1970s and 1980s. The sanitary engineers were further isolated by being organized into large private civil-engineering firms that dealt directly with municipal agencies whose practices were isolated from everyday voter concerns. A small user fee or sewer tax supported these municipal agencies and paid the inter-est on the large bond issues needed for new construction. The financing of sewers thus kept engineers removed from day-to-day politics. Finally, the professions' historical record of success, the seemingly effortless removal of wastes to invisible locations, helped sustain its inertia.

Since the 1920s sanitary engineers preached two major goals: first, building sewage-treatment plants to process sanitary and industrial wastes, and second, constructing dual sewer systems so that sanitary and industrial wastes would go to the treatment plant and storm runoff could be safely shunted to nearby streams. This was the practice of Chicago's post-1930 suburbs.

Such goals have proved an insufficient aspiration. Later generations of voters have wished to maintain or restore the natural systems of their metropolitan regions. Waste-treatment plants were expensive to operate and maintain, and they provided only partial cleanup, so the treatment plants' effluent polluted urban rivers. For example, the sheer volume of the Sanitary District's sewage is such that even on dry days, when the treatment plants remove 85–95 percent of the pollutants, the remainder still pollutes the upper Illinois River.[69]

Also, because post–World War II American cities and suburbs have carried ever heavier chemical burdens, storm runoff itself has proven to be far from harmless. Homeowners took to using strong doses of fertilizers, herbicides, and pesticides, while ever increasing automobile traffic served up a rich chemical soup that ran off highways, streets, and parking lots with every rain. Urban runoff ceased to be merely watered soil and sand and became instead a material requiring careful management lest it pollute groundwaters and streams.[70]

The narrow focus of professional sanitary engineering inevitably influenced the initial federal legislation and the ensuing regulations of the Environmental Protection Agency (EPA). Like most landmark American legislation, the Clean Water Act of 1972 emerged from a joining of popular demands with the concepts of special interests. In this case, conservation demands merged with the ideas of the treatment plant, pipe, and sanitary engineering people.

The new popular consciousness had been long in the making. Since the first days of European settlement, American rivers and streams had served as the dumping grounds for agricultural, industrial, and urban wastes. Now, after World War II, more and more of the metropolitan rivers looked bad and smelled bad. By 1960 the Illinois River had lost its formerly extensive fishery as well as twenty-five species of mussels due to the combined attacks of levee-building farmers, Chicago's sewage discharges, and the industrial and municipal effluent of the cities and towns along its banks.[71] As in the nineteenth century, sport fishermen once again took the lead in calling for conservation, by reporting fish kills in the rivers and lakes to the newspapers. In 1961, the U.S. Public Health Service began compiling and publishing an annual tally of such kills. Private industry, however, fought all attempts to require the reporting of discharges into rivers and streams.

The pollution of overburdened waters grew worse and worse. Like the ever growing patches of abandoned industrial and inner-city lands, these rivers and lakes presented a disheartening contrast both to high levels of suburban housekeeping and to summer memories of favorite vacation spots. This growing tension between the old habits and the new ways, between the despoiled and the attractive, revived and ultimately transformed the nation's conservation tradition. Beginning in 1970 with Earth Day, suburban Americans joined the new environmental movement, which demanded higher standards of conservation and increasing use of natural systems in the management of human affairs.

The Clean Water Act of 1972 thus merged the popular demands for cleanup and restoration with the professional remedies of sewage treatment and dual sewer systems. The goal of the federal legislation looked to "restore and maintain the chemical, biological, and physical integrity of the nation's waters." The EPA called for mandatory reporting of discharges and for state monitoring agencies to issue discharge permits, and required that dischargers install "the average of the best" technology to clean their future outflows. Formerly the intractable enemy of reform, industry now discovered that it could profit by nonpolluting ways, or at least reduce its cleanup costs, through source control, reduction of wastes, and reuse of water and materials. Industrial compliance thus came forward quite rapidly.[72]

Municipalities, however, responded and continue to respond more slowly. Burdened with hundreds of old combined sewer outfalls, thousands of street and highway runoff points, and often inadequate and antiquated treatment plants, they find compliance difficult. For a time a federal grants-in-aid program relieved their task by offering 75 cents on each dollar spent for EPA-approved programs, programs for treatment plants and sewer separation. In these first years the EPA, like the sanitary engineering profession, had not learned of the possibilities of either municipal source abatement or focused on the potentials for employing urban natural systems for onsite or near-site water management.

The Chicago TARP Decision

In 1972 the Sanitary District was all set to leap for an EPA grant. After long study of the limitations of its system, it had prepared another of its heroic engineering "solutions."

Runoff had been identified as the outstanding problem, especially runoff within the 375 square miles covered by the City of Chicago and the old nearby suburbs, all of which used combined sanitary and storm drains.

During the 1960s and 1970s basement flooding became endemic throughout Cook County. This was caused partly by poor maintenance, partly by the cities and towns failing to enlarge their sewers to match the increased paving and building, and partly by the Sanitary District's overburdened capacity. In these years there were one hundred annual occasions when some of the combined sewers of the inner area (375 sq. mi., 54 cities and towns) discharged directly into the Chicago, Des Plaines, or Calumet Rivers. These overflows, and the flooding in the outer, separated-sewer areas, were caused by a complex series of events. But a quick summary would identify "increasing urbanization and flood plain buildup, [and] increased rate of storm runoff" as the causes.[73]

In the face of these changes, the City of Chicago and the Sanitary District backed themselves into a static solution to a dynamic situation. The provenance of an engineering consensus is hard to document years after the event, but the origin of this one seems to lie in a careful calculation of runoff published in 1959 by engineers A. L. Tholin and Clint Keefer. The analysis rested on the assumption that runoff should be estimated from a base of a single inner-city residential block, a block mostly paved and roofed, and fully built out. The authors recognized that the larger suburban house lots had proportionately less roofing and paving, and thereby afforded more permeable surface and possible surface water storage. But their estimates rested on their model block, whose surface could contain only 1/2 an inch of rain during the first hour of any rainstorm.[74]

This technically proficient computerized study headed the Sanitary District and its consultants down an unfortunate path—in the sense that the late 1950s calculations were made just before the process of residential and industrial abandonment in inner Chicago opened up acre after acre that might be employed for storm-water use. The single-block focus, as opposed to an analysis of a square mile, also prevented the authors from seeing the water storage possibilities of parkland and fragments of open space. In short, the pace of metropolitan Chicago's land-use change from 1960 onward presented a wide range of fresh opportunities that far exceeded the purview of either Tholin and Keefer's paper or the commonplace engineering outlook of the times. Instead, a narrow focus led to the proliferation of heroic proposals. For example, in 1958 one firm of consulting engineers suggested pumping the storm waters from the Chicago River into a series of lagoons that would be built offshore in Lake Michigan.[75]

In January 1965 the Chicago *Tribune* carried an announcement by the Sanitary District's chief executive, Vinton W. Bacon, that two local engineering firms had been conducting "intensive preliminary studies" for a new tunnel grid of sewers to control floods. In May 1966 the combined work of the two firms had advanced to a formal public presentation of a proposal: to catch the combined sewer overflow in a modest twenty-one-square-mile area of south Chicago, with possible future additions for the entire city and near suburbs.[76]

The next five years of planning were consumed by a continuing series of advisory committees convened to study deep-tunnel plans. The billion-dollar-plus estimate for construction proved daunting, and the Democrats on the Sanitary District board were reluctant to endorse such an expenditure. The board entertained hopes that the project could be funded as flood control under a "Rivers and Harbors" appropriation in Congress, or that the Army Corps of Engineers might be induced to fund the work. Nothing happened until the Federal Water Pollution Control Act (Clean Water Act) passed on October 18, 1972.[77] On October 27, a few days after passage, the *Tribune* announced that "the Sanitary Board yesterday approved a $1.2 billion plan to eliminate polluted flooding and storm water overflow in Chicago and 50 suburbs in inner Cook County."

The board voted for a remedial Tunnel and Reservoir Plan (TARP). It called for capturing all the waters in the combined sewer area of Cook County (375 sq. mi.) by digging tunnels as large as 30 feet in diameter at depths of 100 and 300 feet beneath the ground. Through sheer volume of empty space these tunnels could store the troublesome "first flush," the heavily laden first rush of water from storm drains. Should a storm continue, then these tunnels would conduct the mixed sanitary and storm overflows to giant limestone quarries that would be fitted out as storage reservoirs (McCook and Stearns quarries and a treatment facility at O'Hare airport). Here the whole mess would be oxygenated to combat any odors. When dry air prevailed, the water would be pumped out and sent through treatment plants that would themselves be enlarged to take the new loads. Of course, like any catch basin in a street, the tunnels would have to be closed down and cleaned of the accumulated sand and dirt every two or three years. The TARP plans estimated that the tunnels and reservoirs would succeed in diverting the rainfall runoff at all levels recorded from 1949–69 except for three peak occasions. They would thus protect Lake Michigan from frequent discharges and stop the occasional flooding of thousands of home basements.[78]

Since the TARP plan proposed no ordinary sewage-treatment plant or sewer separation program, but yet another heroic project that would demand both EPA funding for

its pollution remedies and Corps of Engineers funds for its flood-control aspects, a combined committee of many levels of government was convened by the State of Illinois Institute for Environmental Quality. The City of Chicago was represented, but not the suburban towns. The December 1972 report of this committee, including a checklist of twenty-three alternatives, sanctioned the Sanitary District's decision. All the alternatives, save sewer separation, imagined TARP-like constructions to carry off the combined storm waters for later treatment. The report's significant variations focused on the intensity and volume of storms that any new system might manage.

From hindsight, the rejection of sewer separation, with its many advantages, was unfortunate. As an inevitably slow process, sewer separation would have allowed the Sanitary District and its fifty-four cities and towns to learn about other supplementary programs as the work went forward. It would not have been an all-or-nothing leap like TARP. The work itself would have provided many more jobs than TARP and could have used many small, local contractors. TARP was a big contractor, big machinery job.

The review committee rejected sewer separation for several reasons. The committee guessed that the cost would be $4 billion as opposed to $2.6 billion for TARP's tunnels and treatment-plant enlargements. The $4 billion included estimates of the costs to private home and building owners, who would have to pay for new connections to the dual system. The report also feared the automobile traffic disruptions attendant on the new sewer building. Perhaps these private costs and traffic restrictions suggested a voter rebellion to the committee, but no attempt was made to consult the residents of the metropolis. Finally, the sewer separation would do nothing to relieve either the first-flush pollution or flood control; it would just send runoff into the rivers. It seems likely that flood control was a major concern of the committee at the time since there were hopes that this quarter of the program could attract federal funding.[79]

When the final TARP decision was made in 1972, new environmental approaches to urban water management had not yet been sufficiently developed or demonstrated to be alternatives. Thus the inadequacies of TARP cannot be laid solely at the door of the Sanitary District trustees. The trustees are elected officials. Because Chicago is the largest political unit in Cook County, the political machine of Mayor Richard J. Daley oversaw the nominations for trustee, and thereby controlled the board. And some of the board members participated in the scams of local politics.[80]

Nevertheless, a blue-ribbon board composed of downtown lawyers, bankers, and real estate interests would have been unlikely to have made a superior decision. The engineering firms were the professionals in this process, and they were themselves ignorant of significant alternatives to their proposals.

The first controversy about the TARP decision surfaced over its heavy costs, which the initial public presentations did not fully report. The December 1972 confirmatory state report listed the cost at $2.6 billion. But this estimate included only two of the system's four necessary elements—the tunnels and the expanded sewage-treatment works. "How to Bottle Rainstorms," a citizen brochure prepared for wide circulation, gave an estimate of $2.8 billion, without specifying what the money would be spent on except to indicate that there would be tunnels.[81]

The financial confusions stemmed from the fact that TARP needed all four projects to have the system control floods and manage pollution as the engineers envisioned. The 131 miles of tunnel and the drop shafts might be labeled Element #1, the reservoirs to store

the runoff, Element #2, the improved sewage treatment plants, Element #3, and the enlarged local city and town sewers and sewer connections to the tunnel system, Element #4. Except for the tunnels' ability to store the "first flush" of a storm, the four TARP elements were inextricably intertwined. All had to be built for the system to work. Local sewers had to be expanded and connected to the tunnels to cope with the runoff; the reservoirs had to be fitted out to receive the storm water from the tunnels, and the Sanitary District treatment plants had to be enlarged so that the combined runoff and industrial and sanitary wastes would not pollute the rivers and Lake Michigan.[82]

As work on the tunnels began, the newspapers reported the first fears that local tax rates would double, even though the EPA would pay 75 percent of the tunnel building costs.[83] Then in October 1975 the Army Corps of Engineers offered its first rough estimate for the complete project: $5.7 billion, of which $1.3 billion would be needed for local sewer upgrading in Chicago and the fifty-four suburbs. The Corps of Engineers also added a key fifth element, the interest on the bonds.[84]

Cost issues seemed to lie dormant until June 1977. Then a citizen group, headed by Stanley Hallett and Scott Bernstein of the Northwestern University Center for Urban Affairs, and prominent Chicago architect Harry Weese publicly began to question TARP's basic engineering concepts and to suggest source-reduction alternatives. In a *Reader* interview, Weese specifically mentioned the new opportunities for surface-water management now presented by the acres of inner-city abandoned property. In the same article, Scott Bernstein criticized the Sanitary District for its lack of responsiveness to the needs and wishes of the many city and near suburban neighborhoods. He estimated that TARP construction would be equivalent to spending $10,000 per household, yet no households had been polled for their wishes on this matter. In 1977, at a time when American urbanites called for more local control over neighborhood services, and when Ernst Schumacher's *Small Is Beautiful: Economics as if People Mattered* (1973) exerted a strong influence on popular thinking, TARP remained impervious.[85]

For the next two years the TARP program came under steady attack. Critics questioned its ultimate ability to control floods or to meet the EPA's "swimmable, fishable" goal. They especially attacked its high costs and added the growing list of popular alternatives to their criticism. With local foundation aid, the Northwestern group formed a coalition of civic groups (the TARP Impacts Project) to sponsor a series of careful studies of TARP's likely effects and to offer alternatives. The group published technical papers on pollution, tax, and employment effects, and Bernstein wrote a detailed paper setting forth alternative neighborhood-level water-management and employment possibilities.[86]

Senator Charles Percy (R-Ill.), sensing that the full TARP program would consume billions and perhaps burden suburban taxpayers for the disproportionate benefit of Chicago, requested that the General Accounting Office (GAO) conduct an assessment. On May 24, 1978, the comptroller general of the GAO issued his first report to Congress. It estimated the total bill for all four elements of the TARP project to be about $8 billion. A later study suggested that refitting the plumbing and drains of Chicago's homes would be an inexpensive alternative.[87]

Soon after the second GAO report the *Tribune* called for a halt in the EPA's funding of the program, and it offered a column to Harry Weese. In turn, the *Sun-Times* noted that the tunnels would not control floods unless the reservoirs were built and also suggested that the hoped-for 100 percent Corps

of Engineers funding was very unlikely.[88] The Sanitary District's board chairman Nicholas Melas replied to these attacks by blasting the GAO for including all four elements of the TARP project. He said 47 of the 131 miles of tunnel were under construction or already completed, and that the tunnels could handle 55 percent of the sewage overflow of the Chicago area.[89]

In the end the tunnel project proved to have too much momentum to stop. Senator Percy was defeated for re-election, some say in part due to the efforts of the Sanitary District. In 1996 the tunnels were 85 percent complete, and the TARP expenditures stood at $2.5 billion.[90] It is unlikely, however, that the entire system will ever be completed. The quarry reservoirs are unpopular with their neighbors: both Stearns and McCook have been withdrawn by the trustees.[91] The Corps of Engineers now faces the enormous job of rectifying its years of mistaken management of the Mississippi River system, and Congress seems in no mood for a special Chicago appropriation.[92]

The deep tunnels will help with the frequent small storms by storing the combined sewer overflows underground. They have already reduced basement flooding in Chicago and in suburbs along the Des Plaines. When major storms strike, however, the Metropolitan Water Reclamation District (formerly the Metropolitan Sewer District) engineers will still have to open the locks into Lake Michigan to let the polluted Chicago River discharge. Though not connected to the TARP system, suburbs like Oak Park will still have to pay their share, without any specific benefits.

Stickney and the other treatment plants cannot meet the goal of making the rivers fishable and swimmable unless they institute tertiary treatment, a very expensive undertaking that is probably far beyond the Sanitary District's capabilities. The fifty-four cities and towns of Cook County in the TARP area are continuing to upgrade their local sewers and to make connections to the new tunnel system (forty-seven are already connected). The cost of local sewer-system improvements is high, and no federal funds are available for this work.[93] To pay for the tunnels and for local modernization, sewer rates and property taxes have risen in all fifty-four cities and towns. These tax increases have the unfortunate effect of making the old areas of the metropolis even more expensive, and thereby further encourage the dispersal of metropolitan settlement.

The Metropolitan Water Reclamation District of Greater Chicago is now working in a new climate of water management and urban environmental goals. By 1980 the *New York Times* could already refer to effective land-use alternatives in commenting on the TARP program.[94] The wetlands of the upper Des Plaines River are currently being restored to slow the pace of runoff and flooding. The U.S. Forest Service is proposing that city neighborhoods stop ignoring the Chicago River and that it be made a valuable recreation place. Volunteers are replanting prairie grass in the fields of the Forest Preserve. Neighborhood groups are seeking environmental alternatives within the City of Chicago.[95]

It is now clear that the Metropolitan Water Reclamation District of Greater Chicago must assume a new role within the urban federal hierarchy. It will have to learn to master new, flexible, and small-scale ways to supplement its existing operations. In the future the MWRDGC should learn to work as a partner with the cities and towns in Cook County and with the neighbors and neighborhoods within them to develop and implement local water-management strategies. The big metropolitan utilities have proven able to work with homeowners on energy-saving devices. Surely the MWRDGC can do likewise. It is too expensive and too ineffective for it to continue on its nineteenth-century track as a huge single-purpose engineering bureaucracy.

Conclusion

For many decades a special feature of American urban federalism has been its ability to allow local institutions to respond to local conditions—the "feds" provided funding for interstate highways and public housing, but local agencies made locational decisions. There has been no uniform urban policy at any level. Throughout the country there are likely thousands of examples of localities working out specific challenges within this larger federal-state-local framework. Sometimes local decisions assist the federal agenda; sometimes they stall or ignore it. In the examples discussed in this chapter, the deep tunnel demonstrates the energy, creativity, and power that a local institution can command, and Oak Park's desegregation efforts demonstrate how a local community can customize its response to a larger national trend. For TARP, the federal budget constraints foreclose big engineering experiments for the near future. Presumably the national environmental learning curve will continue to move most metropolitan areas in less-infrastructure-intensive directions in coming decades. On the social side, despite strong efforts to further a once-valued federal agenda, Oak Park and communities like it elsewhere now seem very alone in their pursuit of a common good.

Notes

1. Anne Whiston Spirn, *The Granite Garden: Urban Nature and Human Design* (New York: Basic Books, 1984); Sam Bass Warner, Jr., *The Way We Really Live* (Boston: Boston Public Library, 1977), chs. 5 and 6; Daniel B. Botkin, *Discordant Harmonies: A New Ecology for the Twenty-First*

Century (New York: Oxford University Press, 1990), 11; Rutherford H. Platt et al., *The Ecological City: Preserving and Restoring Urban Biodiversity* (Amherst: University of Massachusetts Press, 1994).

2. In 1990 the African American population of the Chicago Consolidated Statistical Area was 1,548,000 (see Table 10.2).

3. Carl W. Condit, *Chicago: Building, Planning, and Urban Technology* (Chicago: University of Chicago Press, 1973).

4. See Table 10.3 for a partial representation of this process in Chicago.

5. U.S. Department of Transportation, Office of Highway Information Management, Federal Highway Administration, *1990 Nationwide Personal Transportation Study, Early Results* (Washington, D.C.: Federal Highway Administration, August 1991), 21; Elmer W. Johnson, *Avoiding the Collision of Cities and Cars: Urban Transportation Policy for the Twenty-first Century* (Cambridge, Mass.: American Academy of Arts and Sciences, 1993).

6. Reynolds Farley, "The Changing Distribution of Negroes within Metropolitan Areas: The Emergence of Black Suburbs," *American Journal of Sociology* 75 (January 1970), 513–14.

7. An unusually perceptive account of this process as experienced in Mississippi and Chicago is Nicholas Lemann. *The Promised Land* (New York: Knopf, 1991).

8. Frank Harold Wilson, "The Changing Distribution of the African-American Population in the United States, 1980–1990," *Urban League Review* 15 (Winter 1991–92), 56.

9. Karl E. and Alma F. Taeuber, *Negroes and Cities* (Chicago: University of Chicago Press, 1965); Colin Burke, Sam Bass Warner, Jr., et al., "Cultural Change and the Ghetto," *Journal of Contemporary History* 4 (October 1969), 173–87.

10. Arnold R. Hirsch, *The Making of the Second Ghetto: Race and Housing in Chicago, 1940–1960* (New York: Columbia University Press, 1983).

11. Douglas S. Massey and Nancy A. Denton, "Suburbanization and Segregation in U.S. Metropolitan Areas," *American Journal of Sociology* 94 (November 1988), 594; Diana Jean Schemo, "Persistent Racial Segregation Mars Suburbs' Green Dreams," *New York Times,* March 17, 1994, A1, B6.

12. Massey and Denton, "Suburbanization and Segregation," 621; Richard D. Alba and John R.

Logan, "Minority Proximity to Whites in Suburbs: An Individual Level Analysis of Segretation," *American Journal of Sociology* 98 (May 1993), 1388–1427.

13. John F. Kain, "Black Suburbanization in the Eighties: A New Beginning or a False Hope?" in John M. Quigley and Daniel L. Rubinfeld, eds., *American Democratic Priorities: An Economic Appraisal* (Berkeley: University of California Press, 1985), 271; Karen De Witt, "Wave of Suburban Growth Is Being Fed by Minorities," *New York Times,* August 15, 1996, A1, B6.

14. John F. Kain, "Housing Segregation, Negro Employment, and Metropolitan Decentralization," *Quarterly Journal of Economics* 82 (May 1968), 190–97; John D. Kasarda, "Jobs, Migration, and Emerging Mismatches," in Michael G.H. McGeary and Laurence E. Lynn, Jr., *Urban Change and Poverty* (Washington, D.C.: National Academy Press, 1988), 148–98. There are in every city a number of small programs to offset ghetto deficits by moving low-income blacks to the suburbs. The most famous is Chicago's Gautreau Program, begun in 1976 after a protracted lawsuit. See James E. Rosenbaum et al., "Social Integration of Low-Income Black Adults in Middle Class White Suburbs," *Social Problems* 38 (November 1991), 448–61.

15. Judith A. Martin, "The Influence of Values on an Urban Community: The Austin Area of Chicago, 1890–1920" (M.A. thesis, University of Minnesota, 1973).

16. Hirsch, *Making of the Second Ghetto.*

17. Carole A. Goodwin. *The Oak Park Strategy* (Chicago: University of Chicago Press, 1979), 25–44.

18. Goodwin argues (as do many others) that Austin was essentially "sold out" by the Chicago Board of Education in the 1960s and by unchecked blockbusting. Goodwin, *Oak Park,* 59–103.

19. Goodwin, *Oak Park,* 149–63.

20. Goodwin, *Oak Park,* 166–78.

21. Ibid., 167.

22. Roberta Raymond, "Racial Diversity: A Model for American Communities" (Chicago: Illinois Advisory Committee to the U.S. Commission on Civil Rights, 1981), 90.

23. Interview with Robert G. Raymond, July 25, 1994. The OPHC does not charge for its services; most of its funding comes from Community Development Block Grants (CDBG) and grants. There is a time-based fee for landlords; escorts of prospective residents are paid bonuses.

24. W. Dennis Keating, *The Suburban Racial Dilemma* (Philadelphia: Temple University Press, 1994), 212–13.

25. Interview with Cathy Lammski, July 25, 1994. This example was confirmed by a young, white female OPHC staffer, who is herself a building manager and has had exactly this experience in her building.

26. Ellen Burzynski, Lincoln Institute, New Urbanism Symposium, Cambridge, Mass., December 9, 1995.

27. Raymond interview.

28. Raymond interview.

29. Raymond, "Racial Diversity," 1981. Ms. Raymond has long recognized that Oak Park's attraction for black residents ironically holds the potential for the community to become resegregated as a dominantly minority community, following the Austin example.

30. Interview with Mary Ellen Matthies, July 25, 1994. The view of the OPHC is that Oak Park's current success with diversity cannot be maintained unless other suburban locations are also open and welcoming to black clients. They (and the New Directions staff) admit that much of this effort involves "hand-holding" of prospective clients who see the outer suburbs as utterly foreign. They indicate that they have greater success promoting this idea to non-Chicagoans.

31. Matthies interview.

32. Matthies interview.

33. Interview with LaShawne Brundage, July 25, 1994.

34. H. G. Bissinger, "When Whites Flee," *New York Times Magazine,* May 29, 1994.

35. Raymond interview.

36. Agnes Stepniak interview. July 25, 1994.

37. *Oak Park Wednesday Journal,* November 8, 1995.

38. Dan Haley, "A Fine High School Now faces Its Future," *Oak Park Wednesday Journal,* November 8, 1995.

39. *Oak Park Wednesday Journal,* July 20, 1994.

40. Raymond and Stepniak interviews. The term was one used to describe kids who have no support system and who consequently fall into difficulty both academically and socially.

41. *Oak Park Wednesday Journal,* November 1, 1995.

42. Raymond and Stepniak interviews.

43. A scan of local real estate ads for July 1994 and November 1995 revealed home prices ranging from $130,000 to more than $400,000, with most in the $200,000+ range. Condos are less expensive.

44. Goodwin, *Oak Park,* 220–25.

45. Keating, *Suburban Racial Dilemma,* 238–43.

46. U.S. Geological Survey maps. The authors wish to thank the engineers and staff of the Chicago Metropolitan Water Reclamation District for their generous gifts of materials and for their careful, critical reading of an earlier draft of this essay. They are not, of course, responsible for the argument that follows.

47. Horace P. Ramey, "Floods in the Chicago Area" (mimeograph, February 25, 1958, copy in Chicago Public Library), 1–3.

48. Louis P. Cain, *Sanitation Strategy for a Lakefront Metropolis: The Case of Chicago* (DeKalb: Northern Illinois University Press, 1978), 27.

49. Sir John Summerson, *Georgian London* (London: Pelican Books, 1962), 65–67.

50. Cain, *Sanitation Strategy,* 26–31.

51. Homer Hoyt, *One Hundred Years of Land Values in Chicago* (Chicago: University of Chicago Press, 1933), 280.

52. Ramey, "Floods in Chicago," 4–5, 17.

53. Harold M. Mayer and Richard C. Wade, *Chicago: Growth of a Metropolis* (Chicago: University of Chicago Press, 1969), 18–20.

54. Don Coursey, "Environmental Racism in the City of Chicago" (University of Chicago: Harris Graduate School of Public Policy, September 1994), 16; Cain, *Sanitation Strategy,* 39; Metropolitan Water Reclamation District of Greater Chicago (MWRDGC), *Facilities Planning Study, 1992 Update Supplement and Summary* (Chicago: MWRDGC, December 1992), ch. 5, 35.

55. Cain, *Sanitation Strategy,* 37–43, 46–51, 136–137; Max White, "Water Supply Organization in the Chicago Region," (PhD dissertation, Political Science, University of Chicago, 1934), 29.

56. Hoyt, *One Hundred Years of Land Values,* 84–86; Harold Platt, "'A Fountain Inexhaustible': Environmental Perspectives on Water Management and Public Health in Chicago, 1840–1930," (Paper presented to the Graduate Seminar, Technisch Hochschule Darmstadt, Germany, November, 1995).

57. Condit, *Chicago 1910–1929* (Chicago: University of Chicago Press, 1973); Cain, *Sanitation Strategy,* 69–74. The history of nineteenth century Chicago's water supply and sewer system has been gracefully told in the celebratory mode in Donald L.

Miller, *City of the Century* (New York: Simon and Schuster, 1996) 122—31, 423—32. The Sanitary District added much of southern Cook County to its boundaries in 1903 and it was further enlarged November 6, 1956, to its present size of 874 square miles. It now covers all of Cook County plus two additional square miles. MWRDGC, *Facilities Planning Study, 1992,* U91-II-5.

58. "Diversion" is a technical term that sums the amount of water that the river systems would have delivered to Lake Michigan had their flows not been reversed with the amount of direct withdrawal from the lake. MWRDGC, *Facilities Planning Study, 1992,* ch. 4, 35–36.

59. Condit, *Chicago 1910–1929,* 244–46; MWRDGC, *Facilities Planning Study, 1992,* ch. 4, 4, 19.

60. Arthur E. Gorman, "Pollution of Lake Michigan," *Civil Engineering* 3 (September 1933), 519–24.

61. Dalton et al., "Urban Water Management" (Chicago: Metropolitan Water Reclamation District, 1993) 11; U.S. Public Health Service, *The Chicago–Cook County Health Survey* (New York: Columbia University Press, 1949), 135–45.

62. Arthur Evans LeGay, *Improvers and Preservers: A History of Oak Park, Illinois, 1833–1940* (Ph.D. diss., History, University of Chicago, December 1967).

63. Mayer and Wade, *Chicago,* 178–82.

64. All population figures from 1910 onward are from the U.S. Census.

65. Ramey, "Floods in the Chicago Area," 17.

66. U.S. Public Health Service, *Chicago–Cook County,* 132.

67. The Metropolitan Sanitary District engineers estimate that the ordinary soils of Cook County absorb only 10 percent of the precipitation, and that they send 90 percent as runoff. Interview with William A. Macaitis, Assistant Chief Engineer, Collection Facilities Division, MWRDGC, July 21, 1994.

68. Ramey, "Floods in the Chicago Area," 22.

69. U.S. General Accounting Office, Report to the Congress of the United States, "Metropolitan Chicago's Combined Water Cleanup and Flood Control Program: Status and Problems," May 24, 1978, PSAD-78-94, 3.

70. *Journal of Watershed Protection Techniques,* v. 1 (1994), v. 2 (Fall, 1995).

71. Craig E. Colten, "Illinois River Pollution Control, 1900–1970," in Larry M. Dilsaver and Craig E. Colten, eds., *The American Environment,* *Interpreted from Past Geographies* (Lanham, Md.: Rowman and Littlefield, 1992), 193–214.

72. Samuel P. Hays, *Beauty, Health, and Permanence: Environmental Politics in the United States, 1955–1985* (New York: Cambridge University Press, 1987), 76–80.

73. Cook County, North Branch of the Chicago River Steering Committee, *Flood Water Management Plan* (Chicago: MSDGC, October 1974), 2; General Accounting Office, "Metropolitan Chicago's Combined Water Cleanup," 20.

74. A. L. Tholin and Clint J. Keifer, "The Hydrology of Urban Runoff," *Journal of the Sanitary Engineering Division, Proceedings of the American Society of Civil Engineers* 85 (March, 1959, SA2) 51–52, 57–58, 103–4. Keifer later served as an engineer in the Chicago Public Works Department, *Chicago American, Chicago Today,* January 29, 1970.

75. John F. Meissner Engineers, Inc., "Flood Control for the Metropolitan Sanitary District of Greater Chicago," August 1958, copy in the Chicago Public Library, 4.

76. Harza Engineering Co. & Bauer Engineering Co., "Flood and Pollution Control, a Deep Tunnel Plan for the Chicagoland Area, Proposed for the Metropolitan Sanitary District of Greater Chicago," May 1966, copy in the Chicago Public Library, cover letter and IV, 11–12. The following year the Bauer firm proposed building a thousand-foot ski mountain out of rock from the tunnel. Bauer Engineering Co., "Land and Recreational Development through a Rock and Solid Waste Disposal System," September 1967, copy in Chicago Public Library.

77. *Chicago American,* August 25, 1967, and August 28, 1967; "MSDGC Board Split," *Chicago Tribune,* November 10, 1967; *Chicago Daily News,* March 16, 1968, and August 23, 1968; "Plan Revived," *Chicago Sun-Times,* October 6, 1972.

78. MWRDGC, "Facilities Planning Study, 1992," U91-E-3; Frank E. Dalton and P. E. Ramon, "Chicago TARP Problems," *Water and Wastes Engineering* (January 1979), 18–23; Rita Robinson, "The Tunnel That Cleaned Up," *Civil Engineering* (July 1986); William A. Oth, "MWRD Chief Looks Back, and Ahead at Chicago's TARP System," *Construction Digest* (February 4, 1991), 26–35.

79. State of Illinois, County of Cook, Metropolitan Sanitary District of Greater Chicago, City of Chicago, *Development of a Flood and Pollution Control Plan for the Chicagoland Area, The Chicago Underflow Plan* (Chicago: Flood Control

Coordinating Committee, December 1972, copy in Chicago Public Library).

80. For examples, see reports of Chester P. Majewski's plural office-holding and no-show treatment of his job as public defender: *Today,* January 22, 1972; *Daily News,* April 10, 1973; a copy of his November 20, 1973, letter to Mayor Daley as chairman of the Democratic Party of Cook County setting forth his qualifications for nomination, including a mention that Majewski's father had been a precinct captain before him, and that he had served the Thirty-eighth Ward for the past twelve years, is in the Chicago Public Library. For reports of Chairman Nicholas J. Melas's and the Chicago Greek community's campaign contributions to Mayor Daley, see *Daily News,* December 28–29, 1974; for a review of Melas's political career from his beginnings with the Ward 4 Regular Democratic Organization, see *Daily News,* January 1, 1975.

81. State of Illinois et al., *Development of a Flood and Pollution Control Plan for Chicagoland,* 22; Metropolitan Sanitary District of Greater Chicago, "How to Bottle Rainstorms" (Chicago: MSDGC, 1973), 24.

82. TARP Impacts Project, "TARP Summary Description," 1978, copy at the Center for Neighborhood Technology, Chicago, Ill.

83. *Tribune,* November 5, 1974.

84. *Daily News,* October 17, 1975.

85. Denise DeClue, "Deep Tunnel: Monster or Miracle?" *Reader,* June 24, 1977, 22–26; Ernst Schumacher, *Small Is Beautiful: Economics As If People Mattered* (New York: Harper and Row, 1973).

86. Richard L. Robbins, "The Effect of TARP on the Environment of Lake Michigan and the Chicago Waterways"; Nancy S. Philippi, "The Local Tax Impacts of the Deep Tunnel and Reservoir Plan"; Dennis R. Marinno, "The Neighborhood Impacts of the Deep Tunnel and Reservoir Plan"; Scott Bernstein, "Technological Assessment of Waste and Water Management Options for the Garfield Park Community Area in Chicago, Illinois," all TARP impacts project papers published in 1978. Also, Dennis L. Robbins, executive director of the Lake Michigan Foundation, wrote a sum-

mary of the TIP project and its findings: letter and report February 1, 1979. All these materials are located in the files of the Neighborhood Technology Center, Chicago.

87. Comptroller General, "Metropolitan Chicago's Combined Water Cleanup and Flood Control Program: Status and Problems," PSAD-78-94 (Washington, D.C.: General Accounting Office, May 24, 1978); town-by-town sewer analysis, "Combined Sewer Flooding and Pollution—A National Problem. The Search for Solutions in Chicago: A Synopsis of Flooding Problems for Each of the 54 Chicago Area Communities," CED 79-77 vol. 6 (Washington, D.C.: General Accounting Office, May 15, 1979).

88. *Tribune,* May 18, 1979, and June 2, 1979; *Sun-Times,* May 19, 1979.

89. *Tribune,* May 19, 1979.

90. Metropolitan Water Reclamation District of Greater Chicago, *1996 Budget,* (Chicago: MWRDGC, 1996) 4.

91. *Sun-Times,* October 14, 1994.

92. Nancy S. Philippi, "Revisiting Flood Control: An Examination of Federal Flood Control Policy in Light of the 1993 Flood Event on the Upper Mississippi River," (Chicago: Wetlands Research Inc., May 1994).

93. Metropolitan Planning Council (MPC), "Chicago Area MPC, Public Capital Investments: Toward the Year 2000" (Chicago: MPC, December 1972); MPC, "Final Report Infrastructure '84" (Chicago: MPC, May, 1984).

94. *New York Times,* February 3, 1980.

95. Donald L. Hey, "The Des Plaines River Wetlands Demonstration Project: Restoring an Urban Wetland," in Rutherford H. Platt et al., eds., *The Ecological City* (Amherst: University of Massachusetts Press, 1994); Paul H. Gobster and Lynne M. Westphal, "People and the River," (Chicago: USDA Forest Service, North Central Forest Experiment Station, November 1995); Stephanie Mills, *In Service of the Wild: Restoring and Reinhabiting Damaged Land* (Boston: Beacon Press, 1995) 130—49; Don Coursey, "Environmental Racism in the City of Chicago."

Back Bay Fens, Boston, 1904. This seemingly natural environment is in fact the creation of Frederick Law Olmsted, who in the late 19th century transformed a polluted mud flat into a park that combines the beauties of a natural salt marsh with the urban functions of flood control and sewerage. (Frances Loeb Library, Graduate School of Design, Harvard University)

CHAPTER ELEVEN

Reclaiming Common Ground
Water, Neighborhoods, and Public Places

■■
■■

ANNE WHISTON SPIRN

I f cities are to become more livable, it will be by design: not just through the design of built projects—homes and workplaces, gardens and parks, streets and sewer systems—but also through visions that may never be realized. Urban design is a process of envisioning and describing the shape of the future, of posing alternatives from which to choose. Without visions to guide their development, cities will be shaped by the politics of expedience.

For hundreds of years, Bostonians have proposed visions for their city that, built and unbuilt, contributed to the public debate about its future.[1] This chapter was conceived and written in that tradition, at the invitation of the Boston Society of Architects.[2] In its original incarnation, it was an illustrated public lecture given at the Boston Public Library in April 1985, then again in February 1986 at the Boston Atheneum. The lecture and the responses and reflections it provoked were a bridge between my book *The Granite Garden: Urban Nature and Human Design* (1984), my subsequent work in Philadelphia, and the ideas advanced in my most recent book, *The Language of Landscape* (1998).[3] Today some proposals described here have been realized; others remain unfulfilled. My lecture was part of a larger public discussion to which many people contributed. Their efforts over the past two decades have improved greatly the environmental, social, and aesthetic qualities of Boston's public realm.

My proposals were shaped by the some of the most urgent issues of the time— the pollution of Boston Harbor and shrinking water supplies, the deterioration of Boston's inner-city neighborhoods, and the decline in quality of public space downtown. The 1970s had wrought great changes in Boston's built environment, transformations fully felt by 1985. High-rise office buildings, huge parking structures, and deep street canyons—dark, windy, grid-locked by traffic—had made an unpleasant downtown environment. Arson, disinvestment, and illegal dumping had created vast, trash-filled wastelands in inner-city neighborhoods, while deep cuts in the Park Department's budget had led to unkempt parks and playgrounds littered with smashed glass and broken benches. Polluted water and closed beaches mocked plans to turn Boston Harbor into a state park, yet no waterfront neighborhood wanted the new sewage-treatment plant, then under study, located in their vicinity. Widespread dissatisfaction and growing public resistance hampered future plans, but protests against further downtown development, neglect of inner-city neighborhoods, and the proposed sewage-treatment plant all had different constituencies who perceived their concerns as unrelated.

These challenges, despite their apparent diversity, were part of a single, larger failing: the failure to recognize the critical importance of the public realm. This was, and is, not Boston's challenge alone. All across the United States, the neglect and deterioration of the urban public realm threatens to become a pervasive symbol of misplaced priorities and missed opportunities that will characterize the late twentieth century for future generations.

There is growing recognition internationally that solutions to urban problems must integrate economic, social, and environmental issues and must be addressed at local, regional, and national scales. This was the conclusion reached in 1992 at an international conference on the future of cities convened by the Organization for Economic Cooperation and Development (OECD) and attended by ministers in housing, urban development, environment, employment, and education from many countries.[4] The OECD has documented model programs that integrate environmental quality, education, job

creation, and community development. Most entail institutional innovations focused primarily on social and economic issues; few such programs have specifically engaged the built environment or resulted in memorable public spaces. In 1985, my goal was (and still is) to weave together these different sets of concerns (environmental, social, and aesthetic) and scales of intervention to demonstrate how solutions to seemingly intractable, competing problems could address multiple purposes rather than a single, narrowly defined one—and then to imagine how these might be expressed in renewed public places.

The time: April 30, 1985. The place: Boston Public Library at Copley Square. The hall was packed that evening, for there was widespread concern about the future shape of Boston.

Reclaiming Common Ground: The Future Shape of Boston

There is much to admire in the public realm of Boston. Boston Common, the oldest park in the United States, has served a variety of public functions since it was set aside as a common field in 1640. The Public Garden, its swan boats floating on a willow-lined pond, sits at the base of the Common. Commonwealth Avenue, with its shady, urbane mall, is a straight green ribbon that runs through Back Bay, setting off the fine architecture that lines it. The Esplanade, with its lagoons and public harbor, affords views up and down the Charles River. The Emerald Necklace, threading its way from the Back Bay up the Muddy River and out to Jamaica Pond, the Arboretum, and Franklin Park, connects old Boston to the newer suburbs and structured the growth of adjacent neighborhoods. The curving beach of Castle Island and South Boston marks the edge between harbor and city with a graceful arc. This is the public realm—places for public assembly and personal enjoyment that are accessible to all citizens—a testament to the vision of past Bostonians. It was hard-won, achieved through prolonged struggle, protected from encroachment and neglect by the sustained efforts of citizens ever since. Many of the features Bostonians most admire were conceived not as mere ornaments, but as pragmatic solutions to environmental and social problems.

Boston's current challenges seem overwhelming, yet they are not new to Boston, and they are not unique. Many issues confronting Boston face most large American cities: water pollution and dwindling water supplies, deteriorating inner-city neighborhoods, declining environmental quality in downtown streets and plazas. Whether and how these issues are resolved in the next decade will determine the shape of Boston for many years to come. In the nineteenth century, Bostonians forged new urban forms and institutions to meet the challenges of the day; these innovations then became models for the nation. Today Boston could lead once again: in managing urban water resources, in reconstructing inner-city neighborhoods to benefit the people who live there and the region at large, in building a downtown with memorable public spaces.

Water is Boston's greatest problem and its most important resource. The pollution of Boston Harbor by sewage has long been headline news, but the region's shrinking water supply (degraded well water throughout the metropolitan area, in particular) is equally if not more important. Metropolitan sewer and water districts were landmark institutions when founded nearly a century ago, but they need rethinking today. Something is wrong when sewage from as far away as Framingham and Walpole is transported twenty miles to sewage-treatment plants in Boston Harbor, thereby concentrating the sewage of an entire region into a small basin.

Something is wrong when water is piped sixty miles from a reservoir whose water level has been falling, slowly but inexorably, while groundwater resources within the local region are permitted to deteriorate. These are life-threatening problems that affect the health of millions of people dependent on metropolitan water and sewer systems.[5]

Boston's inner neighborhoods are riddled with vacant land, abandoned buildings, and closed fire stations and libraries. The state of these neighborhoods is invisible from downtown, but downtown prosperity, symbolized by gleaming new towers, is clearly visible from the neighborhoods, a stark and disturbing juxtaposition. In the face of unemployment and the decline of local social services, the new towers are a daily reminder to residents of inner-city neighborhoods that they have not shared in Boston's recent economic growth.[6]

Even downtown the boom has been a mixed blessing. Downtown Boston has become a collection of major development projects by private investors, the urban fabric a patchwork of streets and open spaces. The public realm is seen as leftover space, something pieced together, considered only after everything else has already happened, rather than conceived as the frame within which the city evolves. Most of the new buildings that transformed Boston's skyline in the 1970s and 1980s were private projects constructed in a vacuum of public vision. Buildings are designed with more concern for how they look as a part of Boston's skyline than for how people feel in the streets and plazas outside their doors. New office towers have created dark, windy canyons and barren plazas; dusty, gritty winds make sitting and walking outdoors uncomfortable in summer, frigid in winter. Interior atriums do not compensate for the degraded public realm outside their doors. Some, ostensibly public, are really private enclaves guarded by private police. The sumptuous, costly materials lavished on the interiors contrast vividly with potholed, trash-filled streets and narrow, broken sidewalks outside.[7]

Viewed separately, problems seem monumental and compete for meager resources. This need not be, if only they were seen as opportunities to devise solutions that address more than a single, narrowly defined issue.

Restoring Water, Rebuilding Neighborhoods, Reclaiming Public Space

Every problem embodies an opportunity, and crises often provide the greatest opportunities for constructive change. The magnitude of sewer and water problems in Boston is sobering, but there is growing recognition that the current system must be reconstructed. At a time of cutbacks in funds for public spaces and neighborhood redevelopment, millions of dollars are earmarked for new public works related to sewage treatment. This affords a rare chance to exploit new ideas and new technologies and to create new jobs and public amenities at the same time. Water conservation, sewage treatment, neighborhood reconstruction, and renewal of an impoverished public realm should be addressed together with other issues facing Boston. The first step is to focus on issues of primary importance and to analyze each in terms of its essential characteristics and contributing causes. The second step is to look for overlaps and interconnections among the issues; the third step is to devise solutions that accommodate multiple concerns.

There may be as many as fifteen thousand vacant house lots within the city of Boston, amounting to somewhere between three and four thousand acres of vacant land.[8] Viewed together with the social and economic needs of the neighborhoods in which they occur, vacant lands present an opportunity to integrate nature and city in new

ways and to transform the city and the way people live within it. If vacant lands were perceived collectively as part of the city's greater land resource, Bostonians could realize a potential for reshaping the city unmatched since the nineteenth century.

There are many proposals for new development in downtown Boston, but these projects are widely seen as a threat to the quality of life downtown. If there were a vision for what the public realm should be, a vision that incorporated both private development and the welfare of all the city's citizens, development would be welcomed, not feared.

The problem of water, the pollution of surface and groundwater, is paramount, for it threatens the health, even the lives, of all. Pollution in Boston Harbor results both from a centralized system of overloaded, outmoded sewage-treatment plants that flush millions of gallons of untreated sewage per day into the harbor during every breakdown or rainstorm, and from dumping massive amounts of sludge, a byproduct of the treatment process. Two treatment plants in Boston Harbor treat all the sewage from forty-three communities, including some from twenty miles away, so the breakdown of a single plant pours millions of gallons of sewage into the harbor. These two plants plus several wet-weather plants also treat storm water from roof and street drains throughout the region, for unlike in newer cities, many of Boston's sanitary and storm sewers are combined. After rainfalls, storm water enters the system rapidly, mixes with sanitary sewage, and produces tremendous burst of sewage that must be treated or released during and immediately after every storm. Even when Boston's sewage system is functioning well, it produces tons of sludge contaminated with poisonous heavy metals, which is simply dumped back into the harbor. A solution to the pollution of Boston Harbor might therefore include the following strategies: decentralize sewage treatment within the region, prevent sewer overflows after rainstorms by slowing the time it takes for storm water to reach sewers, and reuse rather than discard the resources contained in sewage sludge.[9]

Decentralizing the region's sewage treatment could have many other benefits besides reducing water pollution in the harbor. In suburban communities, wastewater treatment facilities could be combined with parks, using the properties of sunlight, air, plants, and soil to accomplish secondary and tertiary treatment of wastewater. These methods have already been tested elsewhere. Arcata, California, for example, has combined wetlands, parks, and sewage-treatment facilities; funds for sewage treatment also support wildlife habitat and recreation. Secondary effluent from the treatment plant—a lot cleaner than the water in Boston Harbor today—is discharged into the wetland for further treatment. Islands in the center of the marsh are protected feeding and nesting spots for birds; peregrine falcons and migrating birds are now regular visitors to the sanctuary. At Bishop's Lodge resort in Santa Fe, New Mexico, a rocky cascade is part of a man-made system of ornamental waterfalls and pools designed to treat sewage effluent. Sewage receives initial treatment and is then released to a series of cascades; aerated and exposed to sunlight as it falls, the water then irrigates pastures, lawns, and gardens. The effluent is purified further by plants and soil as it seeps through the ground to replenish the underlying aquifer from which the resort draws its drinking water. If subregional sewage treatment were introduced in the Boston area, a treatment facility for communities bordering Fowl Meadow Marsh, like Norwood, Canton, and Walpole, could not only underwrite maintenance of a park, but also recharge the Neponset Aquifer, a potential source of supplementary water for the Boston region.[10]

Sewage sludge poses a major disposal problem for Boston and for most major cities, yet sludge is rich in nutrients, an ideal soil amendment, especially when composted with wood chips and leaves. Philadelphia, a city that produces more than two hundred dry tons of sewage sludge per day, converted its sludge into a marketable resource. The city used one product—"Philorganic"—to fertilize parks and golf courses and to reclaim old landfill sites. "Garden Life," sold in forty-pound bags or in bulk, is made by composting dry sludge with wood chips. Parks in Washington, D.C., have been treated with a similar product called "Com-pro." Boston is prevented from utilizing the nutrients in sludge due to the high concentrations of heavy metals it contains. If treatment facilities were decentralized, sludge from some plants would be low in heavy metals and could be used for fertilizer and soil reclamation.[11]

Currently, Boston's combined treatment system of sanitary sewage and storm water is a liability; with modification, it could be an asset. For some parameters, like suspended solids and coliform bacteria, the quality of storm water running off roads, roofs, and sidewalks is no better than raw sanitary sewage, and it should be treated before entering streams and rivers. A combined system makes it feasible to treat this storm runoff. The issue then is how to prevent sewer overflows after rainstorms. Chicago and Denver employ floodplain parks designed to hold storm water after a rainfall and release it gradually to sewers. Denver also requires that new and renovated buildings in its downtown renewal district detain storm water on site. In downtown Denver, storm water is ponded temporarily on plazas, parking lots, and rooftops. Skyline Plaza, for instance, is a park designed to hold up to several inches of storm water. "Wet roofs" have other benefits besides flood control; they reduce the building's heat gain and energy consumption for air conditioning. Imagine what

Boston might be like if a similar requirement were implemented, and countless rooftops were transformed into gardens with retention pools. Some might look like the Oakland Art Museum, whose rooftop gardens function as a park.[12]

Outside downtown, there is more space to detain storm-water runoff, especially in inner-city neighborhoods where vacant land is concentrated in former floodplains, bogs, and marshes that were sewered and filled in the nineteenth century. Such places are well suited to projects combining storm-water detention and recreation. There are large vacant areas in sections of Dorchester and Roxbury, especially in the Dudley neighborhood where a stream that once marked the boundary between the two towns now flows in an underground sewer. Dudley is one of Sam Bass Warner's nineteenth-century "streetcar suburbs," where public investment in streets and sewers facilitated development by private real estate speculators and builders.[13] The Dudley neighborhood, fully built with homes and businesses by the end of the nineteenth century, is now 30 percent vacant. This statistic is misleading, however, for it conceals a striking pattern: 90 percent of the land within the original floodplain is vacant, with only a few, scattered vacant lots on higher ground. Floodplains and low marshy areas, now vacant, were the last spots developed. They were less favorable locations environmentally, and the houses built on them—many as rental properties for multiple families rather than homes owned and inhabited by a single family—were undoubtedly plagued by wet basements. Some of these properties were already vacant by the early twentieth century, many by the end of the Depression, and most by the 1960s.[14] Although poor drainage probably played an important early role in abandonment, by the 1950s policies like redlining made it difficult to obtain mortgages and home improvement loans in inner-

city neighborhoods like Dudley at a time when federal subsidies for highway construction and mortgages on new suburban homes made suburbs widely accessible and affordable.[15] Yet common wisdom among Bostonians who live outside these neighborhoods holds that the vacant land was the product of civil unrest in the 1960s, that buildings were burned down by rioters, leaving widespread vacancies. This misconception has unfortunate results, for it places blame on the victims of abandonment rather than the perpetrators, on riots rather than poor drainage, shoddy, ill-considered development, long-term neglect, and federal policies that favored suburban development and hindered inner-city investment.[16]

Dudley is not unusual. The same constellation of contributing factors is found in inner-city neighborhoods throughout Boston and other American cities.[17] Land was originally developed, at considerable public expense, without regard for unhealthy or hazardous environmental conditions that contributed to later abandonment. The mistake is being repeated, at great public cost, as public housing, schools, and subsidized homes for families with low incomes are once again built on abandoned, poorly drained land. There are plans to build homes for low-income families on some of the low-lying tracts in the Dudley neighborhood; such plans are well-meaning, but ill-conceived, for maintenance will cost considerably more than in better-drained locations. As neighborhoods like Dudley are rebuilt and repopulated, much of the land now vacant will be built on once again. Some lands, however, should remain open, and now is the time to identify them. Thousands of vacant house lots in Boston are tax-delinquent, the owners absent, many unknown and unaccountable for the condition of their property. The city should decide now which vacant land to acquire. The open floodplain offers an opportunity to detain storm water and provide a linear park for the neighborhood. Reclamation of this common ground could help form a framework for future residential and commercial development to benefit current residents while also contributing to the reclamation of the larger region. And the construction and maintenance of these projects could provide jobs for residents of these inner-city neighborhoods. The cost of this public open space could be borne by funds for regional metropolitan flood control and sewage treatment.[18]

Funds for maintaining public parks are usually among the first to be cut in times of financial crisis. In the 1980s, faced with the destruction of parks and playgrounds within a few years of construction and with declining funds for maintenance, Boston's Neighborhood Development and Employment Agency (NDEA) launched an experimental program in 1983. The Grassroots Program supported neighborhood-initiated projects to convert vacant lots into various types of open space. Funded projects were selected from proposals made by neighborhood organizations and included playgrounds, community gardens, sitting areas, and meadows of wildflowers and clover. Boston Urban Gardeners, a nonprofit organization, helped local groups prepare proposals. Since location, use, design, construction management, and maintenance were all the responsibility of the organization making the proposal, the projects were typically small in scale. The result was a transformation of vacant lots into attractive community open space—playgrounds, sitting areas, and community gardens—that met the needs of local residents. The projects afforded people the opportunity to shape the place they live, to give form to common needs and shared aspirations, to share and care for common ground.[19]

Cooper's Place is a community garden built in 1984 as part of the Grassroots Pro-

gram. Cooper's Place, with its flower garden open to visitors and plots for individual gardeners, has become a neighborhood landmark. It was sponsored by the Roxbury Action Program, Boston Urban Gardeners, and the Highland Park 400, a local senior-citizens' group. The land was purchased by the Boston Natural Areas Fund, the garden designed by my students at the Harvard Graduate School of Design and constructed by unemployed youth enrolled in a four-month program in landscape construction and maintenance at Roxbury Community College. Several years after the garden was constructed, vacant buildings next door and across the street were renovated and occupied. Community landscape projects have had a similar impact in other neighborhoods, including Dudley. A few were part of the NDEA's Grassroots Program, but most were sponsored privately by Boston Urban Gardeners, supported by donations, grants from private foundations, and the vision and energy of neighborhood residents. The most successful recent contributions to the public realm of Boston's inner-city neighborhoods have been local projects achieved, for the most part, by private initiatives.

Small-scale, resident-initiated projects, appropriate at the scale of a neighborhood, are not the answer to improving the public realm downtown. The challenge there is to match the interests of private developers with the needs and desires of those people who live, work, and visit downtown.[20] Recently, major private development has, for the most part, overshadowed and outstripped public investment in its impact on the shape of the city. Many of the decisions that affect the public realm so profoundly are made outside the public forum. In this flood of private projects and with a paucity of major public works, proponents of the public realm are cast in a defensive, negative posture. Their role is restricted to environmental-impact statements and public hearings, to reviews of designs after they are complete, at the point where alterations, even minor ones, are extremely costly. The result is frustration in both camps, among developers who are taking financial risks and among the public who must live with the product. Boston needs a clearly articulated vision for its public realm, a setting within which privately financed improvements can make their contribution, a vision against which citizens can measure proposals and results.

It is paradoxical that Bostonians are not creating for the future what many value from the past. Historic districts like Back Bay were achieved through the construction of the public realm as a framework for private development, not through fragmented assembly of private projects, with the city trying to make the best of leftover space for the public realm. Contrast the nineteenth century's achievements in the public realm, for example, with the results of the past two decades of development, both private and public, in the Back Bay along Boyleston Street and Copley Square. Commercial developments like Prudential Center and Copley Place exploit nostalgic symbols of the nineteenth century's public realm in their interior spaces and turn their backs to the street. Copley Place is a luxurious shopping mall with interior spaces arranged like streets; it even has a "town square" with trees, flowers, park benches, and a white bandstand as a setting for a restaurant. Such symbols of a gracious public realm are limited to the interior. Copley Place offers no such amenities to the public realm immediately outside its walls; the sidewalks alongside are very narrow, uniformed guards stand inside the entrance, and the complex turns its back (loading docks and garbage dumpsters) to the residential neighborhood behind. The 1960s addition to the public library is also fortresslike and forbidding. In contrast, the old library next door

makes a generous addition to the public space of sidewalk and street along Boylston; the base of the building forms a bench, well-used on a sunny day, full of people sitting, waiting for a bus, watching passersby. The juxtaposition of these buildings highlights the difference between the regard that Bostonians of the late nineteenth century had for the public realm and that of their late-twentieth-century counterparts.

There is no vision now for the public realm of Boylston, a street with its source at the Common, its terminus at the Fens; no wonder the developers of Prudential Center and Copley Place chose to focus inward. Why is there no vision for the marvelous street that Boylston could be? It is an active commercial street with all the ingredients for lively success, a street experiencing pressure for large investment of private capital. Boston is not New York and Boylston Street is not Fifth Avenue, but with a new vision for Boylston Street, why couldn't a new Prudential Center (slated for renovation in the near future) offer some of the same amenities that Rockefeller Center in New York gives to the public realm of Fifth Avenue? This might be difficult to achieve, but then so were the projects of the last century that Bostonians admire and take so much for granted.[21]

Boston's Public Realm:
A Hard-Won Legacy

The historic urban fabric of Boston is distinguished not just by the quality of individual buildings, but of entire streets, parks, and districts. For many Americans, these have come to stand as models to be emulated. The Back Bay—framed by the Common and Public Gardens, the Esplanade, and the Fens—is one such district. Many of its prized features are the direct result of solutions to nineteenth-century Boston's environmental and social problems: the need to clean up the foul waters of the Back Bay tidal flats and to prevent the flooding of Stony Brook and Muddy River; the need for more land to accommodate the city's growth; the need for efficient transportation between the old center and growing, outlying towns; and the demand for "breathing spaces" within the city and for access to rural landscapes.

The Back Bay and the Emerald Necklace are two of the most spectacular examples of Victorian urban design in America. Frederick Law Olmsted considered the Fens and the Riverway among the most important projects of his entire career. In their time they served as landmarks for the nation. They remain outstanding examples of collective vision and sustained public energy. But they were not the product of a single genius; they incorporated the ideas of many individuals, their form forged through public dialogue, evolving over decades.

One hundred and eighty years ago, Boston was still a peninsula and the Back Bay was a marsh where high tide lapped at the western edge of the Common. In 1821 a dam was built across the bay to harness the tides to drive mills, but the dam converted the basin, in the words of one critic, into "an empty mud-basin, reeking with filth, abhorrent to the smell, and disgusting to the eye."[22] The Back Bay residential district was a project conceived to provide more building space to accommodate a growing population and eliminate a hazard to public health. Filling the Back Bay was a monumental public undertaking, spanning several decades: "Landfill progressed at the rate of almost two house lots per day, a train of thirty-five loaded gravel cars arriving in the Back Bay on the average of one an hour, night and day, six days a week for almost forty years."[23]

The Back Bay is a human creation forged by the need for new building space and guided by a vision of what a healthy, attractive, urbane neighborhood should be. The public realm as we know it today was established first as the frame: the Public Garden served as the base for the new district and streets were laid out with Commonwealth Avenue planted as a tree-lined mall. This sequence—public investment in an attractive and coherent infrastructure, followed by private investment—is clearly visible in an aerial view of Boston in 1870.

As the new Back Bay residential district neared completion in 1871, the Roxbury tidal flats at its western end were still "the filthiest marsh and mudflats to be found anywhere . . . a body of water so foul that even clams and eels cannot live in it, and that no one will go within a mile of in summertime unless from necessity, so great is the stench."[24] The sewers of Roxbury emptied onto these mudflats, and sewage was carried back into the low-lying streets of lower Roxbury during floods. This nuisance was transformed into a new park called the Fens, designed as an amenity and a basin to store floodwater. Over the next two decades, the Fens was extended into a linked system of parks and parkways up the Muddy River, to Jamaica Pond, the Arboretum, and Franklin Park. This was the nation's first metropolitan-scale park system. It linked the new neighborhood of Back Bay to the center of Boston and to the outlying suburbs and countryside.

Designs for the Back Bay and the Emerald Necklace were not produced overnight, nor did they spring from the mind of a single visionary. Many proposals were made for the layout of the Public Gardens, Back Bay, the Fens, and for Boston at large, from Robert Gourlay's "General Plan for Enlarging and Improving the City of Boston (1844) to Charles Eliot's proposal for a metropolitan park system (1893). These were among Boston's first city plans, produced by professional designers and planners and by private citizens with no design training, presented in published pamphlets, public speeches, and the press. A lawyer named Uriel Crocker, for example, proposed a linear park system of streams, ponds, and hilltops with a continuous parkway between the Charles River and Chestnut Hill Reservoir in 1869. That same year, Robert Morris Copeland, a landscape architect, proposed a metropolitan park system linked by parkways one hundred feet wide and a metropolitan park commission to implement and manage the parks. Several years later, in 1872, Copeland published "The Most Beautiful City in America: Essay and Plan for the Improvement of the City of Boston," a pamphlet outlining how Boston's natural resources might be exploited to meet its economic needs. Copeland's plan featured a new, integrated public infrastructure of open space and sewer and transportation systems designed to shape the future growth of the city. As part of this plan, he proposed a park along a stream on the Roxbury-Dorchester border—the very same area in the Dudley Street neighborhood discussed earlier. That floodplain, open land in Copeland's day, was later built on and is now open again. After Copeland's death in 1874, his associate Ernest Bowditch proposed a plan based on Copeland's ideas, which included a linear park following the upper valley of Muddy River as a link between Back Bay and Jamaica Pond and a system of rural parks to protect the metropolitan water supply. These preceded Olmsted's proposal for the Riverway by six years and Eliot's proposal for a metropolitan park system by nearly twenty years. The future shape of Boston was the subject of continuing debate throughout the last half of the nineteenth century. Though not implemented, the visions of Gourlay, Crocker, Copeland, Bowditch, and dozens of others influenced the course Boston took.[25]

In 1875, the city of Boston passed the Park Act, which established a municipal park commission empowered to prepare a city plan and to take land within city limits. The park commissioners' first action was to advertise for "civil and landscape engineers" and interested citizens to present their views at a public hearing. The majority of those who presented their ideas to the commission were private citizens, many of them petitioning for parks in their own neighborhoods, and property owners who wished to sell land to the city. In the summer of 1876 the commission published a plan of proposed parks and parkways for the city of Boston, which was distributed and read widely. A public meeting was held in June of 1876 in Fanuiel Hall to endorse the plan: its organizers called it "Parks for the People."

The first project to be implemented was the Back Bay Park. The City Council voted an appropriation for the purchase of one hundred acres of land in the middle of mudflats, and the commissioners hired Olmsted to prepare a design. The result was a landmark in city planning and environmental design. A large, masonry storm-water basin had long been part of the city's plan for the Back Bay Park. Olmsted felt that a masonry storage basin big enough to hold floodwaters from Muddy River and Stony Brook would be excessively ugly and expensive. Instead he designed the entire park as a flood storage basin with gently sloping banks covered by marsh grasses and other plants that could tolerate changing water levels. The resulting design was revolutionary, a synthesis of environmental engineering and aesthetics.

By 1881 the Fens was under construction. Tidal flats were scooped out by a dredger, then graded and planted. Olmsted intended the Fens to look like a natural salt marsh around which the city had happened to grow. Never before had anyone attempted to *create* a salt marsh. The planting design required considerable research and a good deal of professional courage. In fact, the first phase of the Fens to be planted was a disaster: most of the plants died, and Olmsted was forced to reconsider the original selection and placement of plants. But within ten years the Fens looked like a landscape that had always been there. In 1881 Olmsted proposed to continue the park up the Muddy River valley. At that time the city's plans for parks and for sewers were separate. The city proposed to connect Back Bay Park to Parker Hill and to convey the waters of Muddy River to the Charles in a straight, masonry conduit, several miles in length. Olmsted proposed instead that the two projects be combined and that the linear park serve as a storm drainage system. Olmsted was critical of the city's plan, which he maintained would be very costly and therefore delayed many years: "Meantime . . . the Muddy River valley will be very dirty, unhealthy, and squalid. No one will want to live in the neighborhood of it. Property will have little value and there will grow up near the best . . . district of the city . . . an unhealthy and pestilential neighborhood."[26] The final proposal incorporated sewer improvements, a park, a roadway connecting the center of the city to the outskirts, and a streetcar line.

The current alignment and shape of the Riverway are the nineteenth century's artificial creation. The banks of the river were regraded, lined with walkways, crossed by bridges for pedestrians and vehicles, and landscaped to form the Riverway as we know it today. Sanitary sewage was intercepted by a new underground sewer and diverted to the Charles, while the Riverway was designed to accommodate the normal stream flow and floodwater of the Muddy River, as well as runoff from adjacent areas. Like the Fens, within a few decades of construction the Riverway had the appearance of a natural floodplain. Depressed below street level, with steep, wooded banks between the roadway above and the path below, it is still a retreat in the middle of modern Boston.

Olmsted described the integrated purposes of the Fens and the Riverway in his report to the park commissioners in 1881. The primary purpose was the abatement of a hazard to public health. In solving this problem he sought to "thriftily turn to account" those essential improvements to provide other benefits as well: improved transportation between adjoining districts; an attractive framework that would encourage private investment, thereby increasing the city's tax base; and finally, the enhancement of natural features to provide a variety of scenery. Putting these multiple purposes into perspective, he concluded that "the continued application of the term *park* to an undertaking of the character thus indicated tends to perpetuate an unfortunate delusion, and to invite unjust expectations and criticisms."[27]

What are the lessons that can be drawn from the story of these civic improvements one hundred years ago? Consider Olmsted's design for the Fens and the Riverway. Originally proposed by the city as parks, they were refashioned by Olmsted to address other issues, some identical to those that face Boston today. Olmsted related these individual projects to a comprehensive vision of the city as a whole and created an attractive public framework to encourage private investment. Environmental problems provoked by the conflict between human activities and natural processes were resolved by adapting to those processes rather than by trying to subdue them.

Not only the tangible products—Back Bay, Fens, and Riverway—are important. The process itself contributed to the success of the solution: a process of open public dialogue that continued over several decades. Visions of people like Robert Morris Copeland contributed to the form the Emerald Necklace and metropolitan park system took, for Olmsted incorporated many ideas initially proposed by others. But their legacy was greater than ideas alone. Vigorous, sustained discussion not only led to widespread acceptance of the proposals, it also generated the support necessary to implement such ambitious projects.

Design is a powerful tool to forge consensus for major public investment. In this tradition, I offer one person's vision of what the future shape of Boston might be.

A Vision: The Future Shape of Boston

From Great Brewster, a craggy outpost at the entry to Boston Harbor, the long arms of Hull and Winthrop embrace the Harbor. Held between a deep blue, watery foreground and blue sky above, Boston is a narrow band along the horizon. Downtown is marked by towers that rise across the water, catching and reflecting the sun. In the foreground, dark humps of Lovell and George's Islands break the water surface. From this vantage, the city is a silent silhouette, seen clearly for what it is: a fragile human construct, supported by the earth, permeated by air and water. Out here in the harbor, the sound is of waves breaking against rocks and of "a distant bell, moving on the groundswell, its clanging marking a time not our time."[28] Out here time is marked by no clock, but by the apparent motion of the sun through the sky vault, the rise and fall of tides, and the daily cycle of the sea breeze, blowing off land in morning, from sea in evening. Approaching the city over the harbor, now a vast state park, cries of gulls and breaking waves begin to mingle with city sounds. The earlier image of the city as a delicate construct recedes as massive buildings fill the horizon, their stolid mass a reassurance of human importance.

Of the city's three great rivers, the Mystic and the Charles have long been dammed to control the rise and fall of water along their banks. Only the Neponset remains a tidal river, its lower course still lined by Neponset Marsh. Further upstream Fowl Meadow Marsh extends from Milton to Canton and Norwood; it overlies the Neponset Aquifer, one source of Boston's water supply. Water purification plants in the southwestern part of the Boston region are located near Fowl Meadow Marsh. After receiving initial treatment, effluent is purified in lagoons and constructed marshes, then released to the larger marsh where it seeps through the soil to replenish groundwater tapped by the city.

The sewage-treatment plant with adjacent composting facility and park along Fowl Meadow is one of many new satellite treatment plants built as a part of the city's renovation of its water system. The former metropolitan sewage district was divided into smaller subregions, their boundaries determined by watershed, each with its own water purification plant and adjoining park. Each facility receives used water from the watershed it serves, and here that water is purified: first in the plant itself, then in the park's lagoons, marshes, and fountains. Formerly all the region's wastewater was treated and dumped into Boston Harbor. The introduction of satellite treatment plants permitted the adoption of innovative technology and the construction and maintenance of parks throughout the region.

Decentralization has also isolated those watersheds whose wastewater contains high concentrations of heavy metals. Formerly, heavy metals mixed with all of Boston's sewage and prevented the city from recapturing the organic nutrients in sewage sludge. Now most of the subregional purification plants process and recycle metal-free sludge. Sludge, mixed with wood chips and leaf mold from the city's parks, is composted to produce a nutrient-rich soil amendment called Metroloam. Metroloam is used within city and region as a replacement for topsoil and packaged and marketed at garden centers.

The benefits have been many: sludge no longer poses a disposal problem or pollution hazard; raked leaves and wood chips harvested from tree work no longer add to the region's sanitary landfills; and the availability of enormous quantities of cheap soil amendment has permitted the reclamation of vast areas of derelict land within Boston at modest cost.

Inner-city neighborhoods have benefited from the renovation of the city's water system. Take the Dudley neighborhood. Twenty years ago, one-third of all properties were vacant; now the neighborhood is rebuilt. The original floodplain of the buried brook is a linear park that threads its way through the neighborhood and beyond. At some points it is quite narrow, at other points it broadens out into shallow basins that hold storm water after a rain. Like the wetlands of the Charles River at the city's outskirts, this park is paid for and maintained as part of the region's flood control and water-treatment system. It has counterparts in other parts of the city, and the form of these parks varies from neighborhood to neighborhood. In some neighborhoods, detention basins form a linear park system, while in others they are discrete elements within the mosaic of buildings, pavement, and private yards. Because of all these basins within the city, the sewers have not overflowed since the Great Hurricane twenty years ago. Many of the storm-water basins are flooded every winter, forming popular skating ponds; experts attribute the phenomenal number of youngsters from Roxbury and Dorchester who now play in the National Hockey League to these neighborhood skating ponds.

The presence of water is pervasive: by harbor and riverbank, permeating public places in the neighborhoods and downtown. The fountain in City Hall Plaza commemorates the reconstruction of the city's water system and celebrates the integration of natural and human cycles. The fountain is showy on a hot summer afternoon, when sun shines through spray and mist sparking rainbows, and water evaporates off wet pavement, cooling the air. In autumn the fountain bubbles softly, feeding still pools; ripples of flowing water reflect the color and activity on the plaza. In winter water freezes into ice crystals as it trickles from the fountain, color varying with thickness, motion captured in ever-shifting forms. The sound of water moving under the ice and the gradually changing color and transparency of the ice as it thaws mark the transition from late winter to early spring. Water leaves the fountain at City Hall Plaza along runnels that irrigate trees on the plaza and feed a series of pools in a stepped basin. Normally only the pools at the bottom are filled, but after a storm runoff from surrounding pavement and rooftops flows into the basin. One can always gauge the magnitude of a rainstorm by which step the water reaches. Only once in the last ten years has water reached the top step.

Besides the pervasive influence of water, the most powerful mark the late twentieth century left on the urban fabric is the great diversity of landscapes and buildings. Boston's tradition of fostering the construction of innovative projects was established during this period. Experimentation was most intense in inner-city neighborhoods. The combination of a relatively inexpensive land resource and the establishment of building funds to promote experimentation in new urban forms made these neighborhoods centers of innovation. They now exhibit an eclectic array of landscape and building forms, products of individual enterprise and invention: houses designed and built by youth, sewage treatment gardens, fish farms, solar streetlights. Some of the models have since been replicated widely, while others remain original, but singular.

Just as the Back Bay and Emerald Necklace are a showcase of nineteenth-century architecture and urban design, so are the neighborhoods of Dorchester and Roxbury showcases of late-twentieth-century architectural exploration.[29] Separated by more than a century, both were a product of intense, sustained, and visionary public efforts. Both represent public investment in the creation of common ground that ordered individual contributions of private citizens. Both addressed environmental nuisances as well as the need for new housing. Both are a source of pride to the city and landmarks in the history of urban design.

These vignettes are one person's vision for the future shape of Boston. The new Boston, however, will result from many people's visions and actions. It should be the product of a collective vision, one that is widely shared by the region's citizens, forged through the consideration of alternatives in a public dialogue. Design is a means to this end.

The cumulative impact of sewer reconstruction, economic growth, and redevelopment of vacant land within Boston will have a profound impact on the future shape of the city. We must decide, before it is too late, whether they will shape Boston by design or default. How we resolve these issues will determine the quality of the future, not just for the next generation, but for many generations to come.

Epilogue

In the audience that April evening in 1985 were many people who had worked on these issues and whose efforts contributed to Boston's transformation by the 1990s. There were several immediate outcomes: an illustrated feature article in the *Boston Globe* and meetings with several members of the governor's cabinet.[30] Ken Kruckemeyer of the Massachusetts Department of Transportation determined to bring these ideas to the attention of then-governor Michael Dukakis, and for several months after the lecture, I presented the proposals to individual members of his cabinet. They were enthusiastic, but nothing further came from these talks. The forces ranged against serious consideration of my proposals were considerable. Though the plans for a new sewage system had not been finalized, firms were already lining up for engineering and design work and to write environmental-impact statements, and construction firms were waiting eagerly in the wings.

More important, my proposals did not fit existing institutional structures for planning and implementing environmental, social, and development programs. Institutional innovations like the Metropolitan District Commission, which, at the turn of the century, enabled Boston to deal with issues of water supply and treatment at the regional rather than the local scale, had become obstacles to alternative approaches. The system that was actually implemented was a massive construction project whose centerpiece is the $3 billion Deer Island facility, the second-largest wastewater treatment plant in the United States.[31] The new plant and related pollution-control facilities have marked a dramatic improvement from the days when raw sewage was discharged directly into Boston Harbor. Nevertheless, the new system represents another example of the highly centralized, engineered systems that Sam Bass Warner, Jr., and Judith Martin have criticized.[32] So far, it has failed to deal adequately with storm-water management and groundwater protection.

By the 1980s, engaging local residents in planning and implementing neighborhood change was an accepted part of the planning process for certain kinds of projects: the Southwest Corridor Project and the Grassroots Program were prime examples. These measures matured in the late 1980s and grew into important new neighborhood planning and development initiatives such as those of the Dudley Street Neighborhood Initiative (DSNI).[33] The DSNI sponsored new housing for owners with low income, which have been popular with residents and recognized with design awards. These homes were clustered around common open space on low-lying ground, thus avoiding flooded foundations and wet basements. But planners involved in grassroots work with local neighborhoods on issues such as housing and local open space did not take part in comprehensive, regional planning of public-works projects such as water supply and sewage treatment, so the billions of dollars spent on Boston's new sewer system did nothing to rebuild inner-city neighborhoods.

Public-private partnerships were embraced in the mid-1980s as the answer to building and maintaining the public realm in downtown Boston; the success of Post Office Square pleased developers and public alike and became a model for other acclaimed public places. It would have cost no more to design these new spaces to detain storm water, but the designers and proponents of these new spaces were unaware of their role in the city's hydrological system, so runoff from pavement still strains the sewer system after heavy rains.

In 1986, I moved to Philadelphia to teach at the University of Pennsylvania, and my direct involvement in the future shape of Boston ceased. Ten years later, much has changed. The public realm is renewed: Boston's beaches are open for swimming, neighborhoods are rebuilding, downtown has many new thriving public places. From this vantage, my lecture "Reclaiming Common Ground: The Future Shape of Boston" was one vision among many that helped launch, sustain, and advance public dialogue, and thereby changed

the course of Boston's future. Like Robert Morris Copeland's "The Most Beautiful City in America: Essay and Plan for the Improvement of the City of Boston," my essay now serves as an example of those many others, most of which were more informal and unpublished. Like Copeland's proposals, mine influenced certain decisions and caused some buildings and landscapes to be built differently, but the idea at the heart—an integrated approach to urgent economic, social, and environmental problems facing the city—remains unrealized in Boston. Much has changed, and much is the same. The proposals were shaped by place and time—Boston 1985—but the challenges and solutions still apply, and not just to Boston.

There are comparable conditions in many other cities, from New York to Cincinnati to Denver to Los Angeles. West Philadelphia's Mill Creek neighborhood, for example, faces challenges closely related to those of Boston's Dudley, and Philadelphia and Boston share the problem of combined sewer overflows that degrade water quality. Since 1987, I have adapted and extended the approach outlined in this chapter to Philadelphia and made similar, more highly developed proposals for Mill Creek.[34] In 1999, the Philadelphia Water Department submitted a grant proposal to the US Environmental Protection Agency for funds to plan, design, and build a demonstration project on vacant land in the West Philadelphia Empowerment Zone, which will combine a storm-water detention facility to reduce combined sewer overflows and an environmental study area for a local middle school. The project will be designed by stormwater engineers, teachers and students at the middle school, my students, and myself. Now, more than fourteen years after the first public presentation of the ideas in Boston, twelve years after I first applied them to Philadelphia, part of this vision may be realized.

Notes

1. See Alex Krieger and Lisa J. Green, *Past Futures: Two Centuries of Imagining Boston* (Cambridge, Mass.: Harvard University Graduate School of Design, May 1985), the catalogue of an exhibit of plans for Boston.

2. This chapter is based on a lecture that was part of a series of three lectures in Boston and two other cities on the future shape of cities sponsored by the American Institute of Architects and the publishers McGraw-Hill; I would like to thank Sally Harkness and the Boston Society of Architects for asking me to give the lecture on the future shape of Boston. Charlotte Kahn was instigator and inspiration in many of the investigations described here and brought me up to date with Boston's accomplishments since 1985. Lorraine Downey, Melvin Colon, Nelson Merced, gardeners at Cooper's Place, and students in my 1984 and 1985 studios at the Harvard Graduate School of Design, especially my research assistant George Batchelor, all helped me understand the context of the issues and solutions. I am grateful to Jack Thomas, who first suggested the inclusion of the Boston lecture as a chapter in this book, and to Mike Lacey, Bob Fishman, Sam Bass Warner, Jr., Judith Martin, Margaret Weir, Arnold Hirsch, James Wescoat, and Carl Abbott for their comments. Greg Watson, John Berg, and Christine Min gave me important material on the present context.

3. Spirn, *The Granite Garden* (New York: Basic Books, 1984), and *The Language of Landscape* (New Haven: Yale University Press, 1998). See also Spirn, *The West Philadelphia Landscape Plan: A Framework for Action* (Philadelphia: Department of Landscape Architecture and Regional Planning, University of Pennsylvania, 1991), and other publications of the West Philadelphia Landscape Project. See also the project's website at www.upenn.edu/wplp.

4. I was chair of the Panel of Experts for the conference and presided at the three-day meeting. A summary of the proceedings was published in OECD, *Cities for the 21st Century* (Paris: OECD, 1994). Although the U.S. representative to the OECD attended a reception, no representative of the U.S. government participated in this meeting.

5. By the late 1990s, the construction of a new sewage treatment plant at Deer Island had greatly improved water quality in Boston Harbor. However, the establishment of the Massachusetts Water Resources Authority (MWRA) in 1985 and the consol-

idation of sewage treatment into a single plant did not resolve the problems associated with scale raised here.

6. Though much remains to be done, there has been significant improvement in neighborhood community development since 1985.

7. While new atriums are still enclaves guarded by private police, there have been many improvements to downtown Boston's public realm since 1985; Post Office Square is an example.

8. At the time of my lecture, the City of Boston did not know exactly how much vacant land there was.

9. The solution implemented by the MWRA was to replace the two old treatment plants with a single plant, thereby increasing centralization and failing to take advantage of alternative approaches to treatment such as those proposed here.

10. Beginning in 1978, as part of the Clean Water Act of 1977, the Environmental Protection Agency (EPA) provided financial incentives for municipalities to implement innovative or alternative wastewater treatment methods: 75 to 85 percent of design and construction costs, plus the cost of revision or replacement should the new system not work properly. Despite widespread advertisement, much of the allocated funding was not used. The EPA staff member who managed this program felt that a major reason was fear of risk on the part of the engineering profession. Robert Bastian, EPA, personal communication, 1985. For descriptions of Arcata, Bishop's Lodge, and other, similar projects, see Ann Whiston Spirn, *The Granite Garden*, 150–54 and "The Poetics of City and Nature: Toward a New Aesthetic for Urban Design," *Landscape Journal* 7:2 (Fall 1988), 119–22.

11. Boston now recycles sludge and markets it as a commercial fertilizer, Bay State Organic.

12. See description of Denver's Urban Storm Drainage and Flood Control District in Anne Whiston Spirn, *The Granite Garden*, 157–62 and "Poetics of City and Nature," 120.

13. Sam Bass Warner, Jr., *Streetcar Suburbs* (Cambridge, Mass.: Harvard University Press, 1962).

14. I have traced the development of these neighborhoods through nineteenth- and twentieth-century fire insurance atlases: Hopkins (1873–74); Bromley (1884, 1906); Sanborn (1943, 1968, 1986).

15. This story has been told elsewhere; see, for example, Kenneth Jackson, *Crabgrass Frontier* (New York: Oxford University Press, 1985).

16. The Dudley neighborhood is the subject of Peter Medoff and Holly Sklar, *Streets of Hope: The*

Fall and Rise of an Urban Neighborhood (Boston: South End Press, 1994). Medoff and Sklar describe how the Dudley neighborhood was plagued by arson in the 1970s (30–32) but show no awareness of the extent to which vacant land in the old floodplain was already present in the '50s and '60s.

17. I have documented the correlation between old floodplains, wetlands, and vacant land in inner-city neighborhoods of other cities, including Philadelphia, New York, Cincinnati, and Washington, D.C. The work in Philadelphia was sponsored by a grant from the J. N. Pew Charitable Trust (1987–91) and was documented in Anne Whiston Spirn, *Vacant Land: A Resource for Reshaping Urban Neighborhoods* (Philadelphia: Department of Landscape Architecture and Regional Planning, University of Pennsylvania, 1991). My work in other cities, including Boston, was sponsored by a grant from the National Endowment for the Arts (1984–85). See description of Philadelphia's Mill Creek neighborhood in Anne Whiston Spirn, *The Language of Landscape* (New Haven, Conn.: Yale University Press, 1998).

18. In 1985, students in my graduate studio in landscape architecture at the Harvard Graduate School of Design met with staff of Alianza Hispana and Nuestra Comunidad Development Corporation, developed designs for the Dudley neighborhood, and presented their proposals to Dudley residents in a public meeting in May 1985. Their work and this public lecture influenced the decision to reserve the lowest-lying land as a town common.

19. The Grassroots Program, now sponsored by Boston's Public Facilities Department, is still functioning in 1998.

20. This was accomplished at Post Office Square, now a popular downtown park with restaurant and underground parking garage.

21. Prudential Center has since been renovated into what a sign calls "Boston's City Under Glass," an interior arcade with stores, food courts, even a chapel, and an entrance to the new convention center alongside. There are terraces facing Boylston Street, and an enclosed escalator invites pedestrians on the sidewalk outside to enter and ascend to the complex. Still, this stretch of Boylston Street remains an unattractive place for pedestrians.

22. Quoted in Walter Muir Whitehill, *Boston: A Topographical History,* 2d ed. (Cambridge, Mass.: Harvard University Press, 1968), 90.

23. Museum of Fine Arts, *Back Bay Boston: The City as a Work of Art* (Boston: Museum of Fine Arts, 1969), 38.

24. Whitehill, *Boston,* 180.

25. For reproductions of these plans, see Alex Krieger and Lisa J. Green, *Past Futures;* Alex Krieger and David Cobb with Amy Turner, *Mapping Boston* (Cambridge, Mass.: MIT Press, 1999); and Cynthia Zaitzevsky, *Frederick Law Olmsted and the Boston Park System* (Cambridge, Mass.: Harvard University Press, 1982).

26. Frederick Law Olmsted, "The Problem and Its Solution," handwritten notes for a lecture to the Boston Society of Architects, 1886, Olmsted Papers, Library of Congress, Washington, D.C.

27. Frederick Law Olmsted, "Seventh Annual report of the Board of Commissioners of the Department of Parks for the City of Boston for the year 1881," reprinted in S. B. Sutton, ed., *Civilizing American Cities: A Selection of Frederick Law Olmsted's Writings on City Landscapes* (Cambridge, Mass.: MIT Press, 1971), 227.

28. T. S. Eliot, "The Dry Salvages," *Four Quartets* in *The Collected Poetry and Plays* (New York: Harcourt, Brace, 1962). The Dry Salvages are a group of rocks in Boston's outer harbor.

29. Sam Bass Warner, Jr. (in a lecture at Harvard Graduate School of Design, Cambridge, Mass., 1984).

30. Steve Curwood, "Profile: Shaping the City to Nature's Laws," *Sunday Boston Globe,* May 26, 1985. In 1986, following the Atheneum lecture, the Boston Aquarium published an abridged version in a publication devoted to Boston Harbor.

31. Charles Button, Ken M. Willis, and Crystal Gandrud, "Managing the Boston Harbor Project," *Civil Engineering Practice* (Spring/Summer 1994), 67 and MWRA, "Facts about BHP Construction" (Boston, Mass.: MWRA, fall 1996).

32. See chapter 10 by Martin and Warner. See also Sam Bass Warner, Jr., "Urban River Management, 1630–1997: The Charles River Case," paper presented at the 20th International Congress of the History of Science, May 1997.

33. Medoff and Sklar, in *Streets of Hope,* describe successful efforts of the DSNI, Alianza Hispana, and Nuestra Comunidad Development Corporation in promoting community development.

34. These are described in Spirn, *Language and Landscape* (see pp. 210–15 and 267–72, especially), *West Philadelphia Landscape Plan.* Designs for the environmental study area/stormwater detention facility by my Penn students and Sulzberger Middle School students can be viewed online at www.upenn.edu/wplp.

Contributors

CARL J. ABBOTT is professor in the School of Urban Studies and Planning at Portland State University. He is the author of numerous books, including *Urban America in the Modern Age, 1920 to the Present* (1987), *Metropolitan Frontier: Cities in the Modern American West* (1993), and *Political Terrain: Washington, D.C., from Tidewater Town to Global Metropolis* (1999).

ALAN BRINKLEY, a former Woodrow Wilson Center Fellow, is Allan Nevins Professor of History at Columbia University. He is the author of *End of Reform: New Deal Liberalism in Recession and War* (1995), *New Federalist Papers: Essays in Defense of the Constitution* (1997), and *Liberalism and Its Discontents* (1998).

ROBERT FISHMAN, a recent Public Policy Scholar at the Woodrow Wilson Center, is professor of history at Rutgers University and author of Urban Utopias in the Twentieth Century: *Ebenezer Howard, Frank Lloyd Wright, and Le Corbusier* (1977) and *Bourgeois Utopias: The Rise and Fall of Suburbia* (1987).

ARNOLD R. HIRSCH is University Research Professor of History at the University of New Orleans. He is the author of *Making the Second Ghetto: Race and Housing in Chicago,* *1940-1960* (1998), and co-editor of *Creole New Orleans: Race and Urbanization* (1992) and *Urban Policy in Twentieth-Century America* (1993).

MICHAEL J. LACEY is director of the American Program at the Woodrow Wilson International Center for Scholars. He is the editor or coeditor and contributor to a number of volumes, among them *Government and Environmental Politics: Essays on Historical Developments Since World War Two,* (1991), *A Culture of Rights: The Bill of Rights in Philosophy, Politics, and Law-1791 and 1991* (1991), and *The State and Social Investigation in Britain and the United States* (1993).

JUDITH A. MARTIN is director of urban studies and professor of geography at the University of Minnesota. She is the author of *Past Choice/Present Landscapes: The Impact of Urban Renewal on the Twin Cities* (1989), *Where We Live: The Residential Districts of Minneapolis and Saint Paul* (1983), and *Recycling the Central City: The Development of a New Town in Town* (1978).

ANNE WHISTON SPIRN, a former Woodrow Wilson Center Fellow, is professor of landscape architecture and regional planning at the University of Pennsylvania, where she has taught since 1986. *She is the author of The*

Granite Garden: Urban Nature and Human Design (1984) and *Language of Landscape* (1998).

JOHN L. THOMAS is professor emeritus of history at Brown University. A former Woodrow Wilson Center Fellow, he is the author of *Alternative America: Henry George, Edward Bellamy, Henry Demarest Lloyd, and the Adversary Tradition* (1983), *Liberator, William Lloyd Garrison: A Biography* (1963), and *Abraham Lincoln and the American Political Tradition* (1986).

SAM BASS WARNER, JR., is visiting professor in the department of Urban Studies and Planning at the Massachusetts Institute of Technology. His numerous books include *Streetcar Suburbs: The Process of Growth in Boston, 1870-1900* (1962), *The Private City: Philadelphia in Three Periods of Its Growth* (1968), and *The Urban Wilderness: A History of the American City* (1972).

MARGARET WEIR is professor of sociology at the University of California, Berkeley. She is the co-editor of *Politics of Social Policy in the United States* (1988) and editor of *Social Divide: Political Parties and the Future of Activist Government* (1998).

JAMES L. WESCOAT, JR., is professor of geography at the University of Colorado at Boulder. He is the author of *Integrated Water Development: Water Use and Conservation Practice in Western Colorado* (1984) and *Evolution of Flood Hazards Programs in Asia: The Current Situation* (1993).

Index